OXFORD IB DIPLOMA PROG

HISTORY OF THE AMERICAS

COURSE COMPANION

Yvonne Berliner
Tom Leppard
Alexis Mamaux
Mark D. Rogers
David Smith

OXFORD
UNIVERSITY PRESS

OXFORD
UNIVERSITY PRESS

Great Clarendon Street, Oxford OX2 6DP

Oxford University Press is a department of the University of Oxford.
It furthers the University's objective of excellence in research,
scholarship, and education by publishing worldwide in

Oxford   New York

Auckland   Cape Town   Dar es Salaam   Hong Kong   Karachi
Kuala Lumpur   Madrid   Melbourne   Mexico City   Nairobi
New Delhi   Shanghai   Taipei   Toronto

With offices in

Argentina   Austria   Brazil   Chile   Czech Republic   France   Greece
Guatemala   Hungary   Italy   Japan   Poland   Portugal   Singapore
South Korea   Switzerland   Thailand   Turkey   Ukraine   Vietnam

Oxford is a registered trade mark of Oxford University Press
in the UK and in certain other countries

British Library Cataloguing in Publication Data

Data available

ISBN: 978-0-19-839015-2
10 9 8 7 6 5 4 3 2 1

Printed in Great Britain by Bell & Bain Ltd, Glasgow

Acknowledgments

The publisher would like to thank the following for permission to
reproduce photographs

Cover image by David Lawrence; P10: Emmwood [John Musgrave-Wood]/British
Cartoon Archive; P17l: Mary Evans Picture Library/Photolibrary; P17r: Richard T.
Nowitz/Corbis; P18: Mexican School, (18th century)/Museo de America, Madrid,
Spain/Giraudon/The Bridgeman Art Library; P19: Mary Evans Picture Library;
P21: Bettmann/Corbis; P24t: Popular Graphic Arts/Library of Congress Prints and
Photographs Division; P24b: Popular Graphic Arts/Library of Congress Prints and
Photographs Division; P25: American School, (18th century)/Private Collection/Pe-
ter Newark American Pictures/The Bridgeman Art Library; P26: North Wind Picture
Archives/Alamy; P31: Thomas Sully/The Bridgeman Art Library/Getty Images; P36:
English School, (19th century) / Private Collection / The Bridgeman Art Library;
P37: French School, (18th century) / Musee de la Ville de Paris, Musee Carnavalet,
Paris, France / Archives Charmet / The Bridgeman Art Library; P40: French School,
(19th century)/Private Collection/Archives Charmet/The Bridgeman Art Library;
P42: Castro, Gil de (19th century)/Private Collection /The Bridgeman Art Library;
P43: Peter Horree/Alamy; P45: Bettmann/Corbis; P46: Subercasseux, Pedro (19th
century)/Private Collection/Index/The Bridgeman Art Library; P50: North Wind Pic-
ture Archives/Alamy; P54t: North Wind Picture Archives/Alamy; P54b: North Wind
Picture Archives/Alamy; P55: North Wind Picture Archives/Alamy; P56: North Wind
Picture Archives/Alamy; P66: MPI/Archive Photos/Getty Images; P68: Ken Welsh/
Photolibrary; P77: Mary Evans Picture Library; P79t: Martín Tovar y Tovar; P79b: Ar-
turo Michelena (1863 - 1898); P87l: National Archives and Records Administration;
P87r: John David Kelly/John David Kelly collection/Library and archives Canada;
P90: Apic/Hulton Archive/Getty Images; P92: T. C. Doane/National Photography
Collection /C-066899/ Library and Archives Canada; P93: Hulton Archive/Getty Im-
ages; P96: L'Ouvrier, Paul (fl.1858)/© Collection of the New-York Historical Society,
USA/The Bridgeman Art Library; P98: National Archives/Archive Photos/Getty
Images; P104t: Bettmann/Corbis; P104b: Hulton Archive/Getty Images ; P105: James
Ashfield/Robert Harris fonds/C-001855/ Library and Archives Canada; P108t: Library
and Archives Canada/A caricature history of Canadian politics : events from the
union of 1841/AMICUS 4606691/nlc001847; P108m: Library and Archives Canada/A
caricature history of Canadian politics : events from the union of 1841/AMICUS
4606691/nlc001843; P108b: Library and Archives Canada/A caricature history of
Canadian politics : events from the union of 1841/AMICUS 4606691/nlc001844;
P110: Ed Lallo/Time & Life Pictures/Getty Images; P 127: Harris & Ewing Collection/
Library of Congress Prints and Photographs Division; P129: Photos 12/Alamy; P134:
Library of Congress Prints and Photographs Division Washington, D.C.; P135:
ClassicStock/Alamy; P139l: Library of Congress Prints and Photographs Division
Washington, D.C.; P139r: Corbis; P140: Superstock/Photolibrary; P146: Niday
Picture Library/Alamy; P149: akg-images/Alamy; P162: Hulton-Deutsch Collection/
Corbis; P163: The Art Archive/Imperial War Museum; P186: Library of Congress
Prints and Photographs Division Washington, D.C.; P187t: The Art Archive; P187b:
The Art Archive; P194: Archive Holdings Inc./Archive Photos/Getty Images; P195:
Rex Features; P196: Hulton Archive/Archive Photos/Getty Images; P201: Fotosearch/
Archive Photos/Getty Images; P204: John Elk III/Alamy; P205: Wikimedia Com-

mons; P206: Photos 12/Alamy; P208: Gjon Mili/Time & Life Pictures/Getty Images;
P209: National Archives of Canada; P213: Hulton-Deutsch Collection/Corbis; P214:
© McCord Museum; P220: National Archives of Canada; P221: Glenbow Archives;
P226: Borderlands/Alamy; P230: Keystone/Hulton Archive/Getty Images; P231: Rue
des Archives/Tall/Mary Evans Picture Library; P233: John Phillips/Time & Life Pic-
tures/Getty Images; P234: Mary Evans Picture Library; P236: Bettmann/Corbis; P237:
Low; David (1891-1963)/British Cartoon Archive; P239: Yrigoyen; P246: Library of
Congress; P252: Library of Congress Prints and Photographs Division Washington,
D.C.; P255: AP Photo; P260: STR New/Reuters; P261: 3LH-B&W/Photolibrary; P266:
Rex Features; P275: Bettmann/Corbis; P276: © Department of National Defence.
Reproduced with the permission of the Minister of Public Works and Government
Services, 2010; P279t: Bettmann/Corbis; P279b: 3LH-B&W/Photolibrary; P280t:
Innes, Tom, Calgary, Alberta/Glenbow Museum; P280bl: © McCord Museum;
P280br: © McCord Museum; P281t: Canadian Flag; P281b: Dusan Po/Shutterstock;
P282: Bettmann/Corbis; P294: © McCord Museum; P296: Hulton Archive/Getty
Images; P297: Claudia Daut/Reuters; P298t: Getty Images; P298b: AP Photo; P305:
Roger Viollet/Getty Images; P306: Ron Frehm/AP Photo; P320: AFP; P323: AP Photo;
P332: OFF/AFP; P342t: INP/AFP; P342b: INTERFOTO/Alamy; P345: APA/Hulton Ar-
chive/Getty Images; P347: Hulton Archive/Getty Images; P358: Authenticated News/
Archive Photos/Getty Images; P360: DOD Media; P362: Frank Scherschel/Time &
Life Pictures/Getty Images; P367: Barbara Kobasuk; P369: Paul Schutzer/Time & Life
Pictures/Getty Images; P376: CBS Photo Archive/Archive Photos/Getty Images; P378:
John Filo/Premium Archive/Getty Images; P384: Getty Images News/Getty Images;
P392: Express/Archive Photos/Getty Images; P394: STF/AFP; P395: TASS/AFP; P396:
El Mercurio; P397: Robert Nickelsberg/Time & Life Pictures/Getty Images; P401:
Courtesy Ronald Reagan Library; P402: Courtesy Ronald Reagan Library; P406:
Nicholas Garland/British Cartoon Archive; P410: INTERFOTO/Alamy; P420t: George
Bush Presidential Library; P420b: peter jordan/Alamy; P427t: Dimitrios Kambouris/
VF1/WireImage/Getty Images; P427b: John Roca/NY Daily News Archive/Getty
Images; P428: Time Life Pictures/ Getty Images; P430: Nicholas Garland/British
Cartoon Archive; P434: William J. Clinton Presidential Library; P437: Diana Walker/
Time Life Pictures/Getty Images; P439: Bill McArthur/British Cartoon Archive; P445:
Bob Pearson/AFP; P453: Mariana Bazo/Reuters; P454: Piero Pomponi/Getty Images
News/Getty Images; P456t: Keith Dannemiller/Alamy; P456b: Anibal Solimano/
Getty Images News/Getty Images; P457t: Ricardo Ceppi/Corbis; P457b: STF/AFP;
P458: AP Photo; P462: Daniel Caselli/AFP; P463: Str Old/Reuters; P466: Julio Etchart/
Alamy; P467: ITV/Rex Features; P468: Chip East/Reuters; P470: Old Visuals/Alamy;
P471t: Doug Wilson/Corbis; P471b: Alex Wong/Getty Images News/Getty Images;
P472: Tom Munnecke/Hulton Archive/Getty Images; P473: Tom Munnecke/Hulton
Archive/Getty Images; P478: Ted Thai/Time & Life Pictures/Getty Images; P480:
David Hoffman Photo Library/Alamy; P486: Missouri School of Journalism; P493:
Photos 12/Alamy; P497t: David Mcgough/DMI/Time Life Pictures/Getty Images;
P497b: Tim Mosenfelder/Getty Images.

We have tried to trace and contact all copyright holders before publication. If
notified, the publishers will be pleased to rectify any errors or omissions at the
earliest opportunity.

Course Companion definition

The IB Diploma Programme Course Companions are resource materials designed to support students throughout their two-year Diploma Programme course of study in a particular subject. They will help students gain an understanding of what is expected from the study of an IB Diploma Programme subject while presenting content in a way that illustrates the purpose and aims of the IB. They reflect the philosophy and approach of the IB and encourage a deep understanding of each subject by making connections to wider issues and providing opportunities for critical thinking.

The books mirror the IB philosophy of viewing the curriculum in terms of a whole-course approach; the use of a wide range of resources, international mindedness, the IB learner profile and the IB Diploma Programme core requirements, theory of knowledge, the extended essay, and creativity, action, service (CAS).

Each book can be used in conjunction with other materials and indeed, students of the IB are required and encouraged to draw conclusions from a variety of resources. Suggestions for additional and further reading are given in each book and suggestions for how to extend research are provided.

In addition, the Course Companions provide advice and guidance on the specific course assessment requirements and on academic honesty protocol. They are distinctive and authoritative without being prescriptive.

IB mission statement

The International Baccalaureate aims to develop inquiring, knowledgable and caring young people who help to create a better and more peaceful world through intercultural understanding and respect.

To this end the IB works with schools, governments and international organizations to develop challenging programmes of international education and rigorous assessment.

These programmes encourage students across the world to become active, compassionate, and lifelong learners who understand that other people, with their differences, can also be right.

The IB learner profile

The aim of all IB programmes is to develop internationally minded people who, recognizing their common humanity and shared guardianship of the planet, help to create a better and more peaceful world. IB learners strive to be:

Inquirers They develop their natural curiosity. They acquire the skills necessary to conduct inquiry and research and show independence in learning. They actively enjoy learning and this love of learning will be sustained throughout their lives.

Knowledgable They explore concepts, ideas, and issues that have local and global significance. In so doing, they acquire in-depth knowledge and develop understanding across a broad and balanced range of disciplines.

Thinkers They exercise initiative in applying thinking skills critically and creatively to recognize and approach complex problems, and make reasoned, ethical decisions.

Communicators They understand and express ideas and information confidently and creatively in more than one language and in a variety of modes of communication. They work effectively and willingly in collaboration with others.

Principled They act with integrity and honesty, with a strong sense of fairness, justice, and respect for the dignity of the individual, groups, and communities. They take responsibility for their own actions and the consequences that accompany them.

Open-minded They understand and appreciate their own cultures and personal histories, and are open to the perspectives, values, and traditions of other individuals and communities. They are accustomed to seeking and evaluating a range of points of view, and are willing to grow from the experience.

Caring They show empathy, compassion, and respect towards the needs and feelings of others. They have a personal commitment to service, and act to make a positive difference to the lives of others and to the environment.

Risk-takers They approach unfamiliar situations and uncertainty with courage and forethought, and have the independence of spirit to explore new roles, ideas, and strategies. They are brave and articulate in defending their beliefs.

Balanced They understand the importance of intellectual, physical, and emotional balance to achieve personal well-being for themselves and others.

Reflective They give thoughtful consideration to their own learning and experience. They are able to assess and understand their strengths and limitations in order to support their learning and personal development.

A note on academic honesty

It is of vital importance to acknowledge and appropriately credit the owners of information when that information is used in your work. After all, owners of ideas (intellectual property) have property rights. To have an authentic piece of work, it must be based on your individual and original ideas with the work of others fully acknowledged. Therefore, all assignments, written or oral, completed for assessment must use your own language and expression. Where sources are used or referred to, whether in the form of direct quotation or paraphrase, such sources must be appropriately acknowledged.

How do I acknowledge the work of others?

The way that you acknowledge that you have used the ideas of other people is through the use of footnotes and bibliographies.

Footnotes (placed at the bottom of a page) or endnotes (placed at the end of a document) are to be provided when you quote or paraphrase from another document, or closely summarize the information provided in another document. You do not need to provide a footnote for information that is part of a "body of knowledge". That is, definitions do not need to be footnoted as they are part of the assumed knowledge.

Bibliographies should include a formal list of the resources that you used in your work. "Formal" means that you should use one of the several accepted forms of presentation. This usually involves separating the resources that you use into different categories (e.g. books, magazines, newspaper articles, Internet-based resources, CDs and works of art) and providing full information as to how a reader or viewer of your work can find the same information. A bibliography is compulsory in the extended essay.

What constitutes malpractice?

Malpractice is behaviour that results in, or may result in, you or any student gaining an unfair advantage in one or more assessment component. Malpractice includes plagiarism and collusion.

Plagiarism is defined as the representation of the ideas or work of another person as your own. The following are some of the ways to avoid plagiarism:

- Words and ideas of another person used to support one's arguments must be acknowledged.
- Passages that are quoted verbatim must be enclosed within quotation marks and acknowledged.
- CD-ROMs, email messages, web sites on the Internet, and any other electronic media must be treated in the same way as books and journals.
- The sources of all photographs, maps, illustrations, computer programs, data, graphs, audio-visual, and similar material must be acknowledged if they are not your own work.
- Works of art, whether music, film, dance, theatre arts, or visual arts, and where the creative use of a part of a work takes place, must be acknowledged.

Collusion is defined as supporting malpractice by another student. This includes:

- allowing your work to be copied or submitted for assessment by another student
- duplicating work for different assessment components and/or diploma requirements.

Other forms of malpractice include any action that gives you an unfair advantage or affects the results of another student. Examples include, taking unauthorized material into an examination room, misconduct during an examination, and falsifying a CAS record.

Contents

Authors 7
Introduction 7
Guidelines for study 8

1 Independence movements   9
Alexis Mamaux

What is meant by the Americas? 10
The New World 12
Origins of revolution 22
Spanish America from the end of the Habsburgs
    to French occupation of Spain 27
The American War of Independence 30
The Caribbean and Latin America: revolution
    and independence 35
Foreign relations in the Americas, 1810–1823 ... 48
Economic and social effects of the revolutions
on the Americas 51
Exam practice and further resources 58

2 Nations and nation-building in the
    Americas, 1787–1867   59
Yvonne Berliner and Tom Leppard

Independence achieved 61
The Articles of Confederation and the
    US Constitution 64
The rise and rule of the *caudillos* in
    Latin America 74
The War of 1812 80
Canada and the road to confederation,
    1837–67 88
The US–Mexican War of 1846–48 95
Canada becomes a nation 104
The plight of Native Americans 109
Exam practice and further resources 114

3 The emergence of the Americas in
    global affairs, 1880–1929   115
David Smith

The United States: setting the stage 116
Ideological reasons for US expansion 117
The Spanish–American War 125
United States foreign policy 133
The United States and the First World War .. 144
Canada and the First World War 160
The impact of the First World War
    on Canada 173
The impact of the First World War on
    Latin America 175

Exam practice and further resources 181

4 The Great Depression and the
    Americas, 1929–39   182
Alexis Mamaux, Mark D. Rogers and
David Smith

The Great Depression in the United States .. 183
The Great Depression in Canada 208
Latin American responses to the Great
    Depression 225
Exam practice and further resources 241

5 Political developments in the Americas
    after the Second World War, 1945–79   242
Yvonne Berliner and Tom Leppard

The domestic policies of US presidents:
    Truman to Nixon 245
Canada's domestic policies: Diefenbaker
    to Clark 270
The Quiet Revolution 290
The Cuban Revolution 295
Populist leaders in Latin America 312
Military regimes In Latin America, 1960s–80s ... 327
Exam practice and further resources 335

6 The Cold War and the Americas,
    1945–81   336
Yvonne Berliner, Tom Leppard,
Alexis Mamaux and Mark D. Rogers

Containment under President Truman 337
The Korean War, 1950–53 355
Eisenhower, Dulles and the New Look 361
US involvement in the Vietnam War 369
US foreign policy towards the Americas 379
The Cold War in Chile, 1945–81 389
Exam practice and further resources 396

7 Into the 21st century, 1980–2000   397
Yvonne Berliner and Mark D. Rogers

The domestic and foreign policies of Reagan,
    Bush and Clinton 398
The restoration of democracy in
    Latin America 445
Into the 21st century: the United States 468
Exam practice and further resources 496

Index 498

Authors

Yvonne Berliner currently teaches world and Latin American history at Washington State University. She taught history, and was IB diploma coordinator, at the International School Nido de Aguilas in Santiago, Chile, until 1997. She has been an IB history examiner, team leader and workshop leader since 1989.

Tom Leppard has been an IB history teacher, examiner, curriculum writer, coordinator, administrator and workshop leader since l983. He recently received a lifetime achievement award from the Alberta Association of IB World Schools, Canada.

Alexis Mamaux currently teaches IB History of the Americas at the United World College in Montezuma, New Mexico, USA. She is also an IB examiner, team leader and workshop leader.

Mark D. Rogers currently teaches history at the J.E.B. Stuart High School in Fairfax County, Virginia, USA, where he was IB diploma coordinator until 2006. His school received an IBNA Inspiration Award in 2004 and he is also a James Madison Memorial Foundation Fellow.

David Smith teaches at the Ecole Lindsay Thurber Comprehensive High School in Alberta, Canada, where he also serves as the IB diploma coordinator. He is an IB workshop leader, examiner, new school application reader and a faculty member for the Online Curriculum Centre.

Introduction

This book is designed to be a companion to the study of the International Baccalaureate Diploma Programme course for Route 2, Higher Level History: Aspects of History of the Americas. It covers the history of the Western Hemisphere from the independence movements of the late-18th century to the onset of the 21st century and the accelerated changes that have taken place in the Americas since 1980. Teachers and schools are instructed to choose three of the topics in the regional option. The recommended focus in this course companion is on the more comparative aspects of the syllabus, including: independence movements and nation building; emergence of the Americas in global affairs; the Great Depression; political developments after the Second World War; the role of the Americas in the Cold War; and the final decades of the century, 1980–2000. In all instances, students are expected to have knowledge of the history of Canada, the United States and Latin America. A case study approach is often suggested for Latin America as it is such a diverse region, and the more focused approach is one way to gain both depth and breadth. The countries considered as examples of political, social and economic developments in the region, during the periods covered, thus vary from chapter to chapter. This is to show flexibility in the approach, rather than presenting a fixed template.

This course companion aims to highlight the uniqueness of the experience of individual countries in the region while also showing the universality of core historical concepts. Students are encouraged to apply the discussion points to a number of areas beyond the Americas as a means of engaging in the core focus of the course on 20th-century world history.

Guidelines for study

Each chapter in this book covers the designated range of themes that make up one entire section of the IB History of the Americas paper. Three chapters/sections must be studied in their entirety in order to be well prepared. The final examination paper will include two questions on each of the 12 sections (this book covers seven) with each question focusing on a designated theme from the section.

Each chapter in this textbook ends with five sample exam questions written by IB examiners. These questions cover the entire range of the type of questions asked on IB examination papers. Use these questions for homework, in school mock exams and revision exercises. Use the IB History guide to familiarize yourself with the meaning of the IB "command terms" in each question.

Read each question carefully. Use the question to structure your answer. Answer the question asked, not the question on the topic for which you have a "prepared" answer. Prepared responses to questions on such popular topics as the civil war in the United States and the Great Depression often fail to score high marks due to this fundamental error.

Questions about "why and with what consequences," require both the "why" and the "consequences" to be addressed in the answer. "Compare and contrast" questions demand a balanced discussion of similarities and differences, in a clearly structured way. If the question states "with reference to any two countries from the region," a maximum of 12 can be achieved if only one country is discussed. A classic mistake is to talk about Germany or Japan in questions about the social, economic or political impact of the Second World War on the Americas. Such a discussion would receive a zero.

The final examination demands three questions to be answered in 150 minutes. Allocate 50 minutes for each question. Spend ten minutes of each 50 minutes planning your response. If you do run out of time, answer the final question as completely as possible in note form.

To improve the quality of your essays, familiarize yourself with the official criteria and markbands used by IB examiners. A series of vague generalizations (claims with no factual support) will score no more than six marks. A response which is simply a descriptive narrative of events, however impressively detailed and accurate, will not score high marks.

The better answers to any question will consist of a series of valid claims, each claim supported by material evidence, or facts. In turn, those claims should be linked together using linking phrases, and woven into a clearly delineated, analytically logical and rhetorically well-structured over-arching argument and counter-argument. The very best responses will also include some discussion of the historiography, an introduction and a conclusion.

1 Independence movements

There are certain dates that become a recognized form of shorthand for the events they represent. Two such dates are 1492 and 1776: the former represents the beginning of the sustained conquest and colonization of the Americas; the latter signifies the conclusion of this period of colonization. Europeans made their way to the Americas in a variety of ways with numerous objectives, but always considered themselves Europeans. Only with the United States Declaration of Independence did the colonizers residing in North America decide to rupture their ties with the mother country and create new, independent states. After 13 British colonies declared independence and achieved a surprising victory against the British Crown, other colonies in the region were encouraged and began their own wars of independence. The first and most brutal of these wars was in Haiti where the slaves had suffered tremendously under French rule and sought to eliminate Europeans from the country. In one of the later movements, Brazil achieved independence from Portugal in a relatively bloodless fashion. In the middle (literally and figuratively) were the wars for independence among the Spanish American colonies: similar, in that they were fighting the same European power, but each distinct due its own history, demography and relation to the Spanish Crown.

The era of independence movements began in the 1760s and lasted well into the 1820s. It covered most of the two continents and involved the European powers. In the beginning there were colonists; by the end of this period, there were Americans, Peruvians, Mexicans, Brazilians and Haitians. It was a turbulent period for the entire region but the different means and methods of independence came to define the countries that were created out of these movements.

The purpose of this chapter is to provide a method for analyzing the causes and developments among the independence movements in the region. By the end of this chapter, students should be able to:

- trace the rise of independence movements in the Americas covering: the political, economic, social, intellectual and religious causes; the role of foreign intervention; conflicts and issues leading to war

- analyze the political and intellectual contributions of leaders to the process of independence including George Washington, Thomas Jefferson, Simón Bolívar, José de San Martín and Bernardo O'Higgins

- explain the processes leading to the United States Declaration of Independence: including the influence of ideas; nature of the declaration; decisive military campaigns and their impact on the outcome (the Battle of Saratoga)

- discuss the rise of independence movements across Latin America: including characteristics of the independence processes; the similarities and/or differences between countries in the region; military campaigns and their impact on the outcome (including the battles of Chacabuco and Maipú)

- evaluate the position of the United States toward Latin American independence, including the events and reasons for the emergence of the Monroe Doctrine
- understand the impact of independence on the economies and societies of the Americas: including economic and social issues; new perspectives on economic development; the impact on different social groups (Native Americans, African Americans, creoles).

What is meant by the Americas?

At face value, the Americas seem homogenous; all countries share the same alphabet, they are all ex-colonies, they achieved independence at roughly the same time, and in all of them Christianity is the prevailing religion. The reality, however, is more complicated. Not only do the Americas cross two continents and the nearby islands, isolated geographically from the rest of the world by two oceans, but they are often isolated from one another. The Americas are defined by mountain ranges that cut across them, making travel difficult. Even today, the best way of getting from one country to the next is often via air travel. And there is little consistency in the heterogeneity of the population of the countries in the region. In some countries, the indigenous population constitutes the majority; in others, it has been all but eradicated. Political systems also vary tremendously. Democracy prevails in some countries, but in others military dictatorships are still dominant and there have even been attempts at monarchies. Some countries have been very right-wing while others are Marxist in their politics.

Discussion point

Rival claims

'America? — yeah, straight ahead, Bud.'

1 What does the cartoon tell us about the discovery of America?
2 Who really discovered America?
3 What is America?
4 Who defined what America is?

The syllabus demands that students and teachers have knowledge of the United States, Canada and Latin America (the Caribbean is implied here even though it is not really Latin or American, and Greenland is excluded, although it is geographically American). The emergence of the Americas as modern, independent states must be looked at as an integral, related unit.

This should be accomplished through adopting a case-study approach where possible. Understanding the individual historical context of a country is just as important as understanding the trends in the region. In any comparative study, there will always be differences, and these often come out in more detailed study. A comparison between two countries that were part of the same colony can yield considerable distinctions. Mexico and Guatemala were both part of New Spain and fought the same war of independence but peacefully split in 1823, reflecting the economic and social differences of two countries, that may not have been so apparent to outsiders.

Another feature that is a necessary component of studying the Americas is the regional dominance of the United States of America. This amalgam of 13 individual colonies—each with its own laws and relationship to the British Crown—became the most powerful American state, if not the largest, and its actions had considerable effects on the rest of the Americas. Thus the United States dominates any regional study not for reasons of ideology or national preference but simply due its status as a world power. No one Latin American state, nor its leadership, has dominated the region in the same way but many have had their moments: Toussaint L'Ouverture's Haiti, the Porfiriato in Mexico, Fidel Castro's Cuba and Juan Perón's Argentina are examples of countries that took center stage in the region for a substantial period of time. Lastly, Canada demands its own examination as its history is very different; it did not fight a war of independence and still retains the British monarchy even though it is constitutionally independent from the British legal system.

Discussion point

Dominant neighbors

Canada and New Zealand suffer from similar fates: both are former British colonies that are often compared or eclipsed by their larger neighbors, the United States and Australia. Canada and New Zealand are treated by many as satellites of their larger neighbors, lacking in a separate history and cultural identity. In both cases, nothing could be farther from the truth, and a quick look at their histories would show just that.

1 Why then, are generalizations made about these two countries?

2 Why are they seen as devoid of their own identities by outsiders?

3 Are there other countries that are treated in a similar manner?

The New World

In 1492, Christopher Columbus, representing the Spanish throne, ushered in a new era of European expansion: overseas conquest. In his attempt to reach India by going west instead of east, he discovered an entire region that was largely unknown to Europe. It proved to be resource rich and populated—in some places densely so.

The Spanish and the Portuguese were the first to engage in conquest, but the other European powers soon followed; from the 15th to the early 18th centuries cartographers filled in maps of what was called "the new world", and by the middle of the 18th century most of the Americas were claimed by European powers; while the Russian, French, Dutch and Portuguese had holdings, the two dominant imperial powers were the Spanish and the British; the French lost most of their power in their losses to Britain in the **French and Indian War** (known as the **Seven Years' War** in Europe).

> **French and Indian War** was the US name for the war fought between France and Great Britain from 1754 to 1763, so-called because the British and British North Americans battled against the French and a number of Native American tribes. In 1756, the American conflict exploded into a global conflict between these European powers called the **Seven Years' War** (1756–63).

There was no clear consensus of how imperial powers treated the lands they took; their attitudes towards the territories, resources and people they encountered varied from empire to empire, according to their own government structure, economic needs and the population density in the colonies. All colonial authorities encouraged settlements of their own populations to control what were seen as wild and underdeveloped regions, inhabited by savage peoples.

The changes in the balance of power in Europe were very real considerations for those who lived in the colonies as the international standing of the mother country often affected relations with other imperial powers and the way people were treated. The colonies were also affected by the economic agendas of their imperial power; demands abroad often had a knock-on effect in the colonies.

As decades of colonialism became centuries, the colonies became increasingly autonomous. The sheer distance of the Americas from Europe meant that constant oversight was not possible. The imperial powers encouraged a certain degree of autonomy, especially regarding defense of the realm, as sending regular military troops to the colonies was very costly, even for the most advanced navies.

Reasons for emigration to the New World varied not only from empire to empire, but from person to person. Not all emigrated willingly; Africans arrived as slaves who had been captured and sold in the lucrative and exploitative transatlantic slave trade. Destitute Europeans often sold themselves into temporary bondage to pay for their passage, in the hopes of making a new start. Still others arrived in the Americas to escape religious persecution, and many accepted political or military appointments overseas because it provided a way to advance their careers at home. Most were men.

The geography of the Americas

Geography was a significant aspect in making any comparison between the colonies of British and Spanish America. Although there were clear geographical differences among the 13 British colonies, the natural environment did not offer major obstacles which isolated them from each other or preclude communications and eventually unification. Within Latin America the steep mountains and wild rivers dividing regions were formidable obstacles. The geography of Latin America helps to explain the differences among its independence movements and its subsequent development into separate nation states, rather than as a Spanish "United States of America". Spanish American colonies had relations with the Crown, rather than each other, due in large part to the physical obstacles that separated them. The Amazon, Orinoco and Paraguay Rivers provide a means of trade and transit via shipping but were so wide in places that they could not be easily crossed. Forming a backbone for South America, the Andes stretched north–south 6,400 kilometers down the continent, with mountain passes over 3,000 meters above sea level. Mexico and Central America have coastal plains on either side but in the middle are the highlands and the Sierra Madre mountain range. These ranges make movement from one side of the region to the other difficult in some instances. British North America, on the other hand, was able to take advantage of river systems that assisted trade and transport; these included the Great Lakes, and the Hudson and Delaware rivers. In comparison with the Andes, the Allegheny mountains in Western Pennsylvania were easily traversed. While North American cities, such as Boston, Philadelphia or Montreal are near the water (on lakes, rivers and at the ocean), Latin American cities like Mexico city, Quito and São Paulo are on mountain mesas, and were not easily accessed in the colonial period.

British and Spanish America before independence

What would eventually become the United States of America formerly existed as 13 colonies of England from 1607 to 1783, a period of 76 years. In contrast, the Latin American colonies had been controlled by Spain from 1492 to 1825: a period of over 300 years. Clearly, colonial traditions were deeper within Latin America. Additionally, Spanish colonization was motivated by initial discoveries of gold and silver; instead, the English colonists found fertile land and wildlife that could employ them as farmers and furriers. All encountered native populations and contributed to their alienation and decimation. Both the Spanish and the British introduced African slaves to their territories. The native populations encountered by the British were smaller in population numbers and less developed than those encountered by the Spanish. Furthermore, attitudes toward the indigenous population were different. While the English occupied the land and forced scattered, disparate tribes to move from coastal to inland territories, the Spanish approach was based upon the subjugation and control of the native population upon whom they were dependent for labour. Furthermore, in many areas of Spanish America the indigenous populations had formed highly organized hierarchical societies such as the Inca, Maya and Aztec which necessitated a period of conquest that was bloody but relatively brief. By the late 18th century, most of these groups in Spanish America had been subdued, but not all. In this period, British North America was still ringed by native tribes who were resentful of British encroachment on their territory.

Activity
Map study
The Americas

The map on the left shows European colonies in the Americas around 1763. Compare it with the current map of the Americas on the right.

Colonial America

1　After studying the map of colonial America, what in your opinion would the strongest imperial power and why?

2　Does extensive geographical reach mean strength? Why or why not?

3　By the late 18th century, the Spaniards had divided their colonies into four administrative areas called viceroyalties—why do you think they did this?

The Americas today

1　Which countries were created out of Spain's viceroyalties?

2　What are Rupert's Land and New France today?

3　Where does most of Argentina's land come from?

4　Which countries gained the most at the expense of other countries or colonies?

5　Which countries lost the most at the expense of other countries or colonies?

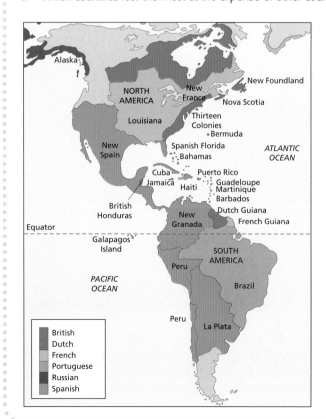

Political control

The administration and government of the British and **Iberian** colonies were in many ways an expression of those of the motherlands. The political organization of the Iberian empires in America reflected the centralized, absolutist regimes of their home countries. From 1516 to 1700, Spain and the Spanish Empire were ruled by the **Habsburg** monarchy. In theory, and to some degree in practice, the authority of the Spanish king was supreme in the Americas. Spain had an extensive body of laws dealing with the administration of the new world, which created an extremely large and complex bureaucratic and legal system. Although these legislative pronouncements tended to work in the major administrative centers, in the outlying areas they were often ignored. Spanish colonies were often known for their noncompliance with the laws of the empire. The senior functionaries in the Spanish colonies were Spanish-born and referred to as *peninsulares*; the **creoles** were virtually excluded from the administration. The only political institution that satisfied local aspirations to some degree was the *cabildo* (town council). In the late 17th century, it became an established practice for the king to sell administrative posts to the highest bidder and the creoles were able to have more input at the local levels of the administration. As the most significant political institution in which the creoles were largely represented, the *cabildos* were destined to play a significant role in the wars of independence. The governmental institutions established by Portugal were, as in the Spanish Empire, highly developed, costly bureaucracies that thwarted local economic initiative and political experimentation. Unlike the Spanish colonies, however, Portuguese rule in Brazil was relatively relaxed. It did not establish the type of colonial administration that Spain held until the 18th century and by then the Portuguese ability to control the Brazilian population was largely mitigated.

As in the Iberian empires, the government and judiciary in the British colonies represented an extension of the English Parliament. The English system was based on common law, and the view that governance was an administrative and judicial system. The English brought with them a tradition of partial representation, and the English colonies had a large degree of self-government. The colonies all had some form of a representative assembly that was voted in by popular support. While only white male landowners could vote, this still constituted some degree of democracy. In some colonies, even the governors were decided by popular vote.

Economic system

The colonial economy adopted by the European empires was **mercantilism**. The basic premise of mercantilism is that national wealth is measured by the amount of capital that a country possesses. Prior to industrialization, gold and silver were the most important resources that a country could own. The mercantile theory is that colonies exist for the economic benefit of the mother country and are useless unless they help to achieve profit. The mother country should draw raw materials from its possessions and sell finished goods back to the subject nations, with the balance favoring the European country. This trade should be monopolistic, so that foreigners would

Iberian Relating to Portugal and Spain, the countries on the Iberian peninsula.

Habsburg European royal family that held the throne for the Holy Roman Empire, Austria, the Netherlands, parts of Italy and Spain. The Habsburgs took the Spanish throne in 1516 under Charles I (Charles V of the Holy Roman Empire) and ruled Spain until the death of Charles II in 1700.

In the Spanish colonies, creoles (*criollos*) were those born in the Americas but descended solely from Spaniards.

Cabildo The local government or municipal council in colonial Spanish America. It was composed of elected officials who were usually landowners and represented the élites in Spanish American society. It was responsible for all aspects of municipal government, including policing, sanitation, taxation, price and wage regulation, land distribution and the administration of justice. Its jurisdiction extended beyond the city to the surrounding villages and countryside. In an emergency the council could choose a governor, lieutenant governor, or captain general.

Mercantilism A form of economic nationalism with the goal of building a wealthy and powerful country. Colonial powers extracted bullion or primary resources from the colonies and exported finished products to the colonies to retain a favorable balance of trade.

not compete with imperial goods; it also meant that when foreigners were allowed to trade in the colonies, protectionist taxes would make imperial goods artificially competitive. Mercantilism guided the imperial powers in their economic relationships with their colonies.

The British passed regulatory laws to benefit their own economy. These laws created a trade system whereby North Americans provided raw goods to Britain, and Britain used the raw goods to produce manufactured goods that were sold on to European markets and back to the colonies. As suppliers of raw goods only, the colonies were not allowed to compete with Britain in manufacturing. English ships and merchants were always favored, excluding other countries from sharing in the British Empire's wealth. England's government implemented mercantilism with a series of **Navigation Acts** (1650 to 1673) which established the rules for colonial trade throughout the entire empire, not just with British America. These were protectionist laws that made the price of imported goods from other parts of the empire much more affordable than foreign goods.

In New England, in particular, many colonists defied the restrictions of the Navigation Acts by smuggling French, Dutch and other countries' goods into the colony. While relations between England and the colonies were strained by these actions the two sides never came to any real conflict. The British government was often lax in enforcing the acts, and its agents in the colonies were known for their corruption. Thus, England developed a policy of **salutary neglect** toward the colonies, which meant that the trade laws that most hurt the colonial economy were not enforced.

Spanish mercantilism was equally restrictive. Unlike England, however, its implementation was tightly enforced and, given the geographic characteristics of colonies, more complex. Spain designated **monopoly ports** on either side of the Atlantic to oversee the collection of taxes. During most of the colonial period, legitimate transatlantic trade was confined to convoys which were supposed to sail annually between Seville and the American ports. The transport and distribution of the goods from Spain to the various administrative centers could take a long time. Moreover, the quantities of manufactured goods were insufficient and the prices inflated. As in the British colonies, smuggling competed with legitimate commerce.

Although its political and economic systems control was more rigid, Spain did not benefit as much from its mercantilist policies as the British did. The problem for the Spanish was that the raw materials shipped to Spain were only a small percentage of the cargo; bullion (mostly silver and some gold) comprised the majority of Spanish colonial exports. Instead of producing finished products in Spain for sale abroad, the Spanish sent the raw materials on to England or the Netherlands for production, and paid for the finished goods with bullion. The long-term result for Spain was a crippling dependence on precious metals, inflation, and a failure to industrialize. Since Spain itself had to rely on finished goods from abroad, it had difficulty supplying its colonies with what they demanded. Mercantilism was resented by the colonists who felt its restrictions and were taxed but saw no benefit from the system. By the late-17th century the inequity,

Navigation Acts A series of laws initiated in 1651 that restricted the use of foreign shipping for trade between England (Great Britain after 1707) and its colonies. This restricted colonial trade in three ways: the colonies could only trade with British merchants; British ships had the exclusive right to transport imports and exports to the colonies; and commodities produced in the colonies could only be exported to British ports.

Salutary neglect The British policy of interfering very little in colonial affairs. It was in place from approximately 1690 to 1760. Colonists were given a high degree of autonomy in local affairs and in turn supported the British government and Crown. After the Seven Years' War, the British reversed this policy, implementing and enforcing tariffs and taxes, much to the objection of its North American subjects.

Monopoly ports A Spanish system whereby only legally recognized ports could engage in trade with the colonies. It also meant that colonies could only trade with Spain, not directly with one another.

shortages and high prices of the Spanish monopoly became more flagrant, prompting the colonists to create their own solutions. Thus, Spanish colonies began to engage in trade among themselves, and intra-continental trade developed a vitality of its own independent of the transatlantic trade. As a result, the colonies saw a rise in new classes of élites in their societies. And with élites, also came the downtrodden.

Social systems

The pattern of settlement and migration into the New World was different for Spanish and British America. Spanish emigrants did not come to the Americas as family units since conditions were more demanding in their colonies, and opportunities were limited. Instead, it was largely single men who came over as soldiers, officials, some as laborers. The Spanish empire also had a much denser indigenous population than British North America. Consequently, there was more intermarriage or interracial relationships, and thus a large percentage of mixed populations in the Iberian colonial regions. In the Spanish colonial territories, racial classifications became very important as the basis of maintaining class and power distinctions. Race was directly

Activity

Research project

The Pirates of the Caribbean

In recent years, piracy in the waters of Southeast Asia and the Horn of Africa (most notably Somalia) has presented challenges for international security and considerable media attention. Interest in the history of piracy has also been fostered by the "Pirates of the Caribbean" films.

Spanish coins and a ring salvaged from the wreck of the pirate ship *Whydah*, which sank along with its captain and most of its crew in 1717, and was recovered in 1984.

A quick Internet search will yield both historical texts and romanticized views of pirates, which brings us to the following questions:

1 Who were the real pirates of the Caribbean?
2 When did piracy hit its apex in the Caribbean?
3 What were they looking for?
4 Was piracy a lucrative profession?
5 What were the dangers faced by people sailing in the Caribbean?
6 How historically accurate are the "Pirates of the Caribbean" films (set in the 1740s according to Disney)?

Captain Kidd on his quarter-deck from a 1907 illustration by Howard Pyle.

linked to social status in a society with a complex racial make-up, and where family connections were important for social advancement. The highest classes were the *peninsulares*—those born in Spain; they had the most privileges, access to the highest political positions and were at the top of the social hierarchy. The creoles, those who were of Spanish blood, but born in the Americas, were denied certain positions and privileges simply due to their place of birth. Since the creoles and *peninsulares* were preoccupied with their own conflicted social status, they did not notice the other social tensions that were developing.

Below the *peninsulares* and creoles were the mixed races or **castas** as they were sometimes called. This group included *mestizos* (mixed European/Native American) and mulattos (European/African) and

> **Peninsulares** are people from the Iberian Peninsula who are of pure Spanish descent.

> **Castas** A Portuguese and Spanish term used in the Americas in reference to all non-whites but especially those who were mixed race such as *mestizos*, mulattos and *lobos*.

The *castas:* Race and social hierarchy

In the period immediately preceding independence, a whole genre of art centered around visual classification of the *castas*, or races, especially in New Spain. These were created almost like modern trading cards, with each card representing a specific marriage and the resultant child.

The image below is just one example of the intricate system that was developed. However, this was not a perfect science; in some respects, the designation given to people was based on visual observations of priests or officials, and not based on actual unions that led to birth. A person's racial designation could be changed through government service or purchase; in the later days of the Spanish Empire (when money was in short supply in Spain), those in the lower *castas* could purchase "certificates of whiteness" that would elevate them. This was only available to those who reached a certain level of affluence, but it showed that there was still an opportunity for upward mobility in Spanish American society.

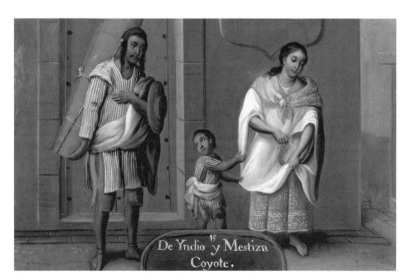

De Yndio y Mestiza 1° Coyote.

A Native American man and his mixed-race wife, from a series on mixed race marriages in Mexico, Mexican school, 18th century.

Spanish + African = **mulatto**
Indigenous (Native American or Amerindian) + mulatto = *lobo*
Spanish + indigenous (Native American or Amerindian) = *mestizo*
Spanish plus *castizo* (*mestizo* + Spanish) = Spanish

> A **mulatto** is a person with one European (or creole) parent and one African parent.

> A *lobo* is a person with one black parent and one indigenous parent.

> A *mestizo* is a person with one European (or creole) parent and one indigenous parent.

formed the majority of the population. Although these groups were relegated to lower jobs and limited opportunities, there were those who achieved wealth and therefore status, especially in cities with sparse creole populations. At the bottom of the social system were the Native Americans and those of African descent, including slaves. They were considered decidedly inferior to the rest of the population and faced brazen discrimination. Social mobility was extremely limited for these groups; although some of them achieved wealth and success, they remained excluded from the upper classes in the Spanish colonies.

Unlike the Spanish, those who migrated to British North America usually came in family groups or even as whole communities, seeking greater personal freedoms and/or greater economic opportunity. Within English colonies, the social structure was largely based on class, but there were always certain ethnicities that were treated as less-than-desirable. In the early stages of colonialism, the Irish and Catholics were seen as threats to colonial security; they were often discriminated against, leading to their further migration westwards.

The class system that developed was based on economics rather than family connections. Wealthy landowners were at the top.

Activity

Discussion point

Race and society

Why did the Spanish develop such intricate ways of categorizing their colonial populations?

TOK Link

What makes race a defining characteristic in some societies and not others?

What happens when race becomes a dominant factor in social hierarchy? Can this be changed in any way?

Activity

TOK Link

The noble savage

The "noble savage" type: Te-Po, Chief of Rarotonga in the Cook Islands, with extensive tattoos and carrying a spear.

Although the idea went back as far as the Roman Empire, colonization once again resurrected the idea of the "noble savage" in Europe. According to this notion, non-Western or "primitive" people are free and equal in a state of nature but become corrupted by society and social institutions that deny them true freedom and equality. Thus, the noble savage is happier and more virtuous than Westerners.

- Why was this concept popularized in the 18th century?
- Why would Europeans and white Americans believe this idea?

In Mexico, Aztec society (12–15th centuries) was divided into local family groups that formed city councils to make decisions that affected the local community. These city councils, in turn, reported to the central government for larger issues, such as warfare (defense).

The Incan government that ruled Perú (1438–1533) had a similar structure to the Roman Empire: the king had senate advisors, a strong army and led the conquest of other South American tribes.

Five North American tribes came together and formed the Iroquois Confederation. As early as 1450 (but certainly by 1525), an oral constitution or "Great Binding Law" was created that included binding ideas such as federalism, separation of duties and checks and balances.

- When did the first constitution appear in Europe?
- When did the ideas of checks and balances first appear in Europe?
- When did religious tolerance first appear in European laws?

 How accurate is the idea of the noble savage for the Americas?

Tradespeople and small farmers formed the majority of the population and they were spurred on by the opportunity to improve their standards of living and attain social advancement through hard work. It is important to remember that two key groups were underrepresented in British colonial society: the aristocracy who rarely emigrated; and the very poor, who could not afford to leave the mother country.

Unlike Spanish America the complex social hierarchy based on racial identity and mixture was absent; the recognized human spectrum was largely white. But, as in the Spanish colonies, the African Americans were at the bottom of the scale with laws that discriminated against them and placed limits on their rights and opportunities. It is often forgotten that even in the northern colonies slaves were an integral part of colonial life, and that the lower white classes based their own sense of social superiority on the slaves who were below them in social status. Native Americans were not even considered to be part of the social spectrum since they remained outside of society; regarded as barbarians or savages, they were not integrated into the class or social system of British North America.

Role of religion

The Americas were colonized by Europeans who wanted to extend the influence of Christianity; while Spanish America was dominated by the Roman Catholic Church, the 13 colonies were mostly—but not entirely—Protestant. Among the settlers were those who sought escape from persecution and those who were driven by missionary zeal. In Spanish America, the Catholic Church played a significant and vital role in the colonies in terms of education, culture and the evangelization of the native population. It also provided social welfare to the general population. The Catholic Church strengthened Spanish imperial control over all segments of colonial society, and was the only faith accepted in the region. Moreover, the church participated in the economy as the leading corporate owner of land, real estate and capital, after the Crown. It also served as a bank, providing laymen with credit and investment capital.

In the British colonies of North America, plurality of faith, although not necessarily tolerance of **dissension**, was the norm. In many ways, what people believed depended on where they lived: The **New England** colonists were largely Puritans, the **Middle colonists** were a mixture of religions, including Quakers, Catholics, Lutherans and Jews. The **Southern colonists** had a mixture of religions as well, including Baptists and Anglicans. This meant that the role of religion and its relationship with the state varied throughout the 13 colonies.

Dissension is a conflict of opinion among those expected to cooperate. In England, dissension was mainly used to describe those who did not participate in the Anglican Church and instead were members of other Protestant sects such as the Puritans.

Making up the original 13 colonies were:

New England
Rhode Island
Connecticut
Massachusetts
New Hampshire

Middle colonies
Delaware
Pennsylvania
New York
New Jersey

Southern colonies
Maryland
Virginia
North Carolina
South Carolina
Georgia

Activity

Case study

The Quaker state

Colonies were sometimes established to protect certain Christian groups from religious persecution. While not unique in this, the founding of Pennsylvania is an interesting case study as it was not just founded but also governed on the basis of ideas of religious freedom and tolerance.

$\rightarrow$

The Society of Friends, or Quakers, had been founded in England in the 1640s with the idea that each individual has his or her own religious experience and relationship with God. As all men and women were regarded as equals, the Quakers did not defer to those of higher social rank, including the monarchy and they saw the clergy as unnecessary. They refused to pay tithes to the Church of England or participate in combat.

In 1681, King Charles II of England granted that land in the American colonies be given to William Penn, a member of a well-connected family and a Quaker. Penn had been jailed frequently due to his outspoken criticism of the Church of England and his demands for religious tolerance. Like many Protestant groups, the Quakers faced persecution in England, but emigration to America had produced further persecution, not relief, until Pennsylvania was founded. Pennsylvania's laws were based on religious freedom and equality and attracted more than Quakers; Mennonites and Amish also settled in the colony.

 Why were Quaker ideas considered treasonous to the British Crown?

Undertake further research to find out what ideas were implemented in Pennsylvania that might later contribute to the ideals of independence?

Activity

Historical role-play

The year is 1765. You are a teenager living in one of the following colonies:

1 New England
2 New Spain
3 Perú
4 Domingue (Haiti)
5 Brazil

Your home life is exactly as it currently is—only in 1765. Your parents have more or less the same professions and you are the same race and possibly religion. Put all of this information in historical context: that is, consider how your life would be in the 18th century in the colony of your choice.

- How would you be treated by others in your society?
- What sort of political affiliations would you and your parents have?
- What would your economic situation be?
- How would you feel about your country's foreign policy goals?
- Would you have a religious affiliation, and if so, what would that mean for you?
- Would you be a dominant or subject nationality?
- How would you feel about your government?

Taking into account these factors, write a 1–2 page analysis of what your life would be like.

An engraving of Stoughton Hall and Massachusetts Hall at Harvard College, c. 1767.

Origins of revolution

In the Americas, discontent emerged as a result of imperial changes in the attitudes towards the colonies. In most cases, events in Europe affected the colonists as their European overlords sought to tighten control and raise revenue. In the British colonies, the French and Indian War brought about the changes; in Spanish America, it was the combination of **Bourbon** reforms and the Napoleonic Wars. In neither case was there one clear event that provided the catalyst; instead, colonists seemed to slip from desires for reform to a war for independence almost unintentionally.

> **Bourbons** The family that assumed the Spanish Crown after the death of Charles II, the last of the Habsburgs, in 1700.

Intellectual foundations: the Enlightenment in the colonies

The role of the Enlightenment was as important in the Americas as it was in Europe. In fact, it could be argued that in the Americas, the educated and élite were more willing to implement the ideas of the Enlightenment than the ruling class of Europeans, who continued to embrace the ideas of divine right, class hierarchy and the supremacy of the church in moral affairs. The Enlightenment's emphasis on human reason appealed to the colonists, who increasingly saw imperial domination as irrational and illogical. Unsurprisingly, the most popular pamphlet in revolutionary America was entitled "Common Sense."

Activity

Historiography

Historical interpretations give an ideological focus to any historical theme. They are based on the facts, as they present themselves, as well as the worldview of the evaluator. It is valuable to read the opinions of a variety of historians with distinct viewpoints. The different perspectives can be based on differences in emphasis, when reviewing the available data, statistics and information on the events of the time, as well as the way information is organized.

Here is an example of how contemporary historian Howard Zinn uses Thomas Paine's pamphlet *Common Sense* (1776) to support his analysis.

Tom Paine's *Common Sense*, which appeared in early 1776 and became the most popular pamphlet in the American colonies … made the first bold argument for independence in words that any fairly literate person could understand:

> Society in every state is a blessing, but Government even in its best state is but a necessary evil.

Thomas Paine dealt with the practical advantages of sticking to England or being separated; he knew the importance of economics: →

I challenge the warmest advocate for reconciliation to show a single advantage that this continent can reap by being connected with Great Britain. I repeat the challenge; not a single advantage is derived. Our corn will fetch its price in any market in Europe, and our imported goods must be paid for by them where we will.

As for the bad effects of the connection with England, Paine appealed to the colonists' memory of all the wars in which England had involved them, wars costly in lives and money:

> But the injuries and disadvantages which we sustain by that connection are without number. … any submission to, or dependence on, Great Britain, tends directly to involve this Continent in European wars and quarrels, and set us at variance with nations who would otherwise seek our friendship.

He built slowly to an emotional pitch:

> Everything that is right or reasonable pleads for separation. The blood of the slain, the weeping voice of nature cries, "TIS TIME TO PART"

In addition, here is an extract in which Howard Zinn explains how *Common Sense* was received by the élites in British North America: →

[Thomas] Paine's pamphlet appealed to a wide range of colonial opinion angered by England. But it caused some tremors in aristocrats like John Adams who were with the patriot causes but wanted to make sure they didn't go too far in the direction of democracy. Paine denounced the so-called balanced government of Lords and Commons [in Britain] as a deception and called for single-chamber representative bodies where the people could be represented. Adams denounced Paine's plan as "so democratical, without any restraint or even an attempt at any equilibrium."

Source: Zinn, Howard. 1980. *A People's History of the United States.* Harper & Row.

Questions

1 What do you think that *Common Sense* is about, based on this text?

2 How does Zinn summarize the main ideas of Paine's text? What do you think is his opinion of the pamphlet?

3 What is your impression of John Adams, based solely on this reading?

4 Do you believe Zinn's interpretation? Why or why not?

5 Is Zinn a valuable source for studying? Why or why not?

The political ideas that are considered to have the greatest impact on New World thinking were John Locke, Jean-Jacques Rousseau and Montesquieu. Their ideas on representative government, popular sovereignty and separation of the powers of the government helped shape regional or local governments prior to independence and central government structures after independence. These ideas presented the American colonists with alternatives to colonial rule and the philosophical justification to reject it.

As they occurred 20 to 30 years earlier, the US and French revolutions also helped shape Latin American independence. The successful overthrow of monarchies, especially by fellow colonists, inspired the leaders in Spanish America to take action.

The 13 colonies and the road to war, 1763–74

Changes began to take place after British success in the French and Indian War. The result of the war was that Great Britain wrested from France most of its North American colonial possessions, and Spain lost Florida (until 1783). Although Louisiana had remained French, it was ceded to Spain as compensation for its support in the war. The war led to a number of conflicts in the relationship between the government in London and the colonists.

An effect of the French and Indian War was that its campaigns gave many colonial officers and men valuable training in war, and enhanced their self-confidence. The war also helped to create an idea of unity among the colonies. So, too, did the spectacle of men from different provinces fighting side by side. State legislatures and officials also had to cooperate intensively, arguably for the first time, in pursuit of a continental military effort.

Colonial troops, although badly equipped and ill-disciplined, found on several fronts that they could fight as well as the British regulars—and in the wilderness could do better. They found many

"*All mankind ... being all equal and independent, no one ought to harm another in his life, health, liberty or possessions.*"

John Locke

"*All men have equal rights to liberty, to their property, and to the protection of the laws.*"

Jean Jacques Rousseau

"*Among the natural rights of the colonists are these: First a right to life, secondly to liberty, and thirdly to property; together with the right to defend them in the best manner they can.*"

Samuel Adams

"*They who can give up essential liberty to obtain a little temporary safety, deserve neither liberty nor safety.*"

Benjamin Franklin

English officers blundering, just as the British labeled many colonials as "incompetent". North Americans from all colonies resented the system whereby any British officer outranked all colonial officers. These lessons would assist the colonists in their push for independence.

Another result of the Seven Years' War that affected the poorer colonists was the agreement the British government made about limits to colonial lands. In the Proclamation of 1763, the British established a western frontier for their colonies and stated that British colonists could not settle west of the Appalachian Mountains. This was done to mollify the Native Americans that fought against them. The establishment of formal relations and regulations regarding trade and land purchases concentrated the colonial population so that British dominion was clearer. This upset colonists, especially frontiersmen who were already beyond the Ohio River valley and land speculators who would no longer have land to broker. It also angered those who felt that it was another method of controlling the British American population by concentrating them along the coastline.

Activity
History painting
Based on the postures and poses of the painting, what do you think was the outcome of the battle? When do you think this image was painted? Why do you think the artist made the British American force appear to be successful? How do you recognize the American soldiers? What was the real outcome of the battle?

This painting by American artist Junius Brutus Stearns shows the future president, George Washington (on horseback), at the Battle of Monongahela in 1755.

George Washington (1732–1799)

George Washington was a general and commander-in-chief of the Continental Army in the War of Independence (1775–83). Subsequently, he was the first president of the United States (1789–97). He was born into a landowning family in the colony of Virginia and was educated privately until the age of 15 at which point he had a brief career as a surveyor. In 1752, Washington inherited his brother's estate (Mount Vernon) and became a landowner and slaveholder himself. He was commissioned as a lieutenant colonel in 1754 and was later made the aide to General Edward Braddock. After Braddock was killed, Washington became the commander of the Virginia regiment in Ohio territory battling against the French and Native Americans in what became the French and Indian War. His service gave him valuable information about the strengths and weaknesses of the British army and he gained a reputation as a capable leader despite a lack of manpower and supplies. Both of these would prove useful to him in the future. In 1759, he resigned his commission to manage his estate and married the widow Martha Dandridge Custis, adopting her children as his own.

He began his political career as a member of Virginia's House of Burgesses (the elected lower house),

1759–74, and as tensions rose with the British he became a proponent of colonial rights. In 1774 he became a representative of Virginia to the Continental Congress, and in 1775 he was elected by the Congress to command the Continental Army against the British. Although he faced several defeats in the War of Independence, he was a successful and supportive leader of the men under his command. Most famously, he held together a malnourished and ill-equipped Continental Army at Valley Forge in the winter of 1777–78. After the British defeat at Yorktown (1781) he once again resigned his commission and returned to Mount Vernon. After the Treaty of Paris he continued his public service as a member of the Constitutional Convention. He was unanimously elected president of the United States by the state electors and was subsequently elected to a second term. By that time there were divisions in the politicians between federalists and democrats and he provided a moderating line that negotiated between the two factions. He declined to serve a third term and retired in 1797. He died at Mount Vernon in 1799.

The war had been very costly for the British; not only did its **national debt** double, but it also recognized that its policy of salutary neglect had given the British Crown very limited control over the colonies. For these economic and political reasons, the government in London decided it needed to tighten its hold on the colonies. A series of punitive laws were passed in the British Parliament to enable this, leading to resentment, hostility and rebellion by the colonists.

Three laws increasing taxes particularly infuriated the colonists. In the 13 colonies, local governments already levied taxes on their citizens to pay local officials and assist in defending the territories. The Sugar, Quartering and Stamp Acts all led to further burdens on the colonists. The Stamp Act of 1765 was seen as particularly offensive; all paper products were to be subject to a tax. Publishers, printers and lawyers objected to this as it affected their professions in particular. At this point, the educated classes found a rallying cry in the argument that they should not be subject to taxes implemented by a parliament in which they were unrepresented. The ensuing riots and boycotts against British imports forced the government to repeal the Act. Nonetheless, the seeds of discontent were sown and groups that could be considered seditionist such as the Sons of Liberty began to emerge.

On the repeal of the Stamp Act, London implemented yet another set of taxes on the colonies through the Townshend Acts (1767). These acts levied tariffs on glass, lead, paint, paper and tea. The Sons of Liberty had moved to boycott all products that were taxed, but the British Parliament still tried to enforce implementation by renaming the taxes "duties". This resulted in even stronger protests and violence. The economic boycott was effective and the Act was repealed with the exception of duties on tea. From protest to economic boycott, the movement advanced.

To coordinate their movements against the British, the individual provinces in the colonies began to convene a series of meetings to collaborate and prevent imperial domination. These "congresses", as they were called, had representatives from sovereign, independent political entities; they were not unitary legislative bodies. The congresses and committees of correspondence coordinated written communication and disseminated information. Here were the beginnings of unified actions and decision making.

Through all of this, many colonists remained loyal to the Crown; while they sought to overturn perceived injustices, they were not looking to break away from the mother country. But the last step towards independence began when the British Parliament passed the Tea Act (1773). Created to prevent the bankruptcy of the British East India Company, the Tea Act put a tax of threepence per pound of tea. This angered colonial merchants and smugglers alike who stood to lose the profits they were making without the taxes. The company granted franchises to certain colonial merchants, creating further resentment among those not granted franchises. Americans in general reverted to the idea born out of the Stamp Act: no taxation without

National debt is the sum of all money that a government owes to investors, both private and public. The British saw an escalation of their national debt after the Seven Years' War as a result of their fighting in North America. The war cost approximately £210,000 at the time or £289 million at current levels (based on average earning levels).

WILLIAM JACKSON,

an *IMPORTER*; at the

BRAZEN HEAD,

North Side of the TOWN-HOUSE,

and *Oppofite the Town-Pump, in*

Corn-hill, BOSTON.

It is defired that the SONS and DAUGHTERS of *LIBERTY*, would not buy any one thing of him, for in fo doing they will bring Difgrace upon *themfelves*, and their *Pofterity*, for *ever* and *ever*, AMEN.

Declaration of the Sons of Liberty, a secret movement founded in 1765 in opposition to British taxes.

Activity

You be the journalist

It is late March, 1770, and the following events have taken place in Boston. The facts:

- British troops first arrived in Boston in 1768 to enforce Townshend Acts.

- Civilians often harassed British soldiers as they walked the streets.

- On March 5, the 29th regiment arrived to relieve the 8th regiment and were met by a taunting crowd.

- Captain Thomas Preston ordered the crowd to disperse.

- The crowd remained and chanted, "Fire and be damned!"

- Preston ordered his troops, "Don't Fire!"

- British soldiers fired into the crowd.

- Five colonists were killed by British regulars.

You are a newspaper writer in either Philadelphia or London. How would you portray the events? What would you emphasize? What would you downplay? What would your headline be? Using these facts as your guide, write a 600–700 word analysis of the events of March 5, 1770, in Boston.

British troops entering Boston to enforce taxation and other colonial legislation before the US Revolution.

representation. The colonists organized a boycott of tea, successfully mobilizing much of the population. This mass protest culminated in the Boston Tea Party of 1773 when colonists, dressed as Native Americans, boarded ships and threw East India Tea into the harbor, costing the company £69,000 pounds (the equivalent of £6.8 million in retail value in 2008).

To compensate the East India Tea Company for its losses, the British Parliament passed the Coercive or Intolerable Acts; these laws closed down Bostonian commerce until the company was repaid for the destroyed tea. To respond in a uniform fashion, the **First Continental Congress** was convened in 1774; it asked King George III to repeal these Acts and coordinated a boycott of British imports and exports. The Continental Congress appealed to the King not as rebels or secessionists, but as loyal citizens who felt they were being treated unfairly. The independence movement was not yet a mainstream idea but the Continental Congress was the beginning of a united political front of 13 colonies in British North America that felt they had common grievances and desires for autonomy from the Crown.

A **congress** is a formal assembly of representatives from sovereign entities to discuss problems common to the entire group. Some British American colonies convened the First and Second Continental Congresses to address the conflicts they were having with Great Britain as a unified body.

Spanish America from the end of the Habsburgs to French occupation of Spain

Spanish America was equally affected by events in Europe. The 18th century saw a change of leadership in Spain: with the death of Charles II in 1700, Habsburg rule came to an end, and after the War of Spanish Succession (1701–14), Spain found itself under the Bourbon monarchy. Whereas the Habsburg rulers had been neglectful of their colonies, the Bourbons sought to tighten the administration of these possessions. Moreover, the French and Indian War had meant that Spain lost Florida, Havana and Manila to the British (albeit temporarily); Spain wanted to reassert its authority as an imperial power. Colonial reforms were part of a larger set of reforms meant to modernize the government and economy of declining Spain.

To achieve these aims the Bourbons introduced a series of reforms in Spanish America in the 1700s. The changes reflected the general concerns of the time, and addressed limiting the power of the Catholic Church, imposing taxes, maintaining royal monopolies, adding to colonial standing armies, limiting powers of the creole elite, and generally consolidating political and economic interests for the improvement of Spain. To a large extent they reversed the economic independence of the colonies. Much like the Intolerable Acts, these laws were a significant source of unrest, and laid the foundations for revolution led by the creole élite.

Administrative reorganization

One clear goal of the reforms was to improve the tax yield from America through restructuring imperial commerce to stimulate the Spanish economy. First, the Crown created two new viceroyalties: one for New Granada in 1717 (based in Bogotá); and the other, in 1776, for La Plata (based in Buenos Aires). The intendancy system was also introduced. Intendants were *peninsulares* who were appointed as officials to oversee military leadership, implement imperial law and collect taxes from the creoles and the native communities alike. Intendants were directly responsible to the Crown, not to the viceroys or generals. The intendancy system proved to be efficient in most areas and led to an increase in revenue collection for the Spanish Crown. The monarchy's need to raise revenue led the imposition of new taxes and the tightening of the tax collection system and a further outflow of bullion thus transferring riches to the Spain. In terms of tightening control over the colonies, this was a success, but the creoles who lost their standing were disgruntled by these changes and looked for opportunities to overturn or circumvent them.

Economic reorganization

In 1779, a free-trade decree was delivered that allowed the Spanish-American ports to trade directly with each other and with most ports in Spain, and forbade the production of certain commodities in the colonies to protect Spanish goods. Although these measures revitalized some sectors of the economy, the benefits to Spain were limited, given the lack of Spanish industrial manufacture. At the same time, many of the colonies began to extract resources that were useful to other European powers and the British colonies in North America and the Caribbean. However, most of this trade was illegal because it was not carried on Spanish ships. The Bourbon administration tried to limit and outlaw this trade but the efforts were largely futile; illegal trade continued. Adding to creole alienation, the Spanish trade monopoly was still dominated by *peninsular* import-export merchants who were given advantage simply by their place of birth.

Religious reforms

To limit the power of the Catholic Church, the Bourbons forced the sale of church lands. This deprived the clergy of rents, which was a significant source of income for parish priests. Unlike the Habsburgs, who often selected clergymen to fill political offices, the Bourbons preferred to appoint career military officers to oversee the colonies which meant that the church lost political authority as well. In 1767, the Jesuits were expelled from the Americas to limit their influence, especially in the field of education. Many of the priests expelled were creoles and thus were deprived of their homelands and missions. The lower clergy were permanently alienated from the Crown, and it was from their ranks that many of the insurgent officers and guerilla leaders were recruited. The church did not actively object or attempt to intervene, but in many cases the clergy were supported by devout laymen who had relations with fellow creoles and saw this as yet another attempt to limit their power.

Military defense

Another concern for the monarchy was the defense of its empire. The colonies barely had an operational military under the Habsburgs and so the Bourbons created a more organized military defense force. At first they tried to rely upon officers deployed straight from Spain but so few were willing to accept commissions in the Americas, so the Crown had to rely on colonial-born men to increase the officer corps. The Spaniards organized the militias along race lines so that there were individual units for whites, blacks and mixed-race people. Furthermore, nearly all the highest-ranking officers were Spanish-born, with creoles occupying the secondary levels of command. This added to racial tensions that would have to be addressed in later years.

While the creoles were most decisively restricted by these changes, all sectors of colonial society were hostile to Bourbon reforms. As in British North America, there was open resistance to the new laws, and in some places, they led to riots and revolts. In Perú, the rebellion of Túpac Amaru II (José Gabriel Condorcanqui Noguera) lasted from 1781 to 1793 and led to 100,00 deaths and tremendous property damage. Also in 1781, the Comuneros—a group of Indians and *mestizos*—rose up in New Granada against the Spanish Crown. These revolts, and the smaller ones that occurred throughout the empire, signaled increasing dissatisfaction with the Bourbon leadership.

In the midst of the turmoil in the colonies Napoleon I of France successfully invaded a weakened Spain and replaced the Bourbon monarchy with his brother Joseph in 1808. France's invasion of Spain had precipitated the abdication of Charles IV, and he was succeeded by his son, who became Ferdinand VII; the creoles throughout the Americas refused to recognize Bonaparte rule and instead claimed loyalty to Ferdinand. As with the British colonists in 1773, the creoles were, at this point, still loyal to the Crown but they saw an opportunity to assert their autonomy. The result was yet another series of revolts that would turn into a number of wars of independence in the viceroyalties.

Activity

The causes of wars of independence

You have been provided with an overview of the conditions in the Americas prior to independence. By examining these and determining how all of these are responsible—and to what degree—you can decide what you think caused these revolutions to take place.

Additionally, the historian must make clear the differences between the long-term causes and short-term causes. Long-term causes tend to be related to conditions; short-term causes concern specific events that may act as catalysts.

Using the chart below, consider the main issues that have been discussed so far and determine their role in revolution. These issues have been discussed in the text, however further research could be useful in order to develop the themes.

	North America	Spanish America
Long-term causes:		
Political	Self-government	Limited political participation of creoles The role of *cabildos* (town councils)
Economic		
Social	Class structure	Ethnic or racial structure
Religious		
Intellectual movements		
Short-term causes:		
Political	Changes to British colonial policies, 1760s	Bourbon reforms (throughout the 18th century) Spanish officials appointed directly by the Crown, territories better divided for administrative purposes
Economic		Free trade policy
Social		
Religious		
International events	French and Indian War (Seven Years' War), 1754–63	Peninsular War and French occupation of Spain

Questions for discussion

1   To what extent was the demand for no taxation without representation the most significant force motivating the North American independence movement?

2   "The grievances that the creoles held against peninsular Spaniards was the most significant cause of the independence movements." To what extent and for what reasons do you agree with this view?

The American War of Independence

Although they were unaware of it at the time, on April 19, 1775, the War of Independence began in Massachusetts. Fearing insurgency, members of the British Regular Army (as opposed to local militias) were sent to the town of Concord to take any military provisions that were being held there. Colonial militiamen resisted in both Concord and Lexington, forcing the British Regulars to retreat to Boston, which was then attacked by colonials.

A Second Continental Congress was convened that appointed George Washington as commander of the Continental army recognizing that he had much work to do with limited resources; this army was composed of untrained soldiers who had not yet been organized. Washington's social status and reputation as a successful officer in the French and Indian War made him the right choice to organize and oversee the army. In March 1776, the Continental army's cannons pointed at Boston and forced the evacuation of the British Regulars to Halifax, Nova Scotia. Knowing that he had the numerical advantage, Washington tried to force a fast victory by attacking the British in Montreal (Quebec). The colonial force lacked the strength for a sustained siege, so once the British retreated into the walled city, the colonials were at a loss. When reinforcements reached the British, the American army had to retreat to New York.

In 1776, it appeared that the British were gaining strength as they took both New York City and Philadelphia. Their strategy was to divide and conquer: the intent was to separate New England from the middle and southern colonies and then tackle one area at a time. Recognizing the military genius of Washington, they wanted him to remain isolated from other strong leaders.

Unfortunately for the British, the colonists used the type of warfare that worked to their advantage: guerrilla warfare. The Americans knew the territory well, and in particular could use the forested areas for refuge and attack. The British were often stumbling across natural barriers such as lakes or rivers that they didn't know of; making it necessary to reroute the soldiers, often into enemy areas where they were then ambushed. In 1777, General John Burgoyne suffered from this calamity and his battalion was forced to surrender at the battle of Saratoga.

While the fighting continued, the British offered conciliatory measures and there were offers for peace. After July 1776, however, the Americans were unwilling to accept any offer that did not include independence. Lexington and Concord were the turning points in which American colonists no longer desired autonomy; they now wanted complete freedom from the British Crown. This was articulated in the Declaration of Independence.

Discussion point

The question was not, whether by a declaration of independence, we should make ourselves what we are not, but whether we should declare a fact that already exists.

Thomas Jefferson on the reason for independence, June 1776.

Nationalism is not the awakening of nations to self-consciousness; it invents nations where they do not exist.

Ernest Gellner. *Thought and Change*, 1964

 Compare and contrast the meanings of the two quotations. Are the ideas presented here contradictory or can they apply to the same case?

Discussion point

Guerrilla warfare

In the colony of South Carolina, Francis Marion, known as the Swamp Fox, used guerrilla warfare against the British. This type of warfare includes:

● fighting a war of attrition (wearing the enemy down);

● using knowledge of the area to ambush larger, better-armed armies;

● employing "hit and run" tactics to minimize casualties.

What other examples of guerrilla warfare do you know of? In what instances is it more successful than conventional warfare? Why?

Declaration of Independence, 1776

At the beginning of the War of Independence, the objectives of the colonists were not entirely clear, even to those fighting. Once again, the Continental Congress was convened to decide the collective war aims for the 13 colonies. It was determined that the colonies had to present a united front, and that unanimity would be necessary for any decision: there were 56 representatives from the colonies with diverse and often disparate viewpoints represented. In June 1776, the Congress named the Committee of Five to write a statement of common action with the understanding that all representatives must approve the document for it to be released. The Committee included John Adams, Benjamin Franklin, Robert Livingston and Roger Sherman, but the true author of the draft would be Thomas Jefferson, a representative from Virginia. The draft was presented to the Congress which debated the terms and edited it so that they could reach consensus. The final product left most of Jefferson's words intact; this was to become the Declaration of Independence, which was approved on July 4, 1776. The Declaration was a formal statement of the liberation of the 13 colonies from Britain and the creation of a new country—the United States of America. The Declaration showed the commitment of these colonies to merge into one political unit that would work collectively to overthrow British rule. It also gave the rationale for independence and explained the grievances that the colonists had against King George III and the mother country.

Thomas Jefferson (1743–1826)

The third president of the United States and main author of the Declaration of Independence was born to wealthy landowners in the colony of Virginia. He attended the College of William and Mary and studied law. In 1772, he married Martha Wayles Skelton and went to his home in Monticello to run the estate.

He was a member of the House of Burgesses and then the Continental Congress; while a quiet member of Congress, he was an eloquent writer who used his talent to sway people to the cause of colonial autonomy. In 1774, he wrote "A Summary View of the Rights of British America" in which he criticized the Coercive Acts and justified colonial actions such as the Boston Tea Party not just on legal grounds but also as part of the natural rights of British Americans. At the age of 33, this "silent member" of the Congress was asked to draft the Declaration of Independence with the assistance of four others.

During the war he served as Governor of Virginia. In 1785, he replaced Benjamin Franklin as the US Minister to France and served as Secretary of State until his endorsement of the French Revolution led to conflict with other members of Washington's Cabinet, so he resigned in 1793.

As American politicians became polarized on the issue of the French Revolution and the nature of government, Jefferson became a supporter of the Democratic-Republicans against the Federalists. He was an opponent of strong central government and wrote vehement articles advocating states' rights. He ran for president in 1796 and lost to John Adams by three votes, becoming vice president, and in 1800 he was elected president by one vote. In his first term, the US acquired the Louisiana Purchase from France (1803) and he supported the Lewis and Clark expedition to explore the territory between the United States and the Pacific Ocean. In his second term, he confronted more pressing domestic issues in the wake of US expansion and sought to avoid his country's participation in the war between France and Great Britain. After his second term he retired to Monticello, selling his books to the US government to form the Library of Congress and founding the University of Virginia, the first non-sectarian university in the United States. He died on July 4, 1826, the 50th anniversary of the document that made him famous.

Activity

Extracts from the Declaration of Independence, July 4, 1776

Source A

When in the course of human events it becomes necessary for one people to dissolve the political bands which have connected them with another, and to assume … the separate and equal station to which the Laws of Nature and of Nature's God entitle them, a decent respect to the opinions of mankind requires that they should declare the causes which impel them to the separation.

Questions

1   In this passage, what is Jefferson explaining?

2   What does Jefferson mean when he wrote that "all men are created equal"?

Source B

We hold these truths to be self-evident, that all men are created equal, that they are endowed by their Creator with certain unalienable rights, that among these are Life, Liberty, and the pursuit of Happiness. That to secure these rights, Governments are instituted among Men, deriving their just powers from the consent of the governed. —That whenever any Form of Government becomes destructive of these ends, it is the right of the People to alter or to abolish it, and to institute new Government … Prudence, indeed, will dictate that Governments long established should not be changed for light and transient causes. … But when a long train of abuses and usurpations, pursuing invariably the same Object, evinces a design to reduce them under absolute Despotism, it is their right, it is their duty, to throw off such Government, and to provide new Guards for their future security. … The history of the present King of Great Britain is a history of repeated injuries and usurpations, all having in direct object the establishment of an absolute Tyranny over these States.

Questions

1   How are people allowed to pursue "unalienable rights"?

2   What are the "repeated injuries and usurpations" that Jefferson refers to?

Source C

We, therefore, the Representatives of the United States of America, in General Congress, Assembled, appealing to the Supreme Judge of the world for the rectitude of our intentions, do, in the Name, and by Authority of the good People of these Colonies solemnly publish and declare, That these United Colonies are, and of Right ought to be, Free and Independent States; that they are Absolved from all allegiance to the British Crown and that all political connection between them and the State of Great Britain is, and ought to be, totally dissolved; and that, as Free and Independent States, they have full Power to levy War, conclude Peace, contract Alliances, establish Commerce, and do all other Acts and Things which Independent States may of right do.

Questions

1   What is Jefferson stating in this concluding paragraph?

2   What rights do the "United Colonies" have?

General discussion

1   How does the Declaration reflect the historical context in which it was written?

2   Who was the primary intended audience?

3   What makes this so revolutionary for the time?

The Battle of Saratoga

The Battle of Saratoga represented a key turning point in the Revolutionary War. The advance of troops began when the British decided to send an army from Canada to take upstate New York and the Hudson River, to divide the Americans in New England from the rest of the colonies. After successfully taking Fort Ticonderoga from the patriots, the 6,000-man royalist army led by Major General Burgoyne advanced to the city of Albany which they found protected by 7,000 Americans led by Major General Gates.

September 19, 1777, marked the first Battle of Saratoga. The British attacked the patriots at Freeman's Farm and drove them into a retreat to Bemis Heights with substantial casualties on both sides. The British kept up their assault on the patriots but this only served to wear them down, so on October 7 the patriots decided to counterattack. The full-on attack stunned the British who were then forced to retreat; when they reached Saratoga, Burgoyne surrendered to the patriots.

The British never managed to sever ties between New England and the rest of the colonies, and seeing the success of the patriots, the French decided to support the cause of American independence. The colonies consolidated their control over the north, and the British switched their efforts to fighting in the south where they thought there was a greater chance of victory.

Foreign intervention: France, Prussia, Spain

At the beginning of the war, the Continental Congress met with the French to try and secure an alliance, although France was eager to reverse the fortunes of the British after their victory in the French and Indian War. In 1776, they began the covert support of the revolutionary forces by providing the Americans with armaments and use of their ports. Seeing the American success at Saratoga, the French were convinced of the viability of the American forces and in 1778 signed treaties of commerce and alliance with the newly-created United States of America. Spain and the Netherlands also joined the war on the side of the United States in 1779 and 1780 respectively.

The French proved to be an especially helpful ally on the high seas where the extent of the British Empire had stretched its navy thin, leaving it unable to patrol all areas. French, Spanish and Dutch navies prevented a British blockade of the United States and allowed provisions to continue to arrive, while also interrupting the flow of trade from the West Indies to Great Britain. In 1776 alone, the amount of sugar shipped to Britain was halved. However, the American victory over the British would prove costly to France, and the French Crown in particular; it cost the French more than the three previous wars

Discussion point

The soldiers returned to France with a feeling of success and victory. Having fought in a war that gave rights and privileges to ordinary citizens, how would these soldiers feel about returning homing to an absolutist regime? How did the US War of Independence affect France?

Discussion point

How has the scorched-earth policy been used in other wars?

it had fought put together. This left the French with a financial crisis that would ultimately end the regime of Louis XVI.

The British also received foreign assistance, with support from the German kingdoms and the Native Americans who feared American expansionism. Various members of the German Confederation provided 30,000 soldiers that served in the US War of Independence. Native Americans attacked frontier settlements in New York and Pennsylvania, often from bases in the Ohio territory to the west. The Continental Army retained control of the highly strategic Fort Pitt (located at the confluence of the Allegheny, Monongahela and Ohio rivers) and pursued a scorched-earth policy against the natives, destroying villages and crops, and making them a negligible force in the war.

The end of the war and the Treaty of Paris

In 1778, the British felt they needed to change their tactics and focused on the southern states instead. They believed that the southern colonies were more loyal and that resistance would collapse once they felt the force of armed combat in their regions. Once again, the British found themselves the target of guerrilla warfare and while they took the cities of Savannah, Georgia and Charles Town in South Carolina, they were unable to penetrate the inland territories. The American forces successfully undertook a policy of attrition, and while they lost most of the battles, they ultimately succeeded in wearing down the British. In 1781, Lord Cornwallis fought what proved to be the final major battle of the war. At Yorktown (Virginia) Washington and the French General Rochambeau trapped the Cornwallis forces on the peninsula of Yorktown with 17,000 soldiers. The French navy prevented British ships from landing and provisioning or reinforcing the British army, and Cornwallis surrendered his army of 7,000 men in October 1781.

The British government determined that it was more costly to continue the war, especially with French assistance to the Americans. The British agreed to a cease-fire with the Americans, but fighting against the French continued until 1782, when the British defeated the French navy in the Caribbean. In the Treaty of Paris (1783), the British formally recognized the independence of the United States of America and ceded all of its territory east of the Mississippi River and south of the Great Lakes. The United States demanded Canada, but the British rebuffed this and maintained its colonial possessions in America north of the Great Lakes. With this, the United States was now independent and could pursue its own destiny as an independent country. Its influence in the region and the world was yet to be established, but a precedent had been set: colonies could overthrow their imperial powers and establish their own state with its own structure of government. The influence of the mother country would be evident in the new state, but direct oversight was gone.

The Caribbean and Latin America: Revolution and independence

The revolution in the United States proved to be the first of a series of revolutions in the Americas that would lead to independence from France, Spain and Portugal, in chronological order. Each revolution had its roots not just in the Enlightenment but in the revolutions that had already occurred. Just like US independence, the Haitian revolution proved to be an important cause of the revolutions in Latin America. More immediately, the French Revolution and subsequent Napoleonic Empire provided the catalysts for change.

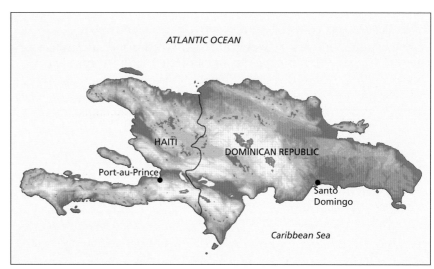

This is a modern map of Hispaniola; on the eastern third of the island is Haiti, or the French colony of Saint Domingue; on the west side was the Spanish colony of Santo Domingo.

The Haitian Revolution, 1791–1804

The Haitian Revolution brought forth ideas of racial equality that proved threatening to the rest of the Americas, especially to those regions that depended on slave labor. The revolution took place in the French colony of Saint Domingue, the eastern part of the island of Hispaniola. The island was important to France; it produced the important commodity of sugar and provided two fifths of its overseas trade. It had a plantation economy that relied on slavery to keep its level of production high. On the eve of the revolution, the population of Haiti was divided by race, legally and socially.

Whites were the dominant group in society, with a population of 40,000 that was divided by class, but equal in legal privileges. Similarly, the 30,000 free non-whites (*gens de coleur*) were also socially diverse and only linked by the legal and societal discrimination that they faced. The overwhelming majority of the population consisted of 500,000 slaves. While this might seem like a homogenous group, ethnically they were diverse, and the rights and privileges they had varied from plantation to plantation; some were even granted the right to farm their own land and sell their produce.

In 1789, the French Revolution provided the catalyst for change in the colony. The whites were divided as the wealthy (*grand blancs*) tried to ensure continued dominance for themselves but the middle and lower classes (*petit blancs*) felt it was their right to rule and formed a National Guard to take action. The *gens de coleur* saw the revolution as their opportunity for equal rights, and in 1790 the National Assembly in France granted them political rights. The whites

Discussion point

As a French colony, St. Domingue was part of an absolute monarchy. In such a society, how can there be differences between legal equality and racial equality?

Toussaint L'Ouverture (born François Dominique Toussaint Bréda) (1743–1803)

"I was born a slave but nature gave me the soul of a free man."

There is little known about his early years as Toussaint was born into slavery and there were few records about slaves beyond birth and death dates. Unlike many slave owners in St. Domingue, his master and plantation bosses were not harsh and violent, and he learned to read and write. At the age of 33 he was given his freedom, when he married and rented land to farm for himself and his family. When the slave rebellion of 1791 began, Toussaint recognized the need for the slaves to have military organization to defeat their overlords. In his rise, he temporarily joined forces with the Spanish in 1793 in adjacent Santo Domingo where he achieved fame and success in battle by finding an opening (*L'Ouverture*) where none seemed possible.

Capitalizing on his success as a military leader he first defeated the French army sent by the new, revolutionary government. At this point he turned his attentions to trying to organize and unite the colony through ousting the whites. Although he personally advocated leniency in the treatment of landowners, he was in the minority, and often had to face opposition within the rebel leadership. In late 1793, the British secured and alliance with the Spanish and, taking advantage of the chaos in the French colony, occupied most of the coastal towns. From 1793 to 1798, the blacks battled and defeated the British forces.

In 1799, the mulattos launched a rebellion against Toussaint and were soundly defeated by his armies. He then turned his attention to Santo Domingo (ceded to France by Spain in 1795) and governed the whole island. He was named the governor-general of St. Domingue and professed loyalty to France but nonetheless issued a constitution for the colony. Although he was a radical who desired change, he governed autocratically rather than democratically. Napoleon feared that Toussaint's constitution and dictatorial manner challenged his authority and renewed warfare against the colony once he concluded peace with the British. In 1802, Toussaint was betrayed by the French who summoned him to a meeting, captured him upon his arrival and bound him. He was put on a ship to France with his family and later imprisoned in the French Alps where he died of apoplexy and pneumonia on April 6, 1803.

"In overthrowing me, you have done no more than cut down the trunk of the tree of the black liberty in St. Domingue—it will spring back from the roots, for they are numerous and deep."

were determined to prevent the implementation of this through their own organization and the development of a colonial assembly. Thus in 1791, when members of the *gens de couleur* organized an armed demonstration to demand that their rights be granted, the leaders were seized and executed by the colonial government. Soon thereafter, the colony faced a series of revolts and riots across racial and class lines. In August 1791, the slaves in the northern part of the island revolted. By November, nearly half of the slaves were in revolt with the goal of ridding the colony of slavery and its white population. They attacked and destroyed the plantations and any whites that they encountered. Slaves who remained loyal to their masters faced a similar fate. The slave revolt eclipsed the conflicts between whites and *gens de couleur*. The whites became equally barbarous in their treatment of slaves and they managed to maintain control of the towns, but not for long. The slaves developed and perfected their use of guerrilla warfare.

A French attempt to restore order through enforcing the rights of the *gens de couleur* met with failure. In 1792, 6,000 French troops were dispatched to Saint Domingue to enforce French law and impose order on the colony. Instead, the fighting intensified as a number of groups battled against one another in a muddied civil war. In desperation, the French commissioner abolished slavery in 1793. While the French attempted to establish control, a leader of the slaves emerged: Toussaint L'Ouverture.

Toussaint proved to be a strong leader who managed to organize the blacks against the invading armies. After defeating the French, Toussaint thought that their fight would be over, but the British soon arrived, seeking to take advantage of the chaos and underestimating yet again the power of colonial armies. The French had declared war on Great Britain and colonial expansion seemed ripe for the taking. Gaining the support of white plantation owners, the British managed to gain control over key coastal areas but then found themselves fighting against multiple black armies. The invasion turned into a war of attrition that dragged on until 1798. The British leadership saw the fighting as futile and negotiated a peace in which they supported Toussaint in exchange for promises to allow trade to continue and to not send revolutionary expeditions to British possessions.

With British withdrawal the colony was in the hands of Toussaint and his blacks and the *gens de coleur*. These two groups turned against one another and engaged in further warfare. The *gens de coleur* were decisively defeated in 1800 and in 1801 Toussaint then turned to conquer the eastern, Spanish part of the island. The new French government—the Consulate—recognized Toussaint as Governor-General and commander-in-chief of the colony. Also in 1801, Toussaint put into place a constitution for the country. While Saint Domingue nominally remained part of the French empire, this was seen as a bid for independence by the French leader Napoleon. In January 1802, Napoleon sent an expeditionary force to the island to prevent it from breaking free from the empire. Toussaint, after initial resistance, attempted negotiations with the French but instead they arrested him and sent him to France where he was imprisoned. Sent to a jail in the Alps, he died of malnutrition and exposure.

While this happened, the French fought against Haitian guerrillas. In May 1803, the French resumed the Napoleonic war with Great Britain and thus lacked the resources to continue fighting against the Haitian revolutionaries. While the guerrillas besieged the coastal towns the French now had to contend with the British navy, too. Keeping Haiti had been very costly for Napoleon and in November he decided to evacuate the remaining French soldiers.

On January 1, 1804, the republic of Haiti was proclaimed, the name change representing a break with Europe and its traditions. Very few whites remained, and the blacks were in power in the new country. It was governed by Jean-Jacques Dessalines, Toussaint's faithful lieutenant who implemented a ruthless military rule and even crowned himself Emperor of Haiti. His brutality included the massacre of all remaining whites on the island and a return to plantation labor to resuscitate the economy. He co-opted the *gens de coleur* to oversee the plantations as Africans once again worked in the fields in harsh conditions. He immediately faced opposition for this and was

The rebellion of the slaves in Santo Domingo, August 23, 1791, French school, 18th century.

assassinated in 1806. Although the whites were gone, Haitian society remained stratified. The *gens de coleur* replaced the whites as the dominant group. The black masses remained below them. Haiti was a beacon of hope for abolitionists in North America, and a warning for the creole population in Spanish America.

Spanish–American wars of independence

The United States War of Independence recognized the unity of 13 of Britain's colonies against a common enemy, but the Spanish Americans who sought independence did not form a similar united front. Instead, they were divided geographically, and not just into the four **viceroyalties**; in most cases they were further divided and fought not only against Napoleonic France and later Spain but also against each other.

These independence movements began more than 30 years after the US Revolution but had much deeper roots; the creoles' social and economic resentments against the Spanish and *peninsulares*, who dominated after the Bourbon reforms were implemented, sought change. Likewise, in many places the *castas* that resented their secondary status saw an opportunity to press for equality. These wars, therefore, were mired not just in the drive for political independence but also the desire for social equality. The resulting wars were long, bloody affairs that often created further tensions rather than allaying them.

Spanish Americans were encouraged and inspired by both the US and French revolutions. Equally, they were terrified by the results of the Haitian revolution and their own wars of independence were informed as much by a desire to prevent such an uprising as to create new, independent republics. Taking into account the local situation, they sought to created political structures that were workable; this meant the creation of a number of new countries out of the viceroyalties; rather than unification, there was balkanization.

Using their historical loyalties to the Bourbon monarchy and not the state, creoles in the viceroyalties refused to recognize Napoleon I's brother Joseph Bonaparte as the king of Spain and began their struggle with an argument that, without a king, the people were sovereign. Much like their North American counterparts, the creole rebellion began as a push for autonomy, not an outward demand for independence. They thus created their own independent governing bodies that would rule until Fernando VII was restored. These **juntas** were rejected or opposed by peninsular officials who did all that they could to block the establishment of creole bodies, further exacerbating resentment and pushing the creoles towards a drive for independence. The creoles subsequently lost what confidence they had in the remnants of imperial leadership and revolted.

While the risings happened concurrently, the nature of the independence wars varied from place to place. Each area had its own leaders with their own philosophies and agendas. In the northern viceroyalty of New Spain, Father Hidalgo sought to bring about a social revolution; in New Granada (modern-day Colombia), the leaders were trying to preempt a potential slave rebellion like the one they had seen

Viceroyalty After the conquest of the Americas, Spain divided the colonies into administrative units led by a viceroy who ran the territory in the name of the monarch.

Discussion point

Balkanization is the fragmentation or division of a geopolitical entity. Why is this term now used to describe this phenomenon?

Junta A group of people controlling a government, especially after a revolutionary seizure of power.

Discussion point

How and why have juntas been put into place in the Americas in the 20th century?

in Haiti. In both cases the creole leaders were addressing the issues that faced their own region's resources, demography and geography.

In 1814, with the collapse of the French Empire, Ferdinand VII was restored to the Spanish throne. This signified an important change, since most of the political and legal changes on both sides of the Atlantic had been done in his name. Ferdinand was an absolutist who disapproved of the political changes undertaken in the Napoleonic period. A similar reverse occurred in the colonies and to address it Ferdinand organized the largest expeditionary force that Spain had ever sent to the Americas up to that time. Ferdinand launched a counterrevolution that, in effect, constituted a definitive break with the autonomous local governments, which had not yet declared formal independence. The governments of these regions, which had their origins in the juntas of 1810, and even moderates there, who had entertained reconciliation with the Crown, now saw the need to separate from Spain.

New Spain and the cause of Mexican independence

The viceroyalty of New Spain had the largest population and was one of the most ethnically diverse colonies. On September 16, 1810, Father Miguel Hidalgo began the Mexican revolution in earnest with his *Grito de Dolores*, a call for independence from Spain that appealed not just to the creoles but to Native Americans, *mestizos*, free blacks and mulattos. He saw not just the political oppression of Spain that the creoles wanted to redress, but also the problems that the lower classes faced: hunger, poverty, lack of land and high taxes. His program called for redistribution of land, abolition of slavery and an end to **Indian tribute**. His plan led to the insurrection of the masses that terrified the creoles and *peninsulares* alike. An estimated 80,000 joined his army, but they were not disciplined or organized and chaos soon reigned. The *peninsulares* and creoles took advantage of this, using both the royal army and local militias to defeat Hidalgo's warriors. Hidalgo himself was captured and executed in 1811.

Indian tribute Resources or taxes that the indigenous populations of Spanish America had to pay to the Spanish Crown.

This did not stop the revolution in Mexico, however. While the royalists managed to control the cities, the countryside was in the hands of a number of insurgent groups. In southern Mexico, another priest became the leader of the revolutionary movement. Father José Maria Morelos fought against the royal army and in 1814 drafted the Constitutional Decree for the Liberty of Mexico, thereby establishing an independent republic. As in the United States, the declaration of independence appeared after the war had begun. Unlike US independence, Mexico's would be infused by Catholicism (the only tolerated religion), and include the abolition of slavery. Like Hidalgo, Morelos was captured and executed, but his ideas helped keep the wars of independence going. Mexico faced years of guerrilla warfare where there were no decisive or clear battles but instead a prolonged war of attrition.

Mexican élites began to recognize that independence was looming and that they could create a state in which they played a dominant role or leave it to the masses. Thus, creoles, the Catholic hierarchy, *peninsulares* and military leaders collaborated to create an independent Mexico. Led by Agustín de Iturbide, they developed the Plan de Iguala which had three clear guarantees: independence from the Spanish Crown, the supremacy of the Roman Catholic Church and equality for *peninsulares* and creoles. In the meantime, Iturbide's forces succeeded on the battlefield and defeated the royalist forces. He then pressured the Spanish political chief Juan O'Donojú to sign the Treaty of Córdoba that recognized an independent Mexico.

The plan preserved the social order in Mexico—which, ultimately, only delayed civil war—and created an independent sovereign state. It also called for the establishment of a monarchy, but the Bourbons refused to send any family members. As a result, Iturbide became Emperor of Mexico in 1822.

Our Lady of Guadalupe

In 1531, the Virgin Mary appeared to converted Mexican native Juan Diego and this image appeared on his cloak. This icon became the symbol of Mexican masses that rebelled against the Spanish Crown and sought independence and social equality during the Mexican War of Independence. The Virgin is the patron saint of Mexico and remains an important symbol; in the Mexican Revolution (1910–20), Zapata's followers carried the Virgin on standards into battle and today it is common to see her in churches, on t-shirts and even as a tattoo in Mexico and the southwestern United States.

The Republic of Venezuela

In Venezuela, as in Mexico, the creoles were united by class interests in addition to a desire for national sovereignty. There had already been localized calls for independence from Francisco de Miranda, a Venezuelan revolutionary who led a war for independence in 1806. On July 5, 1811, the creoles declared an independent Republic of Venezuela that represented their liberal political agenda and the preservation of their power base. They advocated a franchise based on property and the elimination of the slave trade but not slavery. It became very clear that this was a creole revolution and that non-whites were not included. The royalists capitalized on this and recruited non-whites. The Venezuelan war was not just a war against Spain but also a civil war. A Spanish officer, José Tomás Boves, led a largely mixed-race army that was responsible for some of the bloodiest battles against the creole patriots. In 1814, Boves entered Caracas, instituting a reign of terror and bringing down the republic. Spain took advantage of the chaos and dispatched 11,000 soldiers to Spanish America and retook Caracas in May 1815.

Spanish occupation seemed to revitalize the Venezuelan independence movement and united the diverse forces. Its leader, Simón Bolívar, reinforced support for the cause of liberation and he welcomed all races into his armies. The need for more support brought equality; non-whites who supported the royalist cause saw their rights repealed and joined the patriots. Understanding that his own personal attitude set an important example, Bolívar freed his own slaves.

The Spanish were fighting in multiple theaters and had to make decisions on where to fight. Forces were split, there was a deterioration of morale and war-weariness was prevalent in the Spanish army. In 1820, events in Spain once again intervened on the patriots' behalf. An army coup led to the restoration of more liberal laws and a weakened Spanish army had to negotiate with the patriots.

The Spanish withdrew but did not recognize the new states; nonetheless, Venezuela had won its independence, initially as part of **Gran Colombia** (modern Ecuador, Colombia, Panama and Venezuela). In 1830, Venezuela and Ecuador both seceded and became independent republics.

Formerly the viceroyalty of Nueva Granada, **Gran Colombia** was formed in 1819 during the wars of independence from Spain. It dissolved in 1830 with the secession of Venezuela and Ecuador, and also includes the modern states of Colombia and Panama.

Foreign intervention in Spanish America

Foreign assistance was significant but less so than in North America. Although the British had initially supported revolution in Venezuela, Napoleon's invasion of Spain had transformed Spain into an ally of Britain, and the forces pledged to the patriots instead went to fight in the peninsular war. After this, the Venezuelans received no support from Europe or the United States. While individual North Americans provided assistance to Spanish American patriots, and US public sympathy was clearly on their side, there was no official recognition or assistance from the United States government. The patriots did, however, receive support from Haitian president Alexandre Pétion who provided money, volunteers and weapons which enabled the patriots to continue the struggle for independence on the condition that Bolívar expand the fight for independence to include the liberation of slaves, a promise that he kept.

Of greater significance in the armed struggle was the role of foreign volunteers. Fighting under Bolívar's command were the British **Legion** units composed of volunteers that consisted mainly of Napoleonic War veterans as well as some German veterans. In March 1819, Bolívar combined most of his foreign volunteers into a brigade of 250 men with James Rooke as commander. The British Legions consisted of the 1st British Legion led by Colonel James Towers English, the 2nd British Legion led by Colonel John Blossett, and the Irish Legion, led by Colonel William Aylmer. The British Legions played a pivotal role in the Vargas Swamp Battle on July 25, 1819, and Bolívar credited them for the victories at the subsequent battles of Boyaca and Carabobo. Bolívar called them "the saviors of my country".

Foreign legions are small military units composed of foreign volunteers. Numerous foreign legions participated in the wars for independence in the Americas.

Simón Bolívar and José de San Martín

Two men provided military leadership that went beyond the borders of their own nations—Simón Bolívar and José de San Martín. They are considered to be the two leading figures in the struggle for Latin American independence. They both understood that independence for part of Spanish America would mean independence for all, and thus they fought on the battlefields not just in their own countries but throughout the region. They met only once, on July 26, 1822, in Guayaquil (Ecuador) and while they had similar objectives they had very different ideas on the organization, structure and forms of government for the new nation states.

Bolívar's political goal was unity for South America and his acceptance of the leadership of Gran Colombia (Ecuador, Colombia, Venezuela) in 1819, showed this determination. He believed that sovereignty belonged to the majority who were non-white, but feared the tyranny of this dominant class and thus established a dictatorial system that he called "able despotism." He imposed a strong executive to enforce legal equality where racial inequality prevailed. He also rewarded military leaders for their service in the war through allocation of land, giving them local dominance. As he was often away fighting the battles of the continent, he needed to delegate authority to strong men whom he hoped would implement his reforms. Frustrated by his inability to change the interrelated race and class systems in Gran Colombia, and wracked with illness, he was disillusioned by the power he wielded. An assassination attempt in 1828 further weakened him and his government had the problems of debt, a disorganized military and civil discontent.

Simón Bolívar (1783–1830)

It is difficult to provide a chronological account of the military and political leadership of Bolívar as he served in both capacities concurrently. The liberator of northern South America, Simón Bolívar was a wealthy creole Venezuelan who was orphaned early in life and educated by private tutors. Like many members of the Spanish-American élite, he lived and studied in Europe from 1804 to 1807, learning from the ideas of the Enlightenment and rejecting the tyranny of Napoleon Bonaparte whose conquest of Europe he experienced. He also toured the United States and observed what he saw as a successful constitutional democracy that could be implemented in his mother country. Upon his return to Venezuela, he helped mobilize his countrymen who desired independence from Spain (now being ruled by Joseph Bonaparte). When the Venezuelans opted for self-government Bolívar was dispatched to Great Britain to gain the support of its government. Upon his return, he found the country in civil war as royalists battled against patriots. He initially fought for the cause of independence but was forced into exile in Jamaica in

1815 after a defeat at the hands of royalist forces. While in exile he wrote "Letter from Jamaica" which was an exhortation to the British for assistance in the Spanish-American battle for independence.

Bolívar also spent time in Haiti where he received promises of assistance from President Pétion. He then went to New Granada (Colombia) to continue his fight for independence. There he received a commission and 200 soldiers under his command. He attacked royalist forces and battled for independence, first in Venezuela. In 1819 he crossed the Andes and assisted with the conquests of New Granada and Ecuador. This time, he was successful in his battles, steadily taking territory and consolidating northern South America as independent and republican. His final battle was the cavalry battle of Junín, fought for the final liberation of Perú on August 7, 1823.

In 1830, he addressed the Congress, saying, "Fellow citizens, I am ashamed to say it, but independence is the sole benefit we have gained, at the sacrifice of all others." He renounced his presidency and, on December 17, 1830, died from tuberculosis and exhaustion.

> "*Americans; Let us no longer be the object of the sarcasm of those wretched Spaniards who are superior to us only in wickedness, while they do not excel us in valor, because our indulgence is what gives them their strength. If they appear great to us, it is because we are on our knees. Let us avenge three centuries of shame. War alone can only save us through the path of honor!*"
>
> Simón Bolívar,
> October 1812, Cartagena.

José Francisco de San Martín Matorras
(1778–1850)

San Martín, the Argentine son of a Spanish officer, was the liberator of southern South America. Although born in Argentina, he was sent to Spain in 1786 for formal education and military training. He served in the Spanish army, first in Murcia and later against the French invasion after 1808. He served with distinction in the battles of Bailén (1808) and Albuera (1811) but he could not advance further in the Spanish army; even though he had lived most of his life in Spain he was discriminated against because he had been born in America. He then moved to Cadiz where he met other creoles and was introduced to men advocating independence. In 1811, he resigned his commission in the Spanish army so he could return to Argentina after 25 years in Europe.

As a seasoned, experienced military leader San Martín was given a commission and created the cavalry corps for the Argentine army. The Mounted Grenadiers first faced action in 1813 when they were called upon to fight against recently arrived Spanish forces in San Lorenzo, near Montevideo. He was also given command of the northern army after General Belgrano was defeated in Upper Perú. After such difficult battles San Martín felt that it would be best to attack the royalist forces not in Argentina but in Chile and made a difficult trek with his army to reach the other side of the continent. The Army of the Andes succeeded in its task and joined with Chilean patriots led by Bernardo O'Higgins. The combined army defeated the Spanish at the Battle of Chacabuco in 1817 and liberated Chile.

Although he was offered leadership of Chile, San Martín deferred to the Chilean O'Higgins and continued the battle for independence. In 1818 he won the Battle of Maipú, completing the liberation of Chile and moved on to Perú. His army successfully took Lima in 1821 and he was given the title of "protector" over that country. Bolívar was also advancing his army, and the two men met in Guayaquil in 1822. The subject of the meeting remained a secret but San Martín resigned his commission, abdicated from his position of protector and retired from private life, leaving the final conquest of Perú to Bolívar. In 1824 San Martín went to France where he died impoverished and in exile, in 1850. His remains were later transferred to Buenos Aires.

Activity
Leadership

Simón Bolívar, José de San Martín and George Washington

These men provided military and political leadership that was critical to their countries' independence from the mother countries.

Complete the table.

Name	Simón Bolívar	José de San Martín	George Washington
Dates	1783–1830	1778–1850	
Family background	Wealthy creole	Spanish officer	
Country			
Key battles		Chacabuco	Valley Forge
Military leadership		Army of the Andes	
Political leadership			First president of the United States
Quotations			

Learner profile link

Principled

Spaniards and Canadians, count on death, even if indifferent, if you do not actively work in favor of the independence of America. Americans, count on life, even if guilty.

Simón Bolívar, June 15, 1813 in Trujillo, Venezuela

Bolívar's statement represented a full-blown assault on Spaniards. It legitimized death to all Spaniards who did not overtly support the independence movements. Patriots often committed atrocities against the Spaniards and vice versa.

 Can systematic extermination ever be justified?

As Bolívar's forces fought in the north, San Martín's Army of the Andes had crossed into Chilean territory and engaged the royalist army there with the assistance of Chilean leader Bernardo O'Higgins in the Battle of Chacabucho in February 1817. The reason for crossing the Andes was that the strongest of the royalist armies was in Perú and San Martín felt that the liberation of all Spanish America—including his homeland Argentina—was dependent upon expelling the Spanish from the entire continent. Thus, he led his army in a grueling, high-altitude trek through mountain passes, losing one third of his men and over half of his horses.

Realizing that patriot forces had crossed the Andes, royalists raced to the frontier to try to block them from continuing to Santiago. Despite the losses, San Martín's forces outnumbered the royalists 4,000 to 1,500 but the royalists were expecting reinforcements. Royalist strategy was to delay the patriot army until the needed reinforcements arrived.

Bernardo O'Higgins (1778–1842)

Bernardo O'Higgins was the illegitimate son of Ambrose O'Higgins, an Irish-born governor-general of Chile, and Isabel Riquelmes, daughter of wealthy Creoles. Bernardo was first sent to Perú, then Spain and finally England for his formal education. When studying in England, he met Francisco Miranda, one of the earliest proponents of Spanish American independence. Upon his father's death in 1801, he returned to Chile both as a farmer and local politician.

When the Napoleonic wars led to a debate over the future of Spanish America, O'Higgins sided with those who advocated full independence. Lacking in military training, he commissioned Colonel Juan MacKenna to train him, and he formed two cavalry units out of his farmhands. In 1814, his armies were met by defeat at the hands of better equipped and trained royalists and had to retreat to Argentina. At this point he made plans with San Martín as his army regrouped and trained to face the royalists again.

In 1817, San Martín's army crossed the Andes, defeated the royalists and took Santiago. As the highest-ranking member of the Chilean army, O'Higgins was made Supreme Director of Chile (after San Martín graciously declined) and instituted economic, political and social reforms designed to create a new, modern state. He was, however, opposed by the well-connected creoles who resented his changes as he threatened their domination over Chile. In 1823, O'Higgins resigned and left Chile for Perú. Although he was permitted to return to Chile, his health deteriorated substantially and he could not risk the arduous journey. Nonetheless, he remained actively interested in Chilean politics and urged a strengthening of the army and expansion to the Straits of Magellan. He died in 1842 in Lima, and his remains were buried in Santiago, Chile, in 1866.

San Martín knew that he had a narrow window of opportunity and took it. The patriot forces had the assistance of Chilean fighters led by Generals O'Higgins and Soler.

To defeat the royalists, San Martín divided his army in two. The first group, led by O'Higgins, was supposed to divert attention by attacking the left flank of the royalist forces. In the meantime, Soler's group was supposed to attack from the right and encircle the army. By launching simultaneous attacks, they hoped to confuse the Spanish forces. O'Higgins' forces advanced more quickly than expected, but Soler managed to follow through and encircle the Spanish, while O'Higgins continued to hammer away at the front of the army. The royalists suffered 500 dead and 600 captured compared to 12 fatalities for the patriots in battle (although 100 more died of their wounds later). Royalist survivors fled and San Martín and O'Higgins entered Santiago as victors. Although the patriots would have to defeat the Spanish one more time at Maipú in April 1818, this battle gave the Chileans control of their capital and allowed them to being creating a government.

Activity
The Battle of Chacabuco, 1817

The Battle of Chacabuco painted by the Argentinian artist Pedro Subercasseux in the 19th century.

Undertake further research to answer the following questions about the Battle of Chacabuco

1   What is the political importance of this battle?

2   What is the national significance of this battle for Chile?

3   Why is O'Higgins so revered in Chile?

Brazil's path to independence

Brazil's path to independence was somewhat diferent. As in Spanish America, the Napoleonic Wars provided the first engine for change. Unlike the other revolutions of this era, the élites that determined the time for independence was at hand did not face imperial resistance and thus did not need to enlist the masses. This was a revolution from above that brought about reforms yet still maintained the social order, including slavery.

Like Spain, Portugal had adopted mercantilist principals so that the mother country would benefit from colonialism. Laws that prohibited manufacturing in Brazil had been passed, and no foreign ships were allowed in Brazilian ports. In commerce, Portugal had long been dependent on Brazilian goods. In the 18th century it established a positive trade balance with other European countries but had a trade deficit with Brazil. Unlike Spanish America, in Brazil there was no competition between the Portuguese and native-born élites: a sense of unity in the empire was fostered by the events of the early 19th century in Europe.

In 1807, Napoleon invaded and occupied Portugal. The royal family fled to Brazil under the protection of the British navy and established the government in Rio de Janeiro which Prince Dom João (regent for

"O vivir con honor o morir con gloria! El que sea valiente que me siga!" ("*We can live with honour or die with glory! If you have the courage, follow me!*")

Bernardo O'Higgins

Discussion point

Why did Bolívar, O'Higgins and San Martín, all of whom led their countries to victory, end up exiled?

his mother Queen Maria) made the capital of the Portuguese Empire. With the presence of the royal court came privileges and Brazil was provided with a national bank, a library, universities and printing presses. More importantly, Dom Joao opened Brazilian ports to foreign trade and revoked decrees that prohibited certain manufacturing in Brazil.

Even though the British liberated Portugal in 1811, the royal court remained in Brazil. In 1815 Brazil was made a kingdom equal to Portugal and when Queen Maria died, Joao was proclaimed king of both Portugal and Brazil. The élites in society saw real benefits in a dual monarchy in which they were equal to the Portuguese. While the Brazilians seemed complacent with their status, the Portuguese were disturbed and wanted their king to return to Portugal. By 1820, this led to a rebellion that became the Portuguese revolution that created a junta and demanded the return of the king.

Dom João returned to Portugal in 1821 but left his son behind in Brazil as regent. The Portuguese Cortes created wrote a constitution that clearly outlined its plans to re-establish Brazil as a colony. The Cortes then demanded the return of the prince regent, and at that point Brazilians felt that the time had come for independence. They asked Dom Pedro to remain and on September 7, 1822, he declared the independence of Brazil and was crowned emperor in December. In May 1823, he convened a constituent assembly to establish a liberal government.

The assembly created a system of government that limited the power of the emperor more than he liked, so in November he dissolved it and asked his advisors to draft a constitution. The Constitution of 1824 included a bicameral legislature in which the lower house was indirectly elected by male suffrage. The members of the upper house were selected by the emperor and served life terms. The emperor could veto all legislation that was passed by either house and he had the right to dissolve the legislature when he thought necessary. He also appointed the cabinet and could dismiss ministers at will. It created a highly centralized state in which provincial presidents were also appointed by him. Catholicism was the state religion and the emperor was the head of the church. This constitution endured until the end of the monarchy in 1889.

A number of historians have made the argument that Brazilian independence was bloodless, but that is not entirely true. Portuguese troops had been dispatched to reestablish colonial dominance. Their adversaries were generally guerrilla groups whose tactics wore out a numerically superior and better armed army. The situation was so explosive that Dom Pedro asked the British for safe passage and asylum in the event of a full-blown civil war. In the end, there were no major battles in the war, and Dom Pedro turned away subsequent Portuguese soldiers, preventing them from landing in Brazilian ports and sending out supplies so that they could make the return trip.

Discussion points

1   What made Brazil different; how did it avoid the lengthy, costly, bloody struggles of the other independence movements?

2   "A creole élite led by the Crown prince decided it was necessary to secede from the empire." How far do you agree with this assessment of Portuguese independence?

Foreign relations in the Americas, 1810–1823

The United States was surprised and heartened by the independence wars that began in Spanish America. However, its attitude towards the wars was inhibited by its relations with Europe. Just as the Napoleonic wars were the catalyst for these independence movements, so they also brought about perceived opportunities for the United States. But the United States did not take the formal step of recognizing the Spanish American states. Seeking to take advantage of British distractions in Europe, the United States fought and lost the War of 1812 against the British. Its formal reactions to independence were subordinated by its disputes with Britain.

The Spanish American wars were certainly helpful to the United States as they weakened Spanish ties to areas that were of interest to them, such as Florida. The US government adopted a very genial attitude towards the revolutionaries as early as 1810. And, while they did not formally recognize the new governments, the encouraged them and advised them on how to purchase arms, munitions and ships to further the cause of independence. There was, however, no direct involvement of North Americans in Spanish America.

The United States had three sound reasons for this support: expansionist aims, trade with the provinces and ideological sympathy. The first two give evidence of US aims in light of their war with Britain and the changes in trade that they faced after their own independence. The last was equally important; Americans wanted to see the Spanish American independence movements succeed so that other countries could benefit from their form of government and their freedom from empire.

After their loss to the British in 1815, the United States had no desire to fight what might mean another war against a European power. Helping Spanish America to liberate itself was too risky. Thus, the United States adopted a policy of formal neutrality and recognized Fernando VII as leader of Spanish America after his restoration. The US government placed informal agents in all of the main cities of Spanish America rather than the official consuls that were placed in other foreign countries.

Nonetheless, illegal support for the revolutionaries continued, often encouraged by the US government, who counseled the Spanish American patriots on how to purchase arms and munitions. US merchants traded with them, providing them with necessary goods. Ships were built in the United States and then exported to the south (so long as they were unarmed when they left the United States). In fact, US neutrality laws were repeatedly violated by US merchants.

Although the Spanish ambassador Luis de Onís protested against these actions, he realized that the United States would not enforce neutrality unless it stood to gain from doing so. The United States wanted Spain to withdraw from Florida and Texas. Unless the Spanish took this seriously, they would gain no headway regarding violations of neutrality. Taking advantage of Spanish weakness, the

United States invaded Florida in 1818 under the pretext of pacifying natives who had crossed the frontier into the US. The combination of events led to the Adams–Onís Treaty in 1819; both countries agreed to cancel all claims they had on each other and Spain relinquished Florida and the Mississippi River as the US frontier was extended further west.

In the meantime, Spanish American independence was gaining in popularity among US citizens who were intrigued by the battles waged by San Martín and Bolívar. They read about these in local newspapers and began to agitate for their government's recognition of the new countries. Those with influence appealed to the United States government for recognition but events in Spanish America made the administration cautious. In the early 1820s, a rebel victory was an uncertainty and the United States did not want to alienate Spain if in the end they defeated the revolutionaries. Secretary of state John Quincy Adams argued that recognition did not come from the right to independence, but the certainty of it. In 1822, the probability of independence was much higher and so the United States officially recognized the states of Gran Colombia and Mexico. The United States was the first country outside of Spanish America to recognize the new nations.

The Monroe Doctrine

On December 2, 1823, James Monroe, president of the United States, gave his annual message to Congress, and in it he addressed the relationship between the Americas and Europe. This part of his address is now known as the Monroe Doctrine and the core ideas expressed therein became the center of continental relations for over a century.

Just as Spain and Portugal were losing their colonies, other European countries seemed poised to act and expand in the Americas. Most threatening to the United States were the Russians, who had claimed the Pacific coast from Alaska down to the 51st parallel (and coastal waters 100 miles from the Bering Strait), and the French, whom the US feared sought to reassert themselves as a world power through further expansion.

As Latin American countries became independent, the United States saw opportunities for good relations, the formation of other democracies and the spread of commerce all in the Western Hemisphere. At the same time Europe saw the Americas as open territories; all had interests in the region and a certain amount of strength, especially in the Caribbean. North Americans feared that European intervention in the south could lead to intervention in the north.

The British had been hoping to make a joint declaration with the United States that would prevent further European expansion in the Americas but the US decided to act alone. The Monroe Doctrine originated as a statement of the right of self-protection; it was not directed at European possessions in the region but intended to prevent other powers from taking advantage of the newly independent states of Latin America. It was also an attempt at pacification: since its inception the United States had been at war three times and Latin America had been in conflict since 1803.

The Monroe Doctrine warned Europe to stay out of the affairs of the Western hemisphere. It stated that the United States would not tolerate further colonization or puppet governments in the Americas. It further stated that European powers should stay out of hemispheric affairs. There was no clear policy on what the United States would do if the Monroe Doctrine were violated but the European powers accepted it, and it became policy.

Initially, the Latin American countries liked the doctrine; Colombia and Brazil endorsed it themselves. At the end of a long, costly struggle, continental solidarity seemed desirable ideologically and pragmatically. However, it would soon come clear to them that the North Americans were ambitious and openly imperialistic; they sought much of the same territory that they were ostensibly protecting from European encroachment. After initial jubilation, Latin Americans came to view the policy warily. It did not prevent expansion; it warned off the Europeans so that the North Americans could expand themselves.

"That wicked man is going to gobble you up, my child!"

Uncle Sam saying to Cuba "That wicked man is going to gobble you up my child", 1901 cartoon.

 This cartoon was published in 1901. What is the meaning of the cartoon and what does it say about the evolution of the Monroe Doctrine?

Activity

The Monroe Doctrine

The following is an excerpt from the note sent by President Monroe to the US Congress in December 1823 that would later form the basis of the Monroe Doctrine.

Questions

1　In your own words, what does the Monroe Doctrine state?

2　Under what specific situations would the United States, according to the doctrine, take action against European powers?

3　How might the doctrine apply to US policy with regards to 19th-century:

- California
- Oregon
- Canada
- Cuba
- Venezuela

4　Argue against the doctrine from the perspective of a

- British diplomat
- Spanish diplomat
- Argentine nationalist

… that the American continents, by the free and independent condition which they have assumed and maintain, are henceforth not to be considered as subjects for future colonization by any European powers. … we should consider any attempt on their part to extend their system to any portion of this hemisphere as dangerous to our peace and safety. With the existing colonies or dependencies of any European power we have not interfered and shall not interfere. But with the Governments who have declared their independence and maintain it, and whose independence we have, on great consideration and on just principles, acknowledged, we could not view any interposition for the purpose of oppressing them, or controlling in any other manner their destiny, by any European power in any other light than as the manifestation of an unfriendly disposition toward the United States.

Economic and social effects of the revolutions on the Americas

Once again, it is difficult to make generalizations across the entire region; the economic and social effects of the American revolutions were varied and depended upon individual situations. Even in the unified United States of America there were tremendous differences between the states depending on the economic systems in place and the demography of individual states. In the north, the seeds of industrialization were sown; the south remained largely agricultural and was dominated by plantation society.

Spanish America was also diverse, based largely on its racial make-up. In Mexico, the relationship of the indigenous populations and *mestizos* with the dominant creoles created a different situation to that experienced in Venezuela, with its large slave population. Mexico has tremendous population density in the center of the country; the countries of South America tended to be sparsely populated.

What all of these regions had in common, however, was the link between economic and social conditions. One cannot be examined without stumbling into the other. The more egalitarian societies in the United States tended to have greater profits and there were more opportunities for whites, although their advancement was to the detriment of Native Americans who were outside of the boundaries of the state, both geographically and legally. Similarly, the slaves in the southern states of the United States created economic wealth but troubling social issues. One by one, the northern states outlawed slavery but it persisted in the south where it was viewed as economically necessary and socially acceptable.

The United States of America

The economy

The War of Independence had been very costly and left the new government indebted. During the war, bonds were sold to pay troops, but not enough were purchased to pay all salaries. Congress began to print money called Continentals to fund the war effort and replace the British pound. At the end of the war, the national government owed approximately $12 million in foreign and $44 million in domestic debt. Additionally, the state governments were indebted another $25 million. Most of this money was owed to the soldiers (both colonial and foreign) that fought in the war or was owed to suppliers such as the French government. In an attempt to make payments, the government had printed more Continentals that led to inflation and made the currency almost worthless.

Additionally, the United States lost its primary trading partner for raw materials; the demand for the key exports of rice, indigo and tobacco all suffered a serious decline. When trade with the British Empire finally did resume, the United States lost the advantage of being part of a trading unit, and found itself subject to higher prices for British imperial goods. The prices of beef and sugar doubled.

On the other hand, the end of the war meant an end to mercantilism and British restrictions on US commerce and travel. The United States had independence on the high seas and US ships could now legally carry goods to and from other areas. While these ships did not have the protection of the British navy and were susceptible to piracy, the revenue generated from them helped develop US commerce. At this time, France replaced Britain as the main trading partner, and trade with Spanish America escalated; not only did the United States assist patriot revolutionaries there, but it also established commercial relations outside of Spain's boundaries. While much of this was considered contraband during the wars of independence, the United States gained a foothold in Spanish America that it would keep.

The United States was also now free to industrialize and produce whatever it wanted, free of British restrictions. This led to an industrial revolution that would be fueled by abundant natural and primary resources, leading to the establishment of a manufacturing base that would see it to become one of the most important producers of finished goods. Lastly, the Peace of Paris meant the end to the Proclamation Line and settlers could move further west in search of better land to farm.

The end of the war had both positive and negative effects on the economy. While there was inflation and depression immediately after the war, there was also the tremendous potential for growth of the economy as industry and agriculture were both poised to expand.

Social status

When Thomas Jefferson stated that all men were created equal this helped gain the support of a number of potential insurgents who sought political, social and economic advancement. The Revolutionary War was not fought solely by the élites of US society; the lower classes formed the backbone of the army and suffered the most casualties. They fought determinedly in this war to advance their cause and that of their children, but at the end of the war many were back in the same situation, and some people were worse off.

Prior to the war, there had been an élite in US society that was dominated by those loyal to the British Crown. At the end of the war many of the **loyalists** in the 13 colonies went to Canada. Between 1783 and 1800 an estimated 100,000 people emigrated to Canada, but only about half were loyalists who left for political reasons; others emigrated to other parts of the British Empire in search of new opportunities. Loyalists who suffered losses in the war were not compensated and in addition to material losses, they also lost their status as the top of the social hierarchy. This change did not signal a more equal society but led to their replacement at the top of the social hierarchy by patriotic economic élites.

> **Loyalists** were American colonists loyal to Great Britain in the War of Independence. John Adams estimated that one third of colonists were loyalists.

A strong and wealthy group of men emerged out of the Congress and the revolutionary officer corps to form a new upper class in the United States. No sooner was the war over than they began to fear the classes below them as their predecessors had and sought to place limits on the advancement of these groups. Rather than ending social tensions, the war highlighted them and after the common enemy was defeated class conflict began to escalate in the new country.

Farmers in particular were hit hard by the economic troubles of the new country. They faced new taxes that were levied by the states in an attempt to eliminate the debt of the United States. In lean years, their ability to pay was tenable at best and so many farmers faced foreclosure. Such hard times led to a number of rebellions against the states, the most well-known of which is Shays' Rebellion which took place in western Massachusetts in 1786. Daniel Shays, a veteran of the war, organized 1,000 men who marched on the town of Worcester shutting down the supreme court of Massachusetts, before marching on to Springfield to free debtors who had been imprisoned. They also burned the property of a number of wealthy citizens, creating anxiety among Boston's élites. These wealthy men contributed money to form an army that was defeated in January 1787. While Shays managed to escape to Vermont, about 150 men were captured and faced severe sentencing. Since so many of the rebels were veterans, George Washington intervened and asked for leniency at which point they were pardoned for their actions. Massachusetts later changed its laws so that farmers were not so vulnerable to economic distress, but the role reversal of many of the founding fathers was striking as the very men who rebelled against British tax laws urged that actions be taken against the participants in Shays' Rebellion.

This rebellion did not simply change Massachusetts state law; it also led to the creation of the Constitution of the United States which was ratified in September 1878. It also showed the difference in attitudes and lifestyles of the rural farming class that was the majority of the population and the urban merchant classes who dominated American political life.

Similarly, the artisans and tradesmen who willingly took up arms against the British did not find themselves rewarded by economic or social advancement. Those who lived in the cities shared some of the benefits of urban life, but most of the laws passed tended to benefit those with money and property.

The foot soldiers of the US Revolution did not fare very well; they were not paid the pensions they were due and few found the social mobility they were searching for in the areas in which they lived. One way to overcome this was to move, and so many did. Desirous of their own land and a real sense of liberty, settlers moved west beyond the frontiers of the United States. It was there that they often found the material progress and social standing that they could not achieve in their previous homes. This had the knock-on effect of creating profound social disturbances in the native populations they encountered.

Natives were seen as savages and not in possession of basic human rights—they certainly weren't protected by the laws of the United States. Most of the people who moved west brought with them

Activity

Differing perspectives

In the light of Shays' Rebellion, the former radical and revolutionary Samuel Adams wrote:

> Rebellion against a king may be pardoned, or lightly punished, but the man who dares to rebel against the laws of a republic ought to suffer death.

Thomas Jefferson responded:

> A little rebellion now and then is a good thing. It is a medicine necessary for the sound health of government. God forbid that we should ever be twenty years without such a rebellion.

Explain why you think two men so committed to the cause of revolution during the War of Independence would differ in their opinion once a democratic government had been established in the United States.

firearms that could keep the natives at bay unless they were outnumbered or ambushed. Those Native Americans who tried to live in harmony with the settlers failed in the attempt. Either they fought (and in the long run lost) or the tribes had to move.

During the war, most native tribes tried to remain neutral. Although some sided with the patriots, they were more likely to side with the British. Within native communities there were splits in how to proceed, and with whom to negotiate. Warfare along the borders continued long after the war itself had as the tribes (Shawnees and Cherokees in particular) tried to maintain some regional control.

Since some of the tribes fought with the British, the United States claimed that, as losers in the war, they no longer had the right to the lands west of the Proclamation land. Unlike other losing powers, however, the tribes were not represented at Paris and had no part in the negotiations. Some tribes, such as the Cherokees and Shawnees, resisted US advancement but were unsuccessful in the defense of their territories.

What is the image of slavery that is portrayed in the illustrations below? How accurate do you think this perspective was?

The status of slaves

The treatment of African Americans during and after the war depended largely on where they lived. In New England, free blacks joined the patriot militias and fought for the cause of independence. However, in the rest of the 13 colonies, Americans were divided over the issue of the role of slaves. The British used this dilemma to their advantage and promised freedom for all slaves who defended the Empire and approximately 12,000 blacks joined the British in their fight against the patriots who enslaved them. After the British received assistance from German troops there was no longer a military need for the slaves, but the British recognized they could engage in economic warfare by promising freedom to all slaves who escaped from patriot owners. The patriots responded by promising freedom to slaves who escaped from loyalists. In the end, most escaped slaves in the south were not freed, but sold back into slavery by the side that granted them amnesty.

Slave family outside of their cabin on a southern plantation.

In the north, however, slaves were freed for their participation in the Continental Army. This led to a divide in the United States on its views regarding the African population. Dominant in the north was the idea that all men should be free, and seven of the 13 colonies abolished slavery (Vermont, Massachusetts, New York, New Jersey, Connecticut, Rhode Island and Pennsylvania). In the south, slavery continued and was considered necessary for the agricultural and labor-intensive economy. British military leadership did their best to make true their promises and where

Slaves greeting the plantation owner and his family visiting the slave cabins in Virginia, 1700s.

possible blacks were freed and after the war were evacuated to other parts of the British Empire including approximately 3,500 who went to Nova Scotia and New Brunswick. In the south, many black claims for freedom were ignored and even free blacks were sold into slavery at the end of the war. Slavery remained a source of tension among the states and was an unresolved issue that would cause conflict for the new country well into the 19th century. It was the most divisive domestic issue that the United States faced.

Spanish America

The economy

It is difficult to assess the impact of revolution on all of Spanish America but certain generalizations can be made. The wars had devastating effects on the economic resources of the region. The mining industry in particular was harmed by the war—both sides often destroyed extant mines so that they would not benefit the opposing side. Livestock was depleted by hungry armies marching through villages and ranching areas.

Although governments discussed the need to build national economies there were few incentives for those with wealth or ingenuity to do so. Most preferred to purchase imported manufactured goods. They were thus reliant on the continued production and export of raw materials that, in turn, made them dependent on cheap labor. At the same time, without industry, there was little internal demand for the goods they produced, so the logical outcome was export. In the face of such a situation most of the countries welcomed foreign investment and free trade. The results, they would later discover, would not yield the industrial societies that their partners had created; instead they became reliant on foreign investors that established control over most domestic industry in the new countries and often had a stranglehold on key resources.

Social status

Spanish America was in a very different situation to the United States or Haiti, due to the nature of their wars of independence. Unlike their counterparts in the north, the Spanish Americans had to mobilize a substantial number of non-whites to create an army capable of defeating the royalist forces. This meant that at the end of the wars the non-whites would demand key liberties, and while political rights were granted, social status remained a way of subjugating the other races.

Native workers harvesting coffee beans in Costa Rica, 1800s.

Creoles were successful in retaining their control of political and social life. Although independence brought an end to the aristocracy, there was still a class of élites based on race that dominated Spanish American life. They reserved for themselves all bureaucratic positions and made it much easier for their sons to get an education than for others. A European education was still seen as important to social standing, and was difficult for non-whites to attain.

It was still possible for free non-whites to advance socially or economically. They faced discrimination and laws meant to protect them weren't always enforced but they attained more rights than previously. The mixed-race indigenous populations faced even more severe discrimination and often responded with revolts against the governments in power. These revolts were generally suppressed quickly, but there were anomalies. The Yaqui Indians of northern Mexico engaged in nearly a century of warfare against subsequent governments despite receiving the most brutal treatment.

At the end of the revolutions, slavery remained in Spanish America. Although Bolívar outlawed slavery during the wars, it persisted after the war. As in North America, most leaders of the independence movement saw the hypocrisy in their own fight for independence but continued the bondage of others. They were not inclined, however, to act upon these feelings. Reliance on natural resources and primary produce for income also meant continuing an economic system that was reliant on low-paid indigenous and slave labor. This in turn justified the stratified social system that kept the creoles in power.

The situation in Spanish America was by no means homogenous. Just as slavery was not important to the economies of the New England states, it was unimportant in Mexico, Central America and Chile—three countries that abolished slavery shortly after independence. On the other hand, the countries where slavery was more important (Colombia, Venezuela, Perú, Argentina and Ecuador) would continue slavery well into the 1840s and 1850s. Only intensification of slave revolts and a fear of political instability led to emancipation there.

Mexican women making tortillas in the 1800s.

Activity

Indigenous rights

We are not Europeans, we are not Indians. We are but a mixed species of aborigines and Spaniards. …We are disputing with the natives for titles of ownership, and at the same time we are struggling to maintain ourselves in the country that gave us birth against the opposition of the invaders.

Source: Simón Bolívar, Address delivered at the inauguration of the Second National Congress of Venezuela at Angostura, February 15, 1819

In the future the aborigines shall not be called Indians or natives; they are children and citizens of Perú and they shall be known as Peruvians.

Source: José de San Martín, declaring independence for Perú, July 28, 1821.

It was the dispossessed of Latin America who, with spears and machetes, really fought against Spanish power at the dawn of the nineteenth century. Independence did not reward them; it betrayed the hopes of those who had shed their blood. Eduardo Galeano, Uruguayan journalist, writer and novelist.

Source: Galeano, Eduardo. 1997. *Open Veins of Latin America: Five Centuries of the Pillage of a Continent.* p.115.

Questions

1   Do you think that many creoles in Spanish American agreed with the ideas that San Martín and Bolívar expressed? Why or why not?

2   How would these ideas encourage non-creoles to participate in independence movements? Would these ideas be believable to non-whites?

3   Do you agree with Galeano's assessment? Why or why not?

4   Compare and contrast the statements of Bolívar and San Martín to Galeano. Are they contradictory?

Conclusion

By the 1820s, independence had been achieved in most of the Americas. Only some islands in the Caribbean and some coastal colonial outposts remained. European influence was waning and the United States had begun to establish itself as a dominant power in the region.

In general, independence had meant long, bloody, costly wars for these new countries and in addition to creating new governments and writing constitutions they would be plagued by war debt that would inevitably lead to conflicts in the new states. There were also unresolved social issues in all of the new countries that would need to be addressed. Often the élites tried to ignore these hoping to allay the problems. The issues of the day—emancipation, suffrage, taxation—remained and intensified until future generations had to confront them, often with equally terrible results.

Exam practice and further resources

Sample questions

1 Analyze the role of foreign intervention in two independence movements from two countries of the region.

2 "It was military tactics more than ideas which established US Independence." How far do you agree that North American independence from Britain was established through military action, rather than ideology?

3 Compare and contrast the reasons for the rise of independence movements in two Latin American countries.

4 Analyze the impact of independence on the economies and societies of two countries from the Americas.

5 Compare and contrast the contributions of two different leaders to two different processes of independence.

Recommended further reading

E. Bradford Burns & Julie A. Charlip. 2007. *Latin America: An Interpretive History*. 8th edn. New Jersey: Pearson Education Inc.

Alan Brinkley. 1999. *American History: A Survey.* 10th edn. Boston: McGraw-Hill College.

Marshall C. Eakin. 2007. *The History of Latin America: Collision of Cultures.* New York: Palgrave MacMillan.

Eduardo Galeano. 1997. *Open Veins of Latin America: Five Centuries of the Pillage of a Continent.* 25th edn. Monthly Review Press.

Benjamin Keen & Keith Haynes. 2009. *A History of Latin America.* 8th edn. Houghton Mifflin Harcourt Publishing.

Edwin Williamson. 2009. *The Penguin History of Latin America.* London: Penguin Books.

Howard Zinn. 2005. *A People's History of the United States: 1492–Present.* Harper Perennial Modern Classics.

Online resources

History Matters: The U.S. Survey Course on the Web. http://historymatters.gmu.edu.

2 Nations and nation-building in the Americas, 1787–1867

The revolutionary era in the Americas had ended by the second decade of the 19th century but peace was short-lived. The new nations had hastily redrawn the map of the Americas which created new tensions igniting three decades of border conflict from Canada to Argentina. Internally, the newborn nations were challenged to establish peace, order and prosperity. The revolutions brought sovereignty but not stability. The critical issue was adopting and implementing a system of government that promised both political stability and the promotion of revolutionary ideals. Three forms of government would emerge: democratic republicanism, constitutional monarchy, and dictatorship. Canada had a parliamentary confederation responsible to Great Britain. The United States adopted a republican form of federal government. Brazil had a constitutional monarchy. Mexico went from dictatorship to constitutional monarchy to republican government. While there were many variations throughout the Americas, an important point was the division of powers between the states or provinces.

Due to the huge geographical expanse and topography, as well as the variety of European colonial powers and local populations, the situation in Latin America and the Caribbean was far more complex than that of Canada and of the United States. The colonial Spanish viceroyalties and captaincies-general were gone, replaced by new nations or groups of nations, with new borders. The Portuguese colony of Brazil became a monarchy. The French colonies remained, with the exception of Haiti and its violent slave rebellion and independence revolution. Some Spanish colonies seized by the British and the Dutch in the Caribbean remained colonies until well into the 20th century, and some, even to this day. Elaborating a form of government suitable to each nation was a long, arduous process. Much the same as in the northern part of the Americas, people debated on who would hold power and how this power would be distributed, as well as which groups would be excluded from power (like slaves, Native Americans, *mestizos*, immigrants, women, the poor, the illiterate). A few ideologues debated what role revolutionary ideals would play in creating new nations and what influence traditional colonial values and beliefs, notably race, religion and social class would exert in this process.

The tug-of-war in Latin America and the Caribbean between liberals and conservatives would be decisive and in many ways different from the same conflict in the northern part of the Americas. Liberals in Latin America and the Caribbean were influenced by the Enlightenment and the US Revolution and espoused a free-trade economy, a republican form of government, rule of law, hierarchical and limited civil rights and a reduction in the power and influence of the Roman Catholic Church. Conservatives wanted to keep the link between church and state and implement reforms slowly, ensuring traditional colonial institutions and structures that benefited the advantaged position of the élites in the particular nations. The conflict was not easily resolved and the search for stability and prosperity would be long and difficult: in some countries solved for long periods and then upset, in others a balance would not be reached until late in the century and at a great social cost. Still other nations would alternate between the two factions often enough to paralyze any real social or economic progress.

In many new countries in the former Spanish colonies, revolutions were restricted to the political élites regardless of political ideology, as the plight of the slaves and Native Americans remained the same at first. Eleven Latin American nations had freed their African slaves between 1824 and 1869. Where slavery was never a very important economic base for plantations or mines, it was abolished early on; but where it was entrenched in wealth production, like the United States, Cuba, Puerto Rico, and Brazil, it continued, sometimes until late into the 19th century. It is difficult to generalize about the treatment of Indian and mixed-race populations, given the large area and the 20 core nations in question. Countries like Mexico, Guatemala, El Salvador and Honduras (at first part of the nation of Central America), Bolivia and Perú (with large Native American populations), kept them disenfranchised until the 20th century. Argentina and Chile, much like the western United States, engaged in actual wars against Indian populations in the southern cone. Countries with larger *mestizo* populations (like Colombia, Venezuela, Chile, Argentina, Ecuador and others) incorporated these populations into the body politic, although social and cultural restrictions often remained in place. Most countries excluded the poor, landless and illiterates of any color or mix from the power élites.

This chapter will focus on the challenges and problems that came with independence, through an examination of the important developments that took place in the Americas between 1787 and 1867. During this period, the political map of the region was carved out. An examination of the various attempts to bring domestic stability to these new nations and experiments in government and constitution will also be examined. Examples will include Argentina, Brazil, Canada and the United States. The chapter will examine the important wars, major events and key leaders who shaped the Americas during this period.

By the end of this chapter, students should be able to:

- understand the philosophical underpinnings, major compromises and changes in the US political system embodied in the Articles of Confederation (1783) and the Constitution of 1787

- assess the challenges to the establishment of political systems in Latin America through analyzing the conditions for the rise of and impact of the *caudillos*

- address the causes and impact of the War of 1812 on British North America and the United States

- explain the causes and effects on the region of the US–Mexican War, 1846–48

- assess the causes, challenges, events, and leaders in the period 1837–67 that resulted in Canada's confederation; the 1837 rebellions in Canada, the implications of the Durham Report (1839) challenges to the confederation; the British North America Act of 1867; and the effects of various compromises, unresolved issues and regionalism

- evaluate the impact of nation-building on the social position and living conditions of Native Americans, *mestizos* and immigrants in the new nations during the this period.

Independence achieved

The 13 colonies in British North America started the independence movement and ousted the British after a bitter struggle by 1783. The challenge was to create a constitutionally based system of government that enshrined the revolutionary ideals of life, liberty and the pursuit of happiness. The first attempt, the Articles of Confederation, lasted only five years. The issue was determining an acceptable division of power between the **federal government** and the 13 states. Two camps emerged in the debate: The **Federalists** wanted a strong central government, reduced power of the states and opposed a Bill of Rights. The **Anti-Federalists** opposed a strong federal government, believed the states must hold the balance of power and promoted a Bill of Rights. At times the debate was rancorous and polemic but more often it was thoughtful, philosophical and inspiring. Eventually the "Great Compromise" resolved the crisis, a Bill of Rights was added and the constitution was ratified by the 13 states. With the constitutional crisis resolved, a confident United States of America entered an energetic period of economic prosperity, industrialism, immigration and westward expansion. The United States was poised to expand across the continent. Thomas Jefferson's Louisiana Purchase of 1804, one of history's shrewdest land deals, added the Mississippi basin and settlers poured over the Appalachians into the fertile region planting cotton, tobacco and wheat and igniting a new wave of western expansion. Forty years later, the Oregon boundary settlement with Great Britain made the 49th parallel the northern border of the United States. The annexation of Texas (1845) started an unpopular war with Mexico that added the future states of New Mexico, Arizona, Utah, Nevada, California, Colorado and parts of Wyoming. The continental map of the United States increased tremendously. Mexico's territory, on the other hand, was reduced by half upon losing the war.

It is important to point out that independence from European colonial powers was not uniform all over Latin America and the Caribbean. In fact, Caribbean island nations like Puerto Rico and Cuba remained colonies of Spain until the end of the 19th century, and became a haven for royalists escaping South American nations, as did the Dutch colony of Curaçao which held Venezuelan exiles. Today's Dominican Republic was occupied by neighboring Haiti until 1843, and was a Spanish colony again until 1865. Most of the West Indies (French, British and Dutch) remained colonies in the 19th century.

In some newly independent Latin American nations, stability remained elusive. In the former Spanish colonies the revolutionary wars created 18 new nations, but the new borders would not last. By mid-century, the lack of clear boundaries in the former Spanish and Portuguese Empires, in addition to geographical imperatives and different population groups and power élites, resulted in the establishment of 23 nations. In many of these countries, finding an effective system of governance that created consensus between

A **federal system of government** is a division of powers between a central government and local (state or provincial) governments.

The **Federalists** championed a strong federal government with an elected congress and protection of states' rights in the Senate. They opposed a Bill of Rights.

Anti-Federalists wanted the states to control the federal government and an entrenched Bill of Rights.

competing factions and ideologies was elusive, even for the élites. In addition, the destruction caused during the wars of independence, especially in Venezuela, Uruguay and Mexico, was a huge setback for these countries. In Mexico, Uruguay, Argentina and Brazil regionalist disputes escalated to internecine battles between factions grappling for national power. All over the Americas, two powerful ideological groups wrestled for control of the new nations—**liberals** and **conservatives**. Liberals championed the revolutionary ideals of the enlightenment—liberty, fraternity and equality—in theory, but rarely in practice. They believed in republican forms of government, free trade, a market-driven economy, separation of church and state, rule of law and a limited franchise (voting rights). Conservatives, represented the colonial legacy and wanted to keep many of the the old ways; strong ties between the state and the Roman Catholic Church, élite privilege, a hierarchical social structure, tariffs to protect local economic power and colonial landholding laws. It should be noted that most of the discussion and conflict between these two groups was concentrated among the élite, comprising less than 10% of the population in many countries, who were the only part of the population able to wield power.

Across the Americas and most of the Western world, liberal philosophies and ideals could not entirely supplant traditional social structures and systems in the 19th century. In the former Spanish and Portuguese colonies, the American-born creole élite often replaced the Iberian-born élite and set up new governments based on liberal values of *laissez-faire* economics, republican governments with parliaments and a strong executive and rule of law, based on the Napoleonic Code; an exception to this rule were the British colonies or ex-colonies. Their sense of democracy did not include the lower classes, namely rural peasants and indigenous and African peoples, the landless, and women, who comprised the majority of the population. Constitutional influence came from the French and the US constitutions, to be sure, but recent historiography has pointed to the much more powerful influence of the first modern constitution: the Spanish Constitution of Cádiz of 1812. Although most new nations experimented with republican forms of government, Haiti and Mexico unsuccessfully and Brazil successfully tried monarchies. In some countries, such as Ecuador and Mexico, rural uprisings against the servitude of the feudal hacienda system, or slave rebellions in the case of Jamaica, Brazil and Cuba, fanned the fears of the power élites. In other countries, such as Argentina and Uruguay, the promise of order and stability created a new category of leader— the *caudillo*. Building a national consensus that brought stability was difficult, but not impossible. Several nations succeeded: most notably Brazil, Costa Rica and Chile. Here the altercations between liberals and conservatives were held in parliamentary and constitutional debates resulting in a landholder and mercantile élite consensus in the 1840s and 1850s, similar to the situation to the United States and Canada in the 1870s. In other cases, such as Uruguay and Argentina, experiments in republican forms of government failed early on due to conflicts between different provinces; and since no resolution seemed possible through republican institutions, *caudillos* took control at different intervals. These were often charismatic strongmen with

Liberals are middle class intellectuals and revolutionaries who championed *laissez faire* economics, free trade, democratic government and rule of law.

Conservatives maintain the traditional ruling oligarchy of landowners and the Roman Catholic Church. They opposed republican democracy, although some supported constitutional monarchy.

Activity
Liberal vs. conservative

The terms liberal and conservative remain important political concepts, but they had different implications in the 18th and 19th centuries and strong regional and national variants across the globe.

Choose one Latin American country to analyze the enduring impact of liberal and/or conservative traditions, dating from this period, and how they impact on the region today.

Discussion point

Watch *The Price of freedom*, a video documentary written by Carlos Fuentes (Dir. Christopher Ralling) (a Sogetel, S.A. production in association with the Smithsonian Institution, Quinto Centenario España).

How does this video clarify your knowledge of the post-independence leaders and ideologues in Latin America?

Caudillos were local strongmen who emerged in many countries in Latin America after the wars of independence. With military backing, popular support and ruthless dictatorial measures, they ruled for varying time spans, from short periods of months to decades.

the power and money to command private armies. In the early part of the century they were sometimes revolutionary heroes, although they came from different social backgrounds. Often they were rural leaders, with backgrounds as powerful landowners or ranchers, such as Rafael Carrera in Guatemala, Juan Manuel de Rosas in Argentina, Manuel Isidoro Belzú in Bolivia and José Artigas in Uruguay (just to name a few). They key to their power was control of the paramilitary forces and eventually, co-opting part or all of the nation's military forces. The regime of some *caudillos* was short-lived, like Belzú who only lasted seven years. Others were far longer, like that of Carrera (18 years), Rosas (23 years) and José Gaspar Rodríguez de Francia in Paraguay (26 years). The figure of the *caudillo* as a strong military leader would continue to surface in future military dictatorships in Latin America in the 19th and 20th centuries.

There was frequently extensive constitutional discussion between liberals and conservatives. Before 1867, there was much constitutional change: in Perú the constitution was changed eight times, six times in the case of Colombia, and nine times in the case of Ecuador. The constitutions that eventually endured tended to be a compromise of liberalism because they still sharply curtailed power and participation and fostered a strong, centralized executive, as a concession to conservatism. The separation of church and state was also a major dividing factor in these two factions. In both the Spanish and Portuguese ex-colonies, the Roman Catholic Church held powerful landholdings and resources, in addition to a monopoly on education. The influence of the church was felt at all levels of the political hierarchy, but it also represented a cultural confrontation between liberals, who felt that it perpetuated rigid class hierarchies and was too rich and powerful, and conservatives, who felt the church was vital to preserving traditional values that maintained a stable social order. Catholicism, as a religion as well as a cultural icon, was deeply ingrained in Spanish and Portuguese Latin America: both in agrarian communities where the rhythm of the seasons and religious observances where inseparable and in urban communities, of all classes, castes and races. Arguably, the church was the only institution to hold sway over each country's entire population; hence they were reviled by liberals for their stance against modernity and courted by conservatives for being a pacifying influence on potentially volatile sections of society.

Then, there is the case of Canada. Canada's road to nationhood was evolutionary not revolutionary. **British North America** comprised six colonies: five predominantly English-speaking, protestant colonies—Nova Scotia, New Brunswick, Prince Edward Island, Newfoundland and Upper Canada (Ontario)—and Lower Canada (Quebec), which was predominately French speaking and Roman Catholic. The United States had invaded during the Revolutionary wars and the War of 1812. The British questioned the loyalty of French-speaking Lower Canada and transplanted Americans in Upper Canada but these fears proved unfounded. Many fought the invaders or stayed neutral. British North America remained British for different reasons in Quebec. Conservative-minded British political élites known as the "Family Compact" in Upper Canada and the

Discussion point

What is the difference between evolutionary and revolutionary change?

In your view which is preferable and why?

British North America is the term for the British colonies (later provinces) that remained loyal to Great Britain during and after the American Revolution. They include the maritime colonies –Nova Scotia, New Brunswick, Prince Edward Island and Newfound land–as well as Upper Canada (Ontario) and Lower Canada (French-speaking Quebec).

"Château Clique" in Lower Canada controlled the colonial governments. They refused to grant **responsible government** to a politically astute middle class who paid taxes but had no voice in the distribution of public monies. By the 1830s, radical charismatic leaders emerged in both provinces and galvanized protest. Frustrations reached a boiling point in 1837and armed rebellion broke out. The British army made short work of the rebels and the fighting ended by 1838. To prevent further trouble, the British Government sent a respected diplomat and reform politician, Lord Durham, to Canada to sort out the mess. The report that bears his name granted responsible government (a key rebel demand). Less popular was his recommendation that French-speaking Lower-Canada be assimilated. Regardless, Durham's report set British North America on the road to nationhood and on July 1, 1867, Canada became an independent dominion within the British Empire.

> **Responsible government** is a parliamentary term, and requires that the executive (government) in power is responsible to the elected members of the legislature. It must maintain their confidence to be able to raise and distribute tax revenues. If confidence is lost the executive must resign. The term is frequently used these days to refer to accountable government.

The Articles of Confederation and the US Constitution

By 1783, the Revolution was over, the British were defeated and evicted. A new nation emerged, comprised of the original 13 colonies, the United States of America. The first order of business was to "deliberate upon and choosing, the forms of government under which they shall live." From the start, friction existed between those states and delegates who wanted a strong central government and those who wanted power to reside in the states. What they agreed to was a federal system of government with a division of powers between a national (federal) government and the states' governments. In the spirit of the revolution they agreed to create a republic without a hereditary monarchy or system of royalty. They believed political power and the legitimacy of government and political power emanated from an electorate of free people not from an ancient birthright. The difficult part was the division of powers.

The first attempt, the Articles of Confederation of 1783, was unsatisfactory and in 1787, the 13 states gathered in Philadelphia to try again. The result was a new constitution. In this section students will examine and evaluate the weaknesses of the Articles of Confederation, the philosophical and political debate between the Federalists and Anti-Federalists, and the major compromise that paved the way for ratification and the important changes and revisions contained in the new constitution.

Shay's Rebellion and the Philadelphia Convention

Daniel Shay was a farmer and a patriot; an officer in the Continental army he fought bravely for his new country and was wounded. Returning to western Massachusetts, he came home to a bankrupt state that needed funds to pay war debts. New property taxes, that hit farmers hardest, were imposed ruthlessly and those unable to pay were tried in court. Shay watched helplessly as farms were foreclosed and the inhabitants sent to debtors' prison. This was not what he and

The Americans are the first people whom Heaven has favoured with an opportunity of deliberating upon, and choosing, the forms of government under which they shall live.

John Jay, Continental Congress delegate (New York), 1777

Discussion point

An important question facing the men drafting the US Constitution was creating a satisfactory balance of powers between the federal government and the states.

 Do you think the Constitution of 1787 achieved the right balance of powers?

his fellow countrymen had fought and died for—to have their property confiscated by their own government; it was worse than the British!

In Autumn 1786, Shay led about a 1,000 followers, who came to be known as Shayites; armed with pitchforks and carrying the "liberty tree", they marched on the debtor courts. It was more protest than rebellion. No blood was spilled. For six months, Shay roamed the Massachusetts countryside shutting down the hated courts.
In February, the Shayites advanced on the federal arsenal at Springfield where the state militia was waiting. Two cannon shots dispersed the Shayites, killing two and wounding 20, the uprising was over. Shay had gone unchecked, critics argued, because the new republic did not have an army worth mentioning and it took several months to muster the state militia. Shay and his officers were captured and tried, many received the death sentence but most received amnesty and Shay was eventually forgotten but not before he had made his mark.

George Washington, like many in the United States, argued that the insurrection was a direct threat to the revolution's ideals of "life, liberty and property." He believed a political remedy was needed which meant amending the Articles of Confederation. The Articles had been approved by Congress and the state assemblies in March 1781. It contained 13 articles that set-out the division of powers between the federal and state governments. Fearful of an abusive federal government trampling the rights of individuals and the states, the states retained control over the federal government and this was reflected in the Articles. The federal government was virtually powerless, with limited taxation powers. The nation's army and navy were non-existant. Washington and **the Virginians** Alexander Hamilton and James Madison led a group eventually known as "the Federalists" who argued from the start that the Articles did not give the federal government enough power. Events conspired to rapidly convince many citizens of the new republic that these men were right and that the Articles needed to be rewritten. Thomas Jefferson disagreed, arguing that the "Shay" incident was trivial and the Articles were working as intended. His followers were later called "the anti-Federalists". Eventually, however, Washington's views prevailed and the young nation would redraft the articles. Shay's uprising had in the end provided the pretext for action.

James Madison (Virginia) and Alexander Hamilton (New York), joined forces and took centre stage. Hamilton had been questioning the articles even before they were adopted but with little success or support. Hamilton was charismatic and eloquent, Madison was thoughtful, hardworking and respected. The two men used their power and influence with the other states and organized an all-states convention in January 1787 to address the Articles' shortcomings. Only five of the 13 states attended. Some progress on revising the Articles was made but Shay's Rebellion tipped the scales. The next national convention was scheduled for Philadelphia in the spring and every state sent their best delegates. Hamilton wrote that the convention would take the steps "necessary to render the constitution of the Federal government adequate to the exigencies [requirements] of the Union."

The Virginians No group of delegates exercised greater influence (and insight) on the constitutional debates than the Virginians. Educated and intelligent, ideological in outlook, pragmatic in application and from Virginia's landholding and business élite, the delegation included Thomas Jefferson, George Washington and James Madison. There were disagreements over the Constitution. Washington, Hamilton and Madison campaigned for a more powerful federal government. Jefferson advocated for state power, some additional powers to the federal government and a Bill of Rights to protect the individual from the power of the government.

The delegates arrived in Philadelphia in May 1787 to decide the nation's future. It was a heavy burden with Thomas Jefferson in France, John Adams in England and Benjamin Franklin—the nation's conscience—who was in attendance, old and sickly and beyond his prime. The convention, however, brought together the brightest and best of a new generation of patriotic young citizens of the United States. It was a gathering of exceptionally talented, intelligent and like-minded men united in their shared destiny to make the revolution succeed and create in Washington's words "a Government under which life, liberty and property will be secured to us ..." They had been greatly influenced by the ideas of the Enlightenment and expressed growing confidence in reason and the principle of natural "inalienable" rights.

According to historian Hugh Brogan, the problem was difficult but not unsolvable: How to develop a permanent structure that would effectively and efficiently govern the nation and protect the republican ideals of life, liberty and property? The challenge was daunting and would nearly break the strongest delegates. Deliberations were intense and the days were long. The proceedings were kept secret so delegates could speak freely. Washington chaired and Madison took notes that accurately and fairly recorded the debate.

The Signing of the Constitution of the United States, painted by Howard Chandler Christy in 1940. The painting shows Washington standing, Franklin in front (in the grey suit), Hamilton on his left and Madison on his right.

Underscoring the convention were important national issues that many believed required a strong federal government to resolve. The nation's finances were a mess and the current economic crisis could only be resolved, many believed, by a strong central government that had the power to enact its will on the states and on individuals. The country owed Europe money, war debts and foreign loans that it could not repay. France was owed the most and it was important to remember that without the French the US Revolution would have failed. The United States still needed France as an ally and, therefore, needed to repay the debt.

The Articles did not contain the mechanisms necessary for the federal government to raise the funds to pay the debts or run the country.

Activity

Debate

Washington vs. Jefferson

Washington believed Shay's Rebellion showed conclusively that the Articles of Confederation were weak and needed revision. Jefferson disagreed and said the seriousness of the rebellion was being used as justification for giving more power to the federal government.

 Who do you support and why? Which level of government should have the most power?

The Influence of the Enlightenment

The Enlightenment movement challenged the religious and political belief systems of the 18th century. Jefferson, Franklin and other Americans were influenced by the French philosophers, Rousseau, Voltaire and Montesquieu, whom they had known personally. The main tenet of Enlightenment philosophy was the repudiation of the divine right of kings. This, in turn, accepted the truth of inalienable natural rights, extolled democracy and taught that political power came from the people, not a divinity. This led to the principle of the separation of powers between church and state and a system of checks and balances between the executive, legislative and judicial branches of government to insure no branch could supercede another. Most radical of all was the argument for abolishing the monarchy in favour of a republic. The Constitution of the United States gives testimony to the influence of the Enlightenment on the founding fathers.

Under the Articles the federal government requisitioned the states for money but had no authority to enforce payment. It was voluntary taxation. The states rarely paid in full if at all. As a result, foreign debts and war loans were in arrears. The army was a shambles, reduced to 80 soldiers at one point. No money, no guns, no security—this was the lesson of Shay's Rebellion. The navy was in a similar boat. Coastal states fought pirates and smugglers with their own ships. The situation was untenable. What would they do if the British came back? The question was rhetorical but relevant in shaping the debate as Washington would remind delegates.

To make matters worse, a bitter trade war had erupted between the states. For example, New York taxed ships using its waterways to trade in New Jersey and Connecticut. It was the same story up and down the coast. The men who had forged the revolution, men like Madison, Hamilton, Franklin, Jay and Washington, feared they were witnessing the nation's devolution into a loose-knit confederation of semi-independent states. And so they gathered in Philadelphia, unanimous in their desire to stop the drift from the revolution's principles and save the union. What was needed was a new constitution that supported a federal system of government that the states would be keen to ratify.

Federalists vs. anti-Federalists

The delegates attending the Philadelphia Convention had all clearly decided in advance which side they were on: Federalist or anti-Federalist. The Federalists believed the principles of the revolution required a strong federal government that could levy taxes, protect borders and recruit an army and navy. They opposed a **Bill of Rights** arguing that a list of rights could never include all the rights to be protected. Better to leave that work to the courts, similar to the British system. The anti-Federalists believed that any increase of the federal governments' powers should be incremental. They feared a powerful government that could tax, and create a military and undermine the authority of the states. They wanted the states to retain the balance of power and they argued for a Bill of Rights to be enshrined in the constitution to protect the "inalienable" rights of individuals.

The Philadelphia Convention lasted four months, from May to September 1787, and the constitution that emerged was the result of a willingness by delegates to compromise their strongly held personal beliefs in order to advance the national interest. The critical debate centered on whether the states would retain an equal vote in one house of the national legislature, or whether schemes of proportional representation would be devised for both upper and lower chambers. When the small-state leaders like Roger Sherman from Connecticut proved unyielding in opposing the former, after seven weeks of debate, the large states agreed to compromise.

The Virginia caucus had met before the convention and presented their plan on May 29, 1787. It proposed a bicameral (two-house) legislature. Membership in the lower house (the House of Representatives) would be based on representation by population. Members would be selected and elected by the electorate of each

> The **Bill of Rights** are the "inalienable" rights of all citizens protected/interpreted by the Supreme Court. An Example is the First Amendment stipulating freedom of speech.

Discussion point

Who needs a Bill of Rights?

With reference to the US Revolution and philosophy of the Enlightenment period, why do you think Thomas Jefferson believed it essential that the constitution include a Bill of Rights? Do you agree with Jefferson?

Roger Sherman (1721–1793)

Roger Sherman was born in Newton, Massachusetts. Self-educated, he was politically active from an early age. A man of considerable, skill, natural intellect and ambition, he became a lawyer in 1754, and was later a judge, treasurer of Yale University and congressional delegate. Sherman was a key figure in the US Revolution and in shaping the nation afterwards. Elected to the Continental Congress in 1774, he worked so hard his health suffered. In 1783, he served on the committee that wrote the Articles of Confederation. At the Philadelphia convention he was one of the most vocal and persistent members.

Madison's convention notes credit him with speaking 138 times to defend the rights of the smaller states. He is credited with the "Great Compromise." Adams, Jefferson and Madison had great respect for Sherman. He lacked the charisma and eloquence of his peers but was renowned for being pragmatic, stern, taciturn, direct and, as Jefferson quipped, he never said anything foolish.

state. Members of the upper house (later the Senate) would to be nominated by the state legislatures and elected by members of the lower house. Each state received one vote.

The New Jersey Plan of June 15, 1787, offered a uni-cameral (single house) legislature with equal representation for all states regardless of population. The plan retained the Articles of Confederation with some increases in the powers of Congress (federal government). The plan was not popular with the big states. Fortunately, Roger Sherman had another plan.

The Connecticut Compromise, that came to be known as the "Great Compromise," was presented on July 16, 1787: the Connecticut delegation proposed a bicameral legislature with a lower and upper house. Similar to the Virginia plan, each state would elect members to the lower house (House of Representatives) based on a proposed ratio of 30,000 to one. The Upper house (Senate) was the key to Sherman's plan. Each state legislature would elect two members to the upper chamber who would vote independently, not by state. The Great Compromise broke the deadlock, after eleven days of debate, by the narrowest of margins—five to four.

The Philadelphia Convention spawned two sub-committees to write the constitution and the finishing touches were penned by Madison, Sherman and Hamilton. The constitution was almost done but one issue remained: slavery. The issue was how to count slaves when determining the allocation of seats to the lower house (representation by population). The five southern states with the majority of slaves wanted to include slaves in the head count. The northern states argued slaves were property and should be excluded. Of course, the slaves would not be allowed to vote which meant the votes of the electorate in slave states would be more valuable than in non-slave states.

After much debate the convention agreed to the "The three-fifths compromise": each slave was counted as three-fifths of a "free person". If a state had 50,000 slaves, applying the rule equalled 30,000 extra voters and the state received an additional seat in the lower house. The compromise was accepted and the slavery issue was shelved for 20 years but not forgotten. In the short-term,

Discussion point

Roger Sherman was overshadowed by men like Washington, Hamilton and Madison. Does he deserve more credit?

Discussion point

 What does the "three-fifths compromise" tell us about the slavery question in the US in the 1780s?

To what extent does this compromise foreshadow the slavery debate and other slavery compromises such as the 1820 Missouri Compromise and the 1850 Nebraska-Kansas Compromise?

however, the southern states were won over. As predicted, the south was over-represented in the first congress with 45 percent of seats in the house with a voting population of 38 percent, but the advantage proved short-lived following an increase of immigration into the rapidly industrializing northern states that required large reserves of labor. The northern economy grew rapidly reflected in its major cities that became centres of industry, trade and commerce. Industrialization in the south was small by comparison.

Ratification and the Federalist Papers

The language of the constitution was to be simple, precise and elegant. The opening phrase explained the document's purpose: "In order to form a more perfect union ..." Armed with the newly drafed constitution, the delegates returned to their respective state capitals to seek ratification. The ratification process called for each state to elect delegates and convene a ratification convention. Only Rhode Island refused.

In New York, the popular governor, Henry Clinton, stridently opposed the new constitution and without New York all would be lost. The Federalists launched a publicity campaign to convince New York to ratify. Writing under the name "Plubius" Hamilton, Madison and John Jay published 85 essays known as the Federalist Papers. The anti-Federalists fired back, writing under names like "Brutus" and "Farmer". The exchange was nothing short of brilliant but in the end New York ratified largely because other states did so and not because of the Federalist papers.

Virginia was also reluctant but ratified after Thomas Jefferson received assurances from James Madison that a Bill of Rights would be added (which it was in 1791). Why, then, are the Federalist Papers considered important by historians and how much influence did they have during the ratification debates? Historians concur that the influence was more historical than contemporary and did not change the minds of those who opposed the constitution. Ratification came about because of political pressure and additional compromises, most importantly the inclusion of a Bill of Rights which was a key anti-Federalist demand. Nonetheless the Federalist Papers provide an invaluable window into the thoughts and minds of the men who penned the constitution and what they believed and why. It is clear that these beliefs shaped the constitution which, in turn, shaped the United States in years to come.

Between December 1787 and the summer of 1789, 11 of the 13 states ratified the new constitution. Federal elections were held in the fall and George Washington became the first president of the United States, setting out to establish the institutions of the new federal government. By the spring of 1790, the last of the 13 states, Rhode Island, had ratified and the Bill of Rights was added in 1791. The slavery question, was put on hold for two decades. The system of government worked but political issues—slavery and westward expansion—would continue to divide the nation. For the moment, the battle to build a "more perfect union" was over.

Activity

Comparing the Articles of Confederation and the US Constitution

The Articles of Confederation and the Constitution of 1789	Articles of Confederation	US Constitution
Legislature	Unicameral Congress	Bicameral (House of Representatives and Senate)
Members of Congress	2–7 per state	Two per state (Senators) Representation by population (Congressmen)
Voting in Congress	One vote per state	A vote for each Senator and Representative
Selection of Congress:	Appointed by states legislatures in a manner each legislature directed	Congress elected. Senators appointed by State legislature.
Terms of office	One year	Representatives: 2 years Senators: 6 years
Compensation	Paid by states	Paid by federal government
Congress not in session	Powers conferred to a committee of states	President recalls Congress
Chair of Legislature	President	House of Representatives: Speaker Senate: Vice President
Constitutional disputes	Congress	Supreme Court
Admission of new states	Agreement of 9 states	Congress
Amendments	Unanimous agreement of states	Three quarters of the Senate
Armed forces	States fight pirates, Congress requisitions states for troops	Congress establishes and maintains the army and navy
Treasury (power to print money)	Federal government and states mint money	Federal government only
Taxes	Apportioned by Congress, collected by the states	Approved and collected by Congress
Ratification of Constitution	Unanimous consent	Consent by 9 states.
Bill of Rights	No Bill of Rights	Added 1791

Activity

Research on the Enlightenment

Choose one of the following writers and analyze the contribution of their enlightened ideas to the Constitution of the United States.

● Montesquieu

● Jean-Jacques Rousseau

● Voltaire

● Jeremy Bentham

● Adam Smith

Activity

Terminology

Explain the following terms as they apply to a federal government:

Legislative
Executive
Judiciary
Separation of powers
Checks and balances
Separation of church and state
Bill of Rights

Activity

The Federalist Papers

Source A

Federalist paper no. 10 by James Madison, published in *The Independent Journal*, 1787.

.... The valuable improvements made by the American constitutions on the popular models, both ancient and modern, cannot certainly be too much admired; but it would be an unwarranted partiality, to contend that they have as effectually obviated the danger on this side, as was wished and expected. Complaints are everywhere heard from our most considerate and virtuous citizens ... that our governments are too unstable, that the public good is disregarded in the conflicts of the rival parties, and that measures are too often decided, not according to the rules of justice and the rights of the minor party, but by the superior force of an interested and overbearing majority. However anxiously we may wish that these complaints had no foundation, the evidence, of known facts will not permit us to deny that they are in some degree true ... Other causes will not alone account for many of our heaviest misfortunes; and, particularly, for that prevailing and increasing distrust of public engagements, and alarm for private rights, which are echoed from one end of the continent to the other. These must be chiefly, if not wholly, effects of the unsteadiness and injustice with which a factitious spirit has tainted our public administrations ...

Source B

Letter to James Madison from Thomas Jefferson, Paris, December 20, 1787.

... I like much the general idea of framing a government which should go on of itself peaceably, without needing continual recurrence to the state legislatures. I like the organization of the government into Legislative, Judiciary & Executive. I like the power given the Legislature to levy taxes, and for that reason soley approve of the greater house being chosen by the people directly ... I am captivated by the compromise of the opposite claims of the great & and little states, of the latter to equal, and the former to proportional influence. I am much pleased too with the substitution of the method of voting by persons, instead of that of voting by states: and I like *the negative given to the Executive with a third of either house*, though I should have liked it better had the Judiciary been associated for that purpose, or invested with a similar and separate power. There are other good things of less moment. I will now add what I do not like. First the omission of a bill of rights providing clearly & without the aid of sophisms for freedom of religion, freedom of the press, protection against standing armies, restrictions against monopolies, the eternal & unremitting force of habeas corpus laws, and trials by jury in all matters of fact triable by the laws of the land & not by the law of nations ...

Source C

Statement by Richard Henry, representative of Virginia, for the Philadelphia Convention debate concerning the ratification of the constitution, Monday, June 14, 1788.

—Mr. Chairman, the necessity of a bill of rights appears to me be greater in this government, than ever it was in any government, before. I observe already, that the sense of the European nations, and particularly Great Britain, is against the construction of rights being retained, which are not excessively relinquished. I repeat, that all nations have adopted this construction—that all rights not expressively and unequivocally reserved to the people, are impliedly and incidentally relinquished to ruler; as necessarily inseparable from the delegated powers ... let us consider the sentiments which have been entertained by the people of America in this subject. At the revolution it must be admitted, that it was their sense to put down these great rights which ought in all countries to be held inviolable and sacred. Virginia did so, we all remember. She made a compact to reserve, expressly, certain rights.

Source D

Federalist paper no. 30, by Alexander Hamilton, published in the *New York Packet*, Friday, December 28, 1787.

The present Confederation, feeble as it is intended to repose in the United States, an unlimited power of providing for the pecuniary wants of the Union. But proceeding upon an erroneous principle, it has been done in such a manner as entirely to have frustrated the intention. Congress, by the articles which compose that compact ... are authorized to ascertain and call for any sums of money necessary, in their judgement, to the service of the United States; and their requisitions, if conformable to the rule of apportionment, are in every constitutional sense obligatory upon the States. These have no right to question the propriety of the demand; no discretion beyond that of devising the ways and means of furnishing the sums demanded. But though this be strictly and truly the case; though the assumption of such a right would be an infringement of the articles of Union; though it may seldom or never have been avowedly claimed, yet in practice it has been constantly exercised, and would continue to be so, as long as the revenues of the Confederacy should remain dependent on the intermediate agency of its members. What the consequences of this system have been, is within the knowledge of every man the least conversant in our public affairs, and has been amply unfolded in different parts of these inquiries. It is this which has chiefly contributed to reduce us to a situation, which affords ample cause both of mortification to ourselves, and of triumph to our enemies.

Source E

Statement by Amos Singletary, the representative from Massachusetts, for the philadelphia Convention debate concerning the ratification of the constitution. Friday, January 25, 1788.

> ... Mr. President, and I say, that if anybody had proposed such a constitution as this in that day it would have been thrown away at once. It would not have been looked at. We contended with Great Britain—some said for a three penny duty in tea; but it was not that—it was because they claimed a right to tax us and bind us in all cases whatever. Any does not this constitution do the same? Does it not take away all we have—all our property? Does it not lay all taxes, duties, imposts and excise? And what more have we to give? They tell us congress won't lay dry taxes upon us, but collect all the money they want by impost [something imposed or levied] ... and there will always be the same objection; they will be able to raise money enough by impost, and then they will lay it on the land and take all we have.

Complete this chart

On a chart list in point form the origin, purpose, value and limitations of these documents

Sources	A	B	C	D	E
Origin					
Purpose					
Value					
Limitation					

Questions

1 With reference to source B:

    a What is Jefferson referring to? "I like the negative given the executive by a third of either house."

    b What does Jefferson dislike about the new constitution?

2 Compare and contrast source D and E in their views on taxation.

3 Evaluate source A and D as justification for the Federalist positions.

4 With reference to all the sources and your own knowledge, explain why and for what reasons these authors differed on the role and powers of the federal government.

The rise and rule of the *caudillos* in Latin America

In a seminal work on an accurate definition of the figure of the *caudillo* in the history of Latin America, during the first half of the 19th century, Argentine historian Tulio Halperín Donghi points out that it is both simplistic and inaccurate to reduce to a caricature these regional strongmen that were so important in nation-building. Most went far beyond the stereotypical role of military or paramilitary leader merely seeking to obtain power by force rather than democratic means. Regionalism, federalism, foreign intervention, the territorial fragmentation of the former viceroyalties and a general context of insecurity caused strong personalities to emerge and take charge, often representing and counting on the mutual support of different interest groups that varied vastly between Mexico, Central America and South America. The complex social, political and economic panorama that ensued following the independence wars created contexts for these strong leaders to become forceful social actors in building and governing new nations.

Italian political scientist Federica Morelli has pointed to a new analysis of 19th century Latin American *caudillos,* no longer viewed as power-hungry traitors to the cause of democracy in their nascent nations, which has been the prevalent view of historians since the end of the 19th century and beginning of the 20th, as well as the view of many North American and European historians. She proposes the revisionist view, borne out by new evidence, that the personal rural charisma, the military and violent aura has obscured a budding liberalism and republican institution founding in the new political spaces which opened within the new governments. Contrary to what has been written in the past, new evidence has found that many new Latin American nations adopted institutions tending toward democracy, such as wider coverage of suffrage. In fact, with the exception of Ecuador and Chile, most countries extended the vote to Indians and illiterate males. Instead of viewing *caudillos* as tyrants in the midst of political anarchy in which elections played no part, the new Latin American historiography has now found that the *caudillos*, in fact, put forward practices of political modernity alongside traditional conservative roles. The new perspective focuses on petitions, local revolts, other forms of community-based grass-roots political practices that contributed toward nationbuilding in newly independent Latin American countries. In addition, lawyers and jurists in urban areas were responsible for constructing the legal backbone of the state, including provisions for constitutions, codes of law, business and market regulation, and penal codes. Legal professionals often formed the core of the political élites and greatly influenced public opinion. The social actors also contributed to nationbuilding from the salons, literary circles, political clubs, assemblies and congresses, Masonic lodges and the military. The *caudillos* had to negotiate among all of these political and social actors, in addition to local élites, municipal leaders and popular groups, such as peasants, Native Americans and former African slaves.

> ### Discussion point
>
> **The caudillo phenomenon**
>
> In what ways and to what extent was the rule of Spain and, to a lesser degree, Portugal responsible for the political, economic and social upheaval in Latin America during the 19th century that led to the emergence of the *caudillos*?
>
> **In what ways were local and regional issues, as well as geography, foreign intervention and centralism contributing factors?**

This section will provide students with the opportunity to understand why, in some recently independent Latin American countries, *caudillos* of different types emerged. Within the new nations of the former Spanish and Portuguese colonies, a great struggle ensued. Nations were divided by regionalism which challenged the ability of many countries to create stable, effective systems of government and healthy economies. The division also had as an ideological backdrop: conservativism vs. liberalism. Bitter, and less often, bloody and protracted contests for power between these groups dominated Latin American politics, as it did politics in North America and most of Europe, until the end of the 19th century.

Caudillos emerged from both liberal and conservative camps, representing the grievances of different interest groups: ranchers, farmers, merchants, landowners, mine owners and many other groups. Sometimes they represented, or had the support of the lower classes and the Indians. Some were of humble origin, like Rafael Carrera of Guatemala; others were of mixed racial and social origins, like José Antonio Páez of Venezuela. Others, like Martín Miguel de Güemes in northern Argentina, fiercely defended the territory and rights of his native Salta against the centralism of Buenos Aires. José G. Artigas also staunchly defended his region north of the Río de la Plata (River Plate) from Buenos Aires as well as Portuguese encroachment, culminating in the foundation of Uruguay. Juan Manuel de Rosas of Argentina was much absorbed by the diplomatic and military complications with France, Britain, Uruguay, Bolivia, Chile, Paraguay and Brazil.

Local **peons** or former soldiers of the independence armies became the military support for some of the early *caudillos*. The *caudillos* mentioned above were successful and popular officers of the wars of independence. Charismatic, they sometimes employed military justice with impunity to maintain authority and, at times, to eliminate opponents. In other cases, the *caudillos* came to power in the midst of liberal–conservative hostility, such as Rafael Carrera in Guatemala. While Guatemala was still part of the newly independent United Provinces of Central America and early into breaking away from it, Guatemala's government was liberal. The church was especially targeted, as the liberal governments passed reforms to curtail the power of the Roman Catholic Church: this resulted in the expulsion of Dominicans and Jesuits (due mostly to their economic power), the abolition of tithes and recognition of civil marriage and divorce, and the toleration of all religions. Municipalities were especially powerful as sources of local and state power in Guatemala, following not only the colonial tradition of the *cabildo*, or council, but also traditional Indian custom, according to Guatemalan historian Arturo Taracena. Their disagreement with these liberal anti-church moves certainly did much to support the popular *caudillo* Rafael Carrera in his rise to power in 1838. He then, promptly, repealed all the laws against the established church, yet kept toleration of other religions. Carrera also urged the Guatemalan Assembly to allow the Jesuits to return to Guatemala as a boon to education. Carrera eventually signed a concordat with the Vatican in 1852 which strengthened the role of the Catholic Church in

The words **peon** and **peonage** are derived from the Spanish *peón*. It has a range of meanings, but is generally used to describe someone of low social origins, who is in a position of servitude or debt bondage.

Guatemala, making it the exclusive religion and only doctrine taught in schools: a state of affairs which lasted until the liberal revolution in 1871.

A different sort of strong leader emerged in Chile in the 1830s. Businessman Diego Portales was never president, but he formed powerful conservative influence groups as Minister (of the Interior, then of War and the Navy), that changed the political landscape of the country for a century. He was a frequent contributor and commentator for the press and used his powerful influence to control the political anarchy of the previous liberal governments. This austere figure of a public servant of frugal honesty has been enriched by historiography analyzing his defence of the rule of law and stressing social obedience to authority, while maintaining the privileges of the élite and the Catholic Church. He believed in a strong, centralized legal system and judiciary, and wrote that the judicial system must be improved to curb abuses. Democracy was a future ideal to Portales, who believed that first a strong system of law and order was necessary for social control and for the stability required for business to progress. This occurred, and landholders, businessmen and mine owners prospered while the majority of Chileans did not.

Caudillos were important nation-builders in Latin American politics from 1820 into the 1870s, but they were by no means the only social actors demanding or suppressing change. In the newly independent Kingdom of Brazil, according to Brazilian historian Jurandir Malerba, strong conservative élite influence groups exerted their power to maintain their privilege, their monopoly of commerce and the institution of slavery until the end of the 19th century, sometimes supporting local strongmen or *caudillos* in the powerful states of Rio de Janeiro, São Paulo and Minas. The monarchy, like its republican counterparts in most of the rest of Latin America, had a strong social and political influence group in the *salons*, and one of the best known hostesses was the Countess de Barral from the 1850s on. Brazilian writer Wanderley Pinho comments that "No other woman of that era had as much social and political power." Living alternately in Bahia and in Paris, she subtly, but decisively influenced the abolitionist movement, protested imprisonment of Catholic bishops, declared the freedom of her female slaves' children in the 1860's and freed all her slaves in 1880. She often traveled to Rio de Janeiro and the Court in Petrópolis, where she had direct contact with Pedro II and the Brazilian monarchy and often carried missives for him to and from Europe. Her *salon* in Rio was frequented by liberals and conservatives, providing a space for discussion, compromise and decision-making kept civil by the countess's legendary finesse.

Juan Manuel de Rosas of Argentina is a good example of how difficult it is to simply dismiss *caudillos* as stereotypical, crude despots. Rosas ruled for 23 years and was certainly a tyrant, refusing to build republican institutions or a constitution, yet as Argentine historian José Ramos Mejía has written, "In the matter of public funds, Rosas never touched one peso for his own benefit, he lived soberly and modestly and died in poverty." He had been one of the richest

Activity

Film activity

Watch the film *Camila* (1984, Dir. Maria Luisa Bemberg), which deals with life during the Rosas dictatorship in Argentina until 1852.

Examine and discuss the role of the élite in supporting Rosas and the power of the Roman Catholic Church and Rosas in upholding traditional values and customs, as well as curtailing liberal political thought.

conservative landowners in Argentina and he ruled with an iron hand, grievously curtailing free speech and ideas, supported by the Roman Catholic Church. In 1835, he announced a new customs law that was meant to protect agriculture and ranchers, as well as the manufacturing industry, to give the middle-classes a chance to prosper. On the other hand, he did not behave with such largesse toward Argentina's Native American population, and was wary enough of them to say, when offered their support in 1852 against the army that would unseat him: "If we triumph, who will contain the Indians? And if we are defeated, who will contain the Indians?" In addition, revisionist Argentine historian Tulio Halperín Donghi has proposed that Rosas empowered the rural peonage and argues that this makes him "the leader of a bourgeois revolution that has a ranching and rural base, and not, like the metropolitan countries, an industrial and urban base."

Juan Manuel de Rosas (1793–1877)

Juan Manuel de Rosas earned his spurs fighting in a number of wars against foreign and domestic enemies before he came to power as the Governor of Buenos Aires Province (1829–32). He was Caudillo of Argentina from 1835 until his defeat at the Battle of Caseros in 1852. In power, Rosas believed that whatever helped the cattle industry helped the nation. Not surprisingly, he was popular with ranchers, *gauchos*, meat-plant owners and workers. He owned vast tracts of land and was related to Argentina's wealthiest landowning family. He supported the traditional role of the Catholic Church and was no friend of liberal reforms. He was popular with the people who believed he was their benefactor and protector, but also ruthless in putting down his opponents in wars waged against Argentina's domestic and foreign enemies.

Rosas ruled from Buenos Aires yet his support was in the country where he spent many months away from the capital on his ranch. He was suspicious of the Europeans but was popular with the people when he stood up to the English and French on several occasions. The key to his power and longevity was his military prowess. Initially, he recruited an army of *gauchos*, mulattos and *mestizos* and led them to victory after victory. He gave his soldiers land grants and won their loyalty. He maintained the support of the landowning gentry by not initiating land-reforms. The creole élite eventually, however, defeated him in 1852 with the support of the armies of Brazil and Uruguay, after which he fled to England. Rosas's defeat opened the door for liberal values to gain the upper hand. A liberal constitution, capitalism, land speculation and an export-driven cattle industry to feed beef-hungry Europe followed his exile. In the end, his greatest achievement was keeping Argentina united.

Activity

The caudillo: Three historians' views

Read the views of three US and British historians and address the questions at the end of this section

Source A

A few caudillos, however, championed the lifestyles and needs of the dispossessed majority and can be considered "popular" or "folk" caudillos. A highly complex group, they shared some of the characteristics of the elite caudillos, but two major distinctions marked them as unique. They refused to accept unconditionally the elites' ideology of progress, exhibiting a preference for the American experience with its Indo-Afro-Iberian ingredients and, consequently, a greater suspicion of the post-Enlightenment European model. Further they claimed to serve the folk rather than the elite.

A nineteenth century contemporary found that "the people regarded a popular caudillo as 'guardian of their traditions,' the defender of their way of life." And such leaders constituted "the will of the popular masses ... the immediate organ and arm of the people ... the caudillos are democracy."

If the folk obeyed unreservedly those popular leaders, the caudillos in turn bore the obligation to protect and to provide for the welfare of the people. The ruled and the ruler were responsible to and for each other, a personal relationship challenged in the nineteenth century by the more impersonal capitalist concept that a growing gross national product would provide best for all. The popularity of those caudillos is undeniable.

Source: Burns, Bradford E. and Charlip, Julia A. 2007. *Latin America: A Concise Interpretive History*. New Jersey: Pearson-Prentice Hall. pp. 112–13.

Source B

In the conditions prevailing afters the wars of independence there were plenty of opportunities for political buccaneering. Economic depression, the breakdown of law and order, the militarization of society, all contributed to the phenomenon of the caudillo—a charismatic leader who advanced his interests through a combination of military and political skills, and was able to build up a network of clients by dispensing favours and patronage. Caudillos were the major power-brokers and power-seekers in the political world; in fact, they treated politics as a form of economic enterprise, adopting liberalism or conservatism as best suited their strategy for winning control of public funds in order to enhance their capacity to offer patronage and so build up their networks of power.

Source: Williamson, Edwin. 2009. *The Penguin History of Latin America*. Penguin Books. p. 237.

Source C

The Caudillo had three basic qualifications; an economic base, a social constituency and a political project. He first emerged as a local hero, the strong man of his region, whose authority derived from ownership of land, access to men and resources and achievements that impressed for their value of their valor. A caudillo would ride out from his hacienda at the head of an armed band, his followers bound to him by personal ties of dominance and submission and by a common desire to obtain power and weath by force of arms. His progress then depended on the strength of the state. In societies were succession to office was not yet formalized, caudillism filled the gap; political competition was expressed in armed conflice and the successful competitor ruled y violence, not by right of inheritance or election. Such rule would be subject to further competition and could rarely guarantee its own permanence.

Caudillos were thus likely to emerge when the state was in disarray, the political process disrupted, and society in turmoil; personalism and violence took the place of law and institutions, and the rule of the powerful was preferred to representative government.

Source: Lynch, John. 1992. *Caudillos in Spanish America*. Oxford: Clarendon Press.

Questions

Based on the views of these historians answer the following questions:

1 What pre-conditions allowed the *caudillos* to emerge?

2 What were the dominate characteristics of a *caudillo*?

3 Speculate on why *caudillos* did not become a permanent fixture in Latin America

4 Why were *caudillos* most popular with the "folk."?

5 Why did South Americans support the *caudillos* initially?

6 Using the opinions of all three historians, and the Latin American sources mentioned in the text, develop a profile of the *caudillo*.

Activity

The *caudillo* and the Artist

Portrayed as a heroic figure, José Antonio Páez came to prominence because of his bravery and leadership during the wars of independence, serving with Simón Bolívar. In 1830, Páez declared Venezuela independent from Gran Colombia. Nicknamed *El Centauro de los Llanos* (The Centaur of the Plains), Páez served three terms as president.

Examine the two paintings of Páez and answer the questions that follow.

José Antonio Páez, painted in 1874 by Martín Tovar y Tovar.

The Battle of Las Quesearas del Medio, 2 April 1819, painted by Auturo Michelena in 1890. Here, Michelena depicts the moment when Páez ordered his 150 lancers to "Vuelvan Caras!" (Literally to about-face and attack 1,000 Spanish calvary). The Spanish were defeated leaving over 400 dead, while Páez lost six men.

Compare and contrast the messages conveyed in these two paintings.

1 What is the painter of the presidential portrait attempting to convey about José Antonio Páez?

2 Why do you think the lancers obey Páez and turn to face the hard-charging Spanish cavalry despite being outnumbered almost ten to one? How does the painting support your conclusions?

3 Why was it important in wars of independence to portray leaders as heroes?

The War of 1812

Great Britain and the United States went to war for the second time in 20 years in 1812. It was a war that neither side wanted but which both seemed incapable of stopping. War aims on both sides were muddled and public opinion was deeply divided. In the United States support for the war was stronger the further south you got from the Canadian border. In Britain, all attention was on defeating Napoleon on the Continent and the British had ignored the problems that would spark the conflict until it was too late. The war was not avoided, lasted two bloody years and was unpopular with both sides, but the impact of the war created a desire to improve relations between the United States and Britain in the long term. The war also provided enduring historical myths for both sides (Canada and the United States) that became deeply ingrained in the national fabric of both nations. After the war, the United States turned its attention to the slavery issue and westward expansion and British North America (Canada) set itself on the path to nationhood.

The Chesapeake incident

In February 1806, it was reported to the British admiralty that several Royal Navy deserters had joined the crew of the USS *Chesapeake*, a 36-gun frigate. The British requested their return but an investigation by James Madison found that the men were US citizens (albeit only recently naturalized). Meanwhile, the British navy's admiralty issued orders for the men to be returned. The order stated that the *Chesapeake's* crew had many former Royal Navy sailors. The order continued that any British warship encountering the *Chesapeake* was to board and search for deserters.

On June 22, 1807, *Chesapeake* was on its way to the Mediterranean when the 50-gun HMS *Leopard* spotted it. A British messenger rowed to the *Chesapeake* and demanded permission to board and search for deserters. *Chesapeake's* Captain James Barron refused adding that he had no deserters on board. The *Leopard* replied to Barron's refusal with a devastating broadside that killed three and wounded 20. Caught by surprise, the *Chesapeake* immediately "struck the colors" (signalled its surrender by lowering the United States flag). The British boarded and arrested four men. One was hung, one died, the other two were repatriated in 1811. President Jefferson was incensed by this act of war and violation of American sovereignty, writing:

> These aggravations necessarily lead to the policy either of never admitting an armed vessel into our harbours, or of maintaining in every harbour such an armed force as may constrain obedience to the laws, and protect the lives and property of our citizens, against their armed guests.

Pressured by an irate Congress, notably the "War Hawks" from the southern states led by Kentuckian Henry Clay, Jefferson signed the Embargo Act and the United States and Britain moved closer to war.

Causes of the War of 1812

The war resulted from three main causes. First, the search and seizure of neutral North-American trade vessels on the high seas by the French and British navies (mainly by the latter). Cargos were seized and ships impounded. Efforts to convince the British and the French to honor US neutrality through diplomacy and economic sanctions failed. Second was the **impressment** of sailors from US vessels by the Royal Navy. The British were looking for British sailors serving on US ships but that did not stop them from taking US sailors as well. Estimates vary on the actual number of sailors taken but the figure is in the vicinity of 10,000. Unrelated to these maritime causes was the desire for land in the American Midwest, particularly the territories south of the Great Lakes, the headwaters of the Missouri and Ohio rivers. As settlers crossed the Appalachians into the Ohio Valley, the Native Americans lead by Tecumseh and his twin brother the "Prophet" fought back. Many in the United States believed the British supported the natives and supplied them with muskets, shot and powder.

> **Impressment** is a term referring to being forced to serve in the British navy.

Search and seizure

Great Britain began fighting Napoleon sporadically in 1793 and continually after 1803. The Royal Navy had destroyed the combined French and Spanish fleet off the Spanish coast in one of history's most important sea battles, the Battle of Trafalgar, in 1805. Thereafter, Britannia ruled the waves. The Royal Navy set up a blockade to starve France. American trade vessels were stopped and searched, cargos impounded, ships seized and ex-British sailors arrested (impressed). The French responded in kind but were no match for the Royal Navy. The US declared neutrality and demanded the British and French allow US-flagged vessels to cross the respective blockade lines and deliver their cargos. The British and French declined and continued to search and seize US ships. Jefferson called on Congress to ratify the Non-Importation Acts to stop the flow of specific manufactured goods to the United States. US manufacturers would fill the gap. But the Act was delayed pending further negotiations. In a last ditch effort, Jefferson sent trusted colleagues James Monroe and William Pinkney to Britain to negotiate a treaty to respect US neutrality and establish terms of trade between Britain and the United States. The mission failed, the British agreed to some terms but did not follow through and Jefferson signed a different piece of legislation, The Embargo Act, in late 1807 which prohibited the export of all goods from the United States. The Act backfired on US business interests.

At the time, however, the really important issue was impressment. British warships were short of sailors to trim sails and fire cannons. As early as 1803, they began stopping US ships and taking sailors they believed had deserted from the Royal Navy. To the US, this practice was unconscionable, a violation of their sovereignty, and an act of war. The United States demanded the British respect their neutrality and stop the practice but these entreaties fell on deaf ears. In the years leading up to the war, approximately 10,000 sailors were impressed, of whom 1,000 were British. The issue exploded into a full-blown crisis with the *Chesapeake* incident.

The War Hawks demanded action but were a vocal minority at this time. Jefferson proposed economic sanctions. First, he recalled US warships from foreign stations to protect east coast harbours. Next, in December, he convened cabinet to discuss options. Just prior to the meeting he learned of Napoleon's Berlin Decree, the French version of a new British policy requiring ships heading to France to stop at a British port and pay duties. Under the Embargo Act, the US state of New England suffered more than the intended targets but Jefferson countered that economic sanctions were preferable to cannon fire. Congress tried three amendments but these also failed. US business continued to suffer and worse yet, the embargo promoted smuggling notably on the Great Lakes. The British and French maintained their respective blockades and search and seizure continued.

The impasse was broken in 1810 when Napoleon, feeling the effects of the blockade, advised President Madison that France would honour US neutrality. Napoleon's capitulation to US demands was more symbolic than substantial; by this time the Royal Navy had reduced US trade with France to a trickle. The British were winning the economic war.

A house divided

The United States was deeply split. The Southern War Hawk senators demanded "Free Trade and Sailors' Rights" and the annexation of the Ohio-Wabash country. The tribes in that territory had been united under the charismatic leadership of the famous chief of the Shawnee, Tecumseh, and were a formidable obstacle to the white man's idea of growth and westward expansion. Tecumseh's mystical twin brother "The Prophet" had been killed at the Tippecanoe in 1811. Tecumseh vowed to avenge his brother's death and joined the British, rising to the rank of Brigadier-General. The "War Hawks" blamed the British who supplied the Shawnee with arms. Joseph Desha, another War Hawk from Kentucky, argued that "you must remove the cause if you expect to perform the cure."

But why fight Britain and not France who had committed nearly as many maritime offenses? Traditional allegiance to France was partly the explanation. So, too, Canada's rich farmlands along the Great Lakes and the Saint Lawrence River were a valuable prize. Madison was reluctant to even discuss the matter. The Virginia Representative John Randolph opposed the "War Hawks" and stated that the real cause was to grab land:

> If you go to war it will not be for the protection of, or defense of your maritime rights. ... The rich vein of ... land, which is said to be even better on the other side of the lake that on this. Agrarian cupidity, not maritime right urges this war. ... we have heard but on work. ... Canada! Canada! Canada! It is to acquire a preponding northern influence, that you are to launch into war ..."

> **Source:** Debates of the 12th Congress, November 29, 1811.

Seafaring New Englanders opposed the war and would greet its declaration with muffled bells, flags at half-mast and public fasting. Impressment, they said, was an old and exaggerated wrong. New England merchants were still making money trading with the British

A house divided against itself cannot stand.
Abraham Lincoln, June 16, 1858

and many sympathized with the plight of Britain fighting tooth and nail against Napoleon, whom they regarded as the "Corsican butcher" and the "anti-Christ of the age".

Federalists condemned the war as they opposed acquisition of Canada which, in their view, would merely add more agrarian states from the wild northwest. This in turn would increase the voting strength of the party of the west—the Republicans.

James Madison became president in 1810. In May, Congress directed the president to begin trade with either Britain or France if they agreed to respect US neutrality. If either accepted, the United States would forbid trade with the other. The French paid lip service but the British refused.

By 1812, the War Hawks position in Congress was gaining momentum. Henry Clay's influence was at its zenith as speaker of the house and pressured President Madison relentlessly to declare war. On more than one occasion Henry Clay demanded war:

> "It is absurd to suppose that we will not succeed in our enterprise against the enemy's provinces. We have Canada as much at our command as Great Britain has the ocean. ... I would take the whole continent from them and ask no favours. I wish never to see peace until we do."

> **Source:** Sutherin, Victor. 1999. *The War of 1812*. Toronto, Canada: McClelland and Stewart. p. 23.

Historians on both sides of the border agree that attacking Canada was not the primary war aim but a bargaining chip. Jefferson said capturing Canada would be a matter of marching and provide practice for the assault on Halifax which would finally drive the British out of North America. What the US wanted was the British out of the west.

On June 1, Madison told Congress that he was cautiously optimistic that British might would follow the French example and end the blockade. He was right. The new British prime minister, Lord Liverpool, did not want a war with the United States and in late May rescinded the search and seizure orders. Unfortunately, the news took three weeks to cross the Atlantic and Congress had declared war before the mail packet arrived. The vote in Congress reflected the nation's uncertainty: The house voted 79 to 49; the Senate 19 to 13. On June 18, Madison signed the declaration of war.

Opposition to Mr Madison's war was so vociferous that New Englanders lent more money to the British than the federal treasury and sold foodstuffs to the British army throughout the war. New England Governors steadfastly refused to allow the militia to fight out of state. The divided nation went to war with uncertain aims and a Continental army numbering 12,000; the navy numbered 16 frigates (44 guns); fast and agile and capably crewed, these warships were ideal for catching pirates and smugglers. By comparison, the Royal Navy had over one hundred ships with 74 guns or more. The British army was battle-hardened, experienced and boasted many talented officers. One of the top military leaders was Arthur Wellesley, the

Duke of Wellington. Nick-named the "Iron Duke" he had driven the French out of Spain and in 1815 defeated Napoleon at Waterloo. Fortunately for the United States, the British were tied down in Europe and considered the war with the US to be a nuisance, a distraction from the main event in Europe. They would limit the soldiers, ships and guns deployed to defend British North America. American strategy was based on this fact and they took a chance that they could defeat the British before the British defeated Napoleon.

The course of the war

In the spring, the United States launched a three-pronged invasion of Canada that according to Jefferson would be nothing more than "a matter of marching". General Hull would attack at Detroit and head east with about 2,500 men. The second invasion would cross the Niagara, capture the Niagara peninsula and the third and most important, would head up Lake Champlain and secure Montreal. Montreal was the front door to the interior and once in American hands they would choke off the British forces fighting in Upper Canada.

The General in command of the Canadian forces, Sir Isaac Brock, would make short work of Jefferson's pejorative musing. A capable, talented, charismatic officer, he faced long odds. How to defend a long border with a couple of British infantry regiments, a few cannons, undisciplined native allies and poorly trained militia of dubious loyalty and quality. Brock decided to seize the initiative and attack. In a series of rapid manoeuvres, Brock's combined forces captured without firing a shot Fort Michilmackinac which commanded the upper Great Lakes of Huron, Michigan and Superior. Brock surrounded General Hull's forces at Detroit and, fearing a scalping massacre, Hull promptly surrendered.

The defeat shocked the United States who demanded an end to Hull's career. A courts martial sentenced him to hang but President Madison commuted the sentence because of Hull's service record in the Revolution. Further east, Brock turned back the Niagara invasion in the first major engagement of the war, the Battle of Queenston Heights, in which Brock was killed leading the counter-attack. Brock was irreplaceable and thereafter the defense of Canada fell into the hands of the overly cautious and often indecisive Sir George Prevost. After that, the main US effort of 10,000 men driving north from Lake Champlain simply fell apart from bad management. The two sides would continue to stumble about the wilderness for the remainder of 1812.

The US army had learned valuable lessons in training, equipment and leadership. The next invasions in 1813 were more successful, notably the capture and burning of York (present-day Toronto). But the success was short-lived and the invaders were either forced back across the border or grew weary of occupation and returned home for the harvest.

At sea, the US frigates, most famously, the USS *Constitution*, defeated the British in four of five engagements. To the United States these victories signified their naval superiority; to the British they were a source of considerable embarrassment. The US navy's frigates might be able to defeat the Royal Navy's frigates but were no match for British battleships. The American frigates spent most of the war bottled up in port. The Royal Navy blockaded the US coast and put ashore raiding parties without opposition.

The Great Lakes were a different story. The US navy defeated the British in a series of significant major engagements and retained naval superiority on the Lakes until the war's conclusion. At the Battle of the Thames, Tecumseh was killed—breaking the back of Britain's alliance with the Indians. The battles were many all along the border and became increasingly European looking in architecture and tactics. Long lines of disciplined infantry exchanged volley fire at close range with cannons and cavalry adding to the fray.

The good news for the British was the defeat and exile of Napoleon. The US looked eastward and saw the British gaze firmly fixed on them. Events in Europe would no longer restrict British operations. In June 1814, the British launched a three pronged invasion against the top, middle and bottom of the United States. In August, four thousand British troops landed near Washington, defeated six thousand panic-stricken militia at Bladensburg, marched on the capital, burned the White House and looted the city. In one famous incident a British officer "captured" President Madison's love letters to wife Dolly.

Next, the British fleet attacked Baltimore—a haven for US privateers. During the attack on Fort McHenry, Francis Scott Key penned the "Star Spangled Banner." The British fleet was driven off and the invaders boarded ship and left. The next move came in September 1814, when ten thousand British "redcoats" stood ready to invade up-state New York near Plattsburgh but retreated after the US navy defeated the British flotilla.

Meanwhile, the two sides had agreed to start negotiations, bowing to pressure by the Russian Tsar. Both sides wanted to find a way out of the miserable struggle. The Treaty of Ghent was signed on Christmas Eve 1814 ending the war; it was more an armistice than treaty. Both sides agreed to return to pre-1812 borders and the treaty contained nothing about US war aims, such as the acquisition of Native lands in the west, search and seizure or impressments.

The war had ended in a draw lacking the decisive engagement that could have decided the war for one side or the other. For the British there was no equivalent of the Plains of Abraham or for the United States no repeat of Yorktown. Instead the war was a bloody stalemate on land and sea that doled out ample measures of misery, disease and death but no taste of victory. The weary armies went home, but the tragedy had one final act.

The final operation was a British attempt to capture New Orleans by landing an army of 15,000 Napoleonic veterans and seize control of the Mississippi River. Standing behind stacked cotton bales ready to repel the invaders were seven thousand defenders including many frontiersmen from Louisiana, Kentucky and Tennessee. Their commander was "Old Hickory"—General Andrew Jackson—the renowned champion of Indian removals, and supporter of slavery, and future president. The Battle of New Orleans was fought

January 8, 1815, two weeks after the Treaty of Ghent had been signed and was the greatest US victory of the war. The British attack was confused by fog: they advanced on the center of the US line and were shot to pieces suffering 2,000 casualties while US losses were less than 100. The war was over.

News of the triumph reached a jubilant capital but the celebration was short-lived when the treaty arrived. The US Senate quickly approved the treaty with the slogan "Not One Inch of Territory Ceded or Lost". No one mentioned the 1812 slogan "On to Canada".

The battle is important for three reasons. First, it ended British operations against the United States. Second, US folk legend created the frontier myth of the buckskin-clad frontiersmen who had defeated the British army's best and gave the US victory in a second war of independence for US democracy over imperial domination. Third, the battle marked the start of Andrew Jackson's march to the presidency.

The end of the war

What had been gained? The British kept Canada but realized defending it was difficult and moved quickly to repair relations with the United States. In 1819, the Rush-Bagot Treaty reduced the naval forces on the Great Lakes to one ship each. However, to guard against further invasions, the British began fortifying the border with a series of installations at key locations the largest of which was Fort Henry at Kingston. During the 1820s, British engineers constructed the Rideau Canal which connected Montreal to Kingston allowing for the rapid movement of troops and supplies without relying on the St. Lawrence River. The forts were for naught, the United States never launched an invasion. (The post-civil war Fenian raids were not sponsored or condoned by the US government.)

TOK Link

The use of evidence: Mythmaking and the War of 1812

Why do accounts of the same historical event differ? Whose history do we study? Historian Margaret MacMillan contends that history is "not to ... make the present generation feel good but to remind us that human affairs are complicated."

Historians contend that the history is written by the victors. The War of 1812 provides historians with a unique challenge because both sides claimed a qualified victory.

The creation of national myths based on important events provide nations with a common sense of purpose, identity and value. As an example of this, consider these different perceptions on the War of 1812.

Thomas Bailey and David M. Kennedy in *The American Pageant* refer to the War of 1812 as "The Second War for Independence." This suggests that the United States had fought and defeated the British for a second time to gain and retain their freedom. Canadian historians would challenge this claim contending that Canada was the real victim and successfully defended itself from numerous US invasions paving the way for Canadian confederation. For Canadians it was the Battle of Queenston Heights (1812) and for Americans it was the Battle of New Orleans (1815).

Men make their own history ...
Karl Marx

US mythology: The Battle of New Orleans

The Facts: Andrew Jackson's army of 7,000 defeated a veteran British force of 15,000 at The Battle of New Orleans. The US lost less than a hundred men, the British suffered over 2,000 casualties.

Mythology: Freedom-loving frontiersmen volunteered to protect the new nation's liberty and fight the king's army whose ranks were filled with judicial conscripts; paupers, thieves and thugs. The Duke of Wellington called his men "scum" who fought or were hung. Liberty had again defeated Tyranny in this clash of ideology and saved the union for a second time.

The Battle of New Orleans, an engraving after the painting by William Momberger. It shows Andrew Jackson, sword in hand, surrounded by buckskin-clad frontiersmen.

Questions

1 Research the Battles of New Orleans and Queenston Heights.

   a Why did the respective sides win?

   b What was the actual contribution to the battle's outcome of Jackson's frontiersmen and Brock's York volunteers?

Canadian mythology: The Battle of Queenston Heights

The Facts: In 1812, US forces crossed the Niagara River into Canada and met the British at Queenston Heights. The Canadian militia, volunteers loyal to the Crown, fought that day. The Americans were defeated and fled from Canadian soil. The Canadians were led by British General Sir Issac Brock, who was mortally wounded in the fighting.

Myth: Brock's last words, "Push on brave York volunteers", rallied the troops and turned the tide. Brock became a national martyr. The stalwart Canadian militia put down their axe and picked up a musket and defeated the "Yankee" invaders. These brave fellows saved Canada from the nefarious embrace of "Cousin Jonathon" (Canadian slang for the United States). Canada would remain British, "God save the King".

The "militia myth" would remain a Canadian staple for decades

The Battle of Queenston Heights, painted by David Kelly in 1896. It shows Brock, wounded, sword raised as he utters his last words, "Push on brave York Volunteers".

2 Compare and contrast the myths, that is, what are the similarities and differences.

3 Speculate as to why these myths are important to the United States and Canada?

4 Why are national myths important to building a nation's identity? What are the dangers inherent in such myths?

Canada and the road to confederation, 1837–67

The United States turned west and started expanding. Over the next three decades the US would annex Texas, attempt to further subjugate Native Americans, evict the British from the Oregon territory and expel the Spanish and Mexicans from the southwest. The United States could now claim to fill a large part of North America.

The wars of independence had largely swept the Americas clean of colonial masters by the 1830s, except in a handful of Caribbean Islands and British North America (Canada). Canada would follow a different path to independence. Canada's road was evolutionary not revolutionary; the product of public opinion, the popular press, party politics, hard fought elections, ministerial conferences, parliamentary debate, legislation and royal writ. In many respects, confederation was the logical outcome of British rule in Canada. The colonial ruling class were extremely conservative and staunchly British—to a fault, many boasted royal lineage or connection. They unanimously disapproved of the republican values of the United States and believed in the superiority of the British Empire, notably its laws and institutions, personified by loyalty to the Crown. In Quebec (French speaking) it was also a truism but for different reasons. British statutes had protected and preserved the French Canadian way of life; its civil laws, education, land holding (Seigneurial) system and Catholicism since the conquest. Quebec was wary of the United States but for a very different reason—the fear of assimilation.

The path to confederation was about competing visions that would shape the new country. The debate was rarely tranquil, often vicious and always rancorous. This section will examine Canada's path to confederation, starting with the causes and effects of the rebellions of 1837 and the 1839 Durham Report. The challenge to unite the colonies was similar to many of the problems faced by the 13 colonies: notably, creating a federal government with powers entrenched in a viable constitution. This required compromise but several colonies either refused to join or were reluctant to accept leaving the British Empire. External causes were critical in convincing reluctant partners to confederate. These influences will also be examined.

In the end, confederation was achieved July 1, 1867. Founded on the principles of "Peace, Order and Good Government", the new nation was a self-governing dominion within the British Empire, sovereign in the administration of internal affairs. Canada's constitution, the British North America Act (Constitution Act 1982), stipulated a federal system of parliamentary government and laid out the division of powers between the two levels of government: federal powers in section 91 and provincial powers in section 92. Britain retained foreign policy, the Supreme Court and constitutional amendments until the Statute of Westminster gave these to Canada in 1931.

The new federal government set to work building a transcontinental nation across the cold northern half of the continent. Governing this vast nation with its small population divided by geography and climate, culture and language would create regionalism that threatened the nation's survival.

The rebellions of 1837

On September 12, 1759, British General Sir James Wolfe defeated the French forces of Marquis de Montcalm on the Plains of Abraham outside Quebec City. The British victory essentially ended the Seven Years war (French and Indian War) of 1754–63 and gave British control of the much of the continent, but not for long. The US Revolution reduced Britain's holding in the New World to British North America comprised of the independent colonies (from east to west) of Newfoundland, Nova Scotia, New Brunswick, Prince Edward Island, Lower Canada (Quebec—French speaking majority) and Upper Canada (Ontario). Rupert's Land belonged to the Hudson's Bay Company and was eventually sold to Canada in 1869. The newest colony in the mix was Upper Canada.

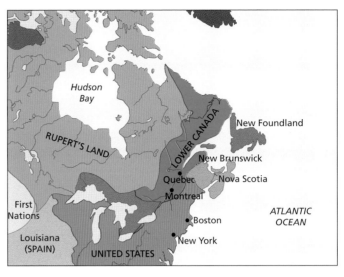

The British North America Act of 1791

Following the US Revolution, large numbers of settlers poured across the porous border into Canada. They fell into two loose categories: farmers lured by vast tracks of fertile farmlands and the more important second group of United Empire Loyalists (also known as Tories), political refugees who fled to remain "Loyal" to the Crown. Many had fought in Tory regiments against the Revolution and had their property confiscated and were forced out of the United States. Influential and motivated by a desire to prevent revolutionary ideas filtering north, they joined forces with Upper Canada's established British merchant class of bankers and business men and became the powerful conservative élite that controlled Upper Canada. Their outlook was patriarchal, class-conscious, anti-democratic and monarchist. Their values would give the colony its pro-British character and abiding distrust of the United States. They were the dominate élite, the "Family Compact", a loose-knit fraternity that opposed any changes which could potentially undermine their privileged status, the British connection or contained the slightest hint of republican ideas and values. The challenge to the Family Compact came from the elected legislative assembly. Notably a group of British reformers (liberals) who landed with a trunk full of radical liberal ideas and political ambitions inspired by the US and French Revolutions and the European rebellions of 1830. They demanded an end to aristocratic and church privilege, advocated responsible government, popular elections and spoke a language of political change that challenged the status quo. They were joined by many immigrants from the United States who added their voice which sounded like republicanism to the Family Compact. Frustrations reached critical mass in 1837 and exploded into gunfire.

The Constitution Act (British North America Act) of 1791 was the problem. The British passed the Act following the US Revolution to establish a system of colonial government in its British North American colonies. Each colony had a lieutenant-governor advised by an appointed legislative (executive) council and a popularly elected legislature. The executive was not responsible or responsive to the elected Legislative Assembly (lower house) and had the power to veto legislation passed by the assembly. The assembly had one significant power and that was to vote "supply" tax money to the executive but had no say over the distribution of this money. In Upper Canada the Lieutenant Governor and council were controlled by members of the influential Family Compact. The same system existed in Lower Canada, which named its controlling élite "The Château Clique".

The rebellion of Upper Canada, 1837–38

The Legislative Assembly was frustrated by the control of the Family Compact. A string of Lieutenant-Governors proved to be nothing more than figureheads willingly doing the Family's bidding. The assembly demanded change, notably an end to political patronage, a public system of education, and an end to clergy reserves; public lands grants to the Anglican Church—but these demands were ignored by the council. The radicals' growing frustration found voice in the caustic pen of newspaper editor and publisher of the *Colonial Advocate*, William Lyon MacKenzie.

A Scottish-born radical, McKenzie crossed the ocean to Montreal in 1820, then moved to York (capital of Upper Canada renamed Toronto in 1834). In 1824 he established the *Colonial Advocate* and took up the grievances and cause of the lower assembly. Initially, he advocated peaceful change through boycotts, strikes and political protest. His editorials became increasingly outspoken in their condemnation of the government and he quickly won loyal friends and powerful enemies but not enough subscribers. The newspaper folded and MacKenzie fled to the United States to avoid his creditors. During his self-imposed exile, a group of young Tories (supporters of the Family Compact) tossed his printing press into Lake Ontario. Local authorities turned a blind eye to the incident. McKenzie returned to York, sued the vandals and was awarded damages. The trial made Mackenzie a celebrity and unchallenged leader of the reformers.

> **William Lyon MacKenzie (1795–1861)**
>
> Born in Dundee, Scotland, William MacKenzie came to Canada in 1820. He was a journalist, newspaper publisher, politician, first mayor of Toronto (1834) and leader of the Rebellion of 1837. An outspoken critic of the "Family Compact" he became increasingly abusive and defamatory in his attacks. He advocated equal rights for US settlers, responsible government and the end of land grants to the Anglican Church. Post-Rebellion, he fled to the United States, returned to Canada in 1850. In 1851 he won a seat in the Legislative Assembly (Haldimand County), which he held until 1858. A reformer to the end he continued to alienate with his acerbic tongue and sarcastic pen.

Shortly afterwards, MacKenzie and his followers established a committee and sent an emissary to London to appeal directly for change. The tactic was initially successful but was matched by the Family Compact who sent their own emissary to London and outflanked the reformers.

What did MacKenzie and his followers want? Most importantly, they desired a system of responsible government that gave more power to the elected assembly. They wanted settlers born in the United States to be given political rights (i.e. the vote) and an end to the system of clergy reserves. The reserves gave public land to the Anglican Church which they sold for profit. A large segment of the population were practicing Methodists or Catholics (mainly Irish) and disapproved of this preferential treatment. MacKenzie was elected to the assembly in 1829 and again in 1831. He began organizing committees to bring about change and reform. He admired US president Andrew Jackson (the hero of New Orleans) and advocated reforms branded as pro-US by his opponents. A Tory-dominated assembly expelled him in November of 1831 and again in 1832. In 1834 Mackenzie became an alderman on the new Toronto City council, who voted him to the Mayor's chair but lost out to a Tory candidate in 1835. He was increasingly frustrated with the failure of these tactics and started to advocate armed revolt. In January 1835 he returned to the assembly with its blessing and was as blustery as ever but lost the seat in the 1836 election. MacKenzie started a new publication *The Constitution* that demanded constitutional reform to rectify colonial grievances. The British response in the House of Commons was the "Ten Resolutions" that removed the few meaningful powers of the legislative assemblies. This was the last straw. MacKenzie demanded rebellion but was upstaged by "Les Patriotes" of Lower Canada who in October 1837 fired the first shots of rebellion and provided MacKenzie with a golden opportunity to strike.

Army units from York were sent to quell the Lower Canada "Patriotes" and their firebrand leader Louis Joseph Papineau. MacKenzie organized his forces and was prepared to establish a provisional government in late november. Paramilitary groups trained in nearby farmer's fields with pitchforks and rakes and a few muskets. In early December, the rebels seized the York armoury and marched down Younge street to Mongomery's tavern and downed ample quantities of alcohol—liquid courage. A British regiment confronted the rebels. The fight was short, less than half an hour. Rebel courage melted with the first cannon shot. The rebels fired a ragged volley and fled. The victorious Tories took revenge and burned the houses of known rebels.

Mackenzie fled with 200 supporters to Navy Island in the Niagara River and declared "The Republic of Canada". The British attacked in January and most rebels fled to the United States and formed the "Hunter Patriots". Several prominent leaders were captured and hung. The "Hunters" raided across the border and were eventually defeated in November of 1838 at the Battle of the Windmill. The rebellion was over in Upper Canada but the matter was not closed. The government's victory ended radical opposition in the colony.

The question now was to determine how best to keep the colony British, not whether or not it should be British.

The rebellion of Lower Canada, 1837–38

Following the War of 1812, English immigration into Lower Canada resulted in English-speaking enclaves in Montreal, Quebec and the eastern townships along the south bank of the Saint Lawrence River. The French-speaking population's growth was due to natural increase promoted by the Catholic church and large families were the norm. Economically, agriculture suffered in the decades prior to the rebellion but the impact differed throughout the colony. Montreal, however, experienced a period of growth and prosperity. Once the center of the fur trade, former fur barons became bankers, merchants and manufacturers. The élite were mainly English-speaking Tories, an urban élite, who controlled the government. Christened the "Château Clique," French Canadians were mainly rural and controlled the elected assembly. Bitterness and resentment between the two major linguistic groups for control of the colony was the backdrop for the rebellion.

The man who would eventually lead the rebellion was Louis Joseph Papineau. He came on the scene as the elected Speaker of the Assembly in 1815. Politically, he supported British rule which protected French-Canadian language, culture, religion and civil laws. He fought against the control of the colony by the British urban élite. For the next 20 years he would try, unsuccessfully, to increase the power and influence of the assembly. The British government adopted a more conciliatory approach in the early 1830s but unforeseen events undermined these efforts, notably a significant drop in agricultural prices and a rapid increase in emigration from the Britain to the urban centres. A cholera outbreak arrived with the immigrants and killed thousands of French Canadians—who blamed the British and fed French-Canadian fears of being outnumbered. By 1830, Papineau had become a "republican reformer"; an advocate of the US-style democracy he demanded responsible government which was similar to the US slogan of "no taxation without representation". He demanded that the elected assembly control the purse strings and direct

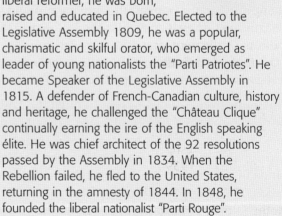

Louis Joseph Papineau (1786–1871)

Louis Joseph Papineau was a leader of the Patriote Rebellion of 1837. A lawyer, wealthy land-owner (seigneur), political activist and liberal reformer, he was born, raised and educated in Quebec. Elected to the Legislative Assembly 1809, he was a popular, charismatic and skilful orator, who emerged as leader of young nationalists the "Parti Patriotes". He became Speaker of the Legislative Assembly in 1815. A defender of French-Canadian culture, history and heritage, he challenged the "Château Clique" continually earning the ire of the English speaking élite. He was chief architect of the 92 resolutions passed by the Assembly in 1834. When the Rebellion failed, he fled to the United States, returning in the amnesty of 1844. In 1848, he founded the liberal nationalist "Parti Rouge".

how the money would be spent. The Château Clique responded by seeking the British government's continued support of the current system. In 1832, three French-Canadiens were killed by British troops during an election riot and further stigmatized the two sides. Papineau's rhetoric became increasingly radical and the Patriote Party became more extreme and published it demands in the 92 Resolutions (1834). The assembly, similar to Upper Canada, refused to vote supply (tax dollars) to the civil service which paralyzed the government. A new player, the so-called British Party opposed these measures and petitioned the British government in London to overturn the Lower Assembly's legislative activism. Extremists on both sides became increasingly dogmatic and refused to budge. The French–English split became entrenched.

In 1837, the British government rejected the Patriotes' demands and authorized the Governor to take funds from the colony's treasury. The Patriotes responded with boycotts, protests, rallies and recruited volunteers who started military training in the countryside. They held out the slim hope that the British might back down and compromise if faced with this threat. They were wrong. The British sent troops from Upper Canada and elsewhere. In November, violence erupted in the streets of Montreal and in the countryside many areas experienced widespread civil disobedience and acts of violence.

On November 16, the rebel leaders were placed under arrest but fled to the countryside. They joined the rebel forces which had been organized into three columns. Between November 23 and November 30, the British forces attacked each column and after several sharp battles the rebellion collapsed. Hundreds of Patriotes were killed or wounded. Papineau escaped with many followers to the United States, determined to continue the rebellion. With the help of US sympathizers they organized the "Hunter's Lodges". In November 1838 the rebels crossed into Canada but were quickly defeated. Over a hundred rebels were captured, 12 were hung and 58 transported to Australia. The rebellion of Lower Canada was over and with it ended the threat to British control of the colonies.

The Durham Report

The British Government was deeply distressed by the rebellions. The unhappy memory of the US Revolution was embedded deeply in their consciousness. They did not want to forfeit any more colonies in the Americas. Parliament moved quickly and approved the immediate despatch of a fact-finding mission headed by Lord Durham. His findings and recommendations would become one of the most famous and hotly debated documents in Canadian history. Durham spent just eight months in Canada before being recalled for overstepping his powers. He spent his time touring the two colonies, interviewing, observing and investigating the causes of the Rebellions. His report was published in 1939 and focused on Lower Canada.

Activity

Compare and contrast

Rebellions and revolutions

What is the difference between them?

Compare and contrast the demands of the rebels and revolutionaries in the following insurrections:

- Canadian Rebellions of 1837
- Hidalgo Revolt, Mexico, 1810
- Bahia Slave Rebellion, Brazil, 1835
- Nat Turner Rebellion, United States, 1831

John George Lambton, first Earl of Durham (1792–1840)

The family of Lord Durham owned a large estate and coal mines employing over 2,000 miners. He was educated at Eton and served briefly in the cavalry. He entered politics in 1812 and remained in office until his death. He received a Cabinet post in 1830 and was Ambassador to Russian (1835–37). He was nicknamed "Radical Jack" because he supported the liberal reforming Whig party. The party's platform included equal rights for Catholics, free trade, better access to education and the voting rights for all citizens. He helped author the famous Reform Bill of 1832 that attempted to correct abuses in the voting system. In 1839, he came to Canada to report on the rebellions and provide recommendations to restore peace and order in the colonies. His findings were published in the famous Durham Report published in late 1839. He suffered from poor health most of his adult life and died suddenly in July 1840.

Activity

The Durham Report

The excerpts from Durham's Report are the three most important and controversial recommendations. Read the excerpts and answer the questions that follow.

Excerpt 1

Responsible government

The system which I propose would, in fact, place the internal government of the colony in the hands of the colonists themselves. ... But the Crown must, on the other hand, submit to the necessary consequences of representative institutions; and if it has to carry on the government in unison with a representative body, it must consent to carry it on by means of those in whom that representative body has confidence.

Excerpt 2

The problem is Lower Canada

Nor do I exaggerate the inevitable constancy any more than the intensity of this animosity. Never again will the present generation of French Canadians yield a loyal submission to a British Government; never again will the English population tolerate the authority of a House of Assembly in which the French shall possess, or even approximate to, a majority.

Excerpt 3

The assimilation of French Canadians

I expected to find a contest between a government and a people: instead I found two nations [English and French] warring in the bosom of a single state: I found a struggle, not of principles, but of races; and I perceived that it would be idle to attempt any amelioration of laws or institutions until we could first succeed in terminating the deadly animosity that now separates the inhabitants of Lower Canada into the hostile divisions of French and English ...

Questions

1 By advocating responsible government, was Durham agreeing with the demands of the rebels? Consider why he might have done so?

2 Do you agree with Durham's assessment that the fundamental cause of the Rebellions was the racial divide between English and French Canadians?

3 Durham's believed that it was "idle" to try and resolve the crisis until the deadly animosity between the English and French was terminated. How do you think Durham proposed to do this? To find clues to your answer research the Act of Union 1840.

4 Speculate as to why Canadian historians still consider Durham's report controversial?

In particular, consider the perspective of French Canadians.

The US–Mexican War of 1846–48

In the 1840s, the territorial ambitions of the United States were embodied in President Polk and the growing belief in the nation's "Manifest Destiny" to rule the continent. Under his leadership the United States would flex its muscles and expand across the continent from "sea to shining sea". The Oregon boundary question with Britain was settled peacefully in 1846 when both agreed that the 49th parallel would divide the United States and Canada. The situation with Texas and Mexico was more complex and not resolved amicably. A war would result that decapitated Mexico north of the Rio Grande and a hegemonic US gained a third of its current continental holdings. The US annexed Texas and in the post-war Treaty of Guadalupe-Hidalgo (*Tratado de Guadalupe Hidalgo* in Spanish) of 1848 gained the former Mexican states of Alta California and Santa Fe de New Mexico (California, Arizona, New Mexico, Utah and portions of Colorado and Wyoming). By the end of the 1840s, the political map of North America, except for a few minor adjustments was defined. This section will examine the causes and effects of the Mexican War of 1846 (*Intervencion estadounidense de Mexico*) on Mexico and the United States.

The road to war

Mexico became independent from Spain in 1821. It was a vast nation covering a third of North America with large tracts of land north of the Rio Grande River (or *Rio Bravo del Norte*). The most interesting area, economically and strategically, was California with is lush valleys and deep harbors. The majority of Mexicans lived south of the Rio Grande. When the war started in 1846 only 75,000 Mexicans lived in a vast territory stretching from California to Texas. It made the territory attractive to Mexico's ambitious and expansionist northern neighbor, the United States.

Post-independence Mexico was swept by a mood of optimism but the society was deeply fragmented between rich and poor, educated and uneducated, rural and urban, élites and peasants, liberals and conservatives. During the first two decades of independence, Mexico searched for stability experimenting with a monarchy, republican government and *caudillos*. Liberals reformers advocated a federal republic while conservatives championed a centralized state, a constitutional Monarchy and the traditional role of the Catholic Church. Describing Mexico during this period, Historian Jesús Velasco-Márquez concludes: "that only the existence of a profound link, beyond that of economics or politics, can explain the survival of the country. ... one can affirm that in Mexico, in contrast with the United States, that yes, a nation existed, but its condition was precarious." Mexico's huge geographical expanse, great range of social and ethnic diversity and, according to some historians, diminished vice-regal status and large debts, mostly to Britain, at the time of independence, made it a special case in newly independent Latin America. The country's precarious condition is illustrated by

Discussion point

Imperialism

Imperialism often happens for very practical reasons, such as economic expansion, desire for resources and geopolitical considerations.

Examine the real reason, as opposed to the justifications for 19th-century imperialism in the Americas: US "Manifest Destiny" against Mexico, Canada and Nicaragua; the Argentina–Brazil War; War of the Pacific (Chile against Bolivia and Perú); Haiti against Santo Domingo the fact that in the first 33 years as a republic, Mexico had 49 presidents, some lasting only months in office. Some presidents were military strongmen, like the *caudillo* Antonio López de Santa Anna, who was president on eight occasions, sometimes for very brief periods. He was a career military officer, who supported various causes, liberal and conservative, as well as fighting against foreign intervention from France and the United States.

Antonio López de Santa Anna (1794–1876)

Santa Anna was a political leader, president and general who greatly influenced Mexico. Ambiguous, ambitious, duplicitous and self-aggrandizing, he was president many times, exiled three times and brought back twice to save the nation. Famously, he stormed the Alamo, then granted Texas independence and was thrown out of office. In 1838, he was brought back to fight the French who had landed at Veracruz. He was successful but lost his leg in the fighting. The Veracruz victory put him back in power as dictator. He was driven out in 1845 and exiled. He came back with the help of US President Polk on the promise he would make peace but instead led his forces against the US. Defeated, he retired to Jamaica in 1847.

The new government of the United States, by contrast, had to deal with a much smaller geographical space and a homogeneous majority population. French, German and even British investment, industrialization and immigration fired the economic engine. Thousands of immigrants—particularly Irish escaping the famine— arrived after 1847 and changed the social make-up of the nation. As land became scarce and expensive along the Atlantic seaboard, US citizens and new arrivals from Europe looked west and began to push across the continent, to the area bought by the US in the 1803 Louisiana Purchase. A growing sense of mission permeated the movement west, a mission to eventually take control of North America—a movement christened as "Manifest Destiny". This mission used the justification to civilize and Christianize the native peoples in order to populate and cultivate the vast tracks of what was then seen as uninhabited lands in the west. By 1840, 4.5 million US citizens had left the Atlantic seaboard, advancing to the Mississippi River forcing Native Americans to migrate farther west. In the way of US southwest expansion was Mexico. The conflict came to a head over Texas.

The state of Texas

In 1824, Stephen Austin, the man credited with bringing the first wave of settlers from the United States into the Mexican northern territory, now known as Texas, was granted permission by the Mexican government to settle 300 families in Texas; known in Texas history as the "Old Three Hundred" they were followed by thousands of US citizens seeking free Texas land grants. Thousands of settlers, mainly from the US southern states, poured into Texas, bringing their slaves with them. This stretch of the country was at the time inhabited by barely 2,500 Mexicans, as the Mexican government considered it a backwater. By 1830, the Mexican government determined that the *Anglos* (as Mexicans called the English-speaking US residents in Texas) outnumbered Mexicans 4 to 1 and tried to end immigration. In addition, a heavy tax was placed on imports and exports in Texas; recognition that economic traffic was mainly between Texas and the United States. Mexican officials and soldiers employed to collect taxes, instead promoted smuggling and friction between the Texas militia and Mexican soldiers. In 1832, Austin, the uncontested head of the US settlers, went to Mexico City to petition the Mexican government but was arrested and jailed for two years, until 1834.

The inhabitants of Texas, both *Anglos* and Mexicans, asked the president of Mexico at the time, Antonio López de Santa Anna, for statehood, in order to have more autonomy regarding taxes and tariffs, as well as land concessions. Santa Anna refused to grant it. Conflict escalated until the Texans declared independence from Mexico in 1836, with the support in arms and resources, from the United States. Santa Anna led the Mexican Army into Texas and after a few initial successes (notably the Alamo) was soundly defeated at the Battle of San Jacinto and imprisoned. To avoid being hanged, he signed the Treaty of Velasco granting Texas independence. But the Mexican government refused to recognize the treaty, declaring that Texas was still Mexican and drove Santa Anna into exile, though they recalled their troops in 1836. A year later, the US recognized Texas as a sovereign state, as did France and Britain, who welcomed a buffer state between the US and Mexico. Between 1836 and 1845, relations between Texas and Mexico remained hostile. Cross-border raids were commonplace. Seaborne Mexican troops sacked coastal towns and attempted a blockade. The Texans responded with privateers and later created a navy that interdicted Mexican trade and supplied Yucatán insurgents.

The Texans had wrongly assumed that the United States would welcome them with open arms, but underestimated the northern anti-slavery lobby which opposed adding another slave state. Mexico had abolished slavery in 1830 but the Texans ignored the law and kept their slaves. The influx of southern slave-owning settlers into Texas was a matter of geographic proximity not a slave conspiracy as many northerners claimed. Regardless, this view of the situation convinced abolitionists to oppose the annexation of Texas until the matter of slave state admission to the union was resolved. Both the US and Mexico made efforts to negotiate, but this was not to be. Meanwhile, Texas was in financial trouble maintaining a costly military. The fledgling Texas government began negotiations with France and England, former supporters of Texan independence, but who were not keen on having it strengthen the US union. On March 1, 1845, outgoing President Tyler adeptly set the annexation table with an annexation bill rather than a treaty which required a two-thirds majority in the Senate. The annexation bill required a simple majority in Congress. Early in 1845, the bill passed and Texas became the 28th state of the union. Mexico had stated that annexation meant war and was confident its 20,000 man regular army could defeat the US army of 7,000. The Mexican newspaper *El Tiempo* summed it up this way "The conduct [of] the American is similar to that of the bandit. ... Mexico must defend itself."

President James K. Polk and "Manifest Destiny"
James Polk was inaugurated as the new president of the United States on March 4, 1845. He had won largely because he was an expansionist, advocated "Manifest Destiny" and insisted on the reoccupation of the Oregon territory and the annexation of Texas.

Annexation carried the day. The Oregon territory dispute was resolved peacefully when the British finally agreed to accept the 49th parallel as the border. The Oregon Treaty of 1846 added the future states of Oregon and Washington to the fold. Mexico was a different problem.

Santa Anna, who had returned to power a few years earlier, was exiled in 1845 and José de Herrera took power. Incensed by Tyler's annexation bill the Minister to the United States was recalled and on June 4 Herrera issued a war proclamation vilifying the United States.

Polk wanted territorial concessions from the Mexicans and, if possible, to avoid war. In October he sent US Commissioner John Slidell to negotiate. Slidell was in fact authorized to offer the Mexican government 25 million dollars for lands north of the Rio Grande. By November, the Mexican press and public opinion had branded Herrera a traitor intent on surrendering Mexican lands. The Mexican press labelled Slidell's mission "a gross trap with [a] Machiavellian and outrageous end." The president bowed to pressure and rejected Slidell's overtures. But it was too late: Herrera was replaced by General Mariano Paredes. On December 29, 1845, Polk signed the annexation bill adding Texas to the union.

Polk's next move was to force the Mexicans to fight or negotiate. The real prize was California, with its lush valleys and the deep harbor of San Francisco. US citizens had, in fact, been immigrating there since 1840. Polk was an opportunist and decided to move into Texas. He ordered General Zachary Taylor to advance with 4,000 men across the Nueces River and drive south to the north bank of the Rio Grande. The Mexicans claimed the Nueces was the border and Taylor's advance was considered an act of war, a violation of Mexican sovereignty. In fact, the area was under dispute.

In Washington, Polk asked his cabinet to support a declaration of war. They hesitated because the president had not convinced the majority of US citizens that the war was necessary and unavoidable. Events now played into the president's hands. Mexican troops ambushed a US patrol on May 8, killing or wounding 16 US soldiers. This was the pretext Polk needed. With the full support of Cabinet he asked Congress for a declaration of war stating that "American blood had been spilled on American soil." On May 13, Congress voted overwhelmingly for war, but the measure was controversial. The south supported the president but influential northerners did not want to admit another slave state. Former president John Quincy Adams described the war as a southern expedition to find "bigger pens to cram with slaves." James Fennimore Cooper disagreed and wrote that the war was a great moral stride in America's "progress toward real independence and high political influence." Walt Whitman was stirred by what he witnessed and captured the nations mood, "There is hardly a more admirable impulse in the human soul than patriotism." The new Congressman Abraham Lincoln opposed the war and challenged the president to provide evidence that the

James Knox Polk
(1795–1849)

James Knox Polk was inaugurated the 11th president of the United States in 1845. He was Governor of Tennessee (1839–1841) before becoming president in 1845. Polk was an imperialist who aggressively expanded the United States across the continent by whatever means necessary. He retired in 1849, fulfilling his promise to serve one term and died of cholera three months later.

"spot" of the skirmish was actually on US soil. The anti-war forces remained a vocal minority throughout the war but the majority of the US supported the president. The pro-war *New York Herald* announced a new role for the nation, a "new destiny" that would ultimately affect "both this continent and the old continent of Europe." Manifest Destiny had taken root.

Historian Karl Bauer suggests "the war was a product of America's romantic age"; a time of "Manifest Destiny", when the US would define her greatness and national character. US citizens believed in the justification that their divine mission was to carry the gospel of liberty to the continent and the world and acquire vast tracts of territory. In fact, upon the US Congress's declaration of war, the US navy blocked Mexican ports in the Pacific and the Atlantic and occupied California and New Mexico, neither of which had purportedly been in dispute over Texas. It is worth commenting that whether pro- or anti-war neither side expressed any sympathy for the Mexican people or that the United States was about to engage in a war of imperial conquest.

The progress of the war

The war lasted longer than expected. Mexico was favoured by the vastness of its territory and communications difficulties for the invading army, but weakened by constant internal conflicts and changes in power. The US army was better organized in armament, discipline and resources. Fighting raged throughout the disputed territories but the war-winning strategy was the two-pronged invasion of Mexico. There were many instances of popular resistance to the US occupation, especially in California. In addition, between 300 and 400 US soldiers, almost all of them Irish, actually joined the Mexican forces as the St. Patrick's Battalion, sharing with them the Catholic faith and hostility for Protestant *Anglos*. On September 14, 1847, culminating a bloody drive across Mexico from Vera Cruz, General Winfield Scott's army entered Mexico City and the fighting was over. Santa Anna resigned. In March 1848, the Treaty of Guadalupe Hidalgo was signed by new president Manuel de la Peña and the war ended.

The United States lost 13,000 soldiers, 1,773 killed in action and about 11,000 from disease, and spent over $100,000 million. Mexico casualties have been estimated at 25,000. Geographically, Mexico lost all lands north of the Rio Grande, the current states of California, Arizona, New Mexico, Utah and portions of Colorado and Wyoming. Mexican historian Juan Brom writes that Mexico lost the war due to its internal affairs:

> "The rivalries between military leaders made difficult and even impeded necessary collaboration; in addition, frequently the troops did not have required supplies in arms and foodstuffs. To this must be added the conflicts between Church and state, as well as the attitude of many governors, who did not support the national struggle. In short, the country lacked the unity and organization that are indispensable for an efficacious defence."

Source: Brom, Juan and Duval, Dolores. 1998. *Esbozo de historia de México*. Mexico D. F.: Editorial Grijalbo. p. 176.

Activity

Saint Patrick's Batallion

Look up David Rovics singing "Saint Patrick's Battalion" on YouTube.com. This song commemorates the Irishmen who fought alongside the Mexican army against the United States in 1846–48.

Questions

1 Why did new immigrants from Ireland join the US army?

2 Why were the new Irish immigrants not taken in by Manifest Destiny?

Mexico's army was decimated and several important Mexican cities and ports had been reduced to rubble, foreign markets and imports destroyed, transportation routes disrupted and thousands of civilians killed. Mexico ceded the northern half of the country, about 800,000 square kilometres (55 percent of Mexico's land area) to the United States. The total doubles to 1.6 million when Oregon and Texas are added. The new border stretched the length of the continent from the Gulf of Mexico along the Rio Grande to the point where the river turns north due west to the Pacific Ocean. The treaty required the US pay Mexico 15 million US dollars for ceded lands and a further 3.25 million in indemnities. Mexicans living in the ceded area (about 75,000), would be granted US citizenship and to keep their lands (later rescinded). The US also promised to guard the border and stop Apache raids into Mexico.

Many Mexicans were aghast at the conditions and wanted to resume the war. The Mexican government, dominated by the creole élite, feared that further fighting would destroy what remained of the nation's shattered economy. They enlisted the support of the Catholic Church and the British who wanted the cash to help repay loans owed to them and Mexico succumbed and plunged into a dark period of economic and political chaos that lasted until the late 1860s. In 1853, Santa Anna was recalled again to establish order and promptly sold another 50,000 kilometers of land bordering New Mexico to the United States for an additional ten million dollars (the Gadsen Purchase of 1853). Santa Anna was exiled—for the last time.

President Polk had fulfilled his campaign promises and expanded the nation. Polk's plan was opportunistic. He was more interested in California than the southwest and would have preferred negotiations to gunfire. He probably just wanted Texas and California; the territories in-between were an added bonus. But when the opportunity presented itself he fought a war of imperial conquest and completed the continental map of the United States from sea to sea: from the Rio Grande to the 49th parallel. Wagon trains of settlers soon filled the Santa Fe Trail. Gold was discovered in California in 1849 and "49er's" flocked west to pan their fortune. Thousands of settlers made the arduous journey to the west. It was a golden age in many respects, but the war had unleashed other forces. Slavery would dominate the national political agenda. Numerous compromises failed to resolve the slavery issue in a nation founded on the "self-evident" principles of inalienable rights and freedoms.

Mexico was weakened and devastated by the war. One of the reasons for the defeat was the unwillingness of the Mexican government to mobilize large numbers of peasants into the army because they feared a long and devastating guerrilla war with the United States. So they concluded a hasty treaty. According to the Mexican historian Leticia Reina, the government "preferred coming to terms with the United States rather than endanger the interests of the ruling class." Mexican politician Manual Rejón predicted the treaty would destroy Mexico's economy and concluded that the Treaty of Guadalupe-Hidalgo was a death sentence for Mexican

Activity

Roundtable discussion

Road to war or conflict resolution

Conflict resolution between countries does not have to lead to war. Why was the territorial dispute between the US and Britain over the Oregon territory resolved peacefully? Why did the dispute between the US and Mexico over Texas lead to war?

Divide the class into two groups, each preparing and answering their response to the questions in a roundtable discussion.

independence. Mexico would be a vassal of the United States. Mexicans living in the conquered territories, Rejón feared, would be treated as second-class citizens and lose their property and civil rights. His fears were soon justified. A group of lawyers known as the "Santa Fe Ring" used long legal battles to exploit the Mexican landholders and acquired lands extending over a million acres. For the next two decades rebellion, revolution and violence were Mexico's national staples. The misfortune finally ended in the 1860s but Mexico had been humiliated by the war and the wounds took a long time to heal.

The US–Mexican War marked an end to the independence period in the Americas and except for British North America and a few Caribbean islands, the colonial powers had been evicted and new, independent nations had emerged. In Canada and the Caribbean nations the road to independence would take a different path.

Discussion point

For the descendants of Mexican landowners and ranchers stripped of their lands by the US courts in violation of the Treaty of Guadalupe-Hidalgo, the treatment of their ancestors remains a contentious issue.

 What impact did the Mexican War have on the ethnic populations of the territories acquired? How is their ethnic mix defined today?

Activity

The US–Mexican War of 1846–48

Source A

Following is an extract from the Monroe Doctrine, President James Monroe's seventh annual message to the Congress on December 2, 1823.

> The American continents, by the free and independent condition which they have assumed and maintain, are henceforth not to be considered as subjects for future colonization by any European powers.
>
> In the wars of the European powers in matters relating to themselves we have never taken any part, nor does it comport with our policy to do so. It is only when our rights are invaded or seriously menaced that we resent injuries or make preparation for our defense. With the movements in this hemisphere we are of necessity connected ... we owe it, therefore, to candor and to the amicable relations existing between the United States and those powers to declare that we should consider any attempt on their part to extend their system to any portion of this hemisphere as dangerous to our peace and safety. With the existing colonies or dependencies of any European power in any other light than as a manifestation of an unfriendly disposition to the United States.
>
> It is still the true policy of the United States to leave the parties to themselves, in hope that other powers will pursue the same course ...
>
> **Source:** "James Monroe: American President: An Online Reference Resource". Miller Center of Public Affairs. University of Virginia. http://millercenter.org/academic/americanpresident/monroe.

Source B

Following is an extract from an article by the US columnist and editor J. O' Sullivan, who approved of the annexation of Texas and is credited with coining the phrase "Manifest destiny".

> The expansive future is our arena and for our history. We are entering on its untrodden space with the truths of God in our minds, beneficent objects in our hearts, and with a clear conscience unsullied by the past. We are the nation of human progress, and who will, what can, set limits to our onward march? Providence is with us, and no earthly power can.

The far-reaching, the boundless future, will be the era of American greatness. In its magnificent domain of time and space, the nation of many nations is destined to manifest to mankind the excellence of divine principles; to establish on the noblest temple ever dedicated to the worship of the Most High, the Sacred, and the True. Its floor shall be a hemisphere, roof the firmament of the star-studded heavens, and its congregation of Union of many Republics, comprising hundreds of happy millions ...

We must onward to the fulfillment of our mission ... This is our high destiny, and in nature's eternal, inevitable decree of cause and effect we must accomplish it. All this will be our future' history, to establish on earth the moral dignity and salvation of man—the immutable truth and beneficence of God. Who, then, can doubt that our country is destined to be the great nation of futurity?

Source C

Following is an extract from a proclamation by the acting president of the Republic of Mexico, José de Herrera, issued June 4, 1845, denouncing the intention of the United States to annex Texas.

That the congress of the United States of the Noorth has, by a decree, which its executive sanctioned, resolved to incorporate the territory of Texas to the U.States tramples on the conservative principle of society, attacks all the rights that Mexico has to that territory, is an insult to her dignity as a sovereign nation, and threatens her independence and political existence; In consequence, the government will call to the arms all the forces of the army, according to the authority granted it by the existing laws; and for the preservation of public order, for the support of her institutions, and in case of necessity, to serve as the reserve to the army, the government, according to the powers given to it on the 9th December 1844, will raise the corps specified by said decree, under the name of "Defenders of the Independence and of the Laws."

Source: "Documents of the US–Mexican War." *Descendants of US–Mexican War Veterans.* http://www.dmwv.org/mexwar/documents/herrera.htm.

Source D

Following is an extract from the inaugural address of President James Polk on March 4, 1845.

I regard the question of annexation as belonging exclusively to the United States and Texas. They are independent powers competent to contract, and foreign nations have no right to interfere with them or to take exceptions to their reunion. Foreign powers do not seem to appreciate the true character of our Government. Our Union is a confederation of independent States, whose policy is peace with each other and all the world. To enlarge its limits is to extend the dominions of peace over additional territories and increased millions ... it is confidently believed that our system may be safely extended to the utmost bonds of our territorial limits, and that as strong as it shall be extended to the utmost bonds of our territorial limits, and that as strong as it shall be extended to the bonds of our Union, so far from being weakened, become stronger.

Nor will it become in a less degree my duty to assert and maintain by all constitutional means the right of the United States to that portion of territory which lies beyond the Rocky Mountains. Our title to the country of the Oregon is "clear and unquestionable," and already our people are preparing to perfect that title by occupying it with their wives and children ... the increasing facilities of intercourse will easily bring the States, of which the formation in that part of our territory cannot be delayed, within the sphere of our federative Union.

Source E

Following is an extract from "Against the Mexican War" by Thomas Corwin, Senator from Ohio, published in 1847.

> Should we prosecute this war another moment, or expend one dollar in the purchase or conquest of a single acre of Mexican land, the North and the South are brought into collision on a point where neither will yield. Who can see or foretell the result! Who so bold and reckless as to look such a conflict in the face unmoved!
>
> ... Let us abandon all idea of acquiring further territory and by consequence cease at once to prosecute this war. Let us call home our armies, and bring them at once within our own acknowledged limits. Show Mexico that you are sincere when you say you desire nothing by conquest. She has learned that she cannot encounter you in the war, and if she had not, she is too weak to disturb you here ... It is your invasion that has made war; your retreat will restore peace ... Let us here, in this temple consecrated to the Union, perform a solemn lustration; let us wash Mexican blood from our hands, and on these altars, and in the presence of that image of the Father of his Country that looks down upon us, swear to preserve honorable peace with all the world and eternal brotherhood with each other.
>
> **Source:** Ravitch, Diane. ed. 1991. *The American Reader: Words that Moved the Nation*. New York: Harper-Collins. pp.77–79.

Questions

1 What is meant by Manifest Destiny in source B?

   a Briefly explain the doctrine outlined by President Monroe in source A.

2 Compare the differing views on the annexation of Texas contained in sources C, D and E.

3 Using sources A, B and D assess why key American leaders advocated expansion.

4 Using your knowledge and with specific reference to the documents, why did Mexico and the United States decide to go to war?

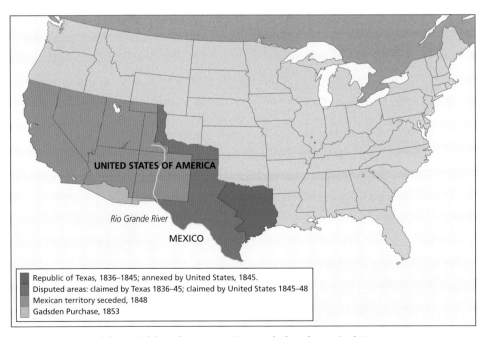

The Treaty of Guadalupe-Hidalgo showing territory ceded to the United States.

Canada becomes a nation

The confederation of the British North American colonies into the Dominion of Canada on July 1, 1867, was the result of fortuitous circumstances, visionary leadership, political compromise, economic realities, cultural imperatives and external pressures. The move to confederate did not gain momentum until the 1860s when it became a serious consideration. The US civil war provided much of the impetus but not all of it. The 1840 Act of Union combined Upper and Lower Canada into a single colony, the Province of Canada and was divided into Canada East (Lower Canada) and Canada West (Upper Canada). Canada East was dissatisfied with the arrangement and wanted its own government to better serve and protect the French Canadian majority. The Maritime colonies of Prince Edward Island, New Brunswick and Nova Scotia were being pressured by the British Colonial office to amalgamate into one big colony with one legislature, a cost-saving measure eliminating three smaller colonial legislatures.

> **A mari usque ad mare** is the Canadian national motto. The phrase comes from the Latin Psalm 72:8, which reads "Et dominabitur a mari usque ad mare, et a flumine usque ad terminos terrae" (King James Bible: "He shall have dominion also from sea to sea, and from the river unto the ends of the earth").

These pragmatic considerations connected with a greater vision of a Canadian nation that would someday stretch from the Atlantic to the Pacific Oceans (*a mari usque ad mare* —Canada's national motto). Led by Sir John A. Macdonald, his French-Canadian colleague—George Étienne Cartier—and George Brown, these "Fathers of Confederation" provided the determination, imagination, dedication and political skill necessary to make confederation a reality.

The move to confederation started gathering steam when the British Parliament adopted the key recommendations contained in Durham's Report in the Act of Union of 1840. Upper and Lower Canada were combined into a single colony—"The Province of Canada" with a single legislature that combined the two districts of Canada East (Lower Canada) and Canada West(Upper Canada) with the intention of assimilated French-Canadians into English Canadian culture. The system of

Sir John A. Macdonald (1815–1891)

Sir John A. Macdonald is known as "The Father of Canada". A brilliant and charismatic politician, Macdonald's "National Dream" was to unite the colonies and create a nation from sea to sea. Born in 1815, in Glasgow, Scotland, he emigrated to Canada in 1820, where he began training for a legal career at 15. He was called to the bar in 1836. He was conservative in outlook but willing to fight for liberal principles. In 1843, he entered city politics, the provincial assembly from 1844. He held several cabinet posts, and was premier of Canada, virtually uninterrupted, from 1856–64. With George Brown, the leader of the Clear Grits (the forerunners to the Liberal Party of Canada) and George-Étienne Cartier (leader of the Parti Bleu, the Conservative Party in Canada East), Macdonald formed the Great Coalition in 1864. Together these three men brought about confederation. Macdonald became Canada's first prime minister in 1867–73 and 1878–91. He lived long enough to witness his dream of a sea-to-sea nation become reality.

George Étienne Cartier (1814–1873)

George Étienne Cartier was a lawyer, railway promoter, politician and a key Father of Confederation. He fought with the Patriotes in 1837, escaped to US and was pardoned in 1838. He ran for office in 1848 and was instrumental in forging the coalition between the Macdonald's Conservative Party and the French-Canadian Parti Bleu, leading to confederation. He was Macdonald's trusted confidant and ally, successfully negotiating the purchase of Rupert's Land (Western Canada). His death in 1873 was a deep blow to the Conservative Party.

The Fathers of Confederation in 1864, Charlottetown Conference painted by Robert Harris in 1884. The man standing rear centre is Sir John A. Macdonald.

government that spawned the rebellions went unchanged until 1849 when the British granted the colonies "responsible government" and ended the control of the appointed legislative council. Government was not the only thing that was changing in British North America. The two decades after the rebellions was a time of rapid growth and economic development that paved the way for nationhood. By the 1860s, the population was 3.5 million. The Reciprocity (free trade) Treaty of 1855 with the United States ushered in a period of rapid economic growth and prosperity and, as a result, the relationship with Britain changed from dependence to self-assurance. Despite the benefits of the Reciprocity Treaty, British North Americans did not trust the United States. The War of 1812 remained the touchstone for Canadian suspicions, along with the later issues raised by the civil war, Mexican War and annexation of its defeated territories, as well as claims of Manifest Destiny, support for slavery, and the potential infection of republican ideals only served further to confirm these doubts. At the same time, British colonial policy changed. Determined to cut the costs of its empire and end preferential trade agreements that benefited the colonies the British encouraged British North America to confederate. British relations with the United States were tense. They had supported the south in the war and decided that a way to ease tensions was to withdraw the British garrison in Canada and leave the Canadians to defend themselves. Yet none of these reasons were singularly compelling enough to bring about confederation. That required a convergence of the events and personalities, fears and passions, politics and policies. And that is exactly what happened at three important conferences held between 1864 and 1867.

The Charlottetown Conference, September 1864

The Charlottetown Conference was held in Charlottetown, Prince Edward Island, on September 19, 1864. The initial momentum came from the British Colonial office. They wanted Nova Scotia,

New Brunswick and Prince Edward Island to unite to reduce costs by amalgamating three legislatures into one. The response from these colonies was apathetic, particularly in Nova Scotia—a colony that was fiercely independent and economically prosperous. The three legislatures passed separate resolutions to have a conference on the subject but nothing was done. Then Macdonald announced that the Canadas would be interested in attending and shocked everyone by proposing they consider a larger union. After overcoming their initial reaction, the Maritime colonies agreed to meet with representatives from the Canadas. The location of Charlottetown (capital of Prince Edward Island) helped to ensure the host's participation in the proceedings. The conference was a success. Maritime union was dropped, replaced by an outline for a larger union. A second conference was scheduled to work out the details for Quebec City in October.

The Quebec Conference, October 1864

The Quebec Conference was held on October 10 to 27, 1864. Thirty-three delegates arrived in Quebec City including two delegates from Newfoundland. The delegates were prepared, in some cases eager, to develop a detailed plan for confederation. Voting would be by delegation with one vote per colony, except the Canadas which received two votes. After two weeks of intense discussions, negotiations and compromise, the Conference adopted the "72 resolutions" which became the basis for confederation. The major stumbling block had been the composition of the federal parliament. Prince Edward Island opposed representation by population fearing its interests would be drowned out by the larger provinces. Compromise was reached by adoption of a bi-cameral parliament. The House of Commons would be popularly elected based on population. The Senate would represent the provinces. Senators would be selected by the Governor-General. The number of Senate seats per province proved a sticking point but eventually a formula was approved.

Further discussions included the agreement to split the Canadas, preserving a French-speaking province (Quebec) that would be able to guarantee French Language, culture and religion. The Catholic Church approved the plan on the eve of confederation. Nova Scotia and New Brunswick reluctantly signed-on but Prince Edward Island and Newfoundland did not join confederation until 1873 and 1949 respectively. Despite the fact that 65 percent of Nova Scotians opposed union, Sir Charles Tupper, Premier of Nova Scotia carried the day, outflanking his opponents by signing the resolutions without asking permission. He received critical support from the British Colonial Secretary, Edward Cardwell.

The final push

Incidents during the US civil war, notably the St. Alban's raid when Confederate soldiers robbed the St. Alban Vermont bank and escaped via Canada ; Secretary of State William Seward's claim "that this whole continent, shall be, sooner or later, within the magic circle of the American union"; the cancellation of the Reciprocity Treaty and the purchase of Alaska; confirmed suspicions that the United States coveted Canada. Then, in 1866, these fears came true, with the Fenian raids.

In the Maritimes the anti-confederationists, led by Nova Scotia newspaper editor Joseph Howe whose slogan was "Confederation—botheration" captured the essence of popular opinion in Nova Scotians. In 1866, the Fenian Brotherhood, invaded Canada and all that changed. The Brotherhood was a para-military organization of Irishmen dedicated to freeing Ireland from British rule. Their strategy was to conquer British North America and trade it for Ireland. Its rank and file was filled with civil war veterans. Several thousand crossed the border into Canada West and New Brunswick. Major battles were fought along the borders before the Brotherhood was defeated. The raids helped convince many Maritimers and other Canadians as well, to support confederation. The failure of the US government to stop the raiders raised questions of collusion and fed Canadian annexation phobia. The Fenians tried again in 1870 and 1871 without success.

The London Conference, December 1866

The Canadians arrived in London armed with the 72 resolutions in December 1866. Deliberations lasted until February 1867. The resolutions formed the basis of the "British North America Act" which was signed into law by Queen Victoria in late April to take effect on July 1, 1867. The Dominion of Canada was born, comprising four provinces: Ontario, Quebec, New Brunswick and Nova Scotia.

The Act gave Canada a federal system of government and outlined the division of powers between the national government and provincial legislatures. The structure was federal, like the United States, but the form of government was parliamentary, like Britain. There was no serious talk of adopting the US congressional model. Residual power was given to the national government to avoid a Canadian version of the US civil war that was fought over states' rights. Provincial governments were comprised of a single elected legislative house without a senate. Quebec was granted special status Canada would have two official languages—French and English. Queen Victoria selected Ottawa for the capital. Sir John A. Macdonald became the first Prime Minister of Canada, and set to work to build a transcontinental railroad to create his vision of a nation stretching from sea to sea.

Unlike its southern neighbour who required two attempts to create its' constitution, Canadians negotiated the powers and structures of federal government first and then were granted self-government in the British North America Act. It would be another 70 years before Canada became entirely free of Britain.

We are the Fenian Brotherhood, skilled in the arts of war, And we're going to fight for Ireland, the land we adore, Many battles we have won, along with the boys in blue, And we'll go and capture Canada, for we've nothing else to do.

Fenian soldier's song

Discussion point

Should the US government have stopped the Fenian's from raiding Canada? Should the British have stopped Confederate soldiers from raiding Maine via New Brunswick (the St. Albans raid) during the US civil war?

Activity

Cartoon analysis

Source A

Britannia: "Is it possible My Dear, thay you have ever given your Cousin Jonathan any encouragement?"

Miss Canada: "Encouragement! Certainly not, Mama. I have told him we can *NEVER* be United?"

Questions

1 Who does Mrs. Britannia represent and why and from what is she protecting Miss Canada?

2 What response is the cartoonist attempting to evoke from readers in his portrayal of the characters? In your answer reference the characterization of Cousin Jonathan, Mrs Britannia and Miss Canada.

Source B

"The way brother Jonathan will astonish the natives." Annexation Comes in by the Rail, While Liberty Flies off in the Smoke, published in *Punch Magazine,* 1849.

Questions

1 Why does the cartoonist fear the "American Eagle"?

2 What recent events could have fueled the fears of annexation?

3 What is the origins, purpose and value of the source? What are its limitations?

Source C

Little Ben Holmes: "And Some naughty Children attempt to pawn their Mother's Pocket-Handkerchief but are Arrested by Policeman Who was stationed around the corner." Published in *Punch Magazine.*

Questions

1 Who do the naughty Children represent and why are they naughty?

2 Cousin Jonathan and Brother Jonathan were the forerunners of Uncle Sam (see sign above door)? Why did British North America depict, characterize and caricature the United States this way?

The plight of Native Americans

No group experienced greater changes during this period than Native Americans. They were conquered and marginalized, denied the rights of citizens, expelled from their ancestral lands and forced to abandon traditional lifestyles, cultures and customs. In the new nations, the ruling élites, whether liberals or conservatives, saw the native peoples as an impediment to the expansion and growth of a Christian-based civilization in the New World. Approaches to the "native problem" varied; oppression came in many forms. For example, Canada established church-run residential schools to educate, assimilate and civilize (often abusively) young native children forcibly removed from their parents. In Latin America, natives were a source of forced cheap labour on the creole-owned haciendas. Other tribes fought back but were defeated and forced onto reservations where they became dependent on the government for the necessities of life and forgotten.

From the Great plains to Patagonia, indigenous peoples were displaced by territorially ravenous European cultures who believed they had been chosen by God to rule the new world and its inhabitants. If the natives of the New World shared one thing—it was this; they were a conquered people, strangers in their own land. To their credit, these cultures proved resilient and adapted to incredible changes and clung tenaciously to their way of life. Yet the cultures that emerged from this crucible of change would have been barely recognizable to previous generations.

Case study: The Trail of Tears

Andrew Jackson became president of the United States in 1830. During the campaign he promised to expel Native Americans from the southern states and elsewhere in the Americas. Jackson claimed to support the native way of life, but not if it impeded expansion. The five nations—the Choctaw, Chickasaw, Creeks, Cherokee and Seminoles—lived in Jackson's home territory and he wanted them moved and soon.

Jackson's plan was to uproot the native people from their ancestral lands and march them west to the "Indian territories" or "Indian country" (present-day Oklahoma). The territory was to be permanently free of white encroachments but he did not take into account the many whites who already lived in the territory, and its appeal as a haven for escaped southern slaves. The region also had its own resident indigenous tribes, who might not react well to their imposed brethren. Jackson created a Bureau of Indian Affairs to administer the territory and keep it free of settlers but within 15 years land-hungry settlers began entering the territory *en masse*. No one stopped them.

Jackson signed the Indian Removal Act in 1830. The tribes were required to sign a treaty that legally ceded their homelands and accepted the compensation of designated lands in the new territory. The Government promised to protect and supply the tribes on their journey, but this did not happen. First to leave were the Choctaws

Activity

Comparative outcomes

Compare the treatment of Canada's *métis* peoples with the *mestizos* in Perú, *ladinos* in Guatemala, *llaneros* in Venezuela, *mestiços* and *mulattos* in Brazil, and other countries of Latin America and the Caribbean.

How do mixed white-indigenous cultures survive in the different nations?

The Trail of Tears, 1988. Tobi & Larry Brown walking along the Trail of Tears with horse-drawn covered wagons reenacting the 1,000-mile journey that the Cherokees traveled 150 years ago.

who left "voluntarily" after signing the Treaty of Dancing Rabbit Creek. The Removal Act encouraged voluntary compliance but left no doubt of the eventual outcome. Fourteen thousand Choctaws marched west, several thousand perished on the trail. Seven thousand stayed behind and suffered untold discrimination. No other tribal group in North America suffered more than the Cherokee. In 1835, they signed the Treaty of Echota, unsuccessfully contested its legality, and were forcibly evicted by the US army in 1838. About 15,000 people started the trek and one third perished on the death march christened the "Trail of Tears".

By 1840, the clearances were complete. Over 46,000 natives had been expelled, ceding 25 million acres of prime agricultural land to the US government.

Discussion point

Clearances

Compare the forced removal of the Cherokees with the expulsion of the Acadians in 1755, Rosas' campaign against Argentine Indians in 1833–34, the Scottish Clearances in the late 18th century, and the Armenian clearances during the First World War. Why were these peoples forced to leave their homes?

Activity

Indian removals

Reading the following documents relating to the Indian Removals of the 1830s and answer the questions that follow:

Source A

President Jackson's second annual address to the nation, given on March 4, 1833, discussing Indian removals.

It will relieve the whole State of Mississippi and the western part of Alabama of Indian occupancy, and enable those States to advance rapidly in population, wealth, and power. It will separate the Indians from immediate contact with settlements of whites; free them from the power of the States; enable them to pursue happiness in their own way and under their own rude institutions; will retard the progress of decay, which is lessening their numbers, and perhaps cause them gradually, under the protection of the Government and through the influence of good counsels, to cast off their savage habits and become an interesting, civilized, and Christian community. What good man would prefer a country covered with forests and ranged by a few thousand savages to our extensive Republic, →

studded with cities, towns, and prosperous farms embellished with all the improvements which art can devise or industry execute, occupied by more than 12,000,000 happy people, and filled with all the blessings of liberty, civilization and religion?

Source: Andrew Jackson: Second Inaugural Address.1833. "Inaugural Addresses of the President of the United States." http://bartelby.com/124/pres24.html.

Source B

The French philosopher Alexis de Tocqueville witnessed the Choctaw removals while in Memphis, Tennessee, in 1831, and later published his observations in his famous "Democracy in America."

In the whole scene there was an air of ruin and destruction, something which betrayed a final and irrevocable adieu; one couldn't watch without feeling one's heart wrung. The Indians were tranquil, but sombre and taciturn. There was one who could speak English and of whom I asked why the Chactas [sic] were leaving their country. "To be free," he answered, could never get any other reason out of him. We ... watch the expulsion ... of one of the most celebrated and ancient American peoples.

Source: de Tocqueville, Alexis. 1835. *Democracy in America*.

Source C

Historian Elisa Frühauf Garcia discussing Native American Indians in Brazil in the 19th century.

... the Indians that were not fully inserted in imperial society, commonly denominated "savages," had to be put in villages, also with the objective of preparing their absorption into the remaining population, or else be implacably fought in case they did not accept being put into villages or if they resisted the expansion fronts. In this way, the Empire projected a homogeneous population, with no space for the permanence of Indians as a differentiated group. It reserved, however, a place of prominence for the natives in the young nation's past. Despite significant differences, the intellectuals involved in building a national identity agreed to grant the Indians an important role in the founding of Brazil, symbolized by their union with the Portuguese.

Source: Frühauf Garcia, Elisa. 2010. *Revista Brasileira de História*. vol. 30, no. 59, June 2010. (A review of the book by Almeida, Maria Regina Celestino de. 2010. *Os índios na história do Brasil*. Rio de Janeiro: FGV).

Source D

Lewis Cass, Governor of Michigan, 1813–31, was considered an expert on the topic of Native Americans. His views were popular with the public and politicians alike.

As civilization shed her light upon them [native Americas] why were they blind to its beams? Hungry or naked, why did they disregard, or regarding, why did they neglect, those arts by which food and clothing could be procured? Existing for two centuries in contact with a civilized people, they have resisted, and successfully too, every effort to meliorate their situation, or to introduce among them the most common arts of life. All this is without a parallel in the history of the world. That it is not to be attributed to the indifference or neglect of the whites, we have already shown. There must then be an inherent difficulty, arising from the institutions, character, and condition of the Indians themselves .... The Indians are entitled to the enjoyment of all the rights which do not interfere with the obvious designs of Providence, and with the just claims of others ... But there are two restraints upon ourselves [the U.S.], which we may safely adopt, —that no force should be used to divest them of any just interest they possess, and that they should be liberally remunerated for all they may cede. We cannot be wrong while we adhere to these rules.

Source: Cass, Lewis. January 1830. "Removal of the Indians." *North American Review.*

Source E

Cherokee letter protesting the Treaty of New Echota from Chief John Ross, "To the Senate and House of Representatives."

With a view to bringing our troubles to a close, a delegation was appointed on the 23rd of October, 1835, by the General Council of the nation, clothed with full powers to enter into arrangements with the Government of the United States, for the final adjustment of all our existing difficulties. The delegation failing to effect an arrangement with the United States commissioner, then in the nation, proceeded, agreeably to their instructions in that case, to Washington City, for the purpose of negotiating a treaty with the authorities of the United States. After the departure of the Delegation, a contract was made by the Rev. John F. Schermerhorn, and certain individual Cherokees, purporting to be a "treaty, concluded at New Echota, in the State of Georgia, on the 29th day of December, 1835, by General William Carroll and John F. Schermerhorn, commissioners on the part of the United States, and the chiefs, headmen, and people of the Cherokee tribes of Indians." A spurious Delegation, in violation of a special injunction of the general council of the nation, proceeded to Washington City with this pretended treaty, and by false and fraudulent representations supplanted in the favor of the Government the legal and accredited Delegation of the Cherokee people, and obtained for this instrument, after making important alterations in its provisions, the recognition of the United States Government. And now it is presented to us as a treaty, ratified by the Senate, and approved by the President [Andrew Jackson], and our acquiescence in its requirements demanded, under the sanction of the displeasure of the United States, and the threat of summary compulsion, in case of refusal. It comes to us, not through our legitimate authorities, the known and usual medium of communication between the Government of the United States and our nation, but through the agency of a complication of powers, civil and military.

Source: Cherokee Nation, September 28, 1836. Red Clay Council Ground.

Questions

1 To what extent do sources A and D support the views expressed in source C?

2 Compare the statements made regarding the nature of Native Americans in sources A and D.

3 Evaluate the points of view expressed in sources B and E on the impact of the expulsion of native peoples.

4 Using the documents and your own knowledge, why do you think the people of the United States overwhelmingly supported the expulsions in the 1830s?

Discussion point

The Canadian push to the west

French and Anglo Canadians lived mostly in the East. First Nations, or aboriginal Canadians, lived in Native Reserves, especially after Confederation in 1867. The spaces were mostly kept separate. As the fur trade caused more white male migration to the prairies and the Canadian West, intermarriage between white men and Indian women became more prevalent. Postcolonial scholarship has explored the mingling of spaces and peoples, particularly J.R. Miller in what has been called "native-newcomer relations."

Source: Wanhalla, Angela. "Women `Living across the Line: Intermarriage on the Canadian Prairies and in Southern New Zealand." *1870–1900. Ethnohistory*. Winter 2008, vol. 55, no. 1. Winter 2008. p. 29–49.

Questions

1 What advantages in access to resources did intermarriage offer for white trappers?

2 What challenges might acceptance of Christian marriages have had for native women?

3 What status was accorded to *métis* or "half-breed" children?

Exam practice and further resources

Sample exam questions

1   Analyze the main compromises which underpinned the US Constitution of 1787.

2   To what extent did colonial political systems bring about their own downfall? Support you answer with reference to two Latin American countries.

3   For what reasons and with what results did war break out in North America in 1812?

4   To what extent was British rule in North America successfully challenged between 1837 and 1867?

5   Assess the social impact of independence with reference to two countries in the Americas.

Recommended further reading

Latin America

Jack K. Bauer. 1992. *The Mexican War l846–l848.* Lincoln: University of Nebraska Press.

Janet Burke & Ted Humphrey. 2010. *Nineteenth-Century Nation Building and the Latin American Intellectual Tradition: A Reader.* Indianapolis: Hackett Publishing Co.

David Bushnell & Neil MacAulay. 1994. *The Emergence of Latin America in the Nineteenth Century.* 2nd edn. New York: Oxford University Press.

Sarah C. Chambers & John Charles Chasteen. 2010. *Latin American Independence: An Anthology of Sources.* Indianapolis: Hackett Publishing Co.

Fernando López-Alves. 2000. *State Formation and Democracy in Latin America, 1810–1900.* Duke University Press.

Pamela S. Murray. 2010. *For Glory and Bolívar: The Remarkable Life of Manuela Sáez.* University of Texas Press.

United States

Constitutional Convention. *TeachingAmericanHistory.org*
http://teachingamericanhistory.org/convention.

The Federalist papers. *Founding Fathers information*
http://www.foundingfathers.info/federalistpapers.

US presidents. *The White House.*
http://www.whitehouse.gov/about/presidents.

US–Mexican War. *Public Broadcasting Service (PBS).*
http://www.pbs.org/kera/usmexicanwar/index_flash.html.

Canada

Robert Bothwell. 2006. *The Penguin History of Canada.* Toronto: Penguin Books.

Victor Suthren. 1999. *The War of l812.* Toronto: McClelland & Stewart.

3 The emergence of the Americas in global affairs, 1880–1929

The end of the 19th century was marked by dramatic global integration. As the countries of the Americas emerged into this new global reality, they were exposed to the benefits and drawbacks of more closely linked national economic and foreign policies. To the profit of expanded trade had to be added the costs and dangers of war and expansion. This was perhaps most evident when the global calamity of the First World War impacted countries throughout the region, even those determined to stay out of it. Of course, the roots of the Americas' emergence into global affairs lay in the mid-century and it is here that we begin.

During the second half of the 19th century, the United States was emerging from a period of bitter civil war and fitful reconstruction into a period of rapid economic expansion. Industries such as railroads, mining, iron and coal production made great advances and in the process created great fortunes. Such economic growth requires ever expanding supplies of resources and ready markets for the finished products. To this end, ambitious settlers from the United States began to look to territory beyond the continental United States. Opposition to the notion of territorial expansion also grew during this period forcing the United States to seriously consider the status and role of the republic in the community of nations.

The status of the United States' northern neighbor also underwent a drastic change from the mid-century. From 1867, the Dominion of Canada was independent in all matters domestic. Foreign policy, however, was still the purview of the United Kingdom. At the same time, Canada was undergoing her own version of territorial and economic expansion that would challenge her dependence on the United Kingdom. While in the United States the debate was whether or not to become an imperial power, in Canada it revolved around whether or not to remain an imperial dependent. The strains of the First World War and Canada's response would help bring some resolution to the question.

South of the United States the countries of South and Central America were likewise caught between the economic and territorial expansion of the United States and Europe and their own ambitions. The internationalization of trade and the increased availability of credit sparked immigration and economic growth in South America, changing both domestic social and economic structures as well as the place of these countries in the global economy. Central American and Caribbean states labored under challenging economic structures and their strategic position in relation to the United States.

Discussion point

US president Harry Truman once said that the *"responsibility of the great states* is to *serve* and *not* to *dominate* the world."

To what extent do powerful countries have an obligation to ensure the stability of the global community? Do they have an economic obligation to countries that are less well-off? To what extent did the powerful countries of the world fulfill any such obligation in the years 1870–1929?

By the end of this chapter, students should be able to:

● analyze the political economic, social and ideological reason for US expansion in the region

115

- understand the causes and effects of the Spanish–American War
- assess the application and impacts of United States foreign policy in the Americas 1890–1914
- demonstrate an understanding of United States involvement in the First World War including its causes, course and impacts
- demonstrate an understanding of Canadian involvement in the First World War including its causes, course and impacts
- analyze the effects of the First World War on Latin America, Canada and the United States.

The United States: setting the stage

The most deadly war in US history came to an end in the spring of 1865. By the time General Robert Lee had surrendered the army of northern Virginia to General Grant and the remaining Confederate armies had laid down their arms, over 620,000 citizens of the United States had died. What lay ahead was the difficult process of **Reconstruction**. How to bring the secessionist southern states back into the union in a meaningful and productive way? At the same time, the northern economy had to adjust to a decline in industrial demand that would accompany the peace. Banking, railways, and other industrial interests had all expanded during the war. In an effort to maintain this growth, government land grants, subsidies and loans flowed to the private sector, most notably to the railway industry. The inauguration of Ulysses S. Grant in 1869 ushered in an aggressive period of Reconstruction that would sweep over the southern United States. Industrial interests became political interests and accusations of political corruption were common.

> **Reconstruction** was the period from 1865–77 during which the states that had seceded from the union were reintegrated into the United States.

The 1870s were also a period of economic dislocation and depression. The rapid industrial expansion of the war years and the early Reconstruction period had caused an expansion of the money supply inducing the Grant administration into a restrictive **monetary policy** as a countermeasure. When Jay Cooke & Company, an important Philadelphia banking firm, collapsed in September 1873 the subsequent panic lead to a cascade of bank failures, plunging the United States into what became known as the **Long Depression**. Grant's monetary policy exacerbated matters, restricting access to capital that could stimulate the stagnating economy. Unemployment and low wages spread across the country and with it labor strife culminating in the Great Railway Strikes of 1877 that further paralyzed commerce, revealing deep class divisions in US society.

> **Monetary policy** is the government policy that controls the supply of money in the economy.

> The **Long Depression** was period of economic stagnation that lasted from 1873 to 1879. The depression was a worldwide phenomenon reflecting the increasingly globalized economy of the late Victorian period.

In 1879, the United States emerged from the Long Depression into yet another period of rapid and immense economic expansion. As capital became more available, industrial enterprises consumed natural and human resources with a voracious appetite. A new wave of immigration brought labor from Southern Europe and Asia to feed this appetite. New supplies of coal, iron, and oil were discovered and exploited. Electricity powered more and more of the country. The efficiency of agriculture, mining, textile manufacture, and steel production dramatically improved, creating new wealth across the country. **Infrastructure** networks multiplied throughout the land led by another wave of railway construction moving raw materials, finished goods and even consumers across all regions of the United States. New business models and financial vehicles accelerated the already dizzying pace of expansion. Terms like **vertical and horizontal integration** began to appear and monopolies, trusts and corporations became powerful archetypes of business organization. Money, legislation, and land from state and federal governments lubricated the entire process and iconic businessmen such as Rockefeller, Morgan, Carnegie, and Mellon arose as commanding figures in American society.

Such expansion must necessarily be accompanied by some dislocation. Rapid urbanization created poor living conditions in areas of many US cities. Workers toiled under poor working conditions, long hours, low wages and no job security. In response, workers began to organize into unions large and small, local and national. With this organization came conflict with those whose profits depended on the status quo. Strikes, demonstrations and riots dotted this period in all major industries from mining, to railways to the steel industry. New political alternatives such as socialism, Marxism and anarchism surfaced in response to worker exploitation.

It is against this backdrop of rapid economic and social change that the United States embarked on an increasingly expansionist foreign policy both within the Americas and around the world. Although this expansion coincided with another wave of European imperialism and shared many motives and elements with it, it was also distinct in its manifestation. It is to this expansion that we now turn.

> **Infrastructure** is those sectors of the economy that assist in the production and distribution of raw materials, labor and goods. Infrastructure includes such things as railroads, telegraphs, roadways, canals, and shipping.

> **Vertical integration** exists when a number of steps in the production of a single product are owned or controlled by a single company.
>
> **Horizontal integration** exists when a single company owns or controls a number of firms in the same stage of production of a single product.

> **Discussion point**
>
> Canada and Latin American countries were developing resource-based economies during this period. How did the Long Depression affect this development? How did these effects compare with those in the United States?

Ideological reasons for US expansion

Monroe Doctrine

By the 1820s, the Spanish and Portuguese empires in the Americas had been replaced by nascent, and largely unstable independent states—states, the legitimacy of which, the United States unilaterally recognized in 1822. The Monroe Doctrine, however, was a product of the situation in Europe as much as it was reflective of the situation in Latin America. In the years following the Congress of Vienna, which rebuilt Europe following the Napoleonic Wars, Russia emerged as a dominant continental force, a European power with definite interests on the North American continent. Ideologically, much of the system set up at Vienna and after was designed to disempower nationalist independence movements of the very kind that were so recently triumphant in Latin America. In such a situation it was easy to conceive of situations in which European powers might feel the need to intervene in the western hemisphere.

Presidents of the United States, 1880–1929		
President	Political Party	Years
Rutherford B. Hayes	Republican	1877–81
James Garfield	Republican	1881
Chester Arthur	Republican	1881–85
Grover Cleveland	Democratic	1885–89
Benjamin Harrison	Republican	1889–93
Grover Cleveland	Democratic	1893–97
William McKinley	Republican	1897–1901
Theodore Roosevelt	Republican	1901–09
William Taft	Republican	1909–13
Woodrow Wilson	Democratic	1913–21
Warren Harding	Republican	1921–23
Calvin Coolidge	Republican	1923–29
Herbert Hoover	Republican	1929–33

With this in mind, President Monroe with his Secretary of State, John Quincy Adams, sent a note to congress outlining what would later become known as the Monroe Doctrine. This doctrine would raise its head throughout the rest of the century, in Mexico, Venezuela and Cuba. Early in the 20th century, President Theodore Roosevelt would expand on the doctrine in what became known as the Roosevelt Corollary. He added to the essentially defensive nature of Monroe's original idea the view that the United States had the right to intervene to manage the independent states of the western hemisphere.

Manifest destiny in the post-Reconstruction period

First coined in the 1840s as a justification for the **annexation** of Texas, "Manifest Destiny" came to mean different things to different people throughout the rest of the 19th Century. At its simplest it was the belief that it was the inevitable mission of the United States to expand beyond its 1840s boundaries and to eventually stretch from the Atlantic to the Pacific. The popularizer of the phrase, John L. Sullivan, took as its evidence the population growth to that point (1845) and used terms like "natural law" and "natural flow of events" and "the spontaneous working of principles." It fit well with other emerging, often equally as malleable ideas, such as American Exceptionalism and Continentalism. With such a broad concept it is not hard to understand that it could be molded to any number of specific worldviews—geographic, racial, economic, religious, practical, or social Darwinian. Although the convulsions of the civil war meant that notions of Manifest Destiny were consumed with more pressing internal issues, it would again emerge in the post-Reconstruction period when the US began again to look beyond its borders.

Expansion as moral duty

We can see two broad impulses to US expansion that developed in the last half of the 19th century. The first has sometimes been broadly characterized as a moral justification and motive for an expanded hegemony of the United States. From 1859, this argument drew increasing energy from the spread of Darwin's powerful ideas. Although Charles Darwin had really only discussed the evolution by means of natural selection of animals in his *Origin of Species* (1859), it did not take long for thinkers from all over Europe and North America to apply this concept to all manner of social constructions, from business to human society, in which the United States saw itself taking a leadership role. Emblematic of the growing popularity of a Darwinian approach to social issues was the growing influence of the British philosopher Herbert Spencer. Spencer, who coined the phrase "survival of the fittest", conceived of society as evolving from a state of undifferentiated homogeneity to one of highly differentiated heterogeneity as exemplified in the modern industrial state driven by relatively unfettered individualism. This became a notion popular with the growing class of US industrialists who sponsored Spencer's tour of the United States in 1882. Spencer

Discussion point

What interests might France, Russia and Great Britain have in Latin America? How realistic were the fears of the United States?

Annexation is the process of attaching territory to an existing country, nation or state that it had not hitherto belonged.

Discussion point

While the Monroe Doctrine might have initially been defensive in nature for the United States, how would it have been perceived by the newly independent countries of Brazil, Argentina and Venezuela?

Discussion point

Darwin's idea referred primarily to biological development. How have these ideas been modified to fit other aspects of society?

seemed to hold out a philosophical if not scientific justification for the continued growth of the United States' industrial economy and therefore the United States itself.

The ideas of Spencer and Darwin and later Francis Galton—the father of the eugenics movement—spread around the world. As Jürgen Buchenau has pointed out, Latin American leaders who read these philosophers developed a view of society as evolving from simple to complex, following the European model. Buchenau goes on to argue that this is reflected in the massive amounts of European migration to Latin America at the end of the 19th century. This migration was encouraged by these leaders to increase the influence of European values and institutions on their "evolving" countries.

In Canada, one of Spencer's chief advocates was historian and journalist Goldwin Smith. Spencer's ideas led Smith to the conclusion that the new country of Canada was not economically developed enough to be viable in the context of the late 19th century. To Smith the only logical solution was to join Canada and the United States.

The ideas of Spencer and Darwin found a supporter in the writings of US historian John Fiske. Fiske's writings and lectures in the 1880s emphasized the evolutionary superiority of the Anglo-Saxon race as evidenced in its population growth, geographic influence and economic strength. He envisioned a day when the world would resemble the United States in institutions, language and religion. Although he stopped short of calling for anything like a crusade of annexation and military expansion, he certainly helped develop an intellectual foundation for US expansion as "natural."

Fiske's position was given a more racial and religious tone by the clergyman Josiah Strong. In his book *Our Country: Its Possible Future and Its Present Crisis* he posited the Anglo-Saxon race, especially as it had developed in the United States, as destined to dominate the globe. In many ways he saw such domination by what he believed to be a superior race as a duty. According to Strong, the combination of liberal democracy and Christianity as expressed in the United States was the chief means by which the world would progress and the vehicle of this progress was to be imperialist expansion—US expansion.

John Burgess, a political scientist from Columbia University argued in *Political Science and Comparative Constitutional Law* (1890) that it was the Teutonic races that had the greatest innate ability to create the modern nation-state and those who resisted the progress toward such states were justly subjugated. Among the most notable of Burgess's students was one who would have the power to act directly on the foreign policy implications of Burgess's ideas—Theodore Roosevelt.

Of course these sentiments were not confined to the United States. European powers were busy parceling out portions of Africa and other territories throughout this period and they too looked to racist theories for justification. Notions of the superiority of the "white races" and its attendant responsibilities appear in the arguments of German, French and British imperialists throughout this period. Perhaps one of the

Discussion point

How "Christian" was the United States at the end of the 19th century?

What other religious traditions existed in the US during this period?

Discussion point

How valid is the concept of "race?"

Does it have a basis in biology? How has the term "race" been used throughout the 19th and 20th centuries? How is the term "race" used in society today?

most famous of these justifications came not in a scholarly work, but rather a popular poem by Rudyard Kipling that leant its title to many a rationalization for imperial expansion at the time. Although published in 1899 and directed at the Philippines annexation debate, "The White Man's Burden" expressed what many had been arguing in various forms for the previous two decades.

Expansion as practical necessity

While vague notions of duty, destiny and race may have inspired the imperial visions of some in the United States, others were more practical in their outlook. This realist approach to US expansion took as its starting point the rapid population, economic, and geographic expansion of the United States in the last half of the century and then looked to what it would take to protect this and ensure further growth. Such concerns naturally revolved around military and economic might.

Foremost among these "realists" was Alfred Thayer Mahan. Mahan was the president of the United States Naval War College whose lectures, magazine articles and books such as *Influence of Sea Power on History, 1660–1783* (1890), popularized the thesis that it was maritime trade and the tools of this trade, ships both merchant and military, that brought national greatness. To Mahan, it further meant secure supplies of coal for these ships be readily available at ports around the world. It also meant control of any advantageous waterways, natural and man-made. In this he was primarily looking to any future canal cutting across the Isthmus of Panama and islands that could potentially protect the approaches to this future waterway. Mahon's thesis found avid readers around the world, perhaps most notably in Berlin. His book was a major influence on Kaiser Wilhelm's decision to embark on a major naval building program that would have such far-reaching consequences. Closer to home his work also found an audience in the likes of Theodore Roosevelt and Henry Cabot Lodge.

Take up the White Man's burden–
Send forth the best ye breed–
Go bind your sons to exile
To serve your captives' need;
To wait in heavy harness,
On fluttered folk and wild–
Your new-caught, sullen peoples,
Half-devil and half-child.

From "The White Man's Burden," Rudyard Kipling, 1899.

Activity

Social Darwinism in action

So influential were the ideas of Herbert Spencer and Francis Galton that many of their ideas found their way into legislation and the press throughout the Americas. Examples included eugenics legislation in Canada and immigration policies throughout the region. Conduct some research and complete the following chart.

Country	Social Darwinian idea	Example
Uruguay		
Argentina		
Brazil		
Canada		
United States		

Economic reasons for expansion

There was a growing economic imperative to national expansion at the end of the 19th century. But even those who saw in expansion a more divine or moral mission, men such as the Protestant clergyman and author Josiah Strong, saw the expansion of the Anglo-Saxon race as inextricably linked to the expansion of its institutions and economic system.

We have already discussed the context of domestic economic expansion in the 1880s. The leaders of this expansion also sought markets beyond North America. Despite the fact that a great deal of European capital was still flowing into the United States, US oil and steel companies sought new markets and resources around the globe, and in so doing came into competition with other economic powers such as the Great Britain and Germany. Other US companies such as Dupont, Colt and Singer also explored foreign markets with their manufactured goods. The depression that hit the world after 1873 meant that businesses, regardless of nationality, had to work that much harder to maintain profits. The move to the **gold standard** by most industrializing powers by the 1870s also placed downward pressure on prices until new gold deposits were discovered at the end of the century. On the other hand, the convertibility that the gold standard provided greased the wheels of international trade by making most currencies easily exchangeable through convertibility into gold. Although the United States had a massive domestic market, importing far less than it consumed domestically, there was a growing sense that by the 1890s, the United States economy was destined to produce more than could be consumed by existing markets, domestic and foreign, and thus these markets had to expand.

Another depression gripped the United States in 1893, bringing with it a sense of social and economic dislocation the solution to which seemed to some the expansion of the United States itself. The Historian Richard Hofstadter contends that the depression affected the country like never before. The depression was radicalizing the working class and this seemed to pose a dangerous threat to what the middle class perceived as the established economic order. Having stretched the republic from sea to sea, there appeared no obvious opportunities to funnel this discontent into North American expansion, as had been the case in the past. Despite the depression, the flow of immigrants continued unabated, as did the growth of urban centers. To Hofstadter, one of the prime expressions of this mood was national self-assertion and aggression.

> The **gold standard** is a monetary policy in which currency is readily convertible to gold. The gold standard requires that a country's supply of currency be tied to its supply of gold.

Activity

Data analysis

United States Economic Expansion, 1865–1898	
Wheat	256%
Corn	222%
Sugar	460%
Coal	800%
Steel Rails	523%

Source: Kennedy, Paul. 1988. *Rise and Fall of the Great Powers: Economic and Military Conflict from 1500 to 2000*. London: Fontana Press p. 312.

Research economic growth in two other countries in the region. How do these numbers compare to those in the United States? What are some reasons for the differences? Who was consuming these goods? Were they exported or consumed within the country? What are the implications for export versus import-reliant economies?

Political reasons for expansion

In some cases of US foreign expansion in the second half of the 19th century, policy and official action seemed hard-pressed to keep pace with the actions of its citizens and officials abroad. In the case of the Samoan Islands, US merchant ships had used the island increasingly as a coaling station for Pacific trade, a trade that had quickened since the transcontinental railroad opened up the Pacific coast to the goods of the US interior. The strategic importance of the islands was not lost on the US navy, which contemplated a naval base at Pago Pago in the 1870s. Despite Congress's rejection of a formal treaty with Samoa at that time, US commercial interests continued and by the end of the decade a treaty established a formal relationship between the Samoans and the United States. Britain and Germany also recognizing the importance of the islands were not about to allow the US a free hand and after some tense encounters agreed to a three-way **protectorate** over the islands. The threat posed by Germany and Britain elicited a great deal of posturing and bellicose rhetoric from politicians and newspapers across the country. By 1899, this arrangement became a two-way split of the islands between Germany and the United States.

Just as the Samoan Islands were an important mid-ocean link between the United States and the South Pacific, the Hawaiian Islands grew into an important way station in the growing China trade. Missionaries, merchants, and sailors settled in the islands throughout the mid century. As the non-native population increased, stories of the islands' commercial potential reached the United States and sugar plantations soon followed providing some evidence for Strong's claim in 1885 that "commerce follows the missionary." And then followed the military. To the growing US navy, Pearl Harbor in the islands seemed to provide an easily defended natural harbor from which it could protect US trade interests.

Hawaii's sugar trade with the United States provided at once a reason and a method by which the US could exert more influence on the islands. In 1875, the United States dropped all tariffs on Hawaiian sugar and guaranteed against any third party influence in its affairs, thus making the Hawaiian Islands a protectorate of the US in all but name. By 1887, the US navy had the use of Pearl Harbor.

The US commercial presence in the islands grew steadily. Fruit and sugar plantations made up the bulk of these enterprises with the United States as their sole destination. When a representative from Ohio named William McKinley introduced a tariff bill that was passed into law in 1890, Hawaiian sugar interests fell through the cracks. While the McKinley Tariff as it became known drastically increased the tariffs on foreign-produced goods it also paid subsidies to US sugar producers. All at once Hawaiian sugar was subject to the tariffs, but ineligible for the subsidy.

Fearing economic ruin, US citizens in the islands took matters into their own hands and overthrew the young Hawaiian queen Liliuokalani early in 1893. Those involved immediately petitioned

> A **protectorate** is a territory that is nominally independent but under the official military and diplomatic protection of another country.

Discussion point

? **What is a protectorate?**

How does it differ from a colony?
For the protectorate?
For the protecting country?
What were the benefits of this situation for the Hawaiians?
What were the benefits for the United States?

Activity

To expand or not

For each of the following groups, write a paragraph taking and defending a position on the annexation of the Hawaiian Islands in 1893.

- Josiah Strong
- Alfred Mahan
- A San Francisco merchant
- A US naval officer
- A US clergyman
- The British Ambassador to the United States
- A US sugar producer

the United States government for annexation—to bring them within the McKinley Tariff wall. The request caught the government and the voting public in the US by surprise. Now they had to confront the reality of the theories of Strong, Burgess, Fiske and Mahan. Did the US really want to be an imperial power?

The immediate answer to this question was ... not right now. The new president, Cleveland, may have been moderately in favor of annexation; he was enough of a politician to understand that the people of the United States and the politicians that represented them, and upon whom he would depend to pass legislation, were split on the issue. He sent a fact-finding mission to the islands and found that the so-called "revolution" was engineered by US business interests in the islands and had little native support. Nevertheless, the provisional government put in place would not be dissuaded and Cleveland was in the unenviable position of having to depose the revolutionaries with force or to find some sort of intermediate status for Hawaii. He chose the latter. It proved only a temporary reprieve for the anti-annexationists. By the time William McKinley had taken office as President of the United States in 1897 the global context had changed considerably and by joint resolution of Congress the US annexed Hawaii in 1898.

Venezuela

The Monroe Doctrine would again emerge as a vital US policy in the mid 1890s when a boundary dispute re-erupted between Great Britain and Venezuela. Gold had been discovered in the border region between Venezuela and British Guiana and this raised the stakes considerably. The relative merits of the gold standard and the free coinage of silver had been building as an important issue, both with politicians and the public for some years. Cleveland and other supporters of the gold standard saw in this discovery a possible source of new gold that could take out some of the fight of the free silver agitators.

Cleveland, on the whole a conservative when it came to matters of foreign policy, was torn between those in Congress, state legislatures and the press who called for a strong response to what was perceived as high-handed British interference in the US sphere of influence and his own beliefs on foreign policy. After studying the somewhat limited information available to him, Cleveland came to the conclusion that the former was indeed the case and advocated for arbitration of the dispute by a third party sending a note saying as much to the British Foreign Ministry. In a letter drafted by his aggressive Secretary of State, Richard Olney, Cleveland reasserted the Monroe Doctrine as he interpreted it applying to the Venezuelan situation. The note also made veiled threats of more aggressive action should the British not heed the US demand for arbitration. The reply from Lord Salisbury was straightforward. Britain would not submit the matter to arbitration and the Monroe Doctrine did not apply nor was it a recognized element of international law.

Discussion point

How had the international situation changed between 1893 and 1898?

What significant foreign events may have affected US foreign policy toward Hawaii? How might these have affected the United States' attitude toward imperial expansion?

When Cleveland's response to the British rebuff came before Congress in December 1895, its bellicose tone and language startled the British and energized **jingoists** in Congress and the press. After a period of negotiation, the US and Britain agreed on an arbitration treaty and eventually the terms of the arbitration itself. On the surface, the aggressive sabre-rattling of Cleveland and Olney seemed to bear fruit. He had reclaimed for himself and the Democratic Party the status of defender of US interests from their Republican Party critics such as Theodore Roosevelt. Further, the Monroe Doctrine seemed to be alive and well as the century drew to a close.

> **Jingoism** is an expression of extreme nationalist or parochial sentiment. It can also manifest itself in an aggressive foreign policy.

Activity

The gold standard

Research the issue of the gold standard at the end of the 19th century.

1 How was coinage minted in the United States prior to the 1890s?
2 Describe how the gold standard worked in the international economic system of the 1890s.
3 Which countries in the world benefited from the gold standard? Which counties were put at a disadvantage by the gold standard? Why was this?
4 What are the advantages and disadvantages of a country adopting the gold standard as a basis for its monetary system?
5 How was this issue resolved in the United States?

Read the following excerpt from a speech by William Jennings Bryan delivered in 1896. Bryan was the Democratic presidential nominee and a supporter of the free coinage of silver.

We say to you that you have made the definition of a business man too limited in its application. The man who is employed for wages is as much a business man as his employer; the attorney in a country town is as much a business man as the corporation counsel in a great metropolis; the merchant at the cross-roads store is as much a business man as the merchant of New York; the farmer who goes forth in the morning and toils all day—who begins in the spring and toils all summer—and who by the application of brain and muscle to the natural resources of the country creates wealth, is as much a business man as the man who goes upon the board of trade and bets upon the price of grain; the miners who go down a thousand feet into the earth, or climb two thousand feet upon the cliffs, and bring forth from their hiding places the precious metals to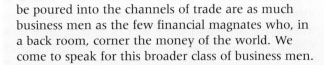

be poured into the channels of trade are as much business men as the few financial magnates who, in a back room, corner the money of the world. We come to speak for this broader class of business men.

It is the issue of 1776 over again. Our ancestors, when but three millions in number, had the courage to declare their political independence of every other nation; shall we, their descendants, when we have grown to seventy millions, declare that we are less independent than our forefathers? No, my friends, that will never be the verdict of our people. Therefore, we care not upon what lines the battle is fought. If they say bimetallism is good, but that we cannot have it until other nations help us, we reply that, instead of having a gold standard because England has, we will restore bimetallism, and then let England have bimetallism because the United States has it. If they dare to come out in the open field and defend the gold standard as a good thing, we will fight them to the uttermost. Having behind us the producing masses of this nation and the world, supported by the commercial interests, the laboring interests, and the toilers everywhere, we will answer their demand for a gold standard by saying to them: "You shall not press down upon the brow of labor this crown of thorns; you shall not crucify mankind upon a cross of gold.

Questions

1 Bryan supports bimetallism as being advantageous to the majority of US workers. To what degree do you agree with him? How does the gold standard help or hurt the working classes?

2 What does this speech tell us about political divisions in the United States at the turn of the century?

3 Draft a response to Bryan from the perspective of a supporter of the gold standard.

Activity

To war?

War over the Venezuelan boundary dispute seemed a definite possibility in December 1895. Evaluate the case for and against war in both Great Britain and the United States. To what degree do you think that war was a real possibility throughout this crisis?

Activity

The Venezuelan Response

In groups, brainstorm possible responses of the Venezuelan government to the British and US positions on the border dispute. Discuss possible outcomes for each response. Use the following chart to help.

Response	Possible US reaction	Possible British reaction

Discussion point

There is some evidence that the British did not initially take the Venezuelan boundary dispute as seriously as the United States did. Why might this have been the case? What other colonial issues were occupying British attention in the mid 1890s?

The Spanish–American War

The Spanish–American War started as a revolution by Cuban nationalists on behalf of a population oppressed by a colonial power. Indeed it was not the first time the Cubans had tried to shake off their Spanish overlords. In the 1870s, Cuban revolutionaries had waged a ten-year struggle for independence. Although there was considerable sympathy in the United Sates for the plight of the revolutionaries, and not a small amount of provocation from Spain, the US government remained neutral.

In 1895, the Cubans rose up against the Spanish colonial administration, which seemed just as determined to retain the island colony as they had been two decades earlier. The most influential Cuban nationalist in 1895 was the poet and writer José Martí. Martí called for an insurrection and in February of that year Cuban guerillas began attacking government installations and troops. In response, General Valeriano Weyler led some 150,000 Spanish troops across the Atlantic to quell the rising. What ensued was a war, the ferocity of which startled many. As in many such wars, civilians bore much of the suffering. In order to deprive the guerillas of food and support, Weyler ordered rural populations into camps without adequate food or sanitation and in which thousands died.

The United States took a keen interest in this war for a number of reasons. The US had invested some $50 million in Cuba and the revolution was threatening this investment and damaging business interests. But this was not enough to explain the growing popular outrage at the Spanish actions in Cuba. By 1895, there were an

Discussion point

What role do civilians play in guerila wars? How does this differ from their role in conventional wars? How have occupying powers tried to defeat guerrilla forces during the 20th century?

125

estimated 20,000 Cubans living in the United States and a number of these organized a committee to agitate in favor of independence, lobby the American government to recognize the revolutionary government organized by the rebels and to raise funds to fight the war. Centered in New York, this committee attempted to gain the support of organized labor, springing from the support of the cigar-makers union. The committee also fed sensational news stories to newspapers across the country. The infamous "**Yellow Press**" of William Randolph Hearst and Joseph Pulitzer capitalized on these stories eventually sending their own correspondents to supply the lurid copy. Mass meetings and demonstrations were held in major cities such as Chicago, New York, Kansas City and Philadelphia. When the issue reached the floor of Congress, many of the ideological arguments for expansion were again voiced. Some argued that a free Cuba would mean expanded markets for US business. Others invoked the Monroe Doctrine in support of the rebels. A friendly Cuba could help the United States navy protect the eastern approaches to the much-heralded canal to be cut across the Isthmus of Panama in the same way that Hawaii could protect its western approaches. Despite this initial furor, interest in the plight of the revolutionaries did not hold the popular US imagination for long and President Cleveland steadfastly refused to intervene. Even during the 1896 election campaign, there was little talk of Cuba. The war, however, was hurting some American interests more than others. By 1897, the revolution in Cuba had significantly affected the sugar market in the United States. Likewise, tobacco imports from the embattled island were shrinking, driving prices higher.

> The **Yellow Press** was originally a group of sensationalist newspapers in the United States at the end of the 19th century. Each newspaper tried to outsell their rivals by printing ever-more shocking stories. The atrocities, real and imagined, during the Cuban Revolution supplied a great deal of material for the yellow press.

Activity

The Yellow Press

In groups of three, choose a current event in your country that has two or more clearly identifiable and opposing positions. One of you write a newspaper article or draw a cartoon keeping as strictly as possible to the established facts of the event. The other two of you write a newspaper article or draw a political cartoon on that event in the style of the Yellow Press, each taking an opposing point of view. There are examples from the Spanish–American War at the PBS site on its series "The Crucible of Empire" (http://www.pbs.org/crucible/frames/_journalism.html).

Use the following chart to help:

Event?	Position?	Facts to emphasize?	Facts to ignore?	Symbols?	Audience?

Discussion questions:

1 How much did the three articles/cartoons differ from each other? Were there facts/ideas that appeared in all three accounts?

2 Analyze the language or symbols used in each of the accounts. To what extent are these used to evoke emotion or appeal to reason?

3 How is the choice of audience important to the writing/drawing of these articles/cartoons?

4 What is the value and limitation for the historian of using Yellow Press articles in understanding the past?

The US diplomatic response

President McKinley, who succeeded Cleveland, was more willing to confront the Spanish diplomatically over their conduct in the war than Cleveland had been, but stopped short of advocating US intervention. Nevertheless, he was torn by conflicting domestic sentiments about the war. The business lobby, on the whole, disliked the idea of war while some politicians of both parties advocated more aggressive action. Much of the public saw intervention in some way, shape or form as a moral duty while diplomats worried about the response of European powers to any sort of US involvement. McKinley attempted to strike a middle ground in his inaugural address by promising a foreign policy that was "firm and dignified … just, impartial and ever watchful of our national honor …" At the same time this foreign policy "want[ed] no wars of conquest." His inaugural address went on to warn against the "temptation of territorial aggression." The Yellow Press, nonetheless, continued to be filled with stories of Spanish cruelty in Cuba. McKinley, again trying to walk a middle line, put the Spanish government on notice that its conduct in Spain was unacceptable and that if it did not remedy the situation the United States would take further action. This threat seemed to have the desired result. The Spanish government recalled General Weyler and proposed some limited reforms. By the end of 1897, the Cuban insurrection again appeared to recede from the public eye in America.

"Ever watchful of our national honor" took on a more immediate meaning in early 1898. The Yellow Press, in this case the *New York Journal*, printed a letter that had been leaked from the Spanish ambassador in Washington, Dupuy de Lôme, to the Spanish government in Madrid in which he derides McKinley as a weak and

William McKinley (1843–1901)

Born in Ohio, William McKinley served a brief tenure as a school teacher and later enlisted as a private in the Union army during the civil war, achieving the rank of major before the end of the war. He studied law and entered into private practice in Canton, Ohio. After entering politics he was elected to Congress in 1877 and served there for 14 years when he left to become governor of Ohio. During and after his years in Congress, McKinley showed himself to be a fervent economic nationalist and protectionist. After becoming president in 1897, he revealed himself to be a skillful politician. The Spanish–American War dominated his presidency. During the first two years of the conflict McKinley tried to steer a cautious course that would not plunge the United States into war, despite growing pressure to do so. After the war, McKinley was persuaded by what he believed public opinion to favor—an extended imperial presence—and with this he acquiesced to the annexation of the Philippines, Guam, and Puerto Rico. In September 1901, McKinley was assassinated while visiting Buffalo, New York, and was succeeded by his vice president, Theodore Roosevelt.

pandering politician. Although his political opponents in the United States made the same accusations, when they came from a foreign country they took on the robes of a national insult. Congress again took up the cause, dormant for some time, of recognition of the revolutionary government. A week later, a more serious and deadly blow to "national honor" occurred when the USS *Maine*, a US battleship, exploded in Havana harbor killing 260 of her crew.

McKinley's response was initially measured. An inquiry was ordered into the causes of the explosion. The inquiry concluded that it had been an underwater mine that had touched off explosions in the ship's magazines. Congress allocated $50 million to the looming war and the press and the public increasingly called for aggressive action against Spain. Although still wary of war, McKinley went to Congress on April 11 for the authority to use force against the Spanish. The Teller Amendment, one of the resolutions that Congress passed authorizing the war, stated that the United States had no intention of annexing Cuba.

The United States invades the Philippines

On April 19, Congress authorized the use of force against the Spanish. Although Spain's colonial holdings included Guam, Puerto Rico, Cuba and the Philippines, the fighting was largely contained to Cuba and the Philippines. The United States navy was well-prepared for the war. It was a modern fighting force that had developed a strategic plan should war with Spain come. Once the war broke, it put this plan into action. Commodore George Dewey assembled a squadron of seven ships of the American Asiatic Squadron in Hong Kong in February and with this force set out for Manila Bay in the Philippines in late April.

The Spanish naval force defending the islands consisted of older ships that were outgunned and out-armored by the US force, although the Spanish commander, Admiral Montojo, had hoped that shore batteries could support his ships in defending the islands against a US naval attack. The Spanish preparations were still underway when Dewey's squadron arrived in the Philippines on April 30. After seeking out Montojo's fleet, the United States attacked at dawn on May 1. After an hour and a half of action, the Spanish force was destroyed. But what to do now? Dewey had enough marines to hold the naval yards in Manila Bay, but not to wrest the city, much less the islands, from the Spanish troops stationed there. The US navy held the waters around the islands and waited for a landing force to arrive, which it had by the end of the summer and by August 13 the Philippines were in US hands. The first major success of the war, the Battle of Manila Bay, had been won half the globe away from the fight to free Cuba.

The United States army was not the modern fighting force that the United States navy was in 1898. At the outbreak of the war, the regular army consisted of 28,000 soldiers and officers spread out across the continent. State militias were estimated to have something under 115,000 additional men, although the federal government's authority to press them into overseas service was debatable. Volunteers would be needed. In this instance, the war fever that had

Discussion point

What did McKinley mean by "national honor?" What type of affront to this honor do you think would provoke a war? What do you think would rouse your country to war?

Activity

President McKinley and war fever

There has been considerable historic debate on the forces that led President McKinley to war with Spain in 1898. Some historians have argued that it was the Yellow Press that incited the public to pressure the government to take action. Others have argued that it was the business lobby that influenced the president. Analyze the arguments of historians such as:

- Walter Lefeber
- Julius Pratt
- Howard Zinn
- Robert C. Hilderbrand
- John Dobson

gripped the country in the preceding months paid dividends. Citizens of the United States responded to the president's call for 125,000 volunteers enthusiastically. It was, however, one thing to call for 125,000 volunteers and quite another one to clothe, arm, equip, train and transport that many men.

US troops crossing over a river, Philippines, 1899.

These problems were soon obvious. As regulars and volunteers assembled in Florida, Tennessee, and Virginia for the anticipated invasion of Cuba, it became evident that the army was not prepared. The camps were rife with disease. Despite the fact that they were going to fight in a tropical climate, the majority of the men were issued with the traditional dark woolen uniforms. While the regular troops were issued with modern repeating rifles, much of the volunteer force had to make do with the Springfield single- shot "Trapdoor" rifle.

Confusion also characterized the early command decisions made by the army. Lacking a coherent strategic plan prior to the Congressional resolutions, the army high command, led by General Nelson Miles, debated how to proceed and where to attack. Havana was considered and then rejected, as the bulk of the Spanish force was stationed there. Eventually, it was decided to launch an attack from the Florida camp, in Tampa, on Santiago. The regular army units were in Tampa as was the volunteer cavalry force that became known as the Rough Riders led by its second in command, Theodore Roosevelt. The Rough Riders, the regular army units and the state militia that embarked at Tampa on June 6 for the invasion numbered some 17,000 men and were led by General William Shafter. This force would face about 125,000 Spanish troops. Spain's land forces were augmented by a squadron of obsolete ships under the command of Admiral Cervera that had managed to elude the US fleet and slip into Santiago Harbor, only to be subsequently trapped.

After a chaotic landing in Cuba, the US forces moved toward Santiago. En route they fought the battles of El Caney and San Juan Hill, defeating the Spanish forces and by early July found themselves in front of Santiago, exhausted and lacking supplies. Within days the Spanish fleet attempted to break through the US naval blockade and was destroyed, leading the Spanish commander to negotiate the surrender of his forces defending Santiago. Meanwhile, a force of 18,000 US soldiers embarked for Puerto Rico, another Spanish Caribbean possession defended by 9,000 Spanish soldiers. After a series of battles in early August, the Puerto Rican campaign was cut short by an armistice signed by Spanish and US officials on August 10. The war had lasted a matter of months and cost the United States about 2,500 dead, only about 16 per cent of which were battle deaths, the remainder perishing from disease.

 Of what strategic importance were the Philippines to the United States in 1899? What challenges did its occupation of the Philippines pose for the United States?

Discussion point

How did the Spanish–American War differ from the other wars that the United States fought in the 19th century? In what ways was it similar? What lesson might the US have taken from the organization and conduct of the war?

The aftermath: The imperial debate

From October to December 1898, US and Spanish representatives negotiated a treaty in Paris. The resulting Treaty of Paris ceded Puerto Rico and Guam to the United States. Cuba would gain her independence as the Teller Amendment prohibited its annexation. It was the Philippines that proved to be a difficult point. The Spanish were less ready to relinquish it than they had been their Caribbean possessions, but had no realistic way of holding them against American demands backed up by a naval squadron in Manila Bay. The United States for its part recognized the strategic importance of the islands to the growing China trade. In the end, the United States agreed to pay $20 million for the Philippines. But the real debate was only getting started.

In the United States, the Treaty of Paris had to be ratified by the Senate with a two-thirds majority. Groups such as the **American Anti-Imperialist League** with prominent members like Mark Twain and Samuel Gompers formed to argue against the annexation of the Philippines. They were joined by many Democrats, sugar growers and isolationists. The Republican Party led by President McKinley, the navy and those who would benefit from increased Asian trade argued in favor of annexation. In early February 1899, the fate of the Philippines was put to the question in the Senate. Annexation carried the day by the narrowest of margins.

While the Teller Amendment ensured Cuba's nominal political independence, the United States still maintained an occupation force on the island until 1902. During this period American capital poured into Cuba. The infrastructure was modernized while the occupiers renovated the financial system and government administration. American fruit and tobacco companies bought up huge tracts of land such that by 1901 much of Cuba's economy and trade was dominated by the US. How, then, to protect these extensive interests while at the same time upholding the Teller Amendment in word if not in spirit? The answer came in the form of the Platt Amendment. Passed in 1901, the Platt Amendment "guaranteed" Cuban independence by forbidding Cuba from entering into any other foreign treaties. The amendment further reserved for the United States the right to intervene in Cuba to protect this independence and to be sold or leased military installations on the island for this purpose. Amid popular Cuban protests, the Platt Amendment became a part of the Cuban constitution.

The status of the Philippines was less complicated; it was part of the United States. In 1899, under the leadership of an erstwhile US ally, Emilio Aquinaldo, Filipinos rose against their colonizers and carried on a brutal guerilla war until 1901. By the time Aquinaldo was captured the US had come to understand the price of empire building—the war had occupied some close to 100,000 soldiers and cost close to 5,000 US lives. It is estimated that over 200,000 Filipinos died in the two and a half years of fighting. When William Taft took over the governorship of the Philippines in 1901 he embarked on a **paternalistic** program of reform that involved the construction of schools and infrastructure to support the US-dominated industry and the creation of a political assembly to practice a limited form of self-rule. Despite this, it would take the severe dislocations accompanying the end of the Second World War to secure Philippine independence.

The **American Anti-Imperialist League** was an organization formed by a wide cross-section of American society to fight against the growing sentiment that favored annexation of the Philippines after the US victory in the Spanish-American War.

Paternalism refers to an unequal relationship between two entities in which one is dominated by the other. In terms of imperialism it is the idea that the colony is not able to make its own decisions and that it is up to the colonizer to act for the colony and take care of it as though it were a child.

Activity

The imperial debate

Source A

The following is an excerpt from an essay written in August 1898 by Andrew Carnegie, a wealthy steel magnate and vice-president of the Anti-Imperialist League.

To reduce it to the concrete, the question is: Shall we attempt to establish ourselves as a power in the far East and possess the Philippines for glory? The glory we already have, in Dewey's victory overcoming the power of Spain in a manner which adds one more to the many laurels of the American navy, which, from its infancy till now, has divided the laurels with Britain upon the sea. The Philippines have about seven and a half millions of people, composed of races bitterly hostile to one another, alien races, ignorant of our language and institutions. Americans cannot be grown there. The islands have been exploited for the benefit of Spain, against whom they have twice rebelled, like the Cubans. But even Spain has received little pecuniary benefit from them. The estimated revenue of the Philippines in 1894–95 was £2,715,980, the expenditure being £2,656,026, leaving a net result of about $300,000. The United States could obtain even this trifling sum from the inhabitants only by oppressing them as Spain has done. But, if we take the Philippines, we shall be forced to govern them as generously as Britain governs her dependencies, which means that they will yield us nothing, and probably be a source of annual expense. Certainly, they will be a grievous drain upon revenue if we consider the enormous army and navy which we shall be forced to maintain upon their account.

Source: Carnegie, Andrew. "Distant Possessions: The Parting of the Ways." *The Gospel of Wealth*. New York: The Century Co. 1901.

Source B

The following is an excerpt of a speech given by Albert Beveridge, a Senator from Indiana.

The Opposition tells us that we ought not to govern a people without their consent. I answer, The rule of liberty that all just government derives its authority from the consent of the governed, applies only to those who are capable of self government We govern the Indians without their consent, we govern our territories without their consent, we govern our children without their consent. How do they know what our government would be without their consent? Would not the people of the Philippines prefer the just, humane, civilizing government of this Republic to the savage, bloody rule of pillage and extortion from which we have rescued them?

Source: Beveridge, Albert J. "The March of the Flag." 1898. *History Tools.org: Resources for the Study of American History*. http://www.historytools.org/sources/beveridge.html.

Source C

President McKinley related the following to General James Rusling in 1899. Rusling recalled the conversation for an interview in 1901.

> When next I realized that the Philippines had dropped into our laps I confess I did not know what to do with them ... I walked the floor of the White House night after night until midnight; and I am not ashamed to tell you, gentlemen, that I went down on my knees and prayed Almighty God for light and guidance. ... And one night late it came to me this way. ...
>
> 1 That we could not give them back to Spain—that would be cowardly and dishonorable;
>
> 2 That we could not turn them over to France or Germany—our commercial rivals in the Orient—that would be bad business and discreditable;
>
> 3 That we could not leave them to themselves—they were unfit for self-government—and they would soon have anarchy and misrule worse than Spain's war;
>
> 4 That there was nothing left for us to do but to take them all, and to educate the Filipinos, and uplift and civilize and Christianize them as our fellow men for whom Christ also died.
>
> **Source:** Rusling, General James. "Interview with President William McKinley." *The Christian Advocate*. 22 January 1903. p. 17. Reprinted in Schirmer, Daniel and Rosskamm Shalom, Stephen. (eds.) 1987. *The Philippines Reader.* Boston: South End Press. pp. 22–23.

Questions

1 What does Carnegie mean by "glory"? (source A)

2 What evidence is there of a practical approach to the issue of imperialism in each of the documents?

3 What evidence is there of ethnocentrism in the documents?

4 Compare and contrast how the people of the Philippines are regarded in sources A and B.

5 What role did religion play in McKinley's decision to annex the Philippines, according to Rusling?

6 With reference to its origin and purpose, evaluate the value and limitations of source C to historians studying McKinley's decision to annex the Philippines.

Activity

Nationalist reaction

In groups of two, research the post Spanish–American War positions of Cuban nationalists and Filipino nationalists. Write a speech from your allocated country's perspective. Come together and write a joint essay, comparing and contrasting postwar nationalism in Cuba and the Philippines.

United States foreign policy

While the United States seemed content to set up a colonial administration in the Philippines, it specifically disavowed such an approach to China. By the end of the 19th century, European powers were taking advantage of a weakening Chinese regime to expand their influence, direct and indirect, in the country. These expanding spheres of influence threatened to leave the United States behind, even though the significant focus of US Asian policies and territorial acquisition in the Pacific has been to protect or further China trade.

The Open Door Policy

John Hay, the US Secretary of State, had to devise a way to assert US trading interests in China without resorting to war. His answer was the Open Door Policy. The Open Door stated that there was to be no discrimination of foreign powers within a country's sphere of influence and that the existing tariff structure as set by the Chinese government was to remain in effect. Hay proclaimed the Open Door in diplomatic notes sent to the major European powers. With no military threat to back it up and no international authority to enforce it, the Open Door could be observed or ignored as the Europeans saw fit. It would take an international incident to give the United States the leverage to press the Open Door into reality.

Chinese nationalists had long bridled at the gradual erosion of their economic and political sovereignty at the hands of European powers. This growing rage erupted in 1900 when a secret nationalist society called the Righteous and Harmonious Fists or Boxers rose against Europeans in China, besieging the foreign diplomatic corps in the British embassy in Beijing. A multinational force, of which over 2,000 were from the United States, eventually relieved the siege. This participation gave the US a say in the resolution to the incident and from which they further pushed the Open Door Policy. Hay further insisted that the resolution must therefore include the territorial integrity of China—that China would stay nominally independent—but that this "independence" must include free trade.

The Big Stick

When an assassin's bullet cut William McKinley's life and presidency short in 1901 it catapulted Theodore Roosevelt into the White House. Roosevelt, in many ways, typified a popular sentiment at the turn of the century. The Progressives and the era that bears their name, was a diverse group of interests within US society that believed that apparent US ascendancy on the world stage depended on a modern, scientific and professional approach in everything from industry to the military and diplomacy. The return of economic prosperity helped fuel this optimism. Under Roosevelt the US military would move from an ad hoc civilian army to a more centralized professional force. The diplomatic corps would be modernized with specialized training and examinations for those who would represent the United States to the world. Roosevelt also believed in the "civilizing"

Theodore Roosevelt (1858–1919)

Born into a wealthy New York family and mostly home schooled, Roosevelt later attended and would graduate from Harvard College. After a period of travel abroad, he entered politics as an elected member of the New York State Assembly. His political style was energetic and he became an ardent proponent of political and social reform, arguing against the power of special interests. After 1889, Roosevelt served in a number of political positions including Commissioner of the New York City Police and Assistant Secretary of the Navy in the McKinley Administration, all the while pushing a "Progressive" agenda. Roosevelt advocated for war with Spain and when this war finally broke on the United States he led a volunteer force in Cuba. In 1898, he was elected Governor of New York State and continued his energetic reforming of the bureaucracy of government and combating the power of big business. He was chosen the Republican vice-presidential candidate in 1900, a position that would catapult him into the White House when President McKinley was assassinated in 1901.

As president, Roosevelt valued action and tended toward autocratic decision-making. He understood that US power must rest on a strong military but also had a sense that the United States must use this power to "civilize" the world. In the western hemisphere this "civilizing" mission generally meant an expansion of US influence backed by US military and economic might and the ignoring of Latin American nationalism. This led to an interventionist approach in Latin America that would become known as Big Stick Diplomacy. Outside of this sphere of influence, Roosevelt generally championed peaceful settlement of disputes between nations. Once out of office, in 1909, he grew disenchanted with Taft's policies. Prior to the 1912 presidential election, Roosevelt spilt with the Republican Party and founded the Progressive Party also known as the Bull Moose Party, effectively splitting the Republican vote and helping Woodrow Wilson's election victory. During the First World War, he would consistently argue for a stronger policy toward Germany.

obligation of the modern countries of the world—that it was their duty to bring the benefits of "civilization," as he saw them, to the "backward" corners of the earth. Inherent in that notion was the principle that the United States would have to become more involved in international affairs.

When Roosevelt's progressive and internationalist inclinations were combined with his deep admiration for the military as an expression of a nation's strength, the result was Big Stick diplomacy—the notion that the United States could achieve its foreign policy goals if it backed its interests with a credible military threat. As an ardent follower of Alfred Mahan, Roosevelt understood this to mean primarily a large and modern navy. Between 1898 and 1913, the US navy constructed 25 battleships and more than doubled its personnel.

In 1907, Roosevelt paraded this portion of his Big Stick around the world. The Great White Fleet made stops at a number of ports around the world including Yokohama in Japan.

The full proverb from which the term Big Stick comes reads: "Speak softly and carry a big stick." On occasion, Roosevelt could speak softly. When Russia and Japan went to war in 1905, it was Roosevelt who helped broker the peace in an attempt to maintain some sort of a balance of power in Asia. Under his leadership the United States grew closer

Warship tonnage of the powers, 1880–1914					
	1880	1890	1900	1910	1914
Great Britain	650,000	679,000	1,065,000	2,174,000	2,714,000
France	271,000	319,000	499,000	725,000	900,000
Russia	200,000	180,000	383,000	401,000	679,000
United States	169,000	240,000	333,000	824,000	985,000
Italy	100,000	242,000	245,000	327,000	498,000
Germany	88,000	190,000	285,000	964,000	1,305,00
Austria-Hungary	60,000	66,000	87,000	210,000	372,000
Japan	15,000	41,000	187,000	496,000	700,000

Source: Kennedy, Paul. *Rise and Fall of the Great Powers: Economic and Military Conflict from 1500 to 2000*. London: Fontana Press. p. 261.

What was the importance of the United States Navy to Theodore Roosevelt's foreign policy? What was the purpose of the Great White Fleet's world tour? To what extent was it successful?

The Great White Fleet, USS *Connecticut* leading North Atlantic fleet off the coast of Virginia, 1909.

to the United Kingdom than it had been in years. Roosevelt also helped to mediate a settlement on Morocco at Algeciras in 1906.

But there was also the Big Stick. Partially on the strength of the enlarged American fleet the Americans and Japanese came to an agreement on the *status quo* in the Pacific. But it was in Latin America that the Big Stick would be the most evident.

The Panama Canal

The prospect of cutting through Central America to join the Pacific and Atlantic oceans had been discussed since the middle of the 19th century. The failure of a French attempt had brought scandal and political disaster to the French Third Republic. The two primary questions surrounding such a massive project were "Who would build it?" and "Where, exactly, would it be built?" The United States and Great Britain had agreed to cooperate in the project, but by the time Roosevelt took office, this had fallen out of favor in the US and the McKinley administration had negotiated away this agreement. Where to locate this colossal project proved more complicated. The two leading contenders were Nicaragua and Panama.

In 1903, Congress and the president decided on the Panama option. The United States, however, had only purchased the rights to build the canal. It now had to acquire the land on which to build the canal, and this would require negotiations with the Colombian government, the country that owned Panama. The US Secretary of State, Hay, negotiated that the United States would lease the land for 100 years, pay $10 million to Colombia for the lease and pay $250,000 a year for the duration of the lease.

The Colombian Senate rejected the treaty favoring as it did US interests. Roosevelt was enraged at the nerve of the Colombian government, standing in the way of his idea of progress and civilization. Since speaking softly had not seemed to work, Roosevelt prepared the "Big Stick." The fear that the United States might abandon the Panama option for the Nicaragua option drove the Panamanians to revolt against their Colombian overlords yet again. The fortuitous arrival of a US battleship and troops, a very real display of Roosevelt's Big Stick foreign policy, prevented the Colombian

Activity

Why Nicaragua? Why Panama?

Research, create and make a presentation to the class on why the Central American Canal should either be dug through Nicaragua or Panama from the point of view of the Panamanians and Nicaraguans. Be sure to include potential economic, military, social, and foreign policy benefits of the canal.

government from crushing the revolt. The United States was only too happy to recognize the newly independent Panama, which agreed to the same payment as had been promised to the previous Colombian government for a strip of land ten miles wide. When the canal opened in 1914, North Americans saw it as a testament to their ingenuity, hard work and industry—a crowning achievement of the Progressive Era. To others in the Americas and indeed the world it was another example of imperialism backed by western technological advances. It also meant that the United States now controlled one of the most important waterways in the world. It needed to secure that ownership to achieve further control of the Caribbean.

Venezuela, Santo Domingo and the Roosevelt Corollary

While the Monroe Doctrine may have stopped European countries from physically intervening in the Americas, it did not stop European capital from flooding into the region through to the end of the 19th century. When early in Roosevelt's presidency Venezuela defaulted on loans to German, British and Italian creditors, these governments used force to secure payment by blockading Venezuelan ports and shelling the port city of Puerto Cabello, something that Roosevelt, the United States and the Monroe Doctrine could not tolerate. To prevent foreign powers from conducting any further debt-collecting incursions, Roosevelt articulated a policy that would come to be known as the Roosevelt Corollary to the Monroe Doctrine. While Monroe's original doctrine had been a warning to European powers to stay out of the United States' sphere of influence, the Corollary was an assurance that if the nations of Central and South America could not keep their financial houses in order and thereby threaten the "civilized" world, the United States would step in and manage their finances for them, even to the point of collecting debts for the European powers. Roosevelt wanted to remove any pretext that European powers might have for military interventions in the Caribbean.

The Corollary was first used in Santo Domingo. To stop France and Italy from forcibly collecting money they were owed by Santo Domingo and thereby threatening American strategic interests in the region, the US sent a financial administrator to manage Dominican finances, collecting duties on imports and using 55 per cent of this revenue to pay foreign creditors. The remaining 45 per cent was remitted to the Dominican government of Carlos Morales.

Responding to extraterritoriality

Extraterritoriality is a principle by which a country enforces its laws outside its own territory. During the later 19th and early 20th centuries this became an important tool of imperialism. Taken to its extreme, this principle held that British or US citizens living in a foreign country would still be governed by British or US laws regardless of the laws of the nation in which they were living. This could prove very handy for foreign businessmen trying to enforce contracts and a serious impediment to a country trying to exercise her sovereignty in the face of imperialism. Two Latin Americans developed doctrines in response to the principle of extraterritoriality. In the late 19th century, the Argentine jurist Carlos Calvo argued that extraterritoriality had no basis in

Activity

The Panama Canal

Research the history of the Panama Canal in the 20th century. Evaluate the effect of the canal on the United States and Panama respectively. List the benefits and drawbacks for each country.

Discussion point

How might the other countries of Central and South America react to the Roosevelt Corollary? What options were open to them?

 What advantages did the Corollary have over simply taking control of Santo Domingo?

international law. Initially, Calvo advocated that debt had to be enforced through the courts of the countries in which the money was lent. He later developed this idea into a doctrine stating that all sovereign countries should be entirely free to treat foreigners within their borders as they saw fit to the extent that there would be very little if any accepted international standards; in a sense, there was no such thing as international law. Argentine foreign minister Luis Drago later developed a more workable and specific doctrine by which counties could not use force to collect debts owed to its nationals. The Hague Conference of 1907 adopted a form of the Drago Doctrine in its conventions.

Activity

TOK Link

Ethics

Extraterritoriality remains an issue in international relations. In recent years, it has been raised in response to the implementation of the death penalty in some countries. Specifically, debates have surrounded the extent to which a country should agree to deport people to countries in which they face a death sentence, despite the fact that the deporting country has no death penalty. Conversely, other instances surround the extent to which a country in which there is no death penalty should seek the release of its citizens under death sentences in other countries, as in the following case.

Canadian on death row in U.S. down to last legal remedy

The Canadian Press
Monday May 17, 2010

CALGARY — It's been a quarter-century of legal battles and court hearings, and now the only Canadian on death row in the United States is about to hit the wall in his fight to stay alive. Ronald Smith's case is to go before the U.S. Supreme Court this fall—the last legal option available to him.

"Frankly our assessment is any time you are asking the U.S. Supreme Court to review a case, and, given the limited number of cases they review, it's probably somewhat of a long shot," Smith's lawyer of many years, Greg Jackson, told The Canadian Press. "That's really from the court system standpoint our last chance ... We've exhausted all state and federal remedies other than the U.S. Supreme Court. If the U.S. Supreme Court does not either hear the petition or grant relief, then basically it will be remanded back to the state of Montana to go forward with an execution date."

Smith, 52, has been living on borrowed time since he was convicted in 1983 of murdering two

cousins, Harvey Madman Jr. and Thomas Running Rabbit, while he was high on drugs and alcohol. He originally requested and was granted the death penalty for his crimes, but he had a change of heart and has been fighting a legal roller coaster for the last 25 years. He has been sentenced to death four times and had the order overturned on three occasions.

Smith, originally from Red Deer, Alta., has spent 23 hours a day in his cell in the maximum-security wing of the Montana State Prison at Deer Lodge. Out behind that wing sits a small trailer, the state's death chamber, where three men have been executed by lethal injection in the last 10 years.

His latest setback came last week when a regional Appeal Court rejected a bid to have his case reheard. Jackson had argued that Smith didn't have effective counsel when he pleaded guilty and the death penalty wasn't warranted. Now Jackson will file the paperwork asking the Supreme Court to review the case. A decision isn't expected until October.

"It's coming down to where the rubber meets the road. It's a position that we all hoped we would never get to," Jackson said. If it goes as expected, and the Supreme Court refuses to hear the case, the final hope will be a request for clemency from Montana Gov. Brian Schweitzer.

"Once a petition is filed, then there is notice published in newspapers throughout the state of the hearing, Jackson explained. "There is a hearing at which the Board of Pardons and Parole listens to comments from the opponents and proponents for clemency. Then they make a recommendation to either grant or deny. "Either way it goes to the governor."

Jackson said the Canadian government will be asked for its support. Ottawa used to routinely lobby for clemency in such cases, but Stephen Harper's Conservatives have brought in a

137

policy that Canada will not get involved if there's been a conviction in a democratic country that honours the rule of law.

But last year a Federal Court justice ruled that Ottawa couldn't arbitrarily end its long-standing approach and ordered the government to try to win clemency for Smith. Liberal MP Dan McTeague, the party's critic for consular affairs, said he will hold the government to its responsibility to follow the federal court decision. "I expect the Canadian government to stand by the law and stand by its conventions and the minister of foreign affairs to do the job to seek to commute the sentence of Ronald Smith," said McTeague. "The reality here is a simple call made

by the Canadian government, through its minister of foreign affairs, to the governor would likely have the effect of sparing Mr. Smith's life."

Source: http://www.ctv.ca/CTVNews/CalgaryHome/20100517/ronald-smith-death-row-100517/.

Class debate

To what extent are ethics universal? Are there some laws that should be applied to foreign nationals and other laws that should not? Is there a case for extraterritoriality? Divide into two groups and debate the following question:

? **To what extent should the laws of a country apply to its citizens beyond its borders?**

Activity

Backing down in Venezuela

Source A

Following is the view of historian Nancy Mitchell on the crisis in Venezuela.

> President Theodore Roosevelt later claimed that it was only his big stick (wielded quietly) that stayed the Kaiser's hand [in Venezuela]. Analysis of German aims and ambitions in Venezuela, however, does not support this interpretation. It indicates that it was a withdrawal of British support, not Roosevelt's stick, that convinced Germans to end the blockade. It also reveals that, US fears and allegations to the contrary, Germany was exceedingly cautious before, during, and after the blockade. Its policy was far from recklessly aggressive. It was timid. ...
>
> Theodore Roosevelt claimed, almost fourteen years after the fact, that he had delivered a secret ultimatum to the Germans that brought them to the bargaining table. The US naval exercises had been planned well in advance and were known to the Germans and the English before the blockade began, yet not one document has been found to confirm the president's assertion, not in the United States, not in Germany, and not in England.
>
> **Source:** Mitchell, Nancy. 1999. *The Danger of Dreams: German and American Imperialism in Latin America*. University of North Carolina Press. pp. 65, 87.

Source B

Following is an alternative view put forward by the historian Edmund Morris.

> The Venezuela incident of late 1902 is the *locus classicus* [classic example] of [Roosevelt's] famously colloquial foreign policy, "Speak softly and carry a big stick."
>
> If Roosevelt expected an answer to his ultimatum of 8 December, he was soon disappointed. That Sunday von Holleben [the German ambassador] seemed interested in talking only about the weather, of all things, and tennis. Losing patience, TR [Theodore Roosevelt] asked if Germany was going to accept President Castro's arbitration proposal transmitted by Secretary of State Hay. The ambassador said no.

Controlling his temper, the president replied that Kaiser Wilhelm must understand that he, Roosevelt, was "very definitely" threatening war.[11] Von Holleben declined to be a party to such peremptory language.

From there [New York], before midnight [16 December], certain words flashed to Berlin. ... The evidence suggests that von Holleben's cable [to Berlin] was burned after reading, in approved German security fashion.

... The reaction in Berlin was immediate [once it received the ultimatum]. On 17 December, the Reichstag decided to accept arbitration, acting secretly and in such haste that urgings from Secretary Hay in Washington and Metternich in London were redundant on receipt.

[11] TR (Theodore Roosevelt), quoted by William Loeb (witness) to Henry Pringle, 14 April 1930, Henry Pringle Papers, Harvard College Library, Cambridge, Mass. (Edmund Morris's citation)

Source: Morris, Edmund. "'A matter of extreme urgency': Theodore Roosevelt, Wilhelm II, and the Venezuela Crisis of 1902." *Naval War College Review.* Spring 2002.

Questions

1 Compare and contrast the views of why the Venezuelan crisis did not result in war in each document. Can you account for the differences?

2 Is it possible for both historians to be correct? Why or why not?

3 According to source A, what was the role of Britain in the resolution to the crisis?

4 With reference to its origin and purpose, evaluate the value and limitations of source B.

Activity

Two views of Roosevelt

Source A

President Roosevelt standing atop Sagamore Hill (his home) wearing wings labeled "Down With Peace" and "Hurrah For War" while carrying a "big stick."

Source B

President Roosevelt "speaking gently" to the Russian Czar and Japanese Emperor in an effort to mediate an end to the Russo–Japanese War in 1905.

Questions

1 Compare and contrast the view of President Theodore Roosevelt in the two sources.

2 How might these two views be explained?

3 How might the domestic context in the United States, when each of these cartoons were published, have affected the cartoonists' opinions of Roosevelt?

Dollar Diplomacy

William Howard Taft succeeded Roosevelt as president in 1908 and sought to hold the same foreign policy course as his predecessor. Taft, however, was less inclined to use the Big Stick. He looked to the apparent success of the Roosevelt Corollary and expanded on what he saw as the lesson gleaned from it. His approach would come to be known as Dollar Diplomacy. Dollar diplomacy sought to replace US military might with the power of its burgeoning economy and the financial know-how of Progressive Era financial wizards. Like the Corollary, Dollar Diplomacy wished to remove any pretext for European intervention in Latin America by managing the financial affairs of countries whose economies were "backward" by US standards and thus ensure that European debts were paid. Loans from US bankers would be used to pay off European creditors. Financial managers would move in and remake the economy, if not in the US model, then to US advantage. Tax collection would become more efficient, budgets regularized, a form of the gold standard adopted.

> ### William Howard Taft (1857–1930)
>
>
>
> A Yale-trained lawyer, Taft distinguished himself in the Republican judicial appointments that he was able to secure while practicing in Ohio. Rather than rise through traditional political channels, Taft proved himself a sound administrator in the Philippines and Cuba and as Roosevelt's Secretary of War. He also handled diplomatic tasks associated with Japanese affairs surrounding the Russo–Japanese War.
>
> Taft can be seen as a reluctant president who nonetheless initially bore Roosevelt's stamp of approval though little of his political skill and stubborn, autocratic style. While in office, Taft was caught between the Progressives and the conservative Republicans. Trying to strike a balance between these two factions pleased few and in the Republican nomination convention of 1912 Roosevelt split with Taft and the Republican conservatives starting the Progressive or Bull Moose Party. Wilson's victory relieved him of the burden of governing and he became a professor of Law at Yale University. He was appointed Chief Justice of the United States in 1921, a post to which he had always aspired.

There developed a marked gap between the theory of Dollar Diplomacy and its practice. As rational and "progressive" as the measures seemed to the United States, Latin Americans could not help but see them as very thinly veiled imperialism. Costa Rica and Guatemala rejected it outright—refusing to sign treaties based on the principles of Dollar Diplomacy. Honduran nationalists persuaded their congress to do the same. This provoked a US-sponsored revolution, which installed a pro-US regime that was more amenable to the dictates of Dollar Diplomacy. The Dominican agreement also broke down in 1912, requiring the US military to restore the obligations of Dollar Diplomacy.

Nicaragua was another trouble spot for US diplomacy. In response to the nationalism of the Nicaraguan leader José Santos Zelaya, US mining interests sponsored a revolution eventually backed by Taft's government and the United States Marine Corps. When the US Senate would not ratify the Dollar Diplomacy treaty with Nicaragua, private US companies and banks acquired controlling interests in Nicaraguan banking and railroads. Such economic imperialism was bound to enrage already tense nationalist sentiments and more marines were called upon to suppress another revolution in 1912. The marines would remain in Nicaragua for another 13 years.

Dollar Diplomacy was not restricted to Latin America. By 1908, Liberia in West Africa was deep in debt. Surrounded as it was by

> **Activity**
> ### Continuity and change
>
> Compare and contrast the administrations of Roosevelt and Taft in the following areas:
>
> - domestic policy
> - foreign policy (Latin America)
> - foreign policy (Europe)
> - economic policy

> ### Discussion point
>
> What were the benefits and drawbacks of Dollar Diplomacy from the perspective of Latin American governments? Latin American businesses?

British and French colonies, the Taft administration feared that a bankruptcy would result in its annexation to one or more of the neighboring colonial empires. To forestall this, Taft approved a loan and the menacing presence of a US warship. Nevertheless, Dollar Diplomacy did not stop Liberia's financial and political problems.

Taft also looked to Dollar Diplomacy as a means to curtail Japanese and Russian influence in China and Manchuria. As in so many other parts of the world, building an effective railroad system was the key to further economic expansion and the US arranged to be an investor in the development of this system in Manchuria. Eventually, Russia and Japan cooperated in dividing the Manchurian economic interests between them and the Chinese government was not strong enough to oppose them. The US, unable to secure the support of France (a Russian ally) or Great Britain (a Japanese ally), settled for more moderate financial intervention in China.

Moral Diplomacy

Despite the aggressive foreign policies of Roosevelt and Taft, there was still anti-imperialist sentiment in the United States and it was to this that Woodrow Wilson appealed as the Democratic presidential candidate in 1912. Publicly repudiating acquisitive foreign policies such as the Big Stick, Wilson promised a foreign policy that would encourage human rights and the development of "constitutional liberty" in the world. Guided by a belief that the Christian precepts of the United States could offer a model to the rest of the world, with little diplomatic experience and a very autocratic nature, Wilson set out to chart a new course for US foreign policy. In light of the actions of his Republican predecessors and the growing tension and later international chaos that would grip the world, this was going to be a difficult course to chart. Wilson, despite his idealistic intentions, would come to understand that like Dollar Diplomacy—his new Moral Diplomacy—would, in the end, depend on its ability to back up good intentions and moral precepts with military force.

There were, however, important elements of continuity between Wilson and his predecessors. He believed in the expansion of international trade and US financial interests and the role that the government can play in that expansion, with or without the consent of trading partners. When this belief was combined with his inability to understand the nature of nationalism and its role in revolutions in places like China and Mexico, a gap emerged between Wilson's perception of the United States in international affairs and the perception of other countries.

Wilson initially supported the Chinese revolution that predated his presidency. As a reformer, he saw it as the birth of a modern state out of the ashes of a corrupt relic of a bygone era. He moved quickly, and unilaterally, to recognize the new government, even though it was by no means clear that this is was the final form that the government would take. He also took the US out of a banking agreement, in the hope of fostering Chinese independence, leaving the other signatories a free hand to benefit from Chinese instability. With the outbreak of the First World War, Japan further expanded its influence in China

TOK Link
Ethnocentrism
Wilson's Moral Diplomacy hinged on his ideas of morality and these in turn were based on his own Christian principles and the established US system of government.

1 What ways of knowing are involved in developing a morality-based foreign policy?

2 What are the strengths and weaknesses of using "morality" as a basis for foreign policy?

3 What might a Chinese version of Moral Diplomacy look like in 1914? What about a Japanese version? In what ways would they be similar and different to Wilson's version?

with little opposition from the US state department. Again, although he sympathized with the revolution, Wilson's idealism was no match for the expansionist self-interest of the Japanese and by 1916 he began to drift to a policy that bore some resemblance to Dollar Diplomacy in that it authorized private loans to China and promised action if the Chinese defaulted.

In the Dominican Republic, Wilson imposed free elections in 1913, but this brought the republic no closer to stability with civil war and revolution constantly simmering just below the surface of Dominican affairs. Efforts by Wilson's Secretary of State, William Jennings Bryan, to appeal to the Dominicans to formally renounce revolution did no good. In 1915, a frustrated Wilson ordered the US military to intervene and establish order. They would occupy the country until 1924. In neighboring Haiti, similar revolutionary upheavals coupled with European financial interests persuaded Wilson to occupy that half of Hispaniola as well. In the case of Haiti, the occupation lasted until 1934.

Likewise, in Mexico, Wilson favored the reforming elements in the 1911 revolution that brought down the regime of Porfirio Díaz. Under Díaz, US oil and railroad concerns had prospered while the Mexican élite profited from this prosperity, alienating Mexican peasants and workers. Francisco Madero's reforming government was itself soon overthrown by General Victoriano Huerta. Wilson, however, was less enamored of Huerta and his regime.

Wilson brought increasing pressure to bear on Huerta, soliciting international support from the likes of Great Britain and offering support to the opposition leader Venustiano Carranza. Carranza, a Mexican nationalist, was hesitant to accept help from the United States. By 1914, the US did not officially recognize the government of Mexico, but had no credible replacement that supported the United States. The quandary was that while recognizing the Huerta government was repugnant to Wilson, if they intervened militarily it would anger, perhaps to the point of war, the Mexican nationalists that opposed Huerta. Moral Diplomacy had again run into the complicated realities of actual diplomacy.

After a minor diplomatic slight, Wilson ordered the US navy to occupy Verecruz in April 1914 precipitating an attempt at mediation by Chile, Brazil and Argentina. Eventually, Carranza's forces forced Huerta from office, but Carranza proved no more able to bring the country together than his predecessor and the country again descended into civil war. During the course of this civil war, Pancho Villa mounted a raid into US territory. The punitive raid ordered by Wilson soon broadened. Wilson did not, however, let these events drag the United States into longer, wider war. As relations with Germany deteriorated and it looked more and more likely that the United States would join the Allies in their war with Germany, Wilson ordered US troops out of Mexico in early 1917.

> ## Discussion point
>
> Often, once in power, leaders find it difficult to implement the principle they held before they were in power. Why is that?
>
> How did Wilson's actions compare to his rhetoric and principles?

Activity
Evaluating US foreign policy, 1900–14

Policy	Proponents	Strengths	Weaknesses	Results
Big Stick Diplomacy				
Dollar Diplomacy				
Moral Diplomacy				

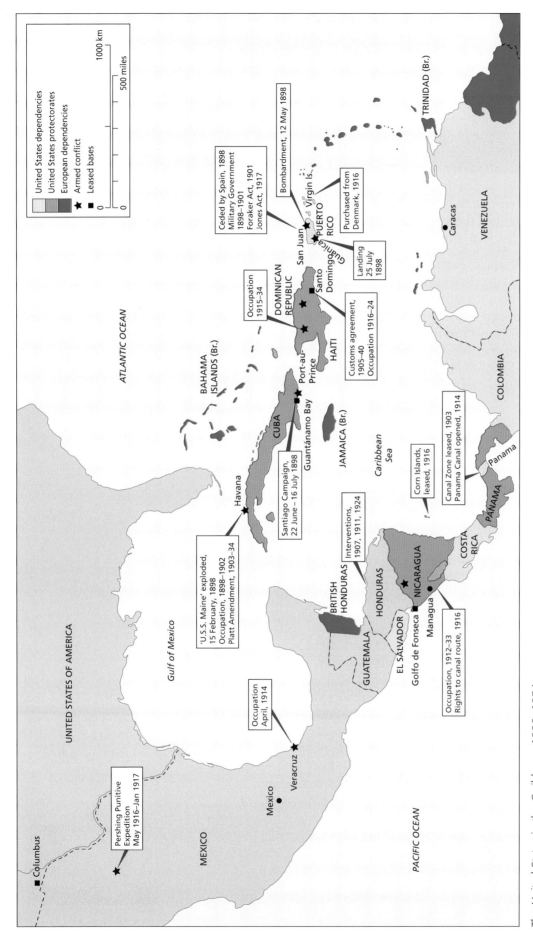

The United States in the Caribbean, 1898–1934.

The United States and the First World War

While President Wilson was trying to craft a foreign policy that looked to morality as a guiding principle, Europe was embracing age-old notions of narrowly defined self-interest and balance of power politics. By 1914, this path saw Europe descend into the catastrophe of the First World War. In the early days of August 1914, European powers committed to war and in the case of the British Empire this commitment stretched around the globe to all the British colonies. The United States did not feel the same gravitational pull of the war. In many ways, Wilson saw it as antithetical to his foreign policy.

The issues that drove Europe over the edge were not American issues. The rival alliance systems that had been developed in mutual fear over the preceding two decades did not include the United States. The nationalism that was hacking at the Austro-Hungarian Empire was of little concern to US interests. While imperialism was an important source of tension to European states, The Monroe Doctrine and Roosevelt's Big Stick combined with Taft's Dollar Diplomacy had kept European interests out of the western hemisphere and US interests in the far east did not significantly run afoul of European interests. Besides, the United States did not see itself as an imperialist power in the same way the Europeans did, especially under Wilson. The militarism that gripped Europe in the decades leading up to the war, was markedly absent from US culture. The United States army, although modernized under Roosevelt, was still a fraction the size of most European nations, with the exception of Great Britain. The United States navy, although gaining in size on European navies, did not pose a major threat to either Germany or Great Britain, its primary naval rivals in the world.

Any sort of official participation in the European convulsions seemed folly to most people in the United States and the case for neutrality strong:

● In 1914, over a quarter of the population of the United States were immigrants. British and Russian immigrants favored the Allies, while German and Austrian immigrants held with the Central powers. Irish Americans would not support any move to join the British. Choosing sides risked tearing the country apart.
● The monstrous appetite that modern war has for industrial goods promised to drag the country out of the depression of 1913, especially if US businesses could trade with both sides.
● The United States had traditionally remained out of European affairs in the same way it hoped that Europeans would stay out of the affairs of the Americas.
● Wilson despised the idea of war as a solution to international disputes and saw the war as an opportunity for the United States to illustrate the benefits of peace and emerge as a world leader.

But, as Belgium had so recently discovered, being neutral is far more complex than simply declaring neutrality. Neutrality, without the ability to enforce it, is only neutrality so long as other states allow it to be so. Belgium was unable to maintain its neutrality even with the guarantee of Great Britain and so was dragged into the war by virtue of her geographic position. The United States would find neutrality difficult for different reasons.

The US had, as we have discovered above, emerged into world prominence in the decades preceding the German invasion of Belgium, Luxemburg, and France in 1914. Her economy was now tied more closely to a world economy than ever before and the disruptions caused by the war were sure to have ramifications in the US economy. US financial institutions caught a glimpse of these disastrous possibilities when the outbreak of the war caused a need for cash in belligerent nations. When these states began to sell off their US securities, Wilson suspended the sale of stocks to prevent a panic.

The Allied blockade

US neutrality was only as good as its ability to force other countries to respect it. Early in the war both sides indicated that they were not willing to do so. This situation laid bare the prejudices of Wilson and most US citizens in favor of the Allies at the same time that the commercial potential of staggering war demand began to dawn on American industry. Although international law prohibited the blockading of non-war material—non-contraband materials—such as food, these restrictions would make the blockade useless as a tool of war and both sides ignored it. The blockade was designed to prevent the importing of goods to enemy ports. Given the geography of the war, this was primarily directed at Atlantic shipping. The Allied blockade, enforced primarily by the surface fleet of the British Royal Navy, proved less deadly than the submarine warfare of the German navy. Regardless, war orders from the Allies were more than enough to keep the US economy producing at capacity especially when credit restrictions were eased and later lifted altogether.

The deadly nature of a blockade enforced by German submarines, without the provision required by international law that adequate measures be taken to ensure the safety of passengers and crew, was brought into sharp focus in May 1915. A single torpedo fired by a U-20 struck the passenger liner RMS *Lusitania* as she steamed off the Irish coast. The *Lusitania* carried passengers as well as US-made munitions destined for Britain. She went down with 1,195 of her passengers and crew, 123 of them US citizens. The Germans claimed that, as well as civilian passengers, the British ship was carrying munitions, which in part was true.

The sense of Allied outrage was partly due to the nature of the attack on a ship carrying civilian passengers. This, despite German warnings printed in US newspapers that such attacks were possible and warning US citizens that they traveled on British ships at their own risk. The outrage was also derived in part from the growing fear that Germany would ignore what the United States saw as its maritime rights as a neutral, regardless of the position of Great

Activity

The sinking of the *Lusitania*

Press coverage

After doing further research on the sinking of the RMS *Lusitania*, write a newspaper article or an editorial on the sinking from one of the following perspectives:

- Brazil
- Germany
- United Kingdom
- United States

Compare your article to those by other students who chose different perspectives. What elements of the event did you choose to emphasize? What elements did other students choose to emphasize? What effect did the sinking of the *Lusitania* have on US public opinion? What effect did it have on Wilson's views on the war? What does this exercise tell us about how historians use newspaper articles and editorials in studying history?

Britain. Again, her neutrality meant nothing if she could not defend it. Having already acquiesced to the British blockade, Wilson felt he could not acquiesce to the German blockade. On the domestic front, Wilson began to feel pressure from Republicans who might use any weakness shown in the face of German aggression to political advantage. After strongly worded warnings from Wilson and after other sinkings the Germans called off unrestricted submarine warfare in May 1916.

The US economy, with its prodigious loans and exports to the Allies, was increasingly dependent on Allied success. The size of the US economic support alone made any blockade attempt that excluded it weak. While the Germans backed down in 1916, they could conceivably get to the point when it would take more than threats to stop them from attacking US ships.

The British were not above aggravating US neutrality. In 1916, Britain banned a number of US firms from doing business in Great Britain on the grounds that they also did business with the enemy. Although this enraged Wilson and many in his administration the US continued to supply the Allied war effort.

Getting ready

Wilson ran for reelection in 1916, partly on his record of keeping the United States out of the war. The reality, however, was that US neutrality was rather one-sided. Further, the first years of the war illustrated that if the United States wanted to maintain what neutrality it had, a credible military threat was going to be necessary. These arguments, anchored by Republicans and industrial interests but also echoed by important members of Wilson's administration, fueled a vigorous debate in the US as to the extent to which a neutral country should militarize. On the other side of the question, pacifists, socialists and organized labor worried that expanding the military could provoke war and should the United States be able to maintain its neutral position would only serve to profit industrialists at the expense of the taxpayer. By the end of 1915, Wilson was coming around to the idea that the war, which was now revealing itself to be the long, bloody stalemate that it would remain until 1918, whether the US was neutral or belligerent, would require a larger and more modern military. Wilson took his argument to Congress and the people. By mid 1916, after difficult legislative wrangling, long debate, and some compromise, Wilson guided his bills through Congress and into law.

National Defense Act, 1916

- Increased the army from 80,000 to 223,000
- Brought state militias under federal control
- Gave the president power to mobilize the National Guard
- Expanded the National Guard to over 400,000
- Established Junior Reserve Officer Training Corps

British recruiting poster. Recruiters in all countries used emotional appeals to encourage men to enlist in the armed forces. Compare and contrast this poster with US recruiting posters you can find online.

Naval Expansion Act, 1916

- Multi-year building plan
- 10 Dreadnoughts
- 16 Cruisers
- 50 Destroyers

Merchant Marine Act, 1916

- Federal government could own ships
- Increased federal power to regulate shipping

The drift to war

The Democrats campaigned in 1916 on Wilson's neutrality record. It is therefore understandable that the Republicans would attack this record and in the process they began to be perceived as the party more likely to guide the country into the war. Wilson did his level best to encourage this perception. On a deeper level, this debate revealed the development of a foreign policy split that would continue for 40 years.

There was of course any number of variations on these two main themes. For example, some internationalists, represented generally by eastern industrial interests, advocated for a strong military to help "police" the world while other internationalists spoke more in terms of universal disarmament and the use of economic sanctions and collective security to enforce the peace. By 1916, Wilson was a committed internationalist. He attempted to bring the belligerents in the European war to the negotiation table to no avail. Early in 1917, he presented his vision for a post-war world, a world in which disputes between countries were negotiated, armaments were greatly reduced, ships plied the seas unmolested, and nations cooperated in a organization to ensure the stability of the international economic and political system.

The realities of the war were, however, conspiring against Wilson's lofty intentions. While he was putting the final touches on this plan, the German Chancellor, Bethmann Hollweg, was meeting with his military commanders. Generals Hindenburg and Ludendorff argued that if the German navy could unleash its fleet of 100 submarines on all shipping bound for her enemies, they could strangle Britain within six months. This timeline was important, because all present at the meeting understood that should Germany resume unrestricted submarine warfare it would entail sinking US

Activity

Debate

"To arm or not to arm?"

Divide the class into two groups, one opposing expanding the US military in 1916 and the other supporting the expansion of the army and navy. Research the arguments of those who supported each position and conduct a class debate on the question.

Against expansion:	**In favour of expansion:**
● Farmers	● Industrialists
● Socialists	● Military leaders
● Organized labor	
● Pacifists	
● Others	

Internationalism	Isolationism
Collective security	Non-involvement
International law	Trade
International organizations	Protection of American interests
American participation/leadership	Uniqueness of American values
Negotiation/arbitration of disputes	
International disarmament	
Freedom of the seas	

vessels and this would likely bring the US into the war against Germany. The German High Command reasoned, however, that it could take up to a year for any US soldiers to materialize on the western front and by this time Britain would have been brought to its knees. On January 31, 1917 the German ambassador in Washington announced that, starting the next day, all ships regardless of country of origin would become targets for their submarines.

While some of Wilson's administration urged an immediate declaration of war, the president could not bring himself to do it. He feared it would further divide his country and wreck prospects for a stable post-war settlement and his role in its construction. Apart from breaking diplomatic relations with Germany, Wilson did little. It would take a curious diplomatic episode to push him and the people of the United States over the edge to war.

Activity

The Zimmermann telegram

The following telegram was sent from the German foreign minister, Arthur Zimmermann, to the German minister in Mexico. It was intercepted by the British and turned over to the United States.

To the German Minister to Mexico

Berlin, January 19, 1917

On the first of February we intend to begin submarine warfare unrestricted. In spite of this, it is our intention to endeavour to keep neutral the United States of America.

If this attempt is not successful, we propose an alliance on the following basis with Mexico: That we shall make war together and together make peace. We shall give general financial support, and it is understood that Mexico is to reconquer the lost territory in New Mexico, Texas, and Arizona. The details are left to you for settlement...

You are instructed to inform the President of Mexico of the above in the greatest confidence as soon as it is certain that there will be an outbreak of war with the United States and suggest that the President of Mexico, on his own initiative, →

should communicate with Japan suggesting adherence at once to this plan; at the same time, offer to mediate between Germany and Japan.

Please call to the attention of the President of Mexico that the employment of ruthless submarine warfare now promises to compel England to make peace in a few months.

Zimmermann

Source: "Primary Documents: Zimmermann Telegram." January 19, 1917. http://www.firstworldwar.com.

Questions

1 How were the Germans "endeavoring to keep neutral the United States of America?"

2 Given the situation of German in January 1917, how realistic was its pledge of support to Mexico?

3 Why might Germany be interested in an alliance with Japan as well?

4 What relationship does this telegram have to the Monroe Doctrine?

5 To what extent do you believe this telegram was an important catalyst for the US entry in the war? Defend your answer.

The Zimmermann telegram

On February 25, 1917, the British turned over to the United States a telegram that they had intercepted. In it, the German foreign minister, Arthur Zimmermann, promised that Mexico might regain territory lost to the US in return for an alliance with Germany.

Regardless of how realistic such a prospect was or was not, it had a serious effect on public opinion. After the telegram was made public, people in the United States who had been ambiguous about the situation in Europe saw Germany as meddling and conniving. More serious than diplomatic intrigues, however, was the fact that German U-Boats were sending US merchant ships to the bottom of the sea throughout February and March. Wilson now believed that the United States would have to enter the war.

On April 2, 1917, Wilson gave a solemn address to Congress in which he outlined his case for war. He understood that it was a "fearful thing to lead this great peaceful people into war. ..."
The extent to which it was a fearful thing that still deeply divided his people was evidenced by the pro-war and anti-war speeches, marches and demonstrations that seemed to appear daily in cities across the country. Four days later, the formal declaration of war was signed.

US Army recruits at Camp Wadsworth South Carolina, 1918. What challenges did the United States face in mobilizing an army to fight in Europe in the First World War? How did it meet these challenges? What were some of the motivations for young men to enlist in the US army in the First World War?

Activity

Declaration of war

Read President Wilson's April 2, 1917, address to Congress in which he asks for a declaration of war. You can find a copy of the speech at http://www.firstworldwar.com/source/usawardeclaration.htm.

Use the following chart to analyze Wilson's reasons for taking the United States into the war.

Immediate reasons for entering the war	Long-term reasons for entering the war

Questions

1 What evidence is there in the speech that Wilson was hesitant to go to war?

2 Why does Wilson say that "Neutrality is no longer feasible ..."?

3 What evidence is there that in asking for the declaration of war, Wilson is already looking to a postwar settlement?

4 What does Wilson mean when he says that "The world must be made safe for democracy?" What implications does this have for the postwar settlement?

5 Write a reply to Wilson's speech from the perspective of the German government.

The Selective Service Act, 1917

In his address of April 2, Wilson had clearly stated that in his view the massive mobilization required by the war must be managed by a strong central government centered in the **executive branch**. It would require a financial commitment that would require higher taxes. Just as wealth would need to be conscripted, Wilson also argued for the draft to swell the ranks of the small US army.

> The **executive branch** is the branch of government concerned with carrying out the laws passed by the legislative branch. The Executive branch of the United States government consists of the president, the cabinet, and the civil service.

Although the National Defense Act of the previous year had provided for an expanded army, the declaration of war required that this be drastically expanded and expedited. Although Wilson's preference would certainly have been a massive volunteer army, he understood that time and sentiment would not permit one. He therefore urged the passing of the Selective Service Act, which would draft young men into the army. The debate that ensued proved that the divisions that had preceded Wilson's April 2 address had not evaporated with the declaration of war. Despite the rancor, the Act was passed in May and by June millions of Americans were registering for the draft.

Discussion point

Apart from how they are constructed, how are conscript armies different from volunteer armies? What are the advantages of conscription? What are the disadvantages of conscription?

Financing the war

Once the United States entered the war it became patently evident to Wilson and the US government how desperate the situation in Europe had become for the Allies who needed money, men and material. The U-boat campaign was biting deeply into Britain's food stores and all belligerents were close to bankruptcy. While Wilson wanted to finance the war with as little recourse to credit as possible, the dire need of his new Allies could not wait for new taxes to make money available for loans while, at the same time, mobilizing and expanding the armed forces. Congress authorized a loan of $7 billion to get mobilization moving and shore up the finances of France and Britain.

The issue of taxation was another that divided the country Wilson was trying to unite behind a war effort. Both the extent of a new tax regime and the distribution of the tax burden were hotly debated. In the end, taxes provided for about 30 per cent of the cost of the war. As in other belligerent countries, to income tax was added a wide variety of duties on a wide variety of goods and services. An extensive Liberty Bond campaign raised money from all quarters of the United States.

The scale of the First World War led all participants to expand government management of national economies to an unprecedented extent. In the United States, this meant the creation of thousands of government agencies to shepherd the economy toward war production.

The Food Administration

Led by future president Herbert Hoover, this agency managed the production and distribution of food through largely voluntary measures. The Administration bought crops at a fixed price that proved profitable to farmers. Hoover encouraged food conservation, while food production increased dramatically under the supervision of the Food Administration.

The War Industries Board

The WIB led by Bernard Baruch coordinated the production and purchase of war materials. All industries involved in war production were subject to its direction in what would be produced and by whom. The Board worked to fix prices and set wages and hours. Factories that had supplied consumer and other peacetime goods were converted to production of war materials.

Fuel Administration

Just as the Hoover had guaranteed a profitable price for grain to encourage increased production, the Fuel Administration did the same thing for coal with a similar effect on production.

National War Labour Front

This organization, with representatives from government, owners and labor sought to regulate labor relations without recourse to lockouts and strikes so as to keep wartime industries producing without interruptions.

Railroad Administration

This board coordinated the transportation of goods from mines, factories and fields by operating the various lines and spurs of US railways as one system. Again, money greased the wheels of coordination. The government provided funds for upgrading existing lines.

The Shipping Board

This body oversaw the expansion of shipbuilding to maintain the merchant fleet in the face of the U-boat campaign. Over the course of the war, US shipping tonnage increased by a factor of ten.

Committee on Public Information

Just as war production was to be coordinated, the Wilson administration also attempted to coordinate public opinion. The CPI published pamphlets, posters and newspapers articles to garner support for the US war effort. Tens of thousands of its speakers trooped around the country presenting the government's case for patriotic support for the war. The propaganda effort extolled the virtues of the Allies and their cause while demonizing the enemy.

Women and the war

As in other Allied countries such as Great Britain and Canada, the jobs vacated by soldiers were filled by an increasing number of women. While women had always played an important role in the industrial production of the United States, the war saw them enter occupations traditionally dominated by men and in numbers never seen before. These jobs were in the industrial sector such as munitions factories and in white-collar positions such as clerks. Women also flocked to more traditionally female occupations such as nursing, many thousands of them serving overseas.

Partially because of the independent income that accompanied these new economic roles, women found themselves with a greater degree of social freedom. While many of these jobs disappeared when the war ended, with the reduction in economic demand and soldiers returning to fill their old jobs, the contribution women had made to the war effort was significant and their social position altered permanently. Women's suffrage activists wished to capitalize on this importance and accelerated their demand for the vote. By 1920, they were successful with the passing and ratification of the **19th Amendment**.

The **19th Amendment** to the United States constitution guarantees the right to vote regardless of gender.

151

Opposition and repression

Opposition to the war continued after Wilson's April 2 address. This resistance could be issue-specific while remaining pro-war, for example there was widespread resistance to the imposition of the draft by many who were generally in favor of the US entering the war. Critics could also be broad and deep in their resistance to the war as a whole. The Socialist Party maintained its opposition to any US participation in the war.

The Espionage Act, passed in June of 1917, provided a powerful club with which to keep dissent in check. The Act allowed for prison sentences of up to 20 years for anyone who, in times of war, willfully caused or attempt to cause insubordination, disloyalty, mutiny or refusal to serve in the military. The Act also stipulated that it could not be used to limit discussion, comment or criticism of the government's policies or actions.

In 1918, the Espionage Act was amended (called the Sedition Act) to include:

> ... whoever, when the United States is at war, shall willfully utter, print, write or publish any disloyal, profane, scurrilous, or abusive language about the form of government of the United States or the Constitution of the United States, or the military or naval forces of the United States, or the flag of the United States, or the uniform of the Army or Navy of the United States ... or by word or act [to] oppose the cause of the United States.

Such an ambiguous, and some would say contradictory, Act was sure to be applied inconsistently and selectively, but the Supreme Court upheld its legality in the face of First Amendment challenges. Those who spoke out against the war, generally, and the draft specifically found themselves in court and often in jail on the force of the Espionage Act. Over 1,500 people were arrested under these acts. Socialist Leader Eugene Debs and hundreds of others were found guilty under the Espionage Act and Sedition Act and went to jail for speaking out against the war.

Other Acts further expanded the government's reach and power over the spread of ideas during the war. The Trading With The Enemy Act of 1917 gave the government the power to censor any communications leaving the country. The Sabotage Act was used to suppress industrial action by organizations like the Industrial Workers of the World (IWW).

By the end of the war, there was also more mainstream opposition to Wilson's handling of the war. There was dissention within his Democratic Party. Eastern Democrats disagreed with measures proposed and occasionally passed by western Progressives in the party. Republicans who had put aside party animosity in the cause of a united war effort emerged from their truce as the end of the war neared. The end result of this inter- and intra-party wrangling was

Activity

Political platforms

Research the platforms of each of the following US political parties active in the First World War period. Be sure to include each party's view on US participation in the war.

Party	Platform
The Democratic Party	
The Republican Party	
The Progressive Party	
The Socialist Party	

that the Republicans took control of both houses of Congress in the 1918 elections. This did not bode well for Wilson as he left for the Peace Conference at the end of the war.

US armed forces overseas

British and French hopes that the United States should be rushed as soon as possible to shore up the existing Allied positions became more acute when the Bolshevik revolution and subsequent **Treaty of Brest-Litovsk** took Russia out of the war and made scores of additional German divisions available for action in France. The near collapse of the Italian army and the French mutinies of 1917 made this situation even more desperate. The US government and army resisted this impulse. General Pershing wanted to enter the war with a US army distinct, intact, and strong enough to fight on its own terms alongside, not mixed in with, her new Allies. In the face of allied pleas, Pershing softened his position somewhat, but it would not be until early 1918 that US troops would move to the front in significant numbers—at about the same time that the German High Command would make one last attempt at breaking the stalemate.

> ### Discussion point
>
> To what extent should the government have the right to restrict personal liberties in times of war? Does war justify this action? Why or why not?

> **The Treaty of Brest-Litovsk** was signed between the new Bolshevik government of Russia and Germany and Austria. It was finalized on March 1, 1918. The treaty provided that Russia would lose parts of Ukraine, the Baltic States and Finland in exchange for an end to hostilities with the Central powers. The treaty allowed the Germans to send troops that had been fighting on the eastern front to the western front.

Activity

The United States in battle

From early 1918, until the end of the war, the American Expeditionary Force contributed to Allied defensive and offensive operations. Research the following battles to complete the following chart.

Battle	Dates	Commanders	Description	Significance
Battle of Cantigny				
Battle of Chateau-Thierry				
Battle of Belleau Wood				
Second Battle of the Marne				
Battle of St Mihiel				
Meuse-Argonne Offensive				

President Wilson and the Peace of Paris

Wilson had advocated for a "peace without victory" before the United States had entered the war. In many ways, Wilson's decision to enter the war was taken with a keen eye to the postwar world system as much as it was to the protection of US shipping. Wilson's notion of internationalism based on liberal democratic ideals, capitalism, freer trade and the dissolution of colonial empires, he believed, required US leadership and to have a guiding hand in the peace required a contribution on the battlefield. Regardless, for these principles to prevail, Wilson believed that Germany had to be defeated. While Wilson had floated a number of these ideas in public since 1917, they were crystallized as the 14 Points in a January 1918 speech.

Activity

The 14 Points

Synopsis of the 14 Points:

1 Open treaties
2 Freedom of the seas
3 Free Trade
4 Universal disarmament
5 Impartial adjustment of colonial claims with consideration of the wishes of the inhabitant and the governments in question
6 Evacuation of all Russian territory
7 Evacuation of Belgium
8 Restoration of all French territory including Alsace-Lorraine
9 Italian border readjusted according to nationality
10 Autonomous development to be offered to the peoples of the Austro-Hungarian Empire
11 Evacuation of Serbia, Montenegro, and Romania; Serbia to be given sea access
12 Autonomous development for the nationalities of the Turkish Empire; the Dardanelles Straits to remain permanently open
13 Establishment of a independent and free Poland with access to the sea
14 A general association of nations must be formed under specific covenants for the purpose of affording mutual guarantees of political independence and territorial integrity to great and small states alike.

Questions

1 On what points would the British have agreed? Which would they have opposed and why? What about the French?
2 What evidence is there of idealism and moral diplomacy in the 14 Points?
3 Analyze the 14 Points in terms of continuity and change in American foreign policy before and after the war.
4 To what degree do these points reflect the principle of collective security?
5 Draft a letter of response from the German government and the French government.

By October 1918, the Germans believed that the 14 Points were the best deal that they could hope for from what increasingly appeared to be an inevitable defeat. They appealed directly to Wilson with a proposition for an armistice based on his peace plan. Wilson found himself in the difficult position of potentially mediating between his enemy and his Allies. Nevertheless, he spent the better part of October 1918 selling the British and French on his 14 Points with some limited success.

As the world limped toward the end of the war on November 11, 1918, it seemed that all parties had taken the 14 Points to be at least the basis for a peace settlement. But there was incredible resentment toward Germany on the part of the Allies and the grudging acceptance of the principles in the 14 Points could not overcome that. After the armistice, Germany evacuated its conquered territory in the west and surrendered her fleet while the Allies maintained the naval blockade. Most significantly, the Allies denied to Germany any role in crafting the peace settlement. If Wilson had envisioned a "peace without victory" the reality certainly appeared as though it would be a victor's peace.

As personally involved as he was in the decision to take the United States into the war, and as closely linked as that decision was to the post-war settlement, Wilson felt the need to negotiate on behalf of the United States personally. He arrived in Europe in late 1918 and would stay for six months with only a brief return to the United States in that time. He left a Congress in the control of the Republicans, a Congress whose approval he would need for any settlement he achieved at the Paris Peace Conference. Aggravating deteriorating domestic party politics, Wilson took no significant Republican politicians with him to Paris, leaving them to fume at the distant president and the treaty he was crafting without them.

The First World War: Armies mobilized and casualties					
Countries	Total mobilized forces	Killed and died	Wounded casualties	Prisoners and missing	Total casualties	Casualties as % of mobilized forces
Allies and Associated Powers:						
Russia	12,000,000	1,700,000	4,950,000	2,500,000	9,150,000	76.3
France	8,410,000	1,357,800	4,266,000	537,000	6,160,800	73.3
British Empire	8,904,467	908,371	2,090,212	191,652	3,190,235	35.8
Italy	5,615,000	650,000	947,000	600,000	2,197,000	39.1
United States	4,355,000	126,000	234,300	4,500	364,800	8.2
Japan	800,000	300	907	3	1,210	0.2
Romania	750,000	335,706	120,000	80,000	535,706	71.4
Serbia	707,343	45,000	133,148	152,958	331,106	46.8
Belgium	267,000	13,716	44,686	34,659	93,061	34.9
Greece	230,000	5,000	21,000	1,000	27,000	11.7
Portugal	100,000	7,222	13,751	12,318	33,291	33.3
Montenegro	50,000	3,000	10,000	7,000	20,000	40.0
Total	42,188,810	5,152,115	12,831,004	4,121,090	22,104,209	52.3
Central Powers:						
Germany	11,000,000	1,773,700	4,216,058	1,152,800	7,142,558	64.9
Austria-Hungary	7,800,000	1,200,000	3,620,000	2,200,000	7,020,000	90.0
Turkey	2,850,000	325,000	400,000	250,000	975,000	34.2
Bulgaria	1,200,000	87,500	152,390	27,029	266,919	22.2
Total	22,850,000	3,386,200	8,388,448	3,629,829	15,404,477	67.4
Overall total	65,038,810	8,538,315	21,219, 452	7,750,919	37,508,686	57.6

Data supplied by the United States War Department, February 1924
Source: Trueman, John et al. 1979. *Modern Perspectives*. 2nd edn. Toronto: McGraw, Hill, Ryerson. p. 411.

The Peace Conference seemed to amplify Wilson's previous tendency toward autocratic decision-making. At various times, he found himself at serious odds with the British prime minister, Lloyd George, and the "Tiger of France", Georges Clemenceau, who at one point threatening to pull out of the negotiations. He did not feel bound by secret treaties concluded by the other Allies such as the Treaty of London with Italy nor to any promises made to Japan. Most of his objections to these agreements, apart from their largely secret nature, were that they amounted to a division of the spoils of war violating his concept of national self-determination. The staggering number of national submissions by countries, territories, national groups complicated matters immeasurably and exposed Wilson's ignorance with regards to European politics—the byproduct of 150 years of US isolationist policies.

As Wilson gradually gave way on some elements of the 14 Points, he seemed to place more and more confidence in his proposed League of Nations to mitigate what he saw as deficiencies in the broader treaty. Rather than creating the League under a separate treaty, Wilson sought to bind the participants more closely to it by insisting the Covenant of the League be included in the actual Treaty of Versailles.

Discussion point

To what extent was the League of Nations a reflection of Wilson's Moral Diplomacy? To what extent does the League mark a departure from US foreign policy?

How do the principles of the League compare to the principles of:

- The Monroe Doctrine?
- Big Stick Diplomacy?
- Dollar Diplomacy?

Back in the United States, the Republican-controlled Senate saw aspects of the League to which they could not agree and political advantage in opposing it. While Wilson acquiesced on some Republican sentiments, such as allowing for the withdrawal of a member nation with two years notice, and the maintenance of the domestic sovereignty of member nations, he stubbornly pressed on.

US support for the League of Nations

A tired and ill Wilson returned from Paris to lay the League, and by association the entire Treaty of Versailles, before the people of the United States. He returned to a country having difficulty adjusting to the new conditions of peace. **The Red Scare** and the impending 1920 presidential election compounded labor strife, unemployment and decreasing economic demand.

Opposition to the Treaty and the League came from a number of quarters. To the pettiness of partisan politics was added the voices of intellectuals worried that the League would serve only to entrench the status quo of balance of power diplomacy in Europe. Some isolationists honestly believed that the interests of the US were best served by disengaging from European matters. Other pragmatists thought the lofty goals of the League unrealistic and the best way to safeguard US interests was a strong military—not disarmament. Many were concerned that a strict reading of Article X of the Covenant of the League would violate US sovereignty and compel her to intervene when other nations' integrity was threatened. Italian Americans were upset at Wilson's stance on the Treaty of London. Irish Americans wondered angrily why "self-determination" did not apply to their homeland. German Americans railed against Germany's humiliation.

A number of Republican Senators—the Reservationists—saw the Covenant as more or less workable with revisions. Most of these agreed that Article X would need some alterations so as to protect what they saw as US freedom of action in the world following its foreign policy traditions.

Those Senators who opposed any form of the treaty with the included League were known as the Irreconcilables and a number of them sat on the Senate Foreign Relations Committee chaired by Senator Lodge. He held weeks of hearings, allowing all manner of dissenters to air their issues with the treaty and the League—all duly reported in the press. For his part, Wilson rapidly became intransigent with regards to the League and especially Article X. His increasingly stubborn defense of the treaty gave ammunition to his opponents who saw him as autocratic and arrogant. Perhaps it was this arrogance that led him to believe that if he could persuade the US public of the righteousness of his cause the recalcitrant Senators would have to yield. To this end, and despite his frail health, Wilson embarked on an exhausting cross-country speaking tour to put his case for the League before the people. The strain proved too much for his health and, after cutting the tour short, Wilson suffered a stroke in early October 1919.

Discussion point

The fate of the 14 Points

What happened to each of the 14 Points in the final peace settlement? Discuss the reason why some of the points were not included in the settlement.

The Red Scare In the aftermath of the First World War and the Bolshevik revolution in Russia, a fear of radical left wing politics gripped the United States. Socialists, Communists, Anarchists and labor organizers were harassed and arrested during this period.

Discussion point

To what extent is foreign policy related to domestic policy? Have there been times in US policy when foreign policy has taken priority over domestic concerns?

Activity

Lodge vs. Wilson on the League

Source A

The following is an excerpt of a speech given by Henry Cabot Lodge in August 1919 addressing the issue of the League of Nations.

National I must remain, and in that way I like all other Americans can render the amplest service to the world. The United States is the world's best hope, but if you fetter her in the interests and quarrels of other nations, if you tangle her in the intrigues of Europe, you will destroy her power for good and endanger her very existence. Leave her to march freely through the centuries to come as in the years that have gone.

Strong, generous, and confident, she has nobly served mankind. Beware how you trifle with your marvellous inheritance, this great land of ordered liberty, for if we stumble and fall freedom and civilization everywhere will go down in ruin.

We are told that we shall "break the heart of the world" if we do not take this league just as it stands. I fear that the hearts of the vast majority of mankind would beat on strongly and steadily and without any quickening if the league were to perish altogether. If it should be effectively and beneficently changed the people who would lie awake in sorrow for a single night could be easily gathered in one not very large room but those who would draw a long breath of relief would reach to millions.

We hear much of visions and I trust we shall continue to have visions and dream dreams of a fairer future for the race. But visions are one thing and visionaries are another, and the mechanical appliances of the rhetorician designed to give a picture of a present which does not exist and of a future which no man can predict are as unreal and short-lived as the steam or canvas clouds, the angels suspended on wires and the artificial lights of the stage.

They pass with the moment of effect and are shabby and tawdry in the daylight. Let us at least be real. Washington's entire honesty of mind and his fearless look into the face of all facts are qualities which can never go out of fashion and which we should all do well to imitate.

Ideals have been thrust upon us as an argument for the league until the healthy mind which ⟶

rejects cant revolts from them. Are ideals confined to this deformed experiment upon a noble purpose, tainted, as it is, with bargains and tied to a peace treaty which might have been disposed of long ago to the great benefit of the world if it had not been compelled to carry this rider on its back? 'Post equitem sedet atra cura,' Horace tells us, but no blacker care ever sat behind any rider than we shall find in this covenant of doubtful and disputed interpretation as it now perches upon the treaty of peace.

No doubt many excellent and patriotic people see a coming fulfilment of noble ideals in the words 'league for peace.' We all respect and share these aspirations and desires, but some of us see no hope, but rather defeat, for them in this murky covenant. For we, too, have our ideals, even if we differ from those who have tried to establish a monopoly of idealism.

Our first ideal is our country, and we see her in the future, as in the past, giving service to all her people and to the world. Our ideal of the future is that she should continue to render that service of her own free will. She has great problems of her own to solve, very grim and perilous problems, and a right solution, if we can attain to it, would largely benefit mankind.

We would have our country strong to resist a peril from the West, as she has flung back the German menace from the East. We would not have our politics distracted and embittered by the dissensions of other lands. We would not have our country's vigour exhausted or her moral force abated, by everlasting meddling and muddling in every quarrel, great and small, which afflicts the world.

Our ideal is to make her ever stronger and better and finer, because in that way alone, as we believe, can she be of the greatest service to the world's peace and to the welfare of mankind.

Source: Henry Cabot Lodge on the League of Nations. 12 August 1919.
http://www.firstworldwar.com/source/lodge_leagueofnations.htm.

Source B

The following is an excerpt of the last speech given by President Wilson in his 1919 tour of the United States promoting the Treaty of Versailles and the League of Nations. ⟶

But the treaty is so much more than that. It is not merely a settlement with Germany; it is a readjustment of those great injustices which underlie the whole structure of European and Asiatic society. ...

It is a people's treaty, that accomplishes by a great sweep of practical justice the liberation of men who never could have liberated themselves, and the power of the most powerful nations has been devoted not to their aggrandizement but to the liberation of people whom they could have put under their control if they had chosen to do so. ...

At the front of this great treaty is put the Covenant of the League of Nations. ...

Unless you get the united, concerted purpose and power of the great Governments of the world behind this settlement, it will fall down like a house of cards. There is only one power to put behind the liberation of mankind, and that is the power of mankind. It is the power of the united moral forces of the world, and in the Covenant of the League of Nations the moral forces of the world are mobilized. For what purpose?

Reflect, my fellow citizens, that the membership of this great League is going to include all the great fighting nations of the world, as well as the weak ones. It is not for the present going to include Germany, but for the time being Germany is not a great fighting country. All the nations that have power that can be mobilized are going to be members of this League, including the United States.

And what do they unite for? They enter into a solemn promise to one another that they will never use their power against one anther for aggression; that they never will impair the territorial integrity of a neighbour; that they never will interfere with the political independence of a neighbour; that they will abide by the principle that great populations are entitled to determine their own destiny and that they will not interfere with that destiny; and that no matter what differences arise amongst them they will never resort to war without first having done one or other of two things—either submitted the matter of controversy to arbitration, in which case they agree to abide by the result without question, or submitted it to the consideration of the council of the League of Nations, laying before that council all the documents, all the facts, agreeing that the council can publish the documents and the facts to the whole world, agreeing that there shall be six months allowed for the mature consideration of those facts by the council, and agreeing that at the expiration of the six months, even if they are not then ready to accept the advice of the council with regard to the settlement of the dispute, they will still not go to war for another three months.

In other words, they consent, no matter what happens, to submit every matter of difference between them to the judgment of mankind, and just so certainly as they do that, my fellow citizens, war will be in the far background, war will be pushed out of that foreground of terror in which it has kept the world for generation after generation, and men will know that there will be a calm time of deliberate counsel.

The most dangerous thing for a bad cause is to expose it to the opinion of the world. The most certain way that you can prove that a man is mistaken is by letting all his neighbours know what he thinks, by letting all his neighbours discuss what he thinks, and if he is in the wrong you will notice that he will stay at home, he will not walk on the street.

He will be afraid of the eyes of his neighbours. He will be afraid of their judgment of his character. He will know that his cause is lost unless he can sustain it by the arguments of right and of justice. The same law that applies to individuals applies to nations. ...

Let us accept what America has always fought for, and accept it with pride that America showed the way and made the proposal. I do not mean that America made the proposal in this particular instance; I mean that the principle was an American principle, proposed by America. ...

Article ten is the heart of the whole matter. What is article ten? I never am certain that I can from memory give a literal repetition of its language, but I am sure that I can give an exact interpretation of its meaning. Article ten provides that every member of the league covenants to respect and preserve the territorial integrity and existing political independence of every other member of the league as against external aggression. . .

It may be that that will impair somewhat the vigour of the League, but, nevertheless, the fact is so, that we are not obliged to take any advice except our own, which to any man who wants to go his own course is a very satisfactory state of affairs. Every man regards his own advice as best, and I dare say every man mixes his own advice with some thought of his own interest.

Whether we use it wisely or unwisely, we can use the vote of the United States to make impossible drawing the United States into any enterprise that she does not care to be drawn into. ...

You will say, "Is the League an absolute guaranty against war?" No; I do not know any absolute guaranty against the errors of human judgment or the violence of human passions but I tell you this: With a cooling space of nine months for human passion, not much of it will keep hot. ...

Source: President Woodrow Wilson's Address in Favour of the League of Nations. 25 September 1919. http://www.firstworldwar.com/source/wilsonspeech_ league.htm

Questions

1 What evidence is there of Wilson's moral diplomacy in source B? What evidence is there of a pragmatic approach to foreign policy?

2 What does Lodge mean when he says "For we, too, have our ideals, even if we differ from those who have tried to establish a monopoly of idealism" in source A?

3 Evaluate Wilson's use of the "neighbor" analogy in making his argument.

4 On what points might have Lodge and Wilson agreed?

5 Evaluate the two arguments. Whose is more convincing? Why?

With Wilson incapacitated and unable to rally more support for the League, the Senate, in a series of votes from November 1919 to March 1920, voted against ratification of the treaty. The end result of this Senate defeat was that the major treaty that concluded the First World War, and was signed by her European wartime allies, was not recognized by the United States.

The impact of the war on the US economy

Wilson would be the last Democratic president for over a decade. The Republicans who won the 1920 election and those that followed, continued on the foreign policy course that had been charted by those who had defeated the Treaty of Versailles in 1920. They vigorously guarded US interests without becoming tangled in alliances and partnerships with other states. They relied on their apparent juggernaut of an economy and the private sector to speak for US interests on the world stage. A small group of Republicans —the Peace Progressives—modified a strictly isolationist stance adopted by others of their party: they opposed the role of business in both domestic and foreign policy while decrying imperialism and militarism. The war had made the United States the single biggest creditor nation on earth. This proved to be a mixed blessing. While, on the one hand, it gave the United States a great deal of influence in the world, it also meant that the US had a huge stake in the economic stability of the world. This ran counter to the growing isolationist sentiments in the country.

Nevertheless, the legacy of the First World War was that the relative strength of the US economy meant that it dominated exports and capital markets around the world. Even with the growing sentiment toward higher tariffs in the US through the 1920s, the United States was still an impressive importer as well. US capital, propping up the German economy and playing a substantial role in many others meant that as went the US economy, so went the world economy. There were elements of continuity with the prewar period. US companies continued to buy and lease huge amounts of foreign land in their voracious search for raw materials for the overheated US economy. The relative weakness of other economies meant that there was limited competition from overseas firms. But again, these "incursions" into foreign countries and markets were piloted by private enterprise, albeit with a helping hand from the US government. **The Washington Treaty** helped short-term relations with Japan—an important trading partner and the **Dawes Plan** helped rehabilitate the German economy such that it could resume payment of reparations to Britain and France, which would then find their way back to the Allies' American creditors.

> **The Washington Treaty** signed in 1922 by Great Britain, the United States, France, Italy, and Japan limited naval armaments including ship tonnage.

> The **Dawes Plan** was an economic recovery plan engineered by Senator Charles Dawes designed to address hyperinflation in Germany. Through this plan, US loans would be used to back the revaluation of the German currency. The plan also facilitated the flow of US capital into the German economy. The recovery was intended to allow Germany to resume its reparation payments to the Allies.

Canada and the First World War

Having gained independence in domestic issues in 1867, Canada still labored under a confusing foreign policy structure in 1914. As a Dominion of the British Empire the British government essentially controlled Canada's foreign policy, which meant she was bound by the course that the British would take in the July Crisis of 1914. Over the course of the preceding 12 years, the Canadian military had been gradually drawn into a more centralized command structure in terms of imperial operations and by 1912 Canadian forces were integrated into imperial defence plans. Despite this integration, there were hints that the issue of British command of Canadian soldiers would prove contentious and in fact would come to a head during the war. In 1904, Wilfred Laurier officially placed the countries militia under the command of a Dominion-born officer. From 1907, however, integration continued with advances in common training and standards among the imperial forces. On paper, Canada had a permanent force of about 4,000 soldiers and about 50,000 militia with some training. The navy consisted of two warships.

Mobilization

In the midst of a heated debate regarding the construction of the Canadian navy, Wilfred Laurier had declared that when Britain was at war, Canada was at war. Although Canada had been debating her place in the British Empire almost since the signing

> ### Discussion point
>
> What were the advantages of Canada integrating her military with British forces? What were the disadvantages? What effect might the position of the United States have played in this decision?

> ### Activity
> #### Canada's economic context
>
> Research the economic situation in Canada in the period 1912–14. Use the following topic headings to guide your research:
> - Manufacturing
> - Unemployment
> - Agricultural production
> - Trade
>
> **Questions**
> 1 How was the economic context related to Canada's ability to fight a war in 1914?
> 2 What effect might the unemployment situation have on recruiting efforts in the autumn of 1914?
> 3 What effect did this economic situation have on government revenues? How might this impact Canada's ability to equip an army and navy? What might be some possible solutions for the government?

of the British North America Act with some advocating greater independence and others arguing caution and the benefits of "Dominion Status", in 1914 the fact remained much as Laurier had characterized it. While it is true that Canada tumbled into the conflict with Britain's declaration of war in August 1914, as the South African War of 1899 had illustrated, the manner of Canada's participation was a matter for the Canadian parliament to decide. That said, there was little debate. Canada and her population of eight million would commit to the total war effort. It would send men and material and mobilize the home front to the war effort. The initial commitment was a contingent of 25,000 men equipped and delivered to the European theatre at Canada's expense—initially estimated at some $50 million. To facilitate this mobilization the government passed the War Measures Act at the outbreak of the war. The Act reserved for the federal government the right to govern by executive decree in times of perceived "war, invasion, or insurrection."

The mobilization effort would be dominated by the character of the minister of militia, Sam Hughes. Hughes operated free from governmental interference, method and scruples. Within a month of the outbreak of the war, over 30,000 men had assembled at Valcartier, Quebec, for training. Assembling men was one thing, but a modern army had to be equipped and clothed and this proved a challenge. Khaki uniforms and the **Ross rifle** were ordered in huge quantities. Ships were contracted and preparations made, albeit at times unorthodox and somewhat haphazard preparations. The embarkation of the first contingent of the Canadian Expeditionary Force bore a marked resemblance to the US army's chaotic departure for Cuba during the Spanish–American War. Nevertheless, the first contingent of 30,000 troops landed in England in mid October 1914, and Robert Borden's Conservative government ordered a second of the same strength be raised.

The volunteer spirit was not limited to those seeking active service in Europe. Organizations such as the YMCA and other existing associations turned their efforts to raising money and material for the war effort. The Canadian Patriotic Fund was chartered to raise money that would bridge the gap between what soldiers would earn in uniform and what they had earned as civilians thus taking some of the financial burden off those who remained behind. Schools, clubs, and mutual benefit societies raised money to buy food, uniforms and even weapons.

Despite the enthusiasm with which most Canadians approached the war effort, there was, from the start some quiet voices of dissent, voices that would grow in volume as the slaughter in France became more apparent and dragged on from year to year. Pacifist religious sects, such as the Mennonites and Doukhobors, remained opposed to the war though quietly so. Even some among the religious groups that opposed the notion of war, such as the Methodists, were won over to support the war effort on the ground that it was becoming a moral crusade against those who would use war to further their national goals, namely Germany.

The **Ross rifle** was the weapon that Sam Hughes decided would be issued to Canadian infantrymen at the outset of the First World War. The rifle proved to be a good target and sniping rifle, but was heavy and jammed regularly, especially in the trying conditions of trench warfare. Persistent criticism by frontline soldiers eventually led to its replacement by the British Lee-Enfield rifle.

Robert Borden (1854–1937)

Born in Nova Scotia, Borden started his professional life as a teacher and later became a lawyer. After practicing law in Nova Scotia, Borden was drawn into political life and was first elected to parliament in 1896. By 1901, he had ascended to leadership of the Conservative Party and spent ten years as leader of the opposition, responding to the more charismatic prime minister, Wilfred Laurier. While in opposition, Borden championed closer ties within the British Empire and defeated Laurier and the Liberals in the 1911 general election.

Once in power, Borden worked to strengthen military and economic ties with Britain. When the First World War erupted, Borden continued this imperial vision to its logical extension and pledged, with vast popular support, unqualified support for the British war effort. As Canada's wartime prime minister he oversaw the dramatic expansion in Canada's military and industrial capacity. He pushed conscription through parliament, developing a Union government and expanding the franchise to women in order to do so. As he managed her expanding war effort, Borden came to realize that the sacrifice in men and material that Canada was making required a greater say in the direction of the war and from 1915 to the end of the war he energetically argued this position. When it came to crafting the peace settlements, Borden continued this position to the end that Canada signed the treaties on her own authority, not that of Great Britain. After his retirement in 1920, he traveled and wrote, serving as the Chancellor of Queen's University from 1924–1929.

Recruiting remained relatively easy throughout 1914 and 1915, with close to 60,000 enlisting by the end of 1914. By June 1915, Canada had a force of over 100,000 soldiers overseas, with a goal of one man in reserve in England for every two at the front. This was in the face of enormous casualty figures, the like of which none of the belligerents had foreseen. By the fall of 1915, Canada had two divisions with a strength of over 40,000 fighting in France. Sam Hughes boasted an ever-expanding Canadian army, with all new recruits forming into new battalions, which in turn would coalesce

Activity

Volunteer motives

The initial volunteers for the Canadian Expeditionary Force came from all over Canada, although in markedly different numbers. For each of the following people, write a letter explaining your motives for volunteering or not.

● A farm boy from Southern Saskatchewan

● A lawyer from Toronto

● A French-Canadian mill worker from Montreal

● A recent German immigrant living in Edmonton

● A Mennonite farmer from Steinbeck, Manitoba

● A logger from New Brunswick whose parents had emigrated from Scotland into new divisions. The brutal arithmetic of the trenches, however, dictated that each division that was fighting would need replacements at a rate of some 15,000 men a year. The decentralized recruiting system continually lowered medical and height standards in order to meet the need for men. Volunteer recruiting peaked in early 1916 and fell off from that point. Nevertheless, when the Battle of Arras erupted in the spring of 1917 and the Canadians began their assault on Vimy Ridge, the Canadian Corps consisted of four divisions in France with a fifth waiting in Britain. But by this time, recruit numbers could not keep up with battle losses.

Canadian Machine gunners in shell hole during the advance at Vimy Ridge, near Arras, France, 1917. The Battle of Vimy Ridge is considered an important event in the development of Canada as an independent nation. How can the experience of war foster nationalist feelings?

 What are some reasons for the decline in volunteers from early 1916? How might the Canadian government have addressed this problem?

Quebec

Recruiting in Quebec had lagged behind English Canada from the beginning of the war. The reasons were numerous. There was one French-speaking regiment—the Royal 22 Battalion "The Van Doos"—but it was primarily led by English officers. Demographically, men married earlier in Quebec and this shrank the available pool of single men as compared to Western Canada and Ontario. Recruiting in the province was organized by a Protestant clergyman, excluding the most influential social institution in the province—The Catholic Church—from the recruitment process. Anti-French education laws in Ontario and Manitoba epitomized an attitude that convinced many French Canadians that this was not their war. The growing employment opportunities afforded by increased war production and the high wages that accompanied them seemed to young Quebecers a more sensible decision than enlisting. Politically, Henri Bourassa was expressing his opposition to the war openly by 1916 as were many of his *nationaliste* allies and this curtailed Quebec recruitment even further.

Activity

Canada's willingness

Source A

The following is an excerpt by historians J. Finlay and D. Sprague.

> At the beginning, mobilization had the effect of unifying the country around a sense of common danger that was far less artificial than anything Canada had experienced in the past. Earlier, in the case of John A. McDonald's attempt to create an atmosphere of national emergency around the building of the CPR, for example, the artificiality of the effort was only too apparent. Or later with the South African war, the episode was only English Canada's adventure.
>
> **Source:** Finlay, J.L. and D. N. Sprague, D.N. 1984.The Structure of Canadian History. Scarborough: Prentice Hall. pp. 298–99.

Source B

Wilfred Laurier, the leader of the official opposition, uttered the following to describe Canada's stance at the beginning of the war.

> ... when the call goes out our answer goes at once, and it goes in the classical language of British answer to the call of Duty: Ready, Aye Ready.

Source C

Stuart Ramsay Tompkins was a young Albertan working for the Department of Education when the war broke out in 1914. The following is an excerpt of a letter he wrote to his wife-to-be in September 1914.

> The whole city [Edmonton] is now astir with a mild form of mobilization. Last night coming down town we passed a squad of citizens marching to the tune of "A Hundred Pipers ...". A whole regiment is being formed to train bellicose citizens. The civil service are forming a squad but in view of the announcement ... there is much less enthusiasm being displayed. Strong exception is being taken to the stand of the government in refusing to allow men any part of their salary while on active service.
>
> **Source:** Stuart Ramsay Tompkins to Edna Christie, September 10, 1914. Cited in Ramsay Tompkins, Stuart. 1989. *A Canadian's Road to Russia: Letters from the Great War Decade*. Doris H. Pieroth (ed.) Edmonton: University of Alberta Press. p. 36.

Questions

1 How does source A contrast the First World War with earlier crises in Canada? Why was it different?

2 Why, according to source C, are members of the civil service hesitant to enlist?

3 Compare and contrast the sentiments of Canadian citizens regarding enlisting as expressed in sources B and C.

4 Using the documents and further research analyze military enlistment in Canada in 1914.

The home front

While the First World War was developing into a human tragedy of catastrophic proportions, it was fundamentally changing the short-term condition and long-term structure of the Canadian economy. Like other countries, Canada entered the war while in the depths of a sharp depression. The increased production required by a European war and the prospect of a vastly expanded army meant that after a period of realignment—and in fact a brief deepening of the depression—unemployment would be a memory. When the massive increase in demand that accompanied a war of this magnitude was combined with the physical devastation and dislocation of established European national economies it meant that Canada, her fields and factories safe on the other side of the Atlantic, could expand into this niche.

Initially, in Canada, this expansion would be in the traditional role of supplier of primary resources. Acreage under cultivation increased dramatically early in the war and this pushed wheat production to new levels. Thereafter, production would stabilize at lower levels. The massive demand created by the disruption to European wheat supplies sent commodity prices higher. The net result was that the value of wheat exports doubled during the war, although it would never match the amount of grain produced per acre in 1915. Wartime necessity also buoyed the Canadian lumber industry, which had been hit hard by the building slump that accompanied the depression of 1913. Dairy products and meat also found new markets. Meat exports increased by some 1400% during the course of the war. Mineral extraction also increased during the war.

Munitions production was certainly not a traditional sector of strength in the Canadian economy. The expanded Canadian army, her British allies, the grinding nature of trench warfare, and the domineering personality of Sam Hughes all demanded that she create one. It was initiated in typical Sam Hughes fashion—ad hoc with a heavy dose of **patronage**. But such a "system" was bound to collapse under the massive demands of a war the scale of which was developing in Europe. Initial war production suffered in both quantity and quality. Hughes' Shell Committee set up in 1914 to manage munitions production proved incapable of keeping up with purchase orders from both the Canadian and British army, plagued by Hughes' meddling, profiteering and old party patronage. The Imperial Munitions Board over which Hughes had no control was created to replace the Shell Committee in 1915. The quantity and quality of munitions improved almost immediately.

> **Patronage** is the practice of giving political positions and economic opportunities to political allies and supporters.

The issues with the Shell Committee and munitions production illustrated the fact that the Canadian government did not have an overall plan for wartime economic coordination. Rather, it responded to issues and situations as they arose. The War Measures Act gave the government a powerful tool with which to address these emergent situations. Nevertheless, as the war progressed, a patchwork of government intervention appeared in Canadian society:

- 1915, Imperial Munitions Board coordinated production of artillery shells and later other materials from ships to airplanes
- 1915, War Purchasing Commission coordinated military procurement
- 1915, Munitions Resources Commission supervised the conservation of natural resources for war production
- 1917, Fuel Controller coordinated fuel import, export, production and distribution
- 1917, Board of Grain Supervisors managed wheat marketing
- 1918, War Trade Board managed import and export licenses
- 1918, Canadian Food Board supervised food distribution,

Financing the war

With a massive war effort comes a massive financial burden. Canada, like all countries had two means at its disposal to meet this burden— taxation and credit. Taxation was anathema to the finance minister, Thomas White, but there really seemed no alternative. A multitude of indirect taxes descended on the Canadian public. Steamship and railroad tickets were taxed, as were items such as coffee, sugar, tobacco, cheques, and telegrams. Tariffs increased. It was clear from the beginning that indirect taxation would not suffice and in 1916 the federal government passed its first direct taxation measure, a power that the **British North America Act** had reserved for the provincial level of government. It was a tax on profits made from war materials. It was not the last such tax and in 1917, with bills mounting, the federal government introduced Canada's first income tax, assuring the public that it was a temporary measure. The new taxation, however, came nowhere near meeting the government's wartime obligations. The rest would have to be raised by borrowing.

Canada was already in debt when the war broke out. Years of railroad construction and subsidies had pushed government expenditures well beyond its income. The problem with wartime debt was where was there money available to borrow? Britain, a traditional source of credit for Canadian enterprise, was strapped beyond her capacity to pay and indeed would become a debtor nation to Canada by the end of the war. The United States was an economy that, free from wartime expenditure and flush with war profits, became one source of credit. The other, more important Canadian source, starting in 1915 and continuing throughout the war, were a series of federal government bonds that would raise Can $2.3 billion. Provincial and municipal governments were also looking for credit during the war and when the resultant burden was added to the federal numbers Canada emerged from the war with a debt of close to $5 billion.

While spending helps create employment it also causes prices to increase. When this spending is undertaken by the government on a scale like that required by the First World War, inflation is bound to be significant. The Borden government had taken Canada off the gold standard early in the war and began to print money. When this was added to the dramatically increased demand in the war years, prices almost doubled. The war also put strains on world supply that exerted an upward pressure on prices.

> **British North America Act** This was an 1867 Act of the British parliament that established and governed self-government in Canada–it, in essence, formed part of the Canadian constitution until 1981 when the constitution became a solely Canadian document.

A question of leadership

The war brought into sharper focus an issue that Canada and her leaders had been grappling with increasingly over the preceding 20 years—namely the dominion's relationship with Great Britain. The simple fact that a declaration of war by the British Parliament committed Canada to war highlighted the limited nature of Canada's independence as did the fact that her constitution was in fact an Act of the British Parliament and would remain so into the 1980s. It is true that when the British Parliament declared war in August 1914, there was no hesitation on the part of both Borden and Laurier, himself somewhat cool to imperial integration. Canada would commit completely to Britain's cause. But as Canada's commitment grew and the war dragged on in its vicious stalemate, questions of dominion sovereignty began to emerge. Nowhere was this more clear than in the matter of the leadership of Canadian troops.

At the outset of the war, the British High Command gave brief consideration as to how the Canadian troops would be distributed among existing British formations, but very early determined to use the Canadians as a division led by a British general. Borden favored the idea that Canadian officers would lead these units. While he was largely successful in these efforts, the Canadian Expeditionary Force (CEF) would become, for operational purposes, part of the British army. Operationally, the Canadian troops would gradually come ever more under the Canadian commanders as the war progressed with Sir Arthur Currie becoming the first Canadian-born commander of the Canadian corps in 1917. But the overall direction of military operations was another matter.

Throughout 1914 and the first half of 1915, Prime Minister Borden began to realize that the Canadian troops had essentially been turned over to the British government to do with as they pleased, short of splitting them up. While this might have been inconsequential had the war been over by Christmas and Canada's contribution remained proportionally small, by the summer of 1915 it was becoming evident that the war was going to be a long, brutal and grinding affair and that the Canadian contribution was growing in significance. Borden found it increasingly difficult to accept that he and the Canadian parliament had no say in the policy and strategy that its troops would execute. Facing staggering casualty figures with no end in sight, Borden traveled to Britain in the summer of 1915 to assess the situation for himself and argue for a more significant decision-making role for his Dominion.

Finding no answers and plenty of condescension from the British government and military officials, Borden returned to Canada determined to raise enough soldiers for the cause that Canada's concerns could not be ignored. It was not until the horrific battles of 1916 decimated Allied ranks and David Lloyd George became the Coalition leader of a new British government that this situation began to change. In January 1917, Lloyd George convened and Imperial War Conference and the Dominion leaders formed into an Imperial War Cabinet. Two things became evident at the Cabinet table: Britain expected even more from her imperial partners and, in turn, the dominions wanted a change in their status.

Discussion point

Canada emerged from the First World War with a greater degree of sovereignty than it had in 1914. Was this the same in the cases of the other dominions -Australia, New Zealand and South Africa?

Quebec

The initial wartime consensus welded together by war fervor and patriotic outpouring soon began to show cracks and as might be expected these were most evident in French–English relations. Wilfred Laurier, ever an eloquent advocate of Canadian unity, never wavered in his exhortations to cooperation. But as the war dragged on, recruiting numbers began to reveal a perceived gap between English volunteers and French volunteers. Lack of distinct French military units and a perceived prejudice against French officers combined with anti-French language legislation in both Ontario and Manitoba to further enflame a tense situation. The Quebec nationalists had furthered their alliance with the Conservatives early in the war by joining Borden's government. The *nationaliste* leader, Henri Bourassa, however, had turned publicly against the war by 1916.

Much of this was brought to a head by the conscription crisis and subsequent 1917 federal election campaign. The Liberal Party under Laurier, whose power stretched across the Quebec/Ontario border, was severely split by the question of conscription. Many Ontario and western Liberals who either supported conscription or recognized the prevailing political winds crossed to join Borden's new Unionist government, leaving the aging Laurier feeling betrayed and with only a few Quebec MPs.

In the streets, conscription proved deeply unpopular in Quebec. Riots and protests spread across the province and with them denunciations of treason by pro-conscription advocates. Order was restored with the help of the War Measures Act. When the dust of the 1917 election settled, Quebec found itself with its MPs in parliamentary opposition and with conscription a reality. While to the community of nation states the First World War helped propel Canada toward nationhood, within its borders Canada was more divided in 1918 than it had been in 1914.

Political unity and division

When the British government tumbled into war in August 1914 dragging her Empire over the edge with her, the news was greeted with pledges of cooperation and support from politicians on both sides of the House of Commons. Wilfred Laurier put aside his pre-war Imperial misgivings and ranged his Liberal Party behind the Borden government. Henri Bourassa, although personally opposed to the war, would not speak against the war as a politician until 1916. His parliamentary followers backed the government, as many had in the years preceding the war. This united front, however, was built more on circumstances than it was on deeper political principles. There was agreement on the ends, but not the means. All could agree if not on the necessity of supporting Great Britain, then at least on opposing the dangers of "Prussianism" and the evils of an unprovoked expansionary war. How that was to be accomplished was another matter.

The government's approach to meeting these ends was to place a great deal of power, money and trust in the controversial minister of the militia. Sam Hughes was a bombastic, stubborn, energetic politician who had little use for the formalities of parliamentary government or his own prime minister. He did, however, have a great deal of use for people who supported him and the quirky ideas that took his fancy. His championing of the Ross rifle, a fine target weapon, but unsuitable for the dirty rigors of trench warfare, left the riding (electoral district) in which it was produced flush with employment and the Ross Rifle Company flush with profits, but Canadian soldiers bereft of a workable rifle in France. His lack of a centralized recruiting system created chaos at the same time as tens of thousands of Canadians signed up. Mounting scandals and criticism finally pushed Borden to fire Hughes in 1916.

The corruption that accompanied Hughes' "system" as well as non-Hughes related scandals, brought political opposition to the Borden government's handling of the war. A number of Liberals had been calling for a coalition government from early in the war and these calls increased in intensity as 1916, with its seemingly endless casualty lists, dragged on. Borden himself began to see that this was going to be necessary before the end of the war. It was the combination of dwindling enlistment numbers and growing casualty lists that would bring about the formation of a Union Government.

The conscription crisis

Unable to maintain voluntary enlistment numbers that could sustain the Canadian Corps in the face of battlefield losses, Prime Minister Borden decided that the only alternative was conscription and in May 1917 announced it to the House of Commons. After announcing it, he approached Laurier with the prospect of forming some kind of coalition government, not necessarily with Borden as prime minister. Laurier, struck by the fact that the prospect of conscription was raised before he was approached, essentially asking his endorsement rather than his input, declined and set himself against conscription.

The Military Service Act was debated throughout the summer of 1917 and passed by August. It would call up single men first and provide for conscientious objectors. Borden hoped it would raise an additional 100,000 men for the Canadian Corps. Borden was unable to persuade opposition leader Laurier into a coalition government and his inability to get the opposition Liberals to consent to a further year's postponement of a general election meant that conscription would be decided largely at the polls. To bolster the chances of victory, the government drafted and passed the Military Voters Act. This Act provided for soldiers serving overseas to cast a vote. As if to underscore the fact that it was essentially a one-issue election, they could either cast a "yes" or "no" vote for the current government. Alternatively, they could write in the name of a candidate if they knew it. A helpful list of government candidates accompanied the ballots. The Wartime Elections Act significantly extended to the franchise to female relatives of serving and deceased soldiers. The same Act removed the franchise from those immigrants who had come to Canada from enemy countries after 1902.

As it became increasingly obvious that the pro-conscription forces would win the looming election, many English-speaking Liberals

Discussion point

To what extent do you think the Wartime Elections Act was based on ideas of gender equality? How did it contribute to the fight for granting the vote to women?

Activity

The Canadians in battle

From their initial blooding in 1915, the Canadians took part in numerous battles on the western front. Research the following battles to complete the following chart.

Battle	Dates	Canadian Commanders	Description	Significance
2nd Ypres				
St. Eloi				
The Somme				
Courcelette				
Vimy Ridge				
Hill 70				
Passchendaele				
The 100 Days				

began to take Borden up on an offer to accept them into what he called a Union Government. Regardless of how these politicians read the prevailing winds, the general election of 1917 was a hard-fought affair that revealed the issue of conscription to be divisive across the country. In an effort to secure the western farm vote, Borden announced that farmer's sons would be exempt from military service. The outcome of the election returned a Unionist government with a 71-seat majority. Closer examination of the returns reflected the divided nature of the country that had emerged in the campaign. Quebec and the Maritimes had gone heavily against the Unionists, but Borden was able to carry the day on the strength of Ontario and Western Canada. In terms of the popular vote, Quebec had voted four to one against the Unionist government while the rest of Canada had voted in favor of it by a margin of almost three to one. Not surprisingly serving soldiers voted overwhelmingly for the Unionists and by association for conscription.

In an effort to win the election of 1917, the Union government had promised a number of conscription exemptions—farmers' sons and Mennonites for example—but the sheer number of those seeking exemption ran the appeals mechanism to a standstill. The conscription machinery in Quebec proved incapable of compelling a largely unwilling population to register for the draft. Faced with the alarming casualties at the beginning of 1918, Borden and his cabinet ended most exemptions causing violence to erupt in Ontario and Quebec. In the west, the violence was often turned on those seeking exemptions. The divisions created by conscription would continue to the end of the war.

Activity

Wartime elections

Compare and contrast the issues, electoral tactics, and results of the following wartime elections:

- Argentina, 1916
- Canada, 1917
- Canada, 1940
- United States, 1944
- United States, 1952
- United States, 1968
- United States, 2004

Activity

The conscription debate

Divide into two groups. One group will take the pro-conscription position and the other will take the anti-conscription position. Conduct a debate on whether or not the Canadian government should pass conscription into law in 1917. In researching your positions be sure to include a representative sample of perspectives including:

- The Maritimes
- The Western Prairies
- British Columbia
- English-speaking Quebecers
- French-speaking Quebecers
- Immigrants
- Families of soldiers
- Members of the Conservative Party
- Members of the Liberal Party
- Labor leaders

By the end of the war, some 24,000 conscripts had made it to the front and were assigned as reinforcements to existing formations within the Canadian corps and many played an important role in the battles that took place in the last three months of the war. While it can be argued that conscription was necessary to maintain Canada's overseas fighting strength, which it did, it was bought at the cost of the national unity that appeared to be forming at the beginning of the war and the division thus engendered would continue throughout the century.

At the front

The first contingent of the Canadian Expeditionary Force arrived in England in October 1914 and soon began a haphazard training at their quarters on the infamous windswept, cold and wet Salisbury plain. While the bulk of Canadian troops would serve as a distinct division and later corps in the British army, some units served in other British formations. The Princess Patricia's Canadian Light Infantry, a unit raised in Canada at the outset of the war consisting of Canadians with British military experience, initially served within a British division. Some Canadian specialist units served in other theatres of war, but the vast majority were stationed at various points on the western front throughout the war.

The Canadians arrived in France in February of 1915. After some minor engagements in March, in April the Canadian brigades were stationed in the Ypres Salient, a bulge in the British line near the ancient cloth-making town of Ypres. On April 22, the Germans opposite the Canadians, who were flanked by French and Algerians, released chlorine gas for the first time on the western front. The ensuing 2nd Battle of Ypres was a chaotic and bloody affair that revealed the Canadians as inexperienced but courageous soldiers.

The shortcomings of the Ross rifle were becoming dangerously evident and Canadian soldiers would abandon them for the more robust Lee Enfield of the British army whenever they could.

With the arrival of the second contingent in mid 1915, the Canadians were formed into a corps commanded by a British general with the component divisions being commanded by Canadian generals. The Canadian Corps began to gain reputation as skillful trench raiders and eventually as shock troops leading larger assaults on German lines. By 1917, the Canadian Corps, by then consisting of four divisions, was given the task of capturing Vimy Ridge, a commanding position that the French army had been unable to wrestle from the German army. This operation, to commence on April 9, was to be Canadian in conception, planning, and execution. General Arthur Currie took note of previous failures and determined not to repeat them had his corps meticulously rehearse the plan behind the lines. Innovations such as platoon tactics, new methods for counterbattery targeting as well as ensuring that all men, especially non-commissioned officers, understood their objectives and how to find them both on a map and in reality helped make the operation a huge success.

The peace

From Borden's first wartime visit to England it was evident that he believed the scale of Canada's commitment entitled her to a share in determining the direction of the conflict. While this was not immediately evident to the British authorities, by the time David Lloyd George formed the Imperial War Cabinet, it was fairly clear that the role of the Dominions would have to be redefined.

The British assumed that the Dominions would be consulted, but submit as subordinate to the British delegation at the Peace Conference. Borden would have none of this; Canada must have a seat at the conference on her own merits and the merits of her contribution to the Allied victory. Canadian delegates sat on committees that decided some aspects of the final treaty. Their position on the whole can be seen as a mixture of US and British sentiments. Borden refused the notion that Canada might benefit from German territorial concessions. While Borden may have seen Canada's new position in the world as ideal to act the middle ground between Britain and the United States, Wilson saw it quite differently. Wilson and other US diplomats preferred to deal with Britain on matters involving Canada. Britain could be counted on to arrive at compromise more quickly than Canada, having little direct interests in much of Canada–US relations. Article X of the League of Nations Covenant providing for international response to aggressive acts, was as much a concern for Borden as it was for US opponents of the treaty. He was worried that this clause might drag Canada into another European war—her hands tied this time by the League as it had been by the British Empire in 1914. Canada also opposed any part of the League of Nations Covenant that might curtail her ability to limit immigration based on race or any other criterion. In the end, Canada became a signatory to the Treaty of Versailles separate from the British delegation. Likewise, she was admitted to the League of Nations as a country.

The impact of the First World War on Canada

Demobilization

Canada had mobilized close to 9% of her total 1914 population for the war effort. Close to 60,000 of these had not returned, but reintegrating those scores who did return into an economy that was no longer buoyed by wartime demand was going to be a difficult task. For the most part, the government made little provision to provide for demobilized soldiers. They were given money for civilian clothing, access to medical care for a year and some help, depending on where they were, in finding a job. Those so inclined and deemed good investments could apply for a low-interest loan to purchase farmland. Remaining free land was made available to veterans, but this was far from prime agricultural land. Beyond this, the veterans were left largely to their own devises. Nevertheless, the veterans were reintegrated into the economy with fewer problems than might have been expected. While the veterans integrated into society, organized labor struggled to adjust to the new ideological and economic landscape. When the Bolsheviks seized control in Russia in 1917, it invigorated left-wing politics in Canada. As in the United States, this prompted a reaction by the Canadian government who worked to shut foreign language newspapers and banned a number of "radical" organizations in 1918. The economic disruption prompted by the end of the war, helped spark a number of radical labor actions in the immediate postwar period, the most significant being the Winnipeg General Strike of 1919 which shut this major western Canadian city down for six weeks, prompting sympathy strikes across the country.

Economic changes

The Canadian economy itself had undergone a significant restructuring during the war. Manufacturing played a far greater role in 1919 than it had in 1914. Not only had existing sectors expanded, but new areas of activity also expanded. Textiles and chemical production had expanded with the wartime demand and the decline of British imports. It would prove far less expensive to convert wartime industries to civilian production than to build these from scratch and thus the war provided and important accelerant to Canadian manufacturing. Despite the advances in manufacturing, expanded land under cultivation, new forests and mineral deposits being exploited, the war had created another important structural shift in the Canadian economy. The relative weakness of the British economy and strength of the US economy meant that, increasingly, the United States replaced Great Britain as Canada's leading trading partner, creditor and foreign investor.

Diplomatic changes

On the world stage, Canada took its independent membership in the League of Nations and the International Labour Organization very

Activity

Labor unrest

Compare and contrast labor unrest in the Americas in the immediate postwar period:

- United States
- Canada
- Argentina
- Brazil
- Central America

seriously. It did not take long after the war, however, for the reality of this independence to be tested. When, in 1922, Turkish forces tested the resolve of the British garrison at Chanak in the Straits, Britain summoned her Dominions to her side once again. Canada's Liberal prime minister, Mackenzie King, discovered the British assumption of Canadian aid in the press before he heard from the British government. King responded by declaring publicly that it would be the Canadian parliament that would decide if Canada would participate, not the British government. While the Chanak crisis was resolved without recourse to arms, it prompted a further clarification of Canada's international position. The conference that assembled at Lausanne to negotiate with the Turks did not include Canada to which King responded by stating that Canada would not be bound by any agreement to which she was not a signatory. The Liberal Mackenzie King continued the course set by the Conservative Borden at Versailles in 1923 when Canada signed the Halibut Treaty with the United States with no participation by the British—the first time that Canada had negotiated and signed a bilateral treaty on her own. By 1927, Canada had appointed a Canadian envoy to the United States who, for the first time, would officially act and work independently of the British embassy. The sovereignty that had begun on the battlefields of Flanders progressed throughout the 1920s.

Activity

Comparing the First World War in the Americas

	Argentina	Brazil	Canada	United States
Reason for involvement/ Noninvolvement				
Nature of Involvement				
Military role				
Economic role				
Diplomatic role				
Impact on society				
Impact on economy				
Impact on hemispheric status				

The impact of the First World War on Latin America

Economic conditions prior to the First World War

The end of the 19th century saw an incredible integration of the world economy. Goods, people and capital moved around the globe with increasing ease and in ever-growing amounts. Technology allowed for a uniform system of commodity prices to exist and thus trade to be more globalized. While this integration allowed consumers and producers around the world to take advantage of foreign markets and prices, it also exposed them to the vagaries of these markets. Changes in livestock prices in Canada could affect the price of Argentine beef and thus the life of Argentine ranchers. A catastrophe the scale of the First World War was bound to have profound effects on this global economy and all its participants whether they were a belligerent or not.

Latin American countries were certainly a part of this global economy. Massive amounts of European capital flowed into the region. By 1914, Great Britain had poured close to four billion dollars-worth of capital into Latin America. Large sums were also invested by France ($1.1 billion) and Germany ($.9 billion). Foreign capital was heavily invested in communication and transportation networks. The British enjoyed a telegraph monopoly in Argentina, Brazil and Uruguay while the US-owned Central and South American Telegraph Company was also heavily invested in the region. British and American banks were scattered throughout the continent facilitating the movement of this capital.

Latin America's major role in this global economy was as an exporter of commodities. Argentina exported wheat, corn, beef, and wool. Foreign capital and technology fueled the Chilean copper mining industry at the turn of the century. Chile's production of nitrates for the world market was also expanding rapidly, as were its wheat and wool industries in the years leading up to the First World War. Although Brazilian coffee production was volatile in the years leading up to the war it was nonetheless an incredibly important part of the Brazilian economy accounting for over half of the value of all Brazilian exports in the years 1870 to 1911. Significantly, for the coming war the primary consumers of Brazilian coffee were the United States, France and Germany. The Mexican export economy grew dramatically until 1911 and tended to be more diversified than other Latin American economies. Ranching, mining, as well as henequen and oil production were important elements in Mexico's export economy.

Latin America in the First World War	
Country	Status
Brazil	Declared War on Germany in 1917
Argentina	Neutral
Colombia	Neutral
Venezuela	Neutral
Perú	Broke diplomatic relations with Germany
Chile	Neutral
Uruguay	Broke diplomatic relations with Germany
Paraguay	Neutral
Ecuador	Broke diplomatic relations with Germany
Bolivia	Broke diplomatic relations with Germany
Nicaragua	Declared War on Germany in 1918
Guatemala	Declared War on Germany in 1918
Mexico	Neutral
Cuba	Declared War on Germany in 1917
Panama	Declared War on Germany in 1917
El Salvador	Neutral
Costa Rica	Declared War on Germany in 1918
Haiti	Declared War on Germany in 1918
Honduras	Declared War on Germany in 1918

Discussion point

What are the uses of nitrates? Why might the world demand for nitrates increased during this period?

Migration was also an important aspect of the prewar global economy. Europeans came to Latin America and these people were increasingly from Germany. Germany was taking an ever more aggressive approach to foreign policy with the Kaiser's imperial desire for "a place in the sun" and this included Latin America. By 1900, well over a quarter of a million Germans had emigrated to Brazil and some 120,000 to Chile. German migrants could be found throughout the region. At the turn of the century, where German people, business and money went, the German army would not be far behind, most notably in Chile where German officers instructed the Chilean army. The Germans also had a military presence in Argentina, Bolivia and Paraguay. The German High Command mapped out contingency plans for a war with the United States during this period which included operations in the Latin American region. German interest in the region raised the ire of the United States and was an important factor in its own ambitions to expand in the region throughout this period.

As war clouds gathered, there were signs that the world economy was beginning to change. Much of this had to do with the ascendance of the United States in international economic importance and the looming comparative decline of the British economy. While the British remained the most important foreign economic power in South America, in Central America the United States had made important inroads. It also had a strong presence in the economies of South American countries, especially those on the Pacific coast. These were changes that were to be accelerated by the outbreak of the First World War. Seen in this light, although there were drastic changes in Latin America as a result of the war, there were also elements of continuity in terms of trends that had begun prior to 1914.

The economic impact of the outbreak of war

The August 1914 outbreak of the war had been preceded by a short sharp world economic recession. Although this represented a dramatic slowdown in economic activity, the war brought things to a near standstill. Part of the reason was that the war immediately affected the physical and the financial apparatus by which world markets operated. Credit was no longer available, and insurance became scarce. There was an immediate impact on shipping as British ships, which carried the bulk of Latin American goods, waited for orders and naval escorts. Thus, shipping rates skyrocketed with the reduction in availability. These effects were fairly immediate but the increased demand that accompanies war had yet to be felt. The end result was that export economies that were dependent on foreign capital and foreign shipping, such as Latin American economies, were hit particularly hard very early in the war.

As they were reliant on foreign credit, predominantly from London, the outbreak of the war in which Great Britain had decided to participate placed immediate pressure on Latin American banks. Loans were called in. There were significant runs on banks and a number of governments responded by declaring "bank holidays" and placing temporary moratoriums on debt. The short-term credit upon which day-to-day business in Latin America and indeed the world depended began to collapse making even small domestic transactions difficult. The Argentine and Brazilian governments were also dependent on long-term loans, as were all the governments that ran deficit budgets as part of their national finances, and these too suffered.

It might be expected that export economies, would fare well in wartime with its dramatically increased demand for everything from food to chemicals and minerals. But this took some time to filter through. For example, Chile was one of the world's leading producers of nitrates (key components in both fertilizer and explosives): two products in particular demand in wartime. But in the early months of the war, other factors conspired to hurt Chilean nitrate sales. The prewar recession and slump in prices meant that many countries carried surplus supplies of nitrates into late 1914. Much of Chile's nitrate sales were to central European countries with close to a third of these sales to Germany. The British naval blockade closed this market creating a nitrate surplus in Chile as well. Only when the incredible destruction of the war continued into 1915 did the massive demand for nitrates among other goods erode the surpluses and increase exports.

By 1915, Latin American economies had begun to recover from the initial shock of the war. The massive demand for the raw materials of war fueled this recovery. Although the volume of exports would not completely recover due to the interruption of shipping and capital, the demand drove prices dramatically higher and therefore the income from exports did recover by 1916. Wartime demand also sparked a rise in international inflation, pushing the price of imports higher. Eventually, as in most other national economies during the war, domestic inflation followed. The price of food in Argentina rose by 50% during the war and clothing in some cases tripled in price. Financial mechanisms such as currency exchange systems also began to improve in Latin America in the second year of the war making it easier to conduct business than it had been when the war broke out. The international value of the US dollar and the pound sterling began to stabilize. Nevertheless, the amount of foreign capital that was directed at infrastructure and capital building projects did not recover. In general, the governments of Latin America responded to the unavailability of foreign loans by curtailing public works and other major projects. Some loans were secured in the United States and others through domestic bonds, but on the whole austerity was the primary response.

The debt problem of many Latin American economies was compounded during the war by the fact that around 50% of states' revenues came in the form of duties. With the slump in imports, this revenue stream was cut dramatically. Some countries, such as Brazil, responded to this revenue shortfall by printing money with the predictable inflationary effects, already extreme, due to supply and demand issues created by the war.

Discussion point

What other minerals and chemicals were needed in the war effort. From where did the Allies and the Central Powers import these goods?

The combination of fiscal austerity and domestic inflation created a volatile labor situation in a number of Latin American countries. By 1917, employment was rising in Argentina, as were consumer prices. Real wages were falling. Consequently labor union activity increased drastically during this period. When the government seemed to side with the workers in these instances they were quickly denounced as pro-German, especially by British business interests. In January 1919, Buenos Aires erupted in a violent general strike that started in the Vesena metal works and quickly spread to other sectors in which a number of strikers and police officers were killed. In this case, the government ordered the army to end the strike and a week of violence, arrests and many deaths followed—a period known as the "Tragic Week." This week was followed by a period of popular reprisals against Russian and Jewish communities in the country, fueled by the belief that the general strike was a prelude to a Bolshevik-like revolution. The war and related events seemed to spark unrest beyond the labor movement in Argentina. Student movements, influenced by the Mexican and Russian revolutions, staged strikes and demonstrations calling for academic reform and these demonstrations did find support from the Yrigoyen government despite its violent suppression of the general strike.

In the end, the effect of the war on the various economies of Latin America depended to a degree on the state of these economies at the outset of the war. Countries such as Brazil and Chile, which had begun to industrialize in the prewar years, used the wartime demand to accelerate industrial output during this period. Perú, Colombia and countries with stronger trade ties with the United States built on these ties during the war and therefore had to substitute for lost imports to a lesser degree than those economies more dependent on European trade. The less industrially developed economies of Central America saw in the war a disruption to their regular economic activity to which they would return at the end of hostilities. Regardless, all these economies would return to export dependence after 1919.

As with Canada, one overarching result of the war in Latin America was the growth in importance of the United States at the expense of European economies, particularly the United Kingdom. US representatives, private and official, advocated this course from very early in the war. The United States government used forums such as the Pan American Financial Conference held in Washington in 1915 to make the point that the outbreak of the war highlighted the problem of relying on European countries economically and to suggest that a more hemispheric approach was desirable. Trade with the United States increased drastically during the war, especially in the west coast economies such as Perú and Chile. The flow of US capital also increased during these years. This increase was not uniform; Brazil and Argentina, for example, did not see much of an increase in US economic activity. In some ways, the United States economy was not predisposed to supplant the British economy either in the region or globally. As Bill Albert has pointed out, the United

States would become increasingly protectionist in the postwar period. The United States also produced a great deal of primary products on its own and was interested in protecting and growing these industries, whereas the domestic British economy produced far less primary goods. These factors meant that although the United States would become more economically dominant in Latin America it would not replace the United Kingdom. Albert also contends that the immediate dislocation caused by the war spurred nationalist sentiments in a number of Latin American countries. In fact, once the United States joined the war, neutrality itself became a point of nationalism as was the case in Colombia.

Noneconomic issues

Throughout the first years of the war, it was Latin America's strategic location that conditioned its role in the war. The terms of neutrality permitted the presence of ships for a 24-hour period in a neutral harbor and both sides availed themselves of this provision in terms of Latin American ports. Naturally, it led to both abuse and accusations of abuse by both sides. German ships were seized on more than one occasion. Latin American goods and ships were subject to the German U-Boat campaign and the British Royal Navy conducted operations in the territorial waters of some Latin American states such as Chile.

Brazil was the only Latin American country to participate in the war beyond a symbolic declaration of war. After the United States entered the war, and after a number of German attacks on Brazilian shipping, Brazil drifted to a more rigorous pro-Ally "neutrality." The April 5, 1917, sinking of the Brazilian ship *Parana* resulted in anti-German rioting in Rio de Janeiro, the expulsion of the German ambassador and the severing of diplomatic ties between the two countries. By late October 1917, Brazil had formally declared war on Germany and the Central Powers. Her main contribution would be to providing naval support in patrolling South American waters and minesweeping activities on the west coast of Africa. By mid-1918, Brazil sent a nominal number of troops to the western front as well as a medical detachment. Brazil's participation in the Paris Peace Conference provided the opportunity to argue for compensation for Brazilian goods confiscated by the Central Powers.

Structure of prewar/wartime exports 1910–14/1915–18		
Country	**1910–12**	**1915–18**
Argentina	Wheat 19.4%	Wheat 12.9%
	Corn 17.9%	Corn 9.6%
	Linseed 10.2%	Linseed 5.4%
	Hides 10.2%	Hides 9%
	Wool 12.9%	Wool 12.9%
	Frozen Beef 7.6%	Frozen beef 15.3%
		Tinned meat 5.9%
Brazil	Coffee 54.2%	Coffee 47.4%
	Rubber 27.9%	Rubber 8.8%
		Hides and skins 7.7%
		Sugar 4.5%
Chile	Nitrates and Iodine 86%	Nitrates and Iodine 74.6%
	Copper 8%	Copper 17.3%
Perú	Sugar 17.5%	Sugar 27.6%
	Cotton 13.8%	Cotton 18.3%
	Copper 20.5%	Copper 26.3%
	Rubber 12.3%	Petroleum 7.5%
	Petroleum 6.3%	Wool 7%

Source: Albert, Bill & Henderson, Paul. 1988. *South America and the First World War: The Impact of the War on Brazil, Argentina, Peru and Chile*. Cambridge: Cambridge University Press. p. 59.

Activity

Brazil's rationale for war

Letter from the Brazilian Foreign Minister Lauro Müller to the Imperial German Government, February 6, 1917.

The unexpected communication we have just received announcing a blockade of the wide extent of countries with which Brazil is continually in economic relations by foreign and Brazilian shipping has produced a justified and profound impression through the imminent menace which it contains of the unjust sacrifice of lives, the destruction of property, and the wholesale disturbance of commercial transactions.

In such circumstances, and while observing always and invariably the same principles, the Brazilian Government, after having examined the tenor of the German note, declares that it cannot accept as effective the blockade which has just been suddenly decreed by the Imperial Government.

Because of the means employed to realize this blockade, the extent of the interdicted zones, the absence of all restrictions, including the failure of warning for even neutral menaced ships, and the announced intention of using every military means of destruction of no matter what character, such a blockade would neither be regular nor effective and would be contrary to the principles of law and the conventional rules established for military operations of this nature.

For these reasons the Brazilian Government, in spite of its sincere and keen desire to avoid any disagreement with the nations at war, with whom it is on friendly terms, believes it to be its duty to protest against this blockade and consequently to leave entirely with the Imperial German Government the responsibility for all acts which will involve Brazilian citizens, merchandise, or ships and which are proven to have been committed in disregard of the recognized principles of international law and of the conventions signed by Brazil and Germany.

Questions

1 What is meant by "the means employed to realize this blockade?"
2 How does this justification compare to the rationale for war in the United States and Canada?
3 Brazil would not declare war until October 1917. Why the delay?
4 With reference to its origin and purpose, assess the value and limitations of this document for historians studying the First World War.
5 Draft a response to this letter from the Imperial German Government.

Activity

Latin America and the First World War

The previous section deals primarily with the economic impact of the war on the Latin American region. Choose a Latin American country and conduct more in-depth research on the impact of the war looking at a variety of factors. This will allow you to come to some conclusions about the important historical theme of continuity vs. change. To what extent did the war represent a continuation of prewar trends or a disruption of those trends? Use the following chart to help organize your research.

	Pre-1914	Post-1918
Economics		
Social structures		
Labor relations		
Domestic politics		
Diplomatic relations		
Culture		

Exam practice and further resources

Sample exam questions

1 "The causes minor, the effects major." To what extent do you agree with this view of the Spanish–American War (1898)?

2 How significant was the First World War for the status of the United States in the region?

3 "The arguments against taking part in the First World War were stronger than those for joining in." Discuss this view with regard to either Canada or one Latin American country.

4 For what reasons and with what results did US foreign policy change between 1880 and 1929?

5 Compare and contrast the political impact of the First World War on two countries of the region.

Recommended further reading

Latin America

Bill Albert & Paul Henderson.1988. *South America and the First World War: The Impact of the War on Brazil, Argentina, Peru and Chile.* Cambridge: Cambridge University Press.

Leslie Bethell (ed). 1986. *The Cambridge History of Latin America.* Cambridge: Cambridge University Press.

United States

George C. Herring. 2008. *From Colony to Superpower: U.S. Foreign Relations Since 1776.* Oxford & New York: Oxford University Press.

Paul A. Kramer, Paul A. 2006. *The Blood of Government: Race, Empire, the United States & the Philippines.* Chapel Hill: University of North Carolina Press.

Edmund.Morris. 2001. *Theodore Rex.* New York: Random House.

Evan Thomas. 2010. *The War Lovers: Roosevelt, Lodge, Hearst, and the Rush to Empire, 1898.* New York: Little, Brown and Co.

G. J. A. O'Toole. 1986. *The Spanish War: An American Epic 1898.* New York: W. W. Norton & Company.

Canada

Desmond Morton & J. L. Granatstein. 1989. *Marching to Armageddon: Canadians and the Great War, 1914–1919.* Toronto: Lester & Orpen Dennys.

4 The Great Depression and the Americas, 1929–39

What became known as the Great Depression was a severe and persistent worldwide economic downturn that began in 1929 and ended in 1941. The economic interconnectedness of nations in a world of increasing trade and investment across oceans resulted in economic distress that included causes beyond the borders of any individual country. Most nations in all six populated continents, whether their economies were based on industry or agriculture, were deeply affected. In the Americas, it was the most serious economic collapse in history. The Depression had many effects, ranging from starvation to the fall of governments. Political leaders from different countries tried a variety of solutions with varying success. In many countries the Great Depression resulted in changes that lasted decades beyond the period itself. Through studies of the United States, Canada, Brazil and Argentina, this chapter is designed to examine the causes, conditions, solutions, and effects of the Great Depression in the Americas 1929–39.

The study will begin with an examination of the Great Depression in the United States with special attention paid to the causes and the steps taken by presidents Herbert Hoover and Franklin D. Roosevelt, examining the New Deal at length. The United States section will also examine how different minority groups were affected, and include a look at the role New Deal programs had in the fine and popular arts. The section ends with a discussion of different theories on the effectiveness of the United States' response to the crisis.

The chapter continues with a study of the Great Depression in Canada, looking at economic, social, and political conditions during the decade of the 1930s. It presents and assesses the responses of Prime Minister Mackenzie King and his successor R.B. Bennett.

The Latin American section continues with case studies of Brazil and Argentina, and the important role of Import Substitution Industrialization (ISI) policies in coping with the loss of international markets, especially those of the United Kingdom and the United States. Each case study concludes with an analysis of the economic and political results.

In reading the chapter, students should look at the Great Depression as a significant economic event that had immediate and lasting effects on the countries and peoples of the Americas. The unit is designed as a comparative one in which candidates are expected to learn about a variety of countries within the Americas and be able to write an assortment of essays employing knowledge from across the region.

By the end of this chapter, students should be able to:

● discuss the political and economic causes of the Great Depression in the Americas

● analyze the nature and efficacy of solutions in the United States, as provided by presidents Hoover and Franklin D Roosevelt, in reference in particular to the New Deal

● assess the response to the Great Depression in Canada of prime ministers William Lyon Mackenzie King and RB Bennett

● evaluate Latin American responses to the Great Depression in Brazil and Argentina and the effects of the policies of Import Substitution Industrialization (ISI)

● recognize the impact of the Great Depression on society, and the particular effects on women and ethnic minorities

● review the impact of the Great Depression on the arts and popular culture.

The Great Depression in the United States

Panics had been a part of US economic patterns from the beginning of the republic. The nation was less than ten years old when the first recession hit, and from 1819 onward there was at least one panic during each decade up to the Great Depression. Economic downturns were frequent in the last decade of the 19th century and the first decade of the 20th century, occurring every three to four years. After the **Panic** of 1911, the economy continued to grow until late 1929, when the stock market crashed and a variety of economic ills quickly followed. The **recession** turned into a depression by the follow year, and lasted a full decade. The Great Depression was the longest and deepest economic downturn in the history of the United States.

> **Panic** A general fear of a stock market crash that results in massive sales of stock, driving share prices quickly downward.

> Economists generally define a **recession** as two or more consecutive quarters (three month periods) of negative growth.

This section will examine the economic and political causes of the Great Depression, the policies and programs of Herbert Hoover and Franklin D. Roosevelt, the effects of the Depression and the efforts at countering it by the government, and the path and uses of the creative arts during the era. The events of the Great Depression had lasting effects of the lives of those who lived through it and future generations.

Causes of the Depression

It is difficult to separate the economic and political causes of the Great Depression. The Depression can be divided into phases and each phase examined for causes. The first phase is the period leading up to and including the crash of 1929. The second phase is the period from late 1929 to 1933 as the country moved from panic to deep depression. The third phase is from 1933 to 1937, which was a period of recovery, and the fourth phase from 1937 to 1941, ended with the United States joining the Second World War.

The 1920s was a time of economic growth and political conservatism in the United States. Calvin Coolidge, a Republican, occupied the White House from 1921 until 1929. A pro-business president, who once said, "The chief business of the American people is business," Coolidge practiced a hands-off policy towards the nation's economy. The businessman was king, regulation was relaxed, and the era of the **Titans of Wall Street** was born. Successful stock brokers and speculators became national celebrities. For eight years stock prices rose and for the first time many ordinary people owned stock. The price rise was fueled by speculation and easy credit. Instead of buying shares with cash, investors borrowed from banks: **buying on margin**. A buyer would put down 10% of the stock price and borrow 90%. The unprecedented extension of credit provided additional stimulus to the market, forcing prices higher and inducing more people into the market. But the market was manipulated by large investors who would combine money to make large purchases of stock, driving prices up. Small investors seeing the price rise bought the stock, hoping to ride the price up and make quick money. When the price reached went high enough, the large investors sold and took profits, leaving only small investors holding stocks.

Expansion of credit also helped fuel consumer demand. Many new household appliances such as washing machines, refrigerators, and air conditioners arrived in stores. The extension of consumer loans allowed manufacturers and retailers to move the new products into homes, but also increased personal debt. The banks' confidence in low-collateral loans followed the common thought of the time that the economy had changed permanently. The patterns of panic and recovery that had been the rhythm of the previous century no longer applied in the new economy. The Federal Reserve Bank, whose responsibility it was to smooth out economic bumps and anticipate problems, stayed on the sidelines, further enabling the expansion of credit. Most economists of the era believed that the economic fundamentals had changed. However, a minority of economists thought differently. They looked at the market fundamentals and saw a large sell-off coming.

There were signs of economic troubles ahead. Farm prices were dropping from overproduction. In the spring of 1929, car sales, steel production, and construction declined. Nevertheless, over the summer months stock prices doubled, their purchase funded by increased debt. High confidence in the market remained. On September 3, the stock market reached its all-time high.

The crash of 1929

Stocks began to fall and the market took wild swings through the rest of the month. Bankers were, however, still convinced that the market was a secure investment. October continued the fluctuations. On October 24, the market crashed and large banks responded by announcing funds would be made available for purchasing stocks. The market appeared to stabilize. On October 29, Black Tuesday, the market crashed and the banks' efforts could not stop the sell-off.

The **Titans of Wall Street** were a group of bankers including J. P. Morgan Jr. and Charles Mitchell.

Buying on margin involved taking a loan for 90% of a stock's value in the belief that the share price would increase. For example, if a share was $100 a buyer could put down $10 and borrow $90, purchasing ten shares worth a total of $100. If the stock price increases to $12 a share, the shareholder could sell the ten shares for $120, pay back the $90, and have a $20 profit on an original investment of $10. A 20% rise in price yielded a 200% profit. But, if prices drop more than 10%, the lending bank issues a margin call when the price of the stock falls below the amount of the loan: the share owner must pay the bank the difference between the current value of the stocks and the loan. If the price continues to fall the owner must again make up the difference.

Activity

Causes of the Great Depression

Set up a table with causes. Suggested sectors include banking, business, government, the environment, and the stock market. After categorizing the causes, assess the relative importance of each in causing the Great Depression or making it more severe.

Causes of the Great Depression		
Sector	Cause	Relative importance

Confidence in the market fell along with stock prices, increasing the sell-off and forcing prices lower. Small investors lost their life savings in a day. Contrary to common thought, the crash alone did not lead directly to the Great Depression.

Several trends occurred in the 1920s that, when combined, can be said to have caused the Great Depression. While gross domestic product increased during the decade, so did income disparity. Uneven distribution of income resulted in wealth becoming concentrated in the upper classes: by 1929, almost one-half of families in the United States lived at subsistence level or below. The declining income of the lower classes reduced their purchasing power. Secondly, much of the economy depended upon the automobile and construction industries and the growing aviation, motion picture and consumer product companies were not large enough to take up the slack when construction fell by 20% in the three years preceding the crash, along with the decline in automobile sales. Productive capacity continued to grow during those same years, as capital flooded the market, eventually outstripping demand, resulting in layoffs and lower wages, which accelerated the decline in the purchasing power of the populace. At the same time that US industries were suffering from domestic economic weaknesses, the market for its products in Europe dropped. A combination of several European countries increasing production while other economies weakened because of turmoil, reparation payments, unpaid war debts and loan obligations caused a decline in the demand for goods from across the Atlantic. All of these developments combined with the unstable underlying economic foundation in the United States to produce an economic free fall.

President Hoover and Federal Reserve monetary policy

The president at the time of the crash was Herbert Hoover, who had been elected the year before, promising to continue Coolidge's policies of minimum government involvement, letting business do business. When the crash occurred, Hoover was unprepared to confront the turn of events. Philosophically, he did not believe in a forceful role for government in the economy. In the months that followed the crash, the actions and inactions of the Hoover administration, legislation passed by Congress, and policies of the Federal Reserve combined to cause a panic to become the deepest depression in the nation's history. Federal Reserve monetary policy, supported by Hoover and government economists, continued to take money out of the economy rather than increase the supply, mistaking deflation for inflation. Initially, Hoover did not try to directly stimulate the economy, believing it was not the business of the federal government to interfere with business. He reduced government spending as well, in the theory that less government involvement would enable the economy to recover. Farms continued to lose money and rural banks continued to fail without government help. Hoover continued in his belief that the people would help each other, that members of communities would fix their own problems. He did not recognize that devastated

Activity

Relevance

Applying history to the present

With the exception of very few countries, there was a worldwide recession that began in 2008 and continued at least until the end of 2010. Research statements made by leading economists, including the governors of the Federal Reserve Bank in the first decade of the 2000s. Then explore the causes of the first major fiscal crisis of this century. Respond to the following question in either an essay or class debate:

"In the decades of the 1920s and the 2000s the economic crisis was mostly caused by unsupported optimism that spurred people to conclude that the rules of the market had fundamentally changed."

communities did not have the resources to save themselves. In addition to mistaken fiscal action and government inaction, legislators reacted to economic distress by trying to protect the home market from foreign goods. In an attempt to save domestic producers Congress passed the Hawley-Smoot Tariff Act in June 1930. Hawley-Smoot, signed by Hoover, established a high protective tariff. The tariff caused other nations to retaliate with their own high tariffs, reducing exports worldwide by more than 50% and causing a deepening of the Depression.

Despite his reluctance to involve the federal government in the economy, Hoover was sensitive to the plight of Americans. Known as Mr. Rescue for his work in assisting postwar Europe and heading relief for the victims of the Great Flood of 1927, he summoned governors to the White House and encouraged them to accelerate infrastructure projects to employ workers. He urged corporations to keep employees on the job despite surplus inventories. He gave monetary assistance to troubled banks. The president established the Reconstruction Finance Corporation, an independent agency that granted loans to banks, railroads, states and local governments, and also spent more money on federal public works projects than any president before him. He hoped to create a solid infrastructure on which a stronger and more resilient economy could rise. Programs to provide credit to farmers and buy excess crops began, but only motivated farmers to grow more crops, consequently prices did not rise. Hoover did not give money to individuals as it was not the government's job to interfere with individual initiative. In fact, job loss and poverty was a sign of individual failure. To give money to the unemployed was to support failure: today that concept is called **moral hazard**. It was resurgent US individualism that would get the country out of the economic downturn.

Herbert Hoover (1874–1964)

Remembered by most Americans as the president who presided over the first years of the Great Depression, Herbert Hoover was an accomplished humanitarian and civil servant before his presidential term. Born in Iowa in 1874, he spent his childhood in Oregon, then earned a degree as a mining engineer from Stanford University in California.

After graduating, Hoover and his wife spent a few years in China, where he worked at his chosen profession. He returned stateside in 1900. In London, at the beginning of the Great War, Hoover organized food, clothing, and transportation home for thousands of stranded Americans. Later that year, and for the next two years he led food relief for Belgium, distributing millions of tons of supplies, becoming a hero to many. When the United States entered the war, Hoover took on administrative responsibilities in the government. After the war, he headed the American Relief Administration, responsible for distributing food to the millions of hungry Europeans. He also extended aid to the Soviet Union, telling his critics, "Twenty million people are starving. Whatever their politics, they shall be fed." Hoover eventually became Warren Harding's commerce secretary and continued serving in the Coolidge administration. When the Great Mississippi Flood of 1927 came, Hoover directed relief, including the eradication of several diseases in areas affected by the flood. Hoover's efforts helped millions of Americans. Hoover was elected president in 1928, having never run or held elective office. Well after his presidency ended, Hoover continued to serve. He went to Germany after the Second World War and organized food distribution for millions of starving children. At the requests of presidents Truman and Eisenhower, Hoover headed commissions to reform the executive branch. He died at the age of 90 in 1964.

A **moral hazard** occurs when a person or party is insured for a certain action. The insurance creates a situation in which the person or party will act in a risky or unproductive way contrary to behavior without the insurance. For example: the contents of a house is insured for loss from fire regardless of cause. A renter who does not pay for the insurance would be less likely to be careful than one whose belongings were not insured.

Social effects of the Depression

The economic downturn affected the entire country. Major cities in the Midwest, their factories stilled, saw unemployment rise above 50% by 1932. In Toledo, Ohio, 80% of workers were jobless.

Despite the shame that accompanied asking for help, increasing numbers asked the government for assistance, because charities could not handle the vast demand for help. Local and state officials were, however, unable to provide relief, as any programs that existed were minimal in the best of times. In cities across the nation men walked the streets looking for work. People searched garbage for food scraps and clothing. Soup kitchens saw lines go for block after block. Families split up as men left to look for work. Families that lost their homes moved to the outskirts of towns and cities. Shanty towns sprung up. The new settlements became known as Hoovervilles, named with anger directed at the ineffective action of the president.

In the heartland

While much of the discussion of the Great Depression focuses on cities, the financial sector, and industry, a long-term drought struck much of the middle part of the country, hitting farmers who were already suffering from a devastating drop in income. The drought began in 1930 and continued for a decade. While much of the United States and Canada was affected, the area of the southern Great Plains was particularly impacted. Years of farming practices, involving the removal of native grasses to be replaced with seasonal crops, deep plowing and failure to rotate crops to replace nutrients, took the deep and fertile top soil for granted. As the drought wore on, crops failed and farm animals were brought to the slaughter house in a desperate attempt to make some money. Many farms in Oklahoma, Texas, Nebraska and neighboring states were abandoned as the drought continued. The winds that often blow across the plains picked up the fine dust that a century before had been held down by tall grasses. The dust formed into massive clouds that darkened the sky, making breathing difficult and fouling farm machinery. The Dust Bowl was born. Over the next few years approximately 100 million acres of top soil blew away. In May 1934, a dust storm darkened skies as far away as Washington, D.C. The condition caused more than two million farmers, shop keepers, and white collar workers to leave the plains for California and other destinations. The Dust Bowl was a terrible ecological disaster that added another dimension to the Great Depression.

Hooverville on the outskirts of Seattle, Washington, on the tidal flats adjacent to the Skinner and Eddy Shipyards, Port of Seattle, June 10, 1937, one of many similar shanty settlements built by Americans who lost their homes during the Great Depression.

Deserted farm in Great Plains region of the United States. As a result of land misuse, erosion and years of drought, the ecological disaster known as the Dust Bowl lasted through the 1930s, resulting in useless farmland and homeless people in their hundreds of thousands.

Activity

Uses of film and the novel in history

The Grapes of Wrath

Read the following passages involving bank representatives foreclosing on tenant farmers from Dust Bowl farms in John's Steinbeck's *The Grapes of Wrath* (1939). Source A is from the novel, and source B is the script from the film version (Dir. John Ford, 1940).

Source A

The owner men sat in the cars and explained. You know the land is poor. You've scrabbled at it long enough. God knows.

The squatting tenant men nodded and wondered and drew figures in the dust, and yes, they knew, God knows. If the dust only wouldn't fly. If the top would only stay on the soil, it might not be so bad.

The owner men went on leading to their point: You know the land's getting poorer. You know what cotton does to the land; robs it sucks all the blood out of it. …

The squatting men raised their eyes to understand. Can't we just hang on? Maybe next year will be a good year … They looked up questioningly.

We can't depend on it. The bank—the monster—has to have profits all the time. It can't wait. It'll die.

Source B

Agent: The fact of the matter, Muley, after what them dusters done to the land, the tenant system don't work no more. You don't even break even, much less show a profit. Why, one man and a tractor can handle twelve or fourteen of these places. You just pay him a wage and take all the crop.

Muley: Yeah, but uh, we couldn't do on any less than what our share is now. Why, the children ain't gettin' enough to eat as it is, and they're so ragged. We'd be ashamed if everybody else's children wasn't the same way.

Agent: I can't help that. All I know is, I got my orders. They told me to tell you to get off, and that's what I'm tellin' ya.

Muley: You mean get off of my own land?

Agent: Now don't go to blamin' me! It ain't my fault.

Muley's son (Hollis Jewell): Who's fault is it?

Agent: You know who owns the land. The Shawnee Land and Cattle Company.

Muley: And who's the Shawnee Land and Cattle Company

Agent: It ain't nobody. It's a company.

Muley's son: They got a President, ain't they? They got somebody who knows what a shotgun's for, ain't they?

Agent: Oh son, it ain't his fault, because the bank tells him what to do.

Muley's son: All right, where's the bank?

Agent: Tulsa. What's the use of pickin' on him? He ain't nothin' but the manager. And he's half-crazy hisself tryin' to keep up with his orders from the East.

Muley: Then who do we shoot?

Agent: Brother, I don't know. If I did, I'd tell ya. I just don't know who's to blame.

Muley: I'm right here to tell you, mister, there ain't nobody gonna push me off my land! My grandpaw took up this land seventy years ago. My paw was born here. We was all born on it. An' some of us was killed on it. (Muley squats down and fingers the dust of the farm he has just lost.) An' some of us died on it. That's what makes it arn. Bein' born on it and workin' on it and dyin', dyin' on it. An' not no piece of paper with writin' on it.

Questions

1   Discuss in groups the effectiveness of using works of fiction to understand an historical period or event.

2   In what ways do these sources evoke the same understanding of the plight of the common man as the lyrics of "Do Re Mi" by Woody Guthrie (See lyrics on page 193) and the photographs of the Dust Bowl?

3   What is the significance of the designation of a company as the antagonist in the scene from the film?

4   What other cultural sources can be used to support the analysis of this period in history?

The effect of the Depression on minorities

An overview of the effect of the Great Depression on Americans must examine the consequences for African Americans, Hispanics, and women. Overall, the 1930s set all groups back, whatever economic gains had come about during the previous decades were lost.

African Americans

In some areas of the United States, African Americans had seen improvements during the 1920s, mostly in the northeast, as the Harlem Renaissance flourished. But in many ways, the 1920s represented stagnation as most African Americans failed to benefit from the economic growth of the decade. Lynchings continued into the decade, although less frequent than the number of killings at the turn of the century. In the economic downturn, African Americans lost the shaky economic status they had obtained. One-half of all blacks lived in the south. Rural southern blacks lost farms as cotton prices and other agricultural products dropped in price. In the cities, blacks lost jobs as white men took the low-pay, low-status jobs such as street cleaners and janitors. The farmers' first move was often into southern cities, where they joined other unemployed African Americans. Some whites formed groups to keep blacks out of work. "No Jobs for Niggers Until Every White Man has a Job!" is representative of the mood and obstacles blacks faced. By 1932, 75% of black people were unemployed compared to the general figure of 25%. Relief programs run by local governments went to whites first, leaving many black families malnourished and homeless. African Americans did benefit from several federal programs including the Public Works Administration, the Works Progress Administration, and the Farm Services Administration Schools. Blacks comprised a quarter of residents in federal housing projects.

Employment in government agencies often, but not always, followed non-discrimination regulations. In fact, Roosevelt appointed several blacks to positions within the administration, including attorney William Hastie, and Mary McLeod Bethune, an important adviser who played a significant role in the **Black Cabinet**. Some divisions harmed African-Americans. The Agricultural Adjustment Administration, whose policy enforcement favored landowners over tenant farmers, penalized blacks, who were mostly sharecroppers. The National Regulatory Authority's industrial non-discrimination wage policy encouraged businesses, especially in the south, to fire African American workers who had been paid significantly less. Federal programs, administered by local whites, often denied relief to African Americans. Intimidation, including lynchings, increased as the Depression deepened. Efforts by the the National Association for the Advancement of Colored People (NAACP) to pass a federal anti-lynching law, in response to the rise in lynchings, foundered as southern Democrats prevented its passage in the Senate. Black women were also affected as jobs as domestic servants went to white women. As a result of the worsening economic and social conditions, close to half a million blacks moved to northern cities to find work (in addition to the millions who moved north during the **Great Migration**

The **Black Cabinet** was a group of African-American leaders in the Roosevelt administration who, with the support of Eleanor Roosevelt, advised the president on a variety of issues.

The **Great Migration** was the movement of African Americans from the South to northern cities beginning in 1915 and continuing in ebbs and flows into the 1970s.

1915–30). When they arrived in the cities, however, there were few jobs available, as the cities were already devastated by factory closings and failed businesses.

African Americans in northern urban cities lost jobs as well. Men and women suffered high unemployment as factories and businesses closed, and as service and domestic work dried up. As elsewhere, job-loss rates for blacks significantly exceeded that for whites. Black women's jobless rates were often greater than that for men.

One bright spot for African Americans was the labor movement. One labor union, the Brotherhood of Sleeping Car Porters, founded by A. Philip Randolph, successfully negotiated the first contract between a black union and a US-based corporation, the Pullman Company, in 1937. Some factory owners attempted to use blacks as strike-breakers. Despite high black unemployment, the NAACP supported the all-white labor unions' job actions. As a result, 500,000 blacks joined labor organizations during the 1930s; in some unions they comprised a fifth of the membership.

Hispanic Americans

The Great Depression devastated Hispanic Americans as well. At the start of the Great Depression there were between one and a half and two million Latinos in the United States. The majority were of Mexican heritage and most lived in the southwest. Other Hispanics traced their heritage to Cuba, Puerto Rico, and the Dominican Republic, among other origins. Latinos lived in many northern cities as well. Though some Mexican Americans were long-established, most Hispanics worked the lowest paying jobs, whether in agriculture or industry. The agricultural jobs were often geographically transient, as workers followed crops, planting and harvesting. Low wages, long hours, and poor working conditions were commonplace. In the southwest United States Hispanics occupied similar socio-economic status to African Americans in the south. When the Depression hit Latinos suffered substantial job losses, as they were "last hired first fired." White program administrators wrongly claimed that many eligible Latinos were not citizens in order to deny them access to relief programs. The ill-treatment went further, as Latin American children were not allowed to enroll in school and hospitals often refused to admit them when ill or injured. There were a few exceptions: for example, the head of the Texas division of the National Youth Administration, Lyndon Baines Johnson, the future president, made sure that Hispanics benefitted from the program. But, because they were often treated as unwelcome aliens, regardless of citizenship status, as well the difficulty they had in creating stable institutions due to labor movement, Latinos frequently had little or no support both outside and within their own communities.

In the face of poverty and ill-treatment by employers, and local and state governments, Hispanics relocated. The mass movement within the United States resulted in a rise in the Latino urban population. The move into cities simply relocated their poverty into urban ghettos. As the city populations swelled, local governments tried to force Mexican Americans out. In raids on their *barrios* US citizens as well as true "illegals" were rounded up in the climate of discrimination and fear that motivated many to move. The intimidation caused close to a half-million Latinos to move to Mexico during the Great Depression. It is estimated that half of all Hispanic Americans relocated during the Great Depression.

Women

The effect of the Great Depression on the lives of women is characterized by a worsening of their circumstances, and increased responsibility, in the need to fend for themselves and their families when their husbands went on the road to find work. In the Dust Bowl region, entire families packed up their belongings and moved west; women fulfilling the traditional role of taking care of the family, even in migrant camps and on the side of the road. Some women became entrepreneurs, but most remained in traditional roles of wife and mother as the prevailing view that jobs should go to men was solidified by the falling economy. During the New Deal, women became more prominent in the federal government, but the changes were incremental rather than revolutionary.

The role of women in the workplace had been changing in the first decades of the 20th century. The percentage of women in the workforce gradually increased to almost a quarter of the workers. Most viewed the spheres of the home and the workplace as separate. The biggest change during the Great Depression was in the working status of married women. The number of working married women increased by 50% during the 1930s. The employment of single women increased by approximately 10% during the same period. The reason for the increase in working married women was economic necessity, but the type of necessity can be divided into two categories: among the poverty-stricken, the need to maintain or attain some kind of level of subsistence forced women to work; for middle-class women the additional income was to maintain an appropriate lifestyle. In fact, according to some data, close to half of employed married women who lived with their husbands (as opposed to families with an absent male head of the household) were of middle class status. It is argued that the consumerism of the 1920s changed the perception of what a middle-class household looked like, raising expectations that necessitated a second wage earner. The push to maintain material comforts was reinforced by women's magazines in which writers gave budget advice on how to cut down needless spending. The advice, often anecdotal, was frequently provided by women in the upper-fifth of household income, so the columns were also the source of ridicule. In fact, it was through the wages of working women that millions of households clung to middle-class lifestyles or, at the very least, had a roof and regular meals. Regardless of economic level, working mothers and wives were seen as a stopgap measure during hard economic times, and the increase should not be viewed as a significant change in their role or status.

Activity

Research presentation and essay

The class is divided into three groups: Each group is assigned a research presentation task. The task is to create a presentation and outline on the following, in preparation for a comparison/ contrast essay discussing the lives of ethnic minorities in the United States during the Great Depression.
Group 1: African Americans
Group 2: Hipanics/Latinos
Group 3: Asians and Asian Americans
(Groups may be subdivided for researching the lives of women, children, rural vs. urban.)

The jobs that most women had during the period were in support roles or domestic work. As jobs became scarce for men, women were pushed out of traditional fields such as education, and took up clerical and retail positions. African American women were forced by circumstances into different endeavors. Black workers lost their jobs in proportionally larger numbers than whites. As middle-class white families cut down on expenses, black women employed as domestic workers were let go. It is estimated that close to 40% of black workers (men and women) lost their jobs during the Depression. Black women took up other means of survival. The choice was often one of **survivalist entrepreneurship.** The two most prominent businesses for black women were boarding houses and beauty parlors. The Great Migration of African Americans to the north provided opportunities for women to run boarding houses for the millions of people looking for places to live. The boarding houses were often within homes, and did not only provide needed funds, but also allowed many families to pay rent and keep their dwellings. African American women also ran salons, whether in storefronts or at home. While many jobs that black women had held were taken by whites during the economic downturn, white-owned beauty salons did not cater to the needs of black women, leaving the field open for entrepreneurs. The demand for beauticians increased as southern women moved north looking for work. Organizations such as the Urban League and the National Council of Negro Women advised women on how to look and what to wear, essentially enhancing the role of the beauty industry. A third but less popular business was running a restaurant or food market. These proprietorships were also run out of homes, and the advantage was that if the investment failed, the stocks could be consumed. African American women, in particular, were limited to the types of businesses that required little or no capital investment. Some women built larger businesses, upgrading from in-home operations to chain storefronts, but for most black women, running a business was about keeping one's home and feeding the family.

> **Survivalist entrepreneurship**
> In response to exclusion from the labor market a person is forced to form his/her own business to provide for herself and her family.

With the New Deal came an increased role for women in the federal government, but not in society as a whole. Franklin Roosevelt's wife Eleanor is credited with increasing the place for women in government. The first female cabinet official in the history of the United States was Frances Perkins, the Secretary of Labor. The government hired scores of other women as well. Still, there was little change for women in general. Just as the Progressives had worked for women's health and safety during the early years of the 20th century, the New Deal period focused on protecting women, while emphasizing that the main wage earner for families was the male head of household. Women were discouraged from taking or remaining in jobs that men could do. Consequently, the Great Depression was a period of temporary change for most women that only served to reinforce the role of men as wage-earners, even while women took on the necessary responsibility of providing for the family.

Activity

Source analysis

The following documents address the lives of people during the Great Depression.

Source A

From *America in the Twentieth Century* by Frank Freidel and Alan Brinkley.

> ... blacks benefitted in significant, if limited ways from New Deal relief programs (in large part because Eleanor Roosevelt, a close friend of relief administrator Harry Hopkins and Harold Ickes worked hard to ensure that the programs did not exclude blacks). By 1935, according to some estimates, nearly 30 percent of all blacks were receiving some form of government assistance. Blacks, who constituted in the 1930s only 10 percent of the population, filled 18 percent of the positions within the WPA. ...
>
> Despite the benefits they received from the New Deal, blacks continued to languish in almost universal poverty and continued to be the victims of brutal racial discrimination ... blacks were the "last hired and first fired"—a pattern that resulted in blacks losing their jobs far more quickly than whites when hard times arrived. ... Two-thirds of black cotton farmers in the 1930s made no money at all from their crops and survived only by hunting, scavenging, begging, or moving to the cities.
>
> **Source:** Freidel, Frank & Brinkley, Alan. 1982. *America in the Twentieth Century*. 5th edn. New York: McGraw-Hill. pp. 266–68.

Source B

The lyrics of the song "Do Re Mi" by Woody Guthrie.

> Lots of folks back East, they say, is leavin' home every day,
> Beatin' the hot old dusty way to the California line.
> Cross the desert sands they roll, gettin' out of that old dust bowl,
> They think they're goin' to a sugar bowl, but here's what they find
> Now, the police at the port of entry say,
> "You're number fourteen thousand for today."
>
> Oh, if you ain't got the do re mi, folks, you ain't got the do re mi,
> Why, you better go back to beautiful Texas, Oklahoma, Kansas, Georgia, Tennessee.
> California is a garden of Eden, a paradise to live in or see;
> But believe it or not, you won't find it so hot
> If you ain't got the do re mi.
>
> You want to buy you a home or a farm, that can't deal nobody harm,
> Or take your vacation by the mountains or sea.
> Don't swap your old cow for a car, you better stay right where you are,
> Better take this little tip from me.
> 'Cause I look through the want ads every day
> But the headlines on the papers always say:
>
> Oh, if you ain't got the do re mi, folks, you ain't got the do re mi,
> Why, you better go back to beautiful Texas, Oklahoma, Kansas, Georgia, Tennessee.
> California is a garden of Eden, a paradise to live in or see;
> But believe it or not, you won't find it so hot
> If you ain't got the do re mi
>
> **Source:** Woody Guthrie Lyrics.
> http://www.woodyguthrie.org/Lyrics/Do_Re_Mi.htm.

Source C

From President Roosevelt's second inaugural address, January 20, 1937.

> ...But here is the challenge to our democracy: In this nation I see tens of millions of its citizens—a substantial part of its whole population—who at this very moment are denied the greater part of what the very lowest standards of today call the necessities of life. I see millions of families trying to live on incomes so meager that the pall of family disaster hangs over them day by day. I see millions whose daily lives in city and on farm continue under conditions labeled indecent by a so-called polite society half a century ago. I see millions denied education, recreation, and the opportunity to better their lot and the lot of their children. I see millions lacking the means to buy the products of farm and factory and by their poverty denying work and productiveness to many other millions. I see one-third of a nation ill-housed, ill-clad, ill-nourished.
>
> **Source:** Inaugural Addresses of the Presidents of the United States.
> http://www.bartleby.com/124/pres50.html.

Source D

Photo of man looking for work in Detroit, Michigan. He holds a placard that says "Work is what I want and not a charity. Who will help me get a job—7 years—in Detroit ..."

Source: Archive Photos, Getty Images.

Questions

1 What is the message of source B?

2 Explain the impact of source D.

3 Compare and contrast the evidence in sources A and C of the difficulties that US citizens encountered in the Great Depression.

4 Referring to the type of document, as well as to the content, explain the values and limitations of sources B and D for historians seeking to understand what life was like in the 1930s.

5 Using the sources and your own knowledge, discuss the harmful effects of the Great Depression on the lives of people from all social groups in the United States in the 1930s.

President Roosevelt and the New Deal

Franklin Delano Roosevelt, New York's Democrat governor, won in a landslide victory over Republican incumbent, Herbert Hoover, in the 1932 elections. Roosevelt ran on a financially conservative platform, not the multitude New Deal programs that were to come over the next four years. Many political observers considered FDR an intellectual lightweight, with little to offer a struggling nation, but Roosevelt would prove them wrong. The new president, working with a sometimes cooperative legislature, tried many different programs over the next two terms, some more successful than others. Roosevelt's public persona was as important as his governmental programs; his warmth and use of the media, especially radio, contrasted greatly with his aloof predecessor. By the end of Roosevelt's first two terms, he and his "Brain Trust" had created a new understanding of the role of government in people's lives, and had been the catalyst behind a realignment of US politics, spearheaded by a group of Democrat politicians who became known as New Deal Democrats. The new coalition lasted as a political force into the 1960s. Roosevelt's administration worked hard to institute beneficial reforms from 1933 to 1941. But what pulled the United States out of the decade-long Depression was the entry of the United States into the Second World War.

The first New Deal

After his inauguration, Roosevelt acted quickly to reform a broken system, providing a foundation for recovery, and much-needed relief for those most affected by the Great Depression in the United States. Building on a theme from his inaugural address, he stated "let me assert my firm belief that the only thing we have to fear is fear itself—nameless, unreasoning, unjustified terror ..." The entire address planted the seeds for immediate and bold presidential initiatives, claiming, "This nation asks for action, and action now." In the first few months, he acted to reform the economic system, stimulate industry, and

Franklin Delano Roosevelt (1882–1945)

The longest-serving president in United States' history, Franklin Roosevelt (also known by his initials FDR) was born in Hyde Park, New York State. His parents were quite wealthy and his mother could trace ancestors back to the Mayflower. Roosevelt was also a fifth cousin of Teddy Roosevelt, who became president when Franklin was attending Harvard. Franklin married a distant cousin, Eleanor, in 1905. His political career began in 1910, when he was elected State Senator. He gained fame by opposing the Tammany Hall political machine. Woodrow Wilson appointed FDR to the position of assistant secretary of the navy only three years after he was elected Senator. In 1920, the Democratic Party nominated Roosevelt as their candidate for vice president, but the Republican ticket, headed by Warren G. Harding, defeated the Cox-Roosevelt team. The following year FDR contracted a disease, thought at the time to be polio, that left him paralyzed from the waist down. Roosevelt refused to believe that the paralysis was permanent. He also refused to let the public see him in a wheelchair, wanting to appear vigorous. In 1928, Roosevelt won the governorship of New York. Four years later he defeated Hoover for the presidency. The US public elected FDR four consecutive times. After holding the nation's highest office, during the Great Depression and most of the Second World War, he died in April 1945, only a few months into his fourth term.

Activity

Leadership qualities

The Italian Renaissance philosopher Niccolò Machiavelli wrote:

> *The one who adapts his policy to the times prospers, and likewise that the one whose policy clashes with the demands of the times does not.*

Explain the role of adaptation in New Deal legislation and administration. Is it better to stick to a philosophy of government or adapt to circumstances? What is the role of political philosophy?

 To what extent should elected leaders act on the promises they made to voters?

develop a sense of confidence in the American people. Two days after taking office, Roosevelt proclaimed a banking holiday, closing all US banks for four days. He subsequently submitted the first of many pieces of legislation: the Emergency Banking Act. Congress passed the bill in one day. The new law stabilized large banks, gave the Federal Reserve Bank additional powers, took the dollar off the gold standard, and mandated inspection of banks by the Treasury Department before they reopened. A second bill, the Economy Act, quickly followed. The new law attempted to balance the federal budget by cutting salaries and reducing pensions.

The two bills reflected Roosevelt's fiscal conservatism and were in no way reflective of British economist John Maynard Keynes' theories on government and the economy. In fact, cutting government spending acted as the opposite of a stimulus. But there was another purpose to the first week's legislation: Roosevelt wanted to rebuild confidence in the economy of the United States after almost four years of decline. He gave his first national radio address in the evening of March 12. Over the radio, Roosevelt explained to the people of the United States how the new laws would work and what they could expect in the upcoming days. It was the first of three-dozen fireside chats over the 13 years of his presidency. The talks played an important part in building support for the president's initiatives and allowing time for the economy to turn around. During 1933, Roosevelt delivered four such talks, speaking in an informal manner as if he was sitting in each family's home by the fire. Each address dealt with an important concept. The May talk explained the New Deal program. The many agencies formed by legislation and executive action became known as the Alphabet Agencies.

US president Franklin Delano Roosevelt speaks into four radio microphones, which sit on his desk during one of his live nationwide 'fireside chats' in 1935.

Activity

Organizing information

Fill in the columns of the table below with evidence of policies, actions, and statements by the three presidents that contributed to the political views of people living in the United States before and during the Great Depression.

President	Cause for concern	Inspired confidence
Coolidge		
Hoover		
Roosevelt		

The Agricultural Adjustment Agency (AAA) was formed in May. The purpose was to raise farm prices so that farmers could survive and put a halt to the abandonment of farms. Even in the midst of the Depression, farmers produced more food than Americans could consume or purchase. The surplus put a downward pressure on prices and, combined with general deflation, resulted in prices well below the cost of producing food. The AAA attempted to reverse the trend by paying farmers to let land lay fallow to reduce production and paying subsidies to farmers to cover the shortfall in market prices. In addition, the AAA slaughtered over six million pigs that year and ordered the destruction of many crops. Some of the pork was distributed to the needy, but the destruction of so much food at a time when millions of people were going hungry was alien to many people. The AAA lent money to farmers as well. These programs tended to benefit large-scale farming operations, although the credit was granted to many small farmers, but rather than helping individuals, the administration was attempting to stabilize and rebuild a critical sector of the economy.

The banking system was also a focus of reform. Congress passed the Glass-Steagall Banking Reform Act which was written to address a main cause of the Depression and to renew confidence in banks. As a significant amount of the money that fueled the stock market speculation of the late 1920s came from banks, the Glass-Steagall Act prohibited banks from underwriting securities. Essentially, financial institutions had to choose between being a lender and a stock underwriter. The Act also created the Federal Deposit Insurance Corporation (FDIC), an organization funded by banks that insured individual bank deposits up to $2,500. The FDIC brought confidence to depositors, inviting trust in banks, which helped to stabilize and rebuild the banking system.

Congress passed the National Industry Recovery Act in 1933 to prompt economic recovery through promoting confidence among workers, industry, and investors. The National Recovery Administration (NRA), directed by General Hugh Johnson, worked to end wage deflation through a minimum wage, establish a maximum limit to weekly hours to promote new hiring, end child labor, and restore competition to the marketplace through business codes that included the elimination of **price fixing**. Perhaps the most famous symbol of the New Deal was the NRA "Blue Eagle," a sticker that cooperating businesses placed in their front window. Many companies agreed to abide by the NRA rules, but not all that professed compliance actually followed the codes. During the two years of the NRA (before it was declared unconstitutional), industrial production rose by 22%.

Price fixing is when manufacturers, wholesalers, or retailers conspire to keep prices at a particular level. The prices may be kept high to increase profits or low to drive competitors out of business.

The third leg of Roosevelt's New Deal concentrated on relief. The Federal Emergency Relief Agency (FERA) was simply a rebranding of the Emergency Relief Agency, formed by Hoover a year before. The original purpose was to create new jobs through loans to states. But FERA did much more. Under the leadership of Harry Hopkins, who would become an important part of the Roosevelt administration's efforts to end the Great Depression and involvement in the Second World War, FERA granted funds to state and local governments. In the two years of its existence, FERA created jobs for more than 20 million workers. Part of FERA was the creation of a sub-agency, the Civil Works Administration (CWA), which accelerated job creation in late 1933 and early 1934. Jobs included building roads, repairing schools, and installing sewers. By mid-January 1934, more than four million people worked at CWA jobs. In addition to jobs through state and local governments, FERA provided funds for adult education, began projects that employed artists and writers, and placed women in jobs along with men. FERA ended when declared unconstitutional by the Supreme Court in 1935.

Activity

Ranking

Make a chronological list of New Deal agencies. Note the activities of each agency under the three purposes: relief, reform, recovery. Organize your list by placing the most effective agency at the top and the least effective at the bottom. What are your criteria for the ranking? Compare your criteria and rankings with your classmates.

New Deal Agencies			
Agency	Relief	Reform	Recovery

The first two years of the New Deal brought more agencies to assist with reform, relief, and recovery. The Tennessee Valley Authority (TVA), established in 1934, brought power and flood relief to the Tennessee River region. The Securities and Exchange Commission (SEC) was created the same year to provide oversight to the stock market to make investing more transparent by curtailing insider trading and market manipulation by large investors. The Public Works Administration, established in 1933 as a result of the National Industry Recovery Act, spent federal funds on building construction projects including dams, bridges and a multitude of public buildings. One agency that is fondly remembered by participants and produced lasting effects on the landscape was the Civilian Conservation Corps (CCC). The CCC was created to offer temporary employment for young men, many of whom were homeless, hungry, and on the road. CCC projects ranged from planting wind-break tree lines across the Dust Bowl to building the Blue Ridge Parkway in the Appalacian Mountains. The CCC paid the young men, but sent the majority of the money to their parents. All told, 1933 and 1934 brought 17 new agencies into the government, many of which, like the FDIC, TVA, SEC, Federal Communications Commission (FCC), Civil Aeronautics Authority (changed to FAA in 1958), and the Federal Housing Administration (FHA) continued throughout the 20th century.

The actual success of the many agencies is debated. There is no doubt that the United States' economy grew during the first two years of Roosevelt's first term. The New Deal programs were criticized as "make-work" **boondoggles**, filled with waste, and an inefficient way to provide relief. Job creation was more expensive than handouts. The programs were also attacked as being anti-capitalist by interfering with the free market, thereby leading to socialism. Finally, in May 1935, a hostile Supreme Court found many of the laws unconstitutional on the grounds that they granted the president powers that violated the intent and words of the Constitution, immediately voiding any program established under the National Recovery Act. The Supreme Court ruled the Agricultural Adjustment Act unconstitutional in January 1936. The court showed itself to be hostile to a large government role in the economy.

A **boondoggle** is a government project, usually expensive and with little practical benefit, that often allowed friends of government officials, as well as the officials themselves, to make money.

Roosevelt and the court system

The court's decisions led the Roosevelt administration to follow two paths. The first was to craft new laws that would meet court scrutiny, and the second was to alter the court itself to being more favorable towards government involvement in the economy than the *laissez-faire* majority. In April 1935, the Works Progress Administration (WPA) was created. Included within the WPA were projects for writers, musicians, artists, and thespians. Among many projects, the Federal Writers Project recorded more than two thousand interviews with former slaves. In June 1935, Congress passed the Wagner Act, a bill guaranteeing labor rights, including the right to collectively bargain. Later that month, the National Youth Administration was created under the WPA. In August, Congress passed a law creating the Social Security System, a retirement contribution program for workers. Many programs continued to operate, and the WPA expanded its programs to include fighting fires and assisting flood victims. But the specter of the court caused Roosevelt to seek major change. After his landslide reelection in November 1936, he prepared to execute a plan to pack the court. The plan he submitted to Congress in February proposed that there be a new justice added to the court for each justice over the age of 70. This meant he would be able to name six new justices who presumably would rule in his favor. Roosevelt's frustration with the court was understood by the public, but even his supporters disapproved of the blatant attempt to weaken the independence of the third branch. The plan languished in Congress during the spring and was allowed to die in July. In the interim, the president's action appeared to have created a change in the court's rulings, specifically Justice Owen Roberts, who began to rule in favor of the administration, whether out of a genuine change of judicial philosophy or, more likely, as a response to avert a possible constitutional crisis or a court damaged by a lack of the public's trust in the fairness of its decisions. Regardless of the reason, the court's rulings upheld the new laws, allowing increased federal involvement in the economy.

Activity

Source analysis

The following documents address Roosevelt's "Court packing."

Source A

On March 9, 1937, in the wake of repeated Supreme Court decisions striking down New Deal legislation and programs, Franklin Roosevelt gave a fireside chat.

> But since the rise of the modern movement for social and economic progress through legislation, the Court has more and more often and more and more boldly asserted a power to veto laws passed by the Congress and by state …
>
> In the last four years the sound rule of giving statutes the benefit of all reasonable doubt has been cast aside. The Court has been acting not as a judicial body, but as a policymaking body.
>
> When the Congress has sought to stabilize national agriculture, to improve the conditions of labor, to safeguard business against unfair competition, to protect our national resources, and in many other ways, to serve our clearly national needs, the majority of the Court has been assuming the power to pass on the wisdom of these acts of the Congress—and to approve or disapprove the public policy written into these laws. …
>
> We have, therefore, reached the point as a nation where we must take action to save the Constitution from the Court and the Court from itself.
>
> **Source:** Fireside Chat on Reorganization of the Judiciary. March 9, 1937. *Oyez, Oyez, Oyez: A Supreme Court Resource.* http://www.hpol.org/fdr/chat.

Source B

Following is a historian's perspective from an article by Richard G. Menaker.

> Shortly thereafter, on "Black Monday," May 27, 1935, the Court issued three destructive decisions—*Schechter Poultry* (the infamous "sick chicken" case) cut the heart out of the NIRA, Louisville Bank struck down the Frazier-Lemke Act limiting mortgage foreclosures, and Humphries' Executor scaled back the President's ability to control the make-up of certain federal regulatory bodies. Each of the decisions was unanimous. Subsequent rulings included the invalidation of the wages-and-hours and price-control mechanisms of the Bituminous Coal Conservation Act (5–4, with Roberts the swing vote), invalidation of the processing tax in the Agricultural Adjustment Act (6–3, with Roberts writing for the majority), and vacatur of a New York State minimum wage law (5–4, Roberts again), a ruling with worrisome implications for a vast area of industrial regulation.
>
> **Source:** Menaker, Richard, G. April 2008. "FDR's Court-Packing Plan: A Study in Irony". *History Now: American History Online.* no. 15. Gilder-Lehrman Institute of American History. http://www.gilderlehrman.org/historynow/04_2008/historian4.php.

Source C

The following extract is from *American History: A Survey*, by Alan Brinkley.

> On one level, the affair was a significant victory for Franklin Roosevelt. The Court was no longer an obstacle to New Deal reforms … But the Court-packing episode did lasting damage to the administration. By giving members of his own party an excuse to oppose him, he helped destroy his congressional coalition. From 1937 on, southern Democrats and other Democratic conservatives voted against his measures much more often than in the past. In combination with Republicans, they constituted a powerful enough force to block many New Deal measures.
>
> **Source:** Brinkley, Alan. 1999. *American History: A Survey*. 10th edn. Boston: McGraw Hill. p. 892.

Source D

Following is a political Cartoon on Roosevelt's court packing, published
February 14, 1937.

Source: Fotosearch/Getty Images.

Questions

1 What evidence is there in source B that the Supreme Court had acted to stop New Deal programs?

2 What is the message of source D?

3 Compare and contrast sources A and B for evidence that Franklin Roosevelt was justified in proposing a significant change to the structure of the Court.

4 With reference to their origin and purpose, what are the values and limitations of sources A and C for historians studying Roosevelt's attempt to "pack" the Supreme Court?

5 Using the documents and your own knowledge and additional research, assess the short- and long-term effects on the New Deal of FDR's attempt to modify the Supreme Court.

Opposition to the New Deal

The Supreme Court's response was disheartening to those who favored Roosevelt's programs, but it was welcomed by opponents to the New Deal. FDR was opposed by those on the left, including the Communist and Socialist Parties, for doing too little to change the economic structure of the country. In fact, the Communist Party gained membership during the 1930s. Greater opposition came from the Republican Party, even Herbert Hoover became a vocal critic of the programs. Many businessmen and bankers felt the New Deal targeted them, got the government too involved in the free market, and weakened their companies by forcing needless and harmful regulations on them. Some conservatives hated Roosevelt so much that decades after the Great Depression they would not even carry a **Roosevelt dime**. Political opposition was also voiced by three charismatic men of vastly different backgrounds, each of whom commanded national attention.

Francis E. Townsend, Father Charles E. Coughlin, and Huey P. Long attracted significant followers in their challenges to the New Deal. Townsend, an elderly doctor from California, proposed his own program, the Old Age Revolving Pension Plan, after seeing many senior citizens living in destitute conditions in his city of **Long Beach**. The central concept of the plan was that the elderly should retire and leave jobs to young people, thus lowering unemployment. The retirees would get a monthly payment from the government of $200. Within two years his organization had more than a million members. Townsend became a significant political force and elements of his program made it to the House floor to be voted on. The bill was defeated, but many congressmen were intimidated by his fame and following; consequently, almost half of the House abstained from the vote. Townsend's influence declined after the bill's defeat, but the popularity of his proposals did lend momentum to expansion of Social Security in later years.

Religious radio broadcasts became popular during the 1920s. Father Charles E. Coughlin was a Catholic priest, originally from Canada, who had a small parish near Detroit, Michigan. Coughlin started broadcasting sermons in 1926. During the late 1920s he gained listeners from an increasing area of the Midwest, and in 1931 CBS signed him to preach on nationwide radio. Eventually, the audience for *Hour of Power* reportedly reached over 40 million listeners each week. As the severity of the Great Depression solidified, Coughlin turned his sermons to economics. He spoke about universal economic rights and the responsibility of people to help those in need within their communities and included proposals to nationalize the banking system and alter the monetary system. During the 1932 election, and the first two years of the Roosevelt presidency, Coughlin voiced strong support. But after being denied the access to the White House that he felt he had earned, and seeing Roosevelt reject many of his economic proposals, Coughlin became a voice of opposition and established the National Union for Social Justice. After Roosevelt's reelection in 1936, Coughlin spoke positively about fascism in Italy and Germany, proclaiming that neither capitalism nor democracy were the answer to the his country's economic

The **Roosevelt dime**, which was first issued in 1946, the year following his death, commemorated his involvement with the March of Dimes. The original name of the March of Dimes was the National Foundation for Infantile Paralysis, started by FDR in 1938. Radio listeners were asked to mail their dimes to the White House to support the cause. The name of the organization officially changed to March of Dimes in 1979.

Long Beach is situated at the south end of the City of Los Angeles across from the port of San Pedro.

problems. He also published a magazine called *Social Justice*. Articles in the magazine and commentaries on the radio became increasingly anti-Semitic. Some radio stations censored his broadcasts or dropped his program as a result. Coughlin, nevertheless, retained a large following, but opposition to his views mounted when he expressed criticism of the entry of the United States into the Second World War, even after the Japanese attack on Pearl Harbor.

The third major opposition figure was the Louisiana Senator Huey P. Long. The "Kingfish" as he was known, rose to power in Louisiana by attacking banks, oil companies, utilities and their supporters. For years, the state's government had been dominated by a small group of conservative and well-connected politicians and Long railed against those in power. Elected governor the year before the stock market crash, he destroyed his opposition with almost dictatorial power. His popularity was built on charisma, reforming the tax code, and the funding of many public works projects, including roads and schools. As a United States Senator taking office in 1931, he opposed Hoover's policies and then supported Roosevelt's run for the presidency. Roosevelt lost Long's support shortly after taking office, and Long proposed an alternative to the New Deal: the Share Our Wealth Plan—a plan to redistribute wealth. Long claimed Share Our Wealth would end the Great Depression, and that by seizing all accumulated wealth over $5 million the government would be able to guarantee every worker an annual wage of $2,500—much higher than the median family income in 1935 of $1,500 per year. The Share Our Wealth Society eventually accumulated a membership list upwards of four million. Long's popularity never reached the heights necessary for his proposals to gain a hold in the Senate, but his voice was a constant reminder to the administration that there was significant support for policies to the political left of Roosevelt's New Deal.

There was significant opposition to the New Deal from the left and the right. While the majority of Americans supported the president's policies, the strength of the forces against the administration did limit New Deal legislation, especially as the Great Depression continued into the latter half of the decade.

The Great Depression and the arts

During the Great Depression, the arts did not disappear. For the first time the federal government took a significant interest in the fine arts as exemplified by Federal Project Number One. Eleanor Roosevelt, the first lady, well known for her promotion of civil rights, was also a strong proponent of the arts. The government launched several programs ranging from theater to music to photography. The private sector, including novelists and movie studios, created many new works, some addressing the Depression while others provided escapism. Other diversions included music and cartoons. Folk music and blues became more visible. The radio also played an important part in popular culture as radio stations penetrated rural heartlands, as well as the cities. The arts expanded the cultural landscape of the United States.

The Federal Government and the arts

There were several federal arts programs. Urged by his wife, Eleanor, who felt that the arts should not be just for the élites, President Roosevelt supported the arts for another reason: it would employ a great many people. Initial involvement began with the Public Works of Art Project division of the CWA. A major focus was the commissioning of murals for public buildings such as schools, libraries, and other public buildings. Artists were commissioned, in the first instance, because they were on relief. But also, of course, for their skills. Artists who participated in the program included Thomas Hart Benton, Jackson Pollock and Grant Wood. The program was short-lived and ended when the CWA was abolished in 1934. The PWAP was followed by a painting and sculpture program housed within the Treasury department under which artists competed for funds. In the short life of the program, more than 1,300 works of arts were commissioned. In 1935, the Treasury Relief Art Program (TRAP) was created. TRAP focused less on relief, not adhering to WPA's standards, and more on the skill of the artist in response to complaints of the established arts community. TRAP continued the placement of art in public buildings, including a mural in at least one post office in every congressional district. The most significant arts program began under the auspices of the WPA.

Activity

Does the US Constitution allow that?

Many critics of Roosevelt have argued that the New Deal went far beyond the intention of those who framed it and the words of the United States Constitution itself.

Read Article 1, sections 8 and 9 of the Constitution.

Does the Constitution allow for arts programs? Does it prohibit Congress from funding such agencies?

For what reasons is it beneficial or harmful for the government to fund the arts?

The Social History of Missouri painted by Thomas Hart Benton in the Missouri State Capitol, Jefferson City, Missouri.

Federal Project Number One

Federal Project Number One (FPNO) began in 1935. The program was much larger than the previous arts programs and would encompass many different art forms including theater, music, writing; it would also contribute to documenting local culture, along with gathering and organizing historical records. A year after the FPNO began, more than 40,000 people were employed in various projects across the country.

FPNO had a significant dramatic arts section that operated until 1939. Not only did it remove over 12,000 people from the relief rolls, but it established community theater in communities, large and small, across the country. Ethnic production companies produced African-American, French, German, Italian and Yiddish dramas. The projects even crossed into CCC camps. Joseph Cotton, **Orson Welles**, and Burt Lancaster were among the participants. The visual arts section contributed more than 20,000 works of art ranging from stained glass to sculpture from artists such as Jacob Lawrence and Mark Rothko. Arts education was an important component of the Federal Arts Project with 100 arts centers that served millions. Writers such as Studs Terkel, **Ralph Ellison** and Margaret Walker were among the thousands of writers who wrote fiction, guidebooks to every state, and collected folklore. One of the most historically significant projects

Orson Welles was a famous film actor and director. His film, Citizen Kane, is often cited as one of the greatest films of all time.

Ralph Ellison wrote the groundbreaking novel *Invisible Man* (1952) about an African American who considers himself invisible to the majority white society around him.

Activity

Using oral history

Visit *Born in Slavery: Slave Narratives from the Federal Writers' Project, 1936–1938* at http://memory.loc.gov/ammem/snhtml/snhome.html. Read several slave narratives. Discuss the content of the narratives, and the role of memory in reconstructing a distant past. Also discuss the role of the person who recorded the narrative in preserving and creating history, and use of the narratives helps you to formulate your understanding of history.

Address the following questions from the ToK Guide, page 29. Form your answers using the narratives and other documents of your own choosing.

1 Does the historian record history or create it?

2 Can the historian be free of bias in the selection and interpretation of material?

3 Could it be reasonably argued that the personal understanding of historians, despite or even because of their possible bias, is necessary of even desirable in the interpretation and recording of history?

was the recording of narratives from former slaves. Additionally, artists created more than 2,000 different posters to publicize theatrical and musical performances and subjects such as health and safety, and education.

An unlikely agency, the Farm Services Administration, was the source of many of the iconic images of the Great Depression. The FSA hired scores of photographers. Included were some of the finest photographers of the era: Esther Bubley, Walker Evans, Dorothea Lange and Gordon Parks. They were sent out to document conditions for workers on the road, in camps and on farms. Dorothea Lange's "Migrant Mother" portrait, for many the image of the displaced Dust Bowl farmer, is but one of thousands of photographs that the FSA used to tell the story of rural life in the United States.

Popular culture

Popular art forms in the 1930s included movies, radio, music, and literature. Two themes

Dorothea Lange (1895–1965)

Known to most students of the Great Depression as the photographer of Dust Bowl migrants, Dorothea Lange was born in Hoboken, New Jersey in 1895. Lange contracted polio at the age of seven, leaving her with a severely weakened right leg and a noticeable limp. When she was 12 her father abandoned the family, forcing her mother to work in New York City. Her mother enrolled Dorothea in New York Public Schools to be near her work. Lange recalled feeling very much the outsider being the only gentile in a school filled primarily with Jewish immigrants. Lange declared her intention to be a photographer at the age of 18, then learned all aspects of the trade for two years as an apprentice. She then moved across the country to San Francisco. Within a few years, she became well-known as a studio photographer. When the Great Depression hit, Lange began taking photographs of people on the streets. Her work caught the eye of Paul Taylor, an economist who was documenting the working conditions of migrant farm workers for the State of California. Taylor hired Lange to provide photographic evidence. Lange and Taylor's combined efforts influenced state and federal policies. Eventually their partnership became romantic, and each divorced their spouses and remarried. Their professional and personal partnership continued throughout Lange's lifetime. Taylor and Lange travelled much of the country, especially the south, documenting conditions in rural areas. Eventually, Lange was hired by the federal government to document conditions in worker camps in California. She spent eight years documenting the lives of many of society's forgotten. Following the Japanese attack on Pearl Harbor, Lange documented the lives of Japanese-Americans who became instant outcasts. She also photographed internment camps. Lange's work continues to have impact on students of the 1930s and 1940s.

emerge: art that addressed the times, or art that allowed audiences to escape for a little while. Authors like John Steinbeck, who portrayed the plight of migrant farmers in *The Grapes of Wrath* (1939), depicted the conditions in fiction. Richard Wright contributed essays, poetry, and novels, and edited *The Left Front*, a Communist Party publication. Movies ranged from Frank Capra's *Mr. Deeds Comes to Town* (1936), a film about a man on the street, to adventure films like *Tarzan the Ape Man* (1932) and *Captains Courageous* (1937) to Busby-Berkeley musicals. The end of the decade brought *Gone With the Wind* and *The Wizard of Oz*, both from 1939, two of the most popular films of all time. For the first time, radio penetrated rural areas and shows such as *The Lone Ranger*, The Adventures of *Superman*, *Dick Tracy*, and comedians Burns & Allen (George Burns and Gracie Allen) and Jack Benny filled the airways. The most popular forms of music that continued into the 1930s, either as live acts or over the radio, included folk, blues and jazz. Folklorist John Lomax (also director of the ex-slave narrative project) made field recordings of thousands of songs, preserving examples of the various musical forms. Lomax is often credited with discovering **Huddie "Lead Belly" Ledbetter**, and elevated folk music as an art form.

Despite the dire living conditions, the federal government stepped in to create a role for the government that brought fine arts to ordinary people and preserved vast amounts of Americana for future generations.

"Migrant Mother," Dorothea Lange's iconic photo of migrant farm workers.

Huddie "Lead Belly" Ledbetter was an influential blues singer. Musicians acknowledging his impact range from Josh White to the Rolling Stones; Bob Dylan to Van Morrison; and Odetta to Kurt Cobain.

Activity

Listening for yourself

Put yourself back in the 1930s by listening to Depression-era radio serials, including *The Lone Ranger*, *Superman*, and a variety of other 1930s radio programs.

You can experience the sound of the past through *America in the 1930s*, a University of Virginia website: http://xroads.virginia.edu/~1930s/RADIO/radiofr.html.

Setback: the recession of 1937

By 1937, the economy had recovered to levels not seen since 1930, and had risen considerably since bottoming out in 1933. GDP was up 80% and private investment went from a low of $1 billion in 1932 to $12 billion in 1937. But beginning in May, the growth of the economy reversed and a recession began. Unemployment was now up to 19% from a low of 14% as more than four million jobs were lost. Manufacturing fell to 1934 levels and private investment fell by 40%. GDP declined a bit over 6% during the recession that lasted until June 1938. The reversal was a stunning setback for the country.

The causes of the recession are still debated. The monetarist school blames the Federal Reserve Bank for taking actions to tighten the money supply. The Fed always feared **inflation**, the result of a growing economy. Trying to anticipate a severe inflationary cycle led the Federal Reserve to clamp down, causing investment to drop and

Inflation is often viewed as a tax on savings. Money in the bank loses real value when currency inflates. The tendency is to remove money from banks and purchase goods before they rise in price even more. The spending increases demand, which accelerates the inflationary spiral. Workers then demand wage increases to maintain purchasing power, further increasing inflationary pressure.

people to stop spending money, which slowed down the economy. The Keynesian school also blames the Central Bank, and Roosevelt for abruptly attempting to balance the budget. FDR was concerned about the build-up of federal debt. Furthermore, the New Deal relief and recovery programs were temporary measures to help the poor and to stimulate the economy. As the economy had grown steadily for four years, Roosevelt and the Congress increased taxes and decreased spending, removing the stimulus. A third possible cause was the reform aspect of the New Deal. Those sympathetic to businesses and favoring an unregulated market blamed the many regulations on the failure of business, despite the Court's limiting of the government's hand.

In response to the downturn, Roosevelt increased government funding to 1936 levels. The recession eased in July 1938 and the economy grew in the second half of the year. By the end of the year, GDP surpassed that of the year preceding the recession. The economy continued to grow in 1939 and 1940, when GDP reached pre-Great Depression levels, but unemployment remained high at 14%. In 1941, the United States economy posted the largest GDP in its history, as output rose by more than 20%. Federal spending, especially defense spending, increased greatly that year. December 7, 1941, brought the entry of the United States into the Second World War and FDR switched from "Mr. New Deal" to "Mr. Win the War."

Were Roosevelt's policies successful?

There are a number of ways to look at the Roosevelt response. Looking at the numbers, the economy recovered over the decade and returned to pre-Depression levels, however, unemployment did not return to 1929 levels until war production absorbed millions of workers. The reform aspects, farm and industrial policy, as well as banking and stock market regulations, encountered significant opposition from interest groups, many members of Congress, and the Supreme Court. The administration's policies were developed to prevent the events that led to the Great Depression. The government programs that lasted well beyond the Depression include Social Security and the SEC. While there was some success in reform, most efforts were watered-down, leaving the agricultural, industrial, and financial sectors with less freedom than in the 1920s, but more freedom than many members of the administration intended. The many relief programs provided work in many fields, from theater to construction and conservation. Millions were employed, housed and fed. A further outcome were the many new parks, schools, hospitals and environmental projects that started many devastated areas on the path to renewal. But benefits to minorities were uneven at best, and some programs caused more harm than good. Historians sometimes criticize Roosevelt for not providing enough stimulus to the economy and for removing it before recovery was complete, as well as for failing to enact major reforms, but his response was pragmatic, rather than ideological. Some historians have even called that approach conservative. The effectiveness and legacy of the New Deal in the United States is still discussed and debated today.

The Great Depression in Canada

To understand how the Depression set upon Canada, its course and consequences, it is important to examine the context of the 1920s. There was significant political fragmentation as a result of the conscription crisis of 1917 that had threatened to tear Canada apart. It pitted English-speaking Canada against French-speaking Canada once again. To this national division was added a rift in traditional party politics. Laurier's Liberals, a party that had largely transcended the linguistic–political divide that had plagued Canada since before confederation, were torn into pro- and anti-conscriptionist factions. Based as it was on a single issue, Borden's Union government could not be expected to outlast the war. With Laurier's death in 1919, and Borden's retirement a year later, it was clear that the political landscape was going to change. Few foresaw just how significant this change would be.

Before they could tackle any of the issues that accompanied the end of the war, the two mainstream national parties had to find new leaders. This was especially delicate for the Liberals. Not only would the new leader have to replace an icon of Canadian politics that had dominated his party since 1887. The more pressing problem was that the new leader had to stitch the party back together. He had to appeal to both the English- and French-speaking elements in the party and the country. The Liberals chose William Lyon MacKenzie King, a previous Minister of Labour, for this role and he, like his predecessor, would dominate both his party and country for 25 years. The Conservatives chose Arthur Meighen to pilot their party in the postwar years. As Borden's Solicitor General, Meighen had been instrumental in developing the War Measures Act, the Military Service Act and the Wartime Elections Act. Meighen had been at the forefront of the most difficult legislation of the war years.

The political situation may have settled down into established prewar patterns had these two parties remained, with nationalists from Quebec, the only political choices for voters. The early 1920s, however, saw

Canadian prime ministers, 1920–48	
Prime minister	**Years**
Arthur Meighen	1920–21
William Lyon Mackenzie King	1921–26
Arthur Meighen	1926
William Lyon Mackenzie King	1926–30
R. B. Bennett	1930–35
William Lyon Mackenzie King	1935–48

William Lyon Mackenzie King (1874–1950)

William Mackenzie King, grandson of Upper Canada Rebellion leader William Lyon Mackenzie, studied economics in Chicago and Harvard and took a job as Deputy Minister of Labour in 1900. Eight years later he entered the House of Commons as an elected member and was appointed Wilfred Laurier's Minister of Labour. After a period of time out of elected office, he succeeded Laurier as the leader of the Liberal Party in 1919 and as such became Prime Minister of Canada in 1921, an office he would hold until 1926. After the briefest of time out of office, he served again in 1926–30 and 1935–48.

In foreign policy King's years were marked by the attempt to solidify the independence won on the battlefields of Europe. This was evidenced in his approach to the Chanak Affair in 1921 and the King–Byng Affair of 1926. In domestic policies he took a cautious approach. He was fond of appointing commissions to study problems before taking any precipitous action. This provoked the ire of those who thought the Depression and other issues such as the Maritime Rights Movement required drastic and immediate action. He charted a cautious foreign policy course in the years leading up to and during the Second World War. His approach to the second conscription crisis was emblematically captured by the masterfully ambiguous slogan "Conscription if necessary, but not necessarily conscription."

a remarkable surge in the popularity of non-traditional parties. Thomas Crerar, a former Minister of Agriculture from Manitoba harnessed a growing sense of western prairie alienation and formed the National Progressive Party with other disaffected western members of parliament in 1919. They would form the official opposition after the federal election of 1921, although they declined the title. This same sense of rural discontent was the chief force that propelled the new United Farmers of Ontario into government in 1919. A similar story played out in Alberta, in 1921, when the United Farmers of Alberta formed the government after the provincial election.

Prairie drought and relief project for a landing-field in Alberta during the Great Depression.

Throughout the 1920s, the Progressives were divided. Moderate Progressives advocated cooperation with the established parties while the more radical members of the party were not so inclined and favored a radical change to the system of Canadian politics. In the mid-1920s a Progressive member of parliament from Winnipeg named J. S. Woodsworth rose to the fore of the Progressives preaching tax reform that shifted the tax burden to business and the wealthy, the development of federal unemployment insurance and old-age pensions.

Regional discontent spread to the Atlantic coast as well. The Maritimes rights movement developed in the early 1920s, arguing for greater subsidies to the Maritime provinces and tariffs to protect their coal and steel industries. When their Liberal members of parliament could not deliver on these demands Maritime voters turned to the Conservatives in the 1925 federal election. Mackenzie King, and his Liberals nevertheless won the election on the strength of their support in the rest of the country. Although this fractured political landscape was short-lived, neutered in large part by the piecemeal compromises of Prime Minister King, it introduced a number of elements into the federal political discussion—the regulation of industry, financial support for farmers, social security, new political parties, federal vs. provincial relations—ideas that would resurface during the difficult years of the 1930s.

 On what other types of projects did people on relief work? Besides giving immediate monetary relief, how did increased incomes help the economic problems of the Depression?

Economic fragility

The roots of the Depression, in Canada and the rest of the world, can be traced to the economic changes that followed the armistice of 1918. The war had beggared most of the major industrial economies of the world. Only the United States would emerge from the First World War in a position of relative economic strength. As such, much of the world owed money to the US. This position of strength spread US economic influence throughout the world to an even greater extent.

In many ways Canada was no different. The economic boom that was gathering pace in the United States throughout the early 1920s

Discussion point

To what extent do you think the United States had an obligation to help rebuild the economies of Europe in the early 1920s? What were the practical advantages in doing so?

 What were the dangers of depending on the US economy for worldwide economic stability?

eventually dragged the Canadian economy out of its postwar slump. The surging demand for consumer goods such as automobiles and electronics, in turn, created a demand for minerals such as zinc and copper, a demand supplied by the Canadian mining industry. Exploration opened new areas of the Canadian Shield to mining interests, many controlled by US investors.

Pulp and paper also became a vital new export. US-demand for newsprint was skyrocketing and it became economical for US paper companies to establish **branch plants** across Canada to feed the appetite of the US newspaper industry. Between 1920 and 1929 Canada had tripled her production of newsprint.

Branch plants are factories operating in Canada, but owned by foreign companies.

The emblematic consumer product of the 1920s was the automobile and its production was an important stimulus to the Canadian economy. By the middle of the decade, the major US carmakers had plants in Canada able to produce half a million automobiles a year. The growing car culture sparked the construction of some 57,000 km of paved roads in the last five years of the 1920s. This, despite the fact that only a quarter of the Canadian population was financially able to purchase a car at the time.

By the last years of the decade agriculture was also recovering from a postwar slump. Prices had recovered and in 1928 Canadian farmers took off a bumper crop of record proportions (close to 600 million bushels). While on the surface, this seemed like good news, it concealed a troubling development. Canada's agricultural sector was not the only one that was recovering in the mid 1920s. Global competition in wheat production from South America and Australia was accelerating and world purchasers could now choose between a number of non-North American grain producers. Such dramatically increased supply could not sustain high prices for long.

A similar story was beginning to play out in other economic sectors. Pulp, paper and mining production were beginning to outstrip demand by 1928. Tertiary industries such as railroads also began to feel the effect of declining trade volume. As economic activity slowed and world prices dropped, the short boom of the 1920s seemed to be coming to an end. Why did the boom end in Canada?

- Increased tariffs across the world meant a decline in trade
- Supply of commodities and manufactured products exceeded demand leading to a decline in world prices for commodities
- Over-dependence on staple products
- Over-dependence on the economy of the United States
- Heavy debt-burden carried by governments and individuals.

The crash of 1929

The previous list points to an important element in the discussion of the causes of the Great Depression. The economic developments that would bring about the Depression were well underway before

1929. There were structural problems in the economic boom that made it inherently unstable, both in Canada and in the United States. The problem was compounded by the world's reliance on the health of the US economy. US capital permeated nearly all aspects of the Canadian economy making Canada vulnerable to instability in the US. This growing instability was dramatically accelerated by the stock market crash of October 1929. Although the Toronto Stock Exchange did not suffer a calamity the scale of that which befell its New York counterpart, the vast amount of US capital invested in the Canadian economy meant that the effects of the New York crash were soon felt north of the 49th parallel, just as they were around the world.

Discussion point

Why was there no panic at the Toronto Stock Exchange of the same scale as that which hit the New York Stock Exchange? Were there comparable panics in other stock exchanges around the world? Why or why not?

The economic impact of the Depression

The Depression of the1930s was not the first economic slump to hit Canada. In 1873, the global economic stagnation had hurt Canada. Just prior to and immediately after the First World War, Canada experienced short, sharp economic downturns. What would set the Great Depression apart from the other slumps was its severity, scope, and length. The fact that it was coupled with one of the most severe droughts in Canadian history only served to spread the misery and make recovery more difficult. In the years between 1929 and 1933:

- Imports fell by 25%
- Exports fell by 55%
- Wheat prices fell by 75%
- Unemployment reached 27%
- 20% of Canadians were on some form of relief.

The Depression manifested itself in different ways across the country. In rural Canada, collapsing prices were not matched by falling production costs. Agricultural and fishing products flowing out of the Maritimes faced slashed commodity prices. Agricultural and manufacturing products from central Canada were met by restricted trade policies. The economic disaster was exacerbated by misguided economic policies around the world. Many countries, like the United States and Canada, had already started building ever-higher tariff walls before 1929. This movement spread around the globe after the stock market crash. Italy, Germany, and France all increased tariffs in an effort to protect their own industries, blocking potential markets for Canadian agricultural and manufacturing products.

The prairie provinces were hit doubly hard in the 1930s as the economic disaster of the Depression was compounded by ecological disaster, as in the United States. The devastating drought that gripped the prairies from 1930 to 1937 turned the fertile land into a Dust Bowl. Scores of farms were simply abandoned, the families that owned them leaving to become part of the growing legions of unemployed in the cities. Those that did remain faced the same depressed commodity prices as all farmers. In Saskatchewan, the total provincial income fell by close to 90% and two thirds of the population was on social welfare.

The picture painted by the Depression in urban Canada was more complex. Factory workers were laid off in droves and those who kept their jobs saw their wages slashed in the absence of any minimum wage legislation to protect them. Wage rates varied across the country, but the growing labor pool meant that they were all headed in one direction—down. But the middle class and those in the professions who managed to maintain a stable source of income during the Depression saw their living standards improve on the back of a falling cost of living. This was, however, not the case for the majority of Canadians.

The social impact of the Depression

While on the surface the Depression was an economic crisis, the reality is that it struck deep into every aspect of life in 1930s Canada. That it was coupled with the worst drought in memory meant that the family farm, often a source of relief during industrial downturns, suffered along with the rest of the economy. In a country that was built largely on the promise of land ownership, losing family farms to foreclosure called into question the identity and character of western Canada. Newfoundland, although not a part of the Canadian Dominion until 1949 and an independent British Dominion at the outset of the Depression, suffered so acutely from the decline of its fisheries that unemployment reached 50%. The instability and ensuing political scandals dissolved its legislature and it was forced to revert to its former colonial status during the Depression.

Accustomed to self-reliance, long-term unemployment struck at workers' sense of self-worth. Marriages were postponed and birth rates declined. Once-prosperous prairie towns ceased to exist. Migration changed the demographics of the country significantly as people moved in search of employment or precipitation. Immigration was sharply curtailed and people lashed out at new Canadians in eruptions of xenophobia. Such divisions bit into the labor movement, pitting English-speaking workers against recent arrivals from eastern and northern Europe in the Maritimes and other parts of the country.

The government's response

The Depression set upon Canada during Mackenzie King's second term in office. King, not unlike his counterpart in the White House, was initially at a loss at what to do about the stagnating economy. Other economic slumps had occurred in King's lifetime, but they had proven temporary. King therefore approached the early stages of the Depression as he approached politics in general—cautiously. When he was pressed for government action to alleviate the growing misery, he hid behind the **British North America Act**. King claimed that the type of action required was constitutionally the responsibility of the provinces. But he then refused to increase subsidies to provincial

Discussion point

While protectionism was a common response to the Depression, how might lowering protective tariffs and encouraging free trade have helped the crisis? What would have been the drawbacks of such an approach?

The **British North America Act** was the Act of the British Parliament that established the Dominion of Canada. Although an Act of the British Parliament it functioned as the written portion of Canada's constitution until it was replaced by a solely Canadian Act, the Constitution Act of 1982.

governments—all but two of which were Conservative. He believed that this fiscally vigilant approach was what prudent Canadians expected of him, and he took this faith to the polls in 1930. King miscalculated. The Conservatives, under the leadership of R. B. Bennett, won a majority government on promises of action and relief.

Richard Bedford (R. B.) Bennett (1870–1947)

Born in New Brunswick, Bennett moved to Calgary after getting his law degree from Dalhousie University. He won election to the provincial legislature in 1909 and was elected to the House of Commons during the 1911 federal election. After serving briefly as the minister of justice in 1921, and even more briefly as minister of finance in 1926, he was elected Conservative leader in 1927.

Bennett campaigned on a platform of aggressively attacking the growing economic crisis in the 1930 federal election and this argument carried the day against the more cautious Mackenzie King. Unable to do much in the face of the economic dislocation of the Depression, however, Bennett became for many suffering Canadians the target of their misery and scorn. Cars hitched to horses because the owners could not afford the gas were dubbed "Bennett Buggies" and the shantytowns that grew up outside

Canadian cities were called "Bennett's Boroughs". During this period he received hundreds of letters from destitute Canadians, many of which he answered by hand and returned with a token five dollar bill from his own pocket. While Bennett may have not been callous, for the most part he believed in the free market system and that it would eventually correct itself. Despite this essential conviction, he proposed a far more interventionist economic policy, Bennett's New Deal, as the 1935 federal election loomed. It was not enough to undo what many voters saw as five years of failure and he and his Conservatives were swept from office in 1935. Bennett finished his days in the United Kingdom where he sat in the House of Lords.

Bennett's response to the Depression

Once in office, Bennett succumbed to conventional wisdom and his campaign promises. He increased tariffs by 50% and allocated $20 million for relief programs. All at once he pushed prices higher with the tariff and gave people money to cope with the higher prices—in broad terms a zero net gain.

The relief "system" that developed in the early 1930s consisted of a patchwork of municipal, provincial, federal and private efforts. Single unemployed men, for instance, were directed to work camps operated by the Department of National Defence and located in the wilderness, far from urban centres. While they toiled in these camps they earned 20 cents a day and the nickname the Royal Twenty Centers. The system of relief, such as it was, consisted of federal and provincial funds making their way into municipal coffers from where they would be redistributed to those in the most need. Initially, most were "work for relief" schemes of public works, but this eventually gave way to direct relief. Nevertheless, federal and provincial funds were rarely enough to sustain the growing numbers of people in need. The economic downturn shrank the tax base in cities across the country drastically at the same time that their costs were ballooning. Cities like Montreal tried to meet the need by raising taxes, but to no avail. The city slid into bankruptcy in 1940. As the Depression deepened, it became evident that its economic costs where to be borne disproportionately by local governments.

At the federal level, Prime Minister Bennett established a number of other measures to fight if not the causes then the symptoms of the Depression:

The Canadian Wheat Board

A marketing board designed to rationalize the marketing of grain on the world market and provide a measure of shelter for prairie farmers.

The Farmer's Creditors Arrangement Act

A law to help debt-ridden farmers restructure their loans.

The Prairie Farm Rehabilitation Act

An act that set up an organization to seek solutions to the devastating ecological conditions of the Dust Bowl

The Bank of Canada

Canada's first central bank. It was designed to coordinate the government's monetary policy.

The Canadian Radio Broadcasting Commission

A body designed to foster the growth of the Canadian Broadcasting industry

In all, despite his personal responses to the letters he received regularly asking for aid and his halting intervention into the economy, Bennett's approach to the economic crisis was largely consistent with his belief in the free enterprise system and that people, not the government, are ultimately responsible for their own wellbeing. As the Canadian economy limped into the fifth year of the Depression, Bennett shocked many in the country and his own party by advocating a more comprehensive and aggressive approach to the crisis. Taking a cue from Roosevelt's plan, this package became known as Bennett's New Deal.

King's response to the Depression

The federal election campaign of 1935 pitted King's Liberals, out of office during the worst years of the Depression, against Bennett and his New Deal, as well as the Cooperative Commonwealth Federation, The Social Credit Party, the remnants of the Progressives and a number of smaller parties. King's Liberals won a huge majority on the slogan "King or Chaos." But now the problem of the Depression was his.

Unemployed men playing ring toss game, Montreal, Quebec, about 1935.

 How would unemployment have affected leisure activities? What activities remained popular during the Depression? Why?

Activity

Bennett's "Deathbed conversion"

Bennett's New Deal came at the end of his tenure as prime minister. His New Deal included the laws to govern the following areas:

● Wages

● Hours of work

● Farm credit

● Natural resource marketing

● Unemployment insurance

Research each of these measures. To what degree do you think Bennett saw them as a repudiation of the free market system or rather temporary measures to correct a defect in the system?

To what extent do you think Bennett genuinely supported these measures or was he rather trying to appease the voting public in the face of the 1935 election?

Sources you can use for your research:

Waite, Peter B. 1992. *Loner: Personal Life & Ideas R.B Bennett*. University of Toronto Press.

Gray, H. James, 1991. *R.B. Bennett: The Calgary Years*. University of Toronto Press.

Boyko, John. 2010. *Bennett: The Rebel Who Challenged and Changed a Nation*. Toronto: Key Porter Books.

The reality is that King had no more of a plan to fight the Depression in 1935 than he had had in 1930. He was not, however, willing to see if Bennett's New Deal would work. He had attacked the New Deal in the election as extravagantly expensive at a time that called for prudence. Not wanting to be the politician to cut this direct aid and risk incurring the wrath of the unemployed, he referred the measures to the Supreme Court, which duly found that most of the New Deal treaded on provincial jurisdiction and thus contradicted the British North America Act. To compound the delay caused by the court challenge, King then struck his own commission to study the extent to which the Act could be altered to accommodate the type of measures pioneered by Bennett.

It was during this period of study that another of King's commissions reported that what the Canadian economy needed was an infusion of government spending and tax cuts. Just as Bennett's relatively radical reforms had split the Conservative Party in 1935, the unity of the Liberal Party was threatened by this revolutionary departure from accepted economic theory during the budget discussion of 1938. A compromise allowed the Liberal Party to remain intact as the Canadian economy stumbled toward the recovery that the Second World War would bring.

Political responses to the Depression

Just as the profound economic dislocation brought on by the Depression led to a radical rejection of liberal democracy in parts of Europe, it brought out ideas for a radical reordering of the political

Discussion point

Politicians seeking election during periods of hard economic conditions often advocate tariffs as a solution. Why?

Discussion point

The British-North America Act, which functioned as the written portion of Canada's constitution from 1867 until 1982, was originally drafted in 1867 to bring New Brunswick, Nova Scotia, Ontario, and Quebec into a Canadian confederation.

As an Act of the British Parliament it could be changed by a majority vote in London.

 To what extent should constitutions be easy to change?

Activity

Keynesian economics

John Maynard Keynes was a British economist who studied the problems of the Great Depression. He formed the opinion that the ultimate issue in the Depression was a lack of overall demand. Although this business cycle of booms and recessions was common, his worry was that the Depression had lasted so long that there was not enough purchasing power left in traditional sources of demand to bring the economy back to close to full employment. He feared that the business cycle might find equilibrium at a lower level of employment. Keynes believed that the only institution with enough purchasing power to boost demand out of the Depression were national governments.

He therefore advocated that governments should spend money on public works and anything that put money in the pockets of potential consumers during periods of economic decline. During times of economic expansion, governments should take in money in the form of increased taxation. Booms would not be as high but nor would recessions be as deep.

Research the economic history of five countries in North, Central, and South America in the decades after the Great Depression, 1936–2000. What evidence is there of Keynesian economics? What are the results of these policies? Are there any patterns to the adoption and or rejection of these policies in the region?

Country	Years	Keynesian policies	Results

economy in North America as well. In Canada, this was expressed in the creation of some new and innovative political parties. In many ways these new parties were a continuation of the populist politics that appeared in Canada during the 1920s.

The Cooperative Commonwealth Federation:

The Cooperative Commonwealth Federation (CCF) was born out of a meeting between labor and farm activists in Calgary in 1932. Within a year there was another meeting in Regina during which the CCF adopted its platform as expressed in the Regina Manifesto. In many ways what separated the CCF and its manifesto from other ideas about how to fight the Depression was its underlying assumption that the system could not or should not be fixed, but rather replaced. It represented a rejection of the basic tenets of the free market system and as such was branded as dangerous socialism or even communism.

The CCF would run as a democratic socialist party in the established Canadian political system—it sought reform not revolution. It chose J. S. Woodsworth, Progressive member of parliament, as its leader and managed to elect five candidates in the 1935 federal election. The CCF ran candidates successfully in provincial and municipal elections as well. This provincial and local success makes sense in that, as King's court challenge to the New Deal would prove, matters of direct relief, unemployment insurance and similar measures were the purview of provincial governments and it was in these areas that the CCF and its policies were most appealing to the voting public. By 1944, the CCF would form the provincial government in Saskatchewan under the leadership of Tommy Douglas, a former Baptist minister. This was the first socialist government elected in North America. The CCF, which merged with organized labor to form the New Democratic Party (NDP) in 1961, governed Saskatchewan for 40 years during the 20th century.

Activity

The Regina Manifesto vs. the Social Credit League of Alberta 10 Plank Platform (1935)

Source A

The Social Credit League of Alberta 10 Plank Platform (1935)

> The following excerpt is from a document that was issued by the Social Credit League of Alberta in 1935 as a summary of its platform.
>
> 1 Finance and the Distribution of Goods
>
>   c The establishment of a Just Price for all goods and services, and the regulation of the price spread [price mark up] on all goods sold or transferred within the bounds of the Province [Alberta].
>
>   →

This Just Price is to be just and fair:

1   To the producers and to the distributors. They should not be required to sell goods for less than the cost of production or of import.

2   To the consumers. They should not be exploited of unduly deprived of fair returns for their purchasing power.

2   The Present Problem of Debt

    a   Private, or Mortgage and Tax Indebtedness

        1   The Distribution of Basic Dividends [Social Dividends] and the Establishment of a Just Price will at once begin to give our citizens the ability to cope with Mortgage Indebtedness at present against their farms and their Homes

Source B

The following is an excerpt from the Regina Manifesto, a founding document of the Cooperative Commonwealth Federation (CCF).

2   Socialization Of Finance

Socialization of all financial machinery—banking currency, credit, and insurance, to make possible the effective control of currency, credit and prices, and the supplying of new productive equipment for socially desirable purposes.

Planning by itself will be of little use if the public authority has not the power to carry its plans into effect. Such power will require the control of finance and of all those vital industries and services, which, if they remain in private hands, can be used to thwart or corrupt the will of the public authority. Control of finance is the first step in the control of the whole economy. The chartered banks must be socialized and removed from the control of private profit-seeking interests; and the national banking system thus established must have at its head a Central Bank to control the flow of credit and the general price level, and to regulate foreign exchange operations. A National Investment Board must also be set up, working in co-operation with the socialized banking system to mobilize and direct the unused surpluses of production for socially desired purposes as determined by the Planning Commission.

Insurance Companies, which provide one of the main channels for the investment of individual savings and which, under their present competitive organization, charge needlessly high premiums for the social services that they render, must also be socialized.

Source: Zakuta, Leo. 1964. *A Protest Movement Becalmed: A Study of Change in the CCF.* Toronto: University of Toronto Press. http://economics.uwaterloo.ca/needhdata/Regina_Manifesto.html.

Questions

1   Explain the following references:

    a   "Basic Dividends" [Source A]

    b   "Socialization of all financial machinery" [Source B]

    c   "socially desired purposes" [Source B]

2   How do "Insurance Companies . . . provide one of the main channels for the investment of individual savings"? [Source B]

3   How do the two documents differ in their approach to debt?

4   **a**   What evidence is there of collectivism in each of the sources?

    b   What evidence is there of individualism in each of the sources?

5   With reference to their origin and purpose, what are the values and limitations of each source for historians studying political responses to the Depression in Canada?

6   What are the strengths and weaknesses of the arguments presented in these two sources?

7   Research the subsequent political history of Saskatchewan and Alberta. How do these sources help explain that history?

Social Credit

While supporters of the CCF looked to collectivism as the solution to the misery of the Depression, others looked to improving the spending power of the individual as the magic bullet. William Aberhart was another Baptist minister who was moved to enter politics by the suffering heaped on the people of the west by the Depression. Aberhart, or "Bible Bill" as he was known, found a solution in the complicated doctrine of Social Credit and brought it to Alberta in 1932, publicizing it on his popular radio program. In short, Social Credit sought to increase consumer spending by issuing credits worth $25 a month to citizens. Not wishing to encourage idleness, these dividends could be suspended if people refused available employment. While Aberhart did denounce the greed of the banking system, Social Credit was designed to operate within the market economy.

It is not hard to understand why Social Credit struck a chord with the impoverished farmers of Alberta. Aberhart seemed to be promising $25 a month to all Albertans and this promise carried them to massive electoral victory in the 1935 Alberta election. The financial mechanics of such a payment, however, delayed its implementation. The Socreds did bring some debt relief to farmers and a reformed farm insurance scheme. When he tried to regulate the banking industry and bring in the $25 social dividends, the laws were struck down as unconstitutional in that monetary policy and banking were federal powers. Nevertheless, with a modified, practical, and largely conservative platform the Social Credit Party would govern Alberta for 36 years until 1971.

Union Nationale

While on the prairies the impulse was to look to either new collectivist models (the CCF) or to modifications on traditional individualist themes (Social Credit), in Quebec the desperation created by the Depression found expression in renewed nationalism. Profiting from an ideological split in Quebec's Liberal Party and the growing popularity of French Catholic social action groups such as Ecole Sociale Populaire, Quebec's Conservative Party leader Maurice Duplessis brought these groups together in a new party called the Union Nationale, which formed the Quebec government after the 1936 election. Strictly provincial and populist, the Union Nationale established a conservative regime that championed Quebec francophone interests against the federal government in Ottawa and a nebulous traditional Quebec Catholic rural ethic. Duplessis ruled Quebec and the Union Nationale as a demagogue, taking aim at political opponents and anyone suspected of socialist or communist sympathies. This hard-line approach to left-wing opponents was best illustrated in the controversial Act Respecting Communist Propaganda, known as the "padlock law," passed by Duplessis's government in 1937. This law empowered the government to shut down any organization deemed by the government to be promoting "communism." The wording was vague enough for Duplessis to use it against any number of moderately left-wing groups.

The Communist Party of Canada

As in other parts of the world, economic crisis bred extremist politics and Canada in the 1930s was no exception. The Communist Party of Canada, founded in 1921, approached the Depression from two angles. It ran, and in some cases elected, members to public office at the provincial and municipal levels, and in the 1940s elected Fred Rose to the federal parliament. The party was also an important force in organized labour and was instrumental in the Workers Unity League and the On To Ottawa Trek. The centralized control of all communist parties imposed by Stalin through the **Comintern**, however, meant that the Communist Party of Canada could not fashion a platform that responded to the Canadian context and its popularity suffered as a consequence. Government repression also bit deep into its popularity. Duplesis used the padlock law liberally against the Communist Party in Quebec. In 1931, the national party's headquarters was raided and its leader, Tim Buck, was arrested and sentenced to five years in prison.

Ontario Liberals

The crisis of the Depression put strains on the relationship between traditional provincial parties and the federal government. In Ontario, Mitchell Hepburn, the Liberal premier clashed regularly with Prime Minister King, a fellow Liberal. Although elected on a moderate reform platform, championing higher wages and business regulation to combat what he described as the privilege of the élite, Hepburn had little time for unionism and governed the province from a fairly traditional centre-right perspective. This perspective was well illustrated in 1937 when he created an army of strike-breakers, "Hepburn's Hussars," to smash a large strike at the Oshawa General Motors plant when Prime Minister King refused to use the Royal Canadian Mounted Police (RCMP) to break the strike.

Unionism

The principles of supply and demand in the labor market generally dictate that unionism is at its weakest during periods of recession and depression and the 1930s more or less bore this out in Canada. There were, however, some important innovations developed by working people to cope with the hardships of the Depression.

Canada's traditional labor organizations, groups like the Trades and Labour Congress (TLC), responded to the Depression by retrenching and turning their attention to what remained of their employed membership. In fact, union membership in Canada only declined by 15% during the 1930s. Much of the militant industrial action that erupted during this period was guided by a new broad-based labor organization led by committed communists.

The Workers Unity League (WUL) was instituted in Canada in 1929 at the behest of the Comintern. Its goal was to organize disparate unions into a larger association and to use this as a weapon for large-scale industrial action. The WUL and its energetic and active organizers led a number of strikes across the country between 1930 and 1940 in both primary industries, such as mining, and secondary

Comintern is short for Communist International, this was an organization developed by the Soviet Union in 1919 to coordinate the activities of national communist parties around the world. From 1928, Stalin was the chairman and used the organization as a tool of Soviet foreign policy.

Discussion point

The Comintern sought to control and coordinate the activities of Communist Parties around the globe. What are the advantages of this approach? What are the disadvantages? Where was the control evident in other parts of the world?

industries such as manufacturing. But the WUL was a tool of international communism and despite its successes in championing the rights of working Canadians, it was denounced and broken up by those in government and rival labor organizations who saw it as a threat to the essential principles of society.

Activity

Industrial action in the 1930s

Industrial action in the 1930s in Canada		
Location	Union	Year
Bienfait, Saskatchewan	Mine Workers Union of Canada	1931
Stratford, Ontario	Chesterfield and Furniture Workers' Industrial Union	1933
Rouyn, Quebec	Mine Workers Union of Canada	1934
Montreal, Quebec	Industrial Union of Needle Trades Workers	1934
Oshawa, Ontario	Committee for Industrial Organization	1935
Vancouver, BC	Vancouver and District Waterfront Workers' Association	1935
Quebec (Province-wide textile industry strike)	Catholic Confederation of Labour	1937

Research the outcome of the strikes listed.

 What generalizations can you make about the effectiveness of industrial action during the 1930s in Canada?

The On To Ottawa Trek

From 1930 to 1935 Bennett's government clung stubbornly to its contention that relief was the business of provinces, municipalities and private charities. For their part, provinces and municipalities preferred to spend their limited resources on the welfare of family breadwinners. The end result of this haphazard and paltry relief system was that as the Depression deepened the legions of single unemployed men swelled to huge proportions. In an effort to find work, these masses of resentful and desperate men took to the rails, hopping on freight cars and traveling across the country in search of what limited employment opportunities might exist elsewhere. Shantytowns grew up outside Canadian cities just as they did outside US cities. While in the United States they were called Hoovervilles, they were the Bennett Boroughs in Canada. These growing encampments and the prospect of throngs of rootless men inundating communities led the Federal government to establish a system of "relief" camps deep in the wilds of Canada, far from urban centres and "respectable" citizens. The work camps were administered by the Department of National Defence with military discipline. The discipline, work

A soup kitchen in Montreal in 1931. With limited government relief, many people had to rely on private charities for food.

 What are the advantages and drawbacks of relying on private relief?

conditions, low wages and sense of hopelessness that permeated the camps made them a natural environment for the growth of radicalism.

The communist WUL recognized this potential to organize and radicalize the unemployed in the relief camps. WUL members soon infiltrated the camps and began to organize and direct the seething discontent in the camps, forming the Relief Camp Workers Union. By the beginning of 1935, men began to leave the camps in British Columbia to descend upon Vancouver. They lived in the streets and supported themselves with handouts, clashing with police regularly. Following their leader Arthur "Slim" Evans, 1,000 of these Royal Twenty Centers climbed aboard trains to take their complaints to the seat of the federal government in Ottawa. As the On to Ottawa Trek passed through the towns and cities of British Columbia and Alberta the number of Trekkers swelled to 2,000.

The threat of thousands, perhaps tens of thousands, of unemployed men invading the capital scared Bennett into negotiating with Evans and other leaders of the Trek. In reality, Bennett was simply buying time while the Trek moved out of his home riding of Calgary. He had already decided that the Trek would be stopped before it reached Winnipeg, the scene of the Winnipeg General Strike of 1919 and hotbed of union activity. Conveniently, the Royal Canadian Mounted Police Training Depot was located between Calgary and Winnipeg in Regina, the next stop on the Trek. On July 1, 1935, police and Trekkers clashed in what became known as the Regina Riot. After a day of bitter fighting, over 100 Trekkers were arrested and the rest dispersed.

Riding the rails. Thousands of Canadian men took to the rails in search of work during the Depression.

 How did local authorities respond to men riding the rails? Why were communities concerned about this practice?

Activity

Canada's Indian Act

The Canadian government passed the Indian Act in 1876. It was designed to identify those First Nations people who were subject to the terms of the various treaties signed by the government and First Nation bands across the country—"status Indians"—and to regulate the relationship between the government and these people. In practice the Indian Act became the chief tool by which the government of Canada sought to assimilate the First Nations people. The Indian Act was amended numerous times between 1884 and 1938 and in the years following the Depression. The Indian Act still exists although not in the form it did throughout the 19th and 20th centuries.

The Act and subsequent amendments to 1938 established the following:

- "Indian Agents" had the power of magistrates and administered Indian affairs in their respective districts
- "Status Indians" could only sell agricultural produce including livestock with the permission of the Indian Agent
- Ceremonial dances and celebrations such as the potlatch were banned
- First Nations people could be removed, without recourse, from reserve land that was close to centers with a population over 8,000 people

- First Nations bands would be compensated up to only 50% for the sale of reserve lands
- Western First Nations people could not appear in ceremonial dress without permission from the Indian Agent
- "Status Indians" people were banned from pool halls
- "Status Indians" were not permitted to vote (They would not be allowed to vote until 1961).

Questions and further research

1   How did the Indian Act try to assimilate First Nations people?

2   In establishing its relationship with the First Nations of what would become Canada, the Canadian government signed a series of treaties with groups of First Nations peoples at the end of the 19th and beginning of the 20th centuries. Use the following website to analyze these treaties and the extent to which the Indian Act reflects or contradicts the provisions of the treaties: http://www.ainc-inac.gc.ca/al/hts/tgu/index-eng.asp.

3   Compare and contrast the treatment of Canada's First Nations people in the 1920s and 1930s with the treatment of African Americans and Native Americans in the United States during this same period.

The role of religion in the Depression

In times of crisis people often turn to traditional sources of comfort. Victims of the Depression looked to established as well as new religious movements for succor. The crisis also politicized religious movements during the Depression. While some saw in the ecological and economic catastrophe divine retribution for the material sins of humans and preached repentance, men like "Bible Bill" Aberhart used their religious pulpits to preach not patience, but rather reform. The Depression gave new life to the Social Gospel movement that had flourished at the end of the previous century. The Social Gospel of the 1930s was the belief that Christian principles such as charity and compassion should be the centre of government action, rather than a fortunate byproduct of a noninterventionist government. This conviction was essential to many of those who helped found the CCF such as J. S. Woodsworth and T. C. Douglas. Tommy Douglas, a Baptist minister, however, did not advocate reckless spending. Instead, they believed that the economy could be actively managed for the equal benefit of all while observing the equally Christian principles of prudence and restraint. The Fellowship of a Christian Social Order brought together Christianity and socialism for members of the United Church. The Catholic Church, especially in Quebec, sought to give its congregation support in the form of charity while at the same time railing against the evils of communism. It saw the Depression as a call to moral rebirth and championed a back-to-the-land movement as a remedy for the wanton consumerism bred by unbridled capitalism.

Activity

Responses across parties

Compare and contrast the policies of Canadian political parties during the Great Depression. To what extent do these policies represent continuity with past policies? To what extent did they represent a break with traditional policy? Use the following chart to help.

	Liberals	Conservatives	CCF	Socreds	Communists
Government ownership					
Relief/welfare					
Monetary policy					
Fiscal policy					
Tariffs					

Depression era culture in Canada

Then, as since, the same forces that formed Canada's economy—colonial heritage, geography and proximity to the United States—have dominated Canada's cultural landscape. In this sense, the Depression represents a good deal of cultural continuity with earlier periods. There was also a continuity with the First World War period in which Canadian nationalism germinated. The growing importance of the radio as a cultural disseminator meant that Canadians were exposed to those elements of US culture that could be broadcast, most notably music. Jazz and country made their way into Canada during the 1920s and this continued throughout the Depression years. Musicians crossed the border in both directions, including popular Canadian Big Bands such as Guy Lombardo and his Royal Canadians. US musical responses to the Depression such as the songs of Woody Guthrie also found an audience in Canada expressing as they did many of the same struggles facing Canadians during this period.

In the years prior to the First World War, a group of Canadian visual artists shared a vision of what could become a particularly Canadian approach to aesthetic representation: The artists Frederick Varley, Franklin Carmichael, and J. E. H. MacDonald came together with Arthur Lismer, Lawren Harris, A. Y. Jackson, and Franz Johnston in the early 1920s to demonstrate their distinctly Canadian sensibility, drawing on an expression of the nationalism that grew out of the participation in the First World War. Known as the Group of Seven, these artists, with a somewhat changing membership, exhibited together into the early1930s. Although the Group of Seven itself did not exist beyond 1931, its influence and nationalist sentiments had an important and lasting impact on those artists grappling with the bitter reality of the 1930s.

The economics of the Depression had a stifling impact on Canadian art during this period. Money for all luxuries dried up and art was certainly no exception. Nevertheless, the Depression was an important context for painters such as Illingsworth Kerr and Carl Schaefer. While, on the one hand, the nationalism of the Group of Seven had an important impact on Canadian painters of the 1930s, the regional character of the Depression also helped foster distinctly local approaches to painting style and subject matter. Much of Kerr's work is rooted in the Saskatchewan prairies and Emily Carr's paintings have become almost iconic of the Pacific coast.

In terms of literature, there were significant Canadian works developed during the Depression. Writers such as Morley Callaghan and Emily Carr (who worked across both art forms) produced period pieces. One of the lasting impacts of the Depression on Canadian literature, however, is its enduring influence on those writers who grew up in this period and later reflected on it: writers such as W. O. Mitchell and Max Braithwaite. Mitchell's *Who Has Seen the Wind?* (1947) offers a deep insight into a boy's coming of age during the years of the Depression in the Canadian prairies and the lives of ordinary Canadians as they responded to the reality of the drought and hardships of rural life told in a distinctively western Canadian voice.

Sporting culture: the emergence of hockey as a national pastime in the Depression

The national passion that hockey would become in Canada during the course of the 20th century was becoming evident early in the century. Like so many other aspects of Canadian society, sports in general and hockey in particular were fundamentally altered by the upheaval of the First World War. Professional hockey, however, as it emerged in the postwar era boomed in much the same way as the broader economy did, both in Canada and in the United States. Hockey franchises appreciated in value dramatically during the 1920s, in some cases by a factor of three. Easy credit, high employment and stable income levels left Canadians with money to spend on entertainment and in many centers this meant the local hockey team. As part of the growing consumer culture, hockey also benefited from the growth of mass media and advertising, which in turn was becoming increasingly national in nature. As such, hockey, which until the 1920s had still largely been dominated by local and regional teams and leagues, became followed on a national scale. By the end of the 1920s, the NHL was the dominant professional hockey league and consisted of ten teams.

The NHL was and is a business and as such was not immune to the economic disaster of the Depression. The NHL expanded, as did many businesses in the 1920s, on easy credit and as this dried up the league would contract into a smaller, but very successful six teams. Cities like New York and Montreal found that they could only financially

> ## TOK Link
>
> What role can works of fiction serve in understanding history? What are the limitations of using historical fiction to discover historical knowledge?

support one team, each losing their second franchise during the 1930s. Other teams found ways to remain and even expand. When Con Smythe tried to build Maple Leaf Gardens in 1930 he garnered some of the building costs by offering shares to the construction trades as partial payment. Tickets sales were but one way a professional hockey franchise made money and when national radio broadcasts began, it opened a number of other revenue streams such as endorsements and advertising that allowed the teams to remain profitable in the Depression.

When Canada slid into economic depression in 1929, and family farms and in some cases whole communities were swept away, Canadians across the country took refuge in what was fast becoming the national pastime—hockey. While comparatively few could afford or even had geographic access to one of the major professional hockey teams, the beginning of national radio broadcasts in 1933 brought the game into the homes of people across Canada and within a year these broadcasts had an audience of over a million. As Richard Gruneau and David Whitson have pointed out, this mass marketing of the game and its incredible popularity in Canada kept hockey a distinctive part of Canadian culture despite the fact that many of the teams were from the United States—albeit with mostly Canadian players. Imbedded within the NHL were two dominant sides of the national culture. The Montreal Canadiens became emblematic of French Canada and later the Toronto Maple Leafs would, to a lesser degree, represent English Canada in ritualized competition on Saturday nights for the whole country to hear. The escapism of *Hockey Night in Canada*, as the national broadcasts were known, allowed Canadians to forget the economic gloom of the 1930s, if only for a couple of hours a week, in the same way that Hollywood musicals did. It did so in a manner that was culturally unifying—the Toronto Maple Leafs, New York Rangers and Detroit Red Wings had fans in Saskatoon, Edmonton, Prince Albert and countless small prairie towns as well as in Toronto, New York and Detroit. In doing this, hockey established itself in the 1930s as an enduring national cultural factor.

Latin American responses to the Great Depression

The conditions that brought the Great Depression to Latin America had their roots in the economic policies of late-19th century political leaders. The first 50 years after independence had seen the creation of largely self-sufficient agriculturally-based units that mirrored the *latifundias* of Spain; here plantations produced the food needed for the immediate surroundings and handicrafts were produced by local artisans, mirroring the feudal systems that existed in Europe. However, with the onset of industrialization in the United States and Europe, Latin American commodities became more valuable. Industrialized countries focused on production and the concentration of labor in factories meant that many of these countries became dependent upon exports to feed the growing urban citizenry in their states.

This was particularly true in the United Kingdom which had established strong trade relations with Latin American states after the wars of independence. They capitalized on pre-existing relations to increase their importation of food; Argentina in particular profited from this exchange, exporting beef and wheat to the UK. There was also a growing market for the tropical fruits that were being produced on US-owned plantations in Central America. The onset of refrigeration on ships allowed this market to flourish and United Fruit Company profited tremendously as it could ship tropical fruits to its home base in the United States. Lastly, the demand for Latin American minerals and natural resources that had dwindled in the post-revolutionary period once again became important; Chilean copper and nitrates were exported to Europe to support its industrial sector.

Women working in the export sector in Honduras.

While the export market for primary produce and natural resources was thriving, Latin American countries were slow to develop their own industries. Textile factories, construction facilities, food processing and beverage industries did thrive on local initiative, but they remained a very small part of the national economy. For most finished goods Latin Americans had to rely on imports. This set up a dual reliance on the export–import trade: Latin American countries were dependent upon the export of resources for income, but they also relied upon foreign imports for industrial goods.

The powerful élites felt that their own countries lacked the educational and technological skills needed to develop a strong industrial base. Rather than nurture a local sector, they encouraged foreign investment and ownership in such endeavors. This was the case in Mexico where the economic liberals called themselves the *científicos* and promoted incentives for overseas investors in Mexico. US investors flocked to the country, buying land for mining and railway construction. While Mexico did benefit from these companies, the majority of the profits went back to the United States, and the government itself had very little to gain as their own incentive schemes granted tax-free or reduced-tax status for foreign companies.

The United States was not the major trading partner for Latin America. In 1913, two thirds of investment in the region came from the United Kingdom. This was followed by the United States, France and Germany. During the First World War, Latin America on the whole benefitted but the weakness of the system was beginning to show. As the European countries faced economic hardships and slow recovery from the war, the wealth that had previously been generated by the export–import model began to fade and most Latin American exports had reached their peak market value even before the crash.

The supply of Latin American goods began to outstrip demand even before the onset of the Great Depression and provided some early warning signs for those who tracked global trade. Since their economies were dependent on the prosperity of those with whom they traded and the policy decisions made overseas, Latin America was very susceptible to the fortunes of its trade partners. Argentina received its peak price for wheat in March 1927; for Cuban sugar, it was March 1928; and Brazilian coffee hit the same apex in March 1929. This shows that the basis of most Latin American countries were already on a downward slope. The Great Depression served to exacerbate existing issues—it did not create them.

The onset of the Depression in Latin America

The initial effects of the Depression were similar to what was seen elsewhere. As the demand for goods declined, there was less inflow of capital. This, in turn, meant internal deflation, the fall in value of Latin American currencies and a rise in unemployment. There was a fall in foreign investment and most countries found themselves in financial trouble as they were significantly indebted to foreign banks. As the banks themselves faced collapse, they also demanded an immediate return of their investments but in most cases this was impossible. Protectionist measures in other countries also made Latin American goods unaffordable. The decline in revenue meant that Latin American countries could not repay their debts or keep governments afloat. There were exceptions: Venezuela's oil and Honduras's bananas kept them solvent, but these were anomalies. Most countries were facing economic collapse.

The immediate effect of the Depression in many countries was political change. Placing blame on the existing governments, there were a number of coups d'etats. In the year after the Wall Street Crash the military took power in Argentina, Brazil, Chile, Guatemala, Honduras and Perú. While their treatment of the population and respect for the rights of individuals were dubious at best, they had at their disposal the mechanisms to change economic policies to address the crisis. From the Depression onwards, state intervention in the economy became the norm.

There were several approaches to addressing the crisis. The first was government regulation to stabilize the local economy; governments set prices and established maximum levels of production (sometimes this included the destruction of surplus goods). This was done to bolster the existing economies and help them regain their strength. The second was Import Substitution Industrialization (ISI). The goal here was to encourage the creation of homegrown industries to replace Latin American dependence on foreign manufactured goods. Lastly, governments tried to keep their international markets open by engaging in bilateral trade agreements with industrialized countries.

In many cases, the policies led to a rapid recovery; mining and agriculture were not as hard hit as the industrial sectors, so these products could be used to bring about recovery. Additionally, the economic model that had been adopted prior to the Depression included a close relationship between banks and the government. Financial reforms of the 1920s included the creation of central banks and regulatory institutions with clearly defined rules. This made government intervention in the financial sector easier than in other countries. Many countries left the gold standard and pegged their currencies to the US dollar, aiding their recovery. Despite difficult financial times, Latin American countries did not default on their loans, and used nonpayment as a temporary measure to bring about recovery and keep faith in their currencies.

Ultimately, these policies brought Latin America out of the Depression but the social inequalities caused by class and racial hierarchies that had plagued the region since independence remained and were in fact heightened by the economic distress. The leaders that came to power as a result of the Depression did not simply have to bring about economic recovery; they also had to address social and labor issues that had languished for over a century. Many leaders adopted a populist stance to co-opt the working and middle classes; the degree of success of these men varied and the results of their rule were contentious.

To make an effective comparison of two countries with striking similarities but also significant differences, the following analysis will focus on two countries: Brazil and Argentina.

Activity

Case study

The two case studies provided, focus on two large countries that were strongly affected by the Depression. But not all countries were hit as hard, nor were all countries so large. To that end, choose a Latin American country—other than Argentina or Brazil—to investigate. Answer the following questions in your case study:

1 What type of government did this country have in place?

2 Was its economy dependent on one crop or was it diversified?

3 Did it have any industry?

4 Who were its main trading partners?

5 What sort of class structure did it have?

6 How hard was it hit by the Depression?

7 How did it get out of the Depression?

Based on your answers to these questions formulate a thesis on how it reflects general trends in Latin America, and its difference to other countries in the region.

Brazil: the coffee economy

Prior to October 1929, the Brazilian economy was dependent on agriculture, particularly coffee. While rubber, cotton and cocoa were also key cash crops, coffee dominated Brazilian exports. In the 1920s, coffee exports were the source of over 70% of the country's revenue. Brazilian producers had to strike a delicate balance to prevent overproduction while having enough to maximize profits; this was not always easy, as the trade was reliant on the vagaries of the international market over which Brazilian producers had no control.

Political leadership of Brazil, 1922–45	
Artur Bernades	1922–26
Washington Luis	1926–30
Júlio Prestes	Did not take office
Getúlio Vargas	1930–45

To take more control, in 1925 Brazil created the São Paulo Institute for Permanent Defense of Coffee. To keep coffee prices high, the institute would purchase and withhold its goods from the world market. To pay for the coffee, the institute received the revenue from a transportation tax and took out loans from foreign banks.

This policy, known as valorization, was potentially dangerous, as Brazilian coffee producers wanted to expand their markets, and other Latin American countries were increasing their production of coffee, thereby limiting Brazil's dominance of the international market. Manipulation of supply might have short-term success, but in the long run it would fail as Brazil would not remain competitive.

The policy was successful in the 1920s. In 1927, Brazil produced an all-time high of 27 million bags of coffee and as world prices began to fall, the institute bought coffee and prevented a substantial decrease in the price. Then, in 1928, when the coffee crop was small, the stocks they had purchased were placed on the market and not only did prices hold, but there were substantial reserves of coffee to be sold.

There was a small, emerging industrial base in several cities, but it was limited; most manufactured goods came from overseas, meaning that most profits from export were spent overseas, and there was a substantial outflow of capital. While some Brazilians advocated protectionist tariffs and tax credits to stimulate domestic industrialization, they were largely ignored by policy makers.

On the eve of the Depression, Brazil's foreign debt was $900 million and the government paid out approximately $175 million per year in repayment of loans, relying on the profits of the export trade to make their annual payments. As long as coffee values remained high, the system worked to Brazil's advantage. But in May 1929 the price of coffee began a very fast decline. In Brazil there had been two years of bumper crops, leading to a huge surplus. Other countries in the region had also achieved a leap in their output, flooding the market. This weakened Brazil's economic standing and foreign lenders began to limit credit to them. Brazilian banks, in turn, began to cut back on their liberal lending to coffee planters. Nonetheless, the institute declared that its policies were sound and no changes would be made, giving Brazilians a false sense of security.

Brazil after the Wall Street Crash

The Wall Street crash of 1929 had a devastating impact on Brazil's export economy, highlighting the problems of the economic system that Brazil had in place. In September 1929, coffee was being sold at 22 cents per pound; by December 1, it had fallen to 15 cents. This dramatic fall meant that national income declined and government revenue was limited. The government tried to curtail the effects by exporting its gold reserves to London and New York, which had the short-term result of preventing a downward spiral.

The state of São Paulo was in especially dire straits and faced bankruptcy. It appealed to the federal government for assistance but this was denied by President Washington Luis. He had been an opponent of coffee valorization earlier in his political career (as governor of São Paulo) but when elected had said that the economy was dependent upon valorization. Following the Wall Street Crash he reverted to his previous outlook and stated that an unhealthy economic situation had been created that would be difficult to recover from. Instead, he favored development of the small commercial and industrial sectors.

This national economic decline had profound effects for local businesses. In an informal report to the São Paulo opposition paper *Diario Nacional* shop owners reported a 40% decline in sales in December 1929. Imports were drastically reduced, trade stagnated and the small industrial sector sat idle. Planters, who often lived in the city, returned to their plantations. They were resentful of Washington Luis's policies, seeing the decline in prices as temporary, and his unwillingness to help them changed their political orientation.

At the same time, a new presidential race was looming between Getúlio Vargas and Julio Prestes—the handpicked successor of Washington Luis. In an astute political move, Vargas both stated support for coffee valorization and the financial propositions of the Washington Luis administration. This increased his popularity among most Brazilians; but even so, in the March 1930 elections Prestes won a narrow victory, which gave an assurance to foreign investors of Brazil's political solvency. Almost immediately, credit was extended to the ailing state of São Paulo which was supposed to use the money that was not borrowed to service debts (almost 50%) to buy coffee surplus and stabilize the price. Instead, a record-breaking 29 million bags of coffee were produced and prices—which had stabilized at 14 cents per pound—dropped anew. Coffee prices fell to 10 cents per pound and the economy was dangerously close to collapsing. At the same time, Brazil's debt had increased to $1,181 million, three quarters of which was owed by the government. Brazil has seriously depleted its gold reserves which stood at $70 million. Additionally, the overthrow of governments in neighboring states made European and American lenders reluctant to invest further in Brazil.

Approximately one million Brazilians were affected by the economic crisis. Most Brazilian rural workers were landless laborers that planters could no longer afford to pay. They began to subsist on food that they planted between coffee trees and faced hunger. Those who could migrated to the cities in search of work, but just as many remained behind, unemployed and disgruntled. Unemployment was also rife among urban workers, including civil servants. Those who retained their positions were often unpaid for months at a time. While there were few civil disturbances, the country seemed poised for a change.

Getúlio Vargas (1882–1954)

Getúlio Vargas served as president of Brazil in 1930–45 and 1951–54. Vargas came from a wealthy family in Rio Grande do Sul and after initially attending military school turned to the study of law and a career as a professional politician. He was elected to the state legislature and then served as a federal representative in the Chamber Deputies beginning in 1922. He quickly became a popular figure and in 1926 was named finance minister by President Washington Luis. He resigned to run for governor of Rio Grande do Sul in 1928 and became a key opposition figure upon his election. Challenging the traditional leadership, Vargas ran for president of Brazil but was narrowly defeated. But his opposition to the ruling government and emerging reputation as a charismatic leader made him the best choice for the role of interim president after the coup d'etat overthrew Washington Luis and Julio Prestes. Although he faced some opposition (and an attempted coup) Vargas governed until 1945, creating a new constitution in 1934 and a new form of governance—the *Estado Novo* (New State)—in 1937. Vargas assumed dictatorial powers in 1938 after an alleged communist plot was discovered and Brazil was declared to be in a state of siege.

In the 1940s, Vargas was known for his policies that improved the lives and working conditions of Brazil's poor. While this increased his popularity in general, it alarmed the upper classes who feared the loss of their own power. His status was further complicated by the Second World War. Initially neutral, Brazil declared war on the Germany and Italy in 1942, to the surprise of many who had called him a fascist dictator. His domestic policies included a relaxation of censorship and a curbing of repressive policies which increased middle-class support but also brought his dictatorship to an end. Elections had been postponed until 1945, at which point Vargas was forced to step down when Eurico Gaspar Dutra became president. In 1951, Vargas once again ran for election and won a second term as president. The postwar policies of Dutra had slowed the growth of the Brazilian economy and the conditions in the country had deteriorated. Vargas once again imposed economic nationalism on Brazil but his import substitution programs were overshadowed by political intrigues and rumors of an impending coup. After the assassination attempt on his political adversary, members of the military leadership tried to force Vargas to resign. In reaction, Vargas committed suicide in 1954 ending his tenure as the populist leader of Brazil.

> *Each drop of my blood will be an immortal flame in your conscience and will uphold the sacred will to resist. To hatred I reply with pardon, and to those who think they have defeated me, I reply with my victory. I was a slave to the Brazilian people, and today I am freeing myself for eternal life. But this people, whose slave I was, will no longer be slave to anyone. My sacrifice will remain forever in their souls and my blood will be the price for their ransom. I fought against the exploitation of Brazil. I fought against the exploitation of her people. I have fought with my whole heart. Hatred, infamy and slander have not conquered my spirit. I have given you my life. Now I offer you my death. I fear nothing. Serenely I take my first step towards eternity and leave life to enter history.*

Getúlio Vargas, suicide note, August 24, 1954.

Political repercussions in Brazil

Vargas took advantage of the situation and, in October 1930, he led a number of revolts. The government could not halt the rebel forces and on October 24 a revolutionary junta was formed. On November 4, Vargas was installed as provisional president. While there were deep-seated political problems that led to this coup d'etat, the economic crisis created the conditions that made it viable. Those who previously advocated democracy saw in him a strong, charismatic leader who could make decisions to improve Brazil's economy. From 1930 to 1945 (and again until 1954) Vargas ruled Brazil. His political dominance was clear and many argue that it was his charismatic personality that created political stability and allowed for a change in economic policies.

Mixing coffee into tar to be used in building new roads and highways.

There were, however, several attempts to overthrow his regime, one of which led to the creation of the *Estado Novo*, or New State, in 1937. Although his policies were largely consistent up to this point, the Constitution implemented at that time gave him authoritarian powers. For the economy that would mean varying degrees of government intervention.

 What was done with the coffee surplus in Brazil in the 1930s?

The economic policies of Getúlio Vargas

To address the economic crisis Vargas implemented a series of policies that both supported the coffee industry while attempting to wean Brazil off of its dependence on this crop. Honoring his promises during his presidential campaign, he created the National Department of Coffee that was under his control but had considerable flexibility. Effective immediately, a reduction in coffee-tree planting was ordered. In 1920, there had been 1.7 billion trees; that figure had since risen to 3 billion, causing in part the glut in production. By 1939, the slow reduction meant there were 2.5 billion trees, curtailing production. In 1931, the government also introduced a program of coffee burning and it is estimated that 60 million bags were burned by 1939. While these were nominally successful, the industry only recovered with the onset of the Second World War.

More importantly, the government tried to diversify the economy. Agricultural incentives were provided that led to significant increases in livestock and cotton production. In the 1920s, cotton was only 2% percent of exports; in the 1930s, it rose to 18%. While coffee would remain an important part of the economy, history and culture of Brazil, its dominance was fading fast. Even in São Paulo, planters diversified their crops and limited coffee production so that they could farm other crops. On the other side, sugar production was reduced; Brazilian sugar could no longer compete on the international market so the government decided to free up the land for more profitable cash crops.

Import Substitution Industrialization

The Brazilian government reduced its imports by 75% between 1929 and 1932—from $416.6 to 108.6 million—and while exports also fell, they did not fall as fast, leaving Brazil with a favorable trade balance despite the economic crisis. Additionally, Brazil's agricultural policies kept a large sector of the society employed. With nowhere else to invest surplus capital, Brazilians (especially the coffee barons) began to invest in the industries which produced goods that had been previously imported. The government assisted through providing tax exemptions and long-term loans with low interest rates. Although most imports were subject to tariffs of up to 40%, exceptions were made for machinery or raw materials that were used to help build new industries.

Vargas strongly supported the growth of industry but it was growing international belligerence and the approaching Second World War that led to the greatest growth spurt of the era. In 1940, the National Steel Commission was established, followed by the National Steel Company which built Brazil's first large steel plant. Similar corporations were founded for the production of iron, aircraft and truck engine production and river valley development. These corporations were funded by a mix of public and private investment. The government reserved the right to intervene directly in the affairs of these corporations if it was considered to be in the national interest.

Another area of economic development was transportation. Recognizing the increasing importance of air transport, due to Brazil's topography, Vargas encouraged commercial aviation and by 1939

"If you were to ask me what is the program of the Estado Novo, I would tell you that its program is to crisscross the nation with railroads, highways and airlines; to increase production; to provide for the laborer and to encourage agricultural credit; to expand exports; to prepare the armed forces so that they are always ready to face any eventuality; to organize public opinion so that there is, body and soul, one Brazilian thought."

Getúlio Vargas,
Speech, July 1938

there were nine Brazilian companies flying routes that covered over 43,000 miles, carrying 71,000 passengers, 223 tons of mail and 490 tons of freight, which accounted for three quarters of all commercial traffic in South America. This nascent industry was encouraged by the military, and in 1941 Vargas created the Air Ministry. Railroad expansion also took place at this time, but there were half as many miles of train track as air routes. Instead, Vargas focused on road construction, leading to the construction of 258,390 miles of roads by 1939.

In addition to a push for industrialization, the government recognized the need to provide more support for and control of labor. The unsuccessful attempt by the communists to overthrow the government in 1935 gave Vargas the opportunity to seize total power through the Congress-approved "state of siege" that was implemented and to recognize the growing threat that labor could play. While still in its early stages of development, urban industrialization was taking place and Vargas felt it best to put in place a new labor code that defined industrial relations. Mirroring other corporatist hybrids, the economy was organized into different industries and worker and employer sectors. A law passed in 1943 permitted unions to organize by plant and industry but not on a statewide or national basis lest their power become too great. A department of labor oversaw union finances and elections, and helped create the labor leadership in the country. Vargas also instituted a minimum wage and a maximum work week for Brazilian labor.

Constitution of 1934: The law will regulate the progressive nationalization of mines, mineral deposits, and waterfalls or other sources of energy, as well as of the industries considered as basic or essential to the economic and military defense of the country." Article 119

> *"The Estado Novo does not recognize the rights of the individual against the collective. Individuals do not have rights; they have duties. Rights belong to the collective!"*
>
> Getúlio Vargas

Changes to Brazil's economy

Import Substitution Industrialization (ISI) policies proved to be successful. Between 1924 and 1939, industrial output grew at an average rate of 6% and the 1930s were marked by very strong increases. In 1941, there were 44,100 plants that employed 944,000 workers, meaning that most work was still done in small-scale factories and plants, and that it was often reliant on hand labor rather than machinery. These industries successfully provided substitutes for goods previously imported, and they helped to diversify the economy. Due to the Second World War, Brazilian goods were also being exported, and a push towards heavy industry was in place.

Men and women polishing Chevrolets on the assembly line at the General Motors Plant, São Paulo, Brazil in 1939.

Economic growth was not evenly spread throughout the country. Most of Brazil's population (40 million) was still land-based and dependent upon cash crops for their livelihoods. Unlike their urban brethren, the rural working class was still subjected to harsh living conditions that included low wages and debt peonage, a condition in which rural laborers, indebted to the plantation owners, worked to

 How did foreign investment help Brazil during the Depression?

pay off an ever-increasing debt rather than for wages. Brazil continued to rely on coffee as a major source of revenue, and foreign reserves. Five states employed three quarters of factory workers, and concentrated most of the industrial wealth; São Paulo alone had 41% of all workers. The interior was largely untouched and untapped; Vargas tried to encourage migration to these areas by offering 50-acre land grants to those willing to populate the west and Amazon Valley.

Activity

You be the journalist

Choose an ideology, a country and a year from the following lists:

Ideological focus: Socialist, National Socialist, Liberal, Conservative

Country: United States, Argentina, Brazil, United Kingdom, Germany

Year: 1933, 1940, 1945

Using your choices to establish the position of the journalist, write an article that explains why, in your opinion, Brazil has become a dictatorship and how it has affected Brazil's economy. Are you excited about or worried by the changes in Brazil? How does your nationality, ideology and the year in which you are writing impact on your perspective? If you are feeling particularly ambitious, do a little research and find out the name of specific newspapers that fulfill your criteria.

Argentina: from democracy to dictatorship

The political leadership of Argentina, 1916–43	
Hipólito Yrigoyen	1916–22; 1928–30
Marcelo Torcuato de Alvear	1922–29
José Félix Uriburu	1930–32
Agustín Justo	1932–38
José María Ortiz	1938–42
Ramón Castillo	1942–43

In 1916, Argentina made a peaceful transition to full democracy with the election of Radical Party leader Hipólito Yirigoyen, ousting the long-term conservative National Autonous Party (PAN) and people were hopeful that Argentine politics would continue in this manner. They did so until 1930 when a combination of forces, including the Great Depression, led to a military coup that would introduce a period of militarism and dictatorship that lasted until the 1980s.

Between 1860 and 1930, Argentina's annual growth averaged 6.3 percent, making it the strongest economy in South America. Although the main source of income came from the export of beef and wheat, the economy was modernizing and diversifying with the development of local industries and handicrafts. Beginning in the 1880s, Argentina embarked on a period of modernization

Argentine *vaqueros* (cowboys) in the 1930s, working in the plains as they had for over a century.

that brought with it social changes that threatened the traditional landowning creole élites. Recent immigrants with an entrepreneurial spirit set up new businesses, challenging the traditional power base. These were the people who challenged the economic system, based on foreign investment (and the UK investments in particular), urging the government to pursue economic nationalism.

The British had dominated the Argentine economy since the late 18th century and in the 1920s little had changed. Most of Argentina's meat exports went to the UK; at the same, it imported coal and petroleum from British companies. This meant that Argentina was particularly susceptible to the British economy and policy decisions made in London. British investors built and owned the railways and the public bus systems in Buenos Aires.

Argentina's economy was far more diversified than Brazil's: while exports were key to its reserves, the country was not reliant on one sole crop. Wheat and beef were the primary exports but they were not the only sources of income; linseed and corn were also key export crops. The industries that developed were logical extensions of its agricultural sector: food processing, meat packing, flour milling and leather tanning are examples. Unlike other Latin American countries, Argentina's industry was largely domestic; there was very limited foreign investment until the 1920s. The First World War had stimulated industrial growth, but after the war the country settled into a depression as its foreign markets dried up. At the same time, trade had been interrupted, creating a need for more domestically-produced goods. This led to a renewed interest in the extractive industries. Prior to the First World War there had been little interest in mining, but it was now seen as an area of potential growth.

With economic growth, the number and power of urban workers increased. Yrigoyen and his Radicals co-opted them as a non-revolutionary alternative to the Socialist Party. Argentina's large immigrant population brought with them revolutionary ideas about the organization of labor and the effectiveness of strike action to secure benefits. Many of the immigrant leaders were expelled, but the movement gained momentum in the 20th century. Many workers also wanted to collaborate with the government and avoid violence. Radical support for labor varied but during its period of dominance, it was a positive turning point for the working class. All parties and social groups were aware of the need to address labor's concerns.

In a show of significant foresight, the Yirigoyen administration sought to wean itself off of dependency on foreign fuels. It was the first country to create a state-run oil company to compete against foreign interests: Fiscal Petroluem Fields (YPF) was created in 1922. The company would source, produce, refine and sell petroleum. In the 1920s, Argentina had one of the largest number of automobiles per capita and consumed considerable amounts of gasoline. YPF helped keep foreign gas prices competitive and would later assist emerging industries.

The impact of the Depression on Argentina

The crash of 1929 had an immediate impact on the demand for Argentine exports. As Europe and America suffered from their crises they implemented protectionist policies to keep their own farmers solvent. For Argentina, this in turn led to an imbalance of trade and a 43% fall in the value of its cash crops that was accompanied by a 40% devaluation of the Argentine peso. At the same time, businesses were forced to lay off workers, creating high unemployment in the cities. Civil servants did not lose their positions but often the government did not have enough money to pay them—customs duties was a main source of revenue for the government and the slowing of export and import made income non-existent.

Most people blamed the Radicals for the dire economic straits. On September 6, 1930, Yrigoyen was overthrown and a military junta under General José Félix Uriburu was established. There was no opposition to the military as they marched to Buenos Aires, and no one supported Yrigoyen, who was placed under temporary house arrest. Uriburu took control of the country and attempted to impose hard-line military rule but a potential rival, General Agustín Justo, was waiting to challenge him. Without consensus among the military, Uriburu was forced to hold election in 1932 and Justo became president, relying on a mix of anti-Yrigoyen Radicals, PAN conservatives and Socialists. This coalition, called the *Concordancia* maintained its power only through electoral fraud and corruption.

While poor economic decision-making appeared to be the catalyst for regime change, the government continued to follow liberal trade policies until the mid-1930s. When the economy hit rock-bottom in 1933 the government responded with policies not meant to change the economy, but to bolster traditional areas of interest and income—livestock and agriculture. The government established a number of agricultural regulatory boards that lobbied for protectionist policies for agriculture that included tariffs. The new government also tried to hold on to the relationship with the UK to boost economic recovery. This resulted in the Roca–Runciman Pact (1933) which put restrictions on Argentina in an attempt to restore positive trade relations with the United Kingdom. According to the terms of this treaty, British markets for Argentine goods would be preserved if Argentina promised to give preference to British manufactured goods and protect British-owned companies from nationalization. This meant the death of a newly-emerged transit sector of private bus companies, based in Buenos Aires, but it was seen as necessary for Argentina to emerge from the Depression.

As in Brazil, Argentine entrepreneurs responded to the lack of imported manufactured goods by trying to replace them. This spontaneous creation of import-substitution industries came out of necessity but quickly found government support. The government

Soldiers in Buenos Aires, Argentina, on September 17, 1930, holding pictures of the new president, General José Félix Uriburu.

provided tax incentives and tariffs to protect new industries. Even while putting protectionist tariffs in place, exceptions were made for those materials and goods needed to assist the creation of domestic industry. Support of ISI would also help create employment opportunities and while factories tended to be small at first, industrialization created jobs.

The state-run oil company YPF continued to expand production in the 1930s with the goal of reducing dependency on oil imports. The oil companies (Shell and Standard Oil) viewed Argentina warily as they had just seen Mexico's nationalization of their oil industry, and in 1934 the private companies dropped their prices substantially to undercut YPF's reforms. After an initial reaction against this, the government reached a favorable agreement with the foreign companies so that half of the Buenos Aires market went to YPF. This allowed for continued expansion that stimulated industrialization.

Unemployment continued to be a problem and the *Concordancia* implemented the solutions that had been put in place in North America: public works. Despite the cost to the government, it was recognized that work-creation schemes would support the domestic market and prevent social strife. Public works projects centered on developing infrastructure and resulted in the construction of 32,000 miles of highways. Prior to 1932, there were only 5,000 miles of roads; this encouraged the expansion of motorized transport and helped Argentina move away from its dependence on British-owned railways.

 How did Argentines react to the overthrow of Yrigoyen? Why do you think this was the case?

This cartoon was first published in London's *Evening Standard* on July 13, 1934.

 What does this political cartoon say about the effect of the Roca–Runciman Pact on the UK's dominions and Argentina?

Activity

Theory of Knowledge (TOK)

Economic theory and history: Raúl Prebisch, the Argentine Depression and ISI

Raúl Prebisch's theories of Import Substitution Industrialization (ISI) gained popularity in the 1950s after he became director of the Economic Commission for Latin America (ECLA). He based his theories on his observations of Argentina during the Depression. Working as a banker, he witnessed the results of free trade on its economy and argued that while it had historically led to development in Europe and the United States, his country's policies were harming its economy and hindering its development.

Despite the wealth of natural resources that Argentina possessed, Prebisch argued that developing countries would never have enough cash to invest in local industry unless they corrected the imbalance of trade that the cycle created:

Raw materials → developed country → finished goods created → developing country

The value added by manufacturing always cost more than the primary products used to create those products. Therefore, developing countries would never earn enough to pay for their imports and an imbalance of trade would always exist. To correct the imbalance, he argued that developing countries should adopt ISI as part of their economic model. They would continue to sell their primary commodities on the world market but would not use their foreign exchange reserves to buy manufactured goods from overseas. Government intervention in the economy would be necessary to protect newly-emerging industries.

When he wrote his report, Argentina and Brazil seemed to provide support for this idea; they had introduced ISI during the Depression. Over the years, however, economists challenged the validity of ISI and Prebisch's prescriptions arguing that they coud not be sustained long term. More moderate critics argued that ISI worked—but only in the larger Latin American countries with a substantial middle class and a working class with purchasing power.

Questions

1 What did Prebisch witness that contributed to his observations?

2 What other policies did government have to implement to make ISI part of its model?

3 What limitations do you see with this idea?

4 Why would "a substantial middle class and working class with purchasing power" be important to the success of ISI?

Argentina's economic recovery

Due to the combination of protecting export industries and ISI Argentina came out of the Depression relatively quickly. The military men that dominated the *Concordancia* saw the opportunities of abandoning liberal free-trade policies in favor of corporatist policies to develop a strong Argentine military. ISI became a dominant economic policy that was developed further during the Second World War, and would remain in place through the 1960s.

The Second World War further accelerated ISI policies and increased dissatisfaction with the government. This set the stage for another coup and in 1943 the United Officers Group (GOU), led by men ranking no higher than colonel, overthrew the government and established another military dictatorship.

For Argentina, the Depression accelerated industry and decreased its dependence on the British market. It also led to the radicalization of the working classes and renewed military intervention in government affairs. Populism and dictatorship would prevail until the 1980s. Lastly, a central bank was created in Argentina that would have sole determination of currency values and the ability to print money. This was seen as necessary so that the government could control the money supply in times of future crisis.

Political changes in Latin America

As in North America, the Great Depression had profound economic effects but those are often overshadowed by the political changes that were brought about, that would have long-term consequences. While a number of countries recovered relatively quickly from the economic distress, it was under newly-established military dictatorships or populist regimes that the economies were directed and controlled.

Traditional agricultural products continued to dominate Latin-American economies, but the economic power of the landowners was waning as a new, urban élite emerged with the onset of ISI. The corporatist policy adopted in the 1930s by Argentina and Brazil would become a popular model for developing countries to escape from economic dependence on the Western, industrialized economies. While ISI prevailed until the 1960s, its success would be challenged and argued by economists and historians alike.

Latin American political systems also shifted over the same time period towards authoritarianism. There were some exceptions to the rule, but from this point forward, military leadership was predominant in the region.

Hipólito Yrigoyen (1850–1933)

Hipólito Yrigoyen 1850–1933 was head of the Radical Party and was twice president of Argentina, during its liberal, democratic period. Early in his career he challenged the ruling oligarchy and conservative parties to embrace true democracy and end their political dominance over the country. Like many of his contemporaries in Latin America, he sought free elections, secret ballots and democratic reforms. The Radical Party's power was limited until 1912 electoral reform brought universal male suffrage and widened the proportion of the population that could vote. In 1916, he won a narrow victory as president of the republic in what is considered the first democratic election in Argentina. He implemented limited changes that included a reform of the universities and the creation of a state-owned petroleum industry. While he had some working-class support, his economic and social reforms were limited; they ignored the social and labor problems that existed at the time.

In 1922 Yrigoyen was succeeded by Marcelo Torcuato de Alvear, whom he would take over from again in 1928, when he was reelected with a significant majority. His second presidency was ended when the Depression brought about the overthrow of his regime. Now seen as elderly—and sometimes accused of senility—he lost his popularity and was replaced by a military junta. After spending time under house arrest he was released and died in Buenos Aires in July 1933.

Activity

Values and limitations

Source analysis

Source A

Conservative responses to the Depression soon branched out in more innovative directions. Led by the Central Bank in 1935, new institutions were established to manage the economy, 'devaluation', 'exchange control' and 'deficit financing' entered the lexicon of economic policy-making, where they have remained ever since. The conservative regime confronted the depression with striking success. Recovery commenced as early as 1934, and by the end of the decade Argentina had regained the prosperity of the 1920s.

Source: Bethell, Leslie. 1993. *Argentina Since Independence*. Cambridge University Press. p. 174.

Source B

Argentina suffered relatively little from the Great Depression. Its urban unemployment, never much above 5 percent, remained far below that in Europe and theUnited States. Despite commercial difficulties with the British, substantial economic recovery was underway by 1934, although another recession followed in 1937–38, mainly caused by adverse weather conditions. Immigration resumed; government spending rose by 27 percent between 1932 and 1937; exports increased, led by grain. …

Imports of manufactured consumer goods, around 40 percent of total imports before 1930, fell to 25 percent by the late 1940s. The 1914 census cataloged some 383,000 industrial workers; by 1935 the number had risen to 544,000, by 1941 to 830,000 and by 1946 to over 1 million. Similarly, the number of industrial firms grew from less than 41,000 in 1935 to more than 57,000 in 1941 and 86,000 by 1946.

Source: Rock, David. 1987. *Argentina, 1516–1982: From Spanish Colonization to the Falklands War.* Taurus. p. 231.

Questions

Both of these sources are used as textbooks.

1 Are these sources consistent? Do they make the same argument?

2 What makes these sources useful in studying the Great Depression in Latin America?

3 Why would a historian find these sources limited in assessing the Great Depression?

4 Is one of these sources more useful than the other? Which one and why?

Exam practice and further resources

Sample exam questions

1 Examine the view that the Great Depression was caused primarily by political rather than by economic factors

2 Analyze the impact of the Great Depression on the arts in one country in the Americas.

3 Compare and contrast the social impact of the Great Depression in two different countries from the region.

4 For what reasons and with what consequences did the governments of either Vargas in Brazil or the Concordancia in Argentina adopt the policies they did in 1929–39.

5 Compare and contrast the role of government intervention in Canada and the United States in 1929–39.

Recommended further reading

Frank Freidel & Alan Brinkley. 1982. *America in the Twentieth Century.* 5th edn. New York: McGraw-Hill Inc.

Winifred D. Wandersee Bolin. "The Economics of Middle-Income Family Life: Working Women During the Great Depression." *The Journal of American History.* vol. 65, no. 1. June 1978. pp. 60–74.

America in the 1930s. http://xroads.virginia.edu/~1930s/front.html.

New Deal Network. http://newdeal.feri.org/index.htm.

New Deal Cultural Programs. *Webster's World of Cultural Democracy.* http://www.wwcd.org/policy/US/newdeal.html.

Farming in the 1930s. *Wessel's Living History Farm.* http://www. livinghistoryfarm.org/farminginthe30s/farminginthe1930s.html.

Barry Broadfoot. 1997. *Ten lost years, 1929–1939: Memories of Canadians who Survived the Depression.* Toronto: McClelland & Stewart.

John English et al (eds). 2002. *Mackenzie King: Citizenship and Community: Essays marking the 125th Anniversary of the Birth of William Lyon Mackenzie King.* Toronto: Robin Brass Studio.

A. E. Safarian. 2009. *The Canadian Economy in the Great Depression.* 3rd ed. Montreal: McGill-Queen's University Press.

Robert Levine. 1998. *Father of the Poor? Vargas and his era.* Cambridge: Cambridge University Press.

5 Political developments in the Americas after the Second World War, 1945–79

This chapter focuses on political developments and the domestic concerns (social, cultural and economic) that dominated the domestic landscape of the Americas in the decades after the Second World War. The response to the domestic issues would vary considerably based on each nation's political structure, national culture and ideology. Despite the large sacrifices made during the Second World War, Canada and the United States emerged with burgeoning economies and stable democratic governments. This was not always true for the other 31 nations in the Americas.

Over the next four decades, domestic policy was overshadowed by the Cold War. Governments throughout the Americas struggled to develop economic policies that would stimulate the economy, reduce poverty and improve prosperity. The United States was the dominant superpower that did not diminish until the 1980s. In Latin America, many nations would struggle to meet basic needs and would fall further and further into debt. The result was often political instability that translated into civil war, military dictatorships and revolution often with foreign support and involvement. A special case was Cuba. Soon after the 1959 revolution, the country became a communist single-party state under the leadership of Fidel Castro.

Overall, the political boundaries of the Americas remained static but this belied the internal turmoil and tumult that took place, to some extent, in every nation. In the United States, the civil rights movement became a legitimate political force and would change the face of the nation. In Canada, the French-speaking province of Quebec would demand a special place in confederation and in Latin America, the search for political stability and social justice would take on many forms.

By the end of this chapter, students should be able to:

- evaluate the domestic policies of the United States under presidents Truman, Eisenhower and Kennedy

- discuss President Johnson's "Great Society" and domestic reforms during the presidency of Richard Nixon

- review the domestic policies of Canadian prime ministers from Diefenbaker to Clark and Trudeau

- assess the causes and effects of the Quiet Revolution in Quebec

- explain the political, social and economic causes of the Cuban Revolution and its impact on the region

- assess the rule of Fidel Castro: his political, economic, social and cultural policies; treatment of minorities; successes and failures

- trace the rise to power of populist leaders in Latin America, and recognize the characteristics of populist regimes in terms of their social, economic and political policies; the treatment of opposition; and their successes and failures using the examples of Getúlio Vargas in Brazil and Juan Perón in Argentina

- recognize the characteristics of Latin-American military regimes: including their rationale for intervention; their challenges and policies; successes and failures.

The United States

The post-war era was a time of incredible economic expansion for the United States, yet the nation faced serious economic and social problems. Rampant inflation, labor unrest, racial segregation, the consumer culture and emergence of suburbia changed the face of the United States. At the top of the government's list was reducing poverty, and the associated development of rural areas, education, healthcare and civil rights. But domestic problems and policies took a back seat to the Cold War. Financing the industrial-military complex would hamper the domestic efforts of all presidents during this period.

A major issue was civil rights. Millions of African Americans endured lives of abject poverty because of legalized discrimination. But for all the inequalities faced by minority groups, the nation prospered. A new managerial middle class of highly skilled and educated workers emerged and gave the United States its competitive edge. It was a time of great expectations and unbridled optimism; a long awaited transformation after the Great Depression's years of sorrow and the sacrifice of war.

Canada

Canadians feared a repetition of the Depression and Prime Minister Mackenzie King's Liberal government responded with a groundbreaking social welfare programs that eventually included family allowances, old-age pensions, workmen's compensation and a national health program. Newfoundland, Britain's oldest colony, joined the confederation in 1949 as the 10th province. Regional alienation between have- and have-not provinces would spark strong debate over the direction of the national agenda. Quebec, a mainly French-speaking province, had by the 1960s undergone a "Quiet Revolution" which emancipated the province from English Canadian domination. Industrialization in central Canada made it the mainstay of the nation's robust economy. The auto industry, in particular, grew rapidly and symbolized the new affluence. The St. Lawrence Seaway was completed in 1959; a joint venture with the United States, it made navigation from the Great Lakes to the Atlantic Ocean a reality.

The postwar era was a time when Canadians trusted their government and expected it to provide solutions to long-standing economic problems and social inequalities. The population grew rapidly, a combination of wartime saving, the baby boom and immigration. The majority of Canadians lived in rapidly growing cities. Some minority groups, especially **First Nations** (aboriginal

The term **First Nations** (most often used in the plural) is used to describe the indigenous people of Canada, except for the Arctic-situated Inuit, and peoples of mixed European-First Nations ancestry called *métis*.

peoples) remained marginalized and the nation ignored its wartime internment of Japanese Canadians. Yet for most Canadians, this was a golden time.

Latin America

Latin American countries experimented with new forms of government and new solutions to the long-standing economic problems of poverty and economic diversification. The results were inconsistent but the common experience was discontent with the status quo. Latin American nations faced unique challenges and yet several patterns emerged. The first was a movement in the 1950s towards greater political participation of disenfranchised groups, such as women. However, it was often difficult to change the deeply rooted political hierarchy supported by a small yet powerful élite. Fidel Castro's leftist revolution in Cuba did not engulf the region as predicted but instead spawned a new trend of right-wing military coups and dictatorships in response. The democratically elected socialist governments of several nations were forced out directly or indirectly by the United States, who feared the spread of communism in the region.

Reform and revolution, dictatorship and democracy, communism followed by corporatist military oligarchies were all represented in different countries in the Americas. Economically, some Latin-American nations struggled with crushing foreign debt, while others suffered from a lack of domestic and foreign investment and still others submitted to too much foreign control. Economies based mainly on one product or resource were vulnerable to the vagaries of world demand. In addition, the profits these commodities generated were seldom distributed equitably. However, due to economic neocolonialism, many nations had difficulties diversifying their economies. This can be seen in the case of Brazilian coffee and sugar, Chilean copper and Nicaraguan bananas, to name a few examples. Attempts to diversify production, through programs like Import Substitution Industrialization (ISI) worked well at first for some countries, like Argentina and Brazil, but more often produced mixed results.

Extended discussion point

Domestic vs. foreign policy

Domestic policy can only defeat us; foreign policy can kill us.

John F. Kennedy

The purpose of a national government is to create laws and policies that promote and advance the national interest. There are two main categories of policies: "domestic" and "foreign". For example, during the Great Depression of the 1930s, many nations in the Americas developed relief programs like Roosevelt's New Deal to jump-start the economy. The United States became isolationist, focused on domestic affairs. But, with the onset of the Cold War, US foreign policy took the lead, military spending grew at the expense of schools and hospitals.

Domestic policy

Attempts to rectify social problems and promote growth within the nation's borders. Domestic policy is concerned with economic growth, prosperity and development; poverty, health and education, law and order, taxation, social welfare and civil rights. Factors that determine the type and nature of domestic policy include political ideology, the system of government (democracy or dictatorship), economic prosperity, history, culture and religion.

Foreign policy

General objectives that guide the activities and relationships of one state in its relations with other nations. Foreign policy promotes the national interest. Diplomacy is the tool of foreign policy. Over the centuries, nations have developed a formal method of recognizing the existence of each other and have developed a set of rules and protocols to promote peaceful and productive relations and resolve disputes. When diplomacy fails, as the German philosopher Carl von Clausewitz stated, nations resort to war—"diplomacy by other means." Factors that define the national interest and thus influence foreign policy include geography, demography, bordering nations, economy, military strength and ideology (e.g. Cold War).

 "The Chicken or the egg?" Domestic policy or foreign policy—which is most important? How do foreign affairs impact on domestic issues?

The domestic policies of US presidents: Truman to Nixon

The period 1945–63 has been called the Golden Era: a time when the economic strength and military might of the United States made the nation the undisputed world leader in the early days of the Cold War. As such, it is easy to overlook the domestic challenges that presidents Truman, Eisenhower and Kennedy faced. Initially, the nation feared a postwar depression but when this failed to materialize other important questions about the role of government in the market place, the inequitable distribution of wealth, the future of organized labor, the fear of communist infiltration and the growing momentum of the civil rights movement would dominate the domestic scene.

Discussion point

What other periods in US history might be called a "Golden Era?"

What assumptions does this term attest to? Do you agree, or disagree with the use of the term for the immediate postwar period in the United States? What issues does it mask?

The accidental president: Harry S. Truman, 1945–53

On April 12, 1945, on the sudden death of Franklin Roosevelt, who had suffered a cerebral haemorrhage, Truman became the 33rd president of the United States. After serving in the post of vice president for only 84 days, this was an unexpected position to be in. Truman had accepted the vice-presidential nomination knowing he was a compromise candidate for the, then, fractious Democratic Party. As a senator from Missouri he had hardly appeared earmarked for higher office. His record was solid but not spectacular. He lacked the charm and charisma of FDR. Relations between President Roosevelt and his new vice president had been distant. FDR did not easily disclose his views and feelings to Truman. What is clear is that Roosevelt considered Truman an outsider and would not give him access to sensitive information. This fact was apparent when, after taking the oath, the Secretary of War, Henry L. Stimson, advised Truman of a "project looking to the development of a new explosive of unbelievable destructive power."

Truman's presidency, 1945–48

The New Deal's reforms and the new promise of advancing civil rights, picked up where Roosevelt had left off. But within a year the momentum for reform had stopped, blocked by a hostile Republican-dominated Congress. Truman faced serious problems with the labor movement. Republicans saw him as soft on communism, and said that he was trying to transform the economy. His popularity waned and initially Truman considered not running for the presidency in the forthcoming election but then changed his mind.

The 1948 election is one of the most storied in presidential history. At the Democratic nominating convention the party was split in three. Henry J. Wallace from Iowa ran on the Progressive Party ticket, advocating an end to segregation, full voting rights for blacks and universal health care. The conservative wing of the party, the Dixiecrats, were southern senators who opposed all of Wallace's platform. Truman, who won the nomination, seemed destined to lose the election. One Truman advisor said that only Truman thought he could win. Against all odds, Truman led a brilliant electoral campaign and became president in his own right.

In 1949, Truman introduced the "Fair Deal"—a reprise of his first attempt at reform in 1945. Again, he met with limited success passing only the government housing initiative. More importantly, the anti-communist movement gained steam and led by Senator Joseph McCarthy attacked Truman, key members of his cabinet and large sections of the government with charges of communist membership, conspiracy and collaboration. The Cold War and foreign affairs dominated the president's time and energy and domestic matters were given low priority.

The State of the Union

Truman's chief task following the war was to convert Roosevelt's "Arsenal of democracy" from the production of tanks to automobiles, and from machine guns to washing machines. Millions of soldiers, back from the war, needed to be retrained. Truman needed to clarify the government's role in the economy after the centralized role of the wartime administration and the New Deal. Republican hard-liners wanted to dismantle the New Deal and get government out of the marketplace entirely, but Truman and the Democrats had a different plan.

Harry S. Truman (1884–1972)

Harry S. Truman, the son of a farmer, was born in Lamar, Missouri, and completed high school in Independence in 1901. After working in various clerical jobs, he took over the farm, following his father's death in 1914. He served in the National Guard and in the First World War was captain of a field artillery unit that saw action at St. Mihiel and the Meuse-Argonne, in France. Returning to the United States in 1919, Truman married Elizabeth Wallace (Bess Truman), whom he had known since childhood. After a failed business venture, running a haberdashery in the 1920s, Truman studied law in Kansas, and was appointed to the position of county judge in 1922. In this position he served two four-year terms, during which he acquired a reputation for honesty and skillful management. In 1934, he was put forward as a candidate in the Democratic primary for a seat in the US Senate. In January 1935, Truman was sworn in as Missouri's junior senator. Truman's friendliness, personal integrity, and attention to the duties of his office soon won him respect among his colleagues. He was responsible for two major pieces of legislation: the Civil Aeronautics Act of 1938, establishing government regulation of the aviation industry, and the Wheeler-Truman Transportation Act of 1940, providing government oversight of railroad reorganization. In 1940, he won a second term in the Senate, and it was during this term that he gained national recognition for leading an investigation into fraud and waste in the US military. Respected by his Senate colleagues and admired by the public, Truman was selected to run as Franklin Delano Roosevelt's vice president on the 1944 Democratic ticket. Truman took the oath of office as vice president on January 20, 1945. His term lasted just 82 days, however, before Roosevelt's sudden death placed him in office as the 33rd president of the United States.

More controversial for his foreign than his domestic policies, Truman set the stage for a strong anti-communist policy of containment in the era of the Cold War. His decision to authorize dropping the atomic bomb on Japan remains one of the most controversial decisions of a US president. Re-elected to office in 1948, against predictions of losing the election, he established a strong program of domestic reform. His commitment to continuing Roosevelt's Fair Deal included proposals for expanded public housing, increased aid to education, a higher minimum wage, federal protection for civil rights, and national health insurance. Despite Democratic majorities in the House and Senate, most Fair Deal proposals either failed to gain legislative majorities or passed in much weakened form. Truman succeeded, however, in laying the groundwork for the domestic agenda for decades to come. His term in office concluded in 1953.

Politically, Truman understood that the Democratic Party was a disparate alliance. The party was not as cohesive as the Republicans and its key constituencies included east- and west-coast Liberals who supported the New Deal and civil rights; ultra-conservative southern Democrats who opposed strong central government, advocated states rights and supported segregation; African American voters in the northern states and the west who advocated civil rights legislation; new immigrants who required government support in settling; and organized labor who supported the New Deal and the Wagner Act

(1935). Truman understood the impossible task of satisfying all these interest groups. The potential for trouble within his own party was also second to the threat he was facing from a Republican-controlled Congress with a long tradition of opposing any president irrespective of party. Creating a national consensus in such an environment would be difficult.

Postwar wage and price controls

In August 1945, the dropping of nuclear bombs on the Japanese cities of Hiroshima and Nagasaki by the United States, forced Japan's unconditional surrender and ended the Pacific war more rapidly than if the US had used conventional warfare. The United States was not prepared for peacetime reconversion. Truman wanted this done quickly and went against the advice of his economic planners and advisors. The military was rapidly demobilized from a wartime peak of 14 million to about half a million by 1947. The fearful predictions that the economy would collapse when the boys came home, never materialized. War workers who had slaved long hours in factories had saved large sums buying war bonds and now demanded consumer goods. Automobiles, appliances and houses topped the list. The problem was that the conversion of factories could not match consumer demand and, as a result, inflation skyrocketed to 25% by the end of 1946. Truman reinstated some wage and price controls, against the wishes of the Republican-dominated Congress, but inflation remained intractable. In one famous incident, in mid-1946, the price of beef doubled in two weeks. Price controls were instituted which angered beef producers who in retaliation reduced the supply, thereby creating an artificial shortage. This was a public relations disaster for the Truman administration. The *New York Daily News* headline blared: "PRICES SOAR, BUYERS SORE, STEERS JUMP OVER THE MOON." Truman took the blame and took a beating at the polls with his approval rating plunging to 32%. Within the Democratic Party itself, many wondered if Truman was the person for the job.

During the 1946 mid-term elections the Republicans, smelling blood, attacked with a vengeance. Their election slogans captured the nation's displeasure: "Had Enough?"; or "To Err is Truman" rang true to many Americans. The Republicans now dominated Congress as never before and Truman was blocked from passing legislation at every turn. But Truman, the old poker player, had them right where he wanted. The opportunity to play his trump card came in 1948. He asked Congress to pass a food price bill to help curb prices and control inflation which had slowed considerably but was still on the rise. He gambled that the Republicans would reject these strong measures. They took the bait and passed a lukewarm bill that was labelled as "pitiful." Robert Taft, Republican Senate Leader, told Americans that they could reduce inflation if they "eat less." Republicans would pay dearly for Taft's arrogance. Truman signed the bill but made it clear that Republicans now owned the inflation problem.

Nevertheless, the US economy was expanding as never before. It was phenomenal, unprecedented and welcomed by the majority in the

United States. Despite inflation, real wages and disposable income grew and would continue to grow to the point it became an expectation, an entitlement. The unemployment rate fell dramatically, full employment seemed possible but Congress blocked any talk of government action to make this a reality. The Gross Domestic Product (GDP) would grow 250 times in the 20 years after the war. More people in the United States were living above the poverty line than ever before. Memories of the Depression dissipated and, for millions, the American Dream had become a reality: a house in the suburbs, a yard full of children, two cars in the garage, a tranquil neighbourhood with churches, schools and stores. It was a bountiful time for the majority of people living in the United States but not for minorities, namely African Americans and Native Americans. Many poor whites lived on farms without electricity or running water, or lived in cramped urban slums and ghettos. Poverty was both democratic and color-blind.

Labor unrest

Compounding Truman's woes was labor unrest. The support of labor was critical to the Democrats. Strikes in major industries caused considerable problems and stifled consumer goods production. There were more than 5,000 strikes in 1946 alone. Truman had to do something and at the same time attempt not to alienate the labor movement. But this proved impossible. Strikes shut down the railroads. Truman threatened to use troops to run the trains. The strike ended. A coal strike threatened to shut down the steel industry. Truman took the United Mine Workers to court and won. The unions in all cases returned to work and the president made certain they did so with more money in their pockets. Yet Truman's hard line came at a price and damaged the Democratic Party's relationship with the labor movement—a key group in the Democratic Party coalition. In his defense, Truman had little choice but to take action. This was one of his strengths. He could set aside political considerations and do what was best for the nation despite the consequences for his presidency; a trait that won him the grudging respect of his most obstinate political opponents.

The Taft-Hartley Act, 1947

The union support that Truman lost was regained thanks to the Republicans' anti-labor legislation, the Labor-Management Relations Act of 1947, more commonly known as the Taft-Hartley Act (supported by Republicans Senator Robert Taft and Congressman Fred Hartley). Labor saw the Act for what it was—an attack on collective bargaining rights gained in the Wagner Act of 1935. The Taft-Hartley Act limited the right to strike by giving the president authorization to obtain an 80-day court injunction against any strike that was deemed a threat to national health, welfare or security. As well, any union threatening strike action was to report the names of any of its members with affiliation to the Communist Party to the government. It was a commonly held belief among Republicans and conservative Democrats that the unions were unpatriotic organizations and a front for communist infiltration and subterfuge. Truman vetoed but the Republican Congress overrode the president. Truman never used the Act. This was yet another example of the Republican-controlled Congress helping Truman out of a tight spot.

The Fair Deal

To many Democrats, Truman's stance on the New Deal was a worry and they feared that he would forfeit the New Deal's legacy. These fears proved unfounded. In September 1945, Truman presented Congress with an ambitious and wide-ranging 21-point program. Congress rejected the program outright but three years later, after his landmark presidential victory in 1948, Truman reintroduced the program as "The Fair Deal" for all Americans. The connection to the New Deal was obvious and included pro-labor reforms, economic controls, a minimum wage increase, expansion of Social Security programs, housing, national health insurance and education. It also contained important civil rights measures and programs. On the agricultural front, Truman produced the "Brannan Plan" to support family farm incomes. The ambitious plan, like the New Deal, floundered because of the intransigence of the conservative Republican Congress. A truncated bill was approved but it fell short of Truman's vision. He had clearly miscalculated the appetite for reform. Congress approved public housing but little else, and polls indicated that the public wanted the New Deal to continue but not expand. Unlike many nations in the Americas that implemented extensive social welfare programs, reforms and philosophies in the 1940s and 1950s, the United States was not ready to shift to the political left. In fact, the opposite was happening. Influenced by the Cold War, that exerted more and more influence over the nation's psyche, the nation would swing inexorably to the political right creating a frenzy of anti-communist paranoia and fear that threatened the very foundations of the US Constitution.

The House Committee on Un-American Activities (HUAC)

The Cold War theater of operations in the United States was the Congressional Senate chambers in which the the House Committee on Un-American Activities (HUAC) met. HUAC was created in 1938 to investigate allegations against private citizens, public employees and organizations suspected of having communist ties. Postwar, HUAC gained momentum from McCarthy's attacks and accusations. Truman announced in November 1946 the need to ascertain the loyalty of federal government employees and root out any security risks. Not all his fears were unfounded. A top-secret counterintelligence operation code-named "Verona" had broken Soviet encryption codes and identified several hundred government employees supplying sensitive information to the Soviets. There were several spectacular spy cases: most famously, the trials of Alger Hiss and Ethel and Julius Rosenberg. Hiss, a former aide to President Roosevelt and a State Department official was accused of spying by the editor of *Time* magazine (and former communist), Whitaker Chambers, in 1948. HUAC investigated the charges and Hiss went to trial. He was given 14 years for perjury because the spying charges wouldn't stick.

The Rosenbergs were allegedly part of a ring passing information about the **Manhattan Project** on to the Soviets. These revelations were all the more shocking when the Soviets successfully tested a nuclear bomb in 1949, ending the A-bomb monopoly of the United States. The Rosenbergs were convicted and hung. A few years earlier, Igor Gozenko, a cipher clerk working in the Soviet Embassy in Ottawa, the Canadian Capital, had turned himself into the Royal Canadian Mounted Police with evidence exposing a Soviet spy ring operating in Canada, the UK and the United States. It is likely his disclosures assisted in the Rosenberg conviction.

In 1949, HUAC doubled its efforts to smoke out the communists. McCarthy (with some justification) claimed communists had infiltrated the highest levels of the US government and the military. On February 9, 1950, McCarthy announced that he had a list of several hundred known communists in the State Department (apparently no such list existed and McCarthy was grandstanding to get publicity—the tactic worked). The witch hunt had begun; his charges were largely unfounded, but that didn't matter. What occurred over the next four years was a steady stream of US citizens being subpoenaed to appear before HUAC. To be summoned was the same as being convicted. McCarthyism became the byword for anti-communist activities.

McCarthy took on the State Department, the army and the presidency with the encouragement of his party. Favorite targets were journalists, diplomats, authors, actors, trade unionists, scientists and scholars. In 1947, HUAC held nine days of hearings into accusations of communist influence and infiltration in Hollywood. The hearings resulted in publication of the "Hollywood Ten", prominent writers and directors, who would be blacklisted and boycotted by the studios. Eventually about 300 artists would be interrogated. HUAC had the power of subpoena and artists who invoked their Fifth Amendment protection were found in contempt. McCarthy learned that once you attacked someone's credibility it was virtually impossible for them to counter the charges. This, despite revelations of his own discredited war record. Nicknamed "Tail-Gunner Joe" he claimed to have flown 32 missions on a bomber but this was later revealed to be false. He was at a desk for most of the war. To add insult to injury, McCarthy won his Senate seat by criticizing his opponent for not enlisting despite the fact that he was too old to enlist. McCarthy won with a good majority. But once in Congress he was quickly isolated for his boorish behavior and limited ability.

Nevertheless, from 1950–53, he had a free hand. As Chair of the Committee on Government operations, he would interrogate hundreds of suspects. In the process, he destroyed many careers though accusation and innuendo. He attacked Truman's secretaries of state—the revered George Marshall and Dean Acheson. When the Democrats attacked McCarthy's own credibility, McCarthy countered that the accusations were orchestrated from Moscow. Yet Truman and then Eisenhower refused to publically condemn McCarthy. Their silence remains a source of historical controversy. Recently, historians

The **Manhattan Project** was the codename for a project conducted during the Second World War to develop the first atomic bomb, before the Germans or the Japanese. The project was led by the United States, and included participation from the United Kingdom and Canada.

have suggested Truman's silence was possibly due to the Verona reports. The Senator's power peaked under Eisenhower. Finally, the Senate came to its senses and in December 1954 voted 67 to 22 to vote McCarthy out.

Truman on civil rights

The civil rights movement was about to become a permanent fixture in US politics. Truman's approach was to steer to the middle of the road. He made history as the first president to address the National Association for the Advancement of Colored People (NAACP) in 1946. Later that year, he established the Committee on Civil Rights and produced the report "To Secure These Rights: The Report of the President's Committee on Civil Rights" in the fall of 1947. Truman's cabinet was split on asking Congress to support civil rights legislation but Truman proceeded and sent a 10-point message calling for a law to prohibit lynching, a federal fair-employment practices committee and protection of voting rights. None of these proposals were enacted but, to his credit, Truman had commenced the process. Truman's decision to desegregate the military and the civil service was controversial and groundbreaking, particularly for the Democrats in the south. These were important developments. Yet in the southern states, blacks remained disenfranchised by **Jim Crow laws**, lynching persisted and the Supreme Court legislation, supporting the segregation of blacks and whites (Plessy vs. Ferguson, 1898), remained uncontested. Truman's approach to civil rights was largely pragmatic. To keep the important urban black vote in the north and California he made bold public statements in support of civil rights yet his do-nothing legislative record suggests he wanted to maintain the support of southern Democratic senators.

The **Jim Crow laws** were state and local laws in the United States, enacted between 1876 and 1965. They legalized racial segregation in all public facilities, with a supposedly "separate but equal" status for African Americans.

Truman finally took a stand on civil rights at the 1948 Democratic Convention, when he stood for nomination. Southern senators stormed out of the convention and formed a splinter group, the "States Rights Democrats." Dubbed the Dixiecrats, and led by South Carolina's governor, Strom Thurmond, the "Dixiecrats" opposed any federal civil rights legislation, seeing it as an intrusion on the authority of the states. Following the election, Truman used executive orders to force compliance with non-discriminatory rules in government contracts, and by the end of the Korean War in 1953, the armed forces had been desegregated.

The reluctant president: Dwight D. Eisenhower, 1953–61

Dwight D. Eisenhower (known as "Ike") returned to the United States in 1946 as the conquering hero, having successfully led the Allied armies in the Second World War. By reaching consensus with British and US generals, Montgomery and Patton, Eisenhower's highly effective command went some way to drawing the war to a conclusion, and led him to stay on as military governor of the US Occupation Zone. Postwar, Eisenhower was held in such high esteem that first the Democrats and then the Republicans pursued him to be their presidential candidate. At first he refused, but in 1951 he changed his mind. In 1952, he ended 20 years of Democratic dominance by soundly defeating Democratic nominee Adlai Stevenson.

Eisenhower takes the middle road

The new president's vision and approach to domestic policy was largely hands-off. At times he appeared uncomfortable with domestic matters preferring foreign policy, which clearly dominated his time in office. Nonetheless, he did attend to domestic matters and believed it was time to slow down what he and many in the Republican Party considered to be the bloated growth of the federal government and its unsolicited involvement in the daily lives of US citizens. He thought that 20 years of interventionist Democrat programs need to be slowed down. The New Deal had impinged on the sovereignty of the states and local government. True to his belief, he would be reluctant to extend the reach of the federal government into these areas. Eisenhower, however, firmly rejected Republicans who wanted to dismantle these programs altogether. Ike told them he was driving down the middle of the road and referred to this as "the New Republicanism." He warned Republicans: "Should any party attempt to abolish social security, unemployment insurance, and eliminate labor laws and farm programs, you would not hear of that party again in our political history."

Eisenhower believed that his government's role was to preserve individual freedom, promote the free market economy and, when necessary, assist the poor, the unemployed and the aged. This would be done selectively, strengthening useful programs incrementally. There would be no Eisenhower corollary of the New Deal.

He would lead the nation from the middle, charting a course between excessive wealth concentrated in the hands of a few and curbing the unbridled power of state intervention. He understood his political future relied on a coalition between business and the burgeoning middle class. Furthermore, he believed US institutions were capable of meeting any new challenges and that reform must be advanced in a thoughtful and gradual manner.

Eisenhower's major economic challenge was to create a climate of continued economic growth. He was fortunate to serve during the greatest expansion of the economy in the 20th century. This approach was aided by several mild recessions that slowed the pace of growth and, more importantly, curbed the inflation that had

Dwight David Eisenhower (1890–1969)

Born in Texas, the third of seven sons, he grew up in Abilene Kansas. In 1911 he entered West Point Military Academy and graduated in 1915. In 1916 he married Mamie Doud of Denver and they had two sons David (1917– 1921) and John (1922). The peacetime army was small and promotion was slow. Eisenhower was a hardworking, diligent and affable officer, dedicated father and husband. His strength was as a staff officer. In 1936, he was promoted to the rank of Lieutenant Colonel after 21 years. Promotions came quicker as the nation prepared for war and in 1940 he became a Brigadier-General and early in 1942 became Major-General. His ability to forge cooperative links between British and US commanders became apparent in 1942 when he moved to England and took command of Allied Forces in North Africa. In December 1943, he was appointed Supreme Commander of the Allied Expeditionary Forces ear-marked to invade north-west Europe. In December of 1944, he was promoted to General of the Army (the highest rank possible). Following the war he became Chief of Staff in 1945, and resigned in 1950 to become president of Columbia University, New York City. In December 1950, he became the first supreme commander of the newly formed North Atlantic Treaty Organisation (NATO). In June 1952 he announced his candidacy for president of the United States. He served two terms as president and twice defeated Democratic candidate Adlai Stevenson, in 1952 and 1956. A heavy smoker he suffered several heart attacks in office. In 1961, he retired to his farm in Gettysburg Pennsylvania where he played golf and wrote his memoirs. He died of a stroke in 1969.

dogged Truman's administration. The economy remained robust, unemployment rates were low and inflation ran at about 2% a year. During the decade, the average family income rose 45% and with cash in their pockets like never before US citizens bought cars, TVs, refrigerators, moved to the suburbs and went on family vacations. To their credit, they also saved significant amounts for investment and retirement. This combination of spending and savings drove the economy. Eisenhower believed the government's role was to balance the budget and create infrastructure to promote continued economic growth. Many Republicans wanted tax cuts but Eisenhower managed to avoid this by keeping the deficit under control.

Supporting the economy required new infrastructure, namely improved transportation networks. The Federal-Aid Highway Act, signed in 1956, became the largest public works project in US history. It became the largest highway system in the world and is named the Eisenhower Interstate System. The highways became, as Eisenhower predicted, the transportation arteries of the modern economy. Trucks crisscrossed the country in days not months and the system served the farthest corners of the continental United States. The second major project was a joint-venture with the Canadian Government—the St. Lawrence Seaway. A system of canals and locks, the Seaway would allow ships to navigate from the Great Lakes to the Atlantic.

Yet against this backdrop of growth and prosperity, one in five Americans (40 million people) still lived in poverty in 1960. Almost half lived in the south but poverty was increasing in northern cities, largely from an influx of African Americans seeking better jobs, notably in the automobile industry. Poverty rates were highest among children and the elderly. While the president's approval rating hovered around 70%, the poor were all but swept under the carpet during the heady days of affluence and wealth that earmarked the 1950s as the most prosperous decade.

If Eisenhower was successful in promoting the economy, which didn't need much help, he was less successful in dealing with Senator McCarthy and civil rights.

McCarthyism under Eisenhower

The Wisconsin Senator's communist-ousting purges reached their climax during the first two years of Eisenhower's presidency. At the start of his second term, Senator McCarthy was given the chair of a relatively minor committee, the Committee on Government Operations, which it was hoped would curb his attacks. On the contrary, he brashly used one of the sub-committees, the Senate Permanent Sub-Committee on Investigations, as a springboard to launch his next round of attacks. He appointed two lawyers, notably including J. F. Kennedy to act as the committee's legal counsel. McCarthy scandalized the majority of middle class US citizens with his unsubstantiated allegations, virulent attacks and blatant disregard for constitutional rights. The hearings were broadcast live on TV and the people of the United States were eventually repulsed by his nasty demeanour and abusive verbal attacks. Rarely did he back his allegations with substantive evidence. Being subpoenaed was to be found guilty. With no due process, and no constitutional protections, the US populace grew critical of the proceedings.

Eisenhower initially supported McCarthy but was outraged by his methods, particularly when he began attacking the loyalty of the US Army. McCarthy's attacks went overboard when he demeaned a serving general and war hero, by saying that he had the intelligence of a five year old and was unfit to wear the uniform. McCarthy then began attacking Eisenhower himself, claiming he had not done enough to expunge known subversives from the federal government or pressure the Chinese to release US pilots captured during the Korean War. No one was safe.

President Eisenhower refused to challenge McCarthy publically, for which he was criticized. But behind the scenes he encouraged the Republican-controlled Senate to investigate the senator. In 1954, a Senate committee brought 46 charges against McCarthy and he was eventually censured on two accounts. McCarthy responded, in characteristic form, by accusing several committee members of deliberate deception and fraud, saying that the committee was simply a lynch mob. The Senate voted 67 to 22 in favour of censure. McCarthy was forced to retreat to the Senate backwaters, dying in 1957 from acute hepatitis most likely brought on by alcoholism. A dark period in US history was over. Eisenhower's administration emerged relatively unscathed. The president quipped that McCarthyism had become "McCarthywasism."

Eisenhower on civil rights

Eisenhower's approach to civil rights was to proceed cautiously. Yet during his presidency the civil rights movement would gain purpose, focus and momentum. The defining moment of the civil rights movement was May 17, 1954, with the Supreme Court's landmark decision in "Brown vs. Board of Education". In this ruling, that supported the 14th Amendment and overturned Plessy vs. Ferguson (1899), Chief Justice Earl Warren declared "separate but unequal" unconstitutional in public schools. Eisenhower had appointed Warren as Chief Justice in 1953 believing him to be a conservative but Warren was, in fact, a liberal and judicial activist. The decision was based on Warren's belief in the Court's responsibility to protect individual rights against the power of the state and a commitment to social justice. If the president was reluctant to proceed with more advanced legislation on civil rights, the Supreme Court had made it clear that it would take the lead. Eisenhower said that appointing Warren was the biggest mistake he made. Nevertheless, the president was in a tight spot. He responded publically that "federal law imposed on the states in such a way as to bring about a conflict. ... would set back the cause of progress in race relations for a long time." He wanted gradual reform rather than imposing federal power on states reluctant to desegregate schools. In this he was wrong.

Unless forced to change, many states simply ignored the decision. As an example of this, in 1957, the president passed a voting rights protection bill, but it was toothless, requiring allegation of voting rights breaches to be adjudicated by jury trial. It was conflict that would eventually accelerate change. That same year, in Little Rock Arkansas, nine black students went to register at Central High School and were stopped by an unruly mob. State officials refused to act and Eisenhower sent in the army. The students went to school and the troops remained the entire school year. In 1958, the graduating class included African Americans for the first time. Most importantly, Eisenhower used executive authority to continue Truman's initiative to desegregate the government and the military. He believed that gradual reform and change would in the long run serve the national interest better than open conflict and federal government fiat. As he put it, nothing good ever came from hitting a man over the head. Yet, at best, he was a half-hearted supporter of civil rights.

Eisenhower's domestic policies: an assessment

Eisenhower's middle of the road approach was the right one for the majority of US citizens in the 1950s. It was a popular approach, as evidenced by Eisenhower's consistently high approval ratings. The hands-off approach to the economy and his motivation to expand and improve the nation's infrastructure were a winning combination.

The new frontier: John F. Kennedy, 1961–63

November 22, 1963: Dallas, Texas. President Kennedy was touring the city in an open Cadillac. Seated beside him was the regal and elegant first lady, Jacqueline Kennedy. Texas governor John Connally sat in

John Fitzgerald Kennedy (1917–1963)

John F. Kennedy was the second of nine children born to Joseph and Rose Kennedy. He was the first Irishman and the first Catholic to hold office as president of the United States. Named after his grandfather, John Francis Fitzgerald, mayor of Boston, he was nicknamed Jack. A sickly child, he contracted scarlet fever and other maladies, and was administered the last rites three times. His father, Joseph Kennedy, was driven to overcome the stigma of being an Irish Catholic. He became a millionaire and wanted his sons to enter public office. The oldest son, Joe Junior, handsome, athletic and personable, seemed like the most likely choice, in comparison to his sickly younger brother Jack who was bookish and withdrawn. Jack attended Choate Boarding School for boys and excelled in history and English, his favourite subjects, but was better known for his unruly behaviour and lack of ambition. His father reprimanded Jack: "I will not be disappointed if you don't turn out to be a real genius, but I think you can be a really worthwhile citizen with good judgment and understanding." Jack attended Princeton University but was forced to withdraw after contracting Addison's disease. He had recovered by 1936 when he joined Joe Junior at Harvard. In 1937 Joseph Kennedy became ambassador to England (an unusual choice considering he was an avowed Anglophobe.) Jack took an instant interest in European politics and when war broke wrote a best seller *Why England Slept* (1940). Joe and Jack enlisted in the Navy. Joe became a pilot and went to Europe hunting U-boats; Jack to the Pacific as the skipper of the torpedo boat P.T. 109; sunk by the Japanese in 1943. Seriously injuring his back he nevertheless managed to avoid capture, saved his crew and was decorated for bravery and leadership. Joe was killed in 1944 flying on a secret mission. Post-war Jack ran for Congress in 1946 and served three terms. In 1952 he was elected as Senator from Massachusetts. In 1953 he married Jacqueline Bouvier. They had two children, Caroline (1957) and John Jr (1960). In 1956 he was nearly selected as vice-presidential candidate. In 1957, recovering from back surgery, he wrote the Pulitzer Prize winning *Profiles in Courage* (although a co-author was confirmed in 2008) In July 1960 he was nominated as the Democratic Party's candidate for the presidency, and became President, defeating Richard Nixon. The election was notable for featuring the first nationally televised debate. President Kennedy (JFK as he was known) was assassinated in Dallas, Texas, on November 22, 1963. The events surrounding JFK's assassination remain a source of historical controversy, speculation and debate 50 years on.

the front seat. The visit had gone very well. Texans seemed to endorse the president's civil rights bill. As the cavalcade swung in front of the Texas library book depository building, shots rang out, Kennedy was killed almost instantly and Connally was seriously wounded.

In 1983, 20 years after that infamous day, polls found that 60% of US citizen considered Kennedy the most appealing of nine presidents since Herbert Hoover (1928–32). Second place was Franklin Delano Roosevelt at 49%. This is hardly surprising. Kennedy's suave demeanour, handsome features, his elegant and beautiful wife and their small children seemed the perfect US family. Pundits called it Camelot, after the Broadway play depicting King Arthur's court—a magical time of love, hope, elegance and opportunity. The same poll also found that people in the United States considered Kennedy to be ahead of FDR as "Best in domestic policy" and that he "Cared most about the elderly, the poor and those in the most economic trouble." Assessing the actual impact and success of the president's domestic policy is difficult because of his early assassination and the sense of unfulfilled promise that surrounds Kennedy's presidency.

Early in his presidency, Kennedy followed in the footsteps of his predecessors Truman and Eisenhower. He was reluctant to advance major reforms preferring to go slowly on important issues like poverty and civil rights. It was only in the third year, following the Cuban Missile Crisis, that he finally displayed the courage and ideological leadership that he had promised in his inaugural address in 1961. In his acceptance speech for the Democratic nomination in 1960, Kennedy set the stage for his presidency:

> We stand on the edge of a New Frontier—the frontier of unfulfilled hopes and dreams, a frontier of unknown opportunities and beliefs in peril. Beyond that frontier are uncharted areas of science and space, unsolved problems of peace and war, unconquered problems of ignorance and prejudice, unanswered questions of poverty and surplus.

The "New Frontier" was Kennedy's catchphrase to chart a new course for the United States and determine the direction of economic and social programs and policies. It represented the New Deal and the Fair Deal and his determination to continue the legacy of Democratic presidents in generating renewal, reform and change. Specifically, Kennedy wanted to alleviate poverty, raise the minimum wage, guarantee equal pay, promote urban renewal, initiate the Peace Corps and provide medical care for the elderly. He reaffirmed the notion of service and duty to the nation and the world; and a belief in social justice. Kennedy's New Frontier promised much but delivered little. He was unwilling to put his popularity at risk over domestic matters.

Kennedy recruited the "brightest and best." Yet, for all their credentials, his administration stumbled on domestic policy. The Cold War, Berlin, Cuba and a host of other foreign entanglements monopolized Kennedy's time and effort. As one former aide said, every day was a new crisis. At the center of this was Kennedy, who unlike Eisenhower, seemed to revel in taking centre

And so my fellow Americans, ask not what your country can do for you, ask what you can do for your country. My fellow citizens of the world, ask not what America will do for you, but what together we can do for the Freedom of Man.

John F. Kennedy,
inaugural address, 1961

stage on every major issue. He was a self-proclaimed "idealist without illusion." Problem-solving, Kennedy style, was to find a technical solution to a problem: establish a program, set up a committee, investigate alternatives. These were his tactics and the tactics of those he recruited to cabinet and as aides. He considered himself a pragmatist and did not champion futile causes. The New Frontier's ideological centerpiece, the Peace Corps, was intended to help improve the image of the United States overseas. The Peace Corps recruited thousands of young people in the US for overseas service in disadvantaged regions of the world. It earned Kennedy the admiration of the first wave of baby boomers.

Kennedy's other measures included an increase in the minimum wage, a federal housing act, a development act for rural areas and a tax cut. His reform efforts, however, experienced limited advance in a conservative Congress. Congress eventually passed about half of the six hundred bills Kennedy proposed in his first two years but these did not represent the important half. Congress raised the minimum hourly wage from $1 to $1.25 and approved $4.9 billion in urban renewal grants. Notably, however, Kennedy's big ticket items were defeated, including Medicare, mass transit and education. Many of Kennedy's programs would find new life in President Johnson's Great Society programs.

Kennedy's new economics

In the Senate, Kennedy had consulted with academic economists and continued the practice as president, appointing several academics as advisors. He ended a period of tight fiscal management and balanced budgets to keep interest rates down and sponsor economic growth. At the time of his inauguration unemployment was at 7%, double the rate during the 1950s. The debate over the reasons for the increase in unemployment was important. Unlike Eisenhower's administration, which attributed spikes to changes in demographics and labor markets, Kennedy's advisors argued that spikes were part of the economy's cyclical nature and resulted from shortfalls in the demand for goods and services. The president's position on the debate determined the methods for recovery. In his first budget, he would side with those advocating a balanced budget and was encouraged by an upturn in the economy. Tax reform was next, and in 1962 he agreed to a tax cut to bolster the economy in an effort to stimulate private investments. The federal deficit was nearly $12 billion, but the tax cut had the desired effect and stimulated the economy. GDP, which had faltered at the end of the Eisenhower years, now averaged 5.5% in 1961–63. As well, industry enjoyed healthy growth, inflation stayed under control and unemployment fell. Yet it remains a matter of debate whether Kennedy's deficit model of financing was beneficial in the long term. The resulting government deficits, carrying with it heavy interest payments and high rates of inflation, together stifled rather than stimulated the economy.

Kennedy on civil rights

There is little doubt that Kennedy owed his electoral victory to his courtship of the African American community by orchestrating the release of Martin Luther King from jail on the eve of the 1960 election. However, at first the best that can be said is that Kennedy postponed taking action on civil rights because he understood that Congress would not support him. He did not want to alienate southern Democratic senators whose support he needed in other areas. Civil rights legislation in 1961 would have failed. His most significant measures had been the appointment of the African American jurist, Thurgood Marshall, to the Supreme Court. Marshall was the lawyer who had successfully argued the Brown vs. Board of Education ruling. Kennedy implemented measures to remove racial discrimination in the federal government and the issuance of federal contracts. The Attorney General, Robert Kennedy, JFK's younger brother, aggressively employed the power of the Justice Department to enforce voter registration legislation. The response in the south was bombings, violence and a resurgence of the Ku Klux Klan. While more interested in advancing the civil rights agenda than Truman or Eisenhower, Kennedy was not moving fast enough for the civil rights movement itself.

By the early 1960s, the civil rights movement had come of age and was gaining momentum. The leadership was experienced, intelligent and dedicated. Under the charismatic Martin Luther King, they were organized and had radicalized the discontent millions of southern African Americans into action. Espousing a philosophy of non-violent political disobedience, they used strikes, marches and sit-ins across the south to foment change. In May 1963, TV coverage of white policemen beating black marchers in Birmingham, Alabama, stunned millions of white Americans and forced Kennedy to take action.

The Alabama governor, George Wallace, was an ardent segregationist and refused to allow African American students to register at the University of Alabama, defying court-ordered desegregation. Kennedy tried to convince Wallace to change his mind and avoid violent confrontation. Wallace publically stated that he would personally stop the students entering the university. Two black students were about to try and register at Alabama. On June 11, 1963, with cameras rolling and the troops watching, Wallace stood by the door and the students entered. Wallace had kept his defiance symbolic, avoided violence and made it appear that he, not the president, was in charge. Hot on the heels of the incident, Kennedy spoke to the nation in a television address that would forever change race relations in the United States.

> The heart of the question is whether all Americans are to be afforded equal rights and equal opportunities, whether we are going to treat our fellow Americans as we want to be treated. If an American, because his skin is dark, cannot eat lunch in a restaurant open to the public, if he cannot send his children to the best public school available, if he cannot vote for the public officials who represent him, if, in short, he cannot enjoy the full and free life which all of us want, then who among us would be content to have the color of his skin changed and stand in his place? Who among us would then be content with the counsels of patience and delay?

National legislation would be enacted to move civil rights from the street to the courthouse. Kennedy proposed a liberal answer—the obligation of the federal government to take action when it was beyond a reasonable doubt that local officials and state governments were unwilling and unable to protect the constitutional rights and freedoms for all citizens. In Kennedy's view, the Bill of Rights took precedence over the sovereignty of local government and he had sworn an oath as president to protect the Constitution. As he stated:

> We preach freedom around the world, and we mean it, and we cherish our freedom here at home, but are we to say to the world, and much more importantly, to each other that this is a land of the free except for the Negroes; that we have no second-class citizens except Negroes; that we have no class or caste system, no ghettoes, no master race except with respect to Negroes?

The civil rights movement had also forced his hand. Black leaders were no longer willing to accept White House calls for restraint and gradual change. No more waiting; they demanded action now. The defining moment of the civil rights movement had come. Kennedy knew his bold speech would have a political price. He had ignored his advisors pleas to soften the speech and by sticking to his guns had effectively lost the south in the next election. He feared that without strong action the civil rights movement would became more aggressive, leading to more violence and damage to property, something average citizens would not tolerate. He wanted to control events, not react to them. The proposed Civil Rights Act reinvigorated Kennedy's administration. In an interesting twist, Congress strengthened the Act giving Kennedy more than he asked. May 1963 was a turning point in Kennedy's presidency showing for the first time on the domestic front the vigorous, intelligent and determined leadership he'd displayed many times on the international stage. He also introduced an economic program to address poverty and other inequalities. He had made the connection

Activity

TOK Link

What knowledge of history might be gained by focusing attention on each of the following?

- the historian
- historical documents and written history
- the readership, and the social, cultural and historical context.

November 22, 1963: It is said that anyone old enough to remember that day knows exactly where they were when they heard the news of President Kennedy's death. Kennedy's assassination is deeply ingrained in the national memory and mythology of the United States. Controversy over the details of his death continues today.

Exercise

Assess the impact of the following events on the memory and national mythology of the United States. Interview people that you know who remember the event, and who may have either witnessed it first hand, or through the media. What about your own experiences? Based on your research, what observations and conclusions can you make about the importance of history in shaping our lives?

- The bombing of Pearl Harbor, Hawaii, December 7, 1941
- Kennedy's assassination, Dallas, Texas, November 22, 1963
- The terrorist attack on the Twin Towers, New York City, September 11, 2001

between political and economic equality and set out to balance both sides of the equation. His new program had three prongs: civil rights; an end to poverty; the promotion of peace at home and abroad. In the final days of his life, JFK had set America on a new course. The tragedy is that he did not live to see it take root.

"The Great Society": Lyndon Baines Johnson, 1963–69

November 22, 1963: Vice President Lyndon Baines Johnson was sworn in as the 36th president of the United States aboard Air Force One, just hours after President Kennedy's assassination. Next to him was the aggrieved widow of the former president. Five days later, President Johnson addressed Congress and the nation "I will do my best, that is all I can do!" Then, he set the stage for what was to come: "We have talked long enough in this country about equal rights. ... It is now time to write it in the books of laws." He was determined to show the nation that he was in charge and prepared to continue Kennedy's work. JFK's untimely death opened a window of opportunity that he was prepared to exploit. In private, he revealed his plan to "take the dead man's program and turn it into a martyr's cause."

In May 1964, five months after taking office, Johnson introduced his program to give a hand-up, not a hand-out to disadvantaged groups. Speaking at the graduation ceremony at the University of Michigan, he used the occasion to declare his vision of the Great Society and present himself as the great reformer.

> The challenge of the next half century is whether we have the wisdom to rich and elevate our national life, and to advance the quality of our American civilization. The Great Society rests on abundance and liberty for all. It demands an end to poverty and racial injustice, to which we are totally committed in our time. But this is just the beginning ...

He identified three issues central to the Great Society: the need to resurrect and reclaim urban life, and achieve a greater quality of life for all its citizens; to update, upgrade and preserve the rural heritage, ensuring future generations enjoyed clean water, clean air, and the natural environment; and to guarantee equal access to a high-quality education from kindergarten to college. President Johnson would build on the legacy of the New Deal and Fair Deal. He would enact Kennedy's civil and voting rights bills that upheld the constitutional rights of all citizens. He would declare war on poverty through education and locally initiated, federally funded, economic improvement plans; head-start classes for pre-school children and tuition loans for high school graduates. He would provide decent housing, medical care for the elderly and take the first steps to cleaning up polluted cities and waterways. It was a bold vision.

Activity

The assassination of a US President

Compare and contrast the assassinations of presidents Lincoln and Kennedy and its relative social, cultural and historical impact on the United States.

Lyndon B. Johnson being sworn-in aboard Air Force One by Federal Judge Sarah T. Hughes. Lady Bird Johnson is on his right and Jacqueline Kennedy on his left.

Lyndon Baines Johnson (1908–1973)

Lyndon Baines Johnson was the first child of Sam and Rebek Johnson, and grew up on the family homestead in Texas, where he was raised in a comfortable setting but surrounded by rural poverty. He graduated from high school at 15 and became a teacher, working in poor neighbourhoods of mainly Mexican descent. In 1934 he married Claudia "Lady Bird" Taylor; and had two daughters Lynda Bird (1944) and Luci Baines (1947). He entered the House of Representatives in 1937 and the senate in 1948. Arguably the most successful US senator of all time, one colleague stated that he never saw Johnson win a debate on the floor of the senate but never saw him lose one behind closed doors. This became known as the "Johnson Treatment" or the "Johnson way". He was able to create consensus behind closed doors, by bullying, blackmailing and charming opponents as required. He could be ruthless one instant and beguiling the next. Tall and lanky, he towered over his target gesticulating with his big hands as a force to be reckoned with. He revelled in power politics and would use any means at his disposal to get his way. Johnson was Senate Minority Leader in 1953, and Senate Majority Leader 1955–61. In 1960 he lost the Democratic Party presidential nomination to Kennedy but became vice-president. He became president of the United States on November 22, 1963 (JFK's assasination). Elected president in 1964, he defeated Republican nominee Barry Goldwater. As president he oversaw the escalation of America's war effort in Vietnam and on the domestic front focused on the implementation of his program for the "Great Society", through declaring a war on poverty. In effect, he lost both wars and did not seek reelection in 1968. Johnson (LBJ as he was also known) died of a heart attack on his Texas Ranch, January 22, 1973, age 64. Johnson's presidential legacy remains a source of great controversy. During one of the most turbulent periods in American history, he tried (and ultimately failed) to defeat communist aggression in South East Asia and defeat poverty and erase racism in America.

Fate had given Johnson the presidency, and he made use of it to pass a frenzy of legislation at a rate never witnessed before or since. In 1964, Johnson had declared war on racism and poverty. He knew how to outflank the Republican Party's penchant for blocking social legislation that they believed expanded the power and reach of the federal government, diminished state sovereignty and expanded the influence of the Democratic Party. Johnson's vision was impressive, ambitious, wide-reaching and ultimately unattainable. For the first time since the end of the Second World War, foreign affairs would temporarily take a back seat to domestic policy. Unlike Roosevelt or Truman, whose initiatives foundered on the Senate floor, Johnson knew how to steer legislation through Congress. Buoyed by his election in November 1964, when he soundly defeated ultra-conservative Republican candidate Barry Goldwater, and with the Democrats in control of Congress Johnson, in 1964 and 1965, worked on over 200 pieces of "Great Society" legislation. The list is impressive for its courage and vision, and included:

- Civil Rights Act (1964) and the Voters Rights Act (1965)
- Medicare and Medicaid
- Social Securty benefits—increased payments
- Elementary and Secondary School Acts (build schools in underpriviledged areas)
- Student Loans (assist High School graduates with college tuition)
- Head Start programs: prepare pre-school children for school
- Affirmative Action: saving a place for historically disadvanted peoples and groups
- Immigration Act of 1965—opened the doors to non-European immigrants.
- Economic Opportunity Act (1965)

- Tax cuts and deficit spending to ensure economic growth and employment
- Environmental protection and regulation; first clean air and water initiatives, created 37 new national parks and reclaimed polluted land
- Established the Corporation for Public Broadcasting and provided support for the arts.

The Civil Rights Act (1964) and Voters Rights Act (1965) were the centerpiece of Johnson's program for reform. Initiated by Kennedy, Johnson was able to improve both Acts by allowing them to foment in Congress. He needed 27 votes to end debate on the Civil Rights Act and used the "Johnson touch" to convince reluctant senators of both parties to join the civil rights movement and vote for the bills. It was a triumph that had eluded Truman and Kennedy.

The Civil Rights Act outlawed dejure (legalized) segregation and discrimination and legislated equal access in restaurants, hotels, bars, and buses. It had been a long time coming but finally the hopes and dreams of African Americans had been realized. Martin Luther King's "dream" had come true. The political cost was high. The Democratic Party, Johnson believed, had lost the south for a generation. The 1965 Voters Rights Act outlawed the pernicious voter registration tactics employed in the south to disenfranchise black voters (such as head taxes and literacy tests). Jim Crow laws were gone and millions of southern African Americans would vote for the first time. The backlash was violent and when a civil rights worker was murdered by the Ku Klux Klan, Johnson warned the "hooded society of bigots" that such acts would not be tolerated.

A century after the civil war, the promise of political and social equality and liberty for all citizens had finally become a reality. It should have guaranteed Johnson's legacy as the man who finished what Lincoln started. But the president's blindspot was that he passed the Great Society legislation often with little regard for the programs the laws would create. "Get it done now" was the adminstration's motto. Johnson knew the honeymoon with Congress had a short shelf life.

One example of the difficulties of implementing these new funding initiatives were the Title 1 Education Grants, targeting school improvement in poor districts. The grants were given to the local school boards who were to use the money for local improvements. But in many cases the monies did not reach the target audience, and was frittered away on minor programs. In Fresno, California, the money was used to purchase a classroom TV system for the entire district. And in Camden, New Jersey, the money was spent on physical education. According to Historian Alan Matusow, Johnson believed that "Title I was an anti-poverty program. The local school districts made sure it was not."

The most controversial program was the Office of Economic Opportunity created under the Economic Opportunity Act (1965). It oversaw a range of programs on poverty, notably Head Start programs, the Community Action Program (CAP), healthcare, housing and unemployment relief. In many ways CAP was a conservative approach to eliminating poverty. It was to be a grass-roots initiative, empowering and encouraging local communities to confront their own economic malaise and work to change the ingrained defeatist attitudes of the urban poor. The programs were to be local, autonomous and self-managed, providing the training, skills, education and assistance for low-income groups to build a better life. This included better housing and schools. But the program ran into a turf war with local governments who resented the presence of the federal government in their communities. Conservatives claimed CAP was the federal government's foot in the door in local matters. Liberals thought Johnson was not doing enough and should simply end poverty. But Johnson wanted not just to ensure equality of opportunity for all citizens of the United States, but to ensure that the initiatives under CAP would guarantee equality of outcome as well. The entitlement age had begun.

Activity

Assessing the Great Society

Success or failure?

Historians continue to debate the merits of LBJ's Great Society. In this activity you will examine the views of historians and contemporary commentators to develop your own assessment of the Great Society, and its impact on:

- poverty
- life expectancy
- public health
- education
- the arts
- voter's rights.

Making an assessment

To what extent do you consider the Great Society to have been a success or a failure? Refer to the areas of focus, the views of the historians quoted here, and undertake additional research on the specific programs.

Historian's views

Source A

Joseph A. Califano, a former Johnson aide and speech writer.

> ... he reminded the American people that God and history would judge us not just on how much the Gross Domestic product grew but on how we spent it. ... Throughout all the distractions of the most serious of times, Johnson never lost focus on the price and promise of the Great Society ...

> No President ever cared more, tried harder or helped more needy americans.
>
> **Source:** Joseph A. Califano quote from: Taking sides: Clashing Views in United States History since 1945. 3rd edition (Boston, McGraw-Hill Higher Education, 2008) p. 249

Source B

George McGovern, Democratic Senator and 1968 presidential candidate, who lost to Nixon.

> If it had been up to Lyndon Johnson we would not have gone to Vietnam in the first place. It would be a historic tragedy if his outstanding domestic record remained forever obscured by his involvement in a war he did not begin and did not know how to stop.
>
> **Source:** George McGovern quote from Madaras, p. 249.

Source C

John Kenneth Galbraith, former White House economic advisor and Harvard Professor of Economics.

> Next only to Franklin D. Roosevelt as a force for a civilized and civilizing social policy essential for human well being and peaceful co-existence between the economically favoured (or financially fortunate) and the poor. ... Lyndon Johnson was the most effective advocate of human and social change in the United States in this [20th] century.
>
> **Source:** John K. Galbraith quote from Madaras, p. 249

Source D

Murray N. Rothbard, Dean of the Austrian School of Economics.

> The cruellest myth fostered by the liberals is that the Great Society functions as a great boon and benefit to the poor; in reality, when we cut through the frothy appearances to the cold reality underneath, the poor are the major victims of the welfare state. The poor are the ones to be conscripted to fight and die at literally slave wages in the Great Society's imperial wars. The poor are the ones to lose their homes to the bulldozer of urban renewal, that bulldozer that operates for the benefit of real estate and construction interests to pulverize available low-cost housing. All this, of course, in the name of "clearing the slums" and helping the aesthetics of housing. The poor are the welfare clientele whose homes are unconstitutionally but regularly invaded by government agents to ferret out sin in the middle of the night. The poor (e.g., Negroes in the South) are the ones disemployed by rising minimum wage floors, put in for the benefit of employers and unions in higher-wage areas (e.g., the North) to prevent industry from moving to the low-wage areas. The poor are cruelly victimized by an income tax that left and right alike misconstrue as an egalitarian program to soak the rich; actually, various tricks and exemptions insure that it is the poor and the middle classes who are hit the hardest. The poor are victimized, too, by a welfare state of which the cardinal macro-economic tenet is perpetual if controlled inflation.
>
> **Source:** Murray N. Rothbard quote from: Murray N. Rothbard, The Great Society: A Libertarian Critique @Len Rockwellll.com (http://lewrockwell.com/rothbard/rothbard40.html).

Source E

The historian Bruce J. Shulman.

> ... for it was Lyndon Johnson himself, more than his aides or opponents or successors, who neglected the Great Society and stunted its growth. ... LBJ made two political mistakes, two fateful errors that utlimately stifled his beloved "child" [Great Society]. ... he covered up the costs of the Asian struggle [Vietnam war], economized on every domestic program and delayed a tax increase as long as possible. This strategy failed. Eventually he had to scale back the Great Soceity to fight the war that took up more and more of his time and energy. Second he did not anticipate the insidious political current that would further undermine [the Great Society]. ... The Civil Rights Act of 1964 had already sacrificed the votes of white southerners, Now the heart of the New Deal coalition [labor and North East ethnic whites] complained about Johnson'sk poverty program and the intensifying demands of African-Americans (i.e Black Panthers).
>
> **Source:** Bruce J. Shulman quote from: William H. Chafe et al.: A History of Our Time: Readings on Post-War America, 7th edition (Oxford University Press, New York, 2008) p. 112

Source F

The historian William H. Chafke.

> No one could gainsay Johnson's achievement. He wanted to be "the greatest of them all, the whole bunch of them," and in many ways he succeeded. ... Yet in the very course of attempting to realize his dreams, Johnson exhibited fatals flaws of personality and political philosophy that contributed to his undoing. ... He alone would make it all happen. ... through personal will, his own brand of dominance on the entire nation. ... The tragedy of Lyndon Johnson was that both his personality and his political assumptions proved inadequate to the dimensions of the foreign policy and domestic tensions that would emerge during his presidency.

In the end, despite Johnson's deep personal commitment, the Great Society became a casualty of the Vietnam War. As he put it: "That bitch of a war killed the lady I really loved—The Great Society." Johnson's believed he could fight two wars simultaneously: the war against poverty and the war in Vietnam. Unfortunately, he was wrong and Vietnam overwhelmed and ultimately undermined the effectiveness of Johnson's presidency.

The New Federalism: Richard Nixon, 1969–74

Richard Nixon effectively and shrewdly created a new conservative coalition built around patriotism, effective law enforcement, and support for middle-class values. He unquestionably had his thumb on the pulse of the nation in his perception that people were fatigued by student radicalism, the civil rights and anti-war movements, and an activist Supreme Court. His domestic policy, however, lacked the moral ascendancy of Johnson's Great Society. Nixon's approach was pragmatic. He was more interested in foreign policy and felt that this was his true calling. Nonetheless, he made advances on the home front that surprised both Republicans and Democrats. Without Watergate, it is likely that his achievements in domestic affairs would have been viewed more favorably by historians.

Nixon did not follow Eisenhower's lead and incrementally maintain or increase Democratic social welfare programs or try to manage them better. He was not interested in creating more government programs but wanted to administer existing programs differently with less federal involvement. His brand was "The New Federalism", a system that would divert money and power from the federal bureaucracy to the states and local governments. The notion was not new, Nixon had believed since arriving in Washington in 1946 that money spent at the local level would be more responsive to local needs and requirements than one-size-fits-all federal programs. His approach was **Jeffersonian**. For example, in 1972, he created the State and Local Assistance Act that initially redistributed four billion federal dollars to the states and local authorities. When the program was cancelled in 1986 by President Ronald Reagan, the total was 83 billion dollars. Not surprisingly, Nixon's plans were supported by the states and local governments and opposed by Washington bureaucrats who

Jeffersonian democracy, named after President Thomas Jefferson, is a political philosophy supporting a federal government with strictly controlled powers (as outlined in the US Constitution). It mandates a strong preference for the rights of state and local governments.

265

Richard Milhous Nixon (1913–1994)

Richard Milhous Nixon was born in Yorba Linda, Orange County, California. From a poor background, he was a hard-working, ambitious and intelligent student. He was awarded a scholarship to Duke University, where he graduated in third place in his law class, subsequently practising law in California where he was called to the bar. During the Second World War, he was a navy lieutenant serving in a transport unit in the Pacific. After the war he ran for Congress as a Republican and was elected to the House in 1946. During the campaign he accused his Democratic opponent of taking money from a communist-dominated action committee. It became a strategy for Nixon to undermine his opponents by accusing them of communist affiliations. In this, he was an ardent cold warrior and supported McCarthy. He earned fame for his unrelenting questioning of Alger Hiss which led to Hiss's conviction for perjury and a 14-year jail term. In 1950, Nixon used smear tactics to discredit his opponents and win a Senate seat. In 1952, he became the youngest vice president in history. President Eisenhower's poor health often required Nixon to chair high-level meetings and make presidential rulings, most notably on the 1957 civil rights bill. In 1960, he won the Republican presidential nomination. During the first-ever televised presidential debate he was overshadowed by the more handsome, witty and charismatic John F. Kennedy. Despite this, he lost the election by a mere 113,000 votes out of 68 million.

He returned to law in California, wrote a best-seller, ran for governor of California in 1962 and lost. Then Nixon moved to New York City to take up a post as senior partner in a law firm. He remained a staunch Republican and gave many speeches around the country supporting Republican candidates and issues. In February 1968, he announced his bid for the presidency. During the campaign he said he had a secret plan to end the war in Vietnam; it is unclear if this plan existed or was an electoral fabrication to gain support. His campaign slogan "Nixon's the one" was very effective against opponents, Democrat Hubert H. Humphrey and independent candidate George Wallace from Alabama.

On November 5, 1968, Nixon was elected president of the United States. He took extreme measures bombing Hanoi, Cambodia and sending ground forces into Vietnam, but was unable to end the war quickly and US troops were not withdrawn until 1973. In 1972, Nixon won a second term defeating George McGovern making him the first vice president since Thomas Jefferson to win two terms as president. His second term came to an unfortunate end with the Watergate scandal. The Senate began impeachment proceedings but Nixon resigned on August 8, 1974. He died of a stroke at the age of 81 in 1994.

feared job losses and congressional politicians wanting to play Robin Hood and deliver federal monies to their constituencies.

Nixon moved quickly to shut-down "Great Society" programs that were unpopular with his party. First to go was the Office of Economic Opportunity (OED), the agency charged with leading the "war on poverty." The Community Action Program (CAP) was reorganized and other programs were shuffled to different departments, their funding reduced or cut entirely. Nixon's war on poverty took two directions. First, he proposed a family allowance program under the direction of the Urban Affairs Council. The plan would replace food stamps and Medicaid and provide a yearly subsidy of $1,600 in direct aid to single-parent families or to a working-poor family of four. The plan was announced on August 8, 1969. It was Nixon's most radical initiative and seemed out of character for a conservative Republican President. Yet, from another vantage point, it aligned with his view that federal government funds should be distributed directly to those who would use the money and avoiding creating an intermediary layer of federal bureaucracy. Recipients would decide how to spend the money without being subject to spending rules imposed by federal case workers. Conservative opponents opposed the plan because it guaranteed an income. Organized labor opposed it because they feared it undermined the minimum wage; liberals argued that $1,600 wasn't enough money to support a family of four and federal case workers feared that they would lose their own jobs. Nixon was unable to get the plan approved, and as the 1972 election approached he dropped it from his agenda. In response, he increased federal support of the Food Stamp Act and Medicaid.

Nixon on civil rights

Nixon wanted to slow down the civil rights movement and earn the trust and support of the south. School desegregation was first up. Nixon proposed federal funds to local districts to build new community schools. He said it was better if students walked to a nearby neighbourhood school rather than take a long bus ride to a strange part of town. For many parents this was an attractive argument, although it was a newer version of "separate but equal"—with an emphasis on equal. Federal courts disagreed and ordered desegregation to continue. Fifteen years after the Plessey ruling was overturned, nearly 70% of black children still attended segregated schools. Nixon complied with the court order and moved the agenda forward with commendable speed; by 1970, less than 10% of black school children attended all-black schools. Nixon was a capable politician. He could assuage the south that his hands were tied by activist courts, and he could show the liberal elements in the nation that he supported the civil rights movement.

The Voting Rights Act of 1965 was up for renewal in 1970 and the president wanted its provisions extended to all states to avoid "discriminating" against the south. Next, he wanted state courts empowered to adjudicate alleged voting-rights violations instead of federal courts. This initiative was scuttled by Republicans on the House Judiciary Committee, but was followed up by the revisions of a bipartisan committee that extended voting rights to 18-year-olds. Despite these apparent setbacks, Nixon's efforts convinced many southerners to support him.

Nixon also supported the women's movement and the Equal Rights Amendment, and despite considerable opposition increased the number of women holding high rank in the government. He created the Presidential Task Force on Women's Rights and ordered the Justice Department to prosecute sexual discrimination cases under Title VII of the Civil Rights Act. Title VII prohibited employment discrimination based on race, color, religion, sex or national origin. In addition, he ordered the Labor Department to add sexual discrimination guidelines to the Office of Federal Contract Compliance.

Finally, the Philadelphia Plan was a Labor Department initiative to provide training and employment opportunities for minorities. Federally funded, the government used racial classifications and quotas in these desegregation programs. Affirmative action, and a liberal program, had been initiated by a Republican president.

Nixon on the environment

On Earth Day, April 22, 1970, millions of people in the United States took to the streets to raise environmental awareness and Nixon the environmental activist was born. Over the next four years, Nixon sent many groundbreaking pieces of environmental legislation to Congress. The centerpiece was the National Environment Policy Act (1969) which gave birth to the Clean Air Act (1970) that for the first time addressed auto emissions and the Water Pollution Act (1972). The Environmental Protection Agency, established in 1970, remains an important agency today. Nixon also created the Consumer Product Safety Commission and the "Legacy of Parks" program (another New Federalist initiative) that transferred federal lands to the states to establish parks, beaches and recreational areas. It was impressive work for a man who previously had shown little or no interest in the environment. Again, it was Nixon the pragmatist. He responded to public opinion and ended up developing a program that was ahead of its time.

Nixon on economics

During his first term in office Nixon had to confront rampant inflation. On several occasions Nixon would impose temporary wage and price controls to slow inflation. The measures were popular with voters tired of **price gouging** but not so with the business sector. The economy was floundering, beset by inflation, and the first trade deficit since the First World War. Unemployment was also on the increase. Economics was not Nixon's favourite area but he came to realize its importance and in 1971 declared his conversion to **Keynesian economics**. First, he took the unusual step of appointing former Texas Democratic governor, John Connally, as Secretary of the Treasury. On Sunday August 15, Nixon announced his "New Economic Policy" that contained wage and price controls, abandonment of the gold standard, depreciation of the dollar and deficit spending. It was a brilliant political move. Whether these measures were in the nation's best interests long term was not Nixon's primary concern. He was concerned about reelection and needed the economy to be running effectively. Specifically, he added a 10% surcharge on import duty—notably on oil imports, which would lead to shortages during his second term. Prices, wages and rents were frozen for 90 days to be followed by a more flexible and lasting system of price controls. The public approved of Nixon's economic measures, deflected the criticism of the Democratic Party, while also confounding Republicans who advocated market-driven solutions and control of the money supply, rather than direct intervention. As his advisors predicted, the effect on the market was immediate and on Monday August 16 the stock market made the biggest single day's gains in its history. The economy took off and Nixon was reelected in 1972. Social Security and Medicaid payments increased significantly during the first term from 6.3% of the **GNP** to 8.9%. This was due in large part to more people applying and qualifying for benefits. At the same time, defense spending dropped from 9.1% to 5.8% of the GNP. Overall, economic growth was sound but not spectacular, inflation remained problematic and unemployment rates remained low. But the improvement in the economy did not last long.

The economy became volatile due to the Yom Kippur War (October 1973) and the artificial oil shortage created by the Organization of Petroleum Exporting Countries (OPEC). The oil nations wanted more money per barrel and so created an artificial shortage that increased the price at the petrol pumps tenfold. Not surprisingly, the stock markets reacted negatively to the continuation of price controls, notably on petroleum. In the final days of his presidency, Nixon was working on a national health insurance program that would have required employers provide employees health insurance and a

Price gouging refers to the practice of raising prices to a level that is not considered reasonable or fair at times of peak or extraordinary demand. It is a crime in some states of the United States if applied to essential goods and services during civil emergencies.

Keynesian economics advocates a greater role for central banks and the government in monetary policy.

GNP is the value of all the goods and services produced by the citizens of a given country, both inside and outside the country.

federal healthcare plan similar to Medicaid. Although Nixon had a think tank of conservative economists, notably Milton Friedman, providing economic advice based on market solutions and monetary policy, many of the programs he implemented were interventionist and seemed more New Deal than the New Deal.

The Watergate scandal

The Watergate scandal was a result of Nixon's desperation to achieve a second term in office. Surrounded by a band of ruthless and loyal operatives, they employed every dirty trick in the book to derail the Democratic campaign. Disguised as the Committee to Re-elect the President (CREEP) millions of dollars were diverted from Republican coffers to finance their defamation campaign and dirty deeds. And they succeeded. Nixon won, destroying the Democratic candidate, George McGovern, by winning 49 states outright. But for a vigilant night watchman at the Watergate Hotel, they might have got away with it.

Members of CREEP planned a break-in of the Democratic campaign headquarters at the Watergate Hotel, an exclusive location in Georgetown. The plan was to install phone wiretaps and listening devices but they were caught and arrested. Two *Washington Post* reporters tracked a trail of hush money that lead to the **Oval Office** aided by a secret White House informant code-named "Deep-throat". The drama reached its peak during the Senate Watergate Committee hearings. This bipartisan committee interrogated Nixon aides and gathered evidence that would lead to the indictment of 40 high-ranking members of Nixon's administration, including his closest and most prominent advisors—Haldeman and Erlichman. Nixon steadfastly claimed his innocence and distanced himself from the guilty. But, eventually, it became apparent that Nixon was privy to the break-in, if not before then shortly after. The infamous White House tapes also revealed a seedy side to Nixon's personality, notably his foul language and bigotry. **Impeachment** proceedings initiated in the House of Representatives forced Nixon's resignation in August 1974.

As a result of Watergate, the presidency was tarnished, some feared permanently. Yet, in another sense, it was a crowning moment for the United States. The constitution had worked as intended and the checks and balances designed to prevent the abuse of executive power eventually overwhelmed Nixon. In later life, he blamed a conspiracy of the left, particularly the media, for destroying his presidency.

The **Oval Office**, located in the West Wing of the White House, is the official office of the president of the United States.

Impeachment is the process of charging a public official over misconduct in office. There are strict terms of what constitutes an impeachable offense or misdemeanor in the US presidential office.

Activity

The domestic policies of presidents Truman, Eisenhower, Kennedy, Johnson and Nixon: 1945–74

Based on your understanding of the domestic policies of the presidents noted above, address the following questions. Further research may be necessary.

	Truman (Fair Deal)	Eisenhower (Middle way)	Kennedy (New frontier)	Johnson (Great Society)	Nixon New Federalism)
Main features of domestic program					
Successes					
Failures and criticism					
Civil rights record					

Questions

Complete the chart before answering the following questions:

1 Compare and contrast the domestic policies of any two US presidents from 1945–74.

2 "McCarthyism, for all its faults and excesses, successfully rooted out the threat of communist infiltration in the US government." To what extent do you agree with this view?

3 "The legacy of government intervention in the daily lives of US citizens is the real legacy of the domestic policies of Truman and Johnson." Assess and evaluate the validity of this statement.

4 "In the 1940s and 1950s the majority of people living in the United States enjoyed an improvement in their standard of living that was unmatched in US economic history. However, this new prosperity did not include all citizens of the United States." With reference to two presidents, analyze efforts to share the wealth across all sectors of US society.

5 Why were Truman and Eisenhower reluctant supporters of the civil rights movement?

6 "Kennedy only began to take domestic policy seriously as he prepared for the election of 1963." What evidence is there to support and to oppose this statement.

7 Without Watergate, Nixon's domestic record would be remembered as more important than Johnson's Great Society." Agree or disagree and explain why.

8 To what extent do you believe the domestic policies of these presidents has made the United States a better place? What else could or should they have done?

Canada's domestic policies: Diefenbaker to Clark

Canadian prime ministers, 1945–84		
William Lyon Mackenzie King	Liberal Party	1935–1948
Louis Stephen Saint-Laurent	Liberal Party	1948–1957
John George Diefenbaker	Conservative Party	1957–1963
Lester Bowles Pearson	Liberal Party	1963–1968
Pierre Elliot Trudeau	Liberal Party	1968–1979; 1980–1984
Charles Joseph Clark	Conservative Party	1979–1980

Six men occupied 24 Sussex Drive, the official residence of the Canadian prime minister in the capital city of Ottawa, between 1945 and 1979. The Liberal Party dominated, holding power for 28 of the 34 years and was only out of office twice. Not surprisingly, they were considered to be "the Government Party" and had come to believe that what was good for the Liberal Party was good for Canada. One Liberal Party prime minister dominated the era, William Lyon Mackenzie King. First elected prime minister in 1922, King held office until 1948, with the exception of the period 1930–35.

King's leadership during the Second World War was the most significant period of his command. In 1939, he led Canada into war, relatively unprepared, and with a small military and an economy still reeling from the Depression. By the end of the war, over one million Canadians had served in the armed forces out of a total population of 12 million. Per capita war production in both the industrial and agricultural sectors equalled the United Kingdom and was ahead of the United States. When the war ended, Canadians feared a return to the low, dishonest days of the Depression, but King had planned for the end of the war and effectively reabsorbed the veterans, converted the economy to peacetime production and set the stage for over two decades of unprecedented economic growth and low unemployment. He retired in 1948, worn out (age 74). He had effectively managed the nation during some of its most trying days. Canada had emerged from the war self-confident, independent, respected and one of the world's most powerful and prosperous nations.

King was succeeded by Louis St. Laurent, who also proved to be a very capable leader at a time in which Canada began to loosen ties with the United Kingdom and strengthen its relationship with the United States. He was also bilingual. St. Laurent had many successes, starting in 1949, when Newfoundland, the UK's oldest colony, became Canada's 10th province. He convinced Eisenhower to agree to the St. Lawrence Seaway project, a joint Canada–US venture, completed in 1959, that allowed ships to navigate up the St. Lawrence River from the Great Lakes to the Atlantic Ocean. To meet the threat of long-range Soviet bombers, the two nations signed a joint air defence arrangement that integrated the command structures of the US and Canadian militaries, the North American Aerospace Defense Command (NORAD) which required the construction of a radar line (DEW Line) across northern Canada.

Nonetheless, St. Laurent's Liberals lost the elections in 1957 and he retired as head of the party. He was replaced by a populist politician, the Conservative John Diefenbaker, who ended the era of Liberal domination. Since confederation, all Canadian prime ministers came from one of the two parties: the Liberal or Conservative parties, nicknamed the Grits and Tories respectively. During the postwar period there was little difference between the platforms of the two parties. They understood that Canadians wanted a social welfare program and full employment. Disagreements on policy tended to focus on level of taxation and processes. However, the appearance of third parties on the political scene injected more serious ideological alternatives into the national debate and effectively challenged the dominance of the Grits and Tories.

In the 1920s, protest political parties, known as third parties, appeared in the west; the result of regional disadvantages and a representation-by-population electoral system that favoured the heavily populated provinces of Quebec and Ontario. The most important of these formed in 1933—the Cooperative Commonwealth Federation (CCF). The more left-leaning CCF advocated nationalization of key industries and the creation of a welfare system. In 1944, they formed the provincial government in Saskatchewan. The next year, the CCF's popular and capable leader, Thomas C. Douglas, went to Ottawa and the CCF won 28 seats. MacKenzie King referred to the CCF as "Liberals in a hurry" but he had to take them seriously. To stave off the threat from the left, the Liberals adopted the CCF's programs as their own and reaped the benefits of their popularity among the electorate. The first was the family allowance program instituted during the war. Taking the wind out of the CCF sails kept the Liberals in power for a decade after the war. By the time Diefenbaker came to power in 1957, the CCF had been joined by the Social Credit Party that also had a Quebec Branch, *le Raillement Creditiste*. These third parties would hold the balance of power in ruling minority governments in the 1960s and 1970s.

Canadian domestic politics, 1957–79

Immediately following the war, Canadians expected their governments (both federal and provincial) to provide solutions and direction in resolving important economic and social problems. The Marsh Report (1943) set the stage for adopting a Keynesian approach to the economy and social welfare programs, notably including a national health insurance scheme. Several key bureaucrats had personally studied under Keynes at Oxford and favored his demand-based economic policies. In the post-war period the federal government ran "Crown corporations" in such areas as rail transportation, air travel and radio and television. Direct involvement of the government in the economy was here to stay. Canada was a large country with a small population and big government was viewed as the best way to ensure regional equality and promote economic development and full employment. Unlike the division of powers in the federal system of the United States, the majority of power was to reside with the federal government. During this period, the provinces demanded more money and more power. Negotiations between these two levels of government would dominate the Canadian political landscape particularly around taxation and constitutional reform. Federal–provincial conferences became an important device to resolve sticky issues.

In Canada, social welfare programs were implemented gradually over three decades. There was no "made-in-Canada" version of Truman's Fair Deal or Johnson's Great Society. The more cautious approach reflected Canada's preference for incremental change based on consensus and compromise rather than radical reform. And it turned out, by the mid 1960s Canadians enjoyed a cradle-to-grave social welfare net that included: family allowances (1945); unemployment insurance (1940); old-age pension (1927, revised in 1951, and incorporating the Canada Pension Plan from 1965); and, most significantly (in comparison with the US model), a national healthcare insurance plan (1965).

It is considered a statement of fact by Canadians that the US Revolution created not one nation but two. Canada was created by men and women who wished to remain loyal to the British Crown. Anti-US sentiment, based on a fear of US domination are as Canadian as maple syrup and the Mounties. Postwar, these tendencies became more pronounced as Canada moved away from the UK and grew closer to the United States. Canadians worried that the nation's distinctive cultural identity was being engulfed by the powerful US media and was becoming a branch of the US economy. Successive governments took action to stem the tide through implementing regulations requiring Canadian content on TV and radio, stopping the sale of Canadian companies and banks to US interests and through providing government grants to promote Canadian culture.

A further cause for special treatment, by the 1960s, was the movement known in Quebec as the Quiet (or Silent) Revolution. A new breed of educated and entrepreneurial Québécois had emerged who demanded that Quebec be given special status and deserved special treatment. "*Maitre Chez Nous*" (masters in our own house), they cried. The Silent Revolution brought about significant changes and reforms to the balance of power between Québéc, the federal government and the other provinces. But by the late 1960s a more radical movement wanted Quebec to secede from Canada. This separatist movement was led by the brilliant orator and former Liberal cabinet minister René Levesque. In 1976, the Levesque-led "Partis Québécois" became the provincial government in Quebec. A darker development in the separatist camp was the appearance of a terrorist group, *Le Front de libération du Québec* (the Quebec Liberation Front, or FLQ). A terrorist cell numbering about 100 members, the FLQ used violence to promote their message of independence. Bombing an armoury and mailboxes they injured a small number of people. In October 1970, the FLQ kidnapped a British diplomat and a Quebec cabinet minister (whom they subsequently murdered). Prime Minister Trudeau implemented the War Measures Act to meet the threat. Previously, the Act had been used during the first and second world wars to give the government emergency powers. Trudeau's implementation was the only time the Act was invoked during peacetime.

In the postwar era, the provinces demanded more power and governments at all levels played an ever active role in the daily lives of Canadians. Taxes increased to pay for these programs and defense spending was slashed as government priorities shifted from guns to butter. The economy, despite a few bumps, continued its upward trend and average household incomes more than doubled. The nation's population exploded with 4.5 million births (the baby boomers) and 1.5 million new immigrants (mainly European), and by 1960 was more than 17 million, expanding to 24 million by 1980. It was a good time for most Canadians. But, despite high employment levels, disadvantage persisted in many areas of the country and the **First Nations** (indigenous) peoples were marginalized and segregated on reservations. Their children were forced to attend church-run residential schools to be converted into Christians and cleansed of their aboriginal heritage. For the first time in its history, equality for all Canadians was about to become a national imperative.

First Nations Aboriginal peoples in Canada comprise the First Nations, or First Peoples, including the inuit and métis. The terms "Indian" and "Eskimo" are these days less frequently used.

The Canadian system of government

Canada is a constitutional monarchy. This means that the powers of the monarch (the British monarch) are administered by an elected assembly named the House of Commons. The monarch's representative is the governor general who carries out the duties of the Crown in Canada. The governor general is the head of state. The prime minister is the head of the government. The federal (central government) is located in Ottawa, the nation's capital. The system of government is parliamentary democracy following the British model. Parliament has the supreme law-making powers in the nation. The provinces and territories are governed by elected assemblies that also follow a parliamentary model.

Parliament is bicameral, meaning it has two legislative bodies. The most powerful is the House of Commons based on representation by population. The political party that wins the most seats in the House of Commons becomes the ruling or "government" party. In the Canadian system, the executive is made up of the prime minister and cabinet who are elected members of the house and directly responsible to the House of Commons. Responsible government is the key to this system and it means that the prime minister and cabinet must maintain the confidence of the house or they are obligated to resign and call an election. This happened in 1979 when the prime minister resigned after his budget was defeated on a vote of no-confidence.

The party in government selects the prime minister who, in turn, selects cabinet ministers who are also members of the house to lead the various departments and government posts. The electorate, therefore, do not vote directly for the prime minister or the cabinet, but will know beforehand who will be prime minister if a particular party wins enough seats to form the government.

The senate is the other house and is appointed based on regional representation. It provides "a sober second look" at legislation passed by the House. Its powers are limited by the fact that members are appointed. Members are appointed for life (to age 75).

Provincial legislatures are unicameral (one house) comprised of an elected assembly based on the same parliamentary principles of responsible government as the federal government.

The Canada Act (1982), originally the British North America Act of 1867, stipulates the division of powers between the federal and provincial governments as contained in sections 91(federal) and 92(provincial) powers. The Supreme Court of Canada rules on jurisdictional disputes between the levels of government and interprets the constitution. A Charter of Rights and Freedoms was added in 1982 to protect and defend individual and collective rights. Unlike the US presidential system, a government may hold office for a maximum of five years before calling an election. However, for a variety of reasons, elections are usually called more frequently. In some cases (as we will see in this section), the prime minister has formed a government without a clear-cut majority in the House of Commons. This is referred to as a minority government. To maintain power, the party with the most seats must work cooperatively with the other parties. On several occasions a minority government has been defeated shortly after taking office and has called an election to secure a majority government. Others have successfully stayed in office by making deals with the opposition parties.

John G. Diefenbaker, 1957–63

John Diefenbaker became the first Conservative prime minister in 22 years after a surprising victory in the 1957 elections, defeating St. Laurent's Liberals and forming a minority government. Even with a minority government, Diefenbaker seemed to be dynamic and decisive, making changes that ensured his popularity with Canadians. He cut personal income tax and raised old age pension payouts at a time when unemployment was low and government revenues were high. Leading in the polls and with the Liberals holding a leadership convention to replace the retired St. Laurent, Diefenbaker called an election with the slogan "Follow John" in 1958. Diefenbaker's Conservative Party won the largest majority in Canadian history taking 208 out of 265 seats. The Liberals got 48 seats, mainly in Quebec. It appeared the era of Liberal dominance was over. Diefenbaker had a clear mandate to bring about meaningful change after decades of Liberal government.

The new government began with significant advantages including a huge majority and tremendous talent in cabinet that included the first female cabinet minister, Ellen Fairclough, who was the Minister of Citizenship and Immigration. Diefenbaker advocated a "Northern dream" to open up the north to development. He promoted regional development that included building dams in his native Saskatchewan and railroad expansion in the hinterlands. He wanted to attend to those sections of the country the Liberals had ignored or forgotten, marginalized by the Liberal focus on central Canada, notably Quebec. He advocated "unhyphenated Canadianism"; a new vision of citizenship that was no longer English-Canadian or French-Canadian but simply Canadian. This fell on deaf ears in Quebec, where it was known that he did not speak French. To Diefenbaker's credit, he offered voters a "made-in-Canada" vision of the future which was a distinctive shift in style from the ad hoc managerial approach of the Liberals. He offered Canadians a future based on equality for all. One of his greatest achievements was granting the franchise to the First Nations.

In the end, however, he was unable to convert ideology into policy. It started in cabinet; he could not build a consensus. Diefenbaker, the prairie populist could preach but was unable to lead. The "Northern dream" was impractical, untenable and too expensive to be realistic.

John George Diefenbaker (1895–1979)

John George Diefenbaker was born in Ontario and grew up in the Canadian prairie province of Saskatchewan, where his father was a teacher. He attended the University of Saskatchewan and earned a BA (1915) and MA (1916). He joined the army and served in England before invalided home in 1917. In 1919 he was called to the bar and practiced law earning a reputation as a stalwart defence attorney opposing the death penalty. He ran for the House of Commons four times between 1925 and 1940, and was finally elected in that year. He remained a member of the House until his death in 1979. In 1956 he became the Conservative Party leader on his third try and formed a minority government in 1957. In 1958 he won the largest majority in Canadian history but thereafter things went badly for Diefenbaker. Combative and stubborn he alienated his party, senior civil servants, the electorate and the United States. By 1963, he had lost the election to Lester Pearson's Liberals. In 1967 he was ousted as Conservative party leader but stayed in the House until his death in 1979.

On March 29, 1958 in his first speech as Prime Minister to the House of Commons, Diefenbaker revealed his vision of the un-hyphenated Canadian:

"*I am the first prime minister of this country of neither English or French origin. So I am determined to bring about a Canadian citizenship that knew no hyphenated consideration. I'm very happy to be able to say that in the House of Commons today in my party we have members of Italian, Dutch, German, Scandinavian, Chinese and Ukrainian origin—and they are all Canadians.*"

For the most part, he maintained St. Laurent's economic programs with minor tinkering. His government was rocked by scandal and infamously bad decisions. Several events contributed significantly to Diefenbaker's demise.

In 1959, Diefenbaker cancelled the Avro Arrow Project. The Arrow was a Canadian designed and built fighter interceptor designed to meet and defeat the threat of Soviet bombers. The fighter was considered the best of its generation but was made obsolete by the advent of long-range nuclear missiles. The cancellation cost thousands of jobs and precipitated an exodus of talented people to the United States from Canada's small but highly developed aerospace industry. The United States pressured Canada to accept anti-aircraft missiles to replace the Arrow. Fifty-six missiles were deployed in northern Ontario and Quebec, designed to carry nuclear warheads, rendering the missiles virtually useless. After the Cuban Missile crisis of October 1962 President Kennedy blamed Canada for failing to deploy nuclear missiles. The Minister of Defence, Douglas Harkness, who had advocated the nuclear warheads, resigned in disgust. Diefenbaker appeared indecisive on both issues and his government looked rudderless. In an effort to slow inflation, improve

The Avro Arrow, Canadian Air Force.

the balance of payments and encourage tourism, Diefenbaker devalued the Canadian dollar to an unheard of 92.5 cents US. The Liberals dubbed it the "Diefenbuck" and made it the election issue in 1962. Diefenbaker could not stem the Liberal tide. The damage done, his majority vanished and he stumbled back into office with another minority government. After more than 20 years in opposition, Diefenbaker and his cabinet were suspicious of the senior civil servants who had loyally served the Liberal Party and had Liberal leanings and connections. Rather than trying to win their loyalty, Diefenbaker tried to govern by avoiding consultation with his senior bureaucrats. He appeared anachronistic, advocating the British connection at a time when the bonds of empire were slipping. His rural background made him an outsider among the urban élites of central Canada.

On a personal level, Diefenbaker had a bad temper and could be vindictive and paranoid, blaming the media for his failures. While the Conservatives appeared to have taken control of the government, things went downhill quickly. After the Cuban Missile Crisis debacle, his minority government was defeated on a vote of no-confidence and the nation went to the polls in April 1963. The Canadian people were tired of Diefenbaker's antics and antiquated rhetoric and the Liberals were returned to power.

Activity

Research and evaluate Diefenbaker's domestic policies

This is an activity to be undertaken before writing an essay on the success and failures of John Diefenbaker's policies. As a representative of Canada's prairies, Diefenbaker implemented a series of policies to assist the shrinking agricultural sector of society and connect the more remote, northern areas with the rest of Canada. Due to these policies the Conservatives enjoyed the largest parliamentary majority in Canadian history, but in retrospect were his policies effective?

Policies implemented	Effect	Success or Failure	Reasons
Built northern railroad			
Expanded Trans-Canada Highway program			
Fixed price for farm products			
Agriculture Reform Act (1961)			
Canadian Bill of Rights (1960)			

Primary sources from the archives of the Canadian Broadcasting Corporation:
Capital Punishment: http://archives.cbc.ca/society/crime_justice/clips/3339/

Canadian Bill of Rights: http://archives.cbc.ca/politics/prime_ministers/topics/1599/

First Nations voting: http://archives.cbc.ca/politics/rights_freedoms/clips/9556/

Highway: http://archives.cbc.ca/science_technology/transportation/clips/13552/

http://archives.cbc.ca/science_technology/transportation/clips/3900/

Conservative Victory: http://archives.cbc.ca/politics/prime_ministers/clips/10963/

Further resources
Library and Archives of Canada: http://www.collectionscanada.gc.ca

Prime Minister of Canada: http://pm.gc.ca

Montreal Gazette: http://www.montrealgazette.com

Lester B. Pearson, 1963–68

Pearson's domestic plans were significantly influenced by his early career as a diplomat and soldier; he saw internationalism and domestic policy as opposite sides of the same coin. His vision was to make Canada an outward-looking nation that would put an end to provincial rivalries that had so defined Canada's national political culture. At the core of his domestic considerations was the idea of establishing a more positive relationship with the United States, where much of its economic and military stock lay. Pearson—like his contemporary, President Johnson in the US—believed in government intervention to improve the lives of average citizens. At the root of Pearson's programs was the principle of "universality" which mandated equal access to government programs for all Canadians, most notably education, welfare and healthcare.

During his five years in office the Liberal Party never enjoyed a majority in parliament but through the support of newly emerging parties he implemented a series of policies favorable to Canadians and contributed to his legacy as a great statesman.

The Auto Pact, 1964

The Canada–United States Automotive Agreement, also known as the Auto Pact, of December 11, 1964, was a free trade agreement that permitted the free trade of automobiles, tires and auto parts across the border. The agreement had more impact in Canada than in the United States in terms of jobs and helped reduce the balance of payments inequity between the two nations. The agreements purpose was twofold: first, to reduce production costs by reducing duplication; and second, related to the first, to reduce the cost to consumers, thereby increasing consumption. It worked. The Canadian balance of payments in the auto industry offset a deficit balance of payments in other sectors of the economy. Car prices dropped, sales increased and Canada's automobile sector increased from 70,000 workers in 1965 to a peak of 125,000 in 1978. Southern

Lester Bowles Pearson (1897–1972)

Lester Bowles Pearson was born in Toronto to parents who were both of Irish descent. His father was a Methodist minister and a Conservative, his mother was a Liberal. In 1913 he entered Victoria College, University of Toronto, at age 16 but his studies were interrupted by the First World War. He volunteered for duty first in a hospital unit and then transferred to the Royal Flying Corps. He was invalided, suffering from physical injuries and psychological trauma, and finished the war an instructor. Returning to university he earned his first degree in 1919. Following two years in private industry he received a two year fellowship at Oxford University where he obtained a BA and MA. In 1924, he joined Canada's most prestigious history faculty at the University of Toronto. In 1928, he was persuaded to join Canada's fledgling Department of External Affairs. He would spend the next 40 years in government service. He held a number of diplomatic posts and participated in The Hague Conference on International Law (1930), the Washington Naval Conference (1930), the Geneva World Disarmament Conference (1933–34), the London Naval Conference (1935) and numerous session of the League of Nations. In 1942, he led the Canadian legation in Washington and was involved in the negotiations leading to the formation of the United Nations (1944–45). Postwar he continued to hold high-ranking positions in foreign affairs including stints as the Chair of Canada's NATO delegation and was Canada's ambassador to the United Nations. In 1957, he brokered the Suez Crisis ceasefire agreement that ended the conflict and earned him the Nobel Peace Prize. He successfully ran for parliament and quickly became the leader of the Liberal Party, replacing Louis St. Laurent. In 1963, he defeated the Conservatives winning a slim minority government. He tried again in 1965 to win a majority but was unsuccessful. He retired from public life 1968 and became president of Carleton University. Diagnosed with cancer in 1970, he wrote his memoirs prior to his death in 1972. Unquestionably Canada's most successful and respected foreign diplomat, he was instrumental in creating Canada's image as a trusted ally, humanitarian and peacekeeping nation. His record as prime minister was considered less successful by his contemporaries, but in retrospect this might not be accurate.

Ontario benefitted more than the rest of the country as the automobile manufacturing sector was concentrated close to the US centers of production with easy access to transportation routes. The pact was critical for increasing domestic support for the Liberal Party.

Defense spending

In the 1950s, Canada rebuilt its military to meet the threat of Soviet expansion. Twenty-five-thousand Canadians fought in the Korean War. And, by the mid-1960s, the armed forces numbered 120,000 with 10,000 permanently stationed in Europe as part of Canada's NATO commitment. However, the Glassco Commission (1963)reported that the military had been very wasteful in its expenditures and recommended that the armed forces become more "flexible, mobile and imaginative" in its structure while maintaining a commitment to international peacekeeping. As a result, Pearson ordered a force size reduction of 20,000 and under

President Johnson and the prime minister of Canada, Lester Pearson, share a laugh. Relations between the two were not always jovial.

the direction of the Minister of Defence implemented unification of the armed forces (the army, navy and air-force) in order to reduce administration expenses. Many senior officers resigned in protest and the debate in parliament and the press revealed deep divisions. Pearson, however, had sufficient support and the bill was passed on February 1, 1968. Pearson understood that Canada's social welfare programs would require an every larger portion of the federal budget and that cuts to the military would go a long way to pay for these costly programs.

Activity

Pearson and Diefenbaker

Adversaries in Parliament for over a decade, they faced each other daily in the House of Commons. When one was the prime minister the other was the leader of the opposition. It was a tempestuous relationship which was the subject of many editorial cartoons. In this activity you will have the opportunity to evaluate the significance of three such cartoons.

You write the caption

For each of the Cartoons, provide your own caption based on your understanding of Canadian politics during the 1960s and explain your caption with reference to the historical context.

Cartoon 1

Diefenbaker is on the left ("John" on his belt), Pearson on the right (with "Mike" on his shorts).

Cartoon 2

Pearson on the left, Diefenbaker on the right; both carry ladders. The damsel on the balcony represents the province of Quebec. The man standing behind her is the premier of Quebec.

Cartoon 3

Tommy Douglas (leader of the NDP), holds the scissors, Pearson is sewing and Diefenbaker holds the British Ensign, c. 1965.

Social welfare programs

Once Pearson cut military spending, that money was allocated for a number of programs that were meant to create equal access to services among all Canadians regardless of income. One of these programs was the Canada Student Loans Program of 1964. This provided loans to students registered in university or technical schools. The goverment developed risk-sharing agreements with the banks in which the federal government acted as the guarantor of the loans and would underwrite defaulted loans and associated costs. The program cost to the federal government was calculated to provide 60% of the assessed financial need to a maximum of $165 dollars a week for full-time students. The remaining 40% was the responsibility of provincial loan schemes.

Another program was an update of the Canada Pension Plan in 1965. Far more comprehensive than its predecessor, it improved the existing old-age pension plan and permitted the provinces to establish their own plans with federal support. Recognizing that the majority of workers did not have a company pension plan, pension benefits were expanded and extended. The program also prescribed survivor benefits.

The 1966 Medical Care Act provided universal healthcare for all Canadians. While all 10 provinces had healthcare programs by 1961, they were unequal. In addition to ensuring basic standards, it also allowed the federal government to provide proportionately more funding to the poorer provinces. Despite some protests by the medical community and the defection of some doctors to the United States, the program, although costly, has proved extremely popular. A further development was Canada's racially-open immigration policy. By the 1960s, European immigration had slowed and Canada most notably encouraged immigration from India and Hong Kong.

Canadian nationalism

The need for a distinctive Canadian flag had been simmering since the 1890s and, under Pearson, it became a reality. Young Canadians, an increasingly vocal force in the nation, wanted something uniquely Canadian that captured the nation's new vitality and autonomy as the Canadian Ensign emphasized colonial ties. A 15-member committee appointed by Pearson vetted over 20,000 submissions before deciding on the red maple leaf with 11 points. But veterans from the Second World War objected to the retirement of the Ensign, as it was a symbol of their participation in war and controversy ensued. In the end, the new flag was enthusiastically accepted by most Canadians as a unique representation of their country.

Similarly, Pearson's government persisted in the approval of "O Canada" as the national anthem and "God Save the Queen" as the royal anthem. Both had been the de facto anthems for decades but this ensured their place as national symbols. "O Canada" became a bilingual anthem with English and French versions.

Pearson led two minority governments with skill and brought about significant and lasting reforms that succeeded in his goal of equality for Canadians, yet the nation faced serious questions about the future of confederation. Upon his retirement from public service in 1968 Canada faced critical and violent challenges as separatists gained support in Quebec.

Activity
The new flag

The Canadian Red Ensign (1921)

The Maple Leaf Flag (February 15, 1965), designed by George F. Stanley.

Compare the two Canadian flags
1 What symbolism do you see in the ensign?
2 Why would young Canadians want to change the flag?
3 What makes the maple leaf uniquely Canadian?
4 There are eleven points on the leaf—why do think it was created that way?
5 There was a proposal for flags with the *fleur-de-lis*; who would be in support of such a flag and why?
6 Based on your knowledge of Canadian history and culture, what would you include on the Canadian flag? Why?

Pierre Elliot Trudeau, 1968–79, 1980–84

Pierre Trudeau was a charismatic leader, a product of the 1960s, who found tremendous support among Canada's young people; they responded to him in a visceral fashion that the press called "Trudeau-mania". Although his opponent, the Conservative leader Robert Stanfield, had more political experience he could not compete with the firebrand oratory, razor wit, wry grin and dynamic persona of Trudeau. Except for a six-month hiatus during Joe Clark's short-lived Conservative government (1979–80) Trudeau was prime minister for the next 16 years (1968–84). Always a controversial figure, he was either loved or hated by Canadians. Many of his policies were a continuation of initiatives begun by Pearson. Proposals based on reports from the previous governments were implemented. He continued unification of the armed forces and further decreased troop levels. He expanded social welfare programs and benefits, adding to existing programs. He made Canada bilingual and multicultural, championed a strong federal government and rejected Quebec's call for special status and separatism. He was despised in the western provinces for his national energy policy, reviled in Quebec for being a traitor and loved elsewhere for his opposition to the separatists and progressive social policies.

Pierre Elliot Trudeau (1919–2000)

Pierre Elliot Trudeau was born in Montreal to a Québécois father and a mother of Scottish descent. His father made a fortune during the Depression. Trudeau attended the prestigious Collège Jean-de-Brébeuf (a private French Jesuit school), where he was affiliated with the ideas of Quebec nationalism. The family toured Europe and Canada frequently. In 1940 Trudeau entered law school at the University of Montreal and joined the Canadian Officers training corps but opposed conscription and did not join the military during the Second World War. He completed an MA at Harvard University in 1946, undertook further studies at the Ecole des Sciences Politiques in Paris and the London School of Economics and later backpacked across Europe and Asia. Politically active from an early age, he supported unions, opposed the Union Nationale and the separatist movement, started a journal that supported new political ideas and criticized Pearson's government. He joined the law faculty at the University of Montreal in 1961 and was elected to the House of Commons in 1965, assuming the post of Minister of Justice in 1967 and became prime minister, replacing Pearson, in 1968. He was prime minister of Canada for 16 years (except for six months in 1979), retiring in 1984. He was married to Margaret Trudeau, had three sons, but divorced and became a single parent in 1977.

On taking office, Trudeau's first major domestic initiative was to achieve Pearson's objective of making Canada officially bilingual and bicultural by ensuring that all Canadians had access to bilingual services from the federal government. At the same time, the pressure of other interest groups was coming to the fore, in particular from representatives of the First Nations of Canada. At first Trudeau resisted these pressures and demands for special status, land claims and a strengthened Indian Act that recognized their historical rights as First Nations gained momentum. Using the courts to their advantage, they won many land claims settlements that derailed Trudeau's desire to stop various groups from attaining special status before the law. These Acts provided a precedent and subsequently blacks, women and homosexuals become increasingly vocal. The Canadian civil rights movement came of age and over the next two decades minority group rights found support in the constitution as Canada became a more inclusive and tolerant nation.

Nearly as controversial for some, was the Liberal government's decision to introduce metric conversion. In the 1970s, temperature was changed from Fahrenheit to Celsius (for several years both measurements were used); kilometers replaced miles; gallons became liters; and yards were converted to meters. Opposition was loud particularly from older Canadians who found the conversion difficult and veterans' groups claimed it was not what they had fought for, although the full change-over was implemented gradually. Nevertheless, by the mid-1980s metrication was a reality in Canada. It was part of Trudeau's vision to make Canada more internationally minded and it distinguished Canada from the United States, one of the few countries in the world to have retained the older system of unit measurement.

In his first term, Trudeau also tried to bring about a repatriation of the constitution and he held a meeting in 1971 in Victoria with the ten provincial premiers to ratify changes that would redistribute the powers of federal and provincial governments. At first he seemed to have consensus but Quebec's premier Bourassa demanded that the provinces be given control over social policy (welfare, unemployment, etc.) with federal funding for these programs. When Trudeau refused, Bourassa left the talks. Shortly thereafter, the meeting ended without agreement; constitutional reform had to wait until the 1980s.

The October Crisis

In 1970, Trudeau faced his most trying moments when confronted with the violent turn that Québécois separatism had taken. In addition to the founding of a parliamentary party in 1968—the Parti Québécois(PQ)—the separatists also created *La Front de libération du Québec* (the Quebec Liberation Front, or FLQ) in 1963. Although the FLQ lacked the support of most Québécois, who viewed them as a fringe movement of dissidents who did more harm than good to the separatist movement, they persisted in trying to bring about a separate state through violent tactics. Although it never numbered more than about 100 members, between 1963 and 1970 the group seats in the 1970 election and planted 95 bombs in government buildings and mailboxes, anything that could be tied to English Canada and the federal government. Canadians, including Québécois, deplored the violence that resulted in three deaths and numerous injuries. The police broke up several terrorist cells and about two dozen FLQ members went to jail.

In October 1970, the FLQ changed tactics, possibly in response to the failure of the Parti Québécois to win more seats in the election, or as a logical expansion of their own campaign. On October 5, they kidnapped British Trade Commissioner James Cross from his home in Quebec City and demanded $500,000 in bullion and the release of 23 jailed FLQ members as a ransom. The government refused to negotiate but did allow the FLQ's manifesto to be read over public radio and TV in both official languages. Upset by the government's refusal to negotiate, the FLQ kidnapped Pierre Laporte, Quebec Minister of Labour, on October 10, 1970. Trudeau responded by ordering the army to patrol the streets and government buildings in Ottawa and invoked the **War Measures Act** (1914), which suspended civil liberties and allowed the police to search and seize without a warrant and arrest suspects without a writ of *habeus corpus*

The War Measures Act (WMA) enacted in 1914 gives the prime minister and cabinet emergency powers during times of "war or insurrection, real or apprehended." It had been invoked during both world wars but resulted in the abuse of minority civil rights. During the First World War, about 8,000 citizens from nations sympathetic to Germany were put in internment camps, as were 22,000 Japanese Canadians in early 1942, following the Japanese attack on Pearl Harbor. Gripped by fear, paranoia and racism and under intense pressure from British Columbia, prime minister Mackenzie King ordered the Japanese to be rounded up. They lost their homes and possessions and spent the war in internment camps or worked as forced labour on farms, mainly in southern Alberta. Post-war about 4,000 Japanese citizens were deported to Japan before the government of Mackenzie King rescinded the internment order.

The October Crisis was the only time the WMA (replaced by the Emergency Act in 1971) was invoked during peacetime. Just under 500 citizens (mainly Québécois) with suspected FLQ connections were detained by the police, some were jailed for three months without being charged. Trudeau's action remains a source of historical controversy today.

(i.e without being charged with an offence or being brought to trial). The leader of the New Democratic Party (NDP), Tommy Douglas, said it was like cracking a peanut with a sledgehammer but overwhelmingly Canadians endorsed the prime minister's actions. The Quebec police were unable to locate the kidnappers despite thousands of tips from the public. Trudeau and Bourassa agreed that they would continue to refuse to negotiate with the FLQ.

Less than 48 hours later the police received an anonymous tip that led them to the lifeless body of Pierre Laporte stuffed in the trunk of a taxi. The FLQ made it clear that the survival of the other hostage was unlikely if the government continued to refuse to negotiate. Trudeau and Bourassa remained steadfast and public opinion polls showed 90% of Canadians supported the prime minister's position. For the next three months the kidnappers avoided detection but in early December their hideout was discovered and surrounded. The kidnappers agreed to release James Cross alive in return for a plane to Cuba. To this request the government agreed and five FLQ members were flown to Cuba. They eventually returned to Canada (as they were not made to feel welcome by Fidel Castro in Cuba) and served time in jail. The crisis was the high-water mark of the FLQ; completely discredited by most Québécois, it no longer had a following. The Parti Québécois was the force to be reckoned with in channelling support for separatism.

> **Discussion point**
>
> Was Trudeau's invocation of the War Measures Act justified under the circumstances or was it an over-reaction? Put yourself in Trudeau's shoes: what would you have done?

Activity

The October Crisis, 1970

Source A

"Canada: 'This Very Sorry Moment'." *Time* magazine. Monday, October 26, 1970.

> THROUGH the week Canada's Prime Minister, Pierre Elliott Trudeau, pondered the most difficult decision of his career. On the surface, the threat that confronted Canada, hardly seemed to merit the label "parallel power." Still, the terrorists of the minuscule Quebec Liberation Front (FLQ), with about 100 hard-core members, had openly defied the government by kidnapping two high-ranking officials and threatening to execute them. First, Trudeau called out thousands of armed troops to stand guard in major cities. Then, because he feared that the Quebec separatist movement would be significantly strengthened and federalism gravely weakened, he decided to move even more forcefully. At week's end, he declared all-out war on the terrorists.
>
> To combat those who "are seeking the destruction of the social order through clandestine and violent means," he invoked Canada's drastic 1914 War Measures Act. Only twice before, during the two world wars, had the act been put in force; it had never been applied in peacetime. Backing up Trudeau's dramatic action was a proclamation by his Cabinet that "insurrection, real or apprehended, exists."
>
> The FLQ evidently saw Trudeau's move as a challenge that could not be ignored. In responding to the challenge, the terrorists amply justified the Prime Minister's description of them as "a new and terrifying type of person." Less than two days after the War Measures Act was proclaimed, the terrorists murdered at least one of their hostages and offered little reason to hope for the survival of the other.

Source B

From the manifesto of the *Front de libération du Québec* (FLQ), 1970.

The *Front de libération du Québec* is not a messiah, nor a modern-day Robin Hood. It is a group of Quebec workers who have decided to use every means to make sure that the people of Quebec take control of their destiny. The Front de libération du Québec wants the total independence of all *Québécois*, united in a free society, purged forever of the clique of voracious sharks, the patronizing "big bosses" and their henchmen who have made Québec their hunting preserve for "cheap labour" and unscrupulous exploitation …

Workers of Quebec, start today to take back what is yours; take for yourselves what belongs to you. Only you know your factories, your machines, your hotels, your universities, your unions. Don't wait for an organizational miracle. Make your own revolution in your areas, in your places of work. And if you don't do it yourselves, other usurpers, technocrats and so on will replace the handful of cigar smokers we now know, and everything will be the same again. Only you are able to build a free society …

Long live Free Quebec!
Long live our imprisoned political comrades.
Long live the Quebec revolution!
Long live the *Front de libération du Québec*.

Source C

Extract of a Letter from Robert Bourassa, Premier of Quebec, to Prime Minister Trudeau, October 16, 1970.

During the last few days the people of Quebec have been greatly shocked by the kidnapping of Mr. James R. Cross, representative of the British Government in Montreal, and the Hon. Pierre Laporte, Minister of Labour and Manpower and Minister of Immigration of Quebec, as well as by the threats to the security of the state and individuals expressed in communiqués issued by the Front de Libération du Québec or on its behalf, and finally by all the circumstances surrounding these events.

After consultation with authorities directly responsible for the administration of justice in Quebec, the Quebec Government is convinced that the law, as it stands now, is inadequate to meet this situation satisfactorily.

Under the circumstances, on behalf of the Government of Quebec, I request that emergency powers be provided as soon as possible so that more effective steps may be taken. I request particularly that such powers encompass the authority to apprehend and keep in custody individuals who the Attorney General of Quebec has valid reasons to believe are determined to overthrow the government through violence and illegal means. According to the information we have and which is available to you, we are facing a concerted effort to intimidate and overthrow the government and the democratic institutions of this province through planned and systematic illegal action, including insurrection. It is obvious that those participating in this concerted effort completely reject the principle of freedom under the rule of law … .

Source D

Government of Canada, War Measures Act, proclaimed October 16, 1970.

EVIDENCE OF WAR

1 The issue of a proclamation by Her Majesty, or under the authority of the Governor in Council shall be conclusive evidence that war, invasion, or insurrection, real or apprehended exists and has existed for any period of time therein stated, and of its continuance, until by the issue of a further proclamation it is declared that the war, invasion or insurrection no longer exists. ...

POWERS OF THE GOVERNOR IN COUNCIL

2 (1) The Governor in Council may do and authorize such acts and things, and make from time to time such orders and regulations, as he may by reason of the existence of real or apprehended war, invasion or insurrection deem necessary or advisable for the security, defense, peace. order and welfare of Canada; and for greater certainty, but not so as to restrict the generality of the foregoing terms it is hereby declared that the powers of the Governor in Council shall extend to all matters coming within the classes of subjects hereinafter enumerated, that is to say:
   (a) censorship, and the control and suppression of publications, writings, maps, plans, photographs, communications and means of communication;
   (b) arrest, detention exclusion and deportation;
   (c) control of the harbours, ports and territorial waters of Canada and the movements of vessels; ...
   (d) appropriation, control, forfeiture and disposition of property and of the use thereof.
   (2) All orders and regulations made under this section shall have the force of law, and shall be enforced in such manner and by such courts, officers and authorities as the Governor in Council may prescribe, and may be varied, extended or revoked by any subsequent order or regulation; ...

Source E

Claude Ryan's editorial in Montreal's *Le Devoir* newspaper, October 17, 1970.

... As for Mr. Trudeau, he may very well succeed, for the time being, in crushing the FLQ. However, he will not succeed in preventing certain ideas from existing and perhaps, with Ottawa's help, from spreading. In the present drama, we must not forget that the "final question" has only temporarily been set aside and that ultimately it will only be solved in Quebec, without outside interference. The man who used to preach mistrust toward established authority has now become a protector of the military. One would search in vain, among the edicts that bear his signature, traces of these virtues of rationality, free will, restraint and respect based on rationality that he once identified with federalism. Mr. Trudeau claims that he was driven to this choice: many will reply that he deserved it.

Those who committed repugnant acts on October 5 and 10, and their allies, are for the time being mainly responsible for the losses of liberty suffered by Quebec. The aggressive and open disdain that they expressed against laws made for all citizens, and many of which were enacted in the respect of basic human rights, and not by a superstructure of domination, justifies the legal banishment that has been pronounced against the FLQ.

We deplore that recourse to do so was made to the War Measures Act; in its possible applications, it far exceeds the scope of the problem that the authorities faced. Further, we deplore that the War Measures Act has already started to be applied in such a spirit, and with such methods, that makes us fear that worse is to come. However, we can only reaffirm the right of a democracy to defend itself and the obligation that it has to judge severely and to put down those that unjustly threaten the freedom and the life of their fellow citizens.

Source F

Prime Minister Trudeau's address to the nation, October 16, 1970.

I am speaking to you at a moment of grave crisis, when violent and fanatical men are attempting to destroy the unity and the freedom of Canada. One aspect of that crisis is the threat which has been made on the lives of two innocent men. These are matters of the utmost gravity and I want to tell you what the government is doing to deal with them. What has taken place in Montreal in the past two weeks is not unprecedented. It has happened elsewhere in the world on several recent occasions: it could happen elsewhere within Canada. But Canadians have always assumed that it could not happen here and as a result we are doubly shocked that it has. Our assumption may have been naive, but it was understandable: understandable because democracy flourishes in Canada; understandable because individual liberty is cherished in Canada. Notwithstanding these conditions, partly because of them it has been demonstrated now to us by a few misguided persons just how fragile a democratic society can be if democracy is not prepared to defend itself, and just how vulnerable to blackmail are tolerant, compassionate people… To bow to the pressures of these kidnappers who demand that the prisoners be released would be not only an abdication of responsibility; it would lead to an increase in terrorist activities in Quebec. It would be as well an invitation to terrorism and kidnapping across the country. We might well find ourselves facing an endless series of demands for the release of criminals from jails, from coast to coast … At the moment the FLQ is holding hostage two men in the Montreal area, one a British diplomat, the other a Quebec cabinet minister. They are threatened with murder.

Should governments give in to this crude blackmail, we would be facing the breakdown of the legal system and its replacement by the law of the jungle. The government's decision to prevent this from happening is not taken just to defend an important principle. It is taken to protect the lives of Canadians from dangers of the sort I have mentioned. Freedom and personal security are safeguarded by laws; those laws must be respected in order to be effective …

Source: "Documents of the October Crisis." *Quebec History*. http://faculty.marianopolis.edu/c.belanger/ QuebecHistory/docs/october/index.htm.

Questions

1 **a** According to source A, why did the Trudeau government take decisive and unprecedented action in October 1970?

 b What is the message of source B?

2 Compare and contrast the attitude and approaches to the crisis suggested in sources E and F.

3 With reference to these sources, assess their origin, purpose, value and limitations for a historian trying to understand and explain the October Crisis of 1970.

4 Using the documents and your own knowledge, to what extent do you agree with the Canadian government's actions to deal with the events of October 1970 in the province of Quebec?

Trudeau's second term

In 1972, Trudeau called an election and the Liberals narrowly defeated the Conservatives, winning 109 seats against their 107. To remain in power, Trudeau had to form a coalition with the NDP. The election results conveyed the message that the government had neglected English Canada and, if they wanted to stay in power, a more balanced and even-handed approach to government was needed. It was clear to most politicians that if changes were not made, the next election would most likely result in a Conservative government. For its part, the NDP agreed to support Trudeau's new legislative program, which included increased spending on social programs and a progressive personal income tax. The new tax plan also included cost-of-living exemptions to protect low-income taxpayers from rising inflation.

The election was a turning point for Trudeau. It ensured his control of the Liberal Party which gave him unfettered control of government policy. Another turn for the better for Trudeau was that Quebec was demanding less of the limelight; his actions in the October Crisis seemed to have brought about the decline and demise of the FLQ. The price of oil was also a significant problem. In the early 1970s, the supply of oil decreased and consequently the price rapidly increased. The government ordered the prices at the gas pumps to be kept below world prices—a policy that made the Liberals unpopular in the oil-producing western provinces but won them the support of Ontario, Quebec and the Atlantic provinces. Using this popularity to his advantage in 1974, Trudeau gave parliament a budget he knew they would reject. Defeated on a vote of no-confidence the Liberals resigned and an election was called. Trudeau again won a majority with the Liberals being elected in 141 of 265 seats.

However, the economy was worsening. Inflation and rising unemployment undermined efforts to effectively plan and manage the economy, improve existing programs or implement new ones. Canada was suffering from "stagflation", a situation where the economy was stagnant and yet inflation kept rising in defiance of the laws of supply and demand. To try and treat the problem, Trudeau announced wage and price controls in October 1975 but made it clear that this was a temporary palliative to reduce some of the current economic pains.

By 1976, the Conservatives held a substantial lead over the Liberals in the polls, and in November of that year the Parti Québécois won the Quebec election. The PQ's election served notice to Canada that separatism was a credible alternative for Quebec. At the same time, Trudeau's reputation for being arrogant and dismissive to the opinions and issues of English Canadians could not be tempered. The popularity of the early days of his leadership had evaporated and when the Liberals' five-year term was up in 1979 Canadians went to the polls looking for a change. Conservative leader Joe Clark did not appear at first glance to be much of a candidate but Trudeau was defeated for the first time in five elections. His time as leader of the opposition was to be short.

> ### Discussion point
>
> Canadian prime ministers are not restricted by the constitution to two terms like US presidents. What are the advantages and disadvantages of these respective systems?

Joe Clark, 1979–1980

On June 4, 1979, Joe Clark was sworn in as prime minister the day before his 40th birthday. Canada's youngest prime minister would have a short-lived government due to continuing economic problems and the challenges of running a minority government. During the campaign, Clark made promises that he could not keep: for example, privatization of government-run oil companies; reduction of personal income tax and of the budget deficit. When none of this happened Clark appeared ineffective and weak-willed. Although he was a bilingual Anglophone, Quebec's support for him was short-lived as they historically supported the Liberals. As with Diefenbaker's cabinet, Conservative Party ministers did not trust the senior federal bureaucrats who were mainly liberals; 16 years out of power made them suspicious of the civil service.

On December 11, 1979, Conservative Finance Minister John Crosby delivered the government's first budget and although he warned that it contained tough measures, the public was aghast at what was presented. The government's intention to raise the price of gasoline by 18 cents per gallon, effective immediately, met with consternation. Even though this measure still left the Canadian price at 85% of the world price for crude oil, the public would not stand for it. On December 13, the Conservative budget was defeated by a vote of 139 to 133 constituting a vote of no-confidence. The nation went to the polls again, and February 1980 the Liberals won another majority taking 146 of 281 seats. Canada's love/hate affair with Pierre Trudeau was not over yet.

Trudeau's final term in office ended in 1984 and in some ways this was his most effective term. Trudeau shifted his gaze again to the constitution, signed by the Queen in 1982. He met the separatist threat head-on by not supporting sovereignty associations with Canada in a referendum. Trudeau characterised Levesque's vision of an independent Quebec that retained economic ties as "Divorce with bed privileges." The PQ remained in power but would not threaten separation again until the mid 1990s.

Activity

Domestic policy in Canada and the United States, 1945–79

Canada and the United States shared similar experiences during the post-war period. Both nations emerged from the Second World War with burgeoning economies and on the verge of an economic expansion that would last two decades. Worried about a "new" depression the respective governments responded with programs to continue economic growth. Government intervention in the economy to create full employment and attack poverty and a social welfare system designed to take the hard edge off capitalism existed in both countries by the end of the 1960s. Both governments faced regional alienation that challenged national unity and other unique challenges. In this activity you will compare and contrast the ways the leaders of their respective countries addressed important domestic issues and the relative merit and success of their solutions.

1 **Social welfare programs** Johnson's Great Society had no Canadian equivalent, yet by the mid 1960s both nations had established cradle-to-grave social welfare programs that endure to this day. Compare President Johnson and Prime Minister Pearson's programs and evaluate their merits and successes. Are there aspects of Johnson's program that you consider better than Pearson's and vice versa?

2 **Protecting minorities** How did the leaders on both sides of the borders address the needs of minority groups: Select two Canadian and two US leaders, and fill out the following chart in point form.

What conclusions can you reach based on the evidence gathered?

Leaders	Civil rights	Women's rights	First Nations
Canada			
United States			
Canada			
United States			

3 Compare the following:

a Trudeau's treatment of Quebec and Kennedy's treatment of the southern states of the USA.

b Diefenbaker's Bill of Rights and Johnson's civil rights legislation?

c Responsible government in Canada and the United States.

4 Speculate on the importance of the St. Lawrence Seaway project and the Auto Pact in developing closer economic ties between Canada and the United States that led to the North American Free Trade Agreement of the mid 1980s.

5 Select the US president and Canadian prime minister that, in your opinion, had the most effective and successful domestic policies? To what extent was their approach similar?

The Quiet Revolution

In the 1960s, Quebec entered a dynamic period of social, economic and political change and transformation, known as *"La Révolution tranquille"* (the Quiet Revolution). Québécois nationalist views were promoted by Union Nationale (Union National Party) under Premier Maurice Duplessis (arguably Canada's most corrupt politician) in the 1940s and 1950s. During the 1960s, young Québécois, irritated by the slow pace of change, demanded fundamental change and reform. These Québécois rejected the conservative Catholic, rural values that had long defined Quebec and instead they sought modernization and secularization that resulted in interventionist government policies that emphasized social policies and an increased bureaucracy to administer new programs. These did not come without a cost, however, Quebec went from being the least taxed province with the least debt to the most taxed and the most indebted in six short years. The Quiet Revolution is said to coincide with the leadership of Premier Jean Lesage, from 1960 to 1966, but the changes continued well into the 1970s, and their effects are still felt.

During the 1950s, a new urban, well-educated, secular and reform-minded middle class had emerged and was gaining influence over traditional, rural, Catholic Quebec. Between 1941 and 1971, the urban population swelled from 55 % to 78% of Quebec's population. At the same time, the number of farms decreased by over 50% and the rural farm population fell from 19.5% to 5.6%. The service sector experienced the greatest economic growth during the period and rose from 37.2% to 59.7%, reflecting the youth movement from farm to city. This new urban class wanted Quebec's institutions modernized and secularized and were tired of Duplessis's brand of nationalism, his corruption, influence-peddling and patronage-ridden style of politics.

Discussion point

Terminology

In Quebec the leader of the provincial government is called the **prime minister**. In the other nine provinces the provincial leader is called the **premier**. The **Legislative Assembly** or **Provincial legislatures** are the names commonly used to describe the legislative bodies of the Canadian provinces, with the exception of Quebec, which has a **National Assembly**.

 Why does Quebec believe it is necessary to use different terms to describe the government leader and the legislative body?

They wanted a new Quebec that took economic control of the province from the wealthy English-speaking minority whose mansions in Montreal's fashionable Westmount district remained a symbol of conquest and subjugation. Influenced by the civil rights movement in the United States and decolonization movements elsewhere, they believed it was time for Quebec to do the same and assert its sovereignty. Finally, they wanted to protect Quebec's distinctive language and culture and expand the province's power and influence in Canada and abroad. "*Maître chez nous*" (Masters in our own house) became the slogan. The stage was set for the Quiet Revolution which according to Canadian Historian J. M. Bumstead transpired faster and with less resistance than anyone imagined or anticipated.

> The Quiet Revolution was less a political movement orchestrated by politicians than an affirmation of an awakening by an entire society and the sudden integration of that society into the middle-class secular world of the twentieth century.

In 1960 the Liberals, led by Jean Lesage, won the provincial elections in Quebec but the results were not so much of an endorsement of the Liberals, as a turn away from the Union Nationale. Nonetheless, Lesage was determined to take advantage of the grass-roots demand for modernization of Quebec's government and institutions. The Liberal campaign had promised two things: an end to government corruption and the adoption of progressive policies. The Liberals had not outlined specific policies, but moved quickly and decisively in two areas that symbolized the Quiet Revolution—electric power and education.

In 1962, the Minister of Natural Resources, René Levesque (eventually leader of the separatist Parti Québécois) decided to nationalize hydro-electricity under a government-run corporation, Hydro-Québec. Levesque acted alone—without the prior knowledge or approval of cabinet. It was a bold move, Lesage and the takeover passed without much opposition in the National Assembly. The majority of power companies in Quebec were privately owned, mainly by English-speaking Canadians and the takeover symbolized that henceforth Quebec would be run by Québécois. It was very popular and costly at Can $600 million. To implement the takeover, the Liberals tripled the provincial budget and demonstrated that they would use this money to pursue their true intentions—to be interventionist, nationalist and statist (this is pro-government solutions to economic and social problems). The Liberals would also assume control of other utility services (water and heating) and would try to promote greater industrialization.

The second area and symbolically more important focus was education, representing a break from Quebec's traditional rural and parochial past. Education had been run by the Roman Catholic Church since the founding of New France. Nuns and priests were the teachers, and teacher training and curriculum development (most notably in math and science) lagged behind the other Canadian provinces. The issue was more than just teaching methods and curriculum but the survival of Quebec in English-dominated Canada. The French press claimed that church-run schools had failed to protect the distinctive and unique language and culture of Quebec from assimilation into North-American (English-speaking) culture.

These issues were brought to the fore in the best-selling novel by Brother Jean-Paul Desbiens, *Les insolences du Frère Untel* (The Impertinences of Brother So and So), published in 1960. The central character was the fictional Frère Untel, a nationalist demanding that education in Quebec should first and foremost protect, defend and ensure the survival of French Canadian language and culture in its purest form. These fears were not without validity. Since the early 1950s, the birthrate in Quebec had fallen by half and consequently the French Canadian portion of the total Canadian population was in sharp decline. Frère Untel had a name for the erosion of language that was taking place: he called it *joual*, a hybrid dialect spoken by Québécois youth that was a style of French liberally laced with English words and phrases. The Frère blamed this on church-run schools that had failed in their duty to teach and protect the French language and culture. The church struck back by condemning Desbiens's novel and recalling him to Rome.

Lesage responded by setting up a provincial education commission called the Parent Commission named after its respected chair, Catholic cleric Monseigneur Alphonse-Marie Parent. Parent's 1963 report formed the blueprint for massive changes to education. In 1964, Bill 60 was passed that gave the provincial government control over education. In rapid order, education standards and teaching qualifications were brought up to national standards. The power of the Catholic Church to exert its influence on the people of Quebec had suffered a setback from which it could never recover.

The Liberals also moved to advance culture through a newly created Ministry of Cultural Affairs. The goal: to encourage, develop and showcase Québécois artists, writers and musicians. It led to a cultural renaissance that reacquainted the province with its proud and distinct cultural history and heritage and reenergized a distinctive arts community dedicated to promoting French Canadian language and culture. Despite instituting a series of popular changes, Lesage was defeated in 1966 by a reinvigorated Union Nationale led by the popular leader Daniel Johnson (who died suddenly in 1968). Johnson had no intention of overturning Liberal reforms, and continued their policies in many instances.

He appointed a commission to investigate French language rights and purity that set the stage for language legislation in the 1970s that made Quebec a unilingual French speaking province, with the passing of the controversial Official Language Act (*Loi sur la langue officielle*) in 1974 that made French the official and dominant language of the province. In 1977, the separatist Parti Québécois government enacted the Charter of French Language (*La charte de la langue francaise*), known as Bill 101. It declared that French was the fundamental and only language of Quebec. It made French the normal and daily language of the workplace. Schools were required to teach in French only and it was made compulsory for immigrants to learn French. All public signs and advertisements were to be in French. The Quebec government replaced Bill 101 in 1988 with Bill 178 that reflected the court decisions particularly regarding unilingual commercial sign, advertising and company names.

Johnson also made advances in women's rights establishing a Royal Commission on the Status of Women. During the Quiet Revolution, the women of Quebec, like women throughout North America and the developed world, rejected the traditional roles of childbearing and childrearing and joined the workforce in ever-growing numbers. This struck at the very heart of Quebec society with its emphasis on traditional family values and was further evidence of the declining influence of the Catholic Church. Large families had been the norm in Quebec, 10 or more children was not unusual. Procreation had a religious and political imperative. The Catholic Church forbade the use of modern contraception, ensuring a birth rate at least twice that of the rest of Canada. But by the 1950s, the use of modern birth control methods had brought about a rapid decline in the province's birth rates and the fear of assimilation prompted the search for new ways of protecting Quebec's unique status in Canada.

The centerpiece to Quebec's new self-image was the 1967 Montreal World Expo that coincided with Canada's centenary celebrations. Over 50 million visitors and foreign dignitaries came to the "Man and His World" exhibition and were impressed by what they saw. In just five years the city of Montreal was had been transformed into a modern city through major public works projects that included an underground metro system, a new international airport, major freeways and sports facilities. An artificial island, Notre Dame, was built in the St. Lawrence River as part of the new metro construction and was the location of many pavilions and exhibitions.

The changes drew notice from the recently restored French president Charles De Gaulle who began treating Quebec as if it were a sovereign nation after his first visit in 1960. He claimed that the spirit of change and revolution in Quebec was an example to France in addressing its own problems. His actions drew the immediate attention of the federal government. During his visit to Expo 67, de Gaulle infamously ended a speech with "Vive le Québec, Vive le Quebec Libres!" (Long live a free Quebec!), causing an uproar among the political leadership in Ottowa. This invocation drew attention to Quebec's growing desire and endless demands to be given special status—a determination that would not abate and would dominate the national scene for the next three decades.

In any revolution there are casualties. In Quebec, it was the English minority. Many could trace their ancestry in Quebec back over two centuries, arriving just after the conquest during the glory days of the Montreal fur trade when the city was Canada's economic centre. The province was their home but they were no longer welcome. As a consequence, thousands moved to English-speaking provinces and took with them their business, expertise and wealth, leaving behind a void that would take time to fill. But their exodus did not stop the revolution. Some of the more radical proponents considered it to be an essential part of the purification process.

By the end of the decade, Quebec had broken out of its traditional stranglehold and modernization had created a new sense of destiny. It was a revolution that dramatically changed Quebec's perception of itself, its identity and its place in confederation. No longer rural, Catholic and parochial, the new Quebec was modern, well-educated, dynamic and autonomous. Relations with the rest of Canada would become increasingly strained during the decade and into the next as the province demanded and received special status and treatment. Yet, for an ever-growing number of young Québécois, this was not enough and a new force would emerge that seemed the logical outcome of this desire for autonomy and cultural purity in separatism.

 Why was it called "The Quiet Revolution"? What else would you call it?

Discussion point

Revolutions

The Oxford English Dictionary defines a social revolution as "a great change in conditions, ways of working beliefs, etc. that affects large numbers of peoples."

 Based on this definition do you agree that what took place in Quebec during the 1960s should be called a "revolution"?

Activity

Cooperative federalism

In the following political cartoon, Prime Minister Pearson is dressed as the referee, Premier Lesage of Quebec is in hockey gear and "The Other Nine" premiers are dressed as baseball players.

What message is the cartoonist trying to convey about the nature of federal–provincial relations in the 1960s in Canada during the time of the Quiet Revolution and, in particular, relations between the federal government and Quebec? What is Quebec's perception of its special status? Who does the waterboy represent and what message is being conveyed? What is meant by the title "Cooperative federalism"?

"Cooperative federalism" by John Collins, first published in the *Montreal Gazette*, c. 1964.

The Cuban Revolution

On January 1, 1959, Cuban dictator Fulgencio Batista boarded a plane and fled Cuba forever. A week later, Fidel Castro led the victorious 26th July revolutionary movement into Havana and took control. For the first time in Cuba in 100 years of revolutionary struggle, Cuba was truly independent. The Cuba Castro inherited was a land with a significant urban and rural divide, promoting the further division between mulatto and Afro-Cubans and the white urban-based élite, driven by the tyranny of a one-crop economy, the sugar cane industry that was Cuba's economic lifeblood. The revolution's success was the result of a historic process that had united Cubans to fight for their independence from foreign control for nearly a century. The overthrow of Spanish rule in the 1898 Spanish–American War, precipitating half a century of US domination and control of its own vested interests in the region, propping up successive administrations that culminated in the notoriously brutal and corrupt final term of Batista. Although Batista started out being progressive and popular, he returned to government following the 1953 coup that was marked by corruption and brutal, military-style dictatorship. Growing unrest, sparked home-grown insurgencies on several fronts, the most successful of which was the 26th of July Movement, led by Fidel Castro, who stepped in to fill the breach on Batista's hasty and final exit.

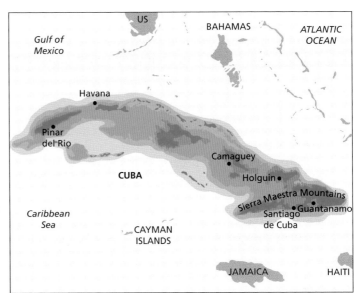

In 1959, Cuba's income from sugar still accounted for four-fifths of export earnings, but a vast income also came from tourism based on Havana's hotels, casinos, and brothels, especially during the years of **Prohibition** in the United States. By the end of the 1950s, Cuba had developed one of the leading economies in Latin America, with an annual income of $353 per capita in 1958—among the highest in the region. Yet there were great economic disparities, and most rural workers earned only about one-fourth the average annual income. The majority of Cubans were illiterate and in poverty (especially in the countryside), suffering from an appalling lack of public services, unemployment and underemployment. Foreign investors controlled the economy, owning about 75% of farming land, 90% of the essential services, and 40% of the sugar production.

> **Prohibition** in the United States was the period from 1919 to 1933, during which the sale, manufacture, and transportation of alcohol were banned nationally. Prohibition laws were also enacted in Canada under several provincial governments in the early part of the 20th century.

The Cuban sugar cane industry

Sugar cane is not indigenous to Cuba and was first planted in the 16th century. It was not until the early 19th that world demand created the conditions for the dynamic expansion of the sugar cane industry, and in a few decades Cuba was annually producing half of the world's sugar supply.

Cheap labor was supplied by the 800,000 African slaves (mainly from the Senegal and Guinea Coast) imported during the late 18th and 19th centuries by Spain to work on plantations. When slavery was abolished in 1888, their descendants continued to be a mainstay of the industry.

Yet, as the industry grew, more labor was required. In the first decades of the 20th century, tens of thousands of black Antillean laborers, nine-tenths of whom were Haitian or Jamaican, arrived as contract laborers, many of them forced to return home when production dropped in the 1930s.

The *zafra* (harvest) came during *la seca* (the dry months) from November to April. Thousands of cane cutters armed with sharp machetes, descended on the *colonias* (cane fields) to cut each stalk individually. It was back-breaking toil. The stalks grow 2–6 meters high and are cut a few centimeters above the ground. The roots of the cane stalk will re-grow several times but require replanting about every five years. The first step in the harvest is to burn the cane. The fields are set on fire burning off all the green leaves and chasing out rodents and snakes. Next, the cane is cut and hauled to a sugar mill.

The work was hard and intense and the *zafra* lasts only four months followed by the *tiempo muerto* (dead months) when there was no work. Hacienda owners built villages for their workforce and encouraged the workers to stay on. These had two purposes: by keeping the workers and families close to the fields, it ensured an available labor force; and it kept large numbers of mulattos and Afro-Cubans out of the major cities. Nevertheless, many workers migrated to the cities looking for work. Sometimes they found manual jobs building roads, digging ditches or laying railroad track, but for most these were idle months living on credit

at the company store, until the next harvest. It was an endless cycle of grueling toil, monotonous unemployment and habitual debt. With the advent of steam engines in the late 19th-century to drive the mills (*ingenios*) and railways, the processing and transportation of sugar was done in ever-larger operations.

One-crop economies are particularly sensitive to world market prices. During the First World War, the price of sugar skyrocketed. Between 1916 and 1919, US companies secured ownership and control of production in half of the sugar mills in Cuba and controlled production of half the sugar crop. In addition, improvements in transportation—mainly railroad construction—and steam-driven sugar presses increased production, leading to larger-scale plantations and output. Wealth was becoming even more concentrated among the Cuban élites and US interests.

Sugar cane train outside a sugar refinery, c. 1900, Cuba.

In comparison to other Caribbean and Latin American countries, Cuba ranked near the top in most economic and social indicators like healthcare and education. The picture was, however, deceivingly cosmetic, a mask that hid the seething frustration and anger of the Cuban people with the social, political and economic structures of the country that had remained virtually unchanged for a century. Frustration had reached the boiling point with the never ending stream of broken promises from corrupt politicians who catered to gangsters and foreign investors. The Cuban government had lost its moral authority with the Cuban people. The Cuban Revolution under Fidel Castro succeeded because he became that authority. His successful revolution made world headlines in 1959 and created the Cuban nation, giving meaning to its struggles for independence and equality, and transforming a troubled but essentially peripheral Caribbean island, once a US protectorate and ally into an independent player on the world stage. He became the most charismatic leader of the Third World, during its heyday, and survived the collapse of the Soviet Union itself as the longest-serving head of a Communist state. Whether for him or against him, successive Latin American generations were profoundly influenced by the figure of Castro and his ability to combine socialism with nationalism, a model based less on Marxism than on the home-grown example of José Martí's *Cuba Libre* (Free Cuba) movement in the late 19th-century.

Revolutionary beginnings

The illegitimate son of a wealthy plantation owner, Castro received the education and status to help him achieve his goals as well as experiencing firsthand the social contradiction of southeastern Cuba, in which a large proportion of the population were Afro-Cuban rural workers. Politicized at university in Havana, where he studied law, Castro's first introduction to activist politics came when, in 1948, he travelled to Bogotá, Colombia, with plans to disrupt the Pan-American Union Conference, when countrywide riots broke out in response to the assassination of the popular leader Jorge Eliecer Gaitán. On returning to Cuba, Castro intended to run for a seat in the Cuban parliament in 1952 but the US-backed coup, that installed Batista for his second presidential term, canceled the election. Sometime during this period Castro the reformer became Castro the revolutionary. For a man with no military background or training and from a wealthy family, the decision was a radical one.

Fidel Castro (1926–)

Castro Fidel Alejandro Castro Ruz was born into the Cuban plantation élite in 1927. He was the third of six children by his father, a *peninsular* and wealthy sugar plantation owner who could not marry Fidel's mother until Castro was 17 at which time he took his father's surname. The region where he grew up in the Oriente province of southeastern Cuba was dominated by the estates of the US-owned United Fruit Company, and Castro's companions were the children of rural workers. In 1945 he went to the University of Havana, entered the law school and entered politics. He became a student activist, joined the Partido Orthodoxo (Orthodox Party) and became a passionate advocate of Cuban nationalism, independence and anti-imperialism. A socialist, he initially denied his more overtly communist sympathies, so as not to offend Ortodoxo Party leader Eduardo Chibas, for whom he had a high regard. In 1948, Castro traveled to Bogotá, Colombia, where he gained firsthand experience of popular uprisings. On returning to Cuba, Fidel married Mirta Diaz Balart. He intended to run for a seat in the Cuban parliament in 1952 but a US-backed coup installed Fulgencia Batista.

On July 26, 1953, at the age of 26, Castro lead a group of 165 students in an audacious attack on the Moncada military barracks near Santiago, intended to spark insurrection against Batista. Poorly armed, with little military training, the attack failed. Castro and his brother Raúl were captured and jailed. The trial and the publication of his speech *History Will Absolve Me* made Castro famous. Castro was released from prison after he had served only two years of his sentence. Batista also promised elections but when it became clear that they would not take place, Castro left for Mexico where he began to plan another attempt to overthrow the Cuban government. After building up a stock of guns and ammunition, Castro, Che Guevara and 81 other rebels arrived in Cuba on December 2, 1956. Met by heavy Batista defenses, nearly everyone in the movement was killed, with merely a handful escaping, including Castro, his brother Raúl, and Guevara. For the next two years, Castro succeeded in gaining large numbers of volunteers. Using guerrilla warfare tactics, Castro and his supporters attacked Batista's forces, overtaking town after town. Batista quickly lost popular support and suffered numerous defeats. On January 1, 1959, Batista fled Cuba. Manuel Urrutia became president of the new government and Castro was placed in charge of the military.

By July 1959, Castro had effectively taken over as leader of Cuba, a role that he would assume for nearly five decades of single-party rule. His regime initiated social and economic reforms, maintaining rigorous opposition to US interests, that saw Cuba established with economic and political ties to the Communist Bloc until the dissolution of the Soviet Union. Castro achieved high standards in literacy, education, healthcare and welfare reform in Cuba, benefiting in particular the large Afro-Cuban population. His legacy is marred by political isolation, unsuccessful economic policies and repression of dissent. Castro retired from government due to ill health in 2006, handing over the leadership to his brother Raúl.

On July 26, 1953, at the age of 26, Castro lead a group of 165 students in an audacious attack on the Moncada military barracks near Santiago. They faced 1000 well-armed soldiers. He hoped the action would precipitate a spontaneous uprising against Batista. He was wrong. Poorly armed, with little military training, the attack failed. The army, initially surprised, recovered quickly, opened fire and many young attackers were killed. Castro and his brother Raúl were captured and jailed to await trial. The trial became a public spectacle. Later, in jail, serving out his sentence, Castro made a record of his courtroom speech, "History will absolve me," later to become the manifesto for the *Movimiento 26 de julio* (the 26th of July Movement) as it became known. After 10, 000 copies of the speech had been distributed, Castro became a national hero. In May 1955, he and his brother Raúl together with 18 followers were released from the Isle of Pines prison under the new General Amnesty law that Batista hoped would restore public favor.

Castro left Cuba in 1955, and went to Mexico to recruit, train and equip an invasion force. Like Martí, he planned to return to Cuba to fight again. His most important recruit was Ernesto "Che" Guevara, who along with Raúl became Castro's most trusted co-revolutionary. Guevara was a young Argentinean doctor, who like Castro was raised in middle-class affluence and was moved to reject his upbringing. Che was convinced that revolution (preferably communist) was the only hope of a better life for the oppressed peoples of Latin America. He became the heroic face of the revolution with his ragged beard and searing dark eyes, framed by his famous red-star beret. He also became its greatest martyr. (He was killed in 1967, fighting in Bolivia).

For the return to Cuba, Castro took exceptional risks, leaving the Mexican port of Tuxpán, Veracruz, on a boat called the *Granma* that was safe to hold

Fidel Castro and Ernesto "Che" Guevara in 1956.

Ernesto "Che" Guevara (1928–1967)

"Che" Guevara was born in Rosario, Argentina, the son of progressive, middle-class parents of Spanish, Basque and Irish descent. An asthmatic all his life, Guevara studied medicine and undertook a trip through the Andes in the early 1950s, while still a student, through which he gained a direct knowledge of peasant conditions and political movements. He was in Guatemala in 1954, in the final months of the reformist government of Jacobo Arbenz, and was witness to the invasion in June by a small group of Guatemalan officers, organized and funded by the US Central Intelligence Agency, which confirmed in him a life-long distrust of the United States. Later in 1954, while living in Mexico City, he met Raúl and Fidel Castro, and joined their 26th of July Movement. Between him and Fidel, he noted on first meeting, there was a "mutual sympathy." Right from the start, they were an effective partnership. Guevara provided Castro with broader horizons, a strong understanding of revolutionary experiments and political theory, as well as considerable first-hand knowledge of Latin America. Castro gave Guevara an immediate political cause. Guevara travelled to Cuba aboard the yacht Granma with the rebel army and became second-in-command to Fidel Castro, playing a major role in the successful two year guerrilla campaign that deposed the Batista regime.

Following the Cuban Revolution, Guevara performed a number of key roles in the new government. These included a focus on agrarian reform as minister of industries, serving as the national bank president, overseeing the revolutionary tribunals and later travelling the globe as a diplomat. He oversaw the training of the militia forces who repelled the Bay of Pigs Invasion and organized the deal to bring the Soviet nuclear-armed ballistic missiles to Cuba in 1962 that sparked the Cuban Missile Crisis. He was an enthusiastic writer and diarist, and published a manual on guerrilla warfare, along with a best-selling memoir about his youthful motorcycle journey across South America. Guevara left Cuba in 1965 to spread revolution abroad, first in Congo-Kinshasa, in Africa, and later in Bolivia, where he was executed by CIA-assisted Bolivian forces.

only 25 people, but carrying over 80 with armaments. On December 2, 1956, it landed in Playa Las Coloradas, not far from Santiago, where the arrival of the rebel army was intended to coincide with planned riots by mainland members of the movement. But after an event-filled voyage in which the boat almost sank, they landed in daylight, and almost immediately were attacked by the Cuban air force, killing most of the rebels. The landing party was split into two and wandered lost for two days, most of their supplies abandoned where they landed. Of the original band, only 12 eventually regrouped in the Sierra Maestra Mountains. Castro and Guevara became international heroes when Herbert Matthews, a reporter from the *New York Times* was brought to the rebel hideout. In a series of articles and photos Matthews described a noble rebel band of freedom fighters, enduring hardships to fight oppression. In the United States, public sympathy for the rebels grew and support for Batista dwindled. Batista had his hands full dealing with the revolutionary unrest in the cities, orchestrated by other members of the movement, most notably Frank País, as well as rival groups. Oriente province was disrupted by strikes and acts of terrorism. Castro's forces were growing and launched a series of raids on the Cuban army, causing heavy causalities. In 1958, the rebels launched a three pronged assault that effectively cut the island in half. The United States government turned its back on Batista's pleas for help, and on January 1, 1959, Batista fled.

The rule of Fidel Castro, 1959–70

On January 1, 1959, Castro triumphantly entered Havana leading the men and women of the 26th of July Movement to the cheers of adoring Cubans. Batista was gone and so was the vision of Cuba as a playground for rich North Americans and their business interests. The revolution had triumphed. Beside him stood the two men that he trusted the most, his younger brother Raúl and Guevara. Together this triumvirate would shape the course and direction of the revolution with Castro as supreme commander. On January 2, Castro began to govern Cuba and the future was uncertain. How long would he last in power if he challenged the United States? In that case, could the revolution succeed? Cubans had high hopes that Castro would bring meaningful change to their country. The 26th of July Movement had promised independence, democracy and an end to social injustice, but what form would it take? What were Castro's true intentions? How would the revolution turn out?

Castro's approach to these questions was based on improvisation and pragmatism. He would dismantle the previous government and create a new structure based on the ideals of the revolution. He appeared a moderate in those early days, installing the respected anti-Batista urban leader Manuel Urrutia as president. Urrutia appointed a cabinet of moderates and a prime minister, José Miró Cardona, and expected a rapid move to free elections. He would be disappointed.

> ### Discussion point
>
> **The Cuban leadership**
>
> President Urrutia and prime minister José Miró Cardona both resigned from the revolutionary Cuban government within six months. Both cited differences with Castro in this period as in their future careers.
>
> What does this say about Castro's leadership goals and the direction of the provisional government appointed in January 1959?

The new government, however, won the approval of the US who responded by officially recognizing the Urrutia government and dispatching a new ambassador. Castro remained in command of the rebel army and maintained an overall right of veto. In February, after Cardona unexpectedly resigned after serving only six weeks, Castro became prime minister—the effective head of the new government. The reasons for the changes in government were cited in the *Revolution* newspaper, regarded as the voice of the 26th of July Movement, as ongoing problems with "the dispersal of power." This was confirmed by the Fundamental Law of the Republic passed in the same month that gave lawmaking power to the executive. In short order, Castro had become the legal leader of Cuba.

In March, Castro implemented three reforms that foreshadowed a move to the left. As a staunch Cuban nationalist, he took over management of the US-owned telephone company and cut rates; he ordered the forced sale of vacant urban lots at reduced prices to end speculation and slashed urban rents by 50%. This was just the start. Within the first two years the *fidelistas* (Castro's inner circle of trusted revolutionaries) had laid the foundation for revolutionary changes to every aspect of Cuba's social, economic, and political structure. By 1970, the socialist (communist) government was in total control with Castro as supreme leader and the last traces of old Cuba were gone. By 1979, Cuba was a communist Caribbean nation with strong economic and political ties to the Soviet Union. National sovereignty, economic independence from foreign control, full employment, equal treatment of all citizens regardless of race or gender; education, healthcare and democracy comprised the first wave of reforms. Castro delivered on all these promises (to some extent) except for democracy, which was permanently shelved after 1961.

Political developments

The new sovereignty would be defended from foreign incursion and counterrevolutionary insurgents by a national militia of part-time soldiers. "Committees for the Defense of the Revolution" were established throughout the country and recruited 500,000 soldiers who owed allegiance to Castro—a huge military considering Cuba's population was 6.7 million. The militia was, in effect, revolutionary and showed their loyalty to the spirit of the 26th of July movement. Like the French Revolution's *levée en Masse* (conscription) it sent a wave of patriotism throughout the island, uniting Cubans to a common cause as never before. In effect, it created a new Cuban sense of shared nationhood. The country was militarized almost overnight. The committees controlled the country and would act as the government's strong arm, keeping order and control during the coming years of change and turmoil, effectively eliminating counterrevolutionary activity, defined broadly as anyone who disagreed with Castro.

 How does the Cuban Revolution compare to the French and Russian revolutions?

A common characteristic of major revolutions is the use of mass execution to purge any trace of the old order as symbolized by the *ancien régime* of pre-revolutionary France. During the French Revolution, thousands of aristocrats died at the guillotine, and in the Soviet Union, millions died under Stalin's purges of counter-revolutionaries (real or imagined). By comparison, the summary execution of 550 Batista supporters and officials seemed restrained by comparison, although still inviting criticism from within Latin America and the United States. Criticism of Castro's refusal to hold elections came from members of the Fidelista. The most famous dissident was Major Huber Matos. A central leader and trusted ally during the revolution, Matos wrote a letter against the growth of communist influence and Castro's cancellation of elections. He resigned from the air force in protest. Fidel resigned the premiership claiming a counterrevolutionary conspiracy. The response was predictable. Castro returned bowing to popular demand. Matos was put on trial and convicted for counterrevolutionary activity. He spent the next 15 years in jail and was often touted as a traitor to the people's revolution. The message was clear, critics of the revolution could expect harsh treatment. For many middle class Cubans, this was a crucial message and resulted in the exodus of hundreds of thousands of Cuba's best-educated and talented citizens to the United States. For Castro, this was just the price of revolution. This event foretold the end of dissent and the growth of censorship. Within the first 18 months the free press was suppressed and the academic autonomy of the University of Havana abolished.

In years to come, it was obvious that eliminating the middle class, though not a direct goal of the revolution was in step with Castro's vision of an egalitarian society. Those who fled, left behind large estates. The *Ministerio de Recuperación de Bienes Malversados* (Ministry for the Recovery of Stolen Property) confiscated the property of Batista and his supporters as well as dissidents (estimated at US$25 million). The haul was lucrative and funded future ventures. Like a modern day Robin Hood, Castro took from the rich and gave to the poor. Lavish houses and mansions were converted into multi-family housing units that helped alleviate housing shortages. With his control assured, Castro called on the people to make the sacrifices needed to correct Cuba's historic wrongs and create a better nation for everyone.

Creating a sovereign Cuba in control of its economy was at the very heart of the revolution. Castro knew that he had to eliminate foreign control, making a clash with the United States inevitable. He made the first moves quickly. When several major oil companies refused to extend the newly installed government credit for oil imports, Castro cancelled Cuba's exclusive contract with these firms and bought Soviet crude oil to be processed in US-owned refineries in Cuba. When their management refused, Castro took over the refineries and sent the US companies packing. In retaliation, the US revoked the Cuban sugar quota that annually bought about 80% of the cane crop. Castro responded, in turn, by seizing all US property and utilities (electricity and telephone), sugar mills and nickel mines. The US responded with an embargo on all US trade to Cuba with a few exceptions like medicine. Next, Cuba's dependence on a one-crop sugar economy had to be changed. Promoting crop diversification and industrialization (ISI) was the responsibility of Guevara who implemented a four year plan to achieve these goals in 1961. A central planning agency was set up but was often ignored by Castro's "special" plans. Guevara's plan unraveled because of high costs and the poor quality of goods produced as well as bad planning. He resigned in 1963 and shortly after departed Cuba to promote revolutions abroad. Meanwhile, the sugar industry had collapsed with crop levels at 50% of pre-1959 levels. Cuba's already meager supply of foreign currency was used up leaving the nation virtually bankrupt. The pace of industrialization could not be sustained. Soviet economic planners advised Castro to resurrect the sugar cane industry. Castro faced a classic economic riddle. To end Cuba's reliance on sugar exports, other areas of the economy required development. But the best source of income to fund diversification was the sugar industry. Any drop in sugar revenues would undermine efforts to end reliance on sugar production. As well, harvesting cane was labor intensive, taking the workforce away from the development of new industries. In 1963, Castro declared that 1970 would be the "Year of Decisive Endeavour." He promised a bumper harvest of 10 million tons, when yearly yields averaged 5.5 to 6.5 million tons. It was a bold move designed to deflect attention from the government's economic shortcomings, a tactic Castro would use often. It was also a national campaign to bring Cubans together under Castro's rule. The issue was how best to motivate Cubans.

Guevara believed that moral incentives should be used to create a new breed of Cubans who understood the need for personal sacrifice to promote the lofty goals of the revolution. Material incentives, wage diversification for example, served only to stunt the growth of the "New Man." Guevara's views were opposed by Carlos Rafael Rodríguez, an economist who argued that for the economy to advance a new prosperity it must offer incentives, sound planning and adopt modern accounting practices. He believed Cuba's policy should be flexible and pragmatic, such as trading with nations who were ideologically different. But Guevara's preference for moral incentive (also distinguishing the Chinese from the Soviet model of material incentive) was, ultimately, to prevail. Guevara's drive to export Marxist revolution throughout Latin America led to his eventual resignation from the government, and search for new revolutions to lead.

The only real solution to Cuba's economic problems was the Soviet Union. The Soviets began wooing Castro in 1960 with a four-year 200 million-dollar deal to trade one billion tons of sugar per year in exchange for Soviet equipment. Castro had never been a Communist Party member and had made a point of keeping his distance. During the revolution, the Communist Party had criticized Castro for his bourgeois adventurism but by 1960 the two sides were holding secret meetings. Castro wanted to take control of the party and did so gradually. On April 15, 1961, shortly after the failed Bay of Pigs invasion, he declared he was leading a socialist revolution under "the very noses of the Yankees."

Next he orchestrated the *Organizaciones Revolucionarias Integradas* (the Integrated Revolutionary Organizations) that brought the *fidelistas* and Cuban communists together formally in 1961. In March 1963 the IRO became the United Party of the Cuban Socialist Revolution (PURSC) and the final step came in 1965 with the creation of the Communist Party of Cuba (CPC). Castro was First Secretary and placed *fidelistas* in key positions. The final act came in 1976, when

Cuba declared itself a communist state with Castro as head of
state, head of the party and in control of key appointments.
In 1960, however, Castro was playing a dangerous game with the
superpowers, moving Cuba into the Soviet sphere at the same time
that the United States was being ousted. This did not sit well in the
White House and eventually led to the Bay of Pigs invasion in April
1961 and a 50-year US trade embargo.

Land reform and nationalization

On May 17, 1959, shortly before signing the trade deal with the
Soviets, the Agrarian Reform Law (ARL) was passed mandating the
expropriation of large agricultural holdings and signaled radical
alterations to Cuba's agricultural sector. The stage had been set by
Guevara who stated in January that land redistribution was high
government priority. The ARL was crafted by him as a means of
dissolving the *latifundios* (large estates) that had been outlawed in
the 1940 constitution but never enforced because of US ownership
and control of the sugar industry, and Cuba's own reliance on cane
profits. The majority of expropriated land belonged to large US
corporations like Coca Cola or Hershey's Chocolate, comprising 70 to
75% of cultivated lands. The *Instituto Nacional de Reforma Agraria*
(National Institute of Agrarian Reform or INRA) was established to
oversee the changes. The ARL set the maximum size of private farms
at 30 *caballerías* (403 hectares or 995 acres). It abolished
sharecropping and restricted foreign ownership. Nearly 100,000
Cubans received 27 hectares and the right to purchase 40 more if
available. Cuba had a mixed farming system of small peasant farms
cultivating 39% of arable land, 19% larger farms and 43% state-
controlled cooperatives. All uncultivated land defaulted to
state ownership. Eventually, all farms became *granjas del
pueblo* (state farms) including 480,000 acres from US companies.

Compensation to foreign land owners was paid in 20-year Cuban
government bonds with an annual interest rate of 4.5% based on
the assessed value of the land at the time of the takeover. In other
words, no compensation would be paid for 20 years based on land
values significantly lower than pre-1959 levels. On June 11, the US
government demanded immediate and fair compensation for US
interests. A year later, in October 1960, in response to the US ending
the sugar quota and imposing an embargo, Castro expropriated all
US landholdings without compensation. This included public
utilities, banking, transportation, sugar refining, mining and tourism
(casinos) totaling over a billion dollars. In effect, in less than two
years, Castro had evicted the United States without compensation
and welcomed the Soviet Union as Cuba's new partner

Large sugar estates and cattle ranches became state cooperatives
rather than being broken into less effective smaller parcels. In 1963,
the Second Law of Agrarian Reform expropriated about 10,000 mid-
sized farms (over 67 hectares) and the state controlled 70% of the
land. Smaller landholders were controlled though a regulatory body
the *Asociación Nacional de Agricultores Pequeños* (National Association of
Small Farmers, ANAP). Members were organized into cooperatives to
control kinds and types of crops, prices and sale of land (only to the

government). The ANAP made these farmers de facto workers of the state and ensured total government control of agriculture. This did not alter Cuba's economic reliance on sugar cane exports, despite efforts to diversify crops. In 1964, the sugar yield recovered, increasing by 9% over the previous year's but was still well below the previous average. Production did not reach pre-1959 levels until the last years of the decade.

The nationalization of property also included the extensive land holdings of the Roman Catholic Church, resulting in the expulsion of the Cuban bishop along with hundreds of clergy. The final part of the initial period was providing a guaranteed wage for all Cubans. This was very popular. One out of every two Cubans worked in the sugar industry which meant that for at least half the year, half the population was unemployed. Now Castro guaranteed them an adequate yearly wage. The unforeseen result was a rise in the demand for food that created severe shortages. In 1962, the government imposed rationing which remained a constant feature.

Castro finished nationalizing in 1968 when he took over 56,000 small Cuban-owned businesses, including restaurants, laundries, garages and beauty parlors. All now became salaried employees of the state. By the end of the 1960s, Cuba had become a communist dictatorship with Castro as supreme commander. Materially, the life of the average Cuban had improved (despite food shortages) but rationing was a vast improvement on chronic starvation. Healthcare, improved nutrition, literacy and education, housing and year-round employment meant a better life for most. The revolutionary movement itself had been transformed from a rugged band of *barbudos* (bearded ones) into a modern authoritarian communist dictatorship supported by a technocratic bureaucracy and an obedient and capable military. The emigration of hundreds of thousands of dissidents meant that Castro's opposition lived in Miami, not Cuba.

Castro's personality cult

Castro's carefully orchestrated persona was as a larger-than-life, paternal populist leader. A man of the people: a ragged, bearded hero in green military fatigues with flashing eyes, often seen puffing a big cigar, he was a man who could be trusted to do what was best for Cuba. By 1970, the revolution had become a powerful, centralized, bureaucracy.

Castro was the all-powerful dictator of a communist regime supported by loyal *fidelistas*, the military and the Soviet Union He had made many improvements to the lives of average Cubans but had yet to significantly improve the economy. A learning curve to correct past mistakes known as *rectificación* was a constant theme during the first decade. The 1970s were a turning point, witnessing a paradigm shift from a revolution serving the people to a people serving the revolution. The next 10 years would be a time of consolidation and expansion of the government's control of the regime domestically. Internationally, Castro would attempt to export revolution throughout Latin America and Africa.

Activity

Cuban Rectificación

The Rectificación Campaign launched by Fidel Castro in 1986 criticized the Soviet model of Marxism. How can it be viewed in relation to Gorbachev's reforms in the Soviet Union?

Analyze Castro's statements from the period 1985–89 to come up with an assessment of his ideological model for Cuban reform.

The much-anticipated 10 million ton sugar harvest would show the world the progress of the socialized Cuban economy. "The year of Decisive Endeavor," as Castro called it, would deliver a 10 million ton harvest that would easily surpass the previous best of 6.5 million tons. The profits would fill Cuba's empty foreign exchange coffers and provide investment funds for industrial development. It was a bold plan. In 1963, Castro had ordered 10 million tons. The quality of the sugar cane was improved, new stalks were planted, new lands appropriated and thousands of volunteers came from the city to cut cane. All efforts were made to reach the goal. But the final tally was 8.5 million tons.

On 26 July 1970, Castro faced the nation, broadcasting before a large crowd in Havana's Plaza de la Revolución: "Let the shame be welcome," he cried. He offered to resign blaming himself for the failure to achieve the target output, but the crowds absolved him and cried no. The crisis passed. Castro had again used revolutionary rhetoric to deflect attention from his economic shortcomings. The failure resulted in closer economic and political ties to the Soviet Union.

The new Cuban bureaucracy

The 1970s was a time of transition as the government adopted a more bureaucratic style of leadership. A new executive committee was formed. The government was reorganized with clearly defined lines of separation between the military, the bureaucracy and the communist party. The common element was that Castro personally controlled all three. The militia was folded into the army which was made into a professional fighting force and would soon find itself fighting in Africa.

The bureaucracy instituted a program of mass involvement in the government which included a larger role for labor unions. Tribunals enforced labor laws and workers rights, and workers were involved in planning production goals and targets. The planning process was computerized and a system of material incentives and merit pay was instituted. The incentives were commonly based on meeting production targets and merit pay was based on the nature of the employment; some jobs were considered more important than others, such as doctors and teachers. The results were encouraging: between 1971 and 1973, productivity increased by 20%. The efforts to systematize economic production combined with merit incentives resulted in a significant rise in the GDP from 3.9% to 10% annually. Subsidies from the Soviet Union played a significant role in funding many of these ventures. Yet all these changes had only reduced not eliminated the sugar one-crop economy. During the last years of the 1970s, economic growth fell to 4%. This was also a reflection of world economic decline during this period, but it also showed that Cuba had a long way to go.

The last major development in this transition came in 1976. A national referendum approved the adoption of a socialist constitution officially replacing the 1940 constitution. It provided for a system of elected municipal and provincial and national assemblies; most representatives were members of the Cuban Communist Party, the top appointments held by Castro and his inner circle.

Castro cutting Cane, 1960.

Social and cultural developments

Many Cubans were opposed to the growing authoritarianism, while others grew tired of the economic problems and Castro's continued call for self-sacrifice. Discontent boiled over in 1980, when over 125,000 abandoned Cuba on a fleet of leaky, overcrowded boats mainly through the port of Mariel to make the 150-kilometre crossing to the United States. Social discontent was on the rise in the 1960s, directed at the increasingly authoritarian, anti-democratic nature of the revolution. As in the 1930s, a counterculture emerged singing *canciones de protesta* (protest songs). Folk artists became popular and were influenced by international protest movements in the 1960s. Artists praised the revolution and its advances but criticized its failures, authoritarianism and the restriction of artistic freedom. Silvio Rodríguez and Haydée Santamaría epitomized the new movement. Rodríguez denounced the faceless bureaucrats for ruining the revolution. His youthful followers dressed like hippies and decried the contradiction of encouraging revolution abroad and stifling expression at home. Santamaria was head of the Casa de las Américas Institute that promoted Cuban music. She tried to protect the young artists from state censure and encouraged them to express themselves. She organized cultural exchanges and music festivals and provided access to state radio and TV for these artists. Some singers were jailed for overtly criticizing the regime.

Following the failure of the 10 million tons, Cubans were given some leeway to vent their frustration through the music of the *Nueva Trova* (new ballad) movement. The government embraced the young musicians who led the movement and allowed them to participate in international music festivals and competitions. There were clearly defined limits to criticism regulated by the *Movimiento Nacional de la Trova* (National Movement of the Ballad, or MNT) and some songs deemed inappropriate or anti-social were banned. The MNT did, however, provide musicians with better equipment, training and recording opportunities. They walked a fine line between supporting and criticizing the revolution in their music.

Creative writers, journalists, filmmakers, visual and performing artists all faced a similar curtailment of their freedom of creative expression, if they were critical of the regime. For many

Heberto Padilla (1932–2000)

In 1968, Heberto Padilla, a respected Cuban poet who had grown disillusioned by the revolution's artistic dogmas and authoritarianism, created an international controversy with his book *Fuera del juego* (Out of the game), a collection of poems that criticized the government's strong-arm tactics. Padilla was awarded Cuba's highest literary prize by the Union of Cuban Writers and Artists. The government was outraged and forced the union to issue an appendix in the book that condemned it as counterrevolutionary. For the next two years, Padilla was under virtual house arrest and was forced to read a humiliating public retraction of his own writings. When it was exposed that he was writing a novel criticizing the government, he and his wife were imprisoned and, most likely, tortured. He became a *cause célèbre* in the international community as a symbol of oppression. His family was allowed to leave for the United States in 1979. International pressure resulted in Padilla's release in 1980. He was called a hero by President Reagan. The result of the affair was an end to the support for the revolution by many important Latin American and European writers. As a writer in exile he continued his criticism of Castro notably in the 1984 novel *En Mi Jardin Pastan Los Heroes* (Heros Graze in my Garden). He never returned to Cuba. Outside of Cuba he became a symbol of oppression but inside Cuba he was an example of what happened to those who were overly critical of the regime.

the only options were to be discredited and imprisoned or a life in exile. One such writer was the poet and novelist Heberto Padilla (1932–2000).

Women and the revolution

Women fought with Castro every step of the way and made significant gains in a society were machismo dominated and controlled relations between the sexes. In 1960, the *Federacíon de Mujeres Cubanas* (Cuban Women's Federation, or FMC) was started under Vilma Espín to bring about a change in the role of women. It started by attacking attitudes and illiteracy and through creating support for a national healthcare system, in which many women might also find employment. Other programs included teaching women vocational farming skills. The FMC has successfully lobbied the government to pass legislation to assist women. In 1975, the egalitarian Family Code was enacted and made sexual equality in a marriage a legal and moral obligation. Both men and women were entitled to education or rewarding employment. The code mandated equal sharing of house chores and child raising and legitimized divorce (which had been virtually forbidden by the Catholic Church). Women started attending universities in growing numbers (by 1990, 57% of university students were women and the percentage is higher in medicine). Cuba's policies towards women remain some of the most progressive and successful in the region.

Throughout the period, the number of women in school and the workplace tripled between 1959 and 1990. Women were, however, under-represented in the ranks of the Communist Party and in government. Yet, compared to other Latin American nations during the same period, Cuba was the uncontested leader in promoting equal opportunity.

Developments in education

Speaking at the United Nations in 1960, Castro boasted that the revolution would get rid of illiteracy within a year, a strategy never-before tried in the developing world. 1961 was proclaimed the "Year of Education." Responding to the inadequacy of schools in the countryside, Castro mobilized 100,000 students to teach in rural areas. They taught a million people to read and write. This gave Cuba one of the highest literacy rates in Latin America. The education of young people was part of Castro's early goals to create a revolutionary nationalism among Cubans: it worked to ensure, in particular, the loyalty of the first generation of the revolution. The results were impressive. In the first decade, the number of new teachers tripled and the number of schools quadrupled. Education was free for all Cubans. Most Cubans completed grade nine, illiteracy disappeared and Cuba became a nation of readers, publishing thousands of books each year. In 1973, for example, 800 new titles and 28 million books were published.

> ### Discussion point
>
> It is a characteristic of single-party regimes to impose limits on the freedom of speech and artistic expression.
>
> **To what extent is it necessary for a successful revolution to control the arts?**

307

Improvements in healthcare

Castro took the revolution in healthcare to the countryside. Healthcare stood beside education as a top priority. Thousands of new doctors (the majority of them female) and medical professionals were trained. Hospitals were opened in the countryside. Infant mortality decreased significantly and when combined with improvements in other areas including nutrition, food supply and housing Cubans enjoyed longer and healthier lives.

Eliminating racism

In 1959, Castro called for an end to racial discrimination in the workplace and in cultural centers. Afro-Cubans were not proportionately well-represented in the early revolutionary movement, despite its progressive, liberal egalitarian agenda. On reason for this was that Castro, unlike Martí, did not forefront "the color question" or devise a political program that targeted this ethnic group, from the outset. Another problem was the high degree of support among Afro-Cubans for Batista, himself a mixed-race mulatto, who employed many blacks in the military and police forces, and supported their cultural organizations, later closed down by Castro, who did not want to encourage a separatist movement. Changes in the law did not, however, put an immediate end to racist attitudes. The growth of the Afro-Cuban and mulatto population, as well as the increase in mixed-race marriages, did contribute to a significant easing of racial tensions. Merit hiring and promotion, notably in the military, meant that Afro-Cubans held important positions in the government. During the 1970s, Cuba guaranteed the entitlement of all citizens regardless of gender and ethnicity to equal wages, education, healthcare and merit hiring. These were important developments in maintaining loyal support for Castro among Afro-Cubans.

Activity

Spreading revolution in Latin America

The spread of revolutionary ideas by Fidel Castro and Che Guevara was promoted through publications and speeches. These included:

- Che Guevara's *Reminiscences of the Cuban Revolutionary War* (1960) and *Guerilla Warfare* (1961).
- Fidel Castro's speech, *The Second Declaration of Havana*, given on February 4, 1962,
- Régis Debray's *Revolution in the Revolution* (1967)

Research these texts and summarize their intention.

Questions

1 How do they serve as historical documents of the Cuban Revolution?
2 How important were they to the development of the revolution and its foreign policies?

Activity

Castro and communism

The historical controversy

In the discussion of Castro's gradual conversion to communism, historians typically fall into three categories. Read each and then answer the questions that follow.

Historian A: Conspiracy theory Castro was always a communist and intended to make Cuba communist all along. He had hidden the fact he was a communist during the revolution to avoid alienating many Cubans and US military intervention under the Platt Amendment. It is uncertain, yet likely, that he had a relationship with the Soviet Union beforehand. He did not reveal his true intentions until he was firmly entrenched in power and knew he could rely on the support of the Soviet Union to counter-balance invasion threats from the United States.

Historian B: Conversion theory Assumes Castro was converted to Marxism. The question is whether he converted to Marxism of his own volition or had his hands forced by the policies and actions of the United States. It seems credible to conclude that active US opposition to Fidel's reforms, notably trade embargos and support for Cuban refugees, drove Fidel to seek an alliance with the Soviet Union. Soviet support was not unqualified and was given only after Castro had implemented a series of pro-socialist programs in the first two years of the revolution.

Historian C: Pragmatism theory Fidel, Guevara and others have acknowledged that the actions of the United States did influence them to a degree but that the reform measures implemented by Castro were Cuban in design and largely unaffected by foreign intervention. Castro and the Fidelistas took advantage of their enormous popularity to swing the revolution in a direction that would eliminate the abuses that the 26th of July movement had fought to eradicate. Fidel's adoption of communism was more pragmatic than ideological, based on the conviction that Cuba's problems could not be solved by capitalism (or democracy) and that Marxism was the best and most viable alternative available. Castro's handling of the situation was "realpolitik" at its best.

Analyzing the evidence

1 What evidence is there to support each of these theories? Provide three facts, and/or statements from the Cuban leaders that historians could use to support each theory.

Theory	Fact 1	Fact 2	Fact 3
Conspiracy theory			
Conversion theory			
Pragmatism theory			

2 Which theory, if any, do you support? Discuss your reasons with reference to your sources and the views of other historians and social commentators. Be aware that historians rarely subscribe to one particular theory when constructing the past, and often like to take a "revisionist" approach.

The impact of the Cuban Revolution on the region

Castro and Guevara both believed that the best way to protect Cuba was to encourage insurrection throughout Latin America. Guevara, the ideologue, believed that communist insurrection was the only hope for the oppressed people of Latin America and the world. He became the recognized face of Latin American revolution and was more popular than Castro. Support organizations sprang up seemingly overnight in virtually every country in the region. A spontaneous continental revolution that united industrial and rural workers, as well as peasant farmers against bourgeois capitalist élites and US hegemony did not materialize. The political élites feared the revolutionary impulses of the people. Some responded with repression, others adopted a mild reform program designed to quell the anger and others combined both approaches (repression and reform).

In reaction to the insurgents, governments, for the most part, adopted a hard-line approach. Armed services took an active role in established military governments that were stridently anti-communist. They were supported in their efforts by sizeable grants from within the region, particularly US, and used these funds to train and arm anti-insurgency forces trained by foreign operatives who were experts in this type of warfare. By 1961, these units were successfully resisting and eliminating guerrilla units that were following the tactics and strategies laid out in Guevara's handbook on guerrilla warfare. He advised taking to the mountains, creating a safe haven and enlisting the support of the peasants as the formula for victory. However, new counterinsurgency strategies that attacked rebel strongholds and the lack of peasant support successfully countered the strategy. The new Cuban government put some of its limited resources—its direct support—into backing campaigns in Argentina, Venezuela and Bolivia without achieving significant results. Successful export of revolutionary socialism had to wait for Allende's Chile (1971), the Sandinistas in Nicaragua and the New Jewel Movement in Grenada (both in 1979). The *fidelistas* were able to agitate reform movements and establish small guerrilla cadres but they were unable to overcome the increasingly well-organized and often US-trained military-backed regimes that took control in many Latin American nations. Between 1960 and 1964, 10 juntas occurred in eight different nations. The fear of another Cuban Revolution was taken seriously and nations moved to suppress and eliminate the threat.

Cuba was isolated, cut-off and contained. Trade with other nation in the region dried up. In 1962, Cuba was expelled from the Organization of American States (OAS). The nations of the region concluded that economic development and prosperity would greatly reduce the appeal of revolution. The 1961 OAS-initiated Alliance for Progress modeled on the Marshall Plan in Europe after the Second World War and an important foreign policy of US president J. F. Kennedy, was one such program aimed at development. But the OAS itself, with its US bias (its headquarters were in Washington DC) promoted vested interests and US-sponsored regimes. The price of stability was compliance. Of the US$100 million in aid intended to improve economic infrastructure and economic development, much of the expenditure went into training police and military recruits in riot control, intelligence gathering and counterinsurgency.

The threat of communism was further complicated by the perception of some military leaders that even minor reform measures like those included in the Alliance for Progress, were communist inspired. Opponents to the government were branded communist. Nonetheless, student protests, workers strikes, revolutionary propaganda condemning the status quo, threats of exile invasions and pro-Castro rallies became an everyday spectacle in Latin America and destabilized many governments but rarely with the intended outcome of establishing a revolutionary government.

For its part, the Cuban government put some of its limited resources—its direct support—into backing campaigns in Argentina, Venezuela, Bolivia and Nicaragua. With the exception of the much later success of the Sandinistas in Nicaragua in 1979, these campaigns were for the most part unsuccessful. By this time, Castro's own allegiances, and cautionary model, had significantly changed, as evidenced by his statement at the annual Moncada celebrations on 26 July, attended by the Sandinistas in their first flush of success, a statement that would rightly be perceived as a caution:

> Each country has its path, its problems, its style, its methods, and its objectives. We have ours and they have theirs. We did it in a certain way—our way—and they will do it in their way … No two revolutions are the same. They cannot be … Our problems are not exactly their problems. The conditions in which our revolution was made are not exactly the same conditions in which their revolution was made … In other words, things in Nicaragua are not going to be exactly the same, or anything like what they are in Cuba.

The Sandinista victory was welcomed by Cuba, but its very existence created additional problems in relation to the United States and the Soviet Union. One similarity with the Cuban experience, was the threat of US intervention (soon to be realized), and Castro cautioned the Sandinistas not to antagonize them. He recommended they establish a mixed economy, a pluralist political system, and maintain good relations with the Catholic Church (more influential than in Cuba). He did not want Nicaragua to go the same way as Cuba and lose a large proportion of middle class support. Under US President Reagan's *contra* insurgency, however, Nicaragua was to experience the full brunt of a CIA-backed insurgency to weaken Sandinista defenses. Castro had promised to send teachers and doctors in his first speech to the Sandinista leaders, but this had to be followed up by military advisors and weapons.

The much less-publicized revolution in Grenada the same year, followed the Cuban model more exactly, and Castro felt a strong and supportive allegiance with its leader Maurice Bishop, who in a dawn raid on the corrupt regime of Eric Gairy invoked comparisons with the Moncada rebellion. The New Jewel Movement that led the revolution of March 1979, on an island with a population of only

---

Activity

The Organization of American States (OAS)

The charter for the OAS, in its current form, was signed in Bogotá, Colombia, in 1948. Research the Organization of American States (OAS) and its membership in 1948–79.

Questions

1 Which regimes did the OAS support? Which countries and political parties were excluded from its intra-regional cooperation and investment programs?

2 What effect did the OAS have on stability in the region?

3 How did the OAS contribute to development goals?

100,000, was closely modeled on the Cuban example, a model, in Bishop's words, "of what socialism can do in a small country—for health, education, employment, and for ending poverty, prostitution and disease." Cuba was true to its word and provided support, also with the construction of an airport at Point Salines to help the small Caribbean nation develop its tourism, much to US concern at what they regarded as a Soviet–Cuban base. These threats and internal divisions within the revolutionary movement saw the end of Bishop's regime at the hands of his own movement in October 1983, and the subsequent US invasion.

Perhaps the most revealing complication of the Cuban model, and its international allegiances, however, was revealed in Cuban relations with Allende's Chile, from 1970. Castro was a long-time friend and supporter of Salvador Allende, the newly elected president and leader of the Chilean Socialist Party, who himself was possibly the warmest supporter of the Cuban Revolution within Latin America. Castro's problem was his newly established allegiance to the Chilean Communist Party that meant he could no longer show support for the revolutionary movement of Allende's. His relationship with Allende became strained and his presence on a state visit to Chile proved unsettling to the country's bourgeois democracy, contributing to internal opposition that ultimately led to the September 1973 coup in which Allende was deposed. As a Soviet-backed state, Cuba became increasingly isolated and turned its attention to the new states and allied regimes in Africa.

Populist leaders in Latin America

Populism, in Latin America, was a response to the political, economic and social conditions and challenges nations faced during and following the Great Depression. It was founded on a charismatic leader who created a multi-class political alliance that represented the significant economic and social changes which had occurred in many Latin America nations because of industrialization and the growth of a prosperous and educated middle class and a rapidly organizing working class. Historian Robert Dix defines populism as:

> … a political movement which enjoys the support of the mass of the working class and/or peasantry, but which does not result from the autonomous organization power of either of these sectors. It is supported by non-working class sectors upholding an anti-status quo ideology.
>
> **Source:** Dix, Robert H. "Populism: Authoritarian and Democratic." *Latin American Research Review.* vol 20, no.2, 1985. p. 29.

In some nations populists challenged the long-standing agricultural elites and the Catholic Church for control of the masses. The military exerted an ever-increasing influence that often stifled meaningful change and in many cases resulted in regime change.

"Give me a balcony and I will become President."

José María Velasco,
President of Ecuador

The key element was a charismatic leader who adopted the "popular" causes of the people, promised immediate rectification and was supported by the military (at least initially). Populism was not as ideologically driven as communism, socialism or capitalism, but should be thought of as a political tactic used to gain and maintain political power in a multi-class political environment relying on mass support. The successful populist was able to continually adjust government priorities and programs to satisfy his supporters, often commanding a coalition government. The appeal of the populists was a new nationalism that promised economic independence from foreign control and a better life for the people. It also fostered a new sense of patriotism. Urban-oriented, and thus less likely to involve land reform, populist regimes promised improvements in social welfare, healthcare, education, wage increases, industrialization and nationalization of resources and public works. The programs, initially at least, offered something for everyone, a panacea and placebo. Higher wages ended strikes and increased productivity. Workers had more money to purchase food, clothes and better housing which put profits in the pockets of businessmen and taxes in government coffers. Such programs created political stability for as long as the prosperity lasted. Populists did not seek the support of the nation's economic élite nor did they challenge their economic dominance. In that sense the populists were more **Mussolini** than Marx, more fascist than communist. They embraced the corporatist state structure that controlled, regulated and directed the economy, including Import Substitution Industrialization (ISI).

The pattern was to provide an immediate stimulus to the economy that often proved unsustainable and, after few years of rapid growth, revenues toppled and the government would be dismembered. When this happened the populist leader had to pick sides in order to stay in power. This generally necessitated a move to the right, seeking support from the military and economic élites against left-wing groups and parties. These authoritarian measures resulted in the violent repression of political opponents and the suppression of civil rights in what was usually to become the final stage in the populist regime. Instead of stifling the opposition, these measures galvanized political dissidents. Strikes, protest marches, riots, kidnapping and political assassinations by urban guerrillas opened the door for the military to step in to restore order. By the mid-1960s, populism had run its course (for now) and was replaced by military juntas supported by wealthy élites (industrial and agrarian) with the tacit support of foreign governments who feared South America would be engulfed by left-wing revolutionary movements inspired by Fidel Castro. The populist era had ended—the era of military dictatorships had begun.

Populism ultimately became unstable because it relied on the leader's popularity. Public opinion and popularity are fickle. As their star became tarnished, the populists were consumed by a virulent form of military dictatorship, determined to eliminate

Benito Mussolini was a European populist who took power in Italy in 1922 advocating a doctrine of corporatism. The doctrine prescribed government regulation and management of the economy. The government would negotiate agreements between the various groups—labor and management for example, which would create social harmony and prosperity for all. The Italian model was based on a political system that managed industry (workers and employers) with a state bureaucracy. It was a method of conscripting the nation to serve the greater good as determined by the leader. In 1932 Mussolini wrote in "The Doctrine of Fascism" that the nature of corporatism was to strengthen the individual and the state through the collective pursuit of common (national) goals.

> Far from crushing the individual, the Fascist State multiplies his energies, just as in a regiment a soldier is not diminished but multiplied by the number of his fellow soldiers.

The model was top down, the message was marital, patriotic and paternal and was popular with Latin American populists like Vargas and Peron.

the threat of communist revolution and create capitalist industrial economies. These juntas opened the doors to foreign corporations and investment, luring them with tax breaks, anti-union policies and security forces. They rolled back wages and reduced social welfare programs. The regimes were oppressive and violent; thousands of dissidents were arrested, tortured and disappeared. By the 1980s, a new era dawned, democracy made a comeback and the military returned to the barracks.

Between 1930 and 1974, Latin America witnessed the rise and fall of a number of populist regimes and leaders including Lázaro Cárdenas of Mexico, José María Velasco of Ecuador, Getúlio Vargas of Brazil and Juan Perón of Argentina. These last two with their unique brand of populism will provide the case studies for this section.

Getúlio Vargas: president of Brazil

Getúlio Vargas was a political chameleon, able to change color and camouflage his true intentions. He once said that he had no political enemies, just people he hadn't made friends with yet. Underneath the wry smile and cherubic face ringed by the smoke of his ever-present cigar, lurked a consummate politician who would run Brazil in 1930–45 and again in 1950–54, putting his mark on the nation as no one had done before (and arguably since). The pinnacle of his power was 1937 to 1945 when he set out to establish the *Estado Novo* (the New State) based on corporatist principles. Shortly after passing the 1937 constitution, Vargas seized power and became a populist *caudillo*. He began to implement the political philosophy laid out in his book *A nova política do Brasil*. It would be a new beginning, making Brazil a modern state by reducing its reliance on coffee, creating modern government institutions, building the infrastructure that could support and encourage industrialization. Fractures in the political framework between right and left, labor and management would be healed by including all views in the corporatist agenda. No one would be left out. At least that was what Vargas said, and to some extent that is what he did.

By the time of the *Estado Novo*, economic changes and modifications were well under way. Import Substitution Industrialization had helped increase industrial output on average by 6% annually. Brazil's industrial sector boasted 44,100 plants and nearly a million workers, tripling in size in just 20 years. Expansion had been funded by foreign investors who provided 44% of Brazil's total investment by 1940.

The regime became increasingly fascist in rhetoric and tactics. Vargas announced that "the decadence of liberal and individualist democracy represents an incontrovertible fact." He became increasingly friendly with Germany, Brazil's biggest buyer of cotton

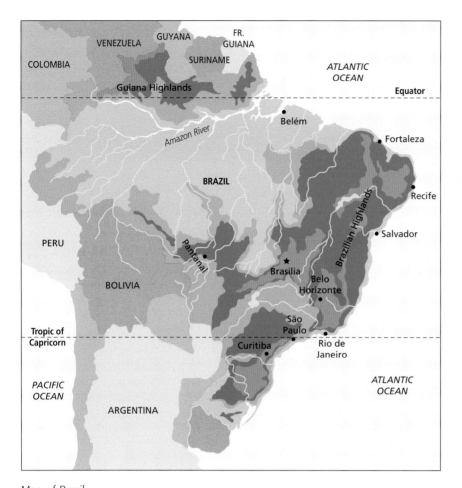

Map of Brazil.

Discussion point

Consider this map of Brazil, to assess the challenges of the infrastructure, and transportation requirements on the development of Brazilian industry and trade.

Refer to section starting p. 225 on "Latin American responses to the Depression," Chapter 4, for further discussion of the Brazilian economy.

and second biggest coffee market. German investment grew and the German military trained and equipped Brazil's Army. This development made the United States and the United Kingdom nervous. Economics aside, Vargas did not support Germany's expansionist agenda and as the nations of Europe marched towards war, Vargas distanced himself from the Germans and Italians and became closer to the United States.

When the Second World War broke out Vargas stayed neutral until German submarines sank several Brazilian ships and Vargas declared war in 1942, sending 25,000 Brazilian soldiers to fight with the Allied armies in Italy. He used this to leverage loans and technical help from the Allies to help build the new state-owned iron and steel plant— the Companhia Siderúrgica Nacional (CSN) in Volta Redonda which was producing about 650,000 tons by 1955.

His focus, however, remained steadfastly on Brazil. In 1940 he implemented a Five Year plan with goals to develop heavy industry and new sources of hydro-electric energy to power the factories and expand the railroads, connecting the vast, often isolated regions of the country. A modern economy needed modern infrastructure and Vargas ambitiously set out to achieve both simultaneously. In 1942, he established the Companhia Vale do Rio Doce (or CVRD), to mine iron ore deposits in the Itabira province. Several of his most important projects were finalized shortly after he was ousted in 1945.

In 1946, the National Steel Company rolled its first steel and the National Motor assembled its first trucks and, together with the National Petroleum Company (established 1938), formed an impressive corporatist triumvirate. But the economy had serious inflationary problems that Vargas was unable to stem. Prices rose 86% in 1940–44.

Vargas also adopted the heavy-handed tactics of a dictator, determined to maintain power by any means necessary. He banned strikes but won labor's approval with generous wage and benefit settlements. The hypocrisy of fighting fascist dictatorship but using fascist tactics at home was a sore point with many Brazilians. Opposition grew and Vargas, ever willing to change course when the political winds changed direction, promised to call an election and end the *Estado Novo* when the war was over. In January 1945, he released all political prisoners and allowed political parties to enter the political arena again. The election was set for December 2, 1945, and would be the first free elections in a decade. Political parties sprang to life. The Social Democratic Party and Brazilian Labor Party were sponsored by Vargas who called him "The Father of the Poor." He signed a decree to stop any practices that were harmful to Brazilians (i.e. the working class) by, for example, ending wage and price controls. Occupying the far right was the National Democratic Party, a conservative coalition of landowners and businessmen. Their platform was pro-American, pro-capitalism and pro- foreign investment to exploit Brazil's untouched resources. On the far left, a well-organized Communist Party emerged.

Other groups made their voices heard and became politically active, employing non-traditional methods. The Women's Committee was a national organization that monitored food prices, demanded social justice and enjoyed wide support. In the machismo Brazil, this was an astounding development. Afro-Brazilians, long the victims of racism and ignored by Vargas, used cultural expressions of discontent such as theater and music to plant and grow cultural consciousness. One of the most popular expressions of protest was the music and dance of the Samba which Vargas tried to marginalize. Other forms of protest included secret worker's groups and spreading absenteeism that became a de facto work slowdown.

Vargas remained above the fray and declared he would not run for president despite the encouragement of his supporters, the *Queremistas* (from the Portuguese verb "to want"). The conservative elements in the military and business were poised to move Brazil into the US Cold War camp and adopt free enterprise economic practices, reduce state intervention and encourage foreign investment and ownership.

The October Coup, 1945
On October 29, 1945, the military forced Vargas to resign and put the Chief Justice of the Supreme Court in office until after the election. Two generals became the front runners for the presidency. When the votes were tallied, General Eurico Gaspar Dutra had won. Vargas drifted into the shadows and worked behind the scenes to plan his return to office.

Dutra adopted a conservative agenda, severed ties with the Soviet Union and outlawed Brazil's Communist Party, expelling Communists elected to Congress. He then attacked organized labor and froze wages. Dutra implemented free enterprise policies and turned his back on the state-run institutions set up by Vargas. A rush of foreign investment, mainly from the United States poured in (US$323 million in 1946 alone) and the total reached over $800 million in 1951. Dutra turned his attention to curbing inflation and did so by restricting credit, lowering social security benefits in addition to maintaining the freeze on wages. Dutra spent the nation's foreign exchange surplus, over $700 million, earmarked by Vargas to fund industrial development, on imported consumer goods including many luxury items. The spending temporarily revived the economy but when the money ran out took a dive.

Dutra did achieve some benefits. He built railroads that connected Salvador and São Paulo and constructed 4,000 new rural schools. In 1951, he set up the National Research Council (still in existence) and implemented a military program to promote domestic arms production, sending young officers to train in the United States.

The return to power, 1950–54

By 1950 Brazil was ready for a return to the style of leadership and government they were used to. Vargas declared his candidacy with the backing of the Social Democratic Party. He had also re-created a coalition of workers groups, industrialists and the middle class. It was the old Vargas at his best, convincing divergent groups to come together to pursue a common cause and that cause was Brazil for Brazilians. He attacked his rivals brilliantly, claiming they wanted to keep the nation chained to producing coffee and cattle to maintain the old power structure of agrarian élites (the Paulistas) and the church. He preached modernization and progress and it was exactly what Brazilians wanted to hear.

He won the election easily but had inherited a bankrupt economy. Vargas needed money so he printed more, increasing inflation. The United States refused to lend Vargas money, going further by withdrawing from a joint commission on economic development. Undaunted, Vargas established a new corporation, the Petróleo Brasileiro S.A (the Brazilian Petroleum Corporation, also known as Petrobras). This joint venture between government and business created a monopoly on oil drilling and new refineries. Next, he created the equivalent electrical corporation, Electrobras. Vargas's supporters hailed these achievements but his opponents became convinced that he was leading the nation in the wrong direction.

Labor unrest also challenged Vargas. He had tried to win them back with a new minimum wage in 1951 but it didn't keep pace. Strikes became a common event, climaxing in 1953 when 300,000 workers walked off the job demanding higher wages and improved benefits. Vargas sacrificed his Minister of Labor, João Goulart, who sided with the workers and recommended doubling the miminum wage. Vargas fired Goulart to pacify the army but then did an about-face and at the **May Day** celebration announced the wage increase and praised his departed minister.

May Day (May 1) is International Workers' Day, also called Labor Day, and is a public holiday in many countries. It is often marked by political demonstrations and celebrations organized by unions and other groups.

The Carlos Lacerda affair

Carlos Lacerda was the editor of the conservative newspaper *Tribuna da Imprensa* and a relentless critique of Vargas's left-wing policies and called for his removal. In early August, a gunman attacked Lacerda, killing his volunteer bodyguard (a major in the air force) and leaving Carlos for dead. But the wounds were minor and Lacerda recovered. The gunman was captured and confessed that he was working for Gregório Fortunato, the head of Vargus's personal security detachment. A search of Fortunato's office exonerated Vargus of any wrongdoing but records were uncovered that detailed rampant corruption, influence peddling and monetary kickbacks. Fortunato was living a luxurious life on a modest government salary. The implications for Vargus's administration were serious. The proximity to the president's office lost Vargas the support of the military. On August 18, it became clear that the military would demand his resignation. Vargas told his staff he would never resign. During the early hours of August 24th the military met several times and concluded there was no alternative but resignation. The ultimatum was delivered to Vargas. Crowds had gathered outside. Vargas gave his aide an envelope, closed his office door and a shot rang out. Vargas was dead. The envelope contained his suicide note and read "I leave life to enter history ..."

Activity

Getúlio Vargas: an assessment

Source A

Ever since, some of Brazil's most successful politicians have proudly defined themselves as disciples of Vargas. They would agree with the opinion of Professor Emir Sader, for whom a typical caudillo like Vargas was just a democratic leader whose only "sin" was to fight against U.S. imperialism. In reality, such "intellectuals" and populist leaders honour Vargas because he much contributed in Brazil to the advance of their xenophobic nationalism, as an ideology whereby the ruling groups can more easily manipulate the popular masses, so as to make them eternally hopeful for a saviour to inaugurate the tropical paradise on earth.

Source: Zimmerman, Augusto. 2005. *Brazil: President Vargas's most enduring Legacy is His Xenophobic Nationalism.* Hispanic American Center for Economic Research.

Source B

Populist rapport does not require tub-thumping demagoguy [sic]: Cárdenas [Mexican populist leader Lázaro Cárdenas] was no more a flamboyant speaker than was Vargas; both acquired support by virtue of their policies, image, and career—and despite (or because of?) their dour personalities. Effective populism, in other words, derived from lived experience rather than rhetorical extravagance.

Source: Knight, Alan. "Populism and Neo-Populism in Latin America, Especially Mexico." *Journal of Latin American Studies.* vol. 30, no. 2. May 1998. p. 237.

Source C

Another benefit of the Vargas period was the temporary breaking of the dominance of the state of São Paulo over the rest of the country. For too long the fortunes of Brazil had been determined by the interests of this very powerful and important state.

What was good for São Paulo was good for the remainder of Brazil. Sometimes this may have been true; often it was not. Often Paulista businessmen made the north of Brazil their own type of colony. The north and the northeast were secure markets and also the source of raw materials for southern Brazil. The Vargas period to a slight degree dislodged the complete power control of São Paulo over the country. Credit should be given to Getúlio Vargas for his conscious attempt to break down the strong regional sentiments that existed before 1930, for Brazil during the Vargas period became more of a unified nation. Regionalism still existed, to be sure, and exists today in Brazil; but for the first time in modern Brazilian history a chief of state had spoken to Brazilians from a non-Paulista base.

Thus, the Vargas epoch was a mixture of gains and benefits in some sectors, setbacks and negative results in others. Nevertheless, by comparison with other Latin American countries during the same time span, in Brazil the era was one of economic and social progress and continuous development.

Source: Young, Jordan. 1967. *The Brazilian Revolution and Aftermath*. Rutgers University Press. pp. 81–97.

Source D

In the elections of 1950, Vargas was returned to office as democratically elected president. If anything, he was more nationalistic in both his pronouncements and his actions during his second administration than in his first. As we have seen, it was during this administration that he created Petrobras and attempted to extend government control over energy and power resources; he also inaugurated his own five-year plan for industrialization.

Ironically, much of Brazil's remarkable industrial progress during these years was due to the mounting investment of foreign capitalists, whom the nationalists, as always, suspected of a variety of evil motives. Vargas became even more outspoken in his criticism of foreign ownership of industry, and he launched a bitter attack against foreign investors, accusing them of "bleeding Brazil." The nationalists cheered each pronouncement. Yet funds continued to flow in from abroad, and industrialization expanded at a rapid pace.

Clearly, Vargas had mastered the rhetoric of the nationalists and adapted it to his own purposes. He relied upon the popular appeal of nationalism more than he had in the past, and these nationalist feelings strengthened his second administration which was less stably anchored than his first.

Source: Burns, Bradford. 1968. *Nationalism in Brazil: A Historical Survey*. New York: Frederick Praeger. pp. 72–89.

Questions

1 According to source A, what the most important contribution made by Vargas? Quote from the document to support your answer.

2 Evaluate the views expressed by historians in sources B and D on the merits of Vargas's economic policy.

3 Compare and contrast the views expressed in sources A and B on the populist characteristics of Vargas.

4 To what extent do you agree that "the Vargas epoch was a mixture of gains and setbacks"?

5 Why and with what success did Vargas use the following approaches to stay in power?
   a Anti-imperialism
   b Nationalism
   c Economic and social progress
   d Anti- Paulista (control by São Paulo)
   e Cult of personality (personal appeal of Vargas)

Populism in Argentina

Juan Perón was an important Argentinean leader for three decades from 1945–74. His popularity peaked during his first term as president (1945–91), when he was married to Eva Perón. Together they captured the hearts and minds of the people with their promise of better days ahead. Perón's rise to power was meteoric and unexpected. In 1941, he had joined the *Grupo de Oficiales Unidos* (the Group of United Officers or GOU) comprised of military officers from middle class backgrounds. Ardent nationalists, they believed in industrialization and modernization and were deeply distressed by the corrupt nature of Argentina's political parties during the 1930s labelled the "Infamous Decade". In 1943, they could no longer tolerate the machinations of President Ramón Castillo and took control. Perón was appointed to a minor cabinet post as Minister of Labor. The government was pro-German and pro-fascist. Perón studied Mussolini's writings, and many officers had been trained by the German military. They had grown to admire the manner in which Germany transformed itself in the 1930s from a vanquished and humiliated nation into a proud and mighty world power. Like Germany, the GUO took control of the unions, censored the media, suppressed opposition and jailed dissidents. As in Germany, the government in Argentina demanded territorial concessions from its neighbours and threatened to destabilize the region. Unlike Germany, however, the tactics failed to intimidate the working classes or neighbouring states.

Juan and Eva Perón in 1946. The glamorous couple became international celebrities.

Perón was gaining power within the GOU. Cunning, capable and charismatic he used his position as labor minister to win the trust and support of organized labor by offering pensions and benefits. In short order he became the Minister of War and then vice president. Rival officers feared his ambition and disliked the "left-wing" programs he implemented and had Perón jailed. But his supporters in the labor movement staged a massive pro-Perón demonstration in the streets of Buenos Aires that forced his release on October 17, 1945.

An election was set for 1946 and Perón ran for the presidency extolling the virtues of democracy. Standing on balcony, above adoring crowds, with his glamorous wife Evita at his side, Perón spreading the message of Argentina for Argentineans, made the election seem like a formality. He was unwittingly aided in his bid by the US Ambassador to Argentina who publically called Perón a fascist. Peron captured 54% of the vote.

Perón's economic plan

Perón called his vision for Argentina "Justicialismo", a political dogma that advocated making accommodations between competing economic and political forces (i.e. capitalism, collectivism and communism). The objective was to attain social harmony, economic prosperity and political stability. Peron's allegiance to Justicialismo had limits and was shelved continually when challenged by the realpolitik of events and practical problems. Perón's success relied on three tactics.

First, creating a coalition of the traditional élites and the working classes; second, extolling patriotism and nationalism by attacking internal and external forces that prevented Argentina from attaining its true destiny (such as nationalizing key industries); and third, provide immediate social benefits (health, education, pensions) to the workers. In the short term, this third tactic paid the biggest dividends creating a cadre of dedicated supporters who remained a force in Argentinean politics long after Perón was removed. His priorities as a populist president are contained in a letter written to newly elected Chilean President Carlos Ibáñez del Campo in 1952.

> Give the people, especially the workers, all that is possible. When it seems to you that already you are giving them too much, give them more. You will see the results. Everybody will try to frighten you with the spectre of an economic collapse. But all of this is a lie. There is nothing more elastic than the economy, which everyone fears so much because no one understands it.

Circumstances now favoured Perón. A postwar export boom of wheat and beef to war-ravaged Europe produced a large foreign exchange surplus which Peron funnelled into industrialization and ushered in a period of significant industrial expansion. By 1948 industrial workers wages had increased by 20% without crimping the profitability of the export sector and industrial profits remained significant even with the wage increases.

Next, the government implemented it's first five year plan that proposed large-scale government intervention in the economy and the reassertion of Argentina's control of its own economy. The first interventionist agency was the El Instituto Argentino de Promoción del Intercambio (the Argentine Institute for Trade Promotion or IAPI), a state trade monopoly to ensure foreign markets bought Argentinean goods and commodities. Next, workers' wages received a boost and the military's budget was increased (Perón never cut military spending). He ensured the loyalty of industrialists with government patronage, for example, government contracts. He then made good on his promise to nationalize foreign companies and expropriated British-owned railroads, the US-controlled telephone network, and the French-owned dock yards. Compensation was high as the government paid the price demanded by the owners; a costly strategy, it avoided a serious international incident with Argentina's main trading and investment partners. He also nationalized the foreign-owned Central Bank which ensured the government's directly control over fiscal policy. Finally, the government paid off the nation's foreign debt in July 1947 followed by Perón's "Declaration of Economic Independence."

1948 was the high-water mark of Perón's success, his "New Argentina" had gone from dream to reality virtually overnight, but it didn't last

Map of Argentina.

long. Two forces conspired to end the prosperity. In 1949, foreign competition in commodities was largely responsible for a trade deficit and inflation began to spiral upward to 31%, twice the 1948 rate. Commodity prices were dropping and prices on imported consumer goods were rising. The situation was further compounded by a drought that lowered production for several years, made worse by the fact that farmers lagged behind in adopting modern technology and techniques. These factors—inflation, trade deficit, deflated commodity prices, lower harvest yields—decreased foreign demand, resulting in real wages falling 20% and, as they fell, so did Perón's popularity.

Something had to be done to stop the economic downturn and the government resorted to tight credit, reduced spending, wage and price controls. But things got worse. By the early 1950s, world commodity prices and demand had dropped sharply and the IAPI's ability to finance industry was eroded. No relief to these problems appeared at hand.

Activity

The Justicialists

Juan Perón wrote this manifesto after losing power in 1955. This was at the height of the Cold War between the United States and the Soviet Union.

On Capitalism and communism

For us, the justicialists, the world today finds itself divided between capitalists and communists in conflict: we are neither one nor the other. We aspire ideologically to stand outside of that conflict between global interests. This doesn't imply in any way that we are in the internationalist camp, dodging the issue.

We believe that capitalism as well as communism are systems already overtaken by the times. We consider capitalism to be the exploitation of the man by capital and communism as the exploitation of the individual by the state. Both "insectify" the individual by means of different systems.

We believe more; we think that the abuses of capitalism are the cause and that communism is the effect. Without capitalism, communism would have no reason to exist; we equally believe that, with the extinction of the cause, there will be the beginning of the end for the effect.

Source: Perón, Juan. (trans. Edsall, T. M.).1958. *La Fuerza es el Derecho de las Bestias* (Force is the Right of the Beasts). Montevideo: Ediciones Cicerón. p. 18.

Questions

1 Perón blames Argentina's problems on two outside forces. Name these forces? What does he believe is the ideological stance for his country?

2 What is his position regarding the superpower struggle based on this excerpt? Is the argument convincing?

3 Based on your knowledge of Perón, what was his approach as president to implementing a "Justicialist" regime in Argentina?

4 Would you agree that, for Perón, pragmatism and maintaining power were more important than ideological considerations?

The second term, 1951–54

Perón wanted a second term as president but the 1853 constitution imposed a one-term limit. Undaunted, Perón amended the constitution so that he could contest the 1951 election. Next, he created a political party, the Perónists and was soundly reelected with 67% of 6.9 million votes, in part due to the extension of voting rights to women in 1947, a move supported by Eva Perón. Eva (Evita) was adored by the workers and urban poor, the so-called *descamisados* (the shirtless ones). She had become indispensible to Perón as the popular face of the regime, the nation's heart and soul. Juan and Eva were inseparable. Perón wanted Eva to be vice president but the military vetoed the move. If anything happened to Perón, a woman would become president and commander in chief. This began a decline in support for Perón from the military.

By 1951, Juan and Eva Perón were firmly in power. Buoyed by their movie star status and the unquestioned loyalty of the people, Perón became increasingly reckless and authoritarian. It started when the government seized the leading opposition newspaper, *La Prensa*, and drove it out of business. In 1952, the tough economic measures seemed to pay off and the economy started to turn around. But a second five year plan was adopted that changed the course of Perón's populist agenda. He could no longer afford lavish wage settlements and actively pursued foreign investment to ingest new funds into industrial development. Over the next three years, he struck a number of deals with foreign companies to drill oil and produce automobiles, borrowing foreign capital to buy technology and increase industrial efficiency and output which would increase profit margins but had the unfortunate consequence of increasing unemployment. Perón further alienated the military when he cancelled a military aviation project in favour of funding automobile production. To make matters worse, the government printed more money increasing supply ninefold and with it inflation. Then tragedy struck: Evita died of cancer at the age of 33 in 1952 and Perón's popularity plummeted.

The legacy of Eva Perón

In a political system dominated by machismo chauvinism, Eva set a powerful example for Latin American women. She told them that "Just as workers could wage their own struggle for liberation, so too could only women be the salvation of women." As the de facto minister of labor, she proved herself to be tough-minded, benevolent and petulant as the situation required which earned her the reputation as the lady with the whip. In 1947, she toured Spain Italy

---

Maria Eva Duarte de Perón (1919–1952)

Eva Duarte was born in rural Argentina to a poor family. At age 15, in 1934, she moved to Buenos Aires and pursued a career in radio and film gaining local fame as a cabaret singer. "Evita" soon joined the society of high-ranking army officers and acquired fine clothes, jewels and a bad reputation. She met Colonel Juan Perón sometime in 1944. The couple were married the following year and during their engagement she became a dedicated Perónist. Thereafter her rise to fame and power was meteoric. In 1946–52 she was one of the most famous celebrity icons in the world. Shunned by the upper classes, she captured the emotional imagination of the Argentinian nation, championing workers' rights and women's suffrage. She founded the charitable Eva Perón Foundation and a female branch of the Perónist Party after women received the vote in 1947, which they exercised for the first time in 1951. Eva received the vice-presidential nomination of the Perónist party in 1951 but was opposed by the military and bourgeoisie. Not long after she withdrew her acceptance of the nomination, also due to declining health. She died of cancer on July 26, 1952, and the nation went into extravagant mourning: clocks were stopped, the grief was palatable and many called for her sainthood. "Don't cry for me Argentina," the haunting anthem from the 1978 musical *Evita* symbolizes her celebrity status for Argentinians, many years after her untimely death.

---

descamisados (the shirtless ones) was a term of affection for the working poor coined by Eva Perón.

and France and was received by the French president and had an audience with the pope. She charmed the Europeans and the trip made her the most visible (and recognizable) female political figure in the world. She returned determined to help Argentina's *descamisados*.

Eva set up the Eva Perón Foundation in 1948 after being snubbed by the socially elite womens' *Sociedad de Benficia*. A presidential decree gave Eva control over charities and the foundation's aim was to provide scholarships, schools, hospitals and orphanages for the underprivileged. Eva provided the first 10,000 pesos from her own purse and donations poured in, eventually totalling hundreds of millions of pesos. At its height, the foundation employed over 14,000 workers, purchased 500,000 sewing machines, 400,000 pairs of shoes and 200,000 cooking pots for distributed to the poor. Homes, schools and hospitals were built and for the first time in Argentina's history healthcare was available to all citizens regardless of race or gender. Pictures of Eva working with the poor, visiting hospitals and schools and dispensing tenderness to all made her the heroine of the people. The foundation's accounting methods were rather slipshod and rumours of fraud and embezzlement, including a Swiss bank account for funnelled funds persisted. Whether these accusations had merit remains a question of historical controversy. Nevertheless, the foundation provided large numbers of low-income Argentineans with a degree of social assistance that did not exist prior to Eva's arrival on the scene. After Perón was ousted from government the foundation fell into disarray.

A womens' branch of the Perónist party was founded by Eva Peron after women received the vote in 1947. By 1951 it had over half a million members. Politically and socially active the party established 3,600 offices nationwide and from these centres dispensed healthcare, legal advice and social services. The party helped women attend university and the number doubled overnight. In 1951 women voted for the first time; 90% of eligible women voted, 65% for Peron. Twenty-four female Perónist candidates were elected as deputies and seven as senators, giving Argentina the distinction of having the most elected female representatives of any Western democracy. The party remained active in the Perónist movement despite the setbacks of Eva's death and Juan's exile and played a significant role in Perón's return to power in 1973.

Perón, realizing his hold on power was becoming increasingly tenuous, went on the attack. He ordered the National Liberating Alliance, Perón's version of the paramilitary Nazi brown shirts, and the federal police were force to intimidate and exile his opponents. The Perón-controlled General Confederation of Labor muzzled dissidents in the ranks of workers and prominent leaders were jailed.

The coalition was breaking up but the government refused to bend to the demands of industrialists to lower wages. In retaliation the business leaders joined with agrarian interests to form an economic

élite that increasingly opposed Perón. The military had already
lost faith in Perón and were further upset with his scandalous
behaviour following Eva's death. Wage and price controls further
contributed to eroding the all-important labor vote. But Perón
wasn't finished yet and his next target was the Roman Catholic
Church. Why he attacked the church remains a mystery but it
sealed his fate with the military. Divorce was legalized, and the
government took control of church-run schools. The Perónists
claim that the church was the last hurdle in the achievement of
Argentinean independence. The military began to plot Perón's
overthrow. The first attempt to oust him in June 1954 failed.
In September another attempt was made and Perón had the choice
to flee or fight. He threatened to arm the *descamisados* but lost his
nerve and fled to Paraguay.

After a decade in power, Perón's personal appeal could no longer
hide the shortcomings of his economic policies and increasing
disconnected from his followers. As Perón transformed from
populist leader to authoritarian dictator he lost the support of the
military which had been the cornerstone of his regime. The regime
that had given millions of Argentineans hope for a better future
was ended, but the legacy lived on. The Perónist Party survived
and paved the way for Perón's triumphant, albeit, brief return to
power 1973.

Populism: the balance sheet

Within weeks of each other, the two most important populist
leaders of the postwar era had been ousted from power and were
replaced by ultra-right-wing military dictatorships that tried to turn
back the clock and roll back the gains made by the working classes
in particular under Perón and Vargas. Why had the populist leaders
failed to survive politically and did they make a difference during
their time in office? Where there countries better off after they left
office? Two problems that were to some extent beyond their control
had contributed to their demise. The state-led ISI policies were
initially successful in helping to create an industrial base, alleviating
the effects of the Great Depression. After the Second World War,
protectionist policies had run their course and the ISI was no longer
viable in the vibrant world economy of the 1950s and 1960s.
The second factor was the new reality of the Cold War and the
pervasive influence of the Cuban Revolution on Latin America in
the 1960s. The major flaw with populism was that it relied on
charismatic and influential leaders to create and maintain the
fragile coalition between groups who were bound to be in conflict
(e.g. workers and industrialists). Populism regimes could not
survive for long without leaders like Perón and Vargas. What
happened subsequently, when the military took control over
the next two decades, remains a dark chapter in the history of
the region.

Activity

Argentina under Perón: an assessment

Source A

It has been said that without freedom there can be no social justice and to that I respond that without social justice there can be no freedom. You, co-workers, have lived in the drawn out times of the so-called freedom of the oligarchies; and I ask you, co-workers: if there was freedom before or if there is freedom now. To those that say that there is freedom in the nations where workers are exploited, I will answer with the words of our workers: what beautiful freedom, the freedom to die of hunger! And to those that accuse us of being a dictator, I will say that the worst of all dictatorships is the foolish ineptness of governments. ... Let us be united, because if we are united, we are invincible; do not let politics divide the workers unions or pitch some against others, because the workers' cause is above all other interests.

Source: Labor Day Speech by Juan Domingo Perón, May 1, 1949, Plaza de Mayo Square, Buenos Aires, Argentina (excerpt translated from Spanish found in http://www.elhistoriador.com.ar/).

Source B

During a historical period in which Argentinean society was socially and politically fractured as a result of, on the one hand, the authoritarian practices of the Peronist government, and, on the other, the conservative political positions of the middle classes, who were not willing to allow a new distribution of the symbolic capital or the social recognition which they felt they deserved, or the value of their cultural capital and the technical skills associated with it, Peronist schoolbooks—innovative in some respects, but transmitters of hierarchic and authoritarian values in others— continued to offer, like their predecessors in earlier decades, an image of social harmony that did not exist. While the schoolbooks of the initial decades of the century ignored the existence of power relations and social conflict, or presented them as something that was natural and therefore morally justified, Peronist schoolbooks related situations of inequality, injustice and denigration to the past.

Source: Rodríguez, Miguel Somoza. "Poverty, Exclusion and Social Conflict in the Schoolbooks of Argentina during the First Peronist Period." *Paedagogica Historica*. Vol. 43, no. 5. October 2007. pp. 633–52.

Source C

Though Evita was the most prominent female political figure in Argentine history, she played a secondary role in addressing housewives during the government's campaign, echoing Perón's call for austerity with few variations. The agony and prostration before her death from cancer in July 1952 only partially explains her lack of involvement, because she continued to work at her foundation and to make public appearances up until her final days. Perón, in contrast, led the campaign personally, talked to housewives directly, and put himself in the position of culinary advisor and shopping consultant, an unexpected role for a man in the 1950s in Argentina and even more unexpected for a president. The way he assumed his role may be peculiar, but the role itself was not: the ubiquitous patriarchal figure who presides over the nation, the aggregate sum of households. In this regard, the national economy depended on women's decisions but Perón was there to guide them in the process. Women were doing the cooking, but Perón still decided what was for dinner.

Source: Milanesio, Natalia. "The Guardian Angels of the Domestic Economy": Housewives' Responsible Consumption in Peronist Argentina." *Journal of Women's History*. vol. 18, no. 3. Fall 2006. pp. 91–117.

Source D

Some parts of the life of Juan Perón read like a radio script, in which, of course, the radio actress Eva Duarte plays herself. There is about both of them a staged quality, contrived, so that in the end there is no sense of tragedy, no inclination toward pity for them, just a feeling that their audience—the "shirtless ones" was the melodramatic phrase—was used for corrupt purposes. Yet Perónismo lives on, representing a strong force among Argentines, a political movement that has outlived the follies of its progenitor. It does so because Juan Perón touched a nerve among working people, one that had been ignored, if not oppressed, by Argentine elites. For that reason, Juan Perón deserves to be remembered.

Source: Adams, Jerome. 1991. *Liberators and Patriots in Latin America*. Jefferson, NC: McFarland.

Questions

1 Look at source A and pick out examples of populism. What message is Perón giving to the workers and their unions?

2 Compare and contrast Perón's patriarchal role represented in sources B and C.

3 Considering origin and purpose, what are the value and limitations of sources A and D to historian's writing about Perón's style of government?

4 Using your own knowledge and the sources, discuss how Perón dealt with traditionally marginalized Argentines: workers, women and children.

Military regimes In Latin America, 1960s–80s

The landscape changed quickly after the Cuban Revolution, and throughout Latin America the military seized control in the first years of the 1960s. There were ten coups alone between 1961 and 1964. Military dictatorships were not new to Latin America but the regimes that appeared in the 1960s were different. Before Fidel Castro, the military took control to restore order or remove corrupt civilian politicians. Following Castro's revolution a more pressing reason to take control was to prevent further Cuban-style revolutions. The military governments were reactionary and anti-revolutionary. They were determined to expel or destroy communist and left-wing movements by any means necessary and establish closer economic and political relations with the West, in particular, the United States. Internally, they were supported by conservative economic and political elites who stood to lose the most if the communists succeeded.

The counterinsurgency strategy adopted by these regimes came from the French experience in Algeria and became a pan-Latin American effort to resist revolution culminating in Operation Condor (1975), a cooperative military effort between Argentina, Bolivia, Chile, Paraguay and Uruguay. The first tactic was to pacify the general populace and eliminate it as a safe haven. Castro, they correctly surmised, had survived because he had earned the trust and support of the people. Without this haven, the insurgents would be exposed and eliminated. The tactics included the rapid expansion of capitalism, a diminution of legal and civil rights, suspension of democracy, control of the media, outlawing trade unions and the wholesale application of violent repression, including incarceration, torture and assassinations. The threat was real and the tactics worked. During the 1960s, 25 communist guerrilla movements appeared across the continent. Many groups were quickly eliminated or dissolved under government pressure. Others waged war for a decade and after limited initial success became more of a nuisance than a *bona fide* threat. Several of the most prominent groups were Fidelista (Cuban) or Soviet supported. They were hunted down by specially trained elite units. Che Guevara was captured and executed in 1967 by one such unit of the Bolivian army. The assumption was that the guerrilla fighters, student protest, trade union activism and media unrest were part of a coordinated effort to destabilize and overthrow the governments of Latin America and were being orchestrated by Moscow. What the military did not know, at least initially, was that the rebels and dissidents were much more fractured than that, and engaged in internecine disputes that undermined any possibility of a coordinated movement.

The Cold War and Castro changed how Latin American generals thought about security and approaches to military training. This shift was most pronounced in the training of a new generation of young officers who studied the social and economic conditions of their own country in addition to the more traditional military curricula. Senior officers, colonels and generals from

Latin-American military coups, 1961–64	
El Salvador	January 24, 1961
Ecuador	March 29, 1962
Perú	July 18, 1962
Guatemala	March 31, 1963
Ecuador	July 11, 1963
Dominican Republic	September 25, 1963
Brazil	March 31, 1964
Bolivia	November 4, 1964.

across Latin America attended the same staff colleges as part of the Inter-American Military System. Small wonder these regimes looked similar in power. The sub-text was that civilian governments were incapable of removing the revolutionary threat. Only the military, they agreed, had the knowledge, skills, personnel and equipment to do the job. The suspension of civilian rule appeared to be the only viable solution to the problem. Once the threat had been removed, consideration could then be given to restoring civilian government. Across Latin America, beginning in early 1960, the military seized control in ten countries including Brazil and Argentina and remained in power until the 1980s. Each coup was unique in its own right according to national circumstances, military traditions, cultural imperatives and the personal qualities of the leaders. Nevertheless, they shared a common cause to eliminate the communist threat and to restore law and order. They also represented a new strain of military intervention, no longer selecting, installing and supporting a chosen civilian leader but taking on the role of government themselves. In the case of leaders like General Pinochet in Chile, this was to evolve into long-term dictatorships.

Once in power, these military governments moved rapidly to eliminate or reduce social welfare programs and workers benefits, lowering wages and outlawing unions. This was designed to attract foreign investment which would be the most expedient way to create a prosperous capitalist economy. These leaders reduced government intervention in the market place in favour of private investment, while also suppressing democracy and democratic institutions and organizations. Individual political rights were subsumed by the collective security of the nation.

These regimes also received considerable support from the United States. This included military equipment, counterinsurgency training and the tacit support of every president from Johnson to Carter in support of containment. They preferred to support repressive ultra-right-wing military dictatorships and turn a blind eye to human rights abuses rather than permit any more successful Cuban style revolutions that would further expand Soviet influence in the Americas. But by the late 1970s the communist threat was over; only in Nicaragua had it succeeded, briefly. Internal and external pressure brought an end to the dictatorships, replaced by new experiments in democracy. Yet the stain and scars of military rule was not easily forgotten. For two decades the military had ruled with an iron fist, resembling in the conquering and subjugation of a people, the tactics of an invading army in reaching far beyond the goal of protecting national security.

Military government in Brazil

Getúlio Vargas committed suicide August 24, 1954, refusing to resign or flee from the military coup. Juscelino Kubitschek was president in 1956–60, promising 50 years of progress in five, but corruption and inflation were rampant and he was replaced. João Goulart took office in 1961. He had been Secretary of Labor under Vargas and initiated populist-like reforms to redistribute wealth. Goulart was popular with workers and the lower classes but the middle-class and powerful business community called for his removal. On March 31, 1964, the military, of whom Goulart had previously been critical, seized power. The agreement was that no leader would stay in power for more than one term. During the 20 years of military rule they installed five presidents.

The first was Marshal Humberto Castelo Branco (1964–67). He set out to purify the economic system by ending Goulart's populist reforms. Castelo coined a new term "manipulated democracy" to defend his regimes policies that were anything but democratic. This initial period has been described as rule by military moderates (terms not usually paired together) because they used existing civilian institutions and bureaucracies to govern on military terms. The subtext, however, was the gradual yet perceptible reduction of political rights and the suppression of dissent. Over the next five years, the military enacted legislation that created an absolute military dictatorship.

The first of these Institutional Acts, passed in 1964, declared that the cleansing of Brazil's corrupt political system had begun. The Act affirmed the 1946 constitution and then did an about-face and cancelled presidential elections. Presidential powers were increased and included the discretion to suspend political rights and remove elected officials for suspected corruption and subversion. The Act had effectively prevented left-wing political parties from contesting elections because anyone elected could be removed for subversion. The government also took control of Labor unions and farmers' organizations which the military considered a safe haven for communist organizers and agitators.

Castelo's government then called for tough economic measures to fight inflation and attract foreign (mainly US) investment. This included a guarantee against expropriation of new foreign companies and ventures. It was an unhappy time for workers; strikes were banned, wages rolled back and social welfare programs reduced. The result was that Brazil's poor got poorer. Not surprisingly, resistance grew and the military responded with a second Institutional Act in October 1965. The Act further reduced democracy, regulated acceptable parties and decreed that only candidates approved by the government could run for office. In addition, the president could dissolve Congress and rule by decree. The President controlled the Supreme Court, appointed pro-military judges and anyone charged with subversion was tried by a military tribunal instead of a civilian court.

Institutional Act no. 3 was passed in February 1966. The military extended its power to the hinterland and ended the election of state governors and city mayors. These changes were codified in the Constitution of 1967. The following year, 1968, was the year of worker and student rebellion, protests and illegal strikes in Brazil as elsewhere. The normally pliant Congress refused to support the president when he ordered the leader of the opposition removed for supporting the students. This led to Institutional Act no. 5 which suspended the 1967 constitution, dissolved Congress and state legislatures, suspended **habeas corpus**, tightened censorship and signalled the end of civil rights and the start of violent oppression.

Habeas corpus literally means "produce the body," and is a time-honoured protection in democratic legal systems against incarceration without being charged or put on trial.

In November 1969, General Emilia Garrastazu Medici (1969–74) took office with significantly more power than Vargas had during the *Estado Novo*. The opposition went underground and began urban guerrilla warfare. The government's counterinsurgency tactics focused on attacking the guerrillas along with their families, friends and associates. Organised crime increased and the police and the military were supplemented by private death squads to whom the government turned a blind eye. It was vigilante justice, instilling a reign of terror.

Brazil's economic turnaround
In 1967, Brazil's economic planners had reduced government spending and instituted wage and price controls to fight inflation. The measures worked, inflation fell, and the economy, fuelled by foreign investment and loans, experienced an average five year growth rate of 10% of GDP. It was called the Brazilian miracle and admirers touted the success as an example for others to follow. The recovery had significant shortcomings. The growth was unequal with the greatest gains in the economically stable and wealthy coffee and industrial sectors. In the rural areas, growth was otherwise

stagnant. Wealth was increasingly concentrated in the pockets of fewer and fewer Brazilians. The earnings of 5% of Brazilians accounted for 39% of the national income while the low-income earners accounted for 12% (a drop of 6% since the military takeover). The plight of the poor was made worse by growing unemployment lines and the rapid reduction of social services. By 1973, the recovery had ended. Brazil was an oil-importing country and with OPEC's price gouging started a worldwide recession that had a big effect on Brazil's export economy. The nation was required to borrow large sums of money to support itself, increasing national debt.

The end of the dicatorship

A few years earlier, President Ernesto Geisel had promised a "distensão," a gradual end of the dictatorship and the return of political rights. Under Geisel, there was less repression and public debate was tolerated to some extent. Geisel's replacement, João Figueiredo, stated publically that it was time for the army to return to the barracks and return government to the civilians. He signed an amnesty that released political prisoners and set to work dismantling the dictatorship. Why, after 15 years in power, did the military decided it was time to relinquish power? The nation was safe from revolution. It was evident that the military's economic plan had not solved Brazil's problems. Despite considerable growth in some areas of the economy, the basic problems of poverty, social injustice, illiteracy, poor healthcare, and regional disparities had been made worse. There was considerable pressure on the government for a return to civilian rule.

The military regime in Argentina, 1976–82

In the spring of 1973, after two decades in exile, Juan Perón made a triumphant return to Argentina. In October he was elected president and his new wife Isabel became vice president. The Perónist Party had made it happen. The Party had been outlawed during the years following Perón's departure but had been an active and influential force in Argentina after the ban was lifted. The euphoria of Perón's return was short-lived. On July 1, 1974, he suffered a fatal heart attack (he was 78). Isabel took over, becoming the first female president in Latin America but her term in office was characterized by political and economic instability. On March 24, 1976, she was ousted by a military junta lead by General Jorge Rafael Videla.

The business community had started the coup when it approached the military to restore order. They were concerned about the growing number of foreign businessmen being kidnapped by urban guerrillas and held for ransom (170 in 1973 alone). The armed wing of the *Ejército Revolucionario del Pueblo* (Peoples' Revolutionary Army or ERP) had exploded dozens of bombs and targeted key government officials including planting a bomb under the bed of the Chief of the Federal Police. These tactics scared off potential foreign investors and the rebels' war chests were brimming with ransom money to buy weapons. To make matters worse, the economy was collapsing, inflation reached 17,000% in 1976. Labor abandoned the Perónists and joined forces with right-wing thugs and death squads. In 1975 alone, 137 soldiers and police were killed by the guerrillas. The country was in a state of anarchy. In September 1975, leaders of the Argentine Industrial Union, comprised of the nation's foremost business leaders, met with the army commander General Jorge Rafael to plan a coup. Six months later, the military was back in power.

The process for national reconstruction

By the time of the takeover, the military had become accustomed to governing and considered themselves the guardians of the nation. They determined that it was their mission to impose order on an unruly and revolutionary civilian population, cleanse the society of communism, populism and collectivism and steer the nation along the path of order and security. They were willing to use any means necessary to achieve these goals. Unlike in Brazil, they did not assume power gradually, but took over the entire nation from the start. The new regime was headed by three officers who held the reins of power until 1981. Generals Jorge Rafael Videla and Orlando Ramon Agosti and Admiral Emilio Eduardo Massera all took a turn at the presidency, effectively running it as a triumvirate.

The ruling triumvirate: (left to right) Massera, Videla and Agosti. These men orchestrated the 1976 coup and "Dirty War." They were later tried and convicted of war crimes.

Shortly after taking power they declared their intentions and promised a fundamental reorganization of the nation, under a plan known as *El Proceso de Reorganización Nacional* (The Process for National Reconstruction). The *Proceso* was based on the model provided by **General Pinochet** in Chile: the economic guide was supplied by **Milton Friedman**, from the Chicago School of Economics, who favoured supply side capitalist solutions; the military tactics were based on the measure applied by the French counterinsurgency in the Algerian civil war. The *Proceso* had three goals: reinstate the essential values of the state (as defined by the military), eliminate subversion, and promote economic development. A military model was imposed on the courts and civil service, and democracy was suspended with opposition political parties and unions outlawed. The constitution was ignored and elected assemblies were dissolved. Admiral Massera became the regime's first president with the self-declared mandate that: "God has decided that we should have the responsibility of designing the future."

Economic policy

The first step was to control inflation and reinvigorate the economy. The goal was to reintegrate Argentina into the world economy, reduce state control and end ISI policies and tariffs. The measures were draconian. Real wages were reduced, social welfare benefits were stopped and foreign investment and loans flooded the economy. Similar to Brazil, the lower classes suffered the most as the standard of living plummeted, unemployment increased and government support dried up. The importation of cheap foreign goods overwhelmed Argentinean industry that had been protected for so long by the ISI and now found they were unable to compete. The government took

General Augusto Pinochet ousted the democratically elected socialist government of Salvador Allende in a coup on September 11, 2003, with the covert support of the CIA. Pinochet's regime was infamous for its brutality and became the example for the "Dirty War".

Milton Friedman was an influential, Nobel-Prize winning economist from the University of Chicago. In the 1960s, he rejected Keynesian economics and argued that it would cause stagflation (high inflation and minimal economic growth). He advocated reduced taxation, privatization and deregulation of industry.

over all institutions capable of challenging its authority: Congress, the courts, political parties, unions and the press.

"The Dirty War", 1976–81

The military's strategy was simple: eliminate dissidents and guerrillas, their families and friends, along with anyone else associated with the guerrillas. The terror would last until Argentina was purified. In that sense, the Dirty War was brilliant in its excesses. Between 10,000 and 30,000 Argentineans vanished. They were called *los desaparecidos* (the disappeared). No records were kept of their arrest, detention, torture, killing or the disposal of their bodies. The majority were unarmed civilians, students, unionists and Perónists who disappeared because they protested against the junta's policies. Over 340 camps and torture centers were secretly constructed throughout the countryside, the most infamous being an abandoned automobile factory where thousands were executed. The government steadfastly denied their existence or any knowledge of whereabouts of the *desaparecidos*.

The second tactic involved special counterterrorist units that hunted and destroyed armed guerrilla groups. The most important being the Soviet-backed *El Proceso de Reorganización Nacional*, (People's Liberation Army) which was responsible for dozens of bombings, kidnappings and murders. The ERP was eventually driven from the cities and fled to the countryside with the army in hot pursuit. They won a few skirmishes early on but was defeated in a series of pitched battles between 1976 and 1979. About 8,600 *detenido desaparecido* (detained disappeared) were eventually released from detention camps. Several thousand had been imprisoned for five years or more.

International attention was aroused by the *Madres desaparacido* (mothers of the disappeared), a grass roots protest movement that met each Sunday in Plaza de Mayo in front of the presidential palace. They demanded the government release information on the whereabouts of their sons and daughters who had disappeared during the dirty war. No information was forthcoming. In fact, the government denied any wrongdoing or knowledge of the "disappeared." Initially, the government ignored the protest movement, but this became increasingly difficult in the face of growing international awareness of the human rights abuses. The *Madres de la Plaza de Mayo* played a significant role in undermining the junta and in bringing those responsible to justice.

The end of the dictatorship

By 1979, the Argentinian military dictatorship had soundly defeated the insurgents but like Brazil had failed to stimulate the economy. In 1981, the GNP had fallen by 11%, stagflation had returned, the national debt had substantially increased and unemployment and poverty seemed unsolvable. A resurgent labor movement took to the streets. The triumvirate had been replaced by General Leopoldo Galtieri, who led the invasion of the *Malvinas* (Falkland) Islands in April 1982. This short but costly war with the United Kingdom ended in defeat and the end of the dictatorship. In 1983, Argentina held its first elections in nearly a decade.

Military regimes: an assessment

Brazil and Argentina were two examples of repressive military regimes that dominated Latin America for two decades during the 1960s and 1970s. These regimes emerged as a direct response to the success of the Cuban Revolution and Fidel Castro's threat to export revolution throughout the region. Following the Cuban Revolution, euphoria swept Latin America among left-wing radicals and dissidents suggesting that political change was inevitable. But the launch of a coordinated pre-emptive strike by the military, supported and to a large extent orchestrated by the United States, put an end to the aspirations of those national groups inspired by the Cuban example, also giving rise to a more deadly Latin American version of McCarthyism. If the anti-revolutionary regimes were successful in stopping communism they did not solve the economic or social disparities. The gap between rich and poor increased and the rights of women, workers and visible minorities made no headway. Moreover, these regimes were willing to suspend democracy and use wholesale, indiscriminate violence, incarceration and torture to prevent opposition and populist movements from gaining root. These regimes still casts a shadow over Latin America. Many of those most responsible for the terror, notably Augusto Pinochet of Chile and the Argentinean triumvirate of Agosti, Massera and Videlo, were given **political amnesty** or died before they were prosecuted. Many of the *Madres de la Plaza de Mayo* died without ever knowing what happened to their children, but 20 years on their fate is no longer in doubt.

Political amnesty After the Second World War, Allied jurists and prosecutors created a new category of international law called "Crimes Against Humanity", defined as the indiscriminate use of violence against civilians. Japanese and German leaders where tried, convicted and executed or sentenced to life imprisonment. The International Court of the Hague is responsible for prosecuting war criminals and recently convicted Serbian leaders who were responsible for the ethnic cleansing of Croatia in the early 1990s. In 2002, the Court decided that forced disappearance constituted a crime against humanity.

The situation in Latin America was different because it was the national governments of Argentina or Brazil that suspended civil rights and murdered their own citizens. In 1985, nine high ranking leaders of the Argentinian junta including Videla, Massera and Agosti were tried and convicted by six Argentine judges and sentence to life imprisonment. In 1989 and 1990 President Carlos Menem granted the generals amnesty. The amnesty laws were overturned by the Argentine Supreme court in 2005 but by then most had died of natural causes. As a consequence, they spent virtually no time in jail for their actions.

Extended discussion point

1 To what extent were the military dictators justified in using the tactics they employed to prevent a Castro-style revolution?

2 How do these tactics compare to the investigations of Senator Joe McCarthy, and the repression of civil liberties for communist sympathisers in the US?

3 How real was the threat of Soviet-style communism taking root in Latin America?

Discussion point

A question of compensation

State sponsored oppression of its citizens takes on many forms. During the Second World War, following Pearl Harbor, the US and Canadian government stripped citizens of Japanese ancestry of their constitutional rights, seized their property and interned them behind barbed wire in camps for the duration of the war. Decades later, the US and Canadian governments apologized and paid compensation to the internees or their families.

Should the *Madres de la Plaza de Mayo* or their families receive an official apology and compensation from the Argentinean government?

Exam practice and further resources

Sample exam questions

1 Compare and contrast the domestic policies of US presidents Truman and Eisenhower.

2 To what extent can it be said that populism succeeded? Discuss this view with reference to two populist leaders in Latin America in 1945–79.

3 Analyze the main developments in the domestic policies of Canadian governments from Diefenbaker to Chrétien.

4 Examine the successes and failures of Fidel Castro's domestic policies in Cuba in 1958–79.

5 For what reasons and with what consequences was there a Quiet Revolution in Canada?

Recommended further reading

Latin America

Tulio Halperín Donghi (trans. John Charles Chasteen). 1993. *The Contemporary History of Latin America.* Palgrave Macmillan.

Richard Gott. 2004. *Cuba: A New History.* New Haven and London: Yale University Press.

Steven Levitsky. 2003. *Transforming Labor-Based Parties in Latin America: Argentine Peronism in Comparative Perspective.* Cambridge University Press.

Thomas E. Skidmore, Peter H. Smith and James N. Green. 2010. *Modern Latin America.* 7th edn. New York: Oxford University Press.

United States

William H. Chafe. 2007. *The Unfinished Journey: America Since World War II.* 6th edn. New York: Oxford University Press.

William H. Chafe, Robert H. Sitkoff and Beth Bailey (eds). 2008. *A History of Our Time: Readings on Postwar America.* 7th edn. New York: Oxford University Press.

Larry Madaras. 2008. *Taking Sides: Clashing views in United States History since l945.* 3rd edn. Boston: McGraw-Hill Higher Education.

Canada

Robert Bothwell, Ian Drummond and John English. 2001. *Canada since l945: Power, Politics and Provincialism.* Rev. edn. Toronto: University of Toronto Press.

J. M. Bumsted. 2008. *The Peoples of Canada: A Post-Confederation History.* Toronto: Oxford University Press.

R. Douglas Francis, Richard Jones and Donald B. Smith. *2008. Destinies: Canadian History Since Confederation.* 6th edn. Toronto: Nelson Education Ltd. Online resources at http://www.destinies6e.nelson.com/faculty.

Don Gillmor, Achille Michaud and Pierre Turgeon. 2001. *Canada: A People's History.* Toronto: McClelland and Stewart.

6 The Cold War and the Americas, 1945–1981

This chapter looks at the Americas between 1945–81, a period that, as stated in the IB Diploma Programme History Guide, "was dominated by the global conflict of the Cold War." The Cold War is often studied as a contest of ideology, diplomatic movements, military activities, and political actions involving two protagonists, the United States and the Soviet Union, locked in a contest for dominance across the Eurasian land mass, focused on Central Europe and far eastern Asia. From its beginnings, the Cold War policies of the two superpowers, especially the United States, had significant and continuing effects on the countries of the Americas, from Argentina and Chile in the south, to the islands of the Caribbean, and to Canada in the north.

While the United States pursued policies designed to solidify the region as a bulwark against the Soviet Union and communism, some nations of the region chose to oppose the US, others to closely ally themselves with their large Northern neighbor, while several charted a neutral path. Regardless, Cold War pressures affected all countries in the Americas, significantly contributing to domestic agendas and the response to international events, from economic policies through to intervention in civil wars.

By the end of this chapter, students should be able to:

- assess the policies of President Truman, containment and its implications for the Americas; the rise of McCarthyism and its effects on domestic and foreign policies of the United States; the Cold War and its impact on society and culture

- discuss the involvement of the Americas in the Korean War: the reasons for participation; military developments; diplomatic and political outcomes of the conflict

- review the policies of President Eisenhower and US Secretary of State John Foster Dulles: the reasons for the New Look, its implementation and repercussions for the region

- understand the United States' involvement in the Vietnam War: the reasons for the conflict, nature of the involvement at different stages; domestic effects and the end of the war.

- evaluate US foreign policies from presidents Kennedy to Carter including, the characteristics of, and reasons for these policies and their implications for the region: Kennedy's Alliance for Progress; Nixon's covert operations and Chile; Carter's quest for human rights and the Panama Canal Treaty

- understand the effects of the Cold War in Chile: the reasons for foreign and domestic policies, and their implementation.

This chapter is organized to cover the Cold War in the Americas across several main areas. A significant focus is placed on the policies and actions of United States' presidents from Harry Truman to Jimmy

Carter. This section looks at specific foreign policies, their repercussions for the region, the actions of the affected countries (including Chile, Guatemala, Panama, and Cuba), and, importantly, the domestic effects of Cold War politics on the United States. A case study of Chile sheds detailed light on domestic and foreign policies of the nation, but will also serve as an example of the effects of the Cold War on Latin American countries. The chapter also examines the involvement of the United States and the Americas in two wars, Korea and Vietnam. It is important to study this chapter with an eye towards the Cold War as a world phenomenon, by seeking to understand the ebb and flow of global tension through its effects on one region as a whole. In addition, this chapter strongly supports and extends Standard Level topic 5 on the Cold War. It also complements topic 1 through its examination of the Korean and Vietnam wars, and other conflicts throughout the Americas, while contributing to a greater understanding of topics 2 and 3 in studying the conduct of both democratic and single-party states.

Containment under President Truman

Looking back 20 years after the dismantling of the Soviet Union, the effectiveness of President Truman's policy of containment as a means of combating the influence of Soviet-style communism appears to be confirmed. The policy of what became known as containment influenced relations between the United States and its hemispheric neighbors, dominating attitudes towards Latin America. The battle against communism was located in not only the official defense and foreign policy of the United States, but also in a multifaceted effort to rid the homeland of any influences of communism, an effort that began with the Red Scares following the First World War, and peaked with the McCarthyist tactics of the 1950s. The fight against communism influenced popular culture, making its way into films, plays, and even television cartoons. The Truman years set the stage for the Cold War abroad and at home.

Activity

Policies of US presidents Truman to Carter.

Create a chart similar to the one below. Expand cells as necessary.

President	Policy	Explanation	Effect in Americas
Truman	Containment		
Eisenhower	New Look		
Kennedy			
Johnson			
Nixon			
Ford			
Carter			

When the Second World War came to a close, the leaders and peoples of the nations of Latin America believed their contributions to the war effort, including subordinating and linking their economies to the needs of the United States, had earned the right to greater recognition and influence in the hemisphere. This was confirmed by the Inter-American Reciprocal Assistance and Solidarity (or Act of Chapultepec) agreement of March 1945. They looked forward to a return to, and enhancement of, Franklin Roosevelt's Good Neighbor policy. The Act of Chapultepec guaranteed each nation's national sovereignty and diplomatic equality. At the same time, the leaders of the United States came to focus on Europe and Asia, treating their Latin American neighbors almost as an afterthought. As the Cold War developed, the Truman administration and the nations of Latin America met diplomatically several times, including at international conferences in Rio de Janeiro (1947) and Bogotá (1948). At these conferences the differences in the views of the United States and its southern neighbors, most significantly in terms of the relationship between economic aid and development and hemispheric defense concerns, became increasingly apparent.

While the countries of Latin America looked at postwar relations with the United States in a hemispheric and global context, for the most part the Truman administration saw them through the lens of the Cold War. Stability, not democracy, became a goal in the fight against communism. The United States would assist Latin America when the US felt threatened in the region. From 1946 to 1950, Latin America received only 2% of US overseas aid, and almost all was military in nature; this, despite the emphasis of the State Department on greater economic support for hemispheric neighbors. Just a year after signing the Act of Chapultepec, the United States violated several provisions by interfering in the internal affairs of Argentina, Bolivia, and Chile. The following year, 1947, the Inter-American Treaty of Reciprocal Assistance (commonly known as the Rio Treaty) was signed. The Rio Treaty seemed to move towards hemispheric military cooperation with a shared vision that was anti-communist, at least from the point of view of the United States, as off-the-record fears of possible communist advances were communicated to US diplomats by Argentina and Brazil. That year Brazil, Chile, and Cuba banned communist organizations and cut off diplomatic relations with the Soviet Union. Over the next year, several South American and Caribbean governments turned away from democratic systems to more autocratic and right-leaning regimes. The United States government interpreted the Rio Treaty as allowing a larger role for itself, essentially rolling back some of the provisions of the Act of Chapultepec. The Truman administration felt it was imperative that Latin America was becoming important as it needed to remain non-communist and friendly to the global goals of the United States. To many people in Latin America, the Rio Treaty was a potential disaster. As Narciso Bassols García, a Mexican jurist and political commentator put it, the worst thing about the treaty signed in Rio de Janeiro was that Latin American countries became "compulsory automatic allies of the United States." In the eyes of many Latin Americans, the nations of the region were falling into Truman's containment plan without any choice, and without receiving any reciprocal benefits.

While Latin American nations were clamoring for economic assistance, the United States continued to press for a united approach to hemispheric defense and paid scant attention to social-economic issues. The Policy Planning Staff of the State Department understood the Latin American perspective, enunciated in a February 1948 anonymous memo that expressed the need for grants in aid, technical assistance, and an easing of the policies of the Export-Import Bank. But despite awareness of these issues, the Truman administration approached the spring 1948 Pan-American Conference in Bogotá, Colombia, with a sole focus on defense issues, leading to the formal formation of The Organization of American States (OAS) as a regional defense pact similar to NATO. In fact, US diplomats attending the conference were advised to avoid any financial commitments. The difference in perspectives was clear in the responses to the riots that occurred in Colombia during the conference. Sparked by the assassination of Liberal leader Jorge Eliecer Gaitán on April 9, violent demonstrations took place across the country. While most Latin American leaders saw the demonstrations as confirmation of the desperate state of the economy, the United States representatives believed that communist instigators were behind the riots.

The overwhelming emphasis on hemispheric defense at the expense of socio-economic advancement and support for democracy within the region might have changed for the better following Truman's inaugural address on January 20, 1949. In what became known as "Point Four programs" (it was the fourth main point of the speech) Truman announced scientific technical assistance and monetary aid to developing nations. Unlike Africa and Asia, however, Latin America received little benefit from Point Four as the administration promoted private enterprise reminiscent of long-discarded and discredited pre-FDR Dollar Diplomacy. Truman's attention was focused on Europe and the victory of the Mao-led communists in China. The monolithic Latin American policy prompted a response from Louis Joseph Halle of the State Department's Policy Planning division, who wrote an anonymous article in the July 1950 issue of *Foreign Affairs*, the same periodical that published George Kennan's Mr X piece. Halle, writing as Mr Y, took the administration to task for its lack of economic support for Latin America. But the article was to have little effect as events in Asia commanded Truman's attention.

On June 25, 1950, North Korea invaded South Korea, resulting in the marginalization of Latin America yet again in US foreign policy while also, paradoxically, intensifying anti-communist assistance to the region. As Truman focused on containing communism in Asia; but the administration feared increased Soviet attempts to penetrate Latin America, using an emergency meeting of the OAS in early 1951 to proclaim communism as a threat to the people of the Americas. A new law, the Mutual Security Act of 1951 provided $38 million of military assistance specifically designated for Latin America. Surplus Second World War weaponry was made available, either as aid or for

Discussion point

1 Why was the Truman administration unresponsive to economic concerns of Latin American countries?

2 To what extent would a focus by the United States on economic assistance have served the purpose of combating communism?

3 Why was economic assistance to Western European countries considered vital by the United States, but not so for the countries of Latin America?

purchase. More emphasis was placed on government stability and internal security, even as public declarations of support for democracy and non-intervention were being issued by the State Department. In the eyes of Latin America, developments in 1951 showed that the United States was continuing to ignore calls for economic assistance and assumed hemispheric support for US Cold War policies.

The last year of the Truman administration saw little change in policy. Following a legitimate election in 1951 in Bolivia that was annulled by the ruling rightist government, and a subsequent revolution in April 1952 to remove the autocracy, the Truman administration withheld formal recognition of the left-leaning Bolivian government of Victor Paz Estenssoro, a government that brought universal suffrage as well as land reform. The threat of a left-leaning government caused concern in the White House. Later the same year, the National Security Council issued the secret document, NSC-141. In line with the earlier NSC-68, defense against communism was the focus, but this time in Latin America.

Activity

Charting US policy

Create a graphic organizer such as the one below to visually organize your understanding of each major United States policy initiative towards countries of the Americas.

Repercussions of US policy

The policy of the United States should "seek first and foremost orderly political and economic development which will make the Latin American nations resistant to the internal growth of communism and Soviet political warfare." The call for stability confirmed Narciso Bassols García's caution following Rio, as NSC-141 continued advising the administration to "seek hemispheric solidarity in support of our world policy." By the end of Truman's term the attitude of the United States toward Latin America, framed within its policy of containment, resulted in weak and increasingly contentious hemispheric relations. In the view of Latin American nations the colossus to the north continued to ignore economic and social needs to the detriment of the region's peoples, while expecting those very same countries to solidly support the United States' mission of combating communism around the world.

McCarthyism and anti-communism

The Red Scare of the late 1940s and early 1950s was not an anomaly; serious historians of anti-communism in the United States must view it in the wider context of a pattern of anti-immigrant sentiments and fears of subversion that began even before the 1917 Bolshevik Revolution in Russia. However, developments in the US Congress that began in 1947 set the stage for Joseph McCarthy's public crusade against communism.

1947 marked the intensification of the actions of the House of Unamerican Activities Committee (HUAC), an organization that was created in 1938 to counteract potential subversives within the United States.

HUAC, with California Congressman Richard Nixon taking a prominent role, began investigating the film industry. Hollywood producers, directors, writers, and actors were accused of imbedding Soviet propaganda in popular films. Hollywood personalities were called to testify publicly before the committee and were asked, "Are you now or have you ever been a member of the Communist Party?" Among those compelled to testify were screenwriters Ring Lardner, Jr. and Dalton Trumbo of the famous Hollywood Ten declared criminally in contempt of Congress for their defiant responses to questions from members of the committee. Witnesses before HUAC often "took the 5th," meaning they chose to remain silent under rights enumerated in the Fifth Amendment to the United States Constitution. While legally permissible, and not supposed to imply any guilt, under repeated questions from committee members and attorneys the witnesses often seemed guilty. Many were tainted by the hearings, but not tried or convicted of subversion. Others chose to cooperate, some because they felt that communism was a real threat to the United States, naming Hollywood colleagues as communists. Well-known director **Elia Kazan**, a member of the American Communist Party in the 1930s, named several members of the Hollywood community as communists, engendering the long-term wrath of many fellow actors and directors, hard feelings that remained even when Kazan received the Oscar for lifetime achievement in 1999. The hearings did serve to intimidate many in the industry as hundreds of movie studio employees and contractors were "blacklisted," meaning studio owners fired and refused to hire anyone so designated.

HUAC did not limit its investigations to Hollywood. Perhaps the most famous case involved Alger Hiss, a mid-level staffer in the State Department. The controversial prosecution and conviction of Hiss

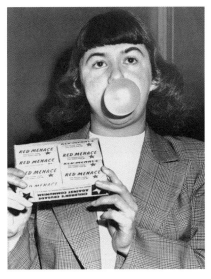

A woman posing with a box of anti-communist chewing gum.

Members of the movie industry not only appeared before HUAC, but prominent actors including Lauren Bacall (left) and Humphrey Bogart (right) demonstrated against HUAC in Washington, DC, in this 1947 protest march. Also seen in the photo is Paul Henreid, who starred as Victor Lazlo in *Casablanca* (1942).

Elia Kazan directed numerous important films, including *On the Waterfront* (1954), starring Marlon Brando and Eve Marie Saint, written by another cooperative witness, Budd Schulberg. Critics of Kazan and Schulberg's testimony saw the film as an attempt at justifying the perceived betrayal.

would be debated into the 21st century. In 1948, a self-identified former communist, Whitaker Chambers, accused Hiss of providing him with classified government documents during the 1930s, knowing that the destination was Moscow. It was not possible, due to the time between the alleged crime of espionage and the charges to prosecute Hiss, but eventually he was charged with perjury for his testimony. The case riveted the nation with testimony of microfilm hidden inside hollowed-out pumpkins in Chambers' garden and a typewriter of Hiss's tested and confirmed to be the origin of several documents. Republican Congressman Richard Nixon took a special interest in the case; his role in pursuing Hiss solidified his credibility as a fierce anti-communist, making him a national political figure, but also led many people, especially Democrats, to regard Nixon as, at best, unprincipled. The conviction of Hiss damaged the Democratic Party establishment, as many, including Illinois governor and future presidential candidate Adlai Stevenson and Secretary of State Dean Acheson, made forceful public statements in Hiss's defense. In fear of being labeled soft on communism or dupes, Democrats learned to speak and act with caution.

Concurrent with this round of HUAC investigations was the Truman administration's persistent prosecution of leaders of the American Communist Party under the Smith Act, resulting in more than 200 jail terms, and the formation and actions of the Federal Loyalty Program, launched by President Truman in March 1947. The program established "loyalty boards" to investigate the influence and infiltration of communists and communist sympathizers in the executive branch. The program authorized the investigation of both applicants to and employees of the federal government to guarantee loyalty because, in the words of the March 21 Executive Order 9835, "it is of vital importance that persons employed in the Federal service be of complete and unswerving loyalty to the United States; and … the presence within the Government service of any disloyal or subversive person constitutes a threat to our democratic processes …" Historian Alan Brinkley attributes Truman's desire to counter Republican attacks and to build support for his foreign policies as the reason for the Federal Loyalty Program, but it is also quite reasonable to take Truman at his stated purpose. The order followed the March 12 speech that established the Truman Doctrine and made the fight against communism, one form of subversion, an essential part of both domestic and foreign policy. Although the program did not specify what constituted disloyalty, within four years, 200 hundred employees were fired and an additional 2,000 resigned. Furthermore, the Federal Loyalty Program was an impetus for other investigations by the Justice Department and gave additional leeway for FBI director, Hoover, to undertake his own inquiries, and use the power of the agency to harm the reputations of many US citizens, including, but not limited to, those suspected of being subversives.

Activity

Seeing from both sides

You are an advisor to President Truman. Prepare two 300–400 word statements with evidentiary support to persuade the president to:

1 Expand the effectiveness of Loyalty Boards in finding and terminating federal employees who show any signs of allegiance or less than absolute opposition to communism.

2 Terminate the program as there is no threat from communists in the government and the process weakens the government by creating an atmosphere of fear preventing the free exchange of ideas.

Activity

Source analysis

The following documents concern the perceived threat to the United States of communist activity.

Source A

BOGOTA, Colombia, April 12 (AP)—Secretary of State George C. Marshall today blamed international Communism for the unsuccessful Bogota revolution. In a statement to other delepates to the Pan-American Conference, which he repeated to the press, Marshall said: "This situation must not be judged on a local basis, however tragic the immediate result to the Colombia (sic) people. The occurrence goes far beyond Colombia. It is the same definite pattern as occurrences which provoked strikes in France and Italy, and that are endeavoring to prejudice the situation in Italy, where elections will take place on April 18.

Source: "Marshall Blames World Communism for Bogota Revolt." *The Philadelphia Inquirer*, April 13, 1948. Full text at http://www.icdc.com/~paulwolf/gaitan/inquirer13april1948.htm.

Source B

I believe I speak for all of the people of the United States when I say that disloyal and subversive elements must be removed from the employ of the Government. We must not, however, permit employees of the Federal Government to be labeled as disloyal or potentially disloyal to their Government when no valid basis exists for arriving at such a conclusion. The overwhelming majority of Federal employees are local citizens who are giving conscientiously of their energy and skills to the United States. I do not want them to fear they are the objects of any "witch hunt." They are not being spied upon; they are not being restricted in their activities. They have nothing to fear from the loyalty program, since every effort has been made to guarantee full protection to those who are suspected of disloyalty. Rumor, gossip, or suspicion will not be sufficient to lead to the dismissal of an employee for disloyalty.

Source: Harry S. Truman. Statement by the president on the Government's Employee Loyalty Program. November 14, 1947. http://teachingamericanhistory.org/library/index.asp?documentprint=853.

Source C

"The great difference between our western Christian world and the atheistic Communist world is not political, gentlemen, it is moral … Today we are engaged in a final, all-out battle between communistic atheism and Christianity. The modern champions of communism have selected this as the time, and ladies and gentlemen, the chips are down—they are truly down. Six years ago … there was within the Soviet orbit, 180,000,000 people. Lined up on the antitotalitarian side there were in the world at that time, roughly 1,625,000,000 people. Today, only six years later, there are 800,000,000 people under the absolute domination of Soviet Russia—an increase of over 400 percent. On our side, the figure has shrunk to around 500,000,000. In other words, in less than six years, the odds have changed from 9 to 1 in our favor to 8 to 5 against us … This indicates the swiftness of the tempo of Communist victories and American defeats in the cold war. As one of our outstanding historical figures once said, "When a great democracy is destroyed, it will not be from enemies from without, but rather because of enemies from within." …

→

> The reason why we find ourselves in a position of impotency is not because our only powerful potential enemy has sent men to invade our shores ... but rather because of the traitorous actions of those who have been treated so well by this Nation. It has not been the less fortunate, or members of minority groups who have been traitorous to this Nation, but rather those who have had all the benefits that the wealthiest Nation on earth has had to offer ... the finest homes, the finest college education and the finest jobs in government we can give.
>
> **Source:** Speech of Joseph McCarthy, Wheeling, West Virginia. February 9, 1950. *History Matters*. http://historymatters.gmu.edu/d/6456.

Source D

Actor Gary Cooper is shown on the witness stand at the House Un-American Activities Committee (HUAC) hearings, Washington, DC, October 24, 1947.

Questions

1   What does source D reveal about the extent of media attention paid to the government efforts to combat the threat of communism?

2   Compare and contrast sources A and C regarding the activities of international communism.

3   With regard to its origin and purpose, how does source B assist historians' understanding of the US government's concerns about communist infiltration in the federal government?

4   Analyze the use of language in sources B and C to determine the appeal to emotion and reason. (TOK link).

5   Using the documents and your own knowledge assess the level, legitimacy, and approaches of the United States political leadership to the influence of communism during the Truman administration.

The active and public pursuit of disloyal citizens increased the fever of the Red Scare. In 1950, it led to the passage of the McCurran Internal Security Act, which became law over the veto of the president. The Act, among other provisions, required the registration of all communist groups with the federal government and determined that their internal documents were not private. The act furthered the intimidation of those who had been involved in legal, but unpopular, political activities. A top-secret program that deciphered Soviet communications, VENONA, provided information that revealed spies within the Manhattan Project. While the source of the information remained secret until 1995, British scientist Karl Fuchs was exposed as having given atomic secrets to the USSR. The uncovering of Fuchs began a trail that eventually led to Ethel and Julius Rosenberg, who were accused of being spies by Ethel's brother, David Greenglass. Greenglass had been exposed as a spy by Harry Gold, who was revealed by Fuchs. Greenglass confessed, turning in his wife, Ruth, as well. In exchange for a sentence reduction and his wife's freedom, Greenlass provided testimony to investigators and prosecutors that played a major part in the conviction of the Rosenbergs.

The Rosenbergs insisted they were innocent of turning over nuclear secrets to the Soviets, but in 1953 became the only US citizens to be executed for espionage during the Cold War. Decades later, in 1996, David Greenglass revealed that he had lied about his sister, Ethel, in order to spare his wife, but continued to insist that Julius Rosenberg was a Soviet spy, a belief, while disputed, that was corroborated by intelligence records and other testimonies. The revelation that allies and US citizens had freely given atomic secrets to Stalin's Soviet Union served to further intensify fears of communist infiltration. Additionally, the victory of Mao Zedong's communists over Chiang Kai-shek's nationalists in China in 1949 seemed to project a rising and threatening communist tide. To the citizens of the United States, only a few years after an Allied victory that was, to them, a triumph of democracy and freedom over totalitarianism, the "loss of China" exacerbated fears of communism.

Senator Joseph McCarthy

By New Year's day, 1950, the federal government's pursuit of domestic communists was well under way. Liberal organizations, including the American Civil Liberties Union (ACLU) and the National Association for the Advancement of Colored People (NAACP) had purged or were actively expelling communists from their ranks. A month later, on February 9, in Wheeling, West Virginia, Wisconsin Senator Joe McCarthy announced "I have here in my hand a list of 205 ... a list of names that were made known to the Secretary of State as being members of the Communist Party and who, nevertheless, are still working and shaping policy in the State Department ..." It was on that date that the hunt for subversives began to reach a level of alarm that seemed to consume much of the United States for the next four years.

During that time most politicians chose to support McCarthy or remain silent about his accusations, regardless of how believable they were, because it was to their political advantage or that McCarthy's accusations had merit. Even General Eisenhower demurred from defending General George C. Marshall when McCarthy accused him of betraying the United States. For the most part, Democrats, often the objects of McCarthy's attacks, stayed silent, fearing being identified with hated communists. Senators who stood up to McCarthy faced withering personal counterattacks and accusations. McCarthy struck fear in much of Washington.

McCarthy's accusations were loud, but also inconsistent. Two days after the Wheeling address, he sent a letter to President Truman claiming to know the identity of 57 communists in the State Department, and demanding that the president hand over evidence to his Senate committee to investigate. Truman refused: the dossiers were often assembled records of uncorroborated testimony and hearsay. Over the next few years, McCarthy used Truman's refusal to turn over executive branch files as an excuse for not revealing the names of those he accused. McCarthy continued to change the alleged number of subversives in the State Department (the next time to 81), and also changed his charge to "loyalty risks." A few weeks after his initial speech, McCarthy began using his committee to investigate many areas of the federal government. Assisted by David Schine and Roy Cohn, who even traveled to overseas offices to investigate, and with information provided by FBI director Herbert Hoover, McCarthy used the Senate Permanent Sub-committee on Investigations to publicly intimidate and often destroy the reputation of government officials. In committee hearings, McCarthy could not be pinned to any specific accusation; when asked to produce a list he claimed secrecy, when challenged on a specific charge he altered his language so that his accusations were moving targets. When challenged to produce one name, in March 1950, McCarthy named Owen Lattimore, a college professor of Asian Studies, who McCarthy stated was a "top Russian agent." Lattimore was not a public figure, and the charges were not supported by solid evidence. Lattimore's closest tie to communism seemed to be a lack of criticism of either the Soviet or Chinese leadership. Lattimore was to be the last person McCarthy accused by name. The failure of the example of Lattimore did not appear to affect McCarthy, who tied the names of Illinois governor Adlai Stevenson (Democrat nominee for president in 1952 and 1956), and Secretary of State Dean Acheson to communists, and further accused George C. Marshall of losing China. In Senator McCarthy's words the entire Democratic Party was responsible for "20 years of treason," and the Truman administration had through its own weaknesses encouraged communist subversion.

North Korea's invasion of South Korea in June 1950 further justified McCarthy's claims and added to the fear of communist encirclement. When the Communist Chinese army assisted North Korean forces that winter and overran US troops, the threat from Bejing and Moscow appeared even greater, coinciding as they did with relentless charges from McCarthy.

President Truman responded to McCarthy, stating that the accusations were untrue, and that McCarthy and his followers were the "greatest asset the Kremlin had." Truman, however, was not running for reelection. In 1952, several incumbent Democratic Senators who had vigorously stood up to challenge McCarthy's charges were defeated at the polls. Few newspapers openly opposed him and most reports accurately detailed his speeches, but few attempted further investigation; McCarthy wisely maintained good relationships with individual reporters. As Haynes Johnson wrote in *The Age of Anxiety: From McCarthyism to Terrorism*, a number of periodicals and several reporters including MaryMcGrory, I. F. Stone, Drew Pearson, Edward R. Murrow and cartoonist Herblock repeatedly tried "admirably to hold him accountable for his falsehoods." But that was a small minority of the press. To Johnson, the press's failure to hold McCarthy accountable was a major contributor to the damage and longevity of McCarthyism.

Senator Joseph McCarthy testifies against the US army during the Army–McCarthy hearings, Washington, DC, June 9, 1954. McCarthy stands before a map which charts communist activity in the United States.

In 1954, McCarthy's downfall came as quickly as his rise. Provoked by accusations from the army,

Activity

The most accurate history?

The same event can take on different meanings when understood through different media. How do historians decide the "truth" of any specific historical moment? You decide. This activity involves understanding the Army–McCarthy Hearings and involves five steps:

1 Go to the link (American Rhetoric: McCarthy–Welch Exchange): http://americanrhetoric.com/speeches/welch-mccarthy.html.

2 Read the transcript and look at the photos. Write down your impressions.

3 Form a group of two or four students, then perform the dialogue out loud. For an extra interpretation, record the reading, then listen to it. Write down your impressions.

4 Watch the 12 minute video on the American Rhetoric website. Write down your impressions as you listen.

5 Compare and contrast the impressions created by the different records of the event. Decide which method provides the most accurate understanding.

that McCarthy's aide Roy Cohn attempted to obtain special treatment for fellow assistant David Schine, who was drafted into the army, McCarthy issued the countercharge that the accusations were in response to McCarthy's inquiries into the loyalty of certain members of the US army. This resulted in the Army–McCarthy hearings from April 22 to June 17, 1954. Although McCarthy was exonerated of assisting Schine (he was found to have no foreknowledge of the actions of Cohn), the nationally televised hearings, revealed an abusive, rude, and evasive Joseph McCarthy to the nation. It was the beginning of a quick end to Joseph McCarthy. Nearing the close of the hearings, Senator Stuart Symington of Missouri told the Wisconsin senator, "The American people have had a look at you for six weeks. You are not fooling anyone." In September, a Senate committee charged with investigating McCarthy's conduct concluded that he was not only "vulgar," but that his behavior as chairman of the Senate Permanent Sub-committee on Investigations was "reprehensible" and inexcusable. In December, the full Senate voted 67 to 22 to condemn him for abuse of power. McCarthyism lost its star protagonist. After the Senate action, McCarthy's drinking increased and health problems from heavy alcohol consumption eventually developed into acute hepatitis. McCarthy died on May 2, 1957. While the boorish, shrill, and shifting tactics of McCarthyism faded when its demagogue was exposed, the government's hunt for subversives continued into the 1960s.

McCarthyism and anti-communism: an assessment

There are many reasons why people in the United States supported the hunt for subversives and McCarthyism. First, postwar events illustrated the strength and aggression of the Soviet Union with salami tactics in Poland, the Berlin blockade, the exploding of atomic and later thermonuclear bombs, Communist victory in the Chinese civil war and support for North Korea's invasion of South Korea. Internal developments such as the theft of atomic secrets by Klaus Fuchs and the exposure of Julius Rosenberg also provided reason for fears of subversion. Additionally, the fact that President

Discussion point

What is the long-term legacy of McCarthyism and anti-communism on the politics and policies of the two main political parties in the United States?

Truman and Congressman Nixon both used the levers of government to attack communism at home, provided a bipartisan affirmation. Politically, McCarthyism proved valuable to Republicans attempting to become the majority party after two decades of Democrat control of the White House. Top Republican officials, including Senator Robert Taft and President Eisenhower, maintained public silence about Joseph McCarthy when he attacked Democrats. Democrats, for their part, were often timid in opposition. Lastly, fears of communism dated back to the second decade of the century and fears of subversion to the beginning of the nation, as demonstrated by Benedict Arnold's defection to the British during the War of Independence. Lastly, there was the demagogue McCarthy himself. None of these factors alone explain the frenetic nature of the McCarthy era. Even when taken as a whole, the relative effects of circumstances and personalities remain difficult to quantify.

Activity

Entertainers, McCarthyism and communism

Many people within the entertainment industry were targeted by HUAC as an industry infiltrated by communists. Below are statements from four prominent representatives, Pete Seeger, Lillian Hellman, Arthur Miller, and John Wayne. HUAC, along with many citizens of the United States, considered the possible infusion of artistic expression with communist ideas to be a significant threat to the "American way of life."

Source A

Following is the testimony of folk singer and song writer Pete Seeger.

> Chairman WALTER: You have only been asked one question, so far.
>
> Mr. SEEGER: I am not going to answer any questions as to my association, my philosophical or religious beliefs or my political beliefs, or how I voted in any election, or any of these private affairs. I think these are very improper questions for any American to be asked, especially under such compulsion as this. I would be very glad to tell you my life if you want to hear of it …
>
> [Later testimony]
> Mr. SEEGER: I have already given you my answer to that question, and all questions such as that. I feel that is improper: to ask about my associations and opinions. I have said that I would be voluntarily glad to tell you any song, or what I have done in my life.
>
> [Later testimony]
> Mr. SEEGER: I have sung for Americans of every political persuasion, and I am proud that I never refuse to sing to an audience, no matter what religion or color of their skin, or situation in life. I have sung in hobo jungles, and I have sung for the Rockefellers, and I am proud that I have never refused to sing for anybody. That is the only answer I can give along that line.
>
> **Source:** Testimony of Pete Seeger before the House Un-American Activities Committee, August 18, 1955. *History Matters*. http://historymatters.gmu.edu/d/6457.

Source B

Following is a letter from the writer Lillian Hellman to HUAC stating her reasons for not testifying.

> But I am advised by counsel that if I answer the committee's questions about myself, I must also answer questions about other people and that if I refuse to do so, I can be cited for contempt. My counsel tells me that if I answer questions about myself, I will have waived my rights under the fifth amendment and could be forced legally to answer questions about others. This is very difficult for a layman to understand. But there is one principle that I do understand: I am not willing, now or in the future, to bring bad trouble to people who, in my past association with them, were completely innocent of any talk or any action that was disloyal or subversive. I do not like subversion or disloyalty in any form and if I had ever seen any I would have considered it my duty to have reported it to the proper authorities. But to hurt innocent people whom I knew many years ago in order to save myself is, to me, inhuman and indecent and dishonorable. I cannot and will not cut my conscience to fit this year's fashions, even though I long ago came to the conclusion that I was not a political person and could have no comfortable place in any political group.
>
> **Source:** Lillian Hellman, Letter to HUAC, May 19, 1952. *History Matters.* http://historymatters.gmu.edu/d/6454

Source C

Following is an extract from an article published by Arthur Miller in *The New Yorker*

> The breathtaking circularity of the process had a kind of poetic tightness. Not everybody was accused, after all, so there must be *some reason why you were* … The more I read into the Salem panic, the more it touched off corresponding images of common experiences in the fifties: the old friend of a blacklisted person crossing the street to avoid being seen talking to him; the overnight conversions of former leftists into born-again patriots; and so on. Apparently, certain processes are universal. When Gentiles in Hitler's Germany, for example, saw their Jewish neighbors being trucked off, or farmers in Soviet Ukraine saw the Kulaks vanishing before their eyes, the common reaction, even among those unsympathetic to Nazism or Communism, was quite naturally to turn away in fear of being identified with the condemned. As I learned from non-Jewish refugees, however, there was often a despairing pity mixed with "Well, they must have done *something*." Few of us can easily surrender our belief that society must somehow make sense. The thought that the state has lost its mind and is punishing so many innocent people is intolerable. And so the evidence has to be internally denied.
>
> **Source:** Miller, Arthur. "Why I wrote "The Crucible." *The New Yorker*. October 21, 1996.

Source D

Following is an extract from an interview with John Wayne published in *Playboy Magazine* in 1971.

> **Wayne:** The articulate liberal group has caused certain things in our country … George Putnam, the Los Angeles news analyst, put it quite succinctly when he said, "What kind of a nation is it that fails to understand that freedom of speech and assembly are one

thing, and anarchy and treason are quite another, that allows known Communists to serve as teachers to pervert the natural loyalties and ideals of our kids, filling them with fear and doubt and hate and down-grading patriotism and all our heroes of the past?"

Playboy: You blame all this on liberals?

Wayne: Well, the liberals seem to be quite willing to have Communists teach their kids in school. The Communists realized that they couldn't start a workers' revolution in the United States, since the workers were too affluent and too progressive. So the Commies decided on the next-best thing, and that's to start on the schools, start on the kids. And they've managed to do it. They're already in colleges; now they're getting into high schools. I wouldn't mind if they taught my children the basic philosophy of communism, in theory and how it works in actuality. But I don't want somebody like Angela Davis inculcating an enemy doctrine in my kids' minds.

Source: Warren Lewis, Richard. "Playboy Interview: John Wayne." *Playboy Magazine.* May 1, 1971. http://www.playboy.co.uk/print/print-article/item64826/.

Questions

1 For what reasons and in what ways are artists qualified to comment on political and social issues?

2 Compare and contrast the approaches taken by sources A and B to HUAC requests for testimony. Which message is more effective? Why?

3 Sources C and D express deep-felt concern over destructive elements to the United States. Referring to both their origin and purpose, what are the values and

limitations of Miller and Wayne's statements for historians US public opinion on fears of communism and responses to it during the Cold War?

4 Actor John Wayne's interview (source D) took place in 1971. In what ways do the sentiments expressed in the interview reflect the policies of the Nixon administration toward communism?

Social and cultural effects of McCarthyism and the Cold War

The Cold War and anti-communist hysteria of the late 1940s and 1950s created a society in which, according to historian Howard Zinn, "The whole culture was permeated with anti-Communism." Still, much of the life in the postwar United States centered around suburbia, the quest for material goods, family, and entertainment of every kind. To assume that North Americans thought about the Cold War constantly is to exaggerate its influence, but to a significant extent it did steer many of the cultural elements of the period. Film, television, education, music, literature, theater, and the role of religion both influenced and reflected the anti-communist mood.

The film industry was affected significantly by the blacklisting of writers and actors. Fame and popularity did not deter the HUAC or the State Department: even film great Charlie Chaplin, a British citizen who had worked in the United States for four decades, was refused reentry into the United States for his alleged sexual immorality and sympathy toward the **Popular Front**, even though he had never been a member of any communist or associated organization. Many writers could no longer work, or had a **front**

Popular Front Groups around the world, usually formed at the instigation of Comintern during the 1930s, that combined communist with other left, but not communist organizations, to oppose fascism.

A **front** was a person who posed as a writer, passing the scripts of those on the Hollywood blacklist to producers. The front received screen credit for the script.

present scripts. Producers were careful not to present any theme that remotely endorsed communism or even a challenge to the existing social order. Films such as *The Grapes of Wrath* that challenged the principles and main components of capitalism were not made in the United States during the 1950s. Victor Navasky, author of *Naming Names* (1980), observes that social-themed films that were common in the 1930s and early 1940s almost completely disappeared in the initial Cold War period and were replaced by either pure entertainment or anti-communist themes. Evil communists were the antagonists of more than 40 Hollywood films, productions of all but one Hollywood studio, during the late 1940s to the fall of Joseph McCarthy in 1954. Titles included *I Married a Communist* (1949), *I was a Communist for the FBI* (1951), *Invasion, U.S.A.* (1952), and the films *My Son John* (1952), and *Big Jim McLain* (1952). *My Son John* featured a communist son and a mother who exposed him. *Big Jim McLain* starred John Wayne and James Arness, both well-known actors in Westerns. In the film, federal agent Jim McLain (John Wayne) hunts down murdering communists and finds romance in Hawaii. The opening scene shows disgust and anger by McLain and his hot-headed partner Mal Baxter as alleged communists refusing to testify are released without punishment. Revealingly, John Wayne expressed particular disdain for the western, *High Noon* (1952.) The film, scripted by soon-to-be-blacklisted Carl Foreman, features a reluctant sheriff, played by Gary Cooper, who is forced to stand alone against bandits because of the cowardice of the townspeople. Wayne, who in a *Playboy Magazine* interview decades later called the movie "the most un-American thing I've ever seen," interpreted *High Noon* as criticism of HUAC's methods and those who cooperated. Films defending the free speech of defenders of leftist political views were few. Instead, Elia Kazan's *On the Waterfront* (1954), a story about mob informers, allegorically defended Kazan's naming names in his HUAC testimony. Taking the opposite point of view, Arthur Miller wrote the play, *The Crucible* (1953) as a Broadway theater production (the Theater was not attacked by HUAC the way Hollywood was and remained mostly free of blacklisting). *The Crucible* addressed the mass hysteria of the Salem Witch Trials in the 1690s to examine and criticize the anti-communist witch hunts in which people were attacked and their lives ruined for being acquainted with a suspected communist, or refusing to name people. Films depicting the dangers of nuclear war were also popular, and included *The Day the Earth Stood Still* (1951).

Although movies attracted significant attention from government officials, by the end of the 1950s it was no longer the dominant entertainment medium. Movie-goers declined by 50% over the decade. Television was on the rise. The penetration of television grew from under 10% of households in 1950 to 90% of US households by 1960. According to Stephen J. Whitfield, author of *Culture of the Cold War* (1996), television also coincided with the decline of radio listenership and magazine readership. As a trustworthy news source, the public rated television equal to newspapers. Entering US homes at a faster pace than any previous technological device, its rate of adoption was only surpassed by the personal computer.

In the 1950s television programming was dominated by comedies, variety shows, theater and dramas, and, as the decade wore on, westerns and game shows. For the 1958–59 season, eight of the top ten most popular shows were westerns. That same year a cartoon, *Rocky and Friends,* featuring a heroic flying squirrel and his sidekick, a moose, battled villains named Boris Badenov and Natasha Fatale. Game shows such as "The Price is Right" and "$64,000 Question" entertained audiences while promoting consumerism, the pursuit of wealth, and, sometimes, displays of intellectual prowess to reinforce the advantages of both capitalism and a US education over the Soviet system. The Cold War's influence was not absent from the small screen, but its day-to-day appearance was often subtle. Dissent was not tolerated in the new, popular medium. Edward R. Murrow, famed for his 1954 denunciation of McCarthy, commented that "Television in the main is being used to distract, delude, amuse and insulate us." Whitfield argues that the primary motivation for avoiding controversial content was due to the desire of program sponsors to attract the largest audience possible. Television was at the same time used to promote anti-Soviet passions and support for US defense and foreign policy. There were live broadcasts of nuclear explosions. News coverage followed administration policy leaders, but rarely examined their statements for accuracy. Murrow's own public affairs show *See It Now* owed its independence to its reliance on a single sponsor, Alcoa. The Columbia Broadcasting System (CBS) did not support the program, alerting FBI director Hoover to its dangers before the famous exposé of Senator McCarthy. Inquisitive television journalists threatened the profits of broadcasting companies and sponsors, and were therefore not encouraged.

The famous quiz show cheating scandal of 1958 caused great consternation among the viewing public, further adding to the climate of retribution. Cheating on the show *Twenty-One* was revealed by a participant, Herb Stempel, whose loss to Charles Van Doren in December 1958 was scripted by the producers. The scandal resulted in Congressional hearings, a public statement of condemnation by President Eisenhower and the immediate loss of public trust in the television industry. Van Doren, who admitted on 2 November that he was a principal part of the fixing of the game show, lost all credibility, his job on national television and his professorship at Columbia University. Several other quiz shows were also found to have been rigged. The dishonesty of the shows revealed that some of the most trusted icons of American entertainment were untrustworthy, in this way pitting honest US citizens against the underhanded, deceitful communists depicted in films such as *Big Jim McLain.*

In the United States, public education has often been viewed as an important avenue for poorer members of society (usually, the most recent immigrants) to climb the social and economic ladder. The system has also served to teach all students the norms of citizenship, United States history, and the thought-to-be common values of the society. For example, school children around the country recited the Pledge of Allegiance daily. Until 1943, schools had the right to compel students to say the Pledge regardless of religion or citizenship. After the Supreme Court decision (West

Virginia Board of Education vs. Barnette), most public schools
conducted a daily flag salute, with pressure to participate from fellow
classmates and school staff commonplace.

With the threat of Soviet "godless Communism" came an increased
effort by some religious groups to emphasize the importance of God
in the lives of US citizens. In 1954, the Catholic organization, the
Knights of Columbus, lobbied to modify the Pledge of Allegiance to
include the words "under God." The US Congress passed a law,
and with President Eisenhower's signature the Pledge included a
government-mandated acknowledgement of a supreme being as
protection against the menace of communism.

After the successful October 1957 launch and orbit of Sputnik, the
faith of US citizens in their system's technological superiority over
the Soviet Union was shattered. If the Soviets could launch a
satellite, why not a missile directed at Washington, DC? One
response was the National Defense Education Act (NDEA) of 1958.
In addition to loans for college education, the NDEA provided $300
million over four years for science, mathematics and foreign
language education in public schools from elementary to high school
to enable a the younger generation to defeat Soviet technological
prowess. NDEA was the first comprehensive federal education law
and presented a challenge to the tradition of state and local control
of schools. The irony of one federal law official decreeing a supreme
being and a second federal law promoting advanced creative and
independent thinking, both to defeat Communism, illustrates the
importance to the majority of elected officials and opinion leaders
of the battle against communism.

The federal government did not just concern itself with educating
children, but also in educating the general public of the dangers of
the Atomic Age. In 1951, the Federal Civil Defense Administration
(FCDA) was created. Its mission was to assure Americans that steps
could be taken to survive nuclear war. The agency contracted with
private film makers to create a series of instructional movies. Many
of these are featured and satirized in *Atomic Cafe,* a 1982
documentary collection of 1940s and 1950s Cold War government-
produced or contracted instructional films. The most famous of the
films was "Duck and Cover," featuring a turtle named Bert.
Produced specifically for school children, the nine-minute film
taught students across the United States to fall to their knees under
their desks and to lower their heads while covering their necks,
whenever the teacher shouted "drop." Part of the logic for the "drop
drills" was to make students feel that in the event of nuclear war
they were not helpless. Survivability was a significant theme for
many other FCDA films for all age groups, designed to convert fear
into a sense of calm.

Popular music of the Fifties seems to be mostly about romance,
failed, flawed or all-consuming, but many pop artists recorded songs
directly related to the Cold War or nuclear disaster. Bill Haley, one of
the first Rock 'n Roll artists, famous for "Rock Around the Clock" and
"See You Later Alligator," recorded "Thirteen Women (and only One

Man in Town)" as the "b" side of "Rock Around the Clock" in 1954.
The lyrics begin:

> Last night I was dreaming,
> Dreamed about the H-Bomb.
> Well the bomb it went off and I was caught
> I was the only man on the ground.
> There was thirteen women and only one man in town.

Haley proceeds to sing his multiple romances and the domestic
benefits of being a man surrounded by women; all due to a nuclear
war. The song was later recorded by Dinah Shore as "Thirteen Men."
Sex symbol/actress Ann-Margret also recorded "Thirteen Men."
In 1963, Bob Dylan released "Talkin' World War III Blues" which
projected a contrasting view of nuclear war:

> Some time ago a crazy dream came to me
> I dreamt I was walkin' into World War Three
> I went to the doctor the very next day
> To see what kind a words he could say
> He said it was a bad dream …
> Well, the whole thing started at 3 o'clock fast
> It was all over by quarter past …

Numerous other musicians recorded songs such as "When They
Drop the Atomic Bomb," "I'm Gonna Dig Myself a Hole," "I'm No
Communist," "Your Atom Bomb Heart," and "Guided Missiles," a
love song by the doo-wop group the Cuff-Links. Music from Country
to Blues to Jazz commented on, and reflected the influence of, the
Cold War.

The Cold War impacted literature and other arts. Modern art was
accused of being communist-influenced. The atomic bomb led to
what Dr Alan Filreis of the University of Pennsylvania called "nuclear
holocaust literature," beginning with John Hersey's *Hiroshima* (1946)
first published in *The New Yorker,* and including British author Nevil
Shute's *On the Beach* (1957). In the mystery genre, writer Mickey
Spillane's hard-bitten detective, Mike Hammer, bragged in *One Lonely
Night* (1951), "I killed more people tonight than I have fingers on my
hands. I shot them in cold blood and enjoyed every minute of it. ...
They were Commies." Novelist Allan Drury published *Advise and
Consent* in 1959, a book of political intrigue over a nominee for
Secretary of State, who is strongly supported by liberals and the
intellectual élite. To some critics, the character appeared modeled
after Alger Hiss, uniting fiction with McCarthyism.

Accelerating consumerism in the United States caught the attention
of researchers. During the 1950s, many significant works of social
commentary were published: *The Organization Man* by William
H. Whyte addressed the conformity of corporate norms and the
willingness of white collar workers to seek comfort within a
community of people similar to them; *The Affluent Society* by John
Kenneth Galbraith addressed income inequality and the influence of
advertising in creating consumer demand; *The Power Elite* by C. Wright
Mills claimed that the voice of the common man was overpowered
by corporate, military, and political élites. Literature that was openly

critical of US society and culture was not subject to the same restraints as films or television, leaving avenues of dissent open, but in a time when increasing numbers of people were getting their information from television programs and sponsors' advertisements, social criticism in book form had limited audience reach.

The culture and society of the late 1940s and 1950s was greatly affected by the Cold War. Society reflected a desire for national unity and fear of communism and nuclear war. The arts, especially film and television, were constrained by the political mood and outright or manipulative governmental pressure of the period. Popular culture, with some exceptions, played to popular themes and did not challenge the prevailing conventional wisdom; challenges to the establishment were commonly viewed as un-American.

The Korean War, 1950–53

On June 25, 1950, 100,000 North Korean soldiers equipped with Soviet battle tanks, artillery and fighter planes crossed the 38th parallel and invaded South Korea, announcing a new phase in the Cold War: one that would be repeated in Vietnam, Afghanistan and a dozen other locations. The North Korean objective was to reunite Korea under the communist government of Kim Il-Sung. They planned for a two month war. The United Nations declared the invasion illegal and authorized the United States to take command of a UN force and restore the borders. Fifteen UN nations committed their military and the Korean War became the first real test of the United Nation's concept of collective security. Intended to be a **"limited war,"** it would drag on for three years, ravaging the Korean peninsula: the Chinese intervened, the United States contemplated using nuclear weapons and millions of Korean civilians became casualties and refugees. The war would end where it started, with no changes to the borders and the lessons learned would dictate US foreign policy and that of other nations in the Americas until the Cold War ended in 1989.

Activity

Limited warfare

Research further definitions of "limited warfare." Which conflicts in the Cold War period conform to this definition? What kind of precedent was set by the Korean War?

A **limited war**, as it came to be known in the second half of the 20th century, is a conflict in which the weapons used, the nations or territories involved, or the objectives pursued are restricted in some way (avoiding, in particular, the use of nuclear weapons).

Background to the Korean War

The Korean peninsula borders China to the north and is relatively close to Japan to the south-east. The Japanese had occupied Korea since 1910. At the end of the Second World War, after Japan had surrendered in August 1945, the Soviet Union and United States divided Korea at the 38th parallel with the Soviets occupying the North and the United States the southern half of the country. The respective populations numbered nine million and 21 million. The occupation was assumed to be temporary but by 1947, with no end in sight, the United States handed the administration of South Korea over to the United Nations. The Soviets suggested that both powers should withdraw and let the Koreans sort it out but the United States rejected this solution, concerned about the build-up of Soviet forces in the North, which the South could not match. On August 14, 1947, the UN created the United Nations Temporary Commission on Korea (UNTCOK) to oversee withdrawal of occupation forces and to supervise elections that would reunify Korea. The North Koreans denied UNTCOK entry. On May 10, 1948, the UN supervised elections in the South and Syngman Rhee was elected president. In the North, the reins of power where firmly held by Soviet-backed leader Kim Il Sung, who refused to hold elections. Korea thus seemed destined to permanent division.

After the elections were held and power consolidated both the Soviet and US forces withdrew from the peninsula. While the Soviets equipped the North Korean army with heavy artillery, tanks and armoured vehicles, the US feared South Korean agression and left them with limited military resources. Both sides claimed they were Korea's legitimate government and North Korean armed incursions into the South became common. UNTCOK warned of a possible civil war.

New archival research reveals that Kim had appealed to Mao Zedong to assist in reunifying Korea.When Stalin was approached he was initially unenthusiastic but changed his mind upon hearing of the Pacific Perimeter speech. In January 1950, the US Secretary of Defense, Dean Acheson, addressed the Washington Press Club and named a "defence perimeter" that the US was committed to protect. Korea was not mentioned as being in the US sphere of defense. Stalin, therefore, thought that the US did not see Korea as in its sphere of influence and he counseled Kim to proceed. The North Koreans crossed the border at 4 a.m. on June 25, 1950. The South Koreans fought bravely but were overwhelmed. Roads became clogged with soldiers and refugees fleeing the communist juggernaut and impeded attempts to move reinforcements north to stop the invasion.

Although he was willing to act unilaterally, President Truman asked the UN Security Council to condemn the North's invasion and give the US command of the UN military response. On June 27, the Security Council passed a resolution that the invasion constituted a "breach of the peace." A Soviet veto would have ended the resolution but the USSR was boycotting proceedings in protest over the UN's refusal to grant a seat to mainland China. On July 8, Truman appointed General Douglas MacArthur as commander of the UN forces, and 15 other UN nations pledged support.

Truman was determined to limit the war to Korea and prevent it from expanding for three reasons. First, to keep the Soviets out and avoid a direct confrontation: the Soviets had successfully tested an A-bomb in 1949 and the nuclear standoff made direct confrontation extremely risky and dangerous. Second, Truman, his advisors, cabinet and allies worried that Korea might be a diversion and the real test would come in Europe. Korea, they opined, was just another in a series of Soviet proves, starting with Greece and Turkey (1947), Czechoslovakia (1948) and the blockade of Berlin (1948–49). Third, Truman had to consider public opinion. The US had sacrificed much during the Second World War and it was unlikely they would support another major conflict on the other side of the world, yet he had been charged with being soft on communism and was determined to change that perception.

Truman was convinced that the US and its allies had to fight to contain communism and the regional conflict to the Korean peninsula. The president was also sensitive to accusations by the Republican-controlled Congress that he was soft on communism and had lost China in 1949. This time he was would take a hard line and stop the communists in their tracks to improve his image and silence his critics. The executive was convinced Stalin was probing the West's defences but this time he had gone to far. No more appeasement. It was a volatile situation trying to keep the confidence and support of the citizens of the United States, as well as the United Nations and keep the conflict localized to Korea. The next move was designed to do it all at once: he did not ask Congress to declare war but instead declared the Korean conflict a "police action." The tactic worked. The military mobilized, the UN gave the United States command and 15 UN nations offered to help.

Military developments

Stage 1: Invasion and Inchon

Four days after the invasion started, the North captured Seoul, South's Korea's capital. The South's army had been routed and was in headlong retreat to Pusan in the southeast corner of the peninsula. US units arrived from Japan but were too few and too lightly armed to make much difference and were brushed aside with heavy losses. The roads were clogged with refugees making reinforcement all but impossible. US air power however, was able to slow the North Korean advance and by late August the invasion had run out steam and, as more US ground forces arrived, the front stabilized around the port of Pusan called the Pusan Perimeter.

On September 15, in a bold and decisive manoeuver, General MacArthur landed two divisions (about 25,000 men) at Inchon on the west coast and moved inland. At the same time, the allied forces broke out of the Pusan Perimeter. Faced with being cut off and surrounded the North Korean army fled retracing their July victory march, this time in retreat. MacArthur's forces quickly recaptured Seoul and crossed the 38th parallel.

Koreans flee the fighting, 1950.

Stage 2: Chinese Intervention

The temptation to reunite Korea was balanced against the likelihood of Chinese intervention. Flushed with victory, MacArthur charged into the North and captured the capital of Pyongyang. By

November, the North Korean army was all but finished. In late November, as US and South Korean forces neared the Yalu River (the border between China and Korea), MacArthur received warnings that the Chinese were coming. He scoffed, believing the Chinese would never dare to fight the US army, and if they did come he would use the opportunity to teach them a lesson. When he and the president had met in October he told the president that the Chinese threat was overblown and did not pose a serious threat. Truman supported his General. MacArthur downplayed a couple of brushes with Chinese units and continued to downplay the threat. On November 27, US troops awoke to the sound of bugles announcing the arrival of 300,000 Chinese soldiers. Taken by surprise, the US suffered one of the worst defeats in its military history. The 1st Marine Division was cut off and barely escaped annihilation, saved by the US and Canadian navies evacuation at Cochin. Within weeks, the Chinese had pushed the UN forces back across the border and recaptured Seoul. Meanwhile, tensions between President Truman and General MacArthur which had been simmering behind the scenes since the war began were about to become public.

Stage 3: Stalemate and Panmunjom

On March 20, 1951, Truman issued a statement that his policy was to continue to fight a limited war and seek a negotiated peace. This seemed wise considering recent indications that the Chinese wanted to start peace talks, which commenced in July. A few days after the president's announcement MacArthur publicly stated his opposition to the policy, threatened to expand the war against China and intimated he might use atomic weapons. This was clear and blatant insubordination. Truman met with his chiefs of staff and on April 11, 1951, fired MacArthur. General Matthew Ridgway took command and quickly mounted a counteroffensive that recaptured Seoul (the fourth time it changed hands during the war) and stopped the advance of the North Koreans at the border. At this point, the war became a stalemate: trench warfare like the First World War, stretched across the hills and valleys of the 38th parallel, from coast to coast. Battles became small engagements to straighten the line here and capture a hill there. The focus shifted to the negotiations. Kaesong, the ancient capital of Korea, was the first venue. Talks commenced on July 10, l951, but broke down in late August when no progress was made. In late October l951, following bitter fighting in September and October, talks resumed and shifted to Panmunjom, on the border in Gyeonggi Province. Negotiations dragged on for another two years, while the fighting continued. During the stalemate, both the US and the USSR had changes in leadership. In November 1952 Dwight Eisenhower was elected president; in March 1953 Stalin died and the USSR was engulfed in yet another power struggle. These new leaders seemed unwilling to continue the fight and a final cease-fire was signed on July 27, 1953. A demilitarized zone roughly along the 38th parallel divided the belligerents. Although the fighting stopped, these negotiations persisted, and in 1954 a permanent armistice was agreed upon without a treaty. Technically, North and South Korea remained at war.

The war had lasted three years and 2 days. The casualties of war included Koreans on both sides of the border, with civilian losses were estimated at 2 to 2.5 million. North and South Korea, respectively, lost 215,000 and 137,00 soldiers. Chinese casualty figures are controversial, depending on the source. Officially, the Chinese report about half a million casualties but US sources contend it was over a million. The United States came next with 36,000 battlefield deaths and the other UN forces lost 3,600 soldiers. The limited war had proved costly totalling over three million lives on all sides.

US trucks crossing the 38th parallel: The Korean War stopped where it started.

Truman was heavily criticized for his handling of the war, particularly his firing of MacArthur and inability to negotiate an end to the fighting. With his popularity at an all time low, he decided not to run for a second term. Dwight D. Eisenhower came home from his NATO command, accepted the Republican nomination and defeated Adlai Stevenson with the slogan "I will go to Korea." Ike fulfilled this objective, when in 1953 he went to Korea and shortly after signed a negotiated settlement. The war ended without a clear victory but with a sense of relief. In the eyes of the United States it was a nasty little war, in a faraway place that cost the lives of too many US soldiers.

Canada and Colombia in the Korean War

Canadian prime minister Louis St. Laurent cautiously brought Canada into the war. He and his cabinet were determined to support the UN and initially offered a token force of three light cruisers and an air- force transport squadron but no ground forces. Following the Chinese intervention, and pressured by the defense minister and Secretary of State, the prime minister authorized the recruitment of a special volunteer force comprising an infantry brigade, tanks and artillery. He decided against using existing standby forces, fearing a Soviet move into Europe. Canada eventually sent 27,000 soldiers, sailors and aircrew to Korea, the third largest UN contingent after the United States and United Kingdom. Over 500 Canadians were killed and 1,500 wounded.

Colombia also sent roughly 6,200 soldiers, many of whom notably participated in the Battle of Pork Chop Hill, the bloodiest battle of the war, from March to July 1953. A regiment of 1,000 men fought with the US forces and suffered heavy losses; almost half of the contingent were killed or wounded. Colombia also sent six warships to assist in the amphibious landings. This was the lone Latin American participant in the war; in a sign of hemispheric solidarity, this force was dispatched and the last Colombian troops did not leave the peninsula until 1955.

Political consequences of the Korean War

Canadian Historian David Bercuson contends that to view the war as futile is incorrect. Korea was the first effort by a communist state to take over a non-communist neighbor. "In a very real sense,

Activity · · · · · · · · · · · · · ·

US public attitudes toward Korea

Research the attitudes of US citizens to the war in Korea and the outcome of the conflict.

 What were the public perceptions of the war, and the region at stake?

the first real victory of the West in the Cold War was won in the bloody hills of central Korea." US historian John Gaddis offers a different lesson.

> The only decisive outcome of the war was the precedent it set: that there could be a bloody and protracted conflict involving the nations armed with nuclear weapons and they could chose not to use them. The lesson was not lost and Vietnam would be next, only this time the ending would be very different.

> **Source:** Gaddis, John. 2005. *Cold War: A New History.* London: Penguin. p. 50.

In Canada, the government's response to Korea was to initiate the most massive and costly peacetime rearmament in the nation's history. By the mid 1950s, 45% of the annual budget went to defense and Canada's NATO contribution in Europe was 10,000 soldiers, sailors and aircrew; a big commitment for a middle power. The contingent was reduced during the 1970s but Canadians stood on guard in Europe for four decades until the Cold War ended. This commitment was a direct result of the Korean War.

In the United States, the Korean War further strained relations with the Soviet bloc. After Truman, President Eisenhower continued to support containment, although he worried about the defense budget's rising costs. He supported the French in Vietnam against Ho Chi Minh's forces. He had little choice: after 1945, the United States became increasingly committed to regime protection against communist forces in Southeast Asia, following the defeat of the nationalist Chinese army of Chiang Kai-shek against Mao's revolutionary army. After three bloody years in Korea, the US remained committed to protecting the fledgling Republic of South Korea, stationing thousands of troops along the 38th parallel.

The political consequence of Korea in the United States was a single-minded commitment to containment by every US president up to the 1990s. In decades to come, this allegiance restricted the freedom of presidents to consider other policy options and alternatives. This monopoly was supported by US public opinion that expected presidents to be tough on communism. Vietnam would begin to change all that. In the short term, Korea helped bring an end to 20 years of Democratic control of the White House, paving the way for Eisenhower. Kennedy, a Democrat, would take a harder line against communism than Eisenhower's Republicans. Johnson would follow Kennedy's lead and the result was the escalation in Vietnam.

Eisenhower, Dulles and the New Look

Most people thought that Eisenhower's foreign policies would be dominated by the Korean War; yet that conflict was resolved, albeit tenuously, by the middle of his first year in office. This gave his administration the opportunity to focus its containment policy elsewhere, and in particular, the US turned its attention to the region. The Arbenz administration in Guatemala was seen as one of the biggest threats; the policies of that democratically-elected president perceived as socialist and pro-Soviet. Guatemala was one among many countries in the region deemed vulnerable to the communist threat in this period. Where socialism and communist governments took hold of power, the US used the skills of the recently-created **Central Intelligence Agency (CIA)** to engage in operations that would undermine those regimes it felt threatened regional stability.

> **Central Intelligence Agency (CIA)** The Central Intelligence Agency, the United States' intelligence service, formed after World War Two by the National Security Act of 1947. According to its website, "The Central Intelligence Agency's primary mission is to collect, evaluate, and disseminate foreign intelligence to assist the president and senior US government policymakers in making decisions relating to the national security."

The core question that arose repeatedly, especially with regard to the so-called banana republics of Central America, is how the Cold War advanced the aims of certain key élites within the United States. For example, it is impossible to address Central America without looking at the debilitating effect that the US-owned United Fruit Company (UFCO) had on the politics, economies and societies in these countries. The Soviet Union argued that it was not containment, but the capitalist interests of US élites that provoked the policies used in the region. In South America the issues were the same, although the United States did not always dominate as completely. In many areas, the wartime policies of the United States had meant that US economic and military dominance replaced former British dominance. In some cases US influence was welcomed by the élites but was increasingly questioned by the emerging middle class.

The United States increasingly supported military regimes that were previously considered anathema to US ideals but tolerated due to the anti-communist positions taken up by such dictators and the economic interests of American élites. This pattern, began under Truman, was clearly supported by Eisenhower and in full force until the late 1970s. The emphasis on human rights under President Jimmy Carter brought about some changes, but these changes in policy were not uniform across the region.

A man carries a stem of bananas over his shoulder at a United Fruit Company plantation, Tiquisate, Guatemala, 1945.

361

President Eisenhower's national security and foreign policies

Dwight D. Eisenhower won the 1952 election, taking the presidency away from the Democrats for the first time since 1933. As a retired general who had led the invasion at Normandy and took command of NATO forces, and a Republican, it was unlikely that he would be perceived as soft on communism (a charge consistently leveled at Democrats), and with John Foster Dulles as his Secretary of State, the two proved to be formidable anti-communists. Their policies were an extension of the containment policies of Truman but Dulles's virulent diatribes against communism and potential communist threats made the administration seem much harsher in its approach. On the other hand, the United States was facing an economic downturn and Eisenhower was looking for ways to curb expenditures. Republican economic policy reflected a free market, *laissez-faire* approach. In foreign policy, this meant limited economic assistance to struggling countries. Specific to the Americas:

- Commodities proposals made during the Truman administration were put on hold, leaving the cacao and coffee producers particularly vulnerable to market fluctuations.

- The creation of an Inter-American Development Bank was halted.

- Latin American states were advised that, in the interest of regional stability and cooperation, they should not discourage private foreign investment (meaning US interests).

The national security policy was called **New Look** as it was supposed to reflect a coming change in military orientation. Developed out of NSC-162/2 (1953), it was a reevaluation of US military priorities, committing the United States to a smaller army and navy while building up nuclear weapons reserves and expanding the air force which would be necessary in the event of nuclear strikes. From his position as a military man, Eisenhower viewed nuclear weapons tactically or strategically. Complementing the military shift, Dulles formulated a rhetoric that stated that the United States was on a moral crusade against communism and it would prevent the spread of communism through the use of all force necessary, including nuclear, to combat aggression. This led to the strategy of brinkmanship: the idea was that, through the threat of massive retaliation, the United States could contain communism by forcing the Soviet (or Chinese) opposition to back down. **Brinkmanship** led to an increase in the number of nuclear weapons the US possessed. During the Eisenhower administration, the US stockpile grew from 1,200 to 22,229.

Despite his investment in this pro-nuclear shift, Eisenhower recognized the danger of nuclear weapons; the US could not simply stockpile weapons as the Soviet Union stood idly by—it, too, was increasing its cache of nuclear weapons. And, indeed, the quest for new forms of weaponry (hydrogen bombs, missiles in outer space) fueled a growing defense industry. Eisenhower recognized that technology brought about the idea of Mutual Assured Destruction (MAD), which theorized that massive retaliation from one side would

New Look President Eisenhower's New Look foreign policy, sometimes called the "New Look Doctrine" was articulated by Secretary of State John Foster Dulles. The New Look was an aggressive change from Truman's policy of containment. The spread of Soviet Communism would be rolled back, countries liberated, and the threat of massive retaliation with nuclear weapons would be used to intimidate the Soviet Union into capitulating.

Brinkmanship A strategy of escalating the consequences of confrontation with one's opponent until one side must back down to avoid potentially catastrophic results. The idea was to force the Soviet Union to back down rather than risk destruction. Brinkmanship differs from massive retaliation in that massive retaliation was thought of as a deterrent to Soviet actions, while brinkmanship would escalate a crisis in which the Soviet Union had already taken aggressive steps. Secretary of State Dean Rusk verbalized brinkmanship during the Cuban Missile Crisis when he remarked, "We're eyeball to eyeball, and I think the other fellow just blinked."

produce the same on the other; this, in turn, led to two US–Soviet summits, in 1955 and 1959, to address the threat of nuclear weapons.

Yet another way of combating communism was developed in the Eisenhower era: covert operations and the use of the CIA. Born out of the Office of Strategic Services from the Second World War, the CIA was created in 1947 as a data-gathering organization to assist policy makers in their decisions. However, its potential was soon recognized by Dulles and Eisenhower; it was an agency that worked mostly overseas, gaining information on those considered enemies of the United States. Headed by Allen Dulles (brother to the Secretary of State), the CIA was soon involved in subversive tactics and paramilitary actions as well as information acquisition. To perform its functions, CIA actions included:

- having foreign leaders on its payroll
- subsidizing anti-communist labor unions, newspapers and political parties overseas
- hiring US journalists and academics to make contact with foreign student leaders
- co-opt business executives who worked overseas to report back on economic circumstances and vulnerabilities
- creation of the US Information Agency to spread US culture, including the funding and programming for the Voice of America and Radio Liberty
- funding Radio Free Europe
- training foreign military officers in counterrevolutionary methods
- conducting covert operations to overthrow regimes hostile to the United States.

A core principle of the CIA is that the US president is removed from its decision-making. According to the principle of **plausible deniability**, the president could arrange for certain actions to take place but the links would be so well concealed that he could later deny knowledge of these actions. This allowed Eisenhower (and subsequent presidents) to disavow US involvement in a number of activities conducted to destabilize, overthrow or even assassinate leaders of hostile regimes. The deniability of such actions was reduced over time, but during Eisenhower's tenure he used this to his advantage in places such as Iran and Guatemala.

Plausible deniability The concept of creating a story or an untraceable connection that provides a believable alibi for those who order the commission of either illegal or embarrassing acts. It usually concerns a senior official of a government agency who orders an act, but for political or other reasons does not want to be held responsible should the action be made public.

Implications of the New Look for the region

Under the New Look policy, defense of the United States was a prime concern and the US military community argued strongly that there needed to be a continental defense policy, not simply a protection of US borders. Canadian politicians were understandably concerned; although they shared US fears of Soviet expansion and understood the destructive potential embedded in massive retaliation, they also feared US encroachment on Canadian territory. Negotiations began in 1953 and finally, in 1958, they reached an agreement, and the North American Aerospace Defense Command (NORAD) was created. NORAD is a bi-national defense organization that provides

"*The ability to get to the verge of war without getting into war is the necessary art. If you cannot master it, you inevitably get into wars.*"

John Foster Dulles,
Life Magazine, 1952

advanced warning of missile and air attacks on the US and Canada and protects the sovereignty of airspace in North America. It also maintains an airborne force to be used in the event of attack.

Dulles constantly stated that communism was on the rise in Latin America and that it remained the largest threat to US security. In his nomination hearings he argued that the conditions there were similar to those of China in the 1930s and that if the US remained non-interventionist, Latin America would meet a similar fate. Added to this was the idea of the domino theory. Although formulated to address the fear of communism in Southeast Asia, the same argument was made for the Western hemisphere: if one country fell to communism, others were sure to follow, especially in the Central American countries which were geographically contiguous. Dulles raised suspicions about the governments in Costa Rica and Guatemala. Although democratically elected, their economic and social policies, and the appearance of known communists in their governments, alarmed him. The reasons for this are not simply founded in anti-communism; US involvement in the region was also clearly based on its economic interests in Central America.

While Marxist thought in Latin America had a long history among intellectuals, the communist parties that had grown in the 1930s had largely been discredited by the 1950s. Until its dissolution, the Comintern and Cominform had directed communist party activities outside of the USSR. As the atrocities of the purges, Five Year Plans and the Soviet army's treatment of civilian populations emerged, these parties were identified as Stalinist and moved to the fringes in most Latin American countries. While socialist ideals were present in many countries, they did not usually appear through a communist party. Nonetheless, links with communism were almost always established.

In reality, many Latin American élites were embracing new models of economic development that more accurately represented their histories and resources. These models didn't always compliment US ideas of the free market; at the same time that Eisenhower entreated Latin America to keep itself open to foreign investment many countries were adopting Import Substitution Industrialization (ISI) as a way to create their own local industries. This was seen as a threat to US economic interests that had dominated the region, especially after the Second World War.

The New Look's focus on minimizing costs was reflected in the support of the military in the Americas and the use of covert operations. To support its ideology and policy decisions, Latin American military men were armed and/or trained by US forces, most notoriously through the Latin American Training Center for US Ground Forces (later known now as the Western Hemisphere Institute for Security Cooperation or School of the Americas), based in Panama before relocating to Georgia in 1984. The training center was a US Department of Defense military academy for Latin American officers to be instructed in the fields of leadership, infantry and counterinsurgency. The New Look's policy was demonstrated by US actions in Guatemala in 1954.

Guatemala and the use of covert operations by the CIA

The most evident source of the US administration's discontent was the situation in Guatemala. Guatemala had suffered under the brutal dictatorship of Jorge Ubico until a 1944 coup d'etat ousted him. Like his predecessors, Ubico endorsed pro-US policies and supported the United Fruit Company in its monopoly over banana production. UFCO not only controlled the main crop but also owned most of the country's infrastructure, including railways, ports and utilities. He was replaced briefly by a military junta until elections were held in December 1944. In 1945, Juan José Arévalo Bermejo became the first democratically-elected president of Guatemala, and a new constitution was written that included provisions for land and labor reform. Arévalo was succeeded in 1951 by Jacobo Arbenz, a center-leftist who pledged social and economic reforms for the country. By all accounts, his election was free, fair and devoid of corruption.

In his inaugural speech, Arbenz articulated three objectives for his people: economic independence, the establishment of a modern, capitalist state, and an increased standard of living for the population. He and his followers felt that the key to achieving these objectives was through agrarian reform. To this end, in June 1952, the Arbenz administration enacted the Agrarian Reform Bill (or Decree 900) that allowed the Guatemalan government to expropriate uncultivated lands from large plantations. The landowners would be compensated through 25-year bonds with 3% interest on the value of the land determined by the taxable worth of the land as of May 1952. After June 1952, 1.5 million acres were distributed to 100,000 families; this included 1,700 acres owned by Arbenz himself.

Much of the expropriated land was owned by UFCO; 85% of this land was unused. Based on the official tax value of the land, the Guatemalan government offered UFCO $627,572 in compensation. But over the years, UFCO had deliberately undervalued its holdings to avoid paying tax and it now complained to the US government that it was not being compensated fairly for the loss of land. As a counteroffer, the US State Department demanded $15,854,849. There was an additional conflict of interests in these negotiations: not only was UFCO a US company, but John Foster Dulles worked for the law firm that represented it and Allen Dulles had been president of the UFCO board.

In this case, the interrelationship of US political and economic interests in the region became very clear. The statements that came out of the US Department of State clearly charged Arbenz with communism, or at the very least, of not stopping a communist insurgency in the country, yet they were coupled with a demand for more money to go to UFCO for the land expropriated. On the issue of UFCO undervaluing its land the State Department was silent.

Once again, the domino theory was applied; the US position was that, if Arbenz could not be stopped, all of Central America and possibly even the US itself could fall to communism. In particular, it was argued, the Panama Canal could become Soviet-controlled, thereby limiting global free trade. It was the duty of the US to act on behalf of all countries that supported free trade.

Despite such accusations, Arbenz continued with his land reforms and refused to oust the four communists in the legislature (of 56). The US responded by appealing to the OAS for assistance, hoping that the group would act collectively against Guatemalan actions. Although a measure for action against Arbenz was passed it did not allow for direct OAS intervention and the US found its hands were tied in this endeavor. And, while most Latin American countries subscribed to the Caracas Declaration of March 1954, that rejected Marxism, there was not much force behind such declarations. The US government resorted to both embargo and covert operations to oppose Arbenz. The US refused to sell military equipment to Guatemala, forcing Arbenz, fearful of invasion to approach Eastern Europe for military support.

The arms shipment from Poland that arrived on May 17, 1954, gave the US the excuse it needed in support of its claims that Arbenz was communist, and in neighboring Honduras the US assisted exiled Colonel Carlos Castillo Armas to lead a group of exiles in an armed insurrection against the Guatemalan government. On June 18, 1954, Castillo and an army of approximately 150 crossed into Guatemala. They were assisted by CIA operatives who provided news reports from the jungles that over-reported the strength of the opposition to Arbenz. At the same time, US pilots raked the capital, causing minimal physical damage but producing the image of a city under siege.

An advertisement for an UFCO product.

The army refused to support the government, fearing the outbreak of a bloody battle, and Arbenz was forced to resign and go into exile. The US ambassador assisted in the transition of power to Castillo who ruled the country for three years without holding elections. Castillo reversed Decree 900, and his rule was marked by a return to the brutality of dictatorship and the dominance of local and foreign élites.

After successfully overthrowing the Arbenz regime, the situation in Latin America seemed to quieten down and throughout 1957 and 1958 the Dulles brothers argued that the threat of communism had been seriously diminished through US actions in the region. State Department policies in the area reflected a diminished fear of communism while crediting and maintaining containment policies. Vice President Richard Nixon's visit to South America in May 1958 would shift the administration's view yet again.

Activity

A recipe

 Write a recipe for a banana republic. What are the essential ingredients? What agents and processes are needed?

Take one democratically elected government … add at least 100,000 acres of fertile land …

Activity

A banana republic

Research definitions of a banana republic. What criteria must be fulfilled for a country to be considered a banana republic? Fill in the following table and answer the questions below.

Country	Guatemala	Jamaica	Norway	Argentina
Dates				
Form of government				
Primary export(s)				
Who controls the primary export(s)				
Type of industry in the country				
Economic élites				
Largest economic class				
Foreign private interest				
Foreign military or political presence				
Main imports				
Size of country				

Questions

1 In coming to a definition of a banana republic, which of the following assumptions are most correct? Which are false? Explain and discuss.

A banana republic is a small country.

A banana republic is a dictatorship.

A banana republic is dependent on a single crop.

A banana republic must be located in the Caribbean or South America.

2 Extending the model, find countries in other regions of the world in which comparable conditions exist that conform to your definition of a banana republic. Discuss your findings with your group.

Nixon's visit to South America

In May 1958, Nixon was dispatched to Latin America to congratulate Argentine president, Arturo Frondizi, on his recent election. He decided to extend his tour throughout Latin America to survey the scene for himself and was surprised by the anti-US sentiment he encountered in city after city. In most cases, he found himself engaged in debates with students and intellectuals who challenged US dominance in the region, and general opposition was respectful. However, in the cities of Lima and Caracas, he met with angry crowds that threatened to turn violent; in Caracas, he was first stoned and then the crowds attempted to pull him from his car.

The US State Department and press portrayed the protestors as an angry mobs of communists; their opposition to the United States was not communicated to the US public. Nonetheless, upon his return, a shaken Nixon reported to Eisenhower that the US had to change its policy directions in Latin America. Eisenhower called in a number of experts and, ultimately, it was agreed that, to keep the region stable and prevent the leftists from coming to power, the US needed to endorse and commit to economic aid. Through the Inter-American Development Bank, Eisenhower's administration provided money for social and economic programs in the region. The problem for the United States was that a downturn in the US economy made it difficult to justify foreign aid when the United States itself was struggling. State Department officials also cautioned that economic aid sent to Latin America would remain in the hands of the oligarchs and dictators, so, the implementation of the revised policies was tenuous at best. In the end, the US committed $500 million to a new program, rather than the $20–30 billion initially envisaged, and the commitment to economic aid lost momentum when Fidel Castro came to power in 1959.

Demonstrators attacking Vice President Nixon's car on May 13, 1958, in Caracas, Venezuela.

Eisenhower and the Cuban Revolution

On January 1, 1959, with former dictator Fulgencio Batista in exile in the Dominican Republic, Cuba's government shifted strongly to the left. Fidel Castro and his followers made a victory tour from one side of the island to another and, upon reaching Havana, Castro made a victory speech that ushered in a new era. He promised free and fair elections once the situation in Cuba had stabilized, and he promised to implement economic and social reforms. The United States viewed the Cuba Revolution with trepidation, also given Cuba's location, 90 miles from the US border. Castro was clearly pursuing socialist policies and, while he did not initiate nationalization or relations with the USSR immediately, his government had ambitious social policies that the Cuban government could ill afford.

In April 1959, Castro went on a press tour of the United States where he engaged journalists, but Eisenhower refused to meet with him. Instead, he was received by Nixon, ending any potential collaboration between the two countries. Shortly thereafter, Eisenhower authorized a CIA plan to train Cuban exiles to overthrow Castro's regime. The program floundered in late 1960 when Vice President Nixon lost the presidential election to John F. Kennedy, but the course of Eisenhower and Dulles remained steady throughout; to the end, they used the New Look policies in an attempt to prevent communism from taking root in the Americas.

US involvement in the Vietnam War

On August 7, 1964, the US Congress passed the Gulf of Tonkin resolution that authorized President Johnson to use conventional military forces in Southeast Asia without a formal declaration of war. US involvement in the Vietnam War can be divided into three stages. The first, in 1945–64, was one of assistance, first to France and then to South Vietnam. The second, in 1964–68, was the escalation of US involvement from 15,000 military advisors to 500,000 soldiers under President Johnson. The last stage, known as Vietnamization, was Richard Nixon's attempt to achieve "peace with honor." US involvement in Vietnam went far beyond containment and the domino theories; it profoundly affected the populace and changed society.

US involvement in Indochina, 1945–65

War in Indochina began immediately after the Second World War. The French wanted to regain control over the Indochinese peninsula (Vietnam, Laos, Cambodia and Thailand), their colonies since the 1880s. During the Second World War, the French ceded control to the Japanese. The United States had supplied guns to Ho Chi Minh, the leader of the tenacious and skilled Viet Minh guerrillas who fought against the Japanese. At war's end, Ho Chi Minh declared Vietnam independent from France. The French, assisted by the British, sent in a joint military force to re-establish French control. President Harry Truman was initially sympathetic to the Viet Minh and was not supportive of the return of French colonial rule. When resistance to the forces of the Viet Minh proved more difficult than they had expected, the French approached the United States to assist them financially but President Truman initially refused. He changed his mind in 1947 but by then everything had changed. The Soviet threat in Europe was real and Truman had responded announcing his containment doctrine. In 1949, Mao Zedong's Chinese communist forces defeated the Nationalist Chinese. The US perception of Vietnam began to change, as they labelled the Viet Minh a communist regime taking its orders from Moscow. Initially, US interest in supporting the French had more to do with securing the situation in Europe than helping to defeat Ho Chi Minh, but that changed in July 1950 at the onset of the Korean War. US soldiers were fighting in the Far East, against an aggressive communist regime with the full backing and support of the Soviet Union. The Truman administration concluded that the situation in Indochina, China and Korea marked a new phase in Soviet expansionism and that nowhere in the world was safe from communism. That same year, Truman gave the French 40 million dollars in economic assistance and military equipment, beginning US involvement in Vietnam. In 1950–54, the United States gave 2.6 billion dollars to the French accounting for half the total cost of the war. In 1954, the French had sent 400,000 troops into Vietnam but were losing the war. The knockout blow came in the spring of 1954 at the Battle of

Dien Bien Phu where 10,000 French troops were surrounded, cut-off and captured by the Viet Minh. The French government pleaded with Eisenhower to send US ground forces to save the situation. Eisenhower stood firm against the advice of Vice President Nixon and his military commanders and refused the request. The defeat ended the French regime. The Geneva Conference was convened to restore peace and unify Vietnam.

In April of 1954, President Eisenhower verbalized his version of containment for Southeast Asia. He claimed that if one nation in the region fell, it was only a matter of time until its neighbours were subjugated one by one by creeping communism. They would fall like dominoes, Eisenhower prophesized, "If the Vietminh won, the remaining countries in Southeast Asia would be menaced by a greater flanking movement," articulating the domino theory of a communist take-over.

When the Geneva Accords were signed in July 1954, South Vietnam and the United States did not sign, but acquiesced to the division of north and south at the 17th parallel. The UN would supervise the terms of the cease-fire: Viet Minh forces below the 17th parallel went north and French forces went south. About 450,000 refugees fled into the south, mainly Roman Catholics who feared a communist government and about 50,000 refugees crossed into the north. The Accords created the independent states of Cambodia and Laos and called for UN-supervised elections in 1956 to form a single government for Vietnam, an election that Ho Chi Minh was certain to win. The United States reluctantly got involved, at this stage covertly. The CIA supported the fledgling government in the South of Ngo Dinh Diem. In 1955, Diem cancelled the elections. Meanwhile eight nations, including the United States, United Kingdom, France and Australia, signed the South East Asia Treaty Organisation (SEATO) that insured collective security of the region against aggression and included specific mention of Cambodia, Laos and South Vietnam, yet excluded all Indochinese states in its membership.

When the elections were cancelled, Ho Chi Minh's guerrilla units, known as the Vietcong, began infiltrating into the South. Diem became president of South Vietnam (The Republic of Vietnam). The Eisenhower administration continued to support the Diem regime and provided equipment, weapons and 1000 US military soldiers as advisors to arm, train and mentor the army of the Republic of Vietnam (ARVN). The direct involvement of the US military in Vietnam had begun. By 1957, the Viet Cong (VC) began active operations in South Vietnam employing the same tactics they used against the French: controlling the jungle and attacking towns, cities and ARVN military bases then melting back into the jungle. By 1959, the VC had killed 2,600 government officials and controlled large portions of the countryside. The US military had little confidence in the ARVN's fighting ability and sent more advisors, about 8,000 by the time President Kennedy took office in 1961. But it didn't help. The majority of ARVN units were badly led, poorly trained and unmotivated. It was increasingly evident to senior US commanders that without the assistance of US ground forces, the South would lose the war.

President Kennedy`s first year in office was a foreign policy nightmare. Despite his guarantee that he would act rather than react to the threat of communism, events undermined his bravado. In 1961, the Bay of Pigs fiasco, the building of the Berlin Wall and a reprimand from Khrushchev in Vienna had made him appear feeble. He needed to change his approach or lose the support of the US public. In November 1961, he committed more forces to Vietnam and sent Vice President Johnson on a fact-finding mission. The result was US covert involvement in the overthrow and murder of the corrupt, authoritarian leader of the South, Diem, who they had originally supported due to his firm anti-communist stance. Although there is some historical debate on the extent of Kennedy's support for actions in Vietnam, it is certain that from this point on, the United States had no other choice but to support the South and start the escalation of its involvement in Vietnam. The course was set when Kennedy went to Dallas on November 22, 1963, and was assassinated. Vice President Lyndon Johnson was sworn in as president of the United States and was thus compelled to follow the unsure path established by the now-dead Kennedy. Shrouded under the pall of the Kennedy tragedy, a little-known war in a Southeast Asian country smaller than Johnson's native Texas was about to take center stage in a drama that would prove the most divisive event in US history since the civil war.

Escalation, 1964–68

Following the Gulf of Tonkin resolution, the US went from assisting South Vietnam to taking control of the war. It was a limited war like Korea, without formal declaration of war and a concerted attempt to keep the conflict localized to the Vietnam. Johnson's decision to escalate the war on the grounds that it was the logical outgrowth of two decades of incremental decisions by his presidential predecessors and it required resolution. Immediately following the Tonkin resolution the military inaugurated "Operation Rolling Thunder", an air campaign to bomb North Vietnam into submission. US bombers flew thousands of missions attacking key North Vietnamese installations, and dropping thousands of tons of bombs. As the air war heated up, so too did the ground war. The US employed helicopters to lift ground forces into remote jungle regions and attack enemy strongholds. The Viet Cong countered by attacking American military installations and ambushing US patrols. US casualties increased and the US public began to question the cost of the war. Johnson questioned the war as well. He wanted to build "The Great Society" that eliminated racism and poverty. He did not want to get dragged into a war that could undermine his domestic agenda. He lamented, "I can't get out, I can't finish with what I've got, So what the hell do I do?"

What he did was try to win the war before the 1968 presidential election so that he could focus on his domestic agenda in a second term. He hoped that the air war would force North Vietnam to negotiate before he committed large numbers of ground troops. By June 1965, the air force was flying 3,600 bombing missions a month and ground forces were increasing incrementally; by the end

Discussion point

War of attrition

The United States military followed a strategy of attrition in Vietnam. Attrition is a strategy that tries to wear down the enemy over a long period rather than defeat them in a decisive battle like Waterloo (1815). It was the strategy employed by General Grant in the US civil war and by Allied generals in the First World War. In Vietnam it was based on the superiority of US technology and a belief that the war could be won by overwhelming fire power. Based on your understanding of the Vietnam War, why did this strategy not work against the Viet Cong?

of 1966, the number was set at 450,000 soldiers. It was evident that the air campaign alone would not win the war. The White House told the people of the United States that they were winning the war and that the sacrifices would soon bring victory but they had to send more ground troops. Johnson was determined to win and refused to be the first US president to lose a war against the communists.

The Tet offensive of January 1968 was the turning point in the Vietnam War. General Westmoreland had told the US public that North Vietnam's forces were being systematically ground down, and it was unlikely they would be capable of launching major attacks against US forces. The reports were more than propaganda, the North was being worn down in a war of attrition and the heavy losses could not be sustained. But the US needed a major victory. Johnson's popularity was fragile and the anti-war movement was gaining momentum. Kennedy had said that the war was for the hearts and minds of the people but support in the US was waning, and a major offensive might turn public opinion against the war. Tet is the Vietnamese New Year and the two sides typically observed a temporary cease-fire. During the lull in the fighting, about 85,000 Viet Cong and North Vietnamese soldiers infiltrated the major cities of South Vietnam. On January 31, the first day of the lunar New Year, they attacked and seized control of important government institutions and even the US embassy in Saigon (Ho Chi Minh City) briefly fell to the North Vietnamese. It took several weeks of heavy fighting to clear out the attackers. Losses on both sides were heavy and in the end the Tet offensive was decisively defeated on the battlefield. However, in the living rooms of the United States, the 6 o'clock news TV broadcast showed uncensored combat footage of desperate fighting and a determined enemy that did not appear on the verge of defeat. Westmoreland asked for another 200,000 soldiers to finish the job. Middle America, the heartland of the United States that had opposed the anti-war movement and staunchly supported the president now began to question US involvement.

The Tet offensive was a huge gamble for the North Vietnamese that turned the tide of the war. General Vo Nguyen Giap, supreme commander of the North Vietnamese army said that "The war was fought on many fronts. At that time the most important one was American public opinion." The US had established a number of large military installations called fire bases, in remote jungle locations close to the North Vietnamese supply routes. Khe Sanh was one such base in Quang Tri province, near the Laotian border, garrisoned by 6,000 US marines and ARVN soldiers. During the Tet offensive, the base was surrounded and besieged by an estimated 15,000–20,000 North Vietnamese soldiers for 77 days. The US military feared another Dien Bien Phu. Khe Sanh was supplied from the air and a relief column eventually finally broke through and relieved the embattled marines and the siege ended. The garrison suffered about 4,400 casualties, and the North's casualties were estimated at double that number. In the United States, people wondered how a guerrilla army that was on the verge of collapse could mount a siege of such magnitude and nearly overrun a major American military installation.

On March 31, 1968, President Johnson went on national television and announced he would not run for a second term. He had achieved considerable milestones notably the passage of civil rights legislation but the escalation of the war had short-changed his domestic ambitions gobbling up a quarter of every tax dollar spent on the Great Society programs. Johnson had tried and failed to fight a war on two fronts. He did, however, suspend the bombing campaign which opened the door to negotiations. Republican candidate Richard Nixon won the November 1968 election promising to restore order on the streets, listen to the silent majority and bring peace with honor and an end to the war.

Vietnamization and withdrawal, 1969–1973

Nixon's policy to turn the war over to the South Vietnamese Army was called Vietnamization. To concurrently increase the ARVN's role in the war and gradually withdraw US ground forces, he sent his chief advisor Henry Kissinger to negotiate a peace treaty that would recognize the permanent division of Vietnam between North and South. Like Korea, the talks dragged on and the United States escalated the war when that happened. The heaviest bombing raids of the war, including the Northern capital of Hanoi and the mining of Haiphong Harbor to stop shipping, leveraged the North Vietnamese back to the table. In 1970, President Nixon authorized secret operations sending ground forces and bombing raids to disrupt North Vietnamese supply routes (the Ho Chi Minh trail) by violating the neutrality of Cambodia and Laos. These tactics worked and the North came back to the negotiation table. Troop withdrawals took place in 1969–72. The last US bombing raid was in August 1972, the Paris Peace Accords were signed in January 1973 and the war was over for the United States. Nixon had been re-elected to a second term in November 1972, hoping to pursue a domestic agenda once the war was ended but the Watergate scandal erupted and ended in his resignation on August 4, 1974. After a brief pause, the fighting began again between North and South in 1975. In early March, the North Vietnamese began a full scale invasion of the South. ARVN forces fought bravely at first, but then collapsed and Saigon was captured on April 30. Vietnam was reunited under the Hanoi government 20 years after the Geneva Accords had split the country.

The domestic impact of the Vietnam War

The 1960s was a period of dramatic change in the United States, and the Vietnam War heightened the growing tensions in US society. This decade witnessed the rise of the middle class, the evolution of the civil rights movement, the women's movement, the rise of the youth culture and government initiatives in social reform. In this atmosphere all was questioned, including the government, and the media—especially television—became a forum for criticism of government policies.

The war became a catalyst for these changes but, more than that, it made the United States reconsider its global image and status. By 1968, the US consensus regarding the containment of communism was weakening and support for the Vietnam War in particular was crumbling. A counterculture had emerged that challenged the status quo and demanded social and political reform.

Discussion point

Compare and contrast the US experience in the Korean and Vietnam wars?

Discussion point

Inequities of the draft

Should all members of a nation be eligible for the draft regardless of education, economic status, gender or race? How was the situation in Vietnam reminiscent of the inequities of the draft during the US civil war?

373

The youth movement took their disquiet to the streets and protests, sit-ins and music festivals became the gatherings that defined this new generation. Universities became centers for dissent. Young men burned their draft cards, and as many as 60,000 draft evaders went to Canada. Muhammad Ali, the heavyweight boxing champion and Olympic gold medalist declared himself a conscientious objector and was jailed after an all-white jury convicted him of draft evasion. He symbolized injustice for millions of young people who opposed the war, also drawing attention to the high proportion of African Americans who were **drafted**. At the same time, it was alleged that the sons of the élite were being protected by their universities who used grade inflation to prevent them from being called up to serve in the military. There were clear racial and class divisions among those who had to serve and those who did not. Then, to make matters worse, the two men who had captured the imagination of young Americans of all races and promised a brighter future were assassinated: Martin Luther King was assassinated on April 4 1968; followed by presidential candidate Robert Kennedy on June 6 of the same year.

The 1968 Democratic National convention in Chicago had turned into a pitched battle between the police and anti-war protestors. TV coverage showed policemen beating young people with batons. There were thousands of marches, sit-ins and rallies across the country. Nevertheless, a significant majority of middle- and working-class people in the United States considered the youth movement an aberration. They did not like hippies, loud music or tie-dyed clothing. Middle America paid its taxes, voted in elections and supported President Johnson and the war. The CBS newsreader Walter Cronkite was Middle America incarnate, always ending his 6 o'clock news programme with the statemenet, "And that's the way it is." So, when he turned around and voiced criticism of the war, in an uncharacteristic departure from his standard objective non-partisan role as news reader, his comments rocked the nation. Cronkite had been in Vietnam during the Tet offensive and on February 27, 1968, he hosted a TV documentary on the war, closing with the words:

> It seems now more certain than ever that the bloody experience of Vietnam is to end in a stalemate. ... But it is increasingly clear to this reporter that the only rational way out then will be to negotiate, not as victors, but as honorable people who lived up to their pledge to defend democracy, and did the best they could.

Cronkite's disenchantment with the war, made public that February night was a turning point, further galvanizing US public opinion against the war. When President Johnson heard Cronkite's comment he lamented, "That's it. If I've lost Cronkite, I've lost middle America."

Things only got worse for Johnson. On March 16, a company of US soldiers deliberately massacred 350–400 villagers in the tiny hamlet of Mai Lai. The military tried to cover it up, but one of the soldiers went to the press. How could this happen? Who was to blame?

The **draft** was not uniformly applied to all US citizens. African-Americans comprised about 11% of the population but made up 12.6 % of the soldiers in Vietnam and suffered 14.9% of combat deaths. More telling overall was the fact that the majority of soldiers were from low-income backgrounds. Young men from poor backgrounds were also twice as likely to serve in front-line combat units and become casualties than men from better educated, higher-income backgrounds. About 10,000 women served in Vietnam, 83.5% were nurses. Women did not serve in combat units. The women who served were volunteers, but the men were drafted.

Walter Cronkite in Vietnam during the Tet offensive.

The reputation of the US army was in tatters. The company commander, Lieutenant William Calley, and several of his men were charged and faced court martial but the stain of the massacre was permanent. Mai Lai provided fresh fodder for the anti-war movement. In October and November hundreds of thousands of protestors gathered in Washington to demand an end to the war, reminiscent of the freedom march of 1963. The rallies were coordinated with similar events across the country. Some radicals called for a general strike. Nixon vowed not to be swayed by the protests. A more radical movement emerged, the most important group being the Weathermen whose slogan was "You don't need a weatherman to tell you which way the wind is blowing." In October 1969, the group launched a campaign against US imperialism and advocated mass violence. The call for violence was unpopular and did not reflect the growing anti-establishment mantra of the youth counterculture.

The Kent State shootings

On April 30, 1970, President Nixon announced the invasion and bombings of Cambodia by US forces. Nixon had been quoted earlier that he would never consider this course of action. Kent State University in Ohio had been a hot-bed of student protest during the war. On the heels of Nixon's announcement the students began four days of protest, starting May 1, and during the first three days some property had been vandalized and a handful of protesters were arrested. A rally was planned for May 4 which university officials tried to cancel. The Ohio National Guard was on campus to keep the peace. About 2,000 protestors gathered and taunted the guardsmen but were dispersed with tear gas. The crowd reformed and a company of guardsmen wearing tear gas masks and with fixed bayonets advanced on the crowd in a line abreast. Without warning, and for reasons which remains a mystery, they then opened fire. Twenty-nine out of 77 soldiers fired 67 rounds at the students. Nine were wounded and four were killed. The country was thrown into a state of civil unrest. Five days after the shooting, over 100,000 protestors descended on Washington. A student strike closed over 900 university campuses. Then, on May 14, two students were killed by police at Jackson State (Mississippi) under similar circumstances. Nixon blamed communist radicals inciting the students, but his comments sounded hollow. New York Mayor John Lindsay denounced Nixon and claimed the country was on the edge of a spiritual and physical breakdown. Nixon responded by organizing a pro-war march by New York construction workers. His defensive attitude only added fuel to the anti-war movement and criticism of the government. No guardsmen were ever convicted for the shootings. Two weeks after Kent State, songwriter Neil Young's hit song "Ohio" hit the air waves and captured the mood of the times. The real enemy to freedom was the president.

"*Tin soldiers and Nixon's comin', we're finally on our own, this summer I hear the drummin'—four dead in Ohio*

Gotta get down to it, soldiers are cutting us down,

Should have been done long ago,

What if you knew her, and found her dead on the ground, How can you run when you know?"

"Ohio," lyrics by Neil Young, recorded May 15, 1970

Kent State shooting, May 4, 1970. Mary Ann Vecchio kneeling over Jeffry Miller. John Filo, a photography student, took the picture.

The conclusion to the Vietnam War

Between 1964 and 1973 over two million US citizens had served in Vietnam and over 500,000 had resisted the draft. The effect of the war on the United States was divisive. The US belief in itself as the protector of freedom and democracy was shattered. No longer was the nation the unquestioned leader of the free world. Postwar, people in the United States tried to make sense of the war but the nation was bitterly divided over the issues. A clear example of this can be seen in the person of Henry Kissinger. While he was awarded the Nobel Peace Prize for his negotations in Paris and lauded by many for those efforts, he is condemned by others for his bombing campaigns in Cambodia and considered a war criminal by other. Just as with the war itself, the verdict has yet to be determined. Historians have struggled to determine the legacy and a historical consensus has yet to emerge on the Vietnam War.

The result of the war, in some respects, proved the fears of ideologues who sought to contain communism and prevent the domino effect from taking place. The clear result of the war in Indochina was that the entire peninsula fell to communism. After the fall of Saigon and unification of Vietnam, Cambodia and Laos both came under communist rule. In the case of Cambodia the results were especially tragic; the Khmer Rouge under Pol Pot killed approximately 1.5 million Cambodians in the pursuit of its extreme version of socialism.

It can be argued that the Vietnam War was a factor that brought the US and the USSR to the bargaining tables, resulting in the Strategic Arms Limitation Talks (SALT), and its link to the beginning of US relations with the People's Republic of China

Activity

Research activity

Photography

How can a photograph change public opinion and influence historical memory? Research other examples of important photographs in the coverage of the Vietnam War.

Write a 100-word caption to support the documentation of an event or a personal story. Present it to your group with a copy of the photograph.

Activity

Hollywood and Vietnam

Write a film review

The following films from the 1970s and 1980s present a critical view of the war in Vietnam. Write a film review of one of them.

Green Berets (Dir. Ray Kellogg and John Wayne, 1968)

The Deer Hunter (Dir. Michael Cimino, 1978)

Apocalypse Now (Dir. Francis Ford Coppola, 1979)

Platoon (Dir. Oliver Stone, 1986)

Full Metal Jacket (Dir. Stanley Kubrick, 1987)

are indisputable. At the same time, the US and Canada had a vehement disagreement over the war; Canadian Prime Minister Pierre Trudeau spoke out against the war and accepted all draft evaders. This is an episode in US history that will continue to be debated.

What cannot be argued is the human cost of the war: approximately 3 million Indochinese civilians died in the war, and military deaths reached nearly 2 million—1.1 million North Vietnamese, 220,000 ARVN, 58,000 US and 2,000 SEATO forces (Australia, New Zealand, the Philippines and Thailand all provided troops). The US was unable to contain communism; in Southeast Asia, the price was too high and even collective security (in the form of SEATO) was ineffective.

Activity

Historiography

The United States and the Vietnam War

Historical opinion remains deeply divided on the lessons, legacy and tragedy of the Vietnam War: Following are the views of five historians that focus on the Vietnam War from the perspective of the United States. Read each and then consider the questions that follow:

Source A

Not ignorance but refusal to credit the evidence and, more fundamentally, refusal to grant stature and fixed purpose to a "fourth-rate" Asiatic country were the determining factors, much as in the case of the British attitude toward the American colonists (during the American Revolution). The irony of history is inexorable. Underestimation was matched by overestimation of South Vietnam because it was the beneficiary of American assistance, and because Washington verbiage equated any non-Communist group with the "free" nations, fostering the delusion that its people were prepared to fight for their "freedom" with the will and energy that freedom is supposed to inspire. Such was the stated anchor of our policy; dissonant evidence had to be rejected or it would have made it obvious that this policy was built on sand. ... A last folly was the absence of reflective thought ... about the balance of possible gain as against loss and against harm both to the ally and to the United States.

Source: Tuchman, Barbara. 1984. *The March of Folly: From Troy to Vietnam.* New York: Knopf.

Source B

The American involvement in Indochina began almost imperceptibly, rather like a mild toothache. At the end, it ran through Vietnam and America like a pestilence. Each president based his policies on exaggerated fears and, later, on exaggerated hopes. Thus each president left the problem to his successor in worse shape than he had found it ... Her leadership lost the respect of an entire generation, universities were disrupted, careers blighted and the economy bloated by war inflation. ... the awesome truth about Vietnam is clear: it was in vain that combatants and civilians had suffered, the land had been devastated and the dead had died.

Source: Stoessinger, John G. 1985. *Why Nations Go to War.* 4th edn. New York: St Martin's Press. pp. 111–12.

Source C

Herein lies Vietnam's most painful but pressing lesson. ... to distinguish between what is desirable and what is possible, ... between what is desirable and what is essential. ... LBJ and his advisers failed to heed this fundamental principle of statesmanship. They failed to weigh American costs in Vietnam against Vietnams' relative importance to American national interests and its effect on overall American power. Compelled by events in Vietnam and, especially, coercive political pressures at home, they deepened an unsound, peripheral commitment and pursued manifestly unpromising and immensely costly objectives. Their failure of statesmanship then proved a failure of judgment and, above all, of proportion.

Source: VanDeMark, Brian. 1991. *Into the Quagmire: Lyndon Johnson and the Escalation of the Vietnam War*. Oxford University Press.

Source D

The war in Vietnam was not lost in the field, nor was it lost on the front pages of the New York Times or on the college campuses. It was lost in Washington D.C., even before Americans assumed sole responsibility for the fighting in 1965 and before they realized the country was at war; indeed, even before the first American units were deployed. The disaster in Vietnam was not the result of impersonal forces but a uniquely human failure, the responsibility for which was shared by President Johnson and his principal military and civilian advisers. The failings were many and reinforcing: arrogance, weakness, lying in the pursuit of self-interest, and, above all, the abdication of responsibility to the American people.

Source: McMaster, HR. 1997. *Dereliction of Duty: Lyndon Johnson, Robert McNamara, the Joint Chiefs of Staff and the Lies that led to Vietnam*. Harper Collins.

Source E

Here then is a provisional verdict. The Vietnam War was a just, constitutional and necessary proxy war ... that was waged by methods that were often counterproductive and sometimes arguably immoral. The war had to be fought in order to preserve the military and diplomatic credibility of the United States in the Cold War, but when its costs grew excessive the war had to be forfeited in order to preserve the political consensus within the United States in favour of the Cold War. The Vietnam War was neither a mistake nor a betrayal nor a crime. It was a military defeat.

Source: Lind, Michael. 1999. *The Genuine Lessons of the Vietnam War*.

Questions
1   Source A describes US involvement in Vietnam as "folly." Assess the other four excerpts and determine whether they agree or disagree.

2   To what extent do you agree with the historians who consider the failure of the Vietnam War to be a failure of leadership?

3   Assess the influence emotion plays in sources B and E?

4   With reference to the origin and purpose of these exceprts, why should we treat the views of these historians cautiously?

5   What is your historical assessment of the war's impact on the development of the United States? Use your own knowledge and these references to support your position.

US foreign policy towards the Americas

The Kennedy administration

Kennedy served as president of the United States for less than three years but his foreign policy legacy was immense. In Vietnam, he began the escalation of US troop involvement; in Berlin, he defused a looming crisis over the sovereignty of West Berlin. But his administration is best known for the resolution of the Cuban Missile Crisis: 13 days of intense negotiation and ultimatums designed to end a standoff between the United States and Soviet Union that, it is argued, brought the world to the brink of nuclear war.

Although the Missile Crisis dominates his administration's political legacy, Kennedy was determined to change the worldview of the other countries in the region through a series of programs to assist them in economic and social change rather than through military intimidation or direct assistance to military regimes. The Alliance for Progress was a program that aimed for the same political stability as other cold war policies but it attempted to achieve it through assistance rather than coercion. Nonetheless, Kennedy's foreign policy concentrated on the US–Soviet rivalry and his presidency was marked by the arrival of a strong Soviet presence in the region.

Flexible response and the Kennedy Doctrine

When John Kennedy assumed the presidency in January 1961 he reiterated the US commitment to contain communism that had marked the Truman and Eisenhower administrations before him. He clearly stated his intention to expand upon both containment and the New Look. Addressing the former, and arguably restating the Monroe Doctrine, the Kennedy Doctrine warned the Soviet Union to stay out of the Americas and pledged to reverse any Soviet incursions into the region that had already occurred. This meant that a key focus of his policy in the Americas would be based on ousting the Soviet Union from Cuba.

The New Look and its core concept of massive retaliation was superseded by the idea of flexible response. This policy did not preclude nuclear war as an option but considered it the choice of last resort. Other options included: negotiation with the Soviets; economic assistance to developing nations; continuation of covert operations; expansion of conventional forces. These policies were articulated in the inaugural address he delivered on January 20, 1961. In this speech he laid out his objectives globally, but also specific to the region. The Kennedy Doctrine showed US commitment to the region even before the events of the early 1960s unraveled and revealed the necessity of a specific policy towards the rest of the region.

The Alliance for Progress

Both Nixon's trip to Latin American in 1958 and Castro's success in Cuba showed the previous administration that there was a need to change US policies in the region. It was left to Kennedy, however, to implement such changes. Returning to the Act of Bogotá (1960), Kennedy fulfilled a pledge to distribute $500 million in assistance to Latin American countries and established a ten-year plan that had six objectives:

- increase per capita income
- diversify trade
- industrialize and increase employment
- bring about price stability
- eliminate adult illiteracy
- bring about social reform.

Kennedy argued that only through prosperity in the region would there be stability, and these two conditions would eliminate the appeal of Marxism and nurture democracy. Participating countries had to develop plans that included redistributive reforms: in most Latin American countries, 5% to 10% of the population controlled 70% to 80% of the land. He recognized that US economic assistance was very limited and could do little to change the situation; nor would a short-term fix be possible. The US—and its Latin American partners—would have to commit to a long-term program for there to be success.

Prior administrations had contributed very little to the economic development of Latin America. Truman had only allocated 3% of US foreign aid, and while Eisenhower increased that amount to 9% there was some question as to how it was allocated. For his part, Kennedy (and Johnson after him) increased assistance to Latin America to 18% of all US overseas aid; this amounted to $22.3 billion throughout the 1960s. Ultimately, however, the Alliance for Progress failed. Despite its ambitions, all of that money only amounted to $10 per person, per year, in the affected countries. Furthermore, planning and allocation of funds was based on a system with a strong middle class, and the reality was that the middle classes in the countries in question were relatively small and tended to support dictatorships rather than progressive ideas. Latin America began the 1960s with a very limited democratic base that only got smaller throughout the decade.

In Kennedy's last year as president there were six coups, forcing him to soften his stance towards dictatorships in the region. Rather than supporting democracies, the change of course supported dictatorships to try to bring about change. Unfortunately, this often strengthened and perpetuated these regimes and the economic development monies rarely reached their intended recipients. By the end of the decade, dictatorships prevailed in the region and while these may have assuaged US fears of Marxist regimes they did little to end the discontent that most Latin Americans experienced.

The Cuban Missile Crisis

Of all countries in the region, Cuba consumed the most of President Kennedy's time. From Eisenhower he inherited an unresolved situation in the Caribbean: Cuban exiles were being trained to overthrow the regime of Fidel Castro. But Kennedy's decision-making would lead to a foreign policy debacle that had farther-reaching consequences than anyone could have imagined. During the 1960 election campaign, Kennedy had taken a hard stance against Castro and accused the Eisenhower government of not doing enough to combat Castro. He promised Cuban exiles in the US that he would take every opportunity to combat communism in the region and restore Cuba as a democracy.

Kennedy was ambivalent about the CIA-directed plan that had been created by Eisenhower and Dulles. According to the plan, the exiles would launch an amphibious invasion of Cuba that would lead to an uprising on the island as it was assumed that many Cubans rejected Castro's rule. With US air support, the exiles would take a beach head, and a government-in-arms would ask for further assistance from the US. The United States would recognize this government and assist it in stabilizing the country and overthrowing Castro.

The plan relied on stealth, a bit of luck and the support of the Cuban population. The exiles had been planning the invasion for over a year, and it is estimated that the US government spent close to $5 million on the project. However, intelligence gathered by the CIA revealed that, despite the propaganda leveled against the Castro regime, most Cubans would not support an armed insurrection. The exiles were largely hated enemies of the Cubans who remained and it was foolhardy to expect them to support the return of those who had exploited the previous system.

Kennedy himself was unsure as to how to proceed. He promised to be hard on communism and to support the exiles yet the plan was not sound. A State Department memo argued for the cancellation of the invasion on legal grounds stating that such an action would violate US commitments to the Organization of American States and the obligations incurred by signing the Act of Bogotá. Congressmen further argued that this was an immoral action that exaggerated Castro's threat to the region and was an invitation for Soviet actions. At a press conference on April 12, 1961, Kennedy said, "I want to say that there will not be, under any conditions, an intervention in Cuba by the United States Armed Forces. This government will do everything it possibly can … I think it can meet its responsibilities, to make sure that there are no Americans involved in any actions inside Cuba … The basic issue in Cuba is not one between the United States and Cuba. It is between the Cubans themselves."

Despite the internal debates on the morality and legality of US support for an invasion, it took place. The invasion was a disaster; at the last moment, Kennedy decided that the US would not provide air support to the invading force, leaving them vulnerable to the Cuban air force, and the exiles lacked supplies. Two hundred rebel forces were killed in the attack and a further 1,197 were captured by the Cuban army. The Cuban people did not rise. For the United States, it was a public relations disaster. US involvement was not covert and thus the administration was guilty not only of violating international law, but also of failing in its attempted coup. Castro, for his part, claimed the success of his revolution over the US operation. But Castro was also shaken by the attempt and went so far as to request assistance from

Activity

Analyzing Kennedy's speeches

Choose one of the documents and with reference to their origins and purpose, assess the values and limitations of the source for historians studying Kennedy's foreign policy in the Americas.

- Kennedy's inaugural address, January 20, 1961, at http://www.yale.edu/lawweb/avalon/presiden/inaug/kennedy.htm.

- Kennedy's Alliance for Progress speech, March 13, 1961, at http://www.fordham.edu/halsall/mod/1961kennedy-afp1.html.

> "*[I]f the nations of this hemisphere should fail to meet their commitments against outside communist penetration—then I want it clearly understood that this government will not hesitate in meeting its primary obligations which are to the security of our nation.*"
>
> President Kennedy, April 20, 1961

US assistance to Latin America under the Alliance for Progress	
Fiscal Year	Budgeted (in millions of $US)
1962	1,400
1963	1,400
1964	1,400
1965	1,400
1966	1,400
1967	500
1968	469
1969	336

the Soviets in the defense of Cuba. This, in turn, led to the Cuban Missile Crisis.

In the summer of 1962, US intelligence began to report heavy Soviet activity in and around the island of Cuba. Agents in Cuba dispatched reports of Soviet trucks hauling machinery into the countryside and U2 spy planes photographed images of cruise-missile launch sites. On the strength of these reports, the US stepped up surveillance and Kennedy warned both the Cubans and the Soviets in speeches that the US would defend itself and its neighbors from hostile attacks.

On October 16, 1962, President Kennedy was informed that a U2 spy plane had taken photos of medium range ballistic missile sites in Cuba. On October 22, Kennedy gave a televised address to the American public informing them of the installations and announced that a quarantine was placed on Cuba and that any violation of the quarantine would be seen as a hostile action that would force the United States to retaliate; on the following day the OAS approved the quarantine. This asserted the policy of brinkmanship in an instant, and the ideas of massive retaliation and mutual assured destruction became potential realities. At the same time, the Soviets dispatched a ship heading to Cuba; the US would consider this an act of war. Subsequent negotiations and compromises, however, resulted in Khrushchev ordering the ship to turn around, and the Crisis was averted. The Soviets agreed to dismantle and remove the weapons under UN supervision. For his part, Kennedy promised that the US would not try another invasion on Cuba; it was also secretly agreed to dismantle and remove nuclear weapons it had in Turkey.

The implications for the Cold War were immense as many citizens were confronted with the possibility of nuclear war. And while Castro was left out of most of the decision-making process, his regime remained unharmed and able to develop. In the future, Cuba would become a center for revolutionary and guerrilla activity in the region and around the globe. This did not end US activities in Cuba; the US continued its boycott on Cuban goods, not allowing trade or travel with Cuba. Additionally, it kept its embassy officials withdrawn although there were unofficial American advisors in Cuba. Covert operations also continued. It was later revealed that the CIA had made several failed assassination attempts on Castro that have passed into legend: exploding cigars and poison-infused shaving cream were two reported methods used to try to kill Castro.

US relations with Cuba during Kennedy's administration show how many aspects of the flexible response policy were used, and the commitment to the Kennedy Doctrine that was articulated so early in his presidency.

A US spy photo taken in October, 1962, of a medium-range ballistic missile base in San Cristobal, Cuba, with labels detailing various parts of the base.

Discussion point

One point in the Act of Bogotá states that "the territory of a State is inviolable; it may not be the object, even temporarily, of military occupation or of other measures of force taken by another state, directly or indirectly, on any grounds whatsoever …"

What does this mean for Cuba regarding US and Soviet actions in the early 1960s?

The Johnson administration

If the Missile Crisis was emblematic of Kennedy's presidency, President Lyndon Johnson's legacy was Vietnam. Assuming the presidency due to Kennedy's assassination maintained Johnson's committment to Kennedy's policies until he could run for election himself. In the Americas, then, he was committed to continuing the Alliance for Progress and containing and eliminating communism. To assist him in Latin America, he enlisted an old friend from Texas, Thomas Mann, who had been the key advisor to Eisenhower in his regional policies. Mann was named Alliance for Progress administrator and Assistant Secretary of State for Inter-American affairs, and he developed a new line in regional affairs. The Mann Doctrine, revealed in March 1964 attempted to redress conflicting US interests in the region. US policies should focus on: economic growth with neutrality towards social reform; protection of US private investments; opposition to communism; and non-intervention. Lastly, the US should have no moral reservations about cooperating with military generals to achieve its policy goals; there should be no preference for democratic states or institutions. It promoted stability over democracy and protected US private investments in the region. Few distinctions were made between anti-US politicians and groups and pro-communist forces.

In April 1964, the US had the first opportunity to implement this new course. The Brazilian president João Goulart was overthrown in a coup that installed a military dictatorship. The United States offered assistance to the regime in the form of $1.5 billion in economic and military assistance (25% of all money that went to Latin America) and, in return, Brazil adopted a pro-US, anti-communist policy. Taking the policies even further, in spring 1965 the US sent 22,000 troops to the Dominican Republic to maintain the pro-US government there. Johnson and Mann also went on to give support to Duvalier (Haiti), Somoza (Nicaragua), Stroessner (Paraguay) and numerous other dictatorships that were anti-communist, if also brutal dictators.

The war in Vietnam was taking a substantial toll on US assistance through the Alliance for Progress. As US military commitments in Southeast Asia grew, there was a need to cut funding elsewhere. As a result, Johnson cut funds for economic assistance—but not military assistance. Even where economic assistance continued, the money rarely reached its intended destination.

El Salvador and Nicaragua: the beginnings of revolution

El Salvador was dominated by dictatorships that early on recognized the value of claiming anti-communism. When a group of moderate officers tried to take power in 1960, the US withheld recognition and forced the junta's collapse. It was subsequently replaced by a right-wing regime. Upon reviewing Alliance statistics, El Salvador seemed to be a model of success: it had high growth rates and its exports increased; however, Alliance monies were usually diverted to the landowning oligarchy, and the peasants ⟶

who were supposed to benefit from the economic assistance remained impoverished and uneducated. The food grown in the country was exported, rather than used for feeding the hunger-stricken peasants. Resistance to the regime was growing, although the CIA reported that there were few revolutionary threats to the regime.

In Nicaragua, the Somoza family ruled the country as its own personal fiefdom beginning in 1937. When the patriarch, Anastasio Somoza, was assassinated in 1956, his sons assumed control over the country. They had the support of US presidents, including Lyndon Johnson and they seemed to have undisputed control over the country, a situation that benefitted US investors in the country, and conformed to the Mann Doctrine. But change was afoot in that country. In 1961, opposition insurrectionists formed the National Sandinista Liberation Front (FSLN) or Sandinistas, a guerrilla group committed to overthrowing the Somozas. Although the CIA reported that the group was no real threat, it began urban warfare in 1966, and by 1967 the US began to commit military advisors to assist Nicaragua's National Guard, and provided military training to officers through the School of the Americas. Despite such measures, support for the FSLN continued to grow, and would lead to revolution in future decades.

> *"A revolution is coming—a revolution that will be peaceful if we are wise enough; compassionate if we care enough; successful if we are fortunate enough—but a revolution that is coming whether we will it or not."*
>
> Senator Robert F. Kennedy

The Nixon administration

Johnson's decision to step down from the presidency led to the election of Richard Nixon, previously the vice president who had witnessed anti-American protests in 1958. At the end of his vice presidency he had counseled a change in course regarding Latin America, and had in some respects sown the seeds for the Alliance for Progress. But it was his administration that would kill the Alliance. Evaluating the aims and outcomes, he determined that the Alliance had not fulfilled its goals, and that it had actually fueled discontent in some areas. While this was an astute observation, he did little to try to remedy the problems and often continued the same policies that had been in place. Like Johnson before him, foreign policy was dominated by Asia —first Vietnam and the promises he made for the withdrawal of US forces, and later by opening the People's Republic of China to the West.

Nixon in Chile

Latin America came to the forefront of US foreign relations when Nixon had to contend with a democratically elected Marxist president in Chile. In 1970, upon the election of Salvador Allende, it was made clear that the US objective was to keep him from taking office; or, in the worst case scenario, to remove him from power as quickly as possible.

US companies had over $1 billion invested in Chile. International Telephone and Telegraph, and the copper conglomerates Anaconda and Kennecott all feared that an Allende presidency would mean nationalization of their companies and the collapse of revenue streams. The United States had intelligence stations in Chile that monitored Soviet submarine fleets and there was fear of a domino effect in South America. Kissinger felt that Chile posed a more serious threat than Cuba as the Marxists in place had been democratically elected in free and fair elections, and ratified by the Chilean congress.

The US used both covert operations and economic measures to try to oust Allende. From 1970 to 1973, an estimated $10 million was spent in trying to bring about his downfall. To do so, the US:

- cut off all economic assistance to Chile, amounting to $70 million
- discouraged foreign private investment
- opposed international credits and loans from the IMF, World Bank and Inter-American Development Bank
- tried to disrupt the international copper market (critical to the Chilean economy)
- put diplomatic pressure on other Latin American countries to oppose Allende
- gave money to the opposition
- used the CIA to bring about a strike of truckers
- organized a break-in of the Chilean embassy in Washington DC.

In reality, the popularity of Allende and his UP had begun to wane. The Chilean military and middle classes strongly opposed his programs for social reform and were willing to take action themselves. The country was in chaos with reforms that were costly and a lack of income to pay for ambitious social programs. In August 1973, Augusto Pinochet was named commander in chief of the Chilean military, sealing the fate of Allende's administration. On September 11, the navy seized the port of Valparaíso and by 4 p.m. armed forces that stormed the presidential palace announced that Allende had committed suicide.

With the benefit of hindsight it seems that Chile was headed towards political change with or without US intervention and in that light the covert operations seem like money unnecessarily spent. However, it is significant that the US was willing to go to such lengths to overthrow a democratically elected government. The US embraced the Pinochet regime and enthusiastically supported it as it brutally repressed the opposition and removed all social reforms that had been put in place to assist the poor. But the Nixon administration was soon embroiled in its own affairs, and while covert actions might have been acceptable overseas they were not only immoral but illegal at home. Nixon resigned, facing impeachment, leaving the affairs of Latin America to Gerald Ford until the 1976 elections.

The Rockefeller report of August 1969 addressed Latin America and assessed that there was potential for political upheaval and a strong Marxist presence in the region; it therefore made sense to collaborate with military rulers to prevent the spread of communism in the region.

Activity

Perception

The following poem was translated from the Spanish and written shortly after the fall of President Salvador Allende of Chile. In it, women of two distinct classes give their views of their lives under the short-lived socialist government.

Two Women

I am a woman.
I am a woman.

I am a woman born of a woman whose man owned a factory.
I am a woman born of a woman whose man labored in a factory.

I am a woman whose man wore silk suits, who constantly watched his weight.
I am a woman whose man wore tattered clothing, whose heart was constantly strangled by hunger.

I am a woman who watched two babies grow into beautiful children.
I am a woman who watched two babies die because there was no milk.

I am a woman who watched twins grow into popular college students with summers abroad.
I am a woman who watched three children grow, but with bellies stretched from no food.

But then there was a man;
But then there was a man;

And he talked about the peasants getting richer by my family getting poorer.
And he told me of days that would be better and he made the days better.

We had to eat rice.
We had rice.

We had to eat beans!
We had beans.

My children were no longer given summer visas to Europe.
My children no longer cried themselves to sleep.

And I felt like a peasant.
And I felt like a woman.

A peasant with a dull, hard, unexciting life.
Like a woman with a life that sometimes allowed a song.

And I saw a man.
And I saw a man.

And together we began to plot with the hope of the return to freedom.
I saw his heart begin to beat with hope of freedom, at last.

Someday, the return to freedom.
Someday freedom.

And then,
But then,

One day,
One day,

There were planes overhead and guns firing close by.
There were planes overhead and guns firing in the distance.

I gathered my children and went home.
I gathered my children and ran.

And the guns moved farther and farther away.
But the guns moved closer and closer.

And then, they announced that freedom had been restored!
And then they came, young boys really.

They came into my home along with my man.
They came and found my man.

Those men whose money was almost gone.
They found all of the men whose lives were almost their own.

And we all had drinks to celebrate.
And they shot them all.

The most wonderful martinis.
They shot my man.

And then they asked us to dance.
And they came for me.

Me.
For me, the woman.

And my sisters.
For my sisters.

And then they took us.
Then they took us.

They took us to dinner at a small private club.
They stripped from us the dignity we had gained.

And they treated us to beef.
And then they raped us.

It was one course after another.
One after another they came after us.

We nearly burst we were so full.
Lunging, plunging—sisters bleeding, sisters dying.

It was magnificent to be free again!
It was hardly a relief to have survived.

The beans have almost disappeared now.
The beans have disappeared.

The rice—I've replaced it with chicken or steak.
The rice, I cannot find it.

And the parties continue night after night to make up for all the time wasted.
And my silent tears are joined once more by the midnight cries of my children.

In pairs, read the poem, with each person taking one part. After reading the poem answer the following questions:

1 What facts do they remember that are similar?

2 What facts do they remember that are different?

3 How do their interests differ?

4 How are their interests the same?

5 Are there any universal experiences here?

Source: http://www.regrettoinform.org/education/html/writing02.html.

The Carter administration

The presidency of Jimmy Carter marked an initial shift away from what had become traditional Cold War foreign policy. When he took office in 1977, Carter asked the US public to put aside their "inordinate fear of communism" and embrace a new program. He promised to: reduce the US military presence overseas and exhort other NATO members to pay more for their own defense; cut back on arms sales that had reached $10 billion per year under Nixon; and slow the arms race with a new round of nuclear weapons talks. Instead, he wanted to address environmental issues and improve human rights abroad through US assistance and pressure. But Carter found shifting the public's perception of foreign policy difficult at best. Part of the problem was a division in his own government: NSC head Zbigniew Brzeshinski was an anti-communist hardliner who was suspicious of Soviet motives; Secretary of State Cyrus Vance, on the other hand, advocated a policy of "quiet diplomacy" and rapprochement. Carter's main foreign policy advisors were often in opposition with one another.

The other problems that Carter faced came towards the end of his presidency from external events. In late 1978 the Soviets began to step up their involvement in Afghanistan, and they eventually invoked the Brezhnev Doctrine and invaded the neighboring country. This led to the deterioration of détente and the arms talks stalled; a US boycott of the 1980 Moscow Olympics further hurt US–Soviet relations. At the same time, revolution engulfed Iran and led to a foreign policy crisis wherein American citizens were held hostage by an incoherent government angered by the sanctuary the US provided the deposed Shah. As a result of the international instability, the defense budget ballooned to over $15 billion.

In the Americas, Carter's policies were focused on human rights and the Panama Canal. In November 1903, the Hay Bunau–Varilla treaty gave the United States the right to build a canal in Panama that would connect the Atlantic and Pacific Oceans. Additionally, the US would lease the land from Panama in perpetuity for $250,000 per year plus $10 million and would reserve the right to use military force if necessary to protect the canal. In September 1977, Jimmy Carter and Panamanian president Omar Torrijos signed two treaties that returned the land and the canal to Panama. According to the terms of one treaty, Panama took control of the Panama Canal on December 31, 1999, with joint protection, management and defense in the interim period. The second treaty emphasized the neutrality of the Canal in times of peace and war, requiring that it remain open to all vessels of all countries.

In an unprecedented move, military and economic assistance could be denied to countries that were seen as obvious human rights abusers. Under this, Guatemala, Chile and Argentina lost their US funding, and support of the Somoza regime in Nicaragua was also withdrawn as the Sandinistas were gaining momentum. It appeared as if, at least in the Americas, US policies were moving away from Cold War domination; that is, until the impact of events in Central Asia reversed this development.

In 1979, the new government of Nicaragua was recognized, given $8 million in emergency relief and promised a further $75 million. However, an October 1979 coup in El Salvador prompted US fears that Central America was mirroring Southeast Asia and soon the whole region would collapse into communism. After fueling support against the right-wing regime, the US soon withdrew support for the younger, more moderate officers and their coalition fell apart. They were replaced by yet another vicious military-backed government that oversaw, among other things, the assassination of Archbishop Oscar Romero in March 1980 and the murder of three North American nuns and a lay worker in December 1980. The US continued to provide military assistance through atrocities in which 10,000 political murders were committed in 1980 alone.

The promises of Carter's inauguration were unfulfilled due to inconsistencies in his administration's policies and events beyond US borders. The events in Central America, the USSR and Iran all led to a reversion to Cold War policies of containment and a fear of the domino effect—policies that had been in place since the onset of the Cold War. In the end, little changed in the outlook of the US, and its attitudes in Latin America were fomenting revolutions that would soon be unleashed.

The Cold War in Chile, 1945–81

After 1945, the period of the Cold War affected the entire world. The South American country of Chile, located in the southern cone of the Americas, provides an interesting study of how Chilean domestic and foreign policies between 1945 and 1981 reflected the global realignments of the Cold War world. The political parties, in a nation that prided itself on its democratic traditions, certainly reflected the bipolar context of this period. Elected governments from the right of the political spectrum represented the conservative oligarchies and co-opted the middle sectors of society, ignoring the working classes. However, the lower classes, sought inclusion and by the 1950s, social malaise was expressed in labor conflicts and strikes. By the presidential election of 1952, Chile had universal suffrage, as women had finally obtained the right to vote in 1949. This certainly helped to elect rightist Carlos Ibáñez to the presidency, claiming 47% of the popular vote. Despite not having a majority, following the precedent set by the Constitution of 1925, he had the mandate.

The new government had to contend with a rise in the cost of living and an annual inflation rate of 51%. Ibáñez had to deal with an enlarged public sector and political incumbents who were manifestly corrupt. The Chilean Constitution allowed the president the power to issue executive decrees and Ibáñez made use of this; however, in the years between 1953 and 1958, the political sphere became increasingly polarized. Part of Ibáñez's foreign policy involved borrowing from the International Monetary Fund (IMF), but this obliged the government to follow strict and unpopular economic austerity measures.

Beginning in 1957, the political parties of the left banded together in the Frente de Acción Popular (Popular Action Front, or FRAP). The government of Ibáñez reacted with harsh repression against communists. Cold War alignments were expressed in the news media, reflecting global political tensions. The left focused on conflicts as part of a historic struggle against systematic exploitation that had to be replaced by a new and more equitable system. The right focused on conflicts as an attack on democracy that had to be defended by upholding principles such as private property and anti-communist "Western" values.

Amidst this right–left polarization, the 1958 elections took place. The new president, the rightist Jorge Alessandri, obtained less than a third of the popular vote, but was confirmed by Congress because he had the highest percentage of the three candidates running. The other two candidates reflected the center and the left, showing how divided the country was. Alessandri was unable to work with a Congress that was politically against him; not even to deal with the devastating

389

Valdivia earthquake of 1960, the strongest ever recorded in the world. The left, encouraged by the recent Cuban Revolution in 1959, fueled protest and gained strength. Alessandri, a conservative, firmly committed to free enterprise and foreign investment, continued to enforce IMF measures to stop the inflation rate of 39% and stabilize the economy. In particular, the government invited an increase in US investment in copper mining and refining. Alessandri's foreign policy included acceptance of the US Alliance for Progress. Alessandri did not rule by decree like his predecessor, but his government was marked by bitter parliamentary debate over an agrarian reform bill in 1962, as well as National Health Service strikes in 1963, which continued to divide public opinion and political parties.

As an alternative to the sharp left–right divide, a centrist party, the Christian Democratic Party (*Partido Demócrata Cristiano*, or PDC) emerged as a strong reformist, but not socialist alternative. To make their point clear, the Party adopted the slogan, a "Revolution in Liberty." The PDC received nearly half of its campaign funds for its candidate Eduardo Frei in the 1964 elections from US and European sources, who viewed the emergence of a non-socialist party with relief. In view of the growing popularity of the leftist coalition, even the rightist parties decided to support Frei.

Activity

The Christian Democratic Party (PDC)

Research the political platform of the Chilean Christian Democratic Party in 1964 to find out what a "Revolution in Liberty" meant. Was it truly revolutionary or just reformist?

Discussion point

Chilean historian Sofía Correa has written that Frei was the first candidate to reach out to young people and to women, and that these two sectors were playing an increasing role in Chilean politics, starting with the election of 1964.

? **Why would these two sectors be so concerned with political events at the time? What would have been their concerns?**

Eduardo Frei (center), Chilean politician and the Christian Democrat candidate for president in 1964, holding two fingers in the air to remind voters that his name is number two on the ballot slip, Chile.

The highly charged and politicized 1964 election, in the aftermath of the Cuban Missile Crisis of 1962, caused the right to focus the election in the stark terms of communism versus liberty and dictatorship versus democracy. Although Frei won 56% of the vote, he encountered the same difficulty as his predecessors: a lack of consensus in the Congress. Strikes continued to plague Chile, now compounded by the implementation of an agrarian reform. While it succeeded in ending the long-term conservative-agrarian hold on political power in Chile, the PDC did not redistribute sufficient land to small farmers.

Frei's term in government was plagued by miners' strikes and student demonstrations for educational reforms. Yet part of Frei's domestic policy included the encouragement of workers' unions, whose membership increased markedly even as the extreme right and left divide continued to grow, with the Christian Democrats in the middle. The left accused the PDC of slowing progress toward a more just Chile and of serving the interests of the upper classes. The right, on the contrary, saw the PDC as encouraging revolutionary changes that seemed in keeping with the left. Extreme parties were born on both sides: the Revolutionary Leftist Movement (the *Movimiento de Izquierda Revolucionario*, or MIR), and the rightist National Party (*Partido Nacional*). Civilian-military relations became tense in 1969 due to low salaries and poor military equipment and armament. Frei's government attempted to improve this situation by providing upgrades. This was an important constitutional reform on the part of the Frei government as a concession to the young people that helped to elect him. After much debate, Congress agreed to lower the voting age from 21 to 18, which meant that by the presidential elections in 1970 there were nearly 1.5 million new voters. Women voters, who also provided support for Frei's government, were strongly encouraged to join 9,000 "Mothers Centers." Nearly half a million women did; they received work training and 70,000 sewing machines with easy credit, to start businesses.

Frei's foreign policy avoided direct confrontation with US hemispheric hegemony. There was internal political pressure to nationalize US-owned copper companies. Frei opted for a middle way, the "Chileanization" of the mines, and with the backing of Congress opted to buy part ownership of these companies and invest profits in improving processing plants. The results of this process were not as profitable as planned, as the US companies retained lucrative contracts. Still, Chile continued in the good graces of the hemispheric leanings in the Cold War, as decidedly pro-US, and was able to receive loans from the World Bank and the Inter-American Development Bank.

By the time of the presidential elections of 1970, Frei had been unable to fulfill all of his campaign promises. The PDC had tried, in a Cold War world, to solve deep-seated political and social issues by finding a middle position between capitalism and communism. It did not work. With the country deeply divided in three camps, the leader of the leftist coalition, Popular Unity (*Unidad Popular*, or UP), received the largest percentage: 36% of the popular vote in the 1970 elections. The traditional Congressional approval of the candidate with the largest share of the vote was bitterly debated this time. The centrist PDC was crucial in supporting the government of Salvador Allende, if he would guarantee respect for constitutional democratic process. US covert pressure to not confirm Allende was unsuccessful.

With Allende as president, the political climate in Chile became highly charged. The upper and middle classes demonstrated their fears of a leftist government with massive removal of capital, creating financial chaos. Some even opted for leaving the country immediately, closing factories and firing employees. Allende and his UP wanted to institute

> **Discussion point**
>
> Discuss the Frei government's views of gender roles when organizing Chilean women's associations in the late 1960s.

391

deep changes in the social, political and economic system of the country and build socialism in Chile. This included a People's Assembly, a replacement of capitalism by more state-owned enterprises in mining and other industries, banks, insurance and foreign commerce. But the years 1970 to 1973 were characterized by deep divisions in the six leftist parties that made up the UP on how and when to implement these radical changes. Although Allende preferred legal and constitutional means, the UP was anything but united and some advocated immediate revolution. The centrist PDC was split in factions and the rightist National Party warned of a socialist takeover. Even the Catholic Church was unable to call for more conciliatory language and debate, to avoid civil war.

President Salvador Allende waves to supporters in Santiago, Chile, a few days after his election on 24 October 1970. The car with Allende is escorted by General Augusto Pinochet.

Allende began to implement a domestic policy that enlarged government social services and the nationalization of key industries to the state, thereby alienating entrepreneurs. He continued the agrarian reform started by his PDC predecessor, Frei. Despite Congressional opposition and the US financial blockade of the Chilean economy, Allende followed through in nationalizing the copper mines and processing plants, as well as many banks and financial institutions. By 1971, however, the lack of coordination within the disparate factions of the UP was evident in the impact of agrarian reform policies, which seriously threatened the role of the private sector in agriculture. The expropriation of large landholdings created violent confrontations. Allende's foreign policy included reaching out to countries in the Soviet bloc, as well as inviting Fidel Castro to Chile. This was during the tense period in the Cold War after the Cuban revolutionary Che Guevara had been killed in Bolivia, in 1967, while exporting the communist revolution. The beginning of the 1970s saw an increasing role being played by Third World countries who challenged the predominance of the two superpowers. Allende also visited the Soviet Union, where he was warmly received. Allende's socialist government in Chile was becoming a focus for the bipolar conflict.

These external pressures were having a strong impact by the end of 1971. As currency reserves diminished and inflation soared, the US blockade was being increasingly felt as Chile was unable to get loans. Agrarian reform and industry expropriations reduced the availability of consumer goods as well as foodstuffs and a black market began to grow despite the government's attempt to fix prices. The opposition staged an increasing number of protest demonstrations against the UP government. The extreme left and the extreme right organized protest groups, who fought against each other in violent street demonstrations. Political polarization and extremism penetrated the entire Chilean society in the cities and in the countryside. It affected

Activity

Music and politics

Quilapayún

Listen to the Chilean left-leaning musical group Quilapayún. In their song "La Batea" (The Basin), they sing about the effect of the Allende election on the rich, as they are leaving the country by road to neighboring Argentina. They are referred to as *momios* or *momiaje* ("mummies") that cling to ancient, dried-out traditions.

Listen to leftist singer Victor Jara's songs *Plegaria a un Labrador* ("Prayer for a peasant") and *El Arado* ("The Plow") in which he dignifies the downtrodden farm worker.

What emotions do these musicians try to evoke? Analyze the lyrics to understand the messages they conveyed to the young people during the period of the Allende government.

schoolchildren and university students, all workplaces and the media, touching every aspect of daily life.

Allende's domestic policies of salary increase and price fixing helped poorer Chileans in particular and brought short-term political benefits. The UP obtained 50% of the posts in the March 1971 municipal elections. With a view to obtain a Congressional majority, in 1972 Allende resorted to populist tactics, creating Neighborhood Supply and Price-control Committees (*Juntas de Abastecimiento y Control de Precios*, or JAP), to dole out basic foodstuffs. In October 1972, the dearth of supplies in the cities was further complicated by a truckers' strike, which was covertly financed by the United States.

Allende's control of his own coalition grew weaker, so that he began to distance himself from them. Even the PDC now became allied with the rightist National Party, presenting opposition candidates to the Congressional election in order to stop Allende's reforms. Like some of his predecessors, Allende resorted to decrees in order to pass laws. One particularly controversial reform, aimed at creating Unified National Schooling (the *Escuela Nacional Unificada*, or ENU), in January 1973, upset the country and its traditional divided education of private and public schools. The demonstrations, all over Chile, were so powerful and violent that the president had to declare a state of emergency in 20 provinces to keep the peace. The ENU did not go through. Even so, by the time the Congressional elections were held in March 1973, 54% of the Congress was pro-UP and 44% opposition. The opposition parties wanted to impeach Allende for violating the Constitution. The copper miners began a long strike for two months, thereby slowing production considerably. Extreme leftist groups continued to call out for revolution. In an effort to alleviate the strained civilian–military relations, Allende installed several officers from the armed forces in his cabinet. The political conflicts, however, did not lessen. The PDC and the National Party argued that Allende had contravened the legislative guidelines, as set out in the Constitution. The UP, especially its most radical sectors, like the MIR, insisted that the process of transferring private enterprises and large landholdings to the state could not be halted.

By August 1973, Allende's government had gone through ten cabinet changes in three years. The media, especially those groups representing the right, spoke increasingly of civil war. The commander-in-chief of the Chilean armed forces, General Prats, came under increasing pressure for his conciliatory stance. Finally, he resigned and General Augusto Pinochet became commander-in-chief.

On a daily basis, Chileans were finding it increasingly more difficult to buy household supplies. Chilean women, in particular, two-thirds of whom were housewives (not in other jobs) at the time, were

President Salvador Allende meets with Soviet premier Alexei Kosygin, General Secretary of the Communist Party Leonid Brezhnev and Chief of State Nikolai Podgorny in Moscow during his visit to the Soviet Union on December 11, 1972.

Activity
Film activity
Machuca (2004, Dir. Andrés Wood)

Watch the film *Machuca* about schoolchildren at a Catholic boys' school during the Allende years. How did the political situation affect the two friends and their families?

Activity
Research activity
US National Security Archives

Divide into groups to search the US National Security Archives for transcriptions of calls between Secretary of State Henry Kissinger and president Richard Nixon on the situation in Chile. These archives can be found online at http://www.gwu.edu/~nsarchiv/nsa/the_archive.html.

 What was the extent of US covert operations in Chile between 1970 and 1973?

incensed at not being able to provide for their families and staged an enormous street demonstration in downtown Santiago. This protest was strongly supported by the coalition of the PDC and the National Party, whose supporters were on the extreme-right, leading to violent confrontations and arrests. The most important newspaper in Chile, the conservative *El Mercurio*, also gave particular coverage to this event, as it was still unusual at this time for women to take an active role in politics.

On September 11, 1973, much to the shock of Chileans, a military coup led by General Pinochet took over the country. It was a bloody, violent end to the conflicted government of Salvador Allende, who shot himself as the presidential palace was being bombed and burned by the Chilean air force. Some Chileans celebrated, some mourned, but the internal political divisions remained and were now suppressed as the presidency was replaced by a military junta of the army, navy, air force and national police. Congress was dismissed and closed. The judiciary were in no position to defend Chileans due to the "state of siege" declared by the military, which suspended the rights of citizens, curtailing the freedom of the press, the right to assembly and so on. All political parties were prohibited, and elections were suspended indefinitely. The supply of food improved, but Chileans now had to get used to curfews every night and censorship of the press, radio and television. Public offices and universities were purged of leftist functionaries and replaced by the military. The judiciary was also purged and many judges opted for silence or open support of the military government. Worse, government became a series of edicts and decrees for the control of the population. Leftists and those thought to be sympathizers of the Allende government were detained, often tortured and sometimes "disappeared." The military organized systematic persecution of "subversives" it considered responsible for the political chaos of Allende's three years in the government. The infamous National Intelligence Direction (the *Dirección de Inteligencia Nacional*, or DINA), also in covert operations with the Argentine and Brazilian military government, searched and detained political activists, murdering people as far away as Argentina, Italy or the US. The director and many officers involved in the DINA were graduates of the US counterinsurgency training School of the Americas at Fort Benning in Georgia.

Activity

Below is a photograph from the front page of *El Mercurio*, from September 6, 1973. Thousands of women congregated, beating pots and pans with wooden spoons or lids, to signify that they had no food to feed their families due to the ineptitude of Allende and his *Unidad Popular* (UP) government. The headline translates as "Women Reject the Government." The two sub-titles say "Marxists attack the [female] demonstrators." and "50 injured in incidents." Why would this female demonstration have been so shocking at the time? How is the right using gender roles to generate support?

Activity

The School of the Americas

Research the formation and objectives of the School of the Americas at Fort Benning in Georgia, USA. What role did it play in the Cold War and Chile in particular?

By 1978, these human rights abuses became public with the discovery of bodies in the rural area of Lonquén. The murder of union leader Tucapel Jiménez in 1982 stunned the labor world and the murder of two teachers from the teachers union in 1985 greatly disturbed educators. These and the burning alive of two university students in 1986, were the most notorious cases of the more than 100,000 Chileans who were tortured or exiled, as well as the approximately 4,000 that "disappeared" when they were killed in military detention camps.

Pinochet acted harshly, yet sought legitimacy to his dictatorship by using *consultas* or plebiscites to document support in response to UN accusations of human rights abuses. In 1978, he claimed 70% support. Under pressure also from the Catholic Church, Pinochet eventually lifted the state of siege and the curfew and declared an amnesty, in an effort to improve his government's reputation abroad. However, the detentions, tortures and disappearances continued. The Church responded by excommunicating the known perpetrators of these crimes. By 1980, the military dictatorship had elaborated a new Constitution, presented to Chileans in a plebiscite for their approval. This included a slow process for the end of military rule that was approved by the population. The new government would remain an authoritarian democracy guarding against what the military considered to be subversive influences. Dismay at the continuing human rights abuses and the changing circumstances of the Cold War eventually turned public opinion against the Pinochet government, which was voted out of office in 1989.

Anti-Pinochet, pro-human rights demonstration in a low-income neighborhood of Santiago, Chile.

Exam practice and further resources

Sample exam questions

1 How and in what ways did McCarthyism affect the domestic and foreign policies of the United States?

2 "The most significant domestic effect of the Vietnam War on the United States was the death of Johnson's 'Great Society.'" To what extent do you agree with this statement?

3 Compare and contrast the impact on the Americas of the foreign policies of US presidents Nixon and Carter.

4 Discuss the view that domestic pressures more than genuine external threats were the cause of US involvement in the Korean War.

5 Evaluate the impact of the Cold War on the foreign and domestic policies of either Canada or one Latin American country.

Recommended further reading

David J. Bercuson. 1999. *Blood in the Hills: The Canadian Army in the Korean War.* Toronto: University of Toronto Press.

Pamela Constable & Arturo Valenzuela. 1993. *A Nation of Enemies: Chile Under Pinochet.* London: W. W. Norton & Company.

John Lewis Gaddis. 2005. *The Cold War: A New History.* New York: Penguin Books.

James T. Patterson. 2005. *Restless Giant: The United States from Watergate to Bush vs. Gore.* Oxford University Press.

Michael Reid. 2009. *Forgotten Continent: The Battle for Latin America's Soul.* New Haven: Yale University Press.

Peter Smith. 1996. *Talons of the Eagle*: *Dynamics of US–Latin American Relations.* Oxford University Press.

John Stoessinger. *2005. Why Nations go to War.* 9th edn. Belmont, California: Thomson & Wadsworth.

Peter Winn. 2006. *Americas: The Changing Face of Latin America and the Caribbean.* 3rd edn. Berkeley: University of California Press.

Thomas C. Wright. 2001. *Latin America in the Era of the Cuban Revolution.* Rev. edn. Westport, CT: Praeger Publishers.

Online resources

Country Studies. Federal Research Division of the Library of Congress. http://countrystudies.us.

The American Presidency Project. University of California, Santa Barbara. http://www.presidency.ucsb.edu.

Top Documentary Films
http://topdocumentaryfilms.com.

US presidential libraries online
Truman: http://www.trumanlibrary.org.
Eisenhower: http://www.eisenhower.archives.gov.
Kennedy: http://www.jfklibrary.org.
Johnson: http://www.lbjlibrary.org.
Nixon: http://www.nixonlibrary.gov/index.php.

7 Into the 21st century, 1980–2000

The final two decades of the 20th century began with few indications of the changes that would occur during those years. In 1980, Ronald Reagan was elected president of the United States to usher in a period of conservatism and reassuring calm differing from the tumultuous previous two decades. The world still seemed to be divided between the USSR and the USA. In Latin America, autocratic regimes were solidifying their power, economies underwent significant changes, and civil wars raged in several countries. If one looked beyond the news headlines, however, changes were underway. The personal computer was already on the market and voices of democracy were already being heard in city squares in South America. In a short 20 years, democratic institutions would flourish across Latin America, the cell phone would change the idea of calling a place to calling a person, using the World Wide Web and sending email would become commonplace. People would talk of "shopping on line." Globalization would become a word of progress, exploitation, and polarization. The Soviet Union disappeared. AIDS and climate change became major concerns in the region and around the globe. It was a time of great change.

This chapter looks at a number of major events, developments, and people during those two decades. The political, economic, technological, cultural, and social changes of the period and region were, in some important ways, both evolutionary and revolutionary. Students reading this chapter should keep in mind the concepts of continuity and change, and cause and effect, to understand the historical processes at work in the 1980s and 1990s.

By the end of this chapter, students should be able to:

- explain the effects of the United States becoming the world's sole superpower

- show an understanding of the similarities, differences, and effects (both at home and in the region) of the domestic and foreign policies of US presidents Ronald Reagan, George H. W. Bush, and Bill Clinton

- explain the causes and evaluate the success of the transition from authoritarian to democratic governments in Perú, Argentina, Uruguay, and Brazil

- be able to discuss and evaluate developments in the United States in terms of:

  –technological developments and their impact on society and politics

  –globalization, political, economic and cultural aspects

  –concerns about HIV/AIDS, climate change, and other important health and environmental issues

  –consistency and changes in popular culture, including music, film, literature, and other forms of entertainment.

The domestic and foreign policies of Reagan, Bush and Clinton

The last two decades of the 20th century hosted three American presidencies: those of Ronald Reagan, George H. W. Bush, and Bill Clinton. In his presidential inauguration speech, January 1981, Reagan announced that, "government is not the solution to our problem; government is the problem," becoming the embodiment of the anti-government politician. Reagan's domestic goals of shrinking both taxes and the size of the government to stimulate the economy contrasted with his desire to rapidly expand the military and present a robust and aggressive anti-communist foreign policy to the world. This two-pronged set of policy directions became known as the Reagan Revolution. During the eight-year Reagan presidency, taxes were lowered and raised, the overall size of the government did not shrink, the military grew, the United States was involved in military and covert action from Lebanon to the Caribbean island of Grenada, Nicaragua and its neighbors and negotiations took place between Reagan and the last leader of the USSR, Mikhail Gorbachev. Yet, by the end of Reagan's two terms he left office as one of America's most popular presidents.

Riding to office on Ronald Reagan's popularity was his vice president, George Bush, a man of vast governmental experience, including ambassador, CIA director, and senator, a member of the Washington establishment, the opposite of Reagan's outsider appeal. Bush ran for office as a kinder, gentler president who would continue his predecessor's policies, but with a more compassionate outlook. When running for president, Bush proclaimed, "Read my lips: no new taxes," a pledge eventually abandoned under the continuing growth of the deficit. More environment-friendly than his predecessor, Bush's domestic achievements included a strengthened Clean Air Act, and civil rights legislation. On the foreign policy front, Bush ordered an invasion of Panama to seize the dictator of that country on drug charges, created and led an international coalition of armed forces to oppose Iraq's invasion of Kuwait, and presided over the United States' response to the breakup of the Soviet Bloc and the dissolving of the USSR into many separate nations. Faced by a recession near the end of his term, President Bush's foreign policy achievements were disregarded by a disillusioned US electorate. Bill Clinton, the first baby-boomer candidate, and the first since Franklin Roosevelt to not have served in the military, broke rank with the experience of previous presidents.

Bill Clinton ran for president portraying the occupant of the White House as out of touch with the people of the United States. Focusing on the economy, the youthful Clinton entered the presidency in January 1993 overflowing with progressive ideas: healthcare, gays in the military, fixes for the economy and many more domestic initiatives. Over the course of his presidency, many of the initiatives faded or failed, some failures due, in large part, to Clinton's personal troubles that ended with him being only the second US president to be impeached, but spared conviction by the Senate. Clinton successfully lowered the ongoing budget deficit through tax hikes and economic growth, spurred by the "dot-com" boom. His political strategies led to seeking a middle ground in legislation, eventually declaring in a Reaganesque way that the era of big government was over. While not originally focused on the outside world, Clinton had to deal with foreign policy issues including involvement in Somalia, a coalition with NATO for military action against Serbia, an AIDS initiative in Africa, and peace talks to end the Serb-Bosnian conflict. Despite his personal travails and almost being removed from office, President Clinton left office in January 2001 as a popular president.

The Reagan years: January 1981 – January 1989

Activity

Note-taking for US presidents

Organize your notes as you take them. Create a simple Presidential Policies Table as below. The three column chart can be drawn in a notebook and expanded as needed. Create a different table for each president. This type of table allows for policy narratives or analysis.

Ronald Reagan: Policies		
Domestic policy	Foreign policy	Comments
		Include your own observations, questions for further research, items that relate to prior study, etc.

Alternatively, create two different tables, one for domestic policy and one for foreign policy:

Foreign policy			
Reagan	Bush	Clinton	Comments

This table allows for comparison and contrast between presidents, as well as narratives and analysis. More information is packed into a confined space, but may be too crowded for some students.

Ronald Reagan entered office after the troubled presidency of Jimmy Carter. Blessed with an optimistic air and fine communication skills honed in acting in many Hollywood films, Reagan projected confidence to a hopeful electorate.

Domestic policies: actions and results

Ronald Reagan began his presidency with four major goals: to revitalize the stagnant economy, lower taxes, balance the budget, and reduce the size and scope of the federal government. Within a couple months, Reagan proposed a series of economic measures that, as a whole, came to be known as Reaganomics. Reagan followed a theory of **supply-side economics**. The premise of supply-side economics is

Ronald Reagan was called "The Great Communicator." Press conferences were often contentious, but Reagan projected friendliness appearing to enjoy the give and take.

Ronald Wilson Reagan (1911–2004)

When Ronald Reagan entered the White House on January 20, 1981, less than two weeks short of his 70th birthday, he became the oldest man ever elected to the presidency. Born in 1911 in the town of Tampico, Illinois, Reagan grew up in modest circumstances in the Midwest, attending Eureka College 1928–32 on a needs-based scholarship. In addition to pursuing a BA in social science and economics, "Dutch" as he was known in college, played football and acted in drama productions. After graduating, Reagan became a sports announcer, a job he recalled fondly, telling of creating play-by-play broadcasts from teletypes of sports events. He accepted a movie studio contract in 1937 after a screen test. He acquired his second nickname "The Gipper" after playing the role of George Gipp in the film *Knute Rockne, All American*. In 1940, he married actress Jane Wyman. In 1942, after several years in the army reserves, Reagan began active duty, serving most of his time in a motion picture unit, and was discharged at the end of 1945. After leaving the army, Reagan resumed his acting career, and became president of the Screen Actors Guild (SAG) in 1947. While SAG president, Reagan became involved in disputes over communists within the film industry with the effect that he shifted from being a political liberal to a conservative. His first marriage ended in 1949, and in 1952 Reagan married Nancy Davis who became an important force in his political career. During the 1950s Reagan was an advocate of conservative causes, and in 1966 he was elected governor of California, defeating "Pat" Brown, the man who had defeated Richard Nixon four years before. Reagan served two terms as governor, increasing his national exposure and popularity. After attempting to win the Republican Party's nomination for president twice previously, he won the nomination in 1980. Reagan served two terms as president of the United States, becoming known for his congenial nature and his conservative policies. After leaving office, Reagan endorsed several causes including the line-item veto and gun control. In 1994 Reagan wrote an open letter to the nation that he had been diagnosed with Alzheimer's disease, sparking some discussion over whether it had affected his presidency. Those close to the former president strongly denied the speculation. Reagan died in 2004 in Bel Air, California.

that by taxing the wealthy and businesses less, they will invest more capital(money). These investments will stimulate productivity, growth and employment, with a growing GDP stimulating greater economic gains for all. Opponents called it "trickle-down" economics. Within weeks of his inauguration Reagan proposed a 30% income tax cut over three years and, according to the *New York Times* (February 5, 1981), "The White House has informed members of Congress that it is aiming for a reduction of $40 billion to $50 billion in the federal budget for the fiscal year 1982, making cuts in virtually every major federal endeavor except the military" The result was a budget cut of about 6%, and increased military spending of approximately 12%. The proposals would reduce government funding for welfare programs and increase private wealth for capital investment, thus stimulating the economy while reducing the size of government.

Supply-side economics is the theory that it is supply that promotes demand and drives the economy. By lowering tax rates on higher incomes and investment, the government does not discourage capital investment. Investment drives the economy.

Reagan's supply-side program was partly based on the Laffer curve: the idea that increased tax revenues could occur with a decrease in tax rates. As Reagan stated on April 29, 1982, in a speech to the nation, "high taxes, destroying incentive, had contributed to reduced productivity and a reduction in savings, which left us without the capital we needed for industrial expansion." In other words, if taxes on income and investment are lowered, people will work harder and take more capital risks, leading to a much greater GDP. In turn, this would lead to increased tax revenues with decreased individual rates. The Reagan administration assumption that lowering tax rates would increase revenues was based on the belief that tax rates were so high that they discouraged working and investment.

In March 1981, the president was shot by John Hinkley, a mentally ill man who thought the he could win actress Jodie Foster's affections by killing Reagan, seemingly confusing Foster's role in the movie, *Taxi Driver*, with real life. Reagan, more badly wounded than he knew and dealing with the trauma with humor, became more popular. When he returned to the White House, his increased popularity helped to push his economic package through Congress—run by a Democrat, Speaker Tip O'Neil. The tax cuts were 25% over three years, not 30%, and the budget didn't cut spending as much as Reagan desired either. It did cut programs to the poor. But the first year was the only year that Reagan would cut taxes. A number of times in the next seven years taxes were raised—1982, 1984, and 1986—all three packaged as tax reform. The taxation rate did not, however, rise close to the rates they were when he took office.

Reaganomics were intended to grow the economy and, in doing so, reduce unemployment. In the quarter preceding Reagan's presidency the GDP grew by 7.6% and in the first quarter of the year, before any budget bills were passed, the economy grew by another 8.2% annual rate. Then the GDP averaged about 1% growth over the next six months, but had two consecutive quarters of over 5% negative growth—the definition of a recession. For the rest of 1982 the economy stagnated, but in 1983 the economy grew by almost 5%, followed by 7.2% growth for 1984. For the rest of Reagan's presidency the GDP grew by a modest 3 to 4%. Based on the GDP data, after the Reagan tax cut took effect, the economy did grow continuously. This was reflected in rising public approval for the president.

However, while the economy grew, unemployment did too. When Reagan took office, 7.5% of workers were unemployed—a disturbingly high figure that went back to May of 1980. During the recession of late 1981 and early 1982 unemployment rose by a little over 1% percent, but kept rising even after the economy began to grow. By September, unemployment had reached the 10% mark and by the end of 1982 was at 11%. Unemployment stayed above 10%

Discussion point

Laffer and Reaganomics

Arthur Laffer, an economist whose ideas influenced Reagan's economic policies, explained how his view of tax rates and revenue:

At a tax rate of 0 percent, the government would collect no tax revenues, no matter how large the tax base. Likewise, at a tax rate of 100 percent, the government would also collect no tax revenues because no one would willingly work for an after-tax wage of zero (i.e., there would be no tax base). Between these two extremes there are two tax rates that will collect the same amount of revenue: a high tax rate on a small tax base and a low tax rate on a large tax base.

Source: Laffer, Arthur. "The Laffer Curve: Past, Present and Future." *The Heritage Foundation*. June 1, 2004. http://www.heritage.org/Research/Reports/ 2004/06/ The-Laffer-Curve-Past-Present-and-Future.

Questions

1 How can Laffer's explanation be used to justify lowering tax rates?

2 For what reasons did Ronald Reagan want to lower taxes? Was maximizing revenue one of the justifications? (For further reference, see Reagan's first inaugural address at http://millercenter.org/ scripps/archive/speeches/detail/3407.)

Discussion point

The standard definition of a recession is two consecutive quarters of negative growth. Should consideration of other economic factors be part of the definition?

 How would you define a recession?

until July of 1983, but did not drop below the 7.5% mark until May 1984. Unemployment continued to drop, interrupted by an occasional minor rise throughout the rest of the Reagan years. Employment growth usually lags behind economic growth, but there was a long period of higher than normal unemployment.

While Reagan pursued his economic agenda, the Federal Reserve Bank tried to bring down the inflation that had plagued the last two years of the Carter administration, reaching above 13% in 1980. Keeping interest rates high, bank chairman Paul Volcker limited the money supply by making borrowing much more expensive, causing grief to farmers, small businesses and much of the middle class. However painful it might be, Reagan supported the Federal Bank's monetary policies, believing that for the economy to grow and investments to be more profitable inflation had to drop significantly. Inflation plummeted to 3% by 1983 and hovered in the 3–4% range for most of his presidency.

The views as to whether Reaganomics promoted economic growth are mixed. Some economists argue that the growth was a normal part of the economic cycle, while others claim that the lowered taxes stimulated a faster, longer, and more vibrant period of economic growth. A third view is that Reagan practiced **Keynesian policies** despite proposing to shrink government. Government spending increased each year, and the gross federal debt soared from 33% of GDP in 1980 to 52% in 1988. Over the eight years 1.6 trillion dollars in deficit spending was injected into the economy. Another factor in the evaluation of Reagonomics is the fact that wages did rise for the lowest quarter of earners, but the wage gap with higher earners increased considerably. Regardless of the view of Reagan's economic programs, the economy did grow.

A significant problem facing the United States during the Reagan years was the Social Security System, which was becoming financially unsound. **Social Security**, known as the "**third rail**" of US politics, was close to impossible for either Congress or the executive to reform. In the United States, the elderly turn out for elections in much higher percentages than voters in their 20s. This makes any changes to Social Security potential political suicide. In this case, Reagan reached across the aisle to the Speaker of the House, Thomas "Tip" O'Neil, a Democrat, to form a commission. The commission came up with a package that assured the viability of the system for decades by raising payroll contributions and the retirement age, and also taxing benefits for the more wealthy. The bill was signed into law in the spring of 1983.

Noneconomic Issues

Labor relations

Despite being the former president of the Screen Actors Guild, Reagan was not a friend of labor. Most labor unions had opposed his election, fearing that Reagan as president would work to enable business owners and enfeeble unions. Early on in his presidency, one of the few unions to support his election went on strike: 12,000 members of PATCO, the air traffic controllers union took action illegally. Reagan fired the striking controllers, filling in the gaps with the few who did not strike, including those in management and

Discussion point

Economies have cycles, as do presidential terms. US presidents often claim, and are assigned responsibility for, improving or harming the economy.

Examining other time periods and places, how much influence have national policies had on economic cycles?

The British economist **John Maynard Keynes** favored demand-based economic policies. As an economy slowed the government could speed up the economy by putting money in, thus increasing demand. Conversely, the government could act to take money out of the economy to ease demand and inflation.

Social Security An income security program, designed primarily to provide financial support for senior citizens. It began as part of the New Deal.

The **Third Rail** is a metaphor referring to the electric rail of a train. In politics, it means that the topic is so charged with importance to a significant part of the electorate that an elected official addressing the topic is taking a huge political risk, possibly leading to being voted out of office.

many new appointments made. Despite fears that flying would be unsafe, the airlines continued to function and the feared accidents did not occur. The dismissals sent a message that the administration would, indeed, be less friendly to unions and emboldened corporations to negotiate from a position of power.

Activity

Reagonomics

The following sources discuss Ronald Reagan's economic policies.

Source A

"They've all sold out, every one of them." That dour assessment came from Jude Wanniski, a fanatic believer in supply-side economics, after a visit to the White House last week. By "they" he meant members of the President's economic team, who in Wanniski's zealous view have all but abandoned supply-side theory—one of the basic Doctrines of Reaganomics.

The economic religion preached by Ronald Reagan has always accommodated the beliefs of two different sects. On one side of the aisle sit the supply-siders, who believe that by slashing taxes Washington can stimulate economic growth: on the other side sit the monetarists, who believe that Washington can slow the inflation rate by tightening the nation's money supply. Now, nagged by persistently high interest rates and the threat of a recession, this uneasy choir of Reagan's economic experts is no longer singing as if with one voice, and the cacophony can be heard from Wall Street to Capitol Hill. True believers in Reaganomics, of course, can justifiably argue that their religion is not a failure, since its trial has only just begun.

Source: Beckwith, David et al. "Reaganomics: Too Many Voices." *Time*. October 19, 1981. http://www.time.com/time/magazine/article/0,9171,924952,00.html.

Source B

The president's persistence paid off in July when Congress passed slightly modified tax and budget bill. Reagan signed both into law on August 13. The tax law … called for a 23 percent cut in federal income taxes over the next three years. It reduced the top marginal rate on individuals from 70 percent to 50 percent, and it cut rates in lower tax brackets. The administration estimated that the reductions would amount to $750 billion—an enormous sum—over the next five years. The budget bill, along with the new regulations that his appointees put into place, gave Reagan many of the cuts in domestic spending—in public assistance, food stamps, and other means-tested programs for the poor—for which he had campaigned.

Source: Patterson, James T. 2005. *Restless Giant: The United States from Watergate to Bush vs. Gore*. Oxford University Press.

Source C

… recession convinced many people, including some conservatives, the Reagan economic program (and thus the Reagan presidency) had failed. In fact, however, the economy recovered more rapidly and impressively than anyone had expected. By late 1983, unemployment had fallen to 8.2 percent, and it declined steadily for several years after that. The gross national product had grown 3.6 percent in a year, the largest increase since the mid 1970s. Inflation had fallen below 5 percent.

Source: Brinkley, Alan.1999. *American History: A Survey*. 10th edn. Boston: McGraw Hill. p. 1119.

Source D

"President's car hit by 'projectile'!" by Nicholas Garland, first published in the *Daily Telegraph*, February 4, 1982.

Questions

1 What does Alan Brinkley (source C) mean by the phrase "the Reagan economic program"?

2 What is the message of source D?

3 Compare and contrast the views of sources A and B in evaluating the success of Reagan's economic program.

4 With reference to their origin and purpose, evaluate the value and limitations of sources A and C to historians studying Ronald Reagan's economic policies.

5 Using these sources and your own knowledge, evaluate the short- and long-term success of Ronald Reagan at implementing his economic program.

Regulations

Another way Reagan wanted to reduce the size of government was to reduce regulations. He felt that the government should be less involved in how people lived and worked. Interestingly, the Carter administration had already deregulated the airlines, trucking, railroads and the financial industries. Major emphasis on deregulation went into the environment and business areas. A look at his environmental and business regulation and enforcement record reveals a mixture of goals and achievements with uneven results. His administration had more success in slowing down the issuing of new regulations than in eliminating existing ones. He did manage to deregulate rules regarding corporate mergers, effectively lessening government anti-monopoly efforts. Many of his other efforts were thwarted by a less than cooperative House of Representatives.

Reagan has been viewed by many as an enemy of environmental protection. His administration made a consistent effort to deregulate or limit the enforcement of existing laws and regulations. Due to lawsuits and congressional action many of these efforts were unsuccessful. For example, he vetoed a renewal of the Clean Water Act in 1987, but was overridden by the House and Senate. But, in Reagan's first year there was more than a two-thirds reduction in the filing of EPA enforcement cases. Additionally, he stopped President Carter's efforts at promoting renewable energy, removing the solar cells from the White House roof and dropping car fleet mileage reductions as well. The administration opened many federal lands to timber harvesting and mining. Personnel changes, mismanagement and a degree of stalemate moderated some

Activity

Choose another country in the Americas. Compare and contrast the activities and influence of labor unions in:

● commercial activities

● government policies.

Activity
Social cost

The total cost of any economic activity is the "Social Cost." The social cost is comprised of private costs and external costs (SC=PC+EC). One view of regulations is that they attempt to turn external costs into private costs, resulting in a more realistic price for any given economic activity. Others argue that regulations unreasonably raise the cost of commerce by burdening businesses beyond the external costs. By what standards, do you think, governments should regulate business activities? Consider these issues and questions in the following case study:

Compare and contrast environmental, financial, or labor regulations of two different countries in the Americas during the 1980s and 1990s. To what extent did the regulations achieve their goals, and to what extent did they cause the harm that opponents predicted?

of these effects, with many of the laws, agencies and public lands surviving the Reagan years mostly intact. Some conservatives are critical of Reagan's record as a lost opportunity to undo the damage of previous administrations, but others argue that he expanded federal wilderness areas by more than 10 million acres and led the international campaign to eliminate ozone damage, resulting in the **Montreal Protocol** of 1987. Additionally, he did sign a number of bills such as amendments strengthening the Safe Water Drinking Act and amendments increasing funding for the Superfund hazardous sites clean-up program. Overall, Ronald Reagan's record on the environment contains efforts consistent with his philosophy of smaller government.

There were a number of other domestic actions by the Reagan administration: the War on Drugs; placing the first woman, Sandra Day O'Connor, on the Supreme Court; and a confused policy on HIV/AIDS that finally resulted in funds for AIDS research. Reagan's approach to further advancement in civil rights was otherwise consistent with the small government approach. He opposed the renewal of the Voting Rights Act, busing for achieving school integration, and affirmative action in employment. Many civil rights leaders claimed that the president was hostile to minority groups, or at best indifferent to their needs. Reagan disagreed, but civil rights were not a focus of the administration.

Activity
Understanding terminology

Reagan's domestic policies were called conservative. Research the terms conservative and liberal as used in the United States. The terms right and left can also described political position. Political tendencies can also range from libertarian or authoritarian. Identify your own political leanings by taking a political test. One political spectrum test is at http://www.gotoquiz.com/politics/political-spectrum-quiz.html; while another is available at www.politicalcompass.org/test (The websites are not endorsed). Or, just do an Internet search for "political typology."

Montreal Protocol A 1987 treaty signed by most nations to reduce the emissions of chemicals that cause the depletion of the ozone layer in the atmosphere. The effort has been largely successful.

TOK Link
Ideology

Presidents are often viewed in terms of faithfulness to a particular ideology. To what extent is pragmatism an ideology? How does pragmatism work in political decision-making? Does pragmatism preclude political ideology?

 Was Reagan an ideologue or a pragmatist?

Foreign policies

Ronald Reagan's entry into the White House followed a period in which many people in the United States perceived a significant fall in the international standing of their country. The loss of Vietnam to communism, the 444-day Iranian Hostage Crisis, the Soviet Invasion of Afghanistan, and the inability of the Nixon or Carter administrations to deal with the oil crises of 1973 and 1979 or with the increasing power of OPEC, only served as evidence that the United States was declining in power and its enemies, including the Soviet Union, on the rise. Central American countries, including El Salvador, with a strong communist themed insurgency and Nicaragua, with a communist government brought the threat of communism close to home. Reagan, believed in **American Exceptionalism** and that the United States was on earth to rid the world of the "Evil Empire." Reagan, projecting the reasoning behind NSC-68 that Moscow was the root of all communist aggression wherever it appeared, stated that communism had to be opposed everywhere it materialized around the globe. The foreign policy ventures of Reagan also dealt with arms control and the Middle East. While Reagan is remembered as a fierce anti-communist, the actions of his administration are quite varied.

American Exceptionalism
While the term was first used by Alexis de Tocqueville, to many Americans it came to mean that the United States was fundamentally different from all other nations as a "bastion of freedom" uniquely blessed by a distinct national character to pursue liberty and material abundance.

Activity

Emotive phrases and national image

In his first Inaugural Address Reagan used the phrase "last and greatest bastion of freedom" to describe the United States. In his farewell address Reagan described the US as "a shining city on a hill." Read through the inaugural address of Reagan, Bush, and Clinton and identify phrases that reinforce the concept of American Exceptionalism.

The USSR and the Strategic Defense Initiative (SDI)

For decades Ronald Reagan had believed that the Soviet Union was the "Evil Empire," a phrase he mouthed publicly in 1983. He strongly distrusted the leadership and assumed their motives were bent on world communist domination. Every indication that the Soviets were violating arms treaties was another reason to read aggression into each action. Acknowledging the effectiveness of **containment**, he was severely disillusioned with the policy of **détente** that had been Nixon's, Ford's and Carter's. Reagan believed that the Soviets had taken advantage of the easing of pressure to greatly increase their military power and influence around the globe. He also believed that the ascendancy of the USSR meant the descent of the United States and the West: that was a state of affairs he could not let stand.

Containment Truman's Cold War policy for not allowing communism to spread beyond the current countries.

Détente Nixon's policy of engaging the Soviet Union and China to lower tensions to lower the threat of war, especially nuclear war.

From the beginning of his presidency Reagan adopted a policy of a massive arms buildup, including a large expansion of the United States Navy to project US power. The idea was to force the Soviet Union into economic collapse. Contrary to intelligence estimates which in retrospect overestimated the strength of the Soviet economy, the president believed that the USSR was in precarious shape. Defense spending had already increased steadily under Jimmy Carter, $102 billion in 1978 (the first year his budgets took effect) to $154 billion in 1981 (the last effective year of Carter budgets). The 50% increase was significant. In Reagan's first four years the US defense budget grew to $245 billion, a 60% increase in spending. Part of the buildup was research into a missile defense system: the Strategic Defense Initiative. SDI, nicknamed **Star Wars** by opponents or doubters, was the idea for a space-based system that would shoot down incoming intercontinental ballistic missiles (ICBMs) in space, creating a defensive umbrella over the United States and allies, rendering the Soviet nuclear threat largely impotent. SDI was only under preliminary research during the Reagan years, but played an important role in arms reduction negotiations between Reagan and Soviet leader, Mikhail Gorbachev.

Confrontation, engagement and arms talks

For the first four years of the Reagan administration, relations with the USSR were tense at best. Beginning shortly after taking office, the announcement of the largest peacetime arms buildup in the history of the United States was announced. Secretly, the military initiated a **PSYOP** operation. The operation, known to very few people in the administration and the Pentagon, mostly consisted of military flights close to the Soviet border or the launching of bombers, testing how the Soviets would react. According to the CIA, the purpose was two-fold: to probe for Soviet defense vulnerabilities and to keep the Kremlin guessing as to what the United States would do, ultimately producing an uneasy Soviet defense establishment. The USSR maintained an outer calm and moderate rhetoric in response to the provocations for the first two years. But to the USSR, the proposed SDI of 1983 was a threat to stability, rendering the strategy of mutually assured destruction (**MAD**) precarious. The Soviets contemplated the increasing possibility of a US or NATO attack. Yuri Andropov responded several days later publicly accusing the United States of preparing a first strike attack, claiming that President Reagan was preparing to start a nuclear war "with the hope of winning it."

PSYOP probes caused deep concern and a heightened alert in the Kremlin. On September 1, a Soviet jet fighter shot down Korean Airline Flight 007, a Boeing 747, killing all 269 people on board. The plane had strayed into Soviet airspace in the vicinity of a US spy plane that had been probing Soviet Air defenses. The Reagan Administration referred to it as deliberate murder, but the US air force wanted the president to hold off on a statement, and eventually intelligence concluded that it was probably a case of mistaken identity and was not premeditated. The USSR insisted that the downed airliner was the United States intelligence platform and not a civilian plane. Historian Richard Rhodes in his book *Arsenals of Folly* and the Fischer report concur that the Soviet military action was likely in response to the PSYOP operation that kept the Soviet air defenses on edge with ever-increasing anxiety.

Tensions continued to grow. Reagan expanded the military and deployed more nuclear missiles in Europe, but he also wanted to rid the world of nuclear weapons. Reagan wanted more than SALT, he wanted to reduce the threat of nuclear war by reducing weapons. Reagan made some moves to bring negotiations back. In 1981, he reversed the Carter wheat embargo imposed after the 1979 Soviet invasion of Afghanistan. In 1982 negotiations

Star Wars was a popular science fiction film released in 1977. The implication was that Reagan was living in a fantasy world where such weapons were only possible.

Discussion point

Dr Strangelove, a character in Stanley Kubrick's 1964 film of the same name, said, "Deterrence is the art of producing in the mind of the enemy ... the fear to attack."

1   How would SDI, if successfully deployed, alter the USSR's nuclear deterrence?

2   Inventors of various weapons have hoped that their invention would create such severe damage that the weapon would prove a deterrent to war, yet the 20th century produced the most deadly wars in history.

?   Is the nuclear deterrent fundamentally different? Why or why not?

PSYOP stands for psychological warfare. Related terms include Psychological warfare (PSYWAR), Psy Ops, Political Warfare, and tactics associated with the phrase "Hearts and Minds." The principle behind such operations is the desire to influence a target audience's value systems and beliefs in order to have an impact on individual and group behavior.

MAD is short for Mutually Assured Destruction, the default nuclear strategy that evolved during the 1960s between the USSR and the US. If both nations possessed sufficient nuclear weapons to destroy each other, even if attacked, then neither side would initiate a strike.

were restarted, but quick changes in Soviet leadership— from Leonid Brezhnev to Yuri Andropov followed by Konstantin Chernenko (who assumed the helm after the death of Andropov in 1984)—all combined to deter negotiations. The Reagan foreign policy team headed by Secretary of State George Schultz met with longtime Soviet ambassador Anatoly Dobrynin in January 1984 to attempt to restart negotiations. Andropov died the next month and Chernenko followed, but appeared to be more willing to engage the United States. In March 1984, Chernenko, the last of the Soviet old guard, died and Mikhail Gorbachev, a protégé of Andropov and the only Soviet leader to be born after the Russian Revolution, became the General Secretary. After British prime minister Margaret Thatcher told Reagan that the new Soviet leader might be amenable to serious negotiations, he sent a letter

Mikhail Gorbachev and Ronald Reagan in Geneva.

proposing a meeting. Gorbachev, who believed that the Soviet economy needed restructuring and desired lower defense expenditures, responded affirmatively, and the two leaders met in Geneva in November 1985. Talks started off well as the two leaders agreed to seek a 50% reduction in strategic weapons, but no agreement was signed because SDI emerged as a sticking point with Gorbachev wanting to observe the traditional Antiballistic Missile Treaty interpretation.

Activity

Reagan's Strategic Defense Initiative (SDI)

Source A

March 27, 1983, Soviet Premier Andropov stated in an interview published in *Pravda* that SDI:

> would open the floodgates of a runaway race of all types of strategic arms, both offensive and defensive. Such is the real significance, the seamy side, so to say, of Washington's "defensive conception." ... The Soviet Union will never be caught defenseless by any threat.... Engaging in this is not just irresponsible, it is insane. ... Washington's actions are putting the entire world in jeopardy.

Source B

In an interview with a US journalist, Marshal Nikolai Ogarkov, First Deputy Defense Minister and Chief of the General Staff in the Soviet Union, interpreted the real meaning of SDI:

> We cannot equal the quality of U.S. arms for a generation or two. Modern military power is based on technology, and technology is based on computers. In the US, small children play with computers. ... Here, we don't even have computers in every office of the Defense Ministry. And for reasons you know well, we cannot make →

computers widely available in our society. We will never be able to catch up with you in modern arms until we have an economic revolution. And the question is whether we can have an economic revolution without a political revolution.

Source: Gelb, Leslie, H. "Foreign Affairs: Who Won the Cold War?," *New York Times.* August 20, 1992.

Source C

Ronald Reagan, in a speech to the nation, March 23, 1983:

After careful consultation with my advisers, including the Joint Chiefs of Staff, I believe there is a way. Let me share with you a vision of the future which offers hope. It is that we embark on a program to counter the awesome Soviet missile threat with measures that are defensive. Let us turn to the very strengths in technology that spawned our great industrial base and that have given us the quality of life we enjoy today.

What if free people could live secure in the knowledge that their security did not rest upon the threat of instant U.S. retaliation to deter a Soviet attack, that we could intercept and destroy strategic ballistic missiles before they reached our own soil or that of our allies?

… I clearly recognize that defensive systems have limitations and raise certain problems and ambiguities. If paired with offensive systems, they can be viewed as fostering an aggressive policy, and no one wants that. But with these considerations firmly in mind, I call upon the scientific community in our country, those who gave us nuclear weapons, to turn their great talents now to the cause of mankind and world peace, to give us the means of rendering these nuclear weapons impotent and obsolete.

Source: Reagan, Ronald. "President Reagan Proposes a Missile Defense System." *Making the History of 1989.* http://chnm.gmu.edu/1989/items/show/59.

Questions

1   What is the central message of source C?

2   Compare and contrast the views on SDI expressed by Soviet Premier Andropov in sources A and B with President Reagan's views in source C.

3   With reference to their origin and purpose, what are the values and limitations of sources A and B for historians studying the difficulty of arms negotiations between the United States and the Soviet Union?

4   Using these sources and your own knowledge access the roles of ideology in arms reduction talks between the United States and the USSR. during the Reagan presidency.

The next summit was in October 1986 in Reykjavik, Iceland. The two settled in for intense negotiations that lasted two days and almost came to agreement on what the *Washington Post* called "sweeping reductions on nuclear arsenals," limiting each side to 1,600 missiles 6,000 warheads. Once again, the sticking point was SDI. There were two more summits between the two leaders. They met next in Washington DC, in December 1987, in a summit that resulted in the signing of an Intermediate Nuclear Force treaty. Another agreement limited strategic ballistic missile warheads to 4,900, while avoiding the SDI issue. Still under discussion was the timing of the Soviet withdrawal from Afghanistan and human rights issues. Both leaders celebrated a successful summit. On June 1, the last official meeting between Reagan and Gorbachev took place in Moscow. No agreement of substance was reached, but it was in Moscow that Reagan made a statement that to a significant degree marked the end of the Cold War. On May 31, while walking through Red Square, Reagan renounced his labeling of the USSR as the "Evil Empire," saying, "I was talking about another time, another era."

Reagan and Gorbachev engaged each other over four years. At the time, there was a great deal of excitement over the positive working relationship and the progress in relations between the two countries that had been enemies since the end of the Second World War. Issues such as human rights and SDI remained sticking points, but nuclear arsenals had been reduced and the two superpowers had turned from limiting strategic nuclear weapons to reducing them.

President Reagan viewed the threat of communism as among the most serious threats to US security. Events in Nicaragua and El Salvador demanded his immediate attention, otherwise communism could spread northward and eventually into Mexico, putting a communist country on the southern border. When the government of the small island of Grenada turned communist, Reagan saw the threat spreading to the Caribbean. With Cuba, already a Soviet ally, only 90 miles off the Florida coast, Reagan sought to reverse and roll back the gains of communism in the Americas.

Nicaragua

In 1979, after three years of civil war, Daniel Ortega and the left-leaning Sandanistas overthrew the longtime dictator of Nicaragua. The brutal Somoza regime, first taking power in 1936, had been supported by the United States. After the revolution, President Jimmy Carter withheld financial support for the new government. Ortega tried to bring social and economic improvements, but denied US dollars sought aid elsewhere, leaving the opening for Cuba to step in with advisors and technicians.

When Reagan became president in 1981, he wanted to get rid of the Sandanista government. Reagan believed that communism anywhere was a threat, but especially in what the United States considered to be its backyard. He directed the government to provide economic and military resources to opponents. In November, he directed the CIA to begin training a counterrevolutionary army who came to be known as the Contras. The secret aid took a group of a few hundred men, including former Guardia Nacional officers, and turned it into an army of 9,000 by 1985 and up to 15,000 soldiers by the end of 1986. According to National Security Advisor Colin Powell, the Contras, who Reagan called "Freedom Fighters," never mounted to more than a "highland fighting force." Additionally, the United States secretly mined Managua harbor, attempting to further destabilize the Sandanista government. During this time the Boland Amendment was passed by the US Congress, making it illegal to provide aid to the Contras. This law caused the Reagan administration to seek a way to get funds to the Contras and ultimately led to the Iran–Contra scandal. Despite the covert aid the Sandanistas stayed in power until

TOK Link

Turning points in history

Ronald Reagan's trip to Moscow is considered to be a turning point in history. Is the concept of turning point historically legitimate? Debate the concept of historical turning points. List other major turning points in the 20th century, with particular reference to the Americas.

Discussion point

To what extent was Eisenhower's policy of roll back more effective than Reagan's?

free elections in 1989, arranged in a settlement created by other Latin American nations, resulted in the election of an anti-Sandanista coalition, and a peaceful transition of power.

El Salvador

Next to Nicaragua in Central America is El Salvador. Political unrest between left and right groups grew throughout the 1970s. The right-leaning government increased its violent repression as a challenge to its power evolved from the FMLN (a group with ties to Cuba) and other opposition, including several leftist guerilla-supported groups and groups established by radical clergy called CEBs (*Comunidades Eclesiásticas de Base*). Additionally, private right-wing death squads including FALANGE and UGB assassinated leftist opponents of the administration. The United States tried to accomplish two seemingly incompatible goals: to keep an anti-communist government in power while at the same time deposing or significantly altering the behavior of the human rights-violating Salvadorian leadership and military in almost every aspect of governance and economic policy.

The Carter administration, having made human rights a significant focus of their foreign policy, and at the same time fearing other communist activities around the globe, had difficulty producing a cohesive policy in El Salvador. Events further fragmented Carter administration policy. On May 9, 1979, the army shot at about 300 peaceful protesters demonstrating in front of the Metropolitan Cathedral in San Salvador. The shootings were filmed by a cameraman from the US TV network CBS. Soon some members of BPR (Popular Revolutionary Bloc) took refuge in the Venezuelan embassy. On May 23, the army killed 14 women and children who were bringing food to BPR members in the embassy. Most walls of downtown San Salvador were covered with graffiti proclaiming the need for El Salvador's liberation from its rulers. President Carter, in the context of a reheating of the Cold War, was loath to lose El Salvador to communists and regarded the preservation of a non-communist government as paramount. The concurrent efforts at reform were mostly ineffective, despite millions of dollars of aid and interruption of that aid after the December 1980 murder of four American churchwomen. The human rights violations continued including the murder of two American reform advisors. Just before Ronald Reagan's inauguration, the FMLN, a communist revolutionary army, attacked, hoping to depose the new government, but President José Napoleón Duarte survived with assistance from the Carter administration.

The Reagan administration, filled with foreign policy professionals including Vice President George Bush, James Baker, Richard "Dick" Cheney, Alexander Haig and George Schultz, steered the ideological president along a course that clarified and accelerated the Carter policy. On March 10, 1983, the president made the reasons for his El Salvador policy clear:

> Central America is simply too close, and the strategic stakes are too high, for us to ignore the danger of governments seizing power there with ideological ties to the Soviet Union. If the FMLN were

to win, El Salvador will join Cuba and Nicaragua as a base for
spreading fresh violence to Guatemala, Honduras, even Costa Rica.
The killing will increase, and so will the threat to Panama, the
Canal, and ultimately Mexico.

Source: Anderson, Thomas P. 1982. *Politics in Central America.*
Stanford, CA: Praeger. p. 2.

The Reagan policy was to provide US military advisors, train the
El Salvadorian armed forces (ESAF), greatly increase material aid,
and offer strategic assistance. With such strong emphasis on fighting
the perceived communist threat, Carter's attention to human rights
receded even more. In fact, to make the massive aid increase
acceptable to the people of the United States, the Reagan
administration took on a policy of exaggerating the human rights
progress of the Duarte regime.

During the first years of the 1980s, more money was pumped into
El Salvador than in the two previous decades. From 1962 to 1979,
the US transferred approximately $50 million in arms grants to the
Salvadorian government, with more than $1 billion in arms grants
from 1980 to 1990. An additional $1.7 billion in economic assistance
accompanied the military grants. The Reagan administration was
not content to support the ruling government without reform. The
administration wanted a more centrist government and preferred
not to have human rights violations. There was still a conflict
between ideology and fighting the Cold War in the Americas.

After elections in 1982, that the CIA spent $2 million to help
conduct, there was a show of popular support for the right-wing
ARENA Party leader Roberto D'Abuisson, a man President Carter's
ambassador called a "pathological killer." Further pressure was
exerted on El Salvador to install a banker, Álvaro Magaña
(considered to be a moderate), as the provisional president.
The Reagan administration also pushed for land reform and greater
democracy. Every six months the administration presented a report
to Congress on the status of human rights, but some media and
political opponents claimed that the administration exaggerated
the progress of El Salvador on that front. While pressuring the
government of El Salvador to reform, the Reagan administration
pursued a policy of not negotiating with the guerilla organizations,
believing it should not provide victories to the left-wing groups that
had not been accomplished on the battlefield. The administration
continued to claim that the anti-government groups were funded by
Cuba, thus any concessions would advance the cause of communism.

By 1985, with ESAF controlling the cities and the FMLN and allies
operating in the countryside, the war was still evolving. The ESAF
began to exert itself on the battlefield, taking the battles to the rural
areas, and the guerillas switched to hit-and-run tactics. Still, there
was a great deal of corruption in the ESAF officer corps and the
military leaders refused to confront the concept that their victory
would not be achieved unless the needs and grievances of
Salvadorians were addressed. The Reagan administration strategy
was to keep the left-wing guerillas at bay while building legitimate

---

government institutions such as courts, police and a structured military. The United States would spend the next several years nation-building, sending in government experts to train Salvadorians with the goal of democratizing and liberalizing all sectors of the government. The policy operated with the assumption that the United States had leverage through military and economic aid to force the compliance of the Duarte government. Duarte offered some degree of compliance and advances in the development of the civil bureaucracy, but there was still corruption and violent repression. The Reagan administration had less leverage than it thought as the Salvadorians knew the US were more concerned about stopping communism than they were about reforming the Salvadorian government, so while some reforms took place, the regime saw little need for major changes.

According to the policy analyst Benjamin Schwartz, a significant reason why Duarte was willing to liberalize institutions was that the death squads operating during the 1970s and the first half of the 1980s were successful in weakening the left-wing opposition. Approximately 8,000 victims were killed by right-wing death squads before Duarte took power and an additional 30,000 were killed in the first term of the Reagan presidency. As a result there was just not enough opposition left to pose a significant threat to government control. The left-wing guerillas would not mount a significant threat to overthrow the government after the coup attempt of 1980. This weakness provided some space for liberalization of the Duarte regime.

Grenada

In late 1983, the leftist regime in Grenada grabbed the attention of Reagan. The island nation, situated near the southern end of the Lesser Antilles, 100 miles north of Venezuela, separating the Atlantic Ocean from the Caribbean Sea, gained independence from Great Britain in 1974. Since 1979, Grenada, a small country with a population of approximately 90,000, had been ruled by Maurice Bishop who headed the people's revolutionary government (PRC), a Marxist government with close ties to Cuba and the USSR. In 1983, Bishop and members of his cabinet were seized and subsequently killed in an intra-party coup. The Bishop government was already in the process of constructing, with Cuban assistance, a 10,000 foot airport runway with the announced purpose of increasing tourism, but which United States officials considered to be primarily of military importance.

The overthrow caused Reagan to intervene, for reasons that included the safety of US medical students living on the island. The Organization of Eastern Caribbean States, a group of former British colonies, also wanted intervention. On October 25, Operation Urgent Fury commenced with the invasion of the island by United States military forces in total numbering 5,000 with a security force of 300 security provided by the OECS. They were opposed by a force of 2,100, including 1,200 Grenadians and 780 Cubans. By October 28 most of the fighting was over and

TOK Link
History and foreign affairs

The foreign activities of nations are based on many factors, including its perceptions of its role in the region and world, judgements of events in other countries, and its capabilities.

To what extent do perceptions of circumstances and events create different versions of reality?

What questions should powerful nations seek answers to before acting to influence events in other countries?

Analyze the Grenada invasion from the point of view of Cuba, as well as the US administration. Refer back to the discussion in chapter 5 (p. 312) to assist you in your research.

on November 3 hostilities were declared over. The only US military intervention of the Reagan years was deemed a success by the administration, with the 599 US citizens rescued and the Marxist government deposed. Operation Urgent Fury was supported by most members of Congress, both Democrats and Republicans, and much of the US public. The quick, decisive action by Reagan was a welcome success after years of perceived US decline. An interim government held power until elections were held in December 1984. The New National Party won 14 of 15 seats and Grenada's constitution, suspended since 1979, was restored.

The Middle East

Ronald Reagan was confronted by a number of issues in the Middle East. Among these was a civil war in Lebanon, a hostile government in Iran, and the Iran–Iraq War. Lebanon and Iran proved especially troubling to the conduct of effective foreign policy. The first direct US military intervention in the region was in Lebanon in 1958 in support of the pro-Western government headed by Camille Chamoun. In the context of the Cold War and the Eisenhower Doctrine, involvement meant stopping the Soviets. The intervention resulted in one US death, and significantly reduced civil disturbances, threats and violence. The United States would again send forces into the country 24 years later.

Lebanon, still a barely a functioning democracy, was in turmoil. Many factions within Lebanon competed for power, among these were the Lebanese Christian Militia, Palestine Liberation Organization and many other armed factions; all had been fighting for power over the last seven years, with the exception of a fragile cease-fire partially engineered by US negotiators in place by July 1981. Syrian and Iranian armed forces also had a Lebanese presence. In June 1982 Israel, a long time American ally, invaded Lebanon in order to stop shellings of Israeli settlements near the border with Lebanon. The invasion had a second purpose: to destroy the PLO and bring about a political order favorable to Israel. After the Israeli bombing of Beirut and the deaths of scores of civilians, Reagan felt strongly that the violence had to stop, and called the Israeli prime minister, Menachem Begin, on August 12 urging him to stop. Begin did. It was after this that a multinational peace force would be assembled to provide stability.

The previous year, the Reagan administration had voiced support for the Lebanese government including writing a public letter backing the Lebanese president Elias Sarkis. Additionally, a special emissary, Philip Habbib, was appointed, signaling an elevation of Lebanon's importance to Reagan's foreign policy. In the same time period, the administration tried to restrain Israeli Defense Force (IDF) activities. In June 1981, Secretary of State Alexander Haig delayed delivery of ten F-16 fighter planes in response to the Israeli bombing of an Iraqi nuclear reactor, but additionally to pressure Israel to reduce violent actions. A favorable policy toward Israel as a bulwark against Soviet expansion in the Middle East was ongoing, but this was a significant act. The United States continued to believe that the Middle East was

Activity

Looking for patterns

The Monroe Doctrine first defined the United States self-determined relationship to the rest of the Americas. The better part of a century later the Roosevelt Corollary announced a more aggressive approach. In the mid-century the US wanted to be a "Good Neighbor."

 Create a data table in chronological order of US military involvement in the Americas. Can you identify a pattern?

vital to US national security. Even as it pursued initiatives in 1981 and into the summer of 1982, the Reagan administration was conflicted about how to act. While Haig and his successor as Secretary of State, George Schulz, both favored deeper involvement, the Secretary of Defense, Caspar Weinberger and the military Joint Chiefs of Staff were quite reluctant about entering what could become another Vietnam. The United States was concerned about the violence in the region for political, military and humane reasons, but in June still had not given serious thought to direct military involvement. After the Israeli bombing of Beirut, involvement was reconsidered.

Beginning August 25, 1982, Reagan sent 800 Marines to Beirut as part of a multinational peacekeeping force (MNF). The purpose was to allow the PLO to withdraw to Syria to be followed by the IDF withdrawal towards the Israel–Lebanon border. Additional justifications by the administration included guaranteeing the safety of Palestinian civilians and restoration of Lebanese government control. The PLO withdrew and the IDF began its pull out, followed by the rapid redeployment of the MNF away from Beirut by September 10. Violence returned later that month, almost immediately upon withdrawal of peacekeeping forces. On September 14 the newly-elected president, Bashir Gamayel, was assassinated by a bomb and the following day IDF moved into West Beirut. On September 16–18, approximately 750 Palestinians were killed in two refugee camps. These developments, especially the massacre of civilians, upset Reagan, as one purpose of the MNF was to guarantee civilian safety. On September 20, Reagan announced a new MNF consisting of American, French and Italian forces.

The Reagan administration had no clear plan. John Kelly, former ambassador to Lebanon in President Reagan's second term, labeled the approach reactive. The marines began deployment on September 29, initially numbering 1,200, but increasing in the next year to 1,800. They were to be an interposition force, but it was never stated between which hostile parties they were interposed. Without a clear mission, the US forces became a bargaining chip for both the Reagan and Gamayel administrations to leverage each other, and came to be seen as supporting Lebanese Christians, the Lebanese government, and Israel to the detriment of all other factions in Lebanon. In March 1983, the United States announced that the MNF would stay in Lebanon until Syrian, PLO, and Israeli forces withdrew. Two months later, Lebanon and Israel signed an agreement stating that Israel would withdraw provided that the PLO and Syrian forces withdrew. However, Syria and the PLO were not party to the agreement. During the following months, there were numerous skirmishes between the US marines and various armed factions. As Israel began withdrawal, violence between factions increased and attacks on the marines continued.

On October 23, a truck carrying a bomb penetrated defenses and exploded close to the US marine barracks at the Lebanon International Airport, killing 241 marines. A second truck exploded near the French barracks killing 56 soldiers. Reagan, suspecting the newly formed Hezbollah for the attacks, ordered the bombing of their headquarters. Initially, Reagan insisted that US forces must remain there, on the advice of Secretary of State George Schulz, as leaving would be a major victory for radical and rejectionist elements. The deaths of so many marines, however, caused anger at home. The administration reassessed its Lebanese policy in the next months, coming to the conclusion that without a sizeable increase in military forces the United States could not significantly influence events. On December 4, US planes attacked a Syrian air defense site that had fired on American planes, and while the administration debated policy, it appeared that the United States was choosing to take sides in the Lebanese conflict. In January 1984, Schulz stated that the United States would continue to pursue the mission in Lebanon, but Defense Secretary Weinberger disagreed and on February 7 Reagan announced that US forces would withdraw to ships off the Lebanese coast. Embassy officials began to leave that day, and by March 5 all US military personnel had been redeployed. On May 17, the government of Lebanon cancelled the IDF withdrawal agreement with Israel. US troops would never be deployed again in the Middle East during the Reagan years.

To John Kelly, the mission was doomed to be a failure from the beginning: "Token military force with a vague mission was probably a recipe for failure. The responsibility rests firmly with the leaders who made the decisions."

The Iran–Contra affair

What came to be known as the Iran–Contra affair resulted from the strange coincidence of the Reagan administration's Middle Eastern policy and the support for anti-government "Contra" forces in Nicaragua. Reagan, who called the Contras the "moral equivalent of the Founding Fathers," was extremely concerned about US citizens held hostage in Lebanon as well as the revolutionary government of Iran. The combination of hostages, secret funding for the Contras, and an ill-fated attempt to sell arms to supposed Iranian moderates in the hope that they would overthrow the radical clerics who took power after the 1979 revolution led to the biggest scandal of the Reagan presidency.

In the 1982 mid-term elections Democrats gained seats in the House and Senate, empowering them to put a legislative halt to the administration's support of the Contras. The Boland Amendment, which passed the House 411 to 0 votes, made it illegal for the CIA and the Defense Department to support the Contras. A stronger second Boland Amendment that banned third-party and any US government funding became law in 1984. The United States, however, secretly mined Managua harbor, which the CIA director William Casey publicly denied. Reagan wanted to keep supporting the Contras. National Security Director Robert "Bud" McFarlane and Lieutenant Colonel Oliver North acquired money from several countries including Saudi Arabia that was transferred to the Nicaraguan anti-government forces. Reagan was pleased when told about the secret foreign-funding sources.

Activity

Looking ahead

Write down the tactics and results of US military involvement in Lebanon. Take note of John Kelly's comment. Be prepared to compare events in Lebanon to the Gulf War and the "Powell Doctrine." Find out the concept of future Secretary of State Colin Powell's doctrine for use of military force.

 Which war laid the foundation for the Powell Doctrine?

In 1985, President Reagan approved a secret plan to sell arms to Iran through Israel to both support Iranian moderates and obtain the release of hostages. More than 1,500 anti-tank weapons were sold to Iran in 1985 and 1986 and several hostages were released. More than $12 million was secretly passed to the rebels. The NSC enlisted the help of Panama's dictator, Manuel Noriega, to assist supplying the Contras. The funding of the Contras was successful. But the arms-for-hostage exchange was in direct contradiction to the publicly stated US policy of not negotiating for hostages. Reagan publicly denied what had happened in 1986. What became known as the Iran–Contra Affair, however, unraveled when a US cargo plane ferrying arms to the Contras was shot down in Nicaragua. November brought newspaper articles in Lebanon reporting the events. Schultz and Vice President George Bush advised the president to publicly admit to the arms-for-hostages deal, but Reagan refused to consider the proposal. Forced by continuing press reports, Reagan approved a commission headed by John Tower to look into the affair, but the pressure continued to build and in December asked for a special prosecutor to be appointed. The House and Senate mounted an investigation. In 1987, Reagan, appeared on national television and stated, "I told the American people I did not trade arms for hostages. My heart and best intentions still tell me that is true, but the facts and the evidence tell me it is not," admitting that he had approved what Secretary of State George Schultz called, "a hostage bazaar." Reagan never admitted and investigators never were able to ascertain specifically what Reagan knew and his level of participation. NSC officials involved in the arms trades and funds diversions testified that they had kept the president out of the loop to insulate him.

The Iran–Contra affair weakened the reputation of the president. Many people were convinced he was lying, while others saw his underlings running wild, enabled to run their own foreign policy initiatives because of Reagan's hands-off delegation style. It was the Iran–Contra affair that combined the Reagan doctrine of fighting communism wherever it appeared with his well-documented compassion for those in need and an ill-understood Middle East policy. The result was a still radical Iran, more hostages taken, and a simmering civil war in Nicaragua.

President George Bush, 1989–93

1988 was the year of the general election to follow Ronald Reagan as president. After falling to an approval rating of 40% when the Iran–Contra affair took its toll, Reagan's popularity in the US increased throughout 1988. By the time of the November election, Reagan, with his regained popularity, paved the way for his vice president, George Herbert Walker Bush, to follow him. In what was predicted to be a close election Bush soundly beat his Democrat rival, Massachusetts Governor, Michael Dukakis, helped by the Democrat's campaign missteps and by promising to continue the policies of Ronald Reagan, but in a kinder and gentler way.

TOK Link

What knowledge issues was Reagan confronting with his statement about trading arms for hostages? How can reason and emotion lead to different truths?

 How should a historian interpret Reagan's remarks?

On January 20, 1989, George Bush took office. When he left office four years later, the Berlin Wall had fallen, the Soviet Union no long existed, the government of China had killed hundreds of its own citizens on Tiananmen Square, the United States had invaded Panama, and sent hundreds of thousands of troops to the Middle East to fight in a war against Iraq. It was a period of major changes in the world for a president who approached the responsibilities of the office with a pragmatic and deliberate style. President Bush took office with the idea of continuing Ronald Reagan's policies, both foreign and domestic. He lacked what he termed, "the vision thing," and appeared to enjoy foreign policy more than the domestic realm. However, he wanted "to make kinder the face of the nation and gentler the face of the world." On the domestic front, he promoted volunteerism, instituted policies to improve the lives of the disabled, and other measures that made the government do its part to encourage a more compassionate nation. Additionally, he had to deal with a savings and loan crisis, a rising federal budget deficit, a massive oil spill along Alaska's coast, and placing two justices on the Supreme Court.

Domestic policies

A major accomplishment of the Bush Administration was the 1990 Americans with Disabilities Act (ADA). The Act extended some of the Civil Rights Act of 1964 to people with disabilities. It prohibited discrimination and required reasonable accommodations in the workplace, as well as expanding public accessibility. The Congress had been working on a bill for several years. Many conservatives opposed the ADA as a betrayal of the Reagan Revolution. They believed that government was the problem, not the solution and that the ADA was a huge intrusion of the federal government into the commercial arena, requiring the expenditure of dollars for a myriad of accommodations and the pursuit of many new regulations. To Bush, the ADA increased freedom. To the ADA's supporters the Act is the single most important accomplishment of the Bush administration.

Bush was not always supportive of civil rights legislation. In October 1990 he vetoed a civil rights bill that the *New York Times* called the "most comprehensive civil rights legislation since the Voting Rights Act of 1965," arguing that it maintained racial quotas. Congress passed another civil rights bill concerning employment discrimination that did become law in 1991. Bush twice vetoed family and medical leave bills because he did not believe that the federal government should mandate companies to provide a specific benefit. The decision

George Herbert Walker Bush (1924–)

George Bush, possibly the most experienced man ever elected president, was born to a well-to-do and well-connected family in Milton, Massachusetts. His father was Senator Prescott Bush. He attended the prestigious Phillips Academy. Upon turning 18 he immediately enlisted in the United States Navy, becoming the youngest fighter pilot in U.S. naval history. He flew 58 missions and was shot down once. The Navy awarded him the Distinguished Flying Cross for bravery. He married Barbara Pierce in 1945. Among their six children is John (Jeb) Bush, the former governor of Florida, and George W. Bush, the 43rd president of the United States. Bush attended Yale and after graduating went to Texas to pursue a career as an oil man. His career in politics began in 1966, when he was elected to Congress from Texas. After four years (1967–71) he became the United States ambassador to the United Nations. He then served a year as chairman of the Republican National Committee, followed by stints as chief liaison officer to the People's Republic of China, CIA director, director of the Council of Foreign Relations, and eight years as Ronald Reagan's vice president. After a four-year term, Bush was defeated by Bill Clinton. George and Barbara Bush retired to Kennebunkport, Maine. In later years he became active with relief efforts, including aid for the victims of the 2004 tsunami in Indonesia, Sri Lanka, Thailand, among other nations.

George Bush speaking at a NATO conference.

Activity

Filling in your chart

As you read, continue to fill in the chart. Highlight similarities between the policies of Reagan and Bush in one color and indicate differences with another.

to support ADA and oppose family and medical leave mandates and a civil rights bill was thought by many to show inconsistency in government intrusion in the workplace.

Environmental regulation

In terms of environmental regulation, Bush was more comfortable with federal regulation of pollution than his predecessor. In June 1990, he proposed major amendment to the 1963 Clean Air Act to specifically reduce pollution in three areas: acid rain, urban air pollution, and toxic emissions. It also strengthened enforcement. The bills, which passed the House and Senate by large margins, also included a phase-out of ozone-depleting chemicals in line with the Montreal Protocol. The new amendments signed by Bush on November 15, 1990, added some significant changes, including encouraging the use of market principles, performance-based standards, and emission trading. Low-sulfur coal and natural gas use were promoted as was energy conservation, and the law effectively reduced oil imports by one million barrels per day, The president's proposal, support and signing of the far-ranging Clean Air Act amendments served to demonstrate his commitment to a healthier environment, but to Reagan conservatives it was more proof that his successor was betraying the less-government theme by introducing increased government interference in the market.

On March 24, just two months after the new president assumed office, *Exxon Valdez*, an oil supertanker, ran aground in Prince William Sound off the Alaskan coast. Within hours millions of gallons of crude oil spilled into the water, eventually contaminating more than 1,100 miles of coastline. The oil spill was the largest in United States history, and caused significant damage to fisheries, shore habitats, wildlife of all types, and recreational areas over a widespread area. Despite the almost immediate response from private clean-up crews and Exxon, the effects of the oil damage continued to be felt into the new millennium. Private companies were responsible for much of the clean-up, but there was significant federal government presence by Coast Guard personnel and the Environmental Protection Agency (EPA). As determined by an EPA report to President Bush later that year, both the private and federal responses were inadequate, resulting in more environmental damage than necessary, but also concluding that prevention is the primary element in protecting the environment from oil spill damage. As a result of the oil spill,

> ## Activity
> ### Presidential decision-making
>
> #### A simulation
>
> You are President George Bush Snr's chief domestic policy advisor. It is the beginning of his term and your job is to create a list of domestic policy initiatives. Create a priority list for the president, based on his political philosophy, the country's needs and wants, and political reality. Present your priority list to the class as if you were making a proposal to the president.

> ## Activity
> ### TOK issues
>
> Discuss the importance, accuracy, and trustworthiness of eye-witness accounts, presidential memoirs, "tell-all" books, and speeches. How does a historian determine intent? Is it the role of the historian to find intent, or simply to present a variety of evidence and let the reader decide?
>
> **How do historians know the reasons for presidential decision-making?**

> ## Activity
> ### Gathering evidence
>
> Research the Reagan and Bush administrations' approaches to and implementation of regulation. After gathering specific evidence in a variety of areas, react to the following knowledge claim:
>
> > Despite his pledge to continue Ronald Reagan's policy of reducing government regulation of business and industry, George Bush greatly increased federal regulations.

Congress passed the Oil Pollution Act of 1990 which required the Coast Guard to strengthen regulations on oil tankers, their owners and operators.

Education

During the 1988 campaign, in a contentious interview with CBS TV network anchorman Dan Rather, Bush stated that he wanted to be the "Education President." Partly spurred on by the 1983 **A Nation at Risk** report that pointed out many weaknesses in public education, President Bush called together the nation's state governors for Education 2000. The Education Summit took place in autumn 1989. Attendees included the future president, then Arkansas governor, Bill Clinton. The summit participants met with directives from the president to meet the rising expectation of US businesses and to change the emphasis from ensuring access through programs such as Title I to improved results based on specific academic outcomes. The proposals that came out of the summit included higher academic standards and federal demonstration grants for **education vouchers** among several proposals. Congress did not turn the initiatives into a bill that could pass, so Bush's educational efforts resulted in increased attention to education, but not immediate federal action.

The economy

Bush took office, succeeding Reagan, with the largest gross federal debt in the history of the United States. The annual deficit had increased in 1988 to over $250 billion. The combination of Reagan era tax cuts and the increases in defense spending while failing to significantly curtail domestic spending is often cited as the causes of the increase. The rising economy failed to overcome the increasing budget expenditures. The gross debt totaled 53% of the nation's GDP, the largest percentage since 1962. Both Congress and the president felt they needed to act. Bush was constrained by his unequivocal promise not to raise taxes during the presidential campaign of 1988. During lengthy and sometimes acrimonious negotiations with the Democrat-controlled Congress for the 1991 budget, Bush came to the conclusion that to get a budget deal he would have to agree to some tax increases. The Democrats wanted to significantly raise taxes on the wealthy, as they claimed that the rich had benefitted disproportionately from Reaganomics over the past decade. Bush issued a statement in June 1990 that back-peddled on his campaign promise by claiming the necessity of revenue increases, a euphemism for increased taxes. Despite the reality of the fiscal and political situation, Bush was harshly criticized by members of his own party for compromising with Democrats on the Omnibus Budget Act of 1990 that cut expenditures and raised taxes. While many looked at the bill as responsible, the act of agreeing to raise taxes, something his predecessor had done several times after the initial tax decreases, caused segments of the US electorate to doubt his word. Even after the budget agreement, yearly deficits increased to more than $300

A Nation at Risk A report on education issued by the National Commission on Excellence in Education, formed by Reagan's Secretary of Education in 1981. The report said that the economic leadership of the United States was threatened by a weak system of public education.

Education vouchers are certificates of financial value provided to students (and by default their parents) who choose not to attend a public school. The state-provided funds would be applied to tuition for a private school.

Discussion point

Presidential terms

After the Roosevelt years, each president was limited to two four-year terms by the 22nd Amendment. This made the president a "lame duck" for the entire 2nd term. How do term limits help or hinder the function of a presidential democracy? How does this differ from a parliamentary system?

billion by Bush's last year in office, and the federal debt totaled more than $4 trillion, rising to two-thirds of GDP.

During the latter half of the 1980s the deregulated **savings and loan associations** (or S & Ls), banking companies that had traditionally made conservative loans for homes, began to feel the results of high-risk investments. Just after his inauguration, Bush announced that the federal government would have to rescue the badly damaged financial institutions. In February 1989, Bush proposed a plan to bail-out the S&Ls. The proposal and negotiations with Congress resulted in the Financial Institutions Reform, Recovery and Enforcement Act of 1989 (FIRREA). As part of the program, the Resolution Trust Corporation was formed to liquidate the insolvent S&Ls. By the end of the Bush administration, close to 600 S&Ls were closed. The total cost to taxpayers for all institutions resolved by the RTC came to $153 billion. Certainly, those costs contributed to the rising federal deficit during the Bush years. In total, the crisis resulted in the closure of a thousand banks. FIRREA was a significant government Act to protect the US economy and gave federal officials greater power than before.

The S&L crisis, along with several crashes in real estate prices, should have been an indicator that the economy was not as healthy when Bush entered the Oval Office as it may have seemed. However, GDP increased around 3% each of the first three quarters of 1989, then dropped to a 1% increase in the fourth quarter, jumped to 4% in the first quarter of 1990, but by autumn the economy was shrinking. The technical recession (two or more quarters of negative economic growth) lasted about six months before a slow return to positive numbers in mid-1991. The recession was relatively mild in terms of production, but unemployment reached just below 8% of the workforce at the peak and stayed at or above 7% from November 1991 to the end of Bush's term of office. These numbers were much lower than the 10.8% unemployment of the Reagan recession a decade before, but Bush was criticized a great deal for his response to the worsening economy. In December 1990, he told reporters that a recession might be possible and that the president should do what he can to lessen the effects. The 1991 State of the Union address began with a discussion of foreign policy, adding to the perception that he cared more about the international scene than domestic problems. He stated that some regions of the country were experiencing economic distress and that some people were hurting badly. That was followed by remarks about the economic success of the previous decade in adding 20 million jobs and lowering inflation. Proposals for helping those suffering from the downturn were slim. The proposed budget included tax-free savings and allowing Individual Retirement Accounts to be used to buy homes for first-time buyers, but remaining consistent with his pragmatic style, he avoided announcing large programs that would increase the federal deficit. Bush discussed federal debt and how a conservative approach would free up dollars for investment. Little of what he proposed offered immediate relief. Additionally, he claimed that the recession would be over soon and that the focus should be on long-term growth.

> **Savings and loan associations** are US financial institutions that accepts savings deposits and makes mortgage, car and other personal loans to individual members; a cooperative venture, they are also known as building societies outside of the Americas.

Activity

Public support

Research the support levels for George H. W. Bush vs. Ronald Reagan during the first terms of their presidencies. To what extent were the levels of support for their economic policies similar? Compare and contrast the responses and results of each administration's economic measures.

Activity

Assessing the presidency

In 1991, Stephen Moore, Director of Fiscal Policy Studies, Cato Institute (a libertarian think tank) wrote:

> During his 1988 bid for the presidency, George Bush distinguished himself from Ronald Reagan by promising to create a "kinder and gentler nation." He also said that he wanted to be known as the "environmental president" and the "education president." By now it is apparent that what Bush meant was that he was eager to spend substantially more money than Reagan had on a wide range of domestic programs.
>
> **Source:** Moore, Stephen. "Policy Analysis: The Profligate President: A Midterm Review of George Bush's Fiscal Policy Performance." *Cato Institute*. February 4, 1991. http://www.cato.org.

Look at the evidence to decide if Moore was correct. Organize a table comparing the two presidents on domestic policy using the following criteria (you may add others if you like):

● taxes

● education

● environment

● civil rights

● healthcare

Foreign policies

President George Bush came into office with a turbulent Central America, the USSR undergoing *perestroika* and *glasnost*, and China in the midst of a small degree of political liberalization. By the time he left office, China had clamped down on dissent but began to modify its communist economic system, peace had come to several warring Central American nations, the Berlin Wall had come down and the Soviet Union ceased to exist. Washington's influence and actions varied according to the situation.

Central America

The administration inherited Reagan's policies in the region, including involvement in El Salvador and Nicaragua. In Nicaragua, the administration continued to support the Contras, but the situation had changed by the time Bush took over because of the Tela Accords of February 1989, in which five Central American presidents agreed to a process which would result in fair elections the next year and called for the demobilization of the Contras. Bush changed the administration's objectives from the Central American equivalent of "roll back" to containment of the Sandinista regime, making sure it kept its promises by maintaining support for the Contras despite the Tesoro Accords. In other words, while Reagan could not abide a communist Nicaragua, Bush could, while working with determination towards a different future.

A peace process had been agreed upon in August 1987 and Nicaraguan elections were scheduled for February 1990. Bush stated that he supported the peace process, but insisted that the Contras, mostly in camps in neighboring Honduras, needed continued support to provide pressure on the Sandinistas to keep to their promises of increased political freedom. Bush and the Congress agreed to the

Activity

Newspapers and history

The Tela Accords

The following passage is the lead paragraph of the *New York Times* article "Contras, Lost Cause?" by Mark A. Uhlig, August 10, 1989:

Source A

TELA, Honduras, Aug. 9—As five Central American Presidents moved toward an agreement Monday on the demobilization of the Nicaraguan rebels, the Bush Administration sent out urgent signals trying to prevent that result. But after eight years of American support for the contra army, diplomats said the logic seemed to have gone out of the fight.

"They themselves couldn't explain what we should be waiting for," a Central American official said, referring to the Americans. "They still have their army, but they had lost their policy."

Source: (http://www.nytimes.com/1989/08/10/world/the-contras-lost-cause-burden-on-the-region-brings-about-accord.html).

Questions

1   To what extent was the unnamed Central American official correct?

2   Based on your own knowledge and research, Why did the Bush administration "send out urgent signals trying to prevent" an agreement?

3   What is the stated purpose of the Accords signed in Tela, Honduras?

4   Does the choice of Central American presidents to work against the wishes of the president of the United States signal a change in power relationships? Explain.

Source B

The following is the text of the Tela Accords signed in the Summit of Central American Presidents on August 7, 1989, in Puerto de Tela, Honduras. The signatories were Oscar Arias Sánchez, president of Costa Rica; Alfredo Cristiani Burkard, president of El Salvador; Marco Vinicio Cerezo Arévalo, president of Guatemala;

They (the presidents) "… have subscribed to the document [called] Collective Plan for the Voluntary Demobilization, Repatriation, or Relocation in Nicaragua and Third Countries of the members of the Nicaraguan Resistance and their dependents as well as the assistance toward the demobilization of all those involved in armed activities in the countries of the region, if they voluntarily request it.

Source: Documentation from the portal of the Central American Integration System (SICA). http:// www.sica.int.

José Azcona Hoyo, president of Honduras; Daniel Ortega Saavedra, president of Nicaragua.

The System of Central American Integration (SICA) is an international organization created by the States of the Republics of El Salvador, Honduras, Nicaragua, Guatemala, Costa Rica and Panama. Its headquarters is in El Salvador.

"Treaty of Washington" in which the Democratic leadership and the president agreed to suspend discussion of differences until after the Nicaragua's February 1990 election. The United States continued to apply diplomatic pressure on the Sandinistas and non-military aid to the Contras. Just before an August 1989 Central American Summit the Sandinistas committed to settling differences with the opposition over election procedures and at the Summit the Central American nations called for demobilization of the Contras by early December. The Bush administration played both sides, announcing support for the agreement but disagreeing over the disarming of the Contras. Its policy can be summed up as continued support for the Contras, tacit but weak support for the agreements, and support for internal opposition. In the months up to the election the administration transferred funds to the United Nicaraguan Opposition (a collection of more than a dozen anti-Sandinista groups, an organization that the administration helped create). The administration also complained of unfair election procedures even before the election took place, hinting that the Sandinistas would not accept election results if the votes did not go their way.

The election took place in February as scheduled and in a welcome surprise to the Bush administration Violeta Chamorro won the election with 55% of the vote and the UNO claimed a majority of seats in the National Assembly. The Contras refused to disband even after the election. Daniel Ortega and the Sandinistas peacefully gave up power, defying the Bush administration's predictions. After inauguration day the Contras agreed to disband and the Bush administration let its economic assistance flow to the new government of Nicaragua with the approval of Congress, led by Democrats who felt that as the United States had significantly contributed to the economic distress of the country, it was obligated to assist in its rebuilding and recovery. The debate was only over how much to spend.

Panama

The Bush administration' focus in Central America continued southward to Panama, which, in December 1989, would become the first major military operation of the Bush presidency. Operation Just Cause would involve Manuel Noriega, the military dictator of Panama, was already under indictment in the United States on drug trafficking charges, specifically cocaine. Previously, Noriega had been a long-time asset of the CIA whose contributions included helping supply the Contras and reportedly allowing the SR-71 Blackbird spy plane landing and take-off rights. . Early in the Reagan years he switched his support to the Sandinistas. In a time of a cocaine epidemic in the cities of the United States, the Reagan administration took steps to control Noriega, including imposing economic sanctions. The sanctions caused serious harm to Panama's financial sector. Still Noriega remained in power, but opposition to Noriega continued to grow in the U.S., especially after the 1988 indictment.

In the first months of the Bush presidency, Panama policy was uncertain as the State Department wanted to remove the Panamanian leader, but was opposed by the CIA and Defense Department, both seeing practical advantages to Noriega. Elections were scheduled in May, featuring Noriega's hand-picked candidate. The United States funneled $10 million to the opposition candidate. When Noriega's candidate lost, he refused to abide by the election results, causing a hardening of U.S. policy against Noriega. The Bush administration upped rhetorical pressure, increased the number of troops in the canal zone, which then engaged in agressive military exercises, and imposed stricter economic measures. Bush worked diplomatic channels to secure condemnation of Noreiga by most western European and, importantly, Latin American nations. To solve the crisis, in July the Organization of American States (OAS), seeking to remove a dictator from power and prevent intervention from the United States, tried to persuade Noriega to leave office and to negotiate with the opposition and form a new government. The efforts yielded no concessions from Panama's leader. An October coup attempt by dissident units of the Panamanian Defense Forces

? Why was the Bush administration surprised at the election result?

(PDF) failed due to flawed planning, weak execution, and steps taken by loyal PDF troops. Bush was criticized for not supporting the coup attempt, but his National Security Advisor, Colin Powell, a serious man whose Vietnam experience contributed to his prudent approach to military action, supported Bush's decision.

During the crisis some conservatives in Congress wanted to use Noriega's criminal activities and illegitimate hold on power as justification to revoke the Panama Canal Treaty President Jimmy Carter had signed, but Bush, echoing Reagan's understanding of the imperialistic image of the United States in Latin America, refused to go along, separating the ill-deeds of Manuel Noriega from the country he ruled.

Children cheering US marines following offensive in Vecca Monte, west of Panama City, during Operation Just Cause, the name given to the US invasion of Panama to remove Manuel Noriega.

December brought critical changes. On 16 December, Noriega declared that a "state of war" existed between the United States and Panama. On the same day members of the PDF shot an unarmed US soldier when he and several friends drove through a roadblock. Two U.S. citizens who witnessed the shooting were beaten. Bush felt the killings and beatings offered more than ample justification for an armed effort to remove Noriega. In a televised speech on 20 December he declared:

General Noriega's reckless threats and attacks upon Americans in Panama created an imminent danger to the 35,000 American citizens in Panama. As President, I have no higher obligation than to safeguard the lives of American citizens. And that is why I directed our Armed Forces to protect the lives of American citizens in Panama and to bring General Noriega to justice in the United States.

The same day 20,000 US troops attacked PDF forces across Panama in the invasion called Operation Just Cause, overcoming opposition in a matter of days. For more than a week Noriega took refuge in the Vatican Embassy in Panama City. He surrendered in early January. Noriega was quickly transferred to the United States where he was placed on trial in September 1991 and and convicted of drug trafficking at the conclusion of the trial in April 1992. He was sentenced to 40 years. The sentence was later reduced to 30 years,

Discussion point

What makes a cause "just"?
Examine several ethical systems for a definition of "justice." Then determine how just the US invasion of Panama was from a variety of perspectives.

Colin Powell (1937–)

Colin Powell's military career began in 1958. In the early 1960s he served as one of the original 16,000 military advisors to South Vietnamese forces. He served two tours in Vietnam and was awarded a number of medals. During the 1970s he moved to the Pentagon, then became a brigadier general. In the early years of the Reagan administration he served as Secretary of Defense, Weinberger's senior military aid. In 1987 Powell was appointed national security advisor by Reagan. In 1991 President Bush appointed him chairman of the Joint Chiefs of Staff (the Joint Chiefs are the highest officers of each branch of the military). Powell retired from the military in 1993. In 2001, when President George W. Bush nominated him for Secretary of State and he was confirmed, Colin Powell achieved the highest government position of any African American to that time.

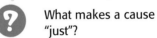

and further reduced for good behavior. (In July 2010 a French Court convicted Noriega of money laundering and sentenced him to seven years in jail. He had also been sentenced in Panama to 60 years in prison on various charges.) During the fighting and the aftermath an estimated 200-300 Panamanian civilians died, 314 PDF soldiers were killed, and 23 US troops lost their lives. Physicians for Human Rights estimated that 15,000 civilians lost homes and businesses. It was not until 1993 that the GDP of Panama returned to pre-invasion levels. Operation Just Cause was popular in the United States. President Bush gained a reputation as a deliberate, firm, and decisive leader. However, the United Nations and the OAS contemned Operation Just Cause as a violation of international law.

The Persian Gulf

On August 2, 1990, Iraq invaded Kuwait. The Iraqi army quickly overwhelmed the Kuwaiti Defenses and seized control of the country. The invasion was caused by a dispute over oil, Iraq having accused Kuwait of both stealing and overproducing oil. The Iraqi army had been massing on the border, and while it is unclear as to what message the Bush administration sent to Iraqi Dictator Saddam Hussein, it is most likely that neither the neighboring Arab states nor President Bush expected Iraq to do more than occupy the oil field in dispute. The day of the invasion the United Nations Security Council approved Resolution 660 demanding Iraq leave Kuwait and imposed economic sanctions four days later. That same day Saudi Arabia gave permission for the United States to put defensive forces in that country to defend against an attack. On August 8, Iraq announced that Kuwait was a province of Iraq. The annexation of Kuwait by Iraq caused great concern by the countries of Western Europe, the United States, and Japan, among other nations. The threat of Hussein controlling the vast oil supply of the Persian Gulf states comprised a large part of that concern.

Colin Powell, Chairman of the Joint Chiefs of Staff, phoning the Pentagon, via satellite, while on duty in the Middle East.

Activity

President Bush and Operation Desert Storm

The following sources are related to Operation Desert Storm in 1991.

Source A

The January 16, 1991, speech by George Bush announcing the commencement of war against Iraq.

Just two hours ago, allied air forces began an attack on military targets in Iraq and Kuwait. These attacks continue as I speak. Ground forces are not engaged.

This conflict started August 2nd when the dictator of Iraq invaded a small and helpless neighbor. Kuwait—a member of the Arab League and a member of the United Nations—was crushed; its people, brutalized. Five months ago, Saddam Hussein started this cruel war against Kuwait. Tonight, the battle has been joined.

This military action, taken in accord with United Nations resolutions and with the consent of the United States Congress, follows months of constant and virtually endless diplomatic activity on the part of the United Nations, the United States, and many, many other countries. Arab leaders sought what became known as an Arab solution, only to conclude that Saddam Hussein was unwilling to leave Kuwait. Others traveled to Baghdad in a variety of efforts to restore peace and justice. Our Secretary of State, James Baker, held an historic meeting in Geneva, only to be totally rebuffed. This past weekend, in a last-ditch effort, the Secretary-General of the United Nations went to the Middle East with peace in his heart—his second such mission. And he came back from Baghdad with no progress at all in getting Saddam Hussein to withdraw from Kuwait.

Now the 28 countries with forces in the Gulf area have exhausted all reasonable efforts to reach a peaceful resolution and have no choice but to drive Saddam from Kuwait by force. We will not fail.

Source: "President George Bush Announcing War Against Iraq." January 16, 1991. *The History Place*. http://www.historyplace.com/speeches/bush-war.htm.

Source B

From American History: A Survey (1999) by Alan Brinkley, a textbook widely used in colleges in the United States.

After some initial indecision, the Bush administration agreed to join with other nations to force Iraq out of Kuwait … Within a few weeks, Bush had persuaded virtually every important government in the world, including the Soviet Union and almost all the Arab and Islamic states, to join in a United Nations-sanctioned trade embargo of Iraq.

At the same time, the United States and its allies (including the British, French, Egyptians, and Saudis) began deploying a massive military force …

And on February 23, allied (primarily American) forces under General Norman Schwarzkopf began a major ground offensive

Source: Brinkley, Alan. 1999. *American History: A Survey*. 10th edn. Boston: McGraw Hill. pp. 1131–32.

Source C

Text from *American President: An Online Reference Resource*, a website run by the Miller Center of Public Affairs at the University of Virginia.

Despite being somewhat caught off guard, the Bush administration went to work immediately trying to assemble a coalition to oppose Iraq. One fortunate turn of events for the administration was that, at the time of the invasion, President Bush was with Prime Minister Margaret Thatcher of Britain at a conference, and Secretary of State Baker was in Siberia with Eduard Shevardnadze, the Soviet foreign minister. This allowed the United States to issue strong condemnations against Iraq with Britain, and most surprisingly, the Soviet Union. James Baker credited this moment, when the United States and Soviet Union issued a joint statement condemning Iraq's actions, as the end of the Cold War because it marked the beginning of unprecedented cooperation between the United States and the Soviet Union.

When the invasion began, Arab countries joined with the United States to form a coalition to convince Iraq to withdraw from Kuwait or face the consequences. When Saudi Arabia became concerned about a possible invasion after Iraqi troops began to mass on the border, President Bush announced the deployment of U.S. troops to the desert kingdom. He also articulated the four principles that guided "Operation Desert Shield": the immediate and complete withdrawal of Iraq from Kuwait; the restoration of the legitimate Kuwaiti government; the stability and security of the Middle East; and the protection of Americans abroad.

On the day of the invasion, the United Nations Security Council passed Resolution 660, which condemned the invasion and demanded that Iraq withdraw "immediately and unconditionally". The United States also quickly moved to freeze Kuwaiti and Iraqi assets. Shortly thereafter, the UN imposed economic sanctions on Iraq designed to try to convince Iraq to withdraw. The Iraqi invasion allowed President Bush to emphasize one of his greatest strengths—personal diplomacy. He had many international contacts, and he personally telephoned world leaders and U.S. allies to start building the coalition that would force Iraq to withdraw. However, the administration did not want Israel to join the coalition because it feared that Israel's involvement would alienate the Arab countries that had already agreed to join the alliance. Israel agreed to stay out of the coalition and not retaliate if attacked in order to allow the coalition's greater resources to deal with Hussein.

Source: "George H. W. Bush. Foreign Affairs." *Miller Center of Public Affairs*. http://millercenter.org/academic/americanpresident/bush/essays/biography/5.

Source D

Cartoon by Nicholas Garland first published in *The Independent* (UK) September 12, 1990.

"SON, WHAT DID YOU DO IN THE GULF WAR?"

Source E

Lucy Webster, at the U.N. Department for Disarmament Affairs, agrees that as a result of the Gulf [War], international law has progressed from the status of "pious norms to norms taken seriously. Law is a question of expectations and enforcement really means the threat of enforcement. There was no reason for Saddam Hussein to expect the response that his invasion provoked. But now the whole context has been changed."

Source: Yost, Jack. "The Role of the U.N. After Desert Storm: Rule of Law or Business as Usual?" *Peace Magazine*. May–June 1991. www.peacemagazine.org.

Questions

1 **a** What evidence is there in source A that the Bush administration made efforts to solve the conflict with Iraq without military action?

   b What is the message of source D?

2 Compare and contrast the level of international involvement in sources B, and E.

3 With reference to origin and purpose, assess the values and limitations of sources A and D for historians studying the Gulf War of 1991.

4 Using the documents and additional research, assess the importance of George Bush in the international action against Iraq in 1990 and 1991.

The invasion was not only condemned by the United States and its allies, but also the Soviet Union, reflecting the budding relationship between the Gorbachev-led USSR and the United States after the 1989 fall of the Berlin Wall and the accompanying collapse of communist rule throughout Eastern Europe. When United States combat forces were deployed, Bush announced the four principles that would guide Operation Desert Shield: the immediate and complete withdrawal from Kuwait, the restoration of the Kuwaiti government, the stability of the region, and protection of US citizens. It was at this time that George Bush began to apply personal diplomacy and work the contacts he had developed over many years.

In the next few months the Kuwaiti government mounted a public relations offensive, spending millions of dollars in the United States to build a case for armed ejection of the Iraqis from Kuwait. Included in the campaign was the appearance of a 15-year-old Kuwaiti girl, identified only by her first name, later identified as the daughter of the Kuwaiti ambassador to the United States, who testified that Iraqi soldiers had gone into a hospital and dumped infants out of incubators, leaving the infants on the floor to die. The story was revealed to be a fabrication. But, it was repeated by the press, Amnesty International, and several times by the president himself. The Kuwaiti government was suspect on human rights, but by painting the Iraqis as purveyors of atrocities, (certainly there was ample evidence of Saddam Hussein's ruthlessness during the Iraq–Iran War and towards his own people) there was enough momentum to gain narrow approval by the Senate for the use of force to expel Iraq. Thanks to an effective PR campaign, presidential pressure, oil, the importance of Middle East stability, the United Nations Security Council's November 29 resolution authorizing "all necessary means," the US Congress approved the use of force on January 12. In the early morning on January 17 the United States began air attacks, including massive bombing, that lasted for more than a month. The ground war commenced on February 23 and on February 27 President Bush announced that Kuwait was liberated. A cease-fire with Iraq was arranged. On March 6 Bush stood before a joint session of the House and Senate declaring, "tonight Kuwait is free." On April 3, the Security Council passed a resolution making the cease-fire permanent. The UN also demanded that Iraq rid itself of chemical and biological weapons and never build weapons of mass destruction in the future. Iraq agreed to the UN's conditions and the war officially ended on April 6.

Discussion point

Leaders and nations

Compare the administration's approach to the actions of Panama's Manuel Noriega and Iraq's Saddam Hussein. How did President Bush distinguish between the citizens of the two countries and their leaders?

Assess the policy statements and discuss the decisions made.

The president's popularity soared at the conclusion of Operation Desert Storm. There were few US casualties. Bush had led a coalition of nations, many providing manpower and some, including Japan, forbidden by its constitution from using its armed forces except for defense, provided significant funds. It was the first major operation of what Bush hoped would become the "new world order." Some were critical of Bush for halting the war before the Iraqi army was destroyed and Saddam Hussein removed, but Bush defended the cease-fire. The Security Council resolutions stated that Iraq had to withdraw to positions held on August 1, 1990, therefore there was no authority for the United States to continue into Iraq. Furthermore, removing Hussein could shift the balance of power in the region to the favor of Iran and if Hussein was removed the United States would be an occupying force for a long time, a state of affairs Bush did not want. Leaving Saddam Hussein in power did cause problems for the United States in future years.

The Soviet Union and Eastern Europe

To many observers the Cold War was already over when George Bush became president. Several increasingly friendly meetings between Mikhail Gorbachev and Ronald Reagan had taken place in the preceding four years, and in 1988 the Soviet occupation of Afghanistan ended. Bush, who practiced caution and exhibited a calm demeanor in domestic affairs, exhibited a similar deliberateness when dealing with the Soviet Union. The slow approach was called *pauza* (meaning pause) by the Soviets. But events in the region proceeded rapidly, seemingly independent of the president. In 1989, the first year of the Bush presidency, Poland, East Germany, Hungary, Romania and the Baltic State gained independence from the USSR. Gorbachev let the satellite states break away, crucially revoking the Brezhnev Doctrine which, since 1968, advocated intervention to prevent any communist state from leaving the fold.

The timing and swiftness of the events of autumn 1989 caught the United States' Defense and Intelligence agencies and President Bush by surprise. While much of the western bloc boisterously rejoiced when the Berlin Wall came down, Bush maintained his typically unflappable demeanor. When criticized for his lack of passion and failure to make a Kennedy or Reaganesque grand speech befitting the fall of the symbol of the Cold War in the city that had been the focal point of more than four decades of tension, Bush explained that he did not want to give the hardliners in the Kremlin an excuse to get rid of Gorbachev and reverse the progress of the previous months by metaphorically dancing on the Berlin Wall.

The collapse of the Iron Curtain that ran through the middle of Germany brought discussions of how Germany would reunite. A number of issues, related to the past and the present affected negotiations. Among those were the Russian fear of a united Germany, the loss of East Germany's economy to the USSR, and the critical question of whether a united Germany would become a member of NATO as was West Germany, or become a neutral nation. The process that became known as "Two-plus-Four" (East and West Germany, plus the United States, France, Great Britain and the

U.S.S.R.) settled the disputes.   The terms agreed upon were: Germany would join NATO but troops would not move onto former East German soil, Red Army units would have several years to leave, and Germany would provide monetary assistance to an economically weak Soviet Union, plagued by the expenses of the Afghanistan War, oil price fluctuations, and the loss of satellite nations.

It was not only the events of Eastern and Central Europe that saw diplomacy between the United States and the Soviet Union. Between the fall of the Berlin Wall and the culmination of negotiations over the future of Germany, Bush and Gorbachev met twice, once in December and again in June to negotiate the final terms of START (Strategic Arms Reduction Treaty). The treaty, signed at the July 1991 Moscow Summit, was a major, concrete step in negotiations that began in Reykjavik, Iceland, 1986, with the earnest discussions of Mikhail Gorbachev and Ronald Reagan.

As hardliners within the Kremlin sought to turn back Gorbachev's reforms, Bush continued to support Gorbachev. A coup attempt in August (a month after the Moscow summit) failed, with Boris Yeltsin emerging as a hero of reform and rule of law. The USSR began to break apart as the Soviet Republics declared independence from the Kremlin. On December 21, the Alma-Ata Protocol was signed by representatives of all the Soviet Republics, declaring the end of the Soviet Union. Bush watched as Gorbachev, the man who thought he could save the communist state, resigned as president of the in-name-only Soviet Union on Christmas Day 1991.

With the Soviet Union no longer an enemy Bush employed his diplomatic skills in the attempt to build a new world order. The idea was to build multinational coalitions to deal with problems around the globe. It was a chance to move beyond the bipolar world that had resulted in destructive alliances based on communist or anti-communist ideology. Some members of the administration wanted Bush to seize the opportunity presented by the collapse of the USSR to assert a hegemony of power. Bush's instinct was to look for diplomatic solutions, but the "peace dividend" did not come about as there was not the expected significant reduction in defense spending. Bush tried to build coalitions to produce peace in the breakup of Yugoslavia, but the effort was fruitless as nationalist sides descended into war. Additionally, the president sent troops into Somalia, a nation in the midst of a civil war. The efforts at creating a new world order fell short as social, political, economic, ideological and cultural concerns and passions proved to be obstacles to an endeavor that recalled the efforts of Woodrow Wilson in Spring 1919.

China

While the Soviet Union was disintegrating, China was encountering problems of its own. The four modernizations had brought some improvements to the economy and in living conditions for the Chinese people. The late 1980s seemed to bring a more open society. But in 1989 the challenge to Deng Xiaoping's regime was too great, which led to the crackdown on a demonstration in Tiananmen Square. President Bush, a former envoy to China, found that a weakening USSR resulted in less leverage for the United States in

Activity
Role play

Create groups of four or five: One person plays George H. W. Bush, one Mikhail Gorbachev, and two or three leaders of other countries (suggestions include, but are not limited to Cuba, Nicaragua, China, France, Egypt, Hungary, Israel, Iran, Nigeria, Poland, the UK etc). Each individual proposes a new world order that their country would support. After sharing proposals, the group creates a working definition and an outline of how it would operate.

An alternative is for each group to represent a nation. The group would create a proposal for a new world order and present it as a PowerPoint. The class would debate the merits and possible results of each proposal.

Activity
Different eras

Compare the policies and actions of President Eisenhower during the CIA-supported coup in Guatemala in 1954 and the Hungarian uprising in 1956 to the US response to the Tiananmen Square demonstrations in 1989. What actions did each president take? How important were the circumstances surrounding each event? Did circumstances dictate actions? Explain.

431

discussions with the Chinese leadership. In the first months of the administration the President had tried to work with the Chinese based on the traditional rivalry with the USSR, but was unsuccessful. Consequently, when Tiananmen occurred, the administration struggled for an effective response. Bush was concerned with the stability of the Chinese leadership and its control of the Chinese armed forces. In China, as opposed to Eastern Europe, force won and democracy lost. The Bush China policy worked with the understanding that cultivating a sound relationship with the Chinese military was critical for regional stability. To the vocal dismay of the Democrats in Congress who saw little reason to tolerate human rights violations on the part of the Chinese government, Bush seemed to abandon the push for democracy. The Bush condemnation of the Chinese crackdown was tepid in their eyes, but to the president, prudence left options that rash statements would have eliminated.

> The United States **electoral system** requires a majority of electoral votes for a candidate to become president. Each state is allotted votes on the basis of number of representatives and senators. Most of the 50 states and the District of Columbia have "winner take all" elections, so it is possible for a candidate to win the majority of electoral votes without obtaining at least 50% of the popular vote.

President Bill Clinton, 1993–2001

Bill Clinton, the Democrat governor of Arkansas, a southern state, was little known outside his region when he began his run for the presidency. Clinton won the the nation's highest office in a three-way contest with incumbent George Bush and Texas billionaire Ross Perot, who ran a folksy campaign focusing on patriotism, deficit reduction and economic issues, but the result was Clinton won an impressive majority of **electoral votes** but received only 43% of the popular votes cast.

Clinton, whose election campaign was based on the phrase, "It's the economy, stupid," was most interested in domestic policy, especially healthcare. Even though he had studied foreign policy at Georgetown, he focused on domestic issues in the light of the first presidential election after the fall of the Soviet Union. His presidency was marked by great failures and great triumphs in foreign policy, domestic policy and personal travails. Included in those episodes were Somalia, Bosnia, Kosovo, healthcare, deficit reduction, gay rights, racial, ethnic and gender diversity, economic prosperity, a technological revolution and market crash, and a presidential impeachment trial for only the second time in the history of the United States.

Domestic policies

Healthcare

Bill Clinton ran for president promising to reform healthcare. The United States was the only developed country in the world without a national healthcare system, and it was estimated that more than 50 million Americans had

> **William Jefferson Clinton (1946–)**
>
> Unlike his predecessor, Clinton did not come from wealth. His father died just before he was born, and his mother was an alcoholic, he was not a war hero (he had avoided the draft), was charismatic, personable, enjoyed domestic policy, and was quite polished. He had a good education: Georgetown University, Oxford University as a Rhodes Scholar, then Yale Law. He became the youngest governor in the country in 1978 at the age of 32, lost his reelection attempt, then came back to serve as governor for four additional terms. Clinton was part of the Democratic Leadership Council, a group of Democrats who were more moderate and tended towards a view that pragmatic policy formulation, combined with moderate liberalism was the way to get elected and to rule. They differed on key points with liberals in supporting capital punishment and championing welfare reform. A risky strategy for primary elections where the left wing of the party was most powerful, Clinton managed to secure the Democratic nomination for the presidency, despite allegations of marital infidelity and being labeled "Slick Willie" by his critics. After serving two terms as president of the United States, Clinton moved to New York and his wife, Hillary, won election to the United States Senate. Bill Clinton worked on many humanitarian projects following his eight years in office, including AIDS and Tsunami relief, joining with his predecessor, George H.W. Bush.

no health insurance. To Clinton this was unacceptable. Additionally, healthcare was taking up an increasingly large portion of the GDP, about 15%, and predicted to keep rising. Unlike many other industries in which technology had decreased costs, technological advances in medicine served to increase demands for new tests and procedures, and even if they reduced some costs, healthcare's share of the economy promised to grow. To Clinton and supporters, reforming heathcare would not only benefit millions of US citizens directly, but controlling costs would make the federal government debt manageable due to reduced Medicare projections in the decades to come. On the private side, it would enable companies to increase profitability and invest in new technologies, making the economy of the nation grow. There seemed to be little downside.

Despite this, there was great opposition to the plan. Republicans saw healthcare reform as a significant expansion of government, a potentially huge victory for the Clinton presidency and a catalyst for the Democrats that could bring "Reagan Democrats" back into the fold. Also, healthcare reform would bring massive change to a system that worked for a majority of the population. But the process of healthcare reform helped to feed the uncertainty. Clinton named his wife, Hillary, an accomplished attorney and former leader of education reform in Arkansas during Clinton's governorship, as head of the task force. The task force—appointed experts in medicine, managed care, and finance—met in private. Hillary Clinton's relationship with the president reportedly caused panel members to mute their criticism of proposals that she favored. To many citizens, it appeared that the Clintons were forming policy in a smoky back room that reminded many of corrupt old-style politics. When the proposal came out, it exceeded 1,000 pages. The president had wanted to present Congress with a complete plan that they could amend, rather than present specific goals and broad principles and let congressional committees hash out the details for months, if not years. A federal court forced the administration to make the records of the task force public, reinforcing the climate of distrust. President Clinton announced the proposal in a September 1993 speech.

Opposition to the healthcare proposal was fierce. Republicans led a coordinated attack. The plan was too big, too complex, and impossible to understand. It was a threat to big and small business alike. It would take away healthcare from those who had it. Americans would no longer get to choose their doctor. The famous "Harry and Louise" commercials, featuring a middle class, elderly couple concerned about losing their healthcare, an ad campaign sponsored by health insurance companies, served to persuade many people that the Clinton plan would make things worse. The suicide of White House aide, Vince Foster, a friend of Hillary Clinton's added to the climate of innuendo around the campaign for the plan. By mid-1994, it was clear that healthcare reform was going nowhere. Congressional mid-term elections were approaching, the Clinton administration was becoming increasingly unpopular and many Democrats up for reelection in both the House and Senate did not want to risk supporting the reform effort. Interestingly, opinion polls showed that the public supported many parts of the plan—except

Discussion point

Looking back in history

Following the First World War, Woodrow Wilson advocated in his 8 January 1918 "Fourteen Points" speech to a joint session of Congress that there should only be "Open covenants of peace, openly arrived at."

How open should governmental processes be in a democracy?

when Clinton's name was part of the question. Clinton had spent whatever political capital he had on reforming healthcare. The failure of the proposal was a huge defeat for his presidency.

The economy

When looked at as a whole, the eight Clinton years brought strong economic growth. There was low inflation, low unemployment and sustained increases in GDP averaging 4% per year. Worker productivity was on the increase. An ever-increasing federal deficit, despite the Bush budget deal, was converted into a budget surplus by the end of Clinton's second term. A look at economic data supports the strong economy of the Clinton era. In January 1993, when Clinton entered office, unemployment stood at 7.3%. Four years later it had dropped to 5.3% and when Clinton left office, unemployment stood at 3.9%.

The question is how much of the economic success was due to Clinton policies. Was he lucky or good or both? One argument is that the deregulation and policies of the Reagan-Bush years set the stage for sustained economic growth. But the legacy also included a massive federal debt. Clinton understood the need to get the federal budget under control. His first budget passed only because Democrats held majorities in both houses. The budget contained aggressive deficit reduction strategies. Several times during his presidency, especially when he was weakened by scandal, Republicans pressed for tax cuts as the deficit receded. Clinton resisted the pressure and pushed a second deficit reduction program in 1997.

The $290 billion deficit that Clinton inherited became a $124 billion surplus when he left. Many economists argue that as the federal government competes for loan dollars when it runs a deficit, decreasing the government's borrowing lowers interest rates by making more capital available for investment. Clinton, following the advice of Treasury Secretary Robert Rubin, followed a controversial policy of a strong dollar. Conventional wisdom said that to increase exports the dollar needed to be weak against other currencies, but the strong dollar allowed for a low-inflation economy and provided options for the inflation-averse Federal Reserve not to raise interest rates to slow the economic expansion.

Clinton also engaged other nations as he looked at the United States as a part of a global economy. Clinton promoted the North American Free Trade Agreement (NAFTA) against the voices of labor (traditionally strong supporters of Democrats), a treaty that George Bush had worked on, and it was approved by the Congress in 1993. He also supported the World Trade Organization (WTO) to encourage increased global commerce. The administration also provided funds to assist the Mexican and Asian economies, as well as through the International Monetary Fund (IMF). The assistance was unpopular domestically, on both the left and the right.

Welfare reform

The 1994 election was a rout in favor of Republicans. Voter anger at the healthcare debacle and ethical questions revolving around the Clinton administration resulted in the Republicans taking over the House and Senate. Newt Gingrich offered a "Contract with America"

Activity
President's policies

Remember to continue adding to the table you created at the beginning of the section on presidents' policies.

Activity
Online activity

"Harry and Louise"

Watch several "Harry and Louise" commercials on YouTube.

1 Identify the message of each advertisement. Then, describe the theme of the campaign.

2 What was the origin of the ads and what was the purpose?

3 Explain the values and limitations of the Harry and Louise campaign for historians studying the failure of healthcare reform during the 1990s.

Discussion point

Economic successes

Answer the following question:

1 To what extent were the economic successes of the Clinton administration the result of
   a The actions of the two previous presidents
   b Clinton's own policies
   c Economic factors beyond the control of the president?

that promised smaller and more ethical government. Clinton was severely weakened and soon after the election he publicly claimed that he was "still relevant." The president's words seemed desperate. Faced with a hostile legislature, he had to change strategy. In 1995, he embraced welfare reform traditionally a Republican issue. Clinton said that it was time to move people from "welfare to work." When campaigning for election, Clinton referred to himself as a New Democrat, one who felt that the era of big government was over, but that government still had a positive role to play. To many Democrats, the promise to "end welfare as we know it" sounded like "blame the poor" rhetoric, but in a growing economy jobs were plentiful. Training was included as part of the legislation. Republicans wrote much of the bill. Federal aid to families with dependent children was replaced with block grants to states. The devolution from federal to state authority was a departure from traditional liberal policy. Clinton succeeded in getting the minimum wage raised. The **Earned Income Tax Credit** was expanded, too. Due to the growing economy and the new laws welfare rolls dropped by half.

> The **Earned Income Tax Credit** provides tax credits (payments by the government even if an individual has not paid income taxes), providing an important additional incentive for workers to stay employed.

Diversity in government appointments

During the 1992 campaign Clinton said that he wanted a presidential cabinet that looked like the United States, meaning his cabinet secretaries would feature racial and ethnic minorities as well as women. Although he ran into trouble with two ill-considered nominees for Attorney General, the heads of the executive departments did indeed differ in background from previous administrations. Women took a prominent place in many parts of his administration: Janet Reno became the first female attorney general, Donna Shallala was appointed Secretary of Health and Human Resources, and Madeleine Albright was the first woman appointed ambassador to the United Nations, later becoming Secretary of State. Hazel O'Leary, the Secretary of Energy was African American, as was Dr Jocelyn Elders, the new surgeon general. Other women also occupied places of prominence in the administration. African American appointees included the Commerce Secretary, Ron Brown, the head of the Department of Agriculture, Mike Espy, and Jesse Brown, the new Secretary of Veterans Affairs. Two Hispanic Americans held cabinet positions: Henry Cisneros, the former mayor of San Antonio, Texas, became the Secretary of Housing and Urban Development and Federico Pena took over the Department of Transportation. Some critics make the point that Clinton's "New Democrat" policies rendered the appointments window-dressing, but the list is extensive and

Activity

Television drama

The West Wing TV series, created by Aaron Sorkin, that was originally broadcast on NBC from September 22, 1999 to May 14, 2006, features a fictional White House administration, loosely inspired by the Clinton era in government.

Choose an episode and reflect on the policies and personalities being discussed in relation to real life policies and issues in government in the 1980s and 1990s.

A White House cabinet meeting in January 1993.

Activity

President Clinton's impeachment

The following sources address issues surrounding the impeachment of President Bill Clinton.

Source A

Foes of the president further complained that he was so absorbed in protecting his hide that he was endangering national security. On August 7, Al Qaeda terrorists blew up the American Embassies in Kenya and Tanzania. On August 20, three days after his televised address, Clinton authorized retaliatory missile strikes in Sudan and Afghanistan, leading critics to charge that he was cynically using military firepower in order to divert attention from his personal excesses. Whether this was so was impossible to prove—Clinton said he acted to thwart terrorism—but there was no doubting his personal problems were consuming much of his time and that partisan battling over sex was hijacking the attention of Washington and the country.

Source: Patterson, James T. 2005. *Restless Giant: The United States from Watergate to Bush vs. Gore*. Oxford University Press.

Source B

I really think the way to think about the political legacy of Bill Clinton is to view it from the lenses of on the one hand and on the other. And let me give you a series of such tensions. I would submit, Bill Clinton is the most gifted American politician since FDR, in every respect, intelligence, policy, knowledge, political skill, capacity to relate to the American people. Yet, he was also the one who was impeached and almost driven from office. As Bob said, Bill Clinton presided over and contributed to a period of extraordinary prosperity, yet leaves office with a widespread sense of squandered opportunities, Belle identified two, the area of health reform, and social insurance reform. On the latter one might argue that the success of fiscal policy has indirectly improved the health of our social insurance system, yet alas he certainly intended to do more and would have, had other matters not overwhelmed him.

Source: Mann, Tom. "Assessing Bill Clinton's Legacy: How will History Remember Him?" *The Brookings Institution*. January 9, 2001. http://www.brookings.edu/events/2001/0109elections.aspx.

Source C

In the process of pursuing an impeachment of the President, the Republicans had seriously overplayed their hand. An indication of what lay ahead came when the party actually lost five seats in the House while gaining no Senate seats in the November 1998 elections conducted just prior to the impeachment vote. Traditionally, the opposition party registers significant gains in the off-year elections of a President's second term, and so the Republican loss was virtually unprecedented.

As the impeachment process unfolded, Clinton's ratings in public opinion polls were at an all-time high, hovering at close to 70 percent. Most Americans gave Clinton low marks for character and honesty. But, they gave him high marks for performance and wanted him censured and condemned for his conduct, but not impeached and removed. Many viewed key Republican attackers as mean-spirited extremists willing to use a personal scandal for partisan goals. In the end, voters were happy with Clinton's handling of the White House, the economy, and most matters of public life. Hillary Clinton's public opinion poll ratings actually exceeded the President's, in large measure because of her dignified demeanor during those trying personal times, thus lifting her popularity to among the highest ever for a First Lady.

Source: "Domestic Affairs: William Jefferson Clinton." *American President: An Online Reference Resource.* The Miller Center of Public Affairs.
http://millercenter.org/academic/americanpresident/clinton/essays/biography/4.

Source D

Cartoon by Bill McArthur, featuring Benjamin Netanyahu, Yasser Arafat, and Bill Clinton. First published in *The Glasgow Herald*. December 14, 1998.

Questions

1 a What evidence is there in Source B that issues surrounding impeachment affected the actions of President Clinton?

b What is the message of Source D?

2 Compare and contrast the views expressed in sources A and C on the effects of the impeachment scandal.

3 With reference to their origin and purpose, assess the values and limitations of sources B and C for historians researching the Clinton presidency.

4 Using the sources and your own knowledge, evaluate the affect of the Whitewater and Lewinsky scandals on the ability of Bill Clinton to carry out his policy goals.

Clinton did change the racial, ethnic, and gender paradigm for presidential appointments.

Impeachment and scandals

Bill Clinton was the only the second president in United States' history to be impeached. The previous impeachment involved Andrew Johnson, Abraham Lincoln's successor, and followed the greatest crisis in the nation's history: the Civil War. The Constitution provides for but one method to remove a sitting president from office, impeachment for "high crimes and misdemeanors." Impeachment by the House of Representatives followed by trial in the Senate is the greatest and ultimate check on the power of the chief executive. Clinton's troubles grew out of a series of allegations that began before the election and ranged from fiscal impropriety, womanizing, the suicide of aide Vince Foster, sexual relations with a White House intern, and perjury to cover up the affair.

The scandals themselves were peripheral to the policies of the president. However, the controversies, which spanned both terms, demanded significant attention from Clinton and his staff, and weakened the president in dealings with the legislative branch. Clinton was accused of attempting to distract the country by launching missile strikes – even his foreign policy initiatives were questioned by critics who citied the scandals.   Many observers of United States politics claimed potential legislative accomplishments had gone unrealized because of the scandals. Thus, the allegations, which became known as *Whitewater,* are critical to understanding the Clinton presidency.

The main scandal, Whitewater, revolved around real estate investment linked with a Savings and Loan that involved close friends of the Clintons. Attorney General Janet Reno, the chief law enforcement officer of the federal government appointed a Republican as an **independent counsel**, but a three-judge panel felt that Reno, a presidential appointee, could not be sufficiently independent. Kenneth Starr, an attorney and former federal judge with numerous conservative connections, was appointed instead. Starr pursued his investigation with vigor and expanding resources. The investigation soon went beyond the limited Whitewater allegations to many aspects of Clinton's public and private life. To Clinton's critics the reach of Starr's investigation was appropriate for a man they believed had committed many crimes and abuses of power, but to supporters the Starr inquiries were a witch hunt. Due to the independent counsel law, people could be prosecuted for crimes unrelated to the original reason for the counsel's appointment. Starr defended the scope of the investigation as necessary for getting to the heart of Clinton's activities.

The investigation continued for several years without charges being brought. But, in 1997 the Supreme Court ruled that a lawsuit by Paula Jones against Clinton for sexual harassment while he was governor of Arkansas to go forward, disregarding arguments that it would distract the sitting president from his duties. Clinton's affair with intern Monica Lewinsky came to light. The independent counsel place Clinton under oath and questioned him, reasoning that his behavior illustrated a pattern of illicit activity. The veracity, or lack thereof, of the president's testimony became the foundation of charges against Clinton. As evidence of Clinton's affair became public knowledge, the tawdriness of the affair affected the president's public standing. On 17 August 1998 Clinton gave a televised address in which he admitted to an affair he had previously adamantly denied, but disavowed directing any cover up.

Starr forwarded his report to the House of Representatives. After heated debate, two articles of impeachment were passed: perjury and obstruction of justice. The Senate trial took place in 1999. At times, the arguments became a surreal discussion of whether lying about sexual activity counted as a high crime or misdemeanor as intended by the Constitution's authors. In the end the Senate failed to convict the Clinton of either charge, with 45 of 100 members in favor of a perjury conviction and 50 voting that he was guilty of obstruction of justice (a two-thirds vote is required for a guilty verdict). There were two years left in the acquitted, but tainted, president's term. In

---

TOK Link
Ethics

1 How are public ethics linked to private ethics?

2 To what extent are ethical codes situational rather than absolute?

3 How do ethics inform our expectations of people in public office? Research the history of issues of impeachment.

retrospect, the Supreme Court's ruling that allowed the sitting president to face a lawsuit greatly underestimated the amount of time, energy and attention the case would demand.

Homosexuals in the military

A discrimination issue that had some parallels to Harry Truman's order to ban racial segregation in the armed forces was Clinton's promise on winning the election to end the ban on homosexuals serving in the military. A court decision, however, forced Clinton to act on his promise early in his administration, before he had established sufficient credibility as a leader. Because Clinton had avoided serving in the military during the Vietnam era, his standing with the military and many veterans was low, and an effort to change the culture of the military needed a careful and timely approach. Clinton was neither afforded the time or the planning. Many other western countries armed forces had openly gay recruits, but the United States armed forces continued to exclude them. Conservatives, numerous veterans, and the military top brass opposed any changes, but after more than six months Clinton proposed "don't ask, don't tell," a policy that allowed homosexuals to serve in secret. A soldier could not reveal and the military could not ask if he or she was gay. The policy pleased few people. A more restrictive bill came out of Congress, but the essential elements of Clinton's compromise became the policy of the armed forces.

Foreign policies

Clinton came to the presidency focusing almost exclusively on the economy. Richard Haass, after counting presidential speeches and broadcasts, reported that the president spent 10% of his efforts on foreign policy. Given that Clinton was the first president elected since 1948 not to face the USSR in the long Cold War contest, it is understandable that his focus was on domestic affairs. For the first time in half a century, there was not a specific international target— no Germany, Japan or USSR—on which to focus. Near the end of his term, George Bush attempted to forge a new world order, and the new president would have an opportunity to create a new US foreign policy. But, as Clinton found out, foreign affairs have a way of becoming unpredictably significant and time-consuming.

The civil war in Somalia, an attempt to oust Haiti's dictator Raoul Cedras, the Bosnian–Serbian and Albanian–Serbian conflicts in the Balkans, and Rwanda's vicious civil war were some of the challenges the Clinton administration faced. There was the opportunity to work with nations of the former Soviet Union to limit and secure nuclear weapons. North Korea's missile and nuclear weapons programs were also a developing threat. Clinton continued the efforts of US presidents to find a solution to the ongoing Arab–Israeli conflict, and was responsible for enforcing sanctions on Iraq's Saddam Hussein. There were terrorist attacks on New York's Twin Towers and a US navy ship in Yemen. Reemerging democracies in Latin America along with trade negotiations and financial interventions were also to occupy Clinton. Along the way, the Clinton foreign policy team developed the doctrine of enlargement: expanding market democracies, free trade, developing and

Ranking the three presidents

Ranking presidents is a favorite activity of many historians.

1 Using the information from your presidential policies table, examine each presidents' successes and failures.

2 Decide the extent to which outside events influence or interfered with presidential actions.

3 Examine the domestic goal of the presidents upon entering office and evaluate the extent to which each accomplished his objectives.

4 Based on those three factors, rank the presidents.

supporting multinational alliances, and a policy of intervention that became known as the Clinton Doctrine. Clinton, explaining why the United States was at times involved in places seemingly beyond the scope of the US national interest, said: "… what are the consequences to our security of letting conflicts fester and spread. We cannot, indeed, we should not, do everything or be everywhere. But where we can make a difference, we must be prepared to do so." For a man elected to fix domestic problems, a full foreign affairs agenda faced the new president.

Africa

Unexpectedly, two nations in Africa, Somalia and Rwanda, became part of the United State's foreign policy portfolio. U.S. policies in each nation were largely unsuccessful and brought a great deal of criticism: involvement in Somalia and a lack of involvement in Rwanda.

U.S. involvement in Somalia began in August 1992, six months before Clinton took office. Beginning with food delivery, the U.S. joined a United Task Force (UNITAF) of almost 40,000 soldiers from twenty countries in December to provide needed security in the war-torn nation. The task force, including 26,000 U.S. troops, operated in Somalia until May 1993. An effort followed to create a manageable situation for Somalis. The United States reduced troops to 4,000, but violence grew in Somalia. Different Somali factions drove through the streets in "techinicals," pick-up trucks armed with a large machine gun or recoilless rifle mounted in the bed, intimidating residents and seizing food intended for distribution. U.S. soldiers attempted to provide protection from the warlords. As violence increased, Clinton added marines, but in a limited mission soldiers were not provided with all the weaponry and equipment necessary for success and safety. In October 1993, in an incident that became known as Black Hawk Down from a book by Mark Bowden (and subsequent 2001 movie), a battle in central Mogadishu resulted in U.S. casualties and images of dead US marines being dragged through the streets.

The United States, along with United Nations forces, withdrew over the next six months. Somalia descended into further disarray with warlords assuming control in the absence of foreign forces. Critics of the president called Somalia a fiasco while supporters, still admitting a failed mission, blamed the previous president for getting into the mess. The first major Clinton foreign policy mission failed to achieve even limited goals.

Trade

Regional and global trade advancement was an important component of Clinton's economic and foreign policies. Important trade negotiations included NAFTA, GATT, WTO, and fast-track action on trade with China. For most of his two terms Clinton advocated removing trade barriers and pushing for increased global commerce with fewer restrictions. This policy antagonized traditional Democratic groups, including labor unions and environmental groups.

Activity

Research

For what reasons did the United Nations Security Council choose to withdraw the vast majority of peacekeeping forces in Rwanda?

TOK Link

Language

What is genocide? In your judgement were the mass killings in Rwanda genocide? Why do labels matter?

Discussion point

To what extent is Tony Lake's statement that the United States could not solve "other people's problems" consistent with US foreign policy in the 20th century?

NAFTA As a presidential candidate Clinton had pledged to support the Bush-initiated North American Free Trade Agreement (NAFTA), a trade agreement between Canada, Mexico, and the United States. Upon entering the White House he did so. Opposition was fierce, and included Ross Perot who claimed that factories would leave the United States for cheaper labor in Mexico, taking millions of jobs with them. Congress approved the pact, a commitment to regional economic integration. NAFTA presented Mexico with the opportunity to attract new foreign investment. Environmental provisions were also included, a concern of environmentalists who felt that polluting industries would simply relocate to the countries with the least restrictive environmental regulations. The administration hoped that NAFTA would stimulate Mexico's economy, stabilizing the Salinas government. NAFTA met with a mixed reception in Mexico as in response the Zapatista National Liberation Army rose up in the state of Chiapas. Overall, NAFTA was an early success, as trade increased more than 20% in the first year alone.

GATT Clinton hoped that NAFTA would provide leverage for the 1994 General Agreement on Tariffs and Trade (GATT) negotiations with Europe and Japan. GATT was a set of international commerce rules with enforcement provisions. The goal was to increase trade between countries by reducing trade barriers in an equitable manner. GATT was to open new markets and reduce the price of imports, allowing the US economy to grow in ways not possible in eras of tariff wars and trade barriers. The result of the negotiations was the creation of the new World Trade Organization (WTO) by 75 GATT members. GATT was ended and the WTO officially began on in 1995.

WTO The WTO was formed as an organization to regulate trade between member nations. It had enforcement powers. But the purpose of the WTO was to stimulate greater international commerce. The third WTO conference, held in Seattle, Washington, started on November 30, 1999. Clinton, in preparation for the meeting issued an executive order that forced the government to review the environmental effects of trade agreements. In line with his executive order, Clinton did emphasize the need for environmental protection, core international labor standards, and for the WTO to open its inner-workings to public scrutiny. But, he informed the public that global trade was expanding and the United States needed to be at the forefront. Clinton told supporters that the United States had 4% percent of the world's population and 22% of its wealth; consequently, it had to offer worthwhile incentives to other countries.

Huge protests of crowds upwards of 40,000 broke out in Seattle during the week of the WTO event. To those who protested, the WTO facilitated a "race to the bottom," and rather than raising standards of living in developing countries it was in the process of lowering standards everywhere. Reinforcing national control over trade united the isolationist right and the liberal left in challenging the president's support for the organization. Clinton angered his advisors with his call for labor and environmental standards. The protests did not shut down the meeting, but in the United States Seattle is viewed as the beginning of a sustained challenge to unfettered globalization.

Discussion point

Economic sovereignty

Two critical components of a nation state's authority are political and territorial sovereignty. In what ways and to what extent is economic sovereignty critical to the survival and success of a state?

441

Clinton, undeterred by Seattle, looked across the ocean to the emerging market of China and, gnoring China's human rights violations, granted Permanent Normal Trading Partner status to China the following year, easing China's entry into the WTO.

Europe

After the breakup of the Soviet empire, many parts of Europe were in turmoil. Economic and political integration caused uncertainty in many former countries of the Soviet Bloc. One such area was the former Yugoslavia. In 1992, Serbia and Bosnia-Herzegovina took up arms against each other. The Serbs quickly gained the advantage and took Bosnian towns, burning homes and killing and raping civilians. As the world watched atrocities, NATO and the United States did little to stop the war. Against the advice of many foreign policy advisors, stating that involvement was not of US national interest, the Clinton administration embarked on efforts to stop the war in the Balkans. The United Nations declared "safe areas" but the Serbian armed forces disregarded enclaves and continued killing. By 1995, the Clinton administration tired of the violence, pushed NATO to act. Led by the United States, NATO repeatedly bombed Serbian positions. The September air raids had the desired effect, driving the Serbian leader, Slobodan Milosevic, to negotiations. The talks took place in Dayton, Ohio, in November and the Dayton Accords were signed in Paris the following month. Clinton sent 20,000 troops to enforce the agreement. The troops succeeded in keeping peace and setting the stage for elections in 1996.

Serbia did not stop its war-making with the Dayton Accords. Serbia entered into a conflict in the province of ethnic Albanian dominated Kosovo. After attacks by the Kosovo Liberation Army (KLA), the superior-armed Serbian army began an offensive, resulting in the deaths of numerous civilians. Atrocities by the Serbians, resulting in thousands of dead Albanians, again came to the attention of the international community. After repeated attempts to come to an agreement with Milosevic to stop the fighting, in 1999, NATO undertook a 79-day bombing campaign against Serbia. Again, Milosevic was driven to negotiate by superior force. With the Russians participating in talks, Serbia agreed to withdraw from Kosovo. The United States, United Kingdom, France and Russia provided troops as peacekeepers.

With the disintegration of the Soviet Union and the Warsaw Pact, the Clinton administration worked for a safer and stable Europe. A topic of great concern was the disposal of nuclear weapons and the stock of weapons-grade material. Working with Senator Sam Nunn, a legislator known for defense expertise, and his Republican counterpart, Richard Lugar, the administration provided for monitoring and securing of nuclear power plants, dangerous materials, and the dismantling of nuclear weapons. Additionally, Clinton supported IMF loans to Russia and Russia's President, Boris Yeltsin, even as Yeltsin faded in popularity and reports of corruption increased. Finally, several former Warsaw Pact countries, Poland, Hungary and the Czech Republic, became members of NATO, with the caveat that no NATO weapons or troops enter those countries. The deal was similar to the Two-Plus-Four agreement over the unification of Germany.

Latin America

The Clinton administration entered office with NAFTA in process and with a military dictatorship in Haiti. The majority of nations in South and Central America were well on their way to establishing, reestablishing and strengthening democratic governments. The new administration appeared more reactive to events than proactive. Some analysts felt Clinton reacted to the pressure of interest groups and media exposure rather than a thought-out plan. Latin America did not command the attention of the administration. Secretary of State Warren Christopher did not visit Latin America until 1996. One exception to the pattern was the Summit of the Americas in December 1994. In addition to NAFTA, the Clinton Presidency can take credit for removing a military dictatorship in Haiti, rescuing the Mexican economy from the "Peso Crisis," and working towards a free trade Americas.

Clinton's foreign policy flexibility was weakened from January 1995, when both the Senate and House were under Republican control. Among the actions of the new congressional leadership was the reduction of foreign aid by more than 20%. Congress added additional conditions: it directed the State Department to certify a country as cooperating in the drug war to be eligible to receive aid. Clinton chose to continue the anti-drug focus of the nation's Latin American policy, but did change emphasis from drug interdiction to eradication and cartel-busting. While the Clinton Doctrine implied a cohesive policy in Latin American to strengthen democracies and expand markets, it can also be viewed as a series of individual events dealt with as circumstances permitted.

Haiti posed a difficult problem for the new president. Haitian refugees floating to the United States on boats and rafts had been prevented from reaching shore by the Coast Guard and returned to Haiti by the Bush administration. The sitting president took no steps to restore Jean-Bertrand Aristide to power. During his election campaign Clinton took the position of restoring Aristide to power, criticizing Bush for denying refugees of the dictatorial regime asylum. But, after winning the election, he reversed his position in response to media reports that thousands of Haitians were about to get in homemade boats to flee to the United States. The United Nations worked out an agreement with the regime to allow Aristide to return. In October 1993, UN and US forces were confronted by Haitian paramilitary forces and not allowed to come ashore. Talks stopped soon after. By June 1994, Clinton realized that diplomacy without the threat of force was useless. It took further pressure from political allies for the president to act. Clinton took the lead in persuading the UN Security Council to pass a resolution authorizing the use of force to restore Aristide to Haiti's presidency.

Clinton also decided that US forces would lead the invasion. In a September speech, Clinton announced that every diplomatic effort had been rejected by the military commander in chief of

An anti-Aristide protester kicks the car carrying US diplomat Vicki Huddleston on 11 October, 1993, in Port-au-Prince, Haiti, after the car was not allowed entry to the sea port to welcome UN troops. The protesters shouted that they would not allow an occupying force in their country.

Haiti, Raoul Cedras. In the same speech he demanded the Haitian ruler and military supporters relinquish power immediately. Within a day, after arrangements by former president Carter, a meeting of the military leaders and Carter, Democratic Senator Sam Nunn, and General Collin Powell took place. Two days later the negotiators reached an agreement that allowed Aristide to return to power. A hitch came when Cedras was informed that US forces were about to invade, but Clinton called off the invasion and the agreement was signed. Eventually, after further negotiations, 20,000 US soldiers came ashore to secure Haiti. On October 15, Aristide was reinstated as president. Clinton's efforts resulted in the restoration of a fledgling democracy. Two years later, US troops left Haiti.

Summit of the Americas

In December 1993, the Clinton administration decided to follow up on NAFTA with a meeting of the heads of the 34 leaders of Latin American democracies—the Summit of the Americas. The meeting took place in Miami a year later, just after the Republican election landslide. To the Clinton Administration, the summit was an advancement of both domestic and foreign policy. The focus on the economy demanded expanding markets for domestically produced goods and the evolving Clinton Doctrine added promotion of democracy to the first priority. The Summit of the Americas was a prime opportunity.

The summit was a gathering of the leaders of 33 democratic states of the Americas and President Salinas of Mexico, a one-party state. By the December 1994 conference, the countries of the region had reduced trade barriers by 80% through a variety of trade pacts. The summit itself resulted in a Declaration of Principles supporting democracy, economic integration, free trade, and sustainable development. There was an agreement to create a Free Trade Area of the Americas by 2005. The goal was an ambitious one, and Clinton was unable to convince the Republican-led Congress to confirm the agreement or work toward the Free Trade Area of the Americas (FTAA).

Bills Clinton's triumphs and setbacks can be viewed as symptoms of an ad-hoc foreign policy, or as a developing policy of enlargement and engagement constrained by an uncooperative Congress. Confronted with wars and violence on several continents, an uncertain economic world, and absence of the stability of a bi-polar world, Clinton's foreign policy legacy is still debated.

Activity
Comparing doctrines

Using a Venn Diagram, compare the foreign policy doctrines of Reagan, Bush, and Clinton. Draw a circle for each president and place policies where they intersect (and with which world regions) and where they do not.

Activity
A poster presentation

Review the human rights policies and actions of the Reagan, Bush and Clinton administrations toward Latin American military dictatorships. Choose one president and, using specific examples, create a poster either praising or criticizing his human rights focus.

Activity
Summing it up

1 Complete the presidential policies table.
2 Review the information. Look for themes in both domestic and foreign policy that carry through two, or all three administrations.
3 Decide on the most significant successes and failures of each president.
4 Outline answers to the following questions:
   a To what extent and in what ways did the foreign policy of the United States change because of the disintegration of the Soviet Union?
   b The domestic policies of the three presidents were more evolutionary than revolutionary. Discuss.

The restoration of democracy in Latin America

In 1977, all but four countries in Latin America were headed by authoritarian regimes, and most of those were military dictatorships. The 1980s and 1990s saw democracy return or come to most of the countries of Latin America. In South America, some constitutions were rewritten or modified among varying degrees of political, social and political disruption. One exception is the case of Chile, which has retained the constitution of 1980, written by the Pinochet government. Many countries in the Caribbean, including Grenada and Haiti, dealt with collapse and then reestablishment of democracy with varying success. Cuba was a notable exception to this trend. Several Central American nations, most after significant periods of war, such as Guatemala and El Salvador, slowly worked their way into democratic forms of government.

Following the Second World War, Import Substitution Industrialization (ISI) proved a success to most Latin American economies through the expansion of industry, improvements in employment and real wages, as well as the transfer of technology into the region. In the political-economic area there were intense struggles over land distribution led by populists such as Gétulio Vargas in Brazil and Mexico under Lázaro Cárdenas, but there was also significant urban expansion and industrialization. ISI fizzled out during the late 1970s, and early 1980s, as capital accumulation was pursued and larger, more highly industrialized Latin American countries, such as Argentina, lost viability and finally collapsed. By the early 1990s, the ISI model had largely been rejected and was replaced by totally different economic strategies.

Countries in the region emerged with working economies, many of them attempting to redistribute wealth through state-dominated programs and financed to a significant extent by foreign loans. As interest rates rose in the United States, the cost of the existing loans in Latin America rose, increasing national debt. Authoritarian governments made attempts to simultaneously contain popular mobilization and increase profitability. Often they were able to rise to power and stay there by fitting into the Cold War world as bastions against communism, such as the cases of US-backed armed forces in El Salvador and Nicaragua.

By the mid-1970s, a new political-economic philosophy of **neoliberalism** emanated from the United States. The Reagan administration popularized the Chicago School of Economics, based on the theories of Milton Friedman. The Chicago School proclaimed the way to a growing economy was through free markets both domestically and internationally, with minimal government involvement in the economy. Essentially, government economic activities distorted the efficiency of markets, therefore the best thing a government could do was to leave the economy alone. This was a direct refutation of the economic policies that had reduced poverty during the previous decade. Authoritarianism often accompanied

> **Neoliberalism** combines a belief in social justice with minimal government involvement in the economy under the idea that freedom of the marketplace is integral to a free society.

the economic changes. A good example is the implementation of similar policies by Chilean dictator Augusto Pinochet between 1973 and 1989, installing as his economic advisors many PhDs who studied with Friedman and were known as the "Chicago Boys." Countries following neoliberalism generally saw steady increases in GDP. This came at a great social cost: higher unemployment, lower wages, and an increase in the number of people living in poverty. Economic disruption, social dislocation, and political violence both on the part of those seeking to maintain control and those challenging the established order generated many changes over the next two decades. In Guatemala, it sparked the birth of revolutionary movements. In Bolivia, it ignited a strong reaction by the coca-growers union in the 1980s. Democracies emerged and retreated; the particular structures of governments were a result of tradition, power relationships, and circumstances on the ground, especially those related to the end of the Cold War. Economic policy changes sometimes accompanied the political transformations, but outside forces often determined the degree of change as globalization increased.

Historical explanations

Some historians have pointed to three significant themes that may explain late-20th century Latin American democracies: neoliberalist economic factors and their impact on democratic institutions, neopopulism, and direct democracy. Often the three existed together. According to professor of Latin American politics Kurt Weyland, neoliberalism both enabled democracy to exist and limited its development. External economic and political pressures restricted the choices the government could make, thus limiting the voters' power, but by empowering economic and political élites also enhanced support for the government. Weyland writes, "The available evidence suggests that neoliberalism has affected Latin American democracy in opposite, even contradictory ways. By exposing the region's countries to greater external pressures and by changing the internal balance of forces so as to preclude threats to domestic elites, market reform has bolstered the survival of democracy."

Neopopulism was also a critical contributor to civilian rule. Neopopulist presidential candidates appealed directly to the voters and promoted themselves as the solution to the nation's problems. They campaigned against the established power-holders. Their political base usually consisted of the rural and urban poor and disaffected city-dwellers, nurtured by the candidate identifying himself as an outsider just like his supporters. The appearance of popular figures promising wholesale reform enabled elections to take place. The charismatic leadership often had to change course when confronted with domestic and international economic realities, but several leaders' popularity enabled them to pursue policies contrary to campaign promises while still holding elections and working with legislatures.

The third element was often the *consulta*. Direct democracy grew as citizens participated in *consultas* in the face of unresponsive legislators

Activity

Neoliberalism

Using search engines and economics reference works, establish a class definition of neoliberalism as government economic policy between 1980 and 2000. The class can be divided in small groups to research different perspectives.

Useful resources for this would be the UN Economic Commission for Latin America (or ECLA, also known by its Spanish acronym CEPAL), with headquarters in Santiago, Chile.

See www.eclac.org and online references such as www. oxfordreference.com available through your school or local library.

Activity

Neopopulism

In groups, or individually, research definitions of neopopulism and compare notes in class to come up with a working definition for your class.

A ***consulta popular*** is a direct vote of the people on an issue of national significance that is sent to the voters by either the president or the legislature.

who were more focused on the interests of the powerful elite than their broader electoral constituents. Voters in many Latin American countries were asked to approve legislation put forward by national legislatures. Constitutions were submitted to referendum as well. Chief executives used *consultas* and initiatives to circumvent strong and uncooperative legislatures, thus becoming an effective tool of neopopulist leaders. In states where democracy was fragile and political leaders were unpopular, the threat of a coup or revolution was often neutralized through a mechanism for voters to express their wishes directly. Consequently, the emerging democracies of Latin America were shaped by a variety of forces that influenced the forms of government.

Latin American scholarship views the resurgence of democracy in the region from different perspectives. Argentine political scientist Enrique Peruzzotti writes that in Argentina, since the end of military authoritarian regimes in 1983, the country has been able to resolve crises using representative institutions. He maintains that human rights abuses by military governments have made the public demand constitutional and institutional solutions. Brazilian political scientist José Maria Pereira da Nóbrega Jr. describes these ruling bodies as hybrid institutions with democratic as well as authoritarian characteristics. Guatemalan sociologist Juan Fernando Molina Meza notes that in his country the institutional model has been too centralized, and has excluded 60% of the population of Native Guatemalans, despite reforms to provide more local power through the 1992 Municipal Code and the Law of Municipal Development Councils. Political **clientelism** and lack of transparency in distributing resources left over from authoritarian governments has not led to a strengthened democracy.

> **Clientelism** is the practice in which a powerful political patron provides economic and government benefits to significantly less powerful and wealthy people in return for political support and economic benefits. Clientelism can occur locally, regionally, nationally.

Factors in the development of Latin American governments

In order to understand the nature of the changes in 1980–2000, this section examines the conditions in Perú, Argentina, Uruguay, and Brazil that led to democracy and sometimes a departure from it. Social, political, and economic developments are looked at, allowing for comparison and contrast between different countries. By 2000, it was by no means clear that the democratic governments were supported by the populace or ruling elites to safeguard against a return to authoritarianism. Yet the transition from authoritarian and often military rule to types of democracy signaled a significant change in a relatively short period of time.

Before examining individual countries, it is important to understand why Latin American countries, like many countries around the world, sometimes failed to sustain democracy. Economic and political development is often tied together when examining power relationships. The uneven political and economic development in Latin America is also based on geography, post-colonial dependencies and the different cultural models.

Activity
Extension map study

Latin America and the Caribbean is an enormous geographical area. From the southern border of Texas in the United States to Cape Horn in Chile, it is a distance of 11,000 kilometers (7,000 miles). It is widest from Perú to Brazil: 5,000 kilometers (3,200 miles). It is double the size of Europe and two and a half times the size of North America. Look at the above map and identify the major:

● mountains

● rivers

● lakes

● jungles and forests

● deserts

● plains

 How have these topographical features posed barriers to development, or functioned to preserve natural habitats?

Geography

The geography of South America does not lend itself to centralization, and the development of strong national bodies or social cohesion. High mountains and rugged coastlines in the west, impenetrable jungles in the equatorial region, and massive rivers in the east make communication and commerce between communities difficult. Efforts to form cohesive legislative bodies that could meet were severely limited by the time, distance, effort and uncertainty of travel throughout the region. Before the opening of the Panama Canal in 1914, the enormous distance from the economic centers of Europe and, from the 20th century, the United States, also influenced the way Latin America felt very much at the periphery of political and social development. Over time, differing cultures and economies developed, making national legislatures into groups of potentially greater numbers of smaller factions. Representative democracy was often impractical and dysfunctional. As a result, autocratic rule developed out of a vacuum of power, notably the *caudillos* of the 19th century, like Argentina's Juan Manuel de Rosas. Dictatorships, often out of reach of the people most negatively affected by government's policies, were able to thrive, survive, or be overthrown by powerful factions placing their support elsewhere, often resulting in the imposition of yet another autocratic regime. Populism and clientelism thrived.

Dependency

Dependency theory comes, in part, from a Marxist analysis, based on the involvement of outside countries in the economic and political affairs of a nation. After independence, Latin American nations, as in times of Spanish and Portuguese rule, were often exploited for their raw materials or unprocessed crops by nations like the United Kingdom, and subsequently the United States. The low-priced raw materials were processed in Europe or the United States, providing jobs along with added value. An economic relationship with some similarities to mercantilism developed. After the Great Depression, and especially in the period following the Second World War, multinational corporations transferred the profits of raw material extraction out of the countries of origin to their own home nations. The continuous exploitation severely limited development, and encouraged monoculture: copper in Chile, coffee in Colombia and Brazil, beef in Argentina, sugar in Cuba, bananas in Nicaragua and so on. As much of the world took part in increasing international trade, Latin America was kept under the control of outside forces, preventing a modern economy from developing. Importantly, the extraction of wealth required a cooperative or compliant government. Dominant countries, like the United States, supported regimes that cooperated with their corporations whether they were involved in mineral extraction, agriculture, transportation, or communication technologies. Democracies do not develop under the exploitive and manipulative direction of foreign powers. Consequently, cooperative dictatorships, supported by landowning elites, developed and sustained power. When internal forces repelled outsiders, those efforts usually resulted in new autocratic regimes.

Culturalism

A third explanation for the authoritarian tradition is based on culture. Spain and Portugal influenced Latin America, not only through economic and governmental control, but through the establishment of the Iberian culture. The Spanish and Portuguese colonies were also under influence of the Catholic Church. A belief in the legitimacy of a rigid hierarchy in which each person has a specific place is the antithesis of economic and social mobility. In many Latin American communities, a stable, unchanging society with respect for authority was valued above the uncertainty of a dynamic one, such as in the United States. Additionally, a ruler who understood the "general will" of the people acted on their behalf. Thus, the cultural combination of faith in hierarchy and preference for stability provided the necessary conditions for dictatorships.

On top of these explanations was the development of the Cold War and, in 1959, the Cuban Revolution and its effect on the Latin American republics. To the United States, the most important component of relations in the Americas was the prevention of another Cuba and establishment of communism in countries to the south. This led the United States to support anti-democratic and often corrupt regimes which violated human rights. Thousands of soldiers from Latin America were trained in counterinsurgency tactics at the School of the Americas in Fort Benning, Georgia. Many officers who trained there were later accused of human rights violations and some became dictators themselves, employing brutal measures to keep opposition at bay. The additional influence the United States exerted post-1945 led to anti-American sentiments and increased nationalism in Latin American countries, both feelings that populist leaders and movements could exploit. The give-and-take activities of legislatures weighing competing ideas were a weak opposition to the strong message of a single voice.

When examining the progress of democratic governments in the final decades of the 20th century, five questions come to mind.

1 To what extent did democratic movements succeed in the face of the many obstacles outlined above?
2 To what extent are the above explanations applicable?
3 What kinds of democracies developed and why?
4 What policy changes did the new governments make and to what effect on the economy and society?
5 What effect did the implementation of government structure and policies have on the level of success and longevity of the democratic government?

Perú: democracy and retreat

Perú was ruled by a military dictatorship from 1968 until 1985. General Juan Velasco Alvarado governed Perú until 1975. He ordered the nationalization of the oil and mining industries from foreign ownership, radical agrarian reform and the promotion of workers' rights to influence and obtain a greater share of the profits of private companies. He also took control of the media. There were some

TOK Link
Language
Why do scholars attempt to categorize explanations? How does labeling affect understanding?

Activity
Democracy chart
Make a chart with each of the five questions as a heading. Add a row for each country examined in this chapter, and take notes as you read through the evidence.

improvements to the wellbeing of local people: food production increased and peasants were freed from serfdom. But the reforms lacked a long-term plan and most benefits ended up in the hands of the few producers and owners of export crops, including sugar, cotton, coffee, and natural resources like oil, gold, copper and lead. His military dictatorship lacked the support of civilian agricultural workers who felt abandoned as the government invested most of its resources trying to increase industrial development. The implementation of programs also forced the government to secure foreign loans that became a burden on the Peruvian economy.

The burden became a crisis and, in 1975, the military replaced Velasco with General Francisco Morales Bermúdez. During his presidency, in a pattern seen in other Latin American countries such as Chile, an austerity program was put in place as forcefully suggested by the IMF. Perú had significant foreign debt, and the IMF imposed conditions for the continuance of loans. The urban working class saw their wages reduced by 40% percent. Morales followed IMF guidelines in attempting to implement a plan of economic decentralization, austerity, and open access of Peruvian economic resources to foreign investment, meaning state-owned industries would be privatized. The economy improved briefly, but the Mexican debt crisis that affected all of Latin America destroyed any economic progress, turning gains into a 12% decline in GDP and significant inflation.

Abimael Guzmán (1934–)

Abimael Guzmán is a Peruvian Marxist, and founder of the splinter group of the Peruvian Communist Party known as the Sendero Luminoso, or "Shining Path," based on Maoist thought and theories of class struggle. Initially the group won favor in mountain villages tired of corruption and military brutality. But Guzmán's own brand of authoritarian brutality lead to whole villages found guilty of collaboration with the military being slaughtered. He eventually alienated the peasants, who ultimately allied with the military to turn him in to the government of Fujimori in 1992. He is currently serving a life-sentence in Callao, Perú. The violent group he led killed about 30,000 people, mainly from the Ayachuco region.

A new constitution modeled on the 1933 version was proposed. Elections took place in 1980 and Fernando Belaúnde Terry won the election with a significant majority and formed a coalition government. Belaúnde was a democrat and politician and made a politician's set of promises: progress and improved living standards through public works while reducing state involvement in the economy and encouraging private investment. Once elected, the new president proposed banning labor actions such as strikes, phasing out economic assistance for food and fuel, and cutting public works projects. A general strike was the result.

A combination of economic deterioration, including rising unemployment, and social tension led to political violence. In the early 1980s two guerilla organizations came to prominence as a reaction to government measures. One, Sendero Luminoso or Shining Path, formed in the highlands, an area that was not benefiting from the economic programs and was becoming a supplier of coca for Colombian drug traffickers (as a result of economic decline). Shining Path used a combination of violence and threats of violence against village elders, as well as protection for coca farmers from police, the Peruvian military, and drug traffickers through the promotion of a Maoist egalitarian utopia. A second group, *Movimiento Revolucionario Tupac Amaru* (MRTA), used kidnapping and ransom, in contrast to killing, to publicize its socialist-Castroist goals and to raise

Activity

Research assignment

Research the two resistance movements, Sendero Luminoso or Shining Path and the *Movimiento Revolucionario Tupac Amaru* (MRTA). What were the differences and similarities in membership, tactics, goals, and achievements?

451

funds. Rising violence caused Belaúnde to use military strikes to suppress the opposition groups. The rise in violence contributed to civil instability, and the military, seeing a lack of popular support, decided to shift Peru's leadership to a civilian presidency.

Belaúnde's presidential term ended in 1985. The charismatic, 36-year-old *Alianza Popular Revolucionaria Americana* (APRA) candidate, Alan García, won the 1985 general election. APRA, a party founded in 1924, also controlled the bicameral legislature. García acted quickly to repair Peru's problems, beginning with the economy. He expanded the government's role in the economy by freezing prices, reducing interest rates and devaluing the Peruvian currency. Wages were increased as taxes were cut. All the changes placed more real "sols" in the hands of consumers, resulting in greater demand. The government, seeing the social unrest in the highland areas where the Shining Path was expanding its influence, began programs to aid small farms. All the changes resulted in a short-term growth in the economy, but also an increased trade deficit. To free the government to pursue his growth policies, García defaulted on foreign debt obligations. The economy soon collapsed as new loans were not available and labor unrest caused entire industries to halt production. Additional actions by the APRA government only accelerated the collapse as GDP declined by a third and inflation rose to 7,500% by the end of the decade. Civilian leadership only seemed to accelerate Perú's social and economic decline.

The 1990 election was an interesting contest between the novelist Mario Vargas Llosa and a little-known agrarian economist, Alberto Fujimori, the face of a new political alliance called *Cambio 90* (Change 90). Spouting populist rhetoric and framing himself as an outsider, Fujimori, a Japanese-Peruvian, promised economic recovery and a halt to civil violence. He won an outright victory.

The election of Fujimori began Perú's retreat from democracy and a return to autocratic leadership. In a program soon known as "Fujishock," he reversed García's approach, eliminating subsidies, lowering tariffs, inviting foreign investment, selling hundreds of state-owned companies, weakened the influence of labor, and generally following a monetarist free-market policy. It was the opposite of the populist approach. Prices rose and money from the drug trade became an integral part of the economy. As opposition mounted, Fujimori moved to consolidate his power. Backed by the military, the democratically-elected Fujimori disbanded the legislature in April 1992 and vigorously eliminated his enemies and potential challengers. Opposition press was silenced. Leaders of the two major guerrilla groups, Shining Path and MRTA, were arrested and the two groups lost momentum without their leadership. Fujimori gained popular support as civil violence subsided, even with the constant violations of human rights and political

> **TOK Link**
> ## Ways of Knowing
> What is political charisma? What is the role of emotion in politics? What is the role of political rhetoric (language) in leadership? In what ways do charisma and rhetoric compliment and distort the workings of democratic states?
>
> **?** Is it preferable that a government make decisions rationally—to the exclusion of emotion?

Alberto Fujimori (1938–)

Alberto Fujimori is a Peruvian agronomist, physicist and mathematician. The son of Japanese immigrants, he was elected to the presidency of Perú in 1990 under his new political movement, *Cambio 90* (Change 90). He instituted harsh and unpopular reforms, following IMF strictures. Two years later, with the support of the army, he temporarily dissolved parliament and ruled by decree, suppressing the Constitution of 1979. His Constituent Assembly, boycotted by traditional parties, was supported by *Nueva Mayoría-Cambio 90* (New Majority-Change 90). He won the elections of 1995 and 2000. His government was authoritarian and guilty of corruption and human rights abuses. He fled for Japan in 2000 and was detained by Chile in 2005 trying to return. He was extradited to Perú in 2007 and sentenced to prison in Callao.

Activity

Data analysis

Coca crops, Perú

The cultivation of coca leaves has been a tradition of the Peruvian and Bolivian highlands for centuries, where it is used for medicinal and religious reasons. Since the 1970s, developed countries in North America and Europe have greatly increased consumption of cocaine, an illegal drug whose raw material is the coca leaf. Therefore, demand for coca has soared, creating a profitable crop for Peruvian and Bolivian farmers, as part of an underground economy. Look at the tables below. What conclusions can you draw from them? What does this say about the presidencies of Alberto Fujimori?

Coca as share of GDP in Bolivia and Peru				
	1985	1988–89	1992	1993
Bolivia	7–11	6–10	4.6–9.0	2–7
Peru	10–14	2–8	1.4–2.1	2.0–3.4

Income, exports and employment in the coca sector, 1993–94		
	Perú	Bolivia
Coca income per capita	1,036–1,585	967–1,383
Income per capita	1,580	760–1,022
Rural income per capita	420–720	390
Direct employment in coca sector (in thousands)	169–178	49
Share of the rural workforce (%)	8.9–9.5	5.2
Hectares planted with coca	159,000–211,000	47,200
Coca exports as share of Licit exports (%)	23–40	27

Sources: Alvares, Elena H. "Economic development, restructuring and the illicit drug sector in Bolivia and Perú: Current Policies." *Journal of Interamerican Studies & World Affairs.* vol. 37, no. 3. Fall 1995. pp.125–49.

killings. A new constitution was adapted by the Fujimori-allied legislature, and approved by popular referendum. It granted the president greater powers, including the right to disband the legislature at will, rule by decree, and to run for reelection.

Fujimori recognized potential threats from a popular uprising. By 1995, social spending was more than double the amount in 1993. The turnabout in government programs brought support from the highlands and victory in 1995. In 1998, Fujimori cemented his authority. Perú's Supreme Court ruled that Fujimori could run for another term as president because he had served only one term under the new constitution. His economic programs tried to be all things, encouraging foreign investment, private enterprise, and ample support for the poor. It worked for a while, reducing the 1993 poverty level of 54% to 44% two years later. GDP grew at almost 5% during the decade, but poverty levels went back to over 50% (income of under $2 per day), showing that the economic

Incumbent President of Perú, Alberto Fujimori, campaigns in a poor neighborhood on the outskirts of Lima during national elections in 1990.

gains went to a select few. Furthermore, the programs had doubled foreign debt and increased the trade deficit, making Perú into a net debtor nation.

As the decade came to a close, Fujimori once more exercised his dictatorial powers. When the Supreme Court ruled that he could not run for president again, he removed the justices. He authorized phone taps on political opponents and whatever opposition press still existed was beaten, kidnapped and tortured. The tactics led to candidate Alejandro Toledo denouncing the elections as fraud and withdrawing. Popular support for Fujimori all but disappeared. There was a general strike and protests in the street. Toledo helped rally Peruvians against the authoritarian regime. The Peruvian Congress finally acted and removed Fujimori from the presidency. He left for exile in Japan.

Discussion point

Important concepts to consider:

1 How did shifting leadership affect the restoration of democracy in Perú?

2 Evaluate the importance of political opposition and economic conditions for democracy in Perú.

3 Why was Fujimori at first able to assume greater powers?

4 What makes populism appealing to voters?

Protests against Fujimori in Perú, October 30, 2000.

Argentina: democracy and expanded presidential authority

Nine years after the death of Juan Perón, in 1974, democracy returned to Argentina in 1983. Following Perón's death, his wife, Isabel, had assumed the presidency. After a violent two years, the military arrested Isabel Perón and established a military dictatorship. Under the leadership of General Jorge Rafael Videla, the military conducted a "dirty war" against the opposition and tens of thousands of people "disappeared." Through violent means the military solidified power and initially weakened the opposition, especially on the left. Seeing a need to address the weak economy, Finance Minister José Alfredo Martínez de Hoz imposed neoliberal economic reforms. The changes resulted in massive inflation and the destruction of many large Argentine corporations. The number of people living in poverty quadrupled. Eventually, the brutality of the government and the worsening economic conditions opened a fissure in the foundation of military rule. There was growing opposition. Community organizations like the Neighbor's Commission, organized protests over taxes, inflated food prices, housing, and health, among other issues. The most

Nora Morales de Cortiñas (1931–)

Nora Morales de Cortiñas is an Argentine housewife and mother, whose 24-year old son, a Perónist, disappeared in 1977. After looking for him in morgues and police stations, she and her family tried appealing to courts of justice, the Church, the Pope and human rights associations. She still has no news of what happened to him. On April 30, 1977, a small group of women got together at the Plaza de Mayo, Buenos Aires' main square and traditional meeting ground for demonstrations. The meetings took place every Thursday afternoon and became bigger, with signs and photographs of their disappeared children. In 1980, they adopted the white kerchief that distinguishes them. Cortiñas is one of the original founders of the Madres de Plaza de Mayo, a human rights association that has been a powerful motivating force to finding out the truth about the military's repressive policies that killed over 30,000 Argentines.

Members of the "Madres de Plaza de Mayo" human rights organization, hold a banner declaring their missing sons and daughters before marching from the Argentine National Congress to the presidential palace, 28 October 1982, in Buenos Aires.

Activity

Assessing historical similarities and differences

Research opposition movements in other countries of the Americas or in other regions.

1 What conditions are necessary for protest movements to succeed?

2 What constitutes success?

famous of the protest organizations was the Mothers of the Plaza de Mayo. The women occupied the central plaza in Buenos Aires and demanded the return of their "disappeared" children and grandchildren. Their courage in the face of the brutal military became a symbol of principled and brave opposition. The combination of protest movements and economic disarray further widened the crack in the foundation.

In 1981 General Videla turned over power to General Roberto Viola, who served for the better part of one year before the commander-in-chief of the army, General Leopoldo Galtieri assumed the presidency. Galtieri, inheriting a worsening economy and a huge foreign debt, saw challenges to the military's rule. He decided to whip up nationalist fever by starting a war against the British over the Malvinas (Falkland) Islands. In April 1982, Argentina attacked the British-held Falklands, 300 miles off the coast of Argentina. The military expected little opposition from the United Kingdom and no interference from the United States. The reality was different, as the British reacted to a challenge to their national honor and fought to maintain their territory. The United States lent support to the British as well. The war lasted over two months with almost a thousand combatants killed, Argentina's forces suffering most of the losses. Argentina suffered a humiliating defeat. The ruling generals were discredited by the failed war, and in the face of military and economic disaster (inflation was up to 400%), along with ongoing

General Leopoldo Galtieri (1926–2003)

was an Argentine Army officer who graduated from the School of the Americas in 1949. He was commander in chief when the military junta took over in 1976 and tried to divert attention from the abysmal state of the country's economy by waging a foreign war. The first attempt was in 1978 against neighboring Chile over three small islands in the Beagle Channel, but the Pinochet government appealed to the pope for arbitration. The second attempt at war was against the United Kingdom over the South Atlantic Malvinas (Falkland) Islands. The war lasted from April to June of 1982 and ended in defeat for Argentina, as the UK rallied to defend the Islands. The United States, in a strong reversal of its Monroe Doctrine, supported the European power. Galtieri resigned and was sentenced to prison in 1986 for military incompetence, but soon released. In 2002 he was convicted of human rights violations in the 1980s. He died under house arrest in 2003.

Activity
Point of view

Martínez de Hoz

Research different points of view on Argentine Finance Minister Martínez de Hoz and the neoliberal economic reforms imposed between 1976 and 1981. He is currently (2010) under house arrest in Buenos Aires, for his implication on the kidnapping and disappearance of Argentine citizens when he was Minister during the military dictatorship of Gral. Jorge Rafael Videla.

Use the following online research services to analyze the effect of economic reforms and human rights abuses on the people of Argentina.

● Academic research databases, such as www.ebsco.com or other subscriber services offered by your school or public libraries.

● Online news services offering differing national and political perspectives: Argentine newspaper *La Nación* (www.lanacion.com.ar) US newspapers, such as the *New York Times* (www.nytimes.com) Cuban newspaper *Granma* (www.granma.cubaweb.cu).

Activity
Ranking importance

Cause and effect

When a historian makes an argument, he or she must decide what evidence is most compelling. This activity will help you to do so.

Make a three column table of the causes of the fall of one or more military regimes between 1980–90 in Argentina, Chile, Brazil, Uruguay, Paraguay, Bolivia, Guatemala, Honduras and El Salvador: Column 1 is "Causes"; column 2 is Level of necessity"; column 3 is "Final order". Rank the factors in terms of importance.

1 Which causes were necessary?

2 Which causes were necessary but not sufficient on their own?

3 Which causes accelerated the transition, but were not strictly necessary?

social unrest, the military allowed the reestablishment of civilian rule in 1983.

Raúl Alfonsín, a human rights activist and member of the Radical Civil Union party, was elected president in 1983, winning a majority of votes against a variety of candidates. The RCU also won control of the lower house of the bicameral legislature, while the rival Perónist *Partido Justicialista* (PJ) won a plurality of seats in the Senate. Alfonsín's major crisis was the ruined economy. By 1985, inflation was over 1,000% per annum. Argentinian industry was technologically backwards where it existed at all. He rejected free market ideology and implemented the Austral Plan. The austral became the new currency, replacing the peso. Wages and prices were controlled by the government. Government spending was reduced to lower the debt. Unions reacted to the stabilization plan by leading 13 general strikes. Inflation dropped dramatically to 25%. Alphonsín's economic remedies did stabilize the economy, but unemployment stayed high, the industrial base was not revitalized, continuing Argentina's reliance on low-revenue exports, and the national debt continued to increase throughout the 1980s. In 1989, there was another economic crisis as GDP fell by 15%. Alfonsín traded his government interventionist policies for neoliberal solutions. In return for loans from the IMF, he enacted deep austerity measures, making further cuts in government expenditures, including social programs, and adopting a free market approach by discontinuing controls over wages. Argentina owed more in interest than it collected in revenue. The debt only deepened and required more foreign loans to stay solvent, which in turn led to greater program cuts. Food rationing and electrical blackouts became the norm, accompanied by peaceful demonstrations and occasional riots; consequently, the government enacted strict security measures to prevent public unrest. In six years of rule and economic policy implementation, a combination of inherited economic weakness, only partially effective initial governmental policies, outside economic pressures and a disastrous turn to neoliberal economics revealed the Alfonsín administration to be a failure.

The economy was not the only problem on Alfonsín's agenda. There were two other significant

Activity
Perónism

Argentina's Perónist Justicialista Party (PJ) underwent important changes between 1980 and 2000. Using the source suggested below or other sources, find out how Perónism's traditional labor participation and clientelist networks were substituted. What is the role of unions in the PJ and what bearing did this have on the election of Carlos Menem in 1989? How did diminishing union influence help to draw middle-class support?

A good source is *Transforming Labor-Based Parties in Latin America: Argentine Peronism in Comparative Perspective* (Cambridge University Press, 2003) by Harvard professor and Argentina expert, Steven Levitsky.

Activity
Linking the regional study with topic 1

The Malvinas–Falklands War is part of the Material for Detailed Study in paper 2, topic 1. Explore the causes of the war, the strategies and tactics of Argentina and the United Kingdom, and the results for both countries. Consider how you would answer the following question in an essay:

 To what extent was the Malvinas (Falklands) War responsible for the establishment of democracy in Argentina?

Activity
Song lines

Listen to Argentine protest songs from the 1970s and 80s by Mercedes Sosa and León Gieco, especially "Solo de Pido a Dios" (I just ask God) and 'La Memoria' (Memory). These popular songs expressed the historical events related here in subtle, poetic ways, in order to avoid repression. Even so, Sosa was detained, forbidden to sing her songs and exiled. Gieco was and still is very popular, although he had to leave Argentina to avoid having his songs censored by the military government.

 What do the lyrics of their songs reveal about the world young Argentines lived in during and after the dictatorships?

issues. The first was a possibility of war with Chile over the Beagle Channel Islands. Even though it was not specifically authorized by the constitution, in 1984 Alfonsín initiated a referendum on a treaty with Chile over the disputed islands. In appealing to the people, President Alfonsín used direct democracy to push his foreign policy. The public voted for the treaty and war was averted. Alfonsín also had to deal with the perpetrators of the violence during the "dirty war." The creation of procedures to punish members of the military for the thousands of people who were kidnapped and tortured, including many deaths, fell to the Alfonsín administration. There were trials and convictions of top military officials who served significant time in prison. Alfonsín did not prosecute low-rank soldiers on the grounds that they had simply followed orders. His refusal to hold the soldiers accountable infuriated many of his supporters. Alfonsín also faced military revolts in 1987 and 1989, neither of which succeeded.

The combination of public anger over insufficient "dirty war" prosecutions and the devastated economy led to the election of the Perónist Partido Justicialista (PJ) party leader Carlos Menem in 1989. Menem was governor of the small province of La Rioja, and used his neopopulist outsider appeal to win the presidency. He took office six months early after Alfonsín resigned. His supporters expected him to repeal the economic policies of his predecessor, but he did the opposite. In fact, Menem appointed many neoliberals and representatives of big business to his cabinet, including economics minister Domingo Cavallo. Menem immediately began to concentrate power in the executive branch. From 1989 to 1994, he issued 336 legislative orders known as "Need and Urgency Decrees". These had the effect of law without legislative action. The concentration of legislative power with the executive was a huge change, as only 25 such decrees had been issued from 1853 until the ascension of Menem. In neopopulist fashion, the democratically elected leader created an overwhelmingly powerful president who acted without interference from the other branches of government. Menem's push for increased presidential authority culminated in a new constitution in 1994 that severely restricted legislative power, provided for *consultas*, and allowed presidential reelection.

The Menem government acted forcefully to stabilize the economy. From the time he took office Menem pursued an austerity program; there was no Perónist nod to labor. Quickly, the new president began a program of privatization of many state-owned enterprises. Electrical power generation was sold off, along with coal, natural gas, shipping, subway systems and the telephone company. In 1991 a peso–dollar parity was established, providing a basis for economic stabilization. Menem's policies resulted in economic growth of approximately 7% per year during the first half of the decade and low inflation, but unemployment doubled.

Spurred by economic stability, Menem won reelection in 1995 with just under 50% of the popular vote, while the closest challenger garnered under 20%. This was despite Menem's 1994 statement supporting the military's behavior in the "Dirty War." However, two years later, the 1997 congressional elections revealed dissatisfaction with the PJ party and the president, attributable to high unemployment, the increased percentage of people in poverty, and disapproval of government corruption. A new party, the Alliance of Work, Justice, and Education (a combination of two older political groups) gained control of the lower house. By 1999, many Argentines were disillusioned with economic progress during the preceding four years. 1995 brought economic problems partially caused by the Mexican peso crisis. The positive economic benefits of Argentina's participation in MERCOSUR, a trade agreement originally between Argentina, Brazil, Paraguay, and Uruguay, began to unravel. Trade, especially with Brazil, became increasingly important for economic growth, so when Brazil devalued its currency in 1999, effectively making Argentine products more expensive and Brazilian ones more affordable, Argentina's trade deficit exploded, causing severe economic distress. The poverty level rose to include more than one out of five Argentines.

The 1999 elections resulted in the election of the Alliance's candidate, Fernando de la Rúa. The new government was, however, restricted by the control of the senate by the PJ party. By 2000, the national debt had risen to $155 billion. In response to international economic pressures, de la Rúa instituted harsh austerity measures including reducing wages and pensions for public workers, cutting total government expenditures by a fifth. Many segments of the public saw increased privatization and reliance on the international economy to the point of perceived subservience to foreign economic powers as the cause of their economic misfortune. President de la Rúa resigned in 2000 as the public lost confidence in his leadership.

By 2001, public disgust with a Senate vote-buying scandal and continued government corruption resulted in an election in which 40% of ballots were submitted unmarked as a protest against the government. As the new century dawned, apathy was on the increase as no political institution appeared both effective and trustworthy. Looking back over the decade of the 1990s, the economy showed periods of growth, but increasing numbers of people faced poverty and the government was still heavily influenced by outside actors, despite ten years of measures to create a modern free-market economy.

Uruguay: return to democracy

Argentina's neighbor across the Río de la Plata delta is Uruguay. A nation of three million people, Uruguay has a history of democracy and a strong two-party system. The two major political parties, the *Blancos* and the *Colorados*, were formed in the 1830s, and while changing political orientation over the course of a century and a half, remained significant players in the region into the latter part of the 20th century. By the time Juan María Bordaberry became president in 1972, Uruguay had come to a point of severe economic and political uncertainty. The military took over the government in 1973 when it felt the civilian leadership could not continue without destroying the country. The military held power for eleven years, using violent repression to maintain power, but also promised to write a new constitution for

Activity

Perú vs. Argentina

Debate the following question:

Which transition to democracy was more successful: Argentina or Perú?

Consider the following factors: Degree of political participation by citizens without fear; numbers of viable political parties; effectiveness of economic policies; effectiveness of foreign policies; human rights.

Activity

The IMF

The International Monetary Fund (IMF) refused to bail Argentina out and the country plunged into economic chaos. What is the role of the IMF in Latin America? How did IMF lending conditions affect Argentina between 1980 and 2000? The Argentine economy went into the steepest drop since the Great Depression. Find out what happened to the country's per capita income, unemployment, exports and other economic indicators. How did this affect the Argentine people?

Activity

Film review

Watch the 1972 film *State of Siege* (Dir. Costa Gavras). How are the *Tupamaros* and the government portrayed?

approval by voters. By 1984, in the face of economic disarray, the military was forced to abdicate power and Uruguay returned to democracy. The reestablishment of democracy confirmed the power of the traditional parties, but a rewritten constitution created the opportunity for the success of the *Frente Amplio* (Broad Front), a leftist coalition. By the end of the century, Uruguay's civilian democracy was solidly in place.

Like other South American countries, Uruguay experienced economic difficulties in the late 1960s. Urban guerilla movements such as the *Tupanmaros,* an armed leftist guerrilla group, contributed to political instability and a highly repressive military regime took power in 1973, the first one in Uruguay's history. The one area that was left to civilian administration was the economic program. The program, run by Alejandro Végh Villegas for the initial two-year phase, was one of free markets, some lower tariffs to protect home industries, significant public investment in infrastructure, the abolition of corporate income tax, and promotion of exports. The economy grew the first six years of the regime's rule. Corporate profits rose, but real wages fell significantly, so that by 1984 real earnings were less than half what they were in 1968. Much of the decline was caused by anti-inflationary measures that followed Végh Villegas' resignation.

The brutal military dictatorship suppressed political activity, and was especially harsh on politicians of the left. In 1976, facing elections, Bordaberry wanted to abolish political parties, but military leaders saw the traditional political parties as an essential stabilizing component of Uruguay. As a result, Bordaberry was forced out and a more cooperative civilian was installed. To protect its power, the military banned 15,000 politicians from participation and a non-elected legislature wrote a new constitution that featured a national security state with the military as the supreme power. It is estimated that nearly 15% of Uruguay's three million people at the time went into exile. In 1980 the proposed constitution came to a national vote, an exercise of direct democracy even within a dictatorial system. The regime controlled all media and used their monopoly of political power to campaign unopposed for the proposed constitution. Despite the fact that opposition politicians and leftists were either in prison or exiled, the regime was stunned when the **plebiscite** lost with 57% "no" vote.

The rejection of the constitution caused confusion in the military. Furthermore, many Uruguayans began to question the legitimacy of the military government. Responding to the challenge, General Gregorio Álvarez assumed power in September 1981. Under his leadership, the government's new plan was to allow the *Blancos* and the *Colorados* to write a new constitution. The new document was to be voted on in 1984. In November 1982, elections took place to select party representatives. The *Blancos* won the election with the

Lucía Topolansky (1944–)

Lucía Topolansky was a Uruguayan politician who in 1967 joined the *Tupamaros*, the leftist *Movimiento de Liberación Nacional* (MLN), when she was in her 20s. An urban guerilla movement, she lived underground (literally, in the sewers), but was arrested in 1970, tortured and imprisoned. She was released in the amnesty of 1985. Topolansky then joined legitimate politics as the leader of the *Movimiento de Participación Popular*, which later joined the *Frente Amplio*, or Broad Front leftist coalition party. She was elected mayor, then to the House of Deputies and finally to the Senate. She became president of the Uruguayan Senate, and first lady of the nation when her husband, José Mujica, also a former *tupamaro*, was elected in 2010.

A **plebiscite** is a national vote to decide a political question.

Colorados 7% behind. In 1983, the new representatives began talks with the regime. The civilian politician vs. military officer rivalry was the source of significant disagreements. Eventually, the *Blancos* withdrew, followed by the *Colorados*. The government responded by suspending all public political activity, and the public responded with a demonstration in Montevideo (the capital) of a quarter million people calling for a return to the 1966 constitution.

The military rulers faced a dilemma. They wanted to withdraw from power and to return to their traditional role within a civilian government as both the political and economic structures unraveled, but they did not want leftist elements to take power. Talks resumed in 1984, as the traditional parties and the military wanted a solution before the radical left gained enough support to win elections. The strategy included legalizing the leftist political coalition known at *Frente Amplio* (Broad Front), and freeing their leader, Líber Seregni, from captivity. But, a prominent leader of the *Blancos*, Wilson Ferreira Aldunate, was arrested trying to enter the country. The military started a rumor that Ferreira Aldunate was attempting to strike a secret deal with the president. The rumor had the desired effect, and Broad Front united with the *Colorados* in talks with the government for a new constitution. The Naval Club Pact that was agreed on in August 1984 returned Uruguay to the 1966 constitution. In an election, mostly free of corruption, that November but with all candidates vetted by the military, *Colorado* candidate Julio María Sanguinetti was elected president.

Due to Uruguay's local and national voting procedure, Sanguinetti was elected with just a third of the popular vote; so, he came into office already weakened. He created a government of national unity and distributed positions to representatives of minority parties and prominent politicians. The administration faced a number of issues: fixing the economy, keeping the military at bay, and effectively reestablishing democracy as a viable and strengthened system for governance. The new administration's economic policy returned to export-based growth. GDP increased significantly in the first two years. Wages increased somewhat, but inflation remained a problem. The economic fixes were, however, viewed as inadequate and late in the term a wave of strikes challenged the administration. The military was kept in check by a new law, Ley de Caducidad, which granted amnesty to members of the military who had violated human rights. The 1986 law was put up to a *consulta* in 1989, and the populace voted to uphold the law. The exercise of direct democracy lent support to the legitimacy of the Sanguinetti presidency. The administration had already shown a willingness to open the machinery of democracy to opposition parties by releasing jailed *Tupamaros* in 1985, the guerrilla group who had

General Gregorio Álvarez (1926–)

General Gregorio Álvarez was a Uruguayan army officer, responsible for waging war against the *Tupamaros*, starting in 1971 under President Bordaberry. In 1973, the military took over, dissolved parliament and General Álvarez headed the nation as president and commander in chief until 1985, when the country returned to elected governments. He retired to the country and the study of history. In 2007, he was charged with the kidnapping and disappearance of Uruguayans and Argentines in support of *Plan Cóndor*, a concerted effort by military dictators across Argentina, Uruguay, Paraguay, Bolivia and Chile in what he called "the war against subversion." He began serving a 25-year sentence in 2007.

Activity

Continuity and change

Case study: Uruguay

1 Why did the military seek to return to its traditional role?

2 To what extent was the Uruguayan restoration of democracy a return to tradition? To what extent was change necessary?

3 Research how the *Blanco* and *Colorado* parties changed over the history of Uruguay. Do parties survive and prosper through consistency or through evolution?

violently opposed the government since 1963, and granting legal political party status to its political arm, the *Movimiento de Liberación Nacional* (MLN) after the Marxist rebel group renounced violence late in the decade. By the end of his term, Sanguinetti had provided a solid basis for the reestablishment of democracy.

In the 1989 elections, a contest of several candidates and parties, a *Blanco* candidate was elected president. Luis Alberto Lacalle was the first *Blanco* to hold the presidency in the 20th century. Elected with only a fifth of the popular vote, Lacalle worked with the traditional rival party to develop economic policies designed to stimulate growth and lower inflation. Lacalle proposed a law that would privatize many government functions, which the legislature approved in 1991. The opposition parties demanded a national referendum, and the following year the law was overwhelmingly rejected by three-fourths of the voters. The 1992 defeat confirmed the electoral weakness of the administration and public rejection of the *Blancos*. The combination of a divided legislature and weak executive led to the frequent use of *consultas* in this time period. Other referendums included approval of cost of living adjustments, a modification of the privatization law, an attempt to increase funding for education, and a reform of the social security system. The elections that followed two years later gave more representation to the Broad Front in the balance of seats of the main three parties within the legislature. *Colorado* leader Sanguinetti took the presidency again and assumed office in 1995.

The *Colorados* and *Blancos* began negotiations to reform the electoral system, motivated primarily by the increasing threat to their primacy by the Broad Front. One significant reform was to require a majority popular vote for presidency and open up the opportunity for the Broad Front to win the highest office. A *consulta* on the issue was held in 1996. The constitutional reform permitted one nominee per political party. If any candidate won at least 40% of the popular vote and outdistanced the nearest competitor by a margin of 10% or greater, they would become president. If no one achieved such a victory, there was to be a runoff of the top two candidates. The *consulta* was approved by a narrow margin, carried by the rural areas, but was not popular in the cities.

The newly structured election procedure came into play in 1999. The Broad Front candidate, ex-socialist Tabaré Vásquez, won the popular vote, but neither his vote percentage nor his margin of victory over *Colorado* Jorge Batlle Ibáñez was enough for first ballot victory. Fearing a leftist victory, the *Blancos* joined with the *Colorados* to elect Batlle by an 8% margin. Batlle took office in March 2000 as the first president elected under the modified constitution.

Uruguay's decade-long dictatorship was an interruption to an otherwise democratic civilian tradition of government. The military takeover was triggered by conditions similar to other South-American countries: economic duress and political turmoil exacerbated by the Cold War context. The military, while harsh in its rule, returned power to civilians in a slow, but mostly orderly fashion. The return to democracy saw an expansion in the role of direct democracy, as the people made critical decisions on the structure of government, as well as its responsibilities and limits. Outsider political parties began to assert more influence as the system became more open in the 1990s, despite the efforts of the two traditional parties. Democracy in Uruguay continued into the next century on a solid foundation of tradition and evolution as it was also forced to deal with the legacy of human rights abuses.

Activity

Uruguay

Source A

URUGUAY: In 1986, a year after the restoration of democracy, the Uruguayan Parliament approved the Ley de Caducidad (roughly translated as the "Expiry Law") which granted amnesty to members of the military or police who were perpetrators of murder, kidnapping, torture and other human rights violations. Starting in 2005 Uruguayans began the process of repealing the law. The Supreme Court finally repealed it in 2009.

Source: Allier, Eugenia. "The Peace Commission: A Consensus on the Recent Past in Uruguay?". *European Review of Latin American and Caribbean Studies*. no. 81. October 2006. pp. 87–96.

Source B

The years between 1985 and 2004 can be broken down into three distinct periods representing separate phases in the history of the struggles to remember or forget the Uruguayan military dictatorship. ...Through the approval of a series of laws, the most important being the Law of Expiry of the Punitive Powers of the State (henceforth the 'Expiry Law'), the state waived its right to judge military or police officers involved in violations of human rights (Ley de Caducidad de la Pretensión Punitiva del Estado, No. 15848, 22 December 1986). In the referendum held 16 April 1989 on the Expiry Law, the voters validated the government's decision not to judge the military with 56.12 per cent in favour of the law, and 43.9 per cent opposing.

The referendum marked the beginning of a second phase in this history: The Repression of the Past: Forgetting Human Rights Violations (1990–1994), which meant the discontinuance of debate from the public space over the military dictatorship during the government of Luis Alberto Lacalle (PN).

Source: Delgado, Maria. "Truth and Justice in Uruguay," *NACLA Report on the Americas*. July/August 2000. vol. 34, no. 1. pp. 37–39.

Source C

The Expiry Law was passed by a public referendum in 1989. Under the current administration of Tabaré Vázquez, Uruguay's president, prosecutions of some of the major players in those crimes have been pursued with the help of testimony from former police and military officials who were involved but had amnesty. But after 20 years with the Expiry Law the country's mood may have changed. Just last week, the Uruguayan supreme court issued a ruling that the Expiry Law was unconstitutional—a decision that legal scholars believe may have broad application.

Source: Khan, Rhiz. "Uruguay poll highlights Expiry Law." October 26, 2009. *Al Jazeera* and the International Center for Transitional Justice at www.ictj.org.

Source D

Relatives of the disappeared marching in Montevideo, Uruguay.

Source: Etchart, Julio & Hopkinson, Amanda (eds.). 1992. *The Forbidden Rainbow: Images and voices*. London: Serpent's Tail.

Questions

1 What evidence is there in source A that Uruguay's military regime committed human rights violations?

2 What conclusion do sources B and C reach about the response of post-dictatorship governments to human rights violations by the military?

3 Referring to origin and purpose, discuss the values and limitations of sources A and B for historians studying the government's approach to human rights violations during the period of dictatorship.

4 Using the documents and your own knowledge, discuss the societal impact of, and the response to, human rights violations by the military during the dictatorship.

Brazil: establishing democracy

Brazil came to democracy after two decades of military and authoritarian rule. When the 1980s began, the military was firmly entrenched in power. The problems of the country were numerous, an economy weakened by the oil crises of the 1970s and a huge national debt, massive poverty, violence, unequal land and income distribution that led to homelessness for the rural poor, and consumer demand so lethargic that it could not support industries. The military regimes sought solutions through neoliberal economic policies and strict political control, along with the support of private militias that controlled unrest in rural areas. As the military dictatorships became more unpopular in the 1980s, the leadership loosened political control slightly. Freer elections eventually took place, a referendum on the structure of government went to popular vote and by the end of the century Brazil settled into a presidential democratic system. However, many of the structural problems that saw the military rulers relinquish power in the 1980s also plagued President Cardoso in a second term that began in 1999.

Last years of authoritarianism

The military regime was in power from 1964 to 1985. In the late 1970s, under the rule of General Ernesto Geisel, Brazil began a move towards democracy. President João Figueiredo followed Geisel in 1979 and continued the liberalization of the government. In 1982, he announced a move to democracy called *Abertura* (literally "opening") that moved to offer limited political freedoms while preserving the military's hold on the government. The economy was in serious decline, and living conditions grew worse for the large majority. Approximately three-fourths of Brazilians lived below the government-established survival level. It was commonplace for children over the age of ten to work. Inflation was over 200% and increased to 500% by mid-decade. Income distribution, always uneven, became more so, limiting the purchasing ability of the middle classes, too. The economy was largely based on exports, and multinational corporations which funneled profits out of the country exercised control over almost half of the major industrial corporations and mines. In addition, foreign debt increased from an already high $55 billion to $85 billion.

Long-running land disputes accelerated. The land-grabbing increased when the Trans-Amazonian Highway and connected roads were completed. Most of the arable farmland was owned by just 3% of the population. Brazil's Amazon Development Agency furthered the interests of agribusiness by subsidizing cattle ranchers. As land became more accessible in the Amazon region, 19 out of 20 new landholdings were granted to existing large farmers and ranchers. The new, mechanized farms employed fewer workers, creating unemployment and pushing subsistence farmers from the land. Some poor families occupied small plots of land; these people became known as *posseiros* or squatters. They raised maize, rice and other food crops. Squatters did have rights under Brazilian law, but large land owners hired gunmen, formed small militias, and through threats and acts of violence forced the *posseiros* off the land. Government officials did nothing to stop the violence, and at times lent support to the perpetrators. Many of the farmers migrated to the city, causing increases in shanty town populations and urban unemployment. But others, often assisted by clergy, formed unions to oppose the removals.

The 1982 election results confirmed significant opposition to the military regime. President Figueiredo initiated the *Abertura*, but the actual changes were minor as Figueiredo retained control not just of the federal budget, but state budgets as well. As the opposition mounted and mobilized and the economy sank further into decline the military agreed to elections, albeit indirect ones, in 1984. An electoral assembly met in January 1985 and, contrary to the wishes of the military, elected opposition candidate Tancredo Neves as president. Neves was popular and thought to be reasonably honest, however he died before taking office. Vice President José Sarney, who had the support of the military, assumed office in his place. Sarney, signed an agrarian reform law passed by the legislature, which sought to distribute land to more than a million farming families during his term in office. But its effectiveness was diluted by the government's failure to oppose the violent attacks on farmers by landowners who hired thousands of soldiers to carry out the attacks. The government further limited the effectiveness by a 1986 decree. To stabilize the economy, Sarney implemented the Economic

Chico Mendes (1944–1988)

Chico Mendes was a Brazilian rubber tapper from the state of Acre. He became head of the rubber tappers union to stop cattle ranchers and developers from their deforestation of the Amazon that would destroy the life of landless rubber tappers and hold them in debt peonage. The public lands worked by the tappers had been sold to private owners with private armies during the military dictatorships that promised road development as well. In 1987, the United Nations environment program honored him with a prize. Mendes was also renowned for his support of the native peoples of the Amazon region. In 1988, a local landowner who wanted to cut down the forest met with resistance from the well-organized tappers and Indians. Mendes reported the rancher, Darly Alves da Silva, who was also wanted for murder in another state, but the federal police did not act on his advice. Mendes was murdered in December, 1988.

Stabilization Plan, commonly called *Plan Cruzado*. The Plan instituted austerity measures including freezing wages and prices, increasing the cost of utilities and raising taxes on alcohol and tobacco. A new currency, the *cruzado*, was introduced to add economic stability.

Brazil under a new constitution

Beginning in 1987 and continuing into the following year a constitutional convention was held to draft a new constitution. The constitution included provisions for direct democracy: only the National Assembly could vote to hold a referendum, but citizens could submit a proposal to the Chamber of Deputies. Citizens, even the illiterate, could vote if they were over 16 years of age. The constitution allowed for the participation of multiple political parties. The constitution was effective as of October 1988. In March 1990, the first democratically elected president took office, Fernando Collor de Mello. A charismatic man and favorite of the elites, Collor de Mello followed policies that helped secure economic interests. As in other Latin American countries, the IMF influenced policies in exchange for loans. Collor de Mello reduced government spending, reduced the negotiating power of unions, and moved to privatize state functions. The economic policies made government more efficient, but GDP dropped, interest rates rose, unemployment rose, and government debt increased. The land disputes in rural areas worsened, but the administration rarely intervened to investigate the murder of hundreds of activists. The Brazilian people became increasingly dissatisfied with Collor de Mello.

Soon a corruption scandal hit the Collor de Mello administration. The president and his associates were accused of taking over 30 million dollars through misappropriation of public funds. As the National Assembly moved to impeach him, in 1992, Collor de Mello resigned, averting a potential national crisis in the fledgling democracy. The office was assumed by vice president Itamar Franco. Franco sought to fix the economy but did not have a particular philosophy, so a debate within the cabinet occurred between those who wanted to correct the social problems of poverty, health, and education and advocates of the neoliberal approach who argued that social advances could not be made unless the economy was first stabilized and productive. Finance minister Fernando Henrique Cardoso eventually prevailed, following a neoliberal program called *Plan Real* that chose stabilization and included large budget cuts, currency reform, and privatization of the government's mining interests. Before the next elections, a *consulta* was scheduled for 1993. The voters were to decide two critical questions: Was Brazil to continue as a democracy or become a monarchy?; Should the country continue with a presidential form of government, or convert to a parliamentary system? During Collor de Mello's scandal crisis, the presidential system became unpopular, but after his resignation presidential

Fernando Henrique Cardoso (1931–)

Fernando Henrique Cardoso was a Brazilian sociologist and academic, accused of being a subversive by the military and forced to go into exile in Chile and France. He was active in prevailing over the military dictatorships in Brazil. Elected Senator in 1982, he was a founding member of the Brazilian Social Democratic Party (PSDB). He was President of Brazil from 1995 to 2003. His government struggled with the legacy of the long rule of a military dictatorship, and its institutionalized impediments to the promotion of justice and human rights despite significant international pressure. His neoliberal economic policies led to privatizations of state enterprises, to attract foreign investment, especially for the mining, telecommunications, oil and gas industries.

government rose in popularity and that form was approved by the referendum.

In the 1994 elections the major campaign issue was whether the government should continue its neoliberal economic policies or switch to greater state control and a rejection of overt cooperation with international financial institutions. The Workers Party candidate Luiz Inaçio da Silva (popularly known as Lula) was up against finance minister Cardoso. Lula ran on a platform of agrarian reform, health improvements, and educational reform and increased funding. Cardoso, a well-respected sociologist, won the election and continued with his program of austerity measures, but did increase education funding by a third. Exports increased during the first years of the Cardoso administration, but unemployment stayed high and most Brazilians still lived in poverty. The weak economy suffered a blow during the Asian financial crisis of 1997 and Cardoso raised interest rates to an astronomical 40% in an attempt to stabilize the currency. He raised taxes and cut spending again in an attempt to put the government's foreign obligations under control. The austerity measures had the predicted effect: the economy slowed and Brazil entered a severe recession. The recession did not spare the rural farming communities, with five million farm families now landless. This homelessness was despite a land reform law passed in 1993 that allowed the government to seize and redistribute land that was largely unused by its owner. Little was done to enact this law in support of landless farmers. The farmers, aided by the Catholic Church, formed the Landless People's Movement. The movement obtained a promise from the Cardoso government to lend assistance to their land claims, but it was never forthcoming despite the threatening treatment and murder of the squatters. Revealing his abiding support for large corporate farmers, Cardoso called the Landless People's Movement a threat to democracy.

When the 1998 elections took place, voters returned Cardoso to office for a second term. His second term began in 1999. As Brazil moved into the next century its new democracy survived a corrupt president and many years of economic programs that failed to lift most Brazilians out of poverty. Violence still plagued the Amazon basin, but there were positive signs as well. Many groups became involved in the democratic process: trade unions, environmental groups, old and new political parties, and groups advocating social reforms. Conservative leadership remained a force as well. The opposition forces showed enough support for the administration to secure from it increased social services while the government simultaneously pursued neoliberal macroeconomic policies. As Cardoso moved into the middle of his second term, many substantial structural hurdles remained for Brazil's second democratically elected president to solve. Lula da Silva, Brazil's first working-class president, would be elected in 2002. Brazil, like many Latin American nations, faced the dilemma of following neoliberal economic strategies and at the same time trying to maintain a democracy in the face of major social challenges.

Activity
Simulation

Direct democracy vs. representative government

1 The class selects an issue such as "How many points an assignment should be," or what food should be served in the school cafeteria. Then, the class is divided into 4 to 6 groups. Each group selects a representative for the class legislature. The class also selects a president.

2 The legislature meets separately to consider the issue and makes a legislative decision without consulting the rest of the class.

3 The President creates a *consulta* on the issue and puts it to a class vote.

4 Compare the results and assess the extent to which the will of the populace was carried out by the two different methods.

Activity
Levels of success

1 Form a group of four people.

2 Decide on the criteria each group will use to evaluate how successful each of the four countries was in restoring democracy.

3 Each group member evaluates all four countries using the agreed-upon criteria.

4 Discuss the extent to which the group agrees or disagrees with each other's judgments. Discuss the reasons.

Into the 21st century: the United States

The last two decades of the 20th century saw significant changes within the United States. The focus of leaders shifted from the Cold War to working within an increasingly multi-centered world. The period was marked by significant technological changes ranging from the introduction and growth of cell phones, personal computers, and the formation and transformation of the Internet from part of the defense industry and scientific community to a commercial World Wide Web. The 1980s and 1990s saw challenges in the areas of health, with the AIDS epidemic, and the environment with acid rain, ozone layer depletion, and an increasing awareness of global climate change. The concept of globalization came to the forefront as the impact of communication technologies increased the flow of information and capital across international boundaries. Popular culture evolved across the diverse geographical regions of the United States. New cable channels such as CNN, ESPN, and MTV challenged to primacy of the big three networks: ABC, CBS, and NBC. The video-cassette and the Compact Disc (CD) began to change the way Americans enjoyed entertainment at home. New trends in music included "hip hop" and "grunge," while self-help books and suspense thrillers were among bestselling books. Films in the 1980s included the Cold War themed *Rocky IV* and *Red Dawn* and in the 1990s Clint Eastwood's western, *Unforgiven*, and the James Cameron blockbuster *Titanic*. Singer and actress Madonna became a cultural symbol in, and of, the 1980s, combining showmanship, artistry, assertiveness, sexuality and materialism. In sports, Magic Johnson, Larry Bird, and Michael Jordan made professional basketball a popular sport, and in the closing years of the 1990s, teenage sisters Venus and Serena Williams re-popularized tennis in the United States. It was indeed a busy 20 years.

Technology

Technological evolution and revolution drove many, but not all of the social and cultural changes of the latter part of the 20th century. Developments in technology changed the way people in the United States worked, communicated with each other and entertained themselves. It also influenced the way entertainment was created and introduced new terms into the vocabulary. Areas worthy of examination are the personal computer, the Internet, and the mobile phone. These two devices and a newly available network system changed the way most people worked and communicated. Because of this, ideas, products and creative arts from around the nation and world were able to come into homes and change the way the world was understood.

In the 1960s and 1970s the mainframe computer was the image most Americans had of the computer.

The computer

The computer had been used in government, universities, and industry for decades. The idea of the mainframe computer was familiar to most people, even though how a computer worked, or what it was used for, beyond a general sense, was not commonly understood. It was when the computer became small enough to sit on a desk and consumers did not have to know how it worked to use it (much like television sets or automobiles) that personal computers became fixtures in offices and homes. The combination of the physical downsizing of the computer to desk size along with user-friendly software made the personal computer almost as commonplace as the television by 2000. During the 1960s and 1970s, various microcomputers—a term that would be replaced by the phrase personal computer (PC)—

Microsoft founders Bill Gates and Paul Allen were all smiles in 1983 just after delivering MS DOS for the Tandy laptop and signing a contract to write MS-DOS for IBM

were invented. Manufacturers such as Hewlett-Packard and Micro Instrumentation and Telemetry Systems (MITS) produced machines. The MITS Altair (1975) featured a programming language called BASIC, the precise Altair Basic was written and licensed by future Microsoft founders, Paul Allen and Bill Gates. The computer sold in kits, at a cost of only $400, but were mainly purchased by enthusiasts. Its functions were still quite limited. The next year brought the Apple I, followed a year later by the Apple II and the Tandy Radio Shack TRS-80, each new development bringing greater capability to do what is now called word processing as well as to play games. The greater capabilities of these machines helped bring more computers into homes. The TRS required no prior knowledge of computers to use, and it sold 10,000 units in the first month.

1981 was an important year for the PC. IBM brought out its first desktop model, the appropriately named IBM PC, and the first portable computer was manufactured by the Osborne Computer Corporation. Osborne 1 weighed only 24 pounds. Soon KayPro brought out a portable computer as well. All the computers offered a

Activity

Analyzing advertising

Go to youtube.com and search 1984 Macintosh Commercial. Watch the advertisement.

1 What is the message of the advertisement?

2 Who or what does the on-screen face and voice symbolize?

3 Who is the gray audience supposed to be?

4 Understanding US culture: For what reasons was the advertisement broadcast during the Super Bowl game?

Bill Gates (1955–)

Bill Gates Grew up in Seattle, Washington. He entered Harvard University as a freshman in 1973. Gates wrote software while at college. In 1975 he formed Micro-soft (later Microsoft) with Paul Allen and left Harvard in his junior year to develop the company. Their stated goal was to have a personal computer on every office desk and in every home. Microsoft grew to become the leader in operating systems and office productivity software used on personal computers, including Windows and Microsoft Office for business and home. With Microsoft's success, Gates became one of the world's wealthiest people, dedicating much of his multibillion fortune to charitable works, both within the United States and abroad.

Steve Jobs (left) and Steve Wozniak, co-founders of Apple Computer Inc, at the first West Coast Computer Faire, April 16–17, 1977.

full array of business software: spreadsheet, database, and word processing. In 1984, the Apple Macintosh, debuting at $2,495, half the $4,997 base price of the "econobox" Chevrolet Chevette or the $5, 249 standard two-door Honda Civic, was introduced by an advertisement broadcast only once, during the Super Bowl football championship game. The "Mac" was the first personal computer to come with "What You See Is What You Get" (WYSIWYG) graphics. The first Microsoft graphical interface was released in 1985, but was limited in capability compared to the Macintosh. The graphical interface made the computer significantly more useable for many computer-illiterate consumers. The evolution of personal computer capability and an increase in affordability shows in the number of PCs in use. In 1981, just over two million were on desks in the United States. In 1985 the number was 25 million, but the growth rate slowed to a doubling by 1990 (54 million PCs). By 2000, there were 161 million personal computers in use in the United States. Computers were in businesses, factories, schools, and homes. Millions of children were exposed to word processing through programs such as Apple Writer and learned about westward expansion by playing *Oregon Trail*. In the office people used WordPerfect or WordStar. Accountants could create financial spreadsheets with Lotus 123 and sales managers kept track of clients with dBase III+. Programs that were considered vital to the industry and drove users to purchase the supporting hardware or software necessary for the programs to run became known as "killer applications." The growth in personal computers brought an entire industry with it: software. Not only were there business applications, but software was created for drawing, music, design, photography (to manipulate scanned photographs) and thousands of games. In the first two decades, the focus seemed to be a dual focus on the physical PC (hardware) and programs (software).

Discussion point

To what extent did the computer revolution differ in its effects on society from the impact of other inventions? What other technological innovations have had significant impact on the way people live?

 Why do some advances in technology have greater impact than others?

The rise of the PC industry produced an economic bonanza for many. Microsoft and Apple are two famous examples of successful companies. Others include Adobe, Lotus (both founded in 1982), and Borland, which started the following year. Collectively, because so many of the companies were located in Santa Clara County, California, and the main ingredient of the computer chip was silicon, the area became known as Silicon Valley. The era also saw the rise and fall of many companies. An example is Ashton-Tate, the creator of dBase, considered a killer application when first released but failing by 1991, when it was bought out by Borland after a lifespan of 11 years. Many people became extremely wealthy: Bill Gates and Steve Jobs were two of the most famous billionaires.

A number of issues grew along with computer sales. By 1990, a rivalry had developed between the IBM PC hardware (and clones) with its MS-DOS (Microsoft Disk Operating System), and the Apple Mactintosh machine and operating platform. Files produced by a DOS-based computer and a Macintosh could not be read or shared cross-platform. Even if conversion was possible, to the average computer user, the compatibility issues forced companies and home users to decide on one or the other. Loyalties developed along with marketing strategies. Consumers used to electronic devices such as televisions and phonographs had difficulty understanding why they were supposed to buy upgrades to computers and software that they'd just spent thousands of dollars acquiring and months learning how to use. Even as capabilities and speed advanced, many consumers used their home computers to keep their accounts, write letters, do school work and play games. To keep sales rising, hardware companies produced more attractive and more **capable machines** and software companies created more advanced versions of programs, along with new capabilities altogether, including the original Photoshop, released for Macintosh in 1990.

The Internet
The expansion of the PC was not only due to improvements in hardware and software, but to a communications network that had developed from the early 1970s into a system that eventually connected users all over the world through the World Wide Web. The network, ARPANET, that became the Internet, started as a connection between 19 computers in 1969. It expanded quickly in the 1970s. A satellite link to Europe expanded the system beyond the United States. During the 1980s, the system grew into 200,000 host computers and email addresses. An email program called Eudora, that made sending and receiving email simpler, came to be used by thousands of advanced computer users. The new users

Steve Jobs (1955–) **and Steve Wozniak** (1950-)

Steve Jobs, the cofounder of Apple Computers with Steve Wozniak, was born the same year as Bill Gates. While in high school in California, Jobs and Wozniak worked as summer employees at Hewlett-Packard, the electronics giant. After college, Jobs and Wozniak got together and formed Apple Computer, with Wozniak as the designer-engineer and Jobs working the business-marketing side of the partnership. Together, the two employed prior inventions, such as the mouse, to develop a user-friendly computer. The Macintosh, known to most people as a "Mac," became a leader in innovative personal computer design. The computer and software became a favorite of creative artists. Apple became known in later years for the iPod, a portable digital music player released in 2001 that became so popular that its name now stands in for any pocket-sized mp3 player.

Computer capability Moore's Law, attributed to Gordon Moore, predicted that the rate of computer processor (chip) capability (the processing speed) would double every two years. Not only did processing speeds increase but computer memory did, too. This enabled increasingly complex software that could perform more elaborate tasks. More storage meant larger files could be produced, including graphics.

connected to the Internet through an Internet Service Provider (ISP) by using a **modem** to dial the ISP and then the modem, with a sequence of beeps and hisses, would negotiate a connection. This allowed home and business computer users to communicate and transfer files via **FTP**, often through programs such as Fetch, a Macintosh program that featured a simple graphic of a dog running as a file was downloaded. At this stage, the user had to know where to go to get the files as there were no search engines. Early adapters signed up with "bulletin boards" where those interested in a particular field could post messages and files. Hundreds of usernet groups, usually open associations of online contributors with common interests, ranging from hobbies to history and mathematics to literature, also found vast numbers of users. The Internet was becoming more than a way to connect and communicate with others—it was becoming cyberspace.

In the early 1990s, the World Wide Web was added to the Internet. ISPs such as Prodigy, America Online (AOL) and MSN made accessing the Web easier. AOL, with its famous email client greeting, "You've got mail," was among the first of a series of ISPs that provided dedicated software to make connecting and using the Internet simple for the new computer user. The AOL platform became so well-known that it featured in the movie of the same name, *You've Got Mail* (1998). Other Internet films from the 1990s included *Hackers* (1993) and *The Net* (1995). The growth of the impact of the Internet is illustrated by the fact that in 1990 the mainstream US media are recorded as using the word "Internet" only 346 times. In 1995 there were 71,000 mentions, and in 1999 over half a million.

The development of the browser made the Internet easier to use. The first widely used browser was Mosaic, developed by the National Center for Supercomputing Applications, University of Illinois in Champaign-Urbana. It allowed the ordinary computer user to access the World Wide Web without needing to know computer commands or learn a specific ISP's interface. The browser let the user subscribe to any ISP, creating room in the ever-widening market. The browser used a language called hypertext markup language (html). HTML enabled web designers, often amateurs, to create web pages that featured both text and graphics. The creative presentation of information became increasingly important. As more information came to be presented on a given page, connection speed became increasingly critical to Internet use. While many large businesses, research facilities, government agencies, and educational institutions acquired broadband (high speed) connections, most home users and small businesses still used dial-up ISPs. Modem connection speeds went from 2,400 to 56,000 **bits** per second, a 25-fold increase in a few short years. Internet use rose to 19 million by 1997 in the United States. The multiplying number and complexity of websites seemed to demand ever-increasing bandwidth. By 2001, there were more than a billion online documents. In 2001, over three million new pages and almost three-quarters of a million images were added every day. But a revealing statistic from 2000 showed that while a full two-thirds of people in the United States used the Internet, only one in 20 had

A **modem** is a modulator-demodulator– a device that transmits and receives digital data from and to a computer.

File Transfer Protocol (FTP), a standard Internet protocol, is the simplest way to exchange files between computers on the Internet. Like the Hypertext Transfer Protocol (HTTP), which transfers web pages and related files, and the Simple Mail Transfer Protocol (SMTP), which transfers e-mail, FTP is an application protocol that uses the Internet's TCP/IP protocols. FTP sites are also commonly used to download programs and other files to your computer from other servers.

Activity

Infrastructures

Research the expansion of previous technologies and supporting/enabling infrastructures: Telegraph and telephone, railroad, electric light, road transport. Can you identify a relationship between government and industry? Compare another country in the Americas to the United States in the development and expansion of three technologies, including the computer (Internet).

A **bit** is one piece of binary information: either a 1 or a 0.

 Why did the use of the Internet expand so quickly?

their own broadband connection, a lower share than a number of other nations. By 2002, the figure had reached 10%, but was less than that of several European nations and paled in comparison with South Korea, where one-in-two users had a high-speed connection. Broadband subscriptions per capita led to a similar conclusion: in the same yeat the United States had 6.9 subscriptions per hundred people, Belgium 8, Canada 11.7 and South Korea 21.4.

A study undertaken by the University of California, Los Angeles (UCLA) found that two-thirds of the population of the United States had Internet access, 76% of those used email daily, and just upwards of half of Internet users had made an online purchase. In 2000, e-commerce totaled $150 billion, up from just $2 billion three years earlier. In fact, a quarter of Internet shoppers bought online once a month. The search engines Magellan, Exite, Lycos, AltaVista and Ask Jeeves, all Google predecessors, started to take the place of directories. The study also revealed that children enjoyed the World Wide Web to such a degree that they were denied access as punishment. The Web intruded on time spent watching television, as Web users reported 25% less viewing time. Spending time on the World Wide Web had become a commonplace activity in less than a decade.

The flurry of Web activity spawned the **dot-com** bubble. Beginning with the **IPO** of Netscape in 1995, investors saw Internet and tech companies as good investments with the potential for high yields. The peak years of 1998–2000 saw billions of dollars invested in new offerings, creating a speculative bubble. In 1998, the average first day increase in share value on a dot-com IPO was 22%. In 1999, the first day increase averaged 71%, meaning that a dollar in company value at the beginning of the day was worth $1.71 several hours later. The bubble burst on March 10, 2000. In two years, the NASDAQ index fell from 5133 to 1114 (a 78% drop). Hundreds of companies failed and thousands of investors lost fortunes.

The amazing growth of the Internet and increasing public reliance on it for information and commerce led to issues around access. Would those without access to the Internet, either due to geography or income, be denied the educational, commercial, and informational opportunities that the rest of the United States already took for granted? Education, income, race, and geographic location were all factors. The UCLA study found that people with a college degree were almost three times as likely to use the Internet as those without a high school diploma. The Department of Commerce's National Telecommunications and Information Administration found that individuals with household incomes of less than $25,000 a year used the Internet at a rate less than half of those above $50,000. Nevertheless, between 1997 and 2001 the percentage of computer and Internet users with family incomes below $15,000 grew from 9% to 25%. The large differential in Internet use is often what is called the Digital Divide. The study also showed that Internet use increased in all racial classifications at faster rates for Hispanics and African Americans than for whites, Asian Americans, and Pacific Islanders. Significant differences in computer availability and Internet use remained at the beginning of the new millennium.

TOK Link
Search engines
How do search engines direct knowledge acquisition?

1 Choose five terms (may be multiple words) to search.
2 Enter the terms into at least three different search engines.
3 Record the top ten results of each search engine. Analyze the results in terms of consistency and direction.
4 Go to search results #101–10. Assess the similarities and differences in the results when compared to #1–10.
5 How do search engines direct knowledge?

Dot-com refers to the ".com" affix to web addresses for businesses and corporations.

An **Initial Public Offering (IPO)** is when a private company first offers shares to the public. It is used as a way to acquire capital for research, expansion, etc.

Activity

The Digital divide

The following documents relate to the alleged disparity in the availability of computer technology between different racial and socioeconomic groups in the United States in the 1990s.

Source A

Internet use among Hispanics differs considerably depending on whether Spanish is the only language spoken in the household, which is the case for about one in nine of Hispanic households. In September 2001, 14.1 percent of Hispanics who lived in households where Spanish was the only language spoken used the Internet. In contrast, 37.6 percent of Hispanics who lived in households where Spanish was not the only language spoken used the Internet.

Source: The National Telecommunications and Information Administration report: "Falling Through the Net II: Data on the Digital Divide." http://www.ntia.doc.gov/ntiahome/net2/falling.html.

Source B

Then there are times when the digital divide looks unfathomably deep. The phrase has become mired in the blurry realm of cliche, applied variously to women, the disabled, seniors, ethnic minorities, rural and inner-city populations. But the underlying threat is real. Technology has moved so fast that a new upper class—composed largely of the same white, affluent, college-educated males that made up the old upper class—has spurted ahead of the rest of society, mostly because they have the time and money necessary to acquire and understand the tools of the digital revolution.

Source: Taylor, Chris et al. "Digital Divide." *Time*, December 4, 2000. http://www.time.com/time/magazine/article/0,9171,998678,00.html.

Source C

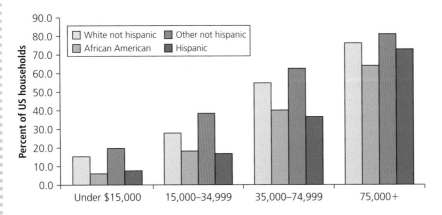

Percentage of US households with a computer by income, race or origin.
Source: "Falling Through the Net II: Data on the Digital Divide."
National Telecommunication and Information Administration.
http://www.ntia.doc.gov/ntiahome/net2/Image13.gif.

Source D

The gap between high- and low-income Americans is increasing. In the last year, the divide between those at the highest and lowest income levels grew 29%. Households with incomes of $75,000 or higher are more than *twenty times* more likely to have access to the Internet than those at the lowest income levels, and more than *nine times* as likely to have a computer at home.

Whites more likely to be connected than African-Americans or Hispanics. The digital divide is also persistent and growing along racial and ethnic lines. Whites are more likely to have access to the Internet from home than African-Americans or Hispanics have from *any* location. African-American and Hispanic households are roughly *two-fifths* as likely to have home Internet access as white households. The gaps between white and Hispanic households, and between white and African-American households, are now more than six percentage points larger than they were in 1994. However, for incomes of $75,000 and higher, the divide between whites and African-Americans has narrowed considerably in the last year.

Source: "From Digital Divide to Digital Opportunity: The Importance of Bridging the Digital Divide." From President Bill Clinton's White House Web site.
http://clinton4.nara.gov/WH/New/digitaldivide/digital3.html

Questions

1 What evidence is there in source D that there is a digital divide?

2 What is the message of source B?

3 What are the similarities and differences between sources C and D?

4 What is are the values and limitations of sources A and B for historians researching access to computer technology in the 1990s?

5 Using the documents and your own knowledge, assess the severity of the digital divide in the 1990s.

The cell phone

Another important advance in technology and communication was the cell phone. The first available cell phone was the Motorola DynaTAC 8000, launched in 1983. The phone was priced at $3,995 and talk time was a maximum of one hour for the 13-inch long "brick." Cell phones were the province of the wealthy, but by 1985 there were some 340,000 cell phone subscribers in the United States. As cell phones grew smaller and less expensive, subscriptions increased to just over five million in 1990. Ten years later, more than 100 million of 281 million Americans used cell phones.

Aside from the rapid growth, spurred on by telecommunications companies such as Sprint, Cingular, AT&T and many more, the cell phone changed the nature of communication. Until its use became commonplace, a phone call was placed from one permanent location to a second permanent location. Essentially, one called a phone, not a person. The cell phone reversed the dynamic: a call was placed to a person, regardless of where the person was. Mobile phones enabled people to be just that—mobile. Business could be conducted almost any place, friends were available when they were not at home or work. Socially, the cell phone caused letters to be

Activity

Globalization and the mobile phone

Cell phones may have changed the way people in developed nations communicate.

What has been the impact of people living in less developed countries in both rural and urban areas?

written to newspapers about etiquette. When was it okay to talk on the phone? In a restaurant? At a bus stop? Being available more of the time was sometimes a positive, but it became more difficult to ignore a call.

The computer, the Internet, and the cell phone were not the only technological advances in the last two decades of the 20th century. Integrated circuits (chips) became commonplace in automobiles, household appliances, even toys. The Sony Walkman first accompanied **early adapters** in 1981, making music both portable and personal. The video cassette recorder (VCR) could be found connected to television sets, freeing viewers from the time constraints of network broadcast schedules and providing the movie industry with an entirely new way of distributing films. The compact disc (CD) replaced the vinyl long-playing (LP) record album, provoking arguments over sound quality and issues of copyright infringement. Unlike audio cassettes' analog degradation, CD "burners" made exact copies of digitized music; it was impossible to tell a copy from the original. DVDs appeared at the end of the 1990s, doing for video what the CD had done for audio. Millions of homes had several, if not all, of the VCRs, CD players, DVD players, internet-connected computers, and computerized game units, in living rooms, family rooms and bedrooms. Many of the manufacturers of the new electronic products were Japanese (for example, Sony), and South Korean (Samsung), supplanting or buying US companies such as RCA, Zenith and Motorola. By 2000, many devices that had not been invented or affordable for common use decades earlier were a part of the everyday life of the average consumer.

Photo shows the comparative size of a Sony Walkman cassette player and a pack of cigarettes. The Walkman was among the first of many Japanese electronics products to dominate the US market in the 1980s. Coincidentally, as portable-personal music players expanded in popularity, cigarette sales declined.

> The term **early adopter** came to mean people who first used new technologies, whether the technologies were hardware (computers, cell phones, DVD players) or software (browsers, image processing, gaming).

The effects of globalization on the United States

Many discussions of globalization involve consideration of the impact of US governmental policies and corporations on economies, environments, and peoples, in lesser developed countries (LDCs). Since the Second World War, the United States has generally pursued a policy of trade liberalization, allowing for expanding markets for American goods around the world. As the world's largest economy during the 1980s and 1990s, the dollar was the world's currency, involved in most of the major international trade and financial transactions around the globe. The United States promoted increased trade (to many observers, mainly on its own terms), and exported products from Coca Cola to garbage. It follows that the people and businesses of the United States were the major beneficiaries of the increased economic activity. A number of factors, however, test the validity of this assumption.

This section turns the gaze around and examines the effect of globalization on the United States. A number of factors influenced the growing awareness of globalization, even if the term was unfamiliar. Increased trade volume and new goods from new places

Discussion point

The format war over the video cassette is similar to the format battle between HD and Blu-Ray. Why do consumers and manufacturers seem to settle on one format rather than welcoming a variety?

Globalization is a process of interaction and integration among the people, companies, and governments of different nations. It is a process driven by international trade and investment and aided by information technology.

Globalization101.org

landed on store shelves. Manufacturing jobs dropped in important sectors such as steel and automobiles at the same time imports of the same products became increasingly familiar. It seemed that more languages were spoken on the streets of US towns and cities as immigrants arrived from Latin America, East Asia, southwest Asia, the Caribbean, and the Horn of Africa. Unfamiliar clothing, food, music, and ideas arrived with the million new people each year. By 2000, one in ten residents was of foreign birth—and most of them were not of European ancestry. The globalization process of interaction and integration was visibly taking place in communities across the country, and the process was accelerating, partially due to advances in technology, including the Internet.

Positive effects

Globalization resulted in a number of positive outcomes in the United States. During the period of increased globalization, the number of jobs in the United States increased, as did GDP. In the last quarter of the 20th century, employment for college-educated women and men increased 400%. The 1980s and 1990s brought significant and almost continuous economic growth. Consumers benefitted enormously from the sheer variety of imports. Economists Christian Broda and David Weinstein argue that Americans underestimate the economic gains from increased foreign trade. They argue that the economy experienced a net gain of $260 billion from 1972 to 2001 due to the increase in the variety of products available in the United States. During those same years, the quantity of different kinds of imported products more than doubled, and the total variety of products grew from 75,000 to 259,000. It follows that, for consumers, greater choice leads to many benefits. The gains are higher quality, lower price, and the expansion of choices from new fruits and vegetables, to clothing, washing machines and automobiles. Essentially, most people in the United States experienced a higher standard of living due, in part, to accelerated globalization. In addition, people in the US had greater access to new forms of music, art, and literature. For example, the documentary, *The Buena Vista Social Club* (Dir. Wim Wenders, 1999), a film about a group of Cuban musicians from the 1950s and 1960s who reunited, made $7 million in the first six months of its release in the United States, exposing US audiences to a new sound from only 90 miles south of Florida. The cultural landscape of the United States in 2000 would have been quite different without the products and cultural contributions from around the world.

Globalization's downside

The overall good economic times of the Reagan and Clinton years was not good for everyone in the United States. Many view those years in which globalization accelerated, as symptomatic of an economic, political, and cultural decline for the nation as a whole. Opposition to globalization came from both the political right and the political left. To many US citizens, the increased interaction with the companies, institutions, and people of different countries signaled the decline of their country. Several factors contributed to this view.

Activity

Class debate

Is globalization good or bad?

1   Divide into groups by topic: economics, environment, religion, health, conflict and any additional topics the class would like to discuss.

2   Each group researches their chosen topic for different countries from the Americas, Asia, Africa, and Europe. There should be as many countries as group members.

3   As a class, discuss the benefits and disadvantages of globalization for each topic and decide whether globalization is, on balance, beneficial or harmful.

The increase in global trade and the accelerating shift of capital that allowed for multinational corporations opening new factories an ocean away from the factory that was closing, caused significant worker dislocation, especially among well-paid blue collar workers. Factory workers in the **Rust Belt** lost their jobs as Japan, Korea and other nations exported steel and automobiles that had previously been made in places like Pittsburg, Pennsylvania and Detroit, Michigan. US automobile companies had produced half of the world's cars in 1960; by 1994 the figure was 25%. Garment factories in the south closed as clothing manufacturing moved to Mexico and Malaysia. Nike opened a shoe factory in Vietnam in 1995. As a share of the total labor force, manufacturing jobs fell by more than a third from 1980 to 2000. Even white collar jobs were exported to countries such as India. As it became easier for corporations to make products in places with lower wages and fewer governmental regulations, to sell in more affluent markets, the **comparative advantage** of the United States in manufacturing and agriculture was declining. Government officials watched as the trade deficit grew from a few billion dollars and 0.7% of GDP in 1980 to approximately$400 billion or 3.6% of GDP in 2000. It seemed that, economically, the United States was losing its world power status. Interestingly, people on both ends of the political spectrum saw downsides in the evolving world system. Unions, environmentalists, isolationists, small businesses, among others felt that the increasing power of multinational corporations and international financial institutions was causing a decline in the political and economic status of the ordinary citizen, as well as the degradation of the environment. The willingness to embrace globalization worked against the interests of many workers and communities in the United States and overseas. The opposition resulted in a variety of protests exemplified by massive protests against the World Trade Organization summit in Seattle, Washington, in 1999.

> The **Rust Belt** is the region of the United States near the Great Lakes. Once known as the industrial heartland, factories producing steel, automobiles, and other goods once dominated the economies of the states of Indiana, Ohio, Pennsylvania, and Michigan, but beginning in the 1970s and accelerating into the 1980s, they shut down and the chained shut, rusting gates became the symbol of the region.

> **Comparative advantage** is the ability of one country to produce a specific product at a lower cost than another country.

Additionally, especially in the latter years of the Clinton administration, the United States saw many other nations challenging its global political position. Conservatives, including Patrick Buchanan, claimed that the United States was losing national sovereignty to international institutions such as the International Criminal Court and the United Nations. Leading up to the 2000 Republican primary election campaign, Buchanan said: "This then is a millennial struggle that succeeds the Cold War: It is the struggle of patriots of every nation against a world government where all nations yield up their sovereignty and fade away." Others, including an organization called the Project for a New American Century, wrote of the necessity of US leadership in the century to come. In their view, the United States could not relinquish its 20th-century hegemony. The decline of US power would mean the decline of the United States itself and an increase in crises around the world. They saw Clinton's internationalist foreign policy as furthering that decline.

Protest march against the World Trade Organisation (WTO) through Capitol Hill, Seattle, before talks begin, November 27, 1999.

The results of globalization

Economically and politically, globalization had mixed results in the United States. The 1980s and 1990s did see the decline of manufacturing jobs. As presidents Bush and Clinton moved to embrace international coalitions and organizations, the economy continued to grow. Job growth continued in the United States even as the manufacturing sector declined. As economist Russell Roberts reported, the proportion of manufacturing jobs as a part of the economy had fallen steadily since the Second World War. In the ensuing 55 years, the manufacturing output rose at a slightly faster rate than the rest of the economy. He argues that a more educated workforce requiring the use of more technologically advanced machinery caused the decline in manufacturing employment—not globalization itself. Still, the shifts in employment sectors caused dislocation and forced many to move or accept a lower standard of living. Job retraining was encouraged, but for middle-aged workers going to school was a challenge. It was also difficult to anticipate what job sectors held the most potential in a quickly shifting economy. The 1990s saw the United States working with international coalitions to solve problems. Solutions to environmental problems, in particular, became more international with the approved Montreal Protocol regarding ozone depletion in the 1980s and the unratified Kyoto Treaty concerning climate change in the 1990s. By 2000, the impact of the many aspects of globalization was still a hotly debated topic.

Activity

Change or continuity?

Research the practice of protectionism by the United States government in earlier historical periods. How similar or different was the reaction of groups such as labor to international trade in the late 20th century compared to earlier times?

As a variation on the above, you could research the prevalence of protectionism in a country of your choice in the Americas. How have various interest groups reacted to international economic pressures?

New concerns in health and the environment

The last 20 years of the century brought new concerns in both healthcare and the environment. The two decades in this case study began with President Reagan, who removed solar panels from the roof of the White House, and ended with the close defeat in the presidential election of 2000 of sitting vice president Al Gore, author of the 1992 best seller *The Earth in Balance*. But, to view environmental concerns through the lens of the White House is to minimize the sheer quantity of issues. In a country as geographically diverse as the United States the environmental issues were both local and national. Logging of old-growth forests provoked confrontations in the Pacific northwest and brought legislative action concerning forests in Alaska. Pollution of land and water by toxic chemicals in areas with unexplained high incidences of cancer and other detrimental health conditions brought headlines in local and nationally influential papers, and were popularized by films such as *Erin Brockovich* (2000, Dir. Steven Soderbergh). Studies showed that some pesticides used in agriculture caused illness in consumers and agricultural workers. Concerns regarding water quality were many. On the East Coast, watermen, recreational boaters, and environmentalists watched and worked for solutions as the Chesapeake Bay was contaminated by nutrients from agricultural run-off and sewage. Ocean fisheries suffered from over-fishing. Safe drinking water was a concern in cities across the country, leading to national legislation. Water shortages in the arid southwest led to debates about water allocation between farmers, the residents of fast-growing cities, industry, and environmentalists. Even the beaches of

Long Island brought fears of a spoiled ecosystem when medical waste washed up on the sands. Air pollution, often a local concern of smoggy automobile-dominated cities such as Los Angeles in California and industrial municipalities such as Gary in Indiana, garnered national attention. The location of high levels of pollutants and concerns over the effectiveness of government regulation enforcement caused some activists to level charges of environmental racism. Lead from gasoline was deemed a health hazard and acid rain that was the result of the burning of sulfur-rich fossil fuels damaged not only watersheds in Canada and the northeastern United States, but also caused building damage, including pitting the monuments on the National Mall in Washington DC. Awareness of a quickly growing "ozone hole" above the Antarctic followed by growing concern of the effect of greenhouse gasses on the global climate added to the plethora of environmental issues that confronted the United States during the two decades.

Health concerns

During the 1980s and 1990s, life spans of the average person in the United States increased. In fact, most health indicators showed improved health for Americans. Deaths from heart disease declined by 50%, and smoking fell by a quarter. Many recent technological advances including coronary stents, improved arthroscopy, Magnetic Resonance Imaging, and Lasik eye surgery improved the daily lives of those who could take advantage of the medical advances. But, not for all: these and other expensive treatments were not available to the millions who could not afford them. While most people had health insurance through their employer or the programs of Medicare and Medicaid, the proportion of the population with no health coverage persisted just above 15%. The reliance of the majority of people on employer-supplied or supplemented health insurance was a concern as insurance premiums rose, increasing the financial burden on employers or on employees when the costs were passed onto them. The coverage concerns resulted in the effort by the Clinton administration to attempt comprehensive healthcare reform. Other health concerns that challenged the United States included the rise of eating disorders, both overeating and under-eating, reflected in the rising rates of obesity and anorexia. Food health became an important topic of discussion. Two concerns that caused public alarm, and gained massive media attention, connecting social issues to health issues were the rise in cocaine use and the HIV/AIDS epidemic.

The AIDS crisis

On July 3, 1981, the *New York Times* carried a story about 41 men who had been diagnosed with a strange disease that left eight of them dead within two years. The men exhibited a rare form of skin cancer and soon became ill from several other diseases. The men were homosexuals, and as the number of victims of this malady grew, AIDS was thought to be limited to homosexual men. It even acquired the moniker GRID (gay-related immune deficiency). In September 1982, the Centers for Disease Control (CDC) named the illness Acquired Immune Deficiency Syndrome (AIDS). Intravenous drug users also came down with AIDS. This combination of victims contributed to making the public discussion of AIDS taboo. The death of the movie legend Rock Hudson from AIDS and a famous photograph of Elizabeth Taylor holding a gaunt Hudson's hand helped promote public discussion and action. Another AIDS case, 13-year-old Ryan White, provoked a strong reaction. White, a hemophiliac, contracted AIDS through a transfusion. When his school found out, he was banned from campus, but in time a court ordered the school to allow him to attend. Classmates made fun of him, but Ryan White helped change common perception of the disease.

By the time of Hudson's death and White's diagnosis, more than 10,000 people had died of AIDS in the United States. The number of deaths per year increased during the 1980s from 130 in 1981 to 51,000 in 1994. In 1993, AIDS was the leading cause of death for men aged 25–44, reaching a quarter of all deaths for that age group. AIDS rates among minority groups increased in the early 1990s: it accounted for a third of deaths of African American men (in the same age group) and 22% of African American women—the most affected groups in the United States. 1996 brought the introduction of anti-retroviral drugs and death rates plummeted. The phrase "People living with HIV/AIDS" became commonplace. 1996 marked the year that **HIV/AIDS** changed from being thought of as a death sentence to being a manageable disease, albeit with many side effects and great expense in healthcare provision.

The disease was a taboo subject throughout most of the 1980s and those with AIDS carried a stigma, often invoking fear and discriminatory treatment. For example, a 1990 survey of primary care physicians showed that a third felt no duty to treat someone with HIV/AIDS. Some well-known religious leaders called AIDS a punishment for sin. Jerry Falwell, the founder of the Moral Majority, said that AIDS was not only a punishment to homosexuals, but also a punishment to societies that tolerate homosexuality. Some African American activists, seeing the increasing occurrence of HIV/AIDS in their communities, discussed the possibility that AIDS was a creation of the United States Government. In 1992, film director Spike Lee wrote an essay that appeared in *Rolling Stone* magazine, stating his belief that AIDS was a "government-engineered disease" designed to kill "gays and minorities." A 1993

Activity
Working with a graph

The graph above is from the Centers for Disease Control. It details the prevalence of HIV infections and the number of people living with HIV/AIDS.

Source: http://www.cdc.gov/hiv/topics/surveillance/images/infections-lg.jpg

Questions
1 What does the solid blue line stand for?
2 When did people living with HIV/AIDS cross the 600,000 mark?
3 What was the peak year for new infections? Why?
4 Using your own knowledge and the graph, for what reasons did the number of people living with HIV/AIDS continue to rise from 1994–90, when new infections declined?

HIV is the retrovirus that causes the disease AIDS. AIDS is the disease caused by HIV.

survey revealed that one-third of African Americans agreed with that conclusion. But the 1990s also brought a shift among many people to compassion. At the 1991 **Tony Awards**, participants wore red ribbons to illustrate awareness and concern for people living with AIDS. The red ribbon is often cited as the first time that public pressure worked to promote action on health issues. Also in 1991, Magic Johnson, a basketball star for the Los Angeles Lakers, announced his retirement because of HIV, bringing an upbeat celebrity face to the fight against the disease. The rap and cross-over group Salt' n Pepa included a public service announcement on their new CD, and the popular MTV show *The Real World* added a cast member with HIV/AIDS. *Angels in America* (1991), a play by Tony Kushner on the subject of AIDS, won a Tony Award. The 1993 film *Philadelphia* (Dir. Jonathan Demme), starring Tom Hanks and Denzel Washington, two major Hollywood stars, focused on the case of an attorney who was fired because he had AIDS. In the 1990s, many school districts added AIDS education to their curriculums, often invoking heated debate within communities. Discussions of illness and sexuality became more open and homosexuality appeared to gain greater acceptance, as evidenced by the popular television show *Will and Grace* broadcast on NBC 1998–2006.

HIV/AIDS did not stop at the end of the 1990s. By then, many nations around the world were affected to a much greater degree than the United States. During the Clinton administration, an important part of foreign policy was foreign aid directed towards several African nations. HIV continued to infect tens of thousands of people each year in the United States at the beginning of the new century, while thousands living with AIDS died.

The cocaine epidemic

The cocaine and crack cocaine epidemic of the late 1970s and the 1980s was the most visible of the illegal drug crisis. By the middle of the 1980s crack cocaine was linked to a rise in sexually transmitted diseases, increased violence, especially in the inner-city, and safety problems caused by drug use in the workplace. Cocaine use and drug-related violence became nightly stories on evening news broadcasts, including the new cable news channel, CNN.

Tony Awards Annual awards for the theatrical productions in the US.

Activity

Ethics and public health

A 1990 survey of African American church-attendees in five cities revealed that a third believed that AIDS was an artificial disease. Why might some Americans have suspected that HIV/AIDS was a government conspiracy? Research the Tuskegee Syphilis Study (1930–72), and its impact on African American perceptions of public healthcare conspiracies.

Activity

Does music affect behavior?

Listen to a recording of "Cocaine Blues" by T. J. Arnall. Johnny Cash recorded a version in 1968 in his album *At Folsom Prison*, as did George Thorogood.

1 What are the messages of the song?

2 Other songs that talk about cocaine, including "Casey Jones" by the Grateful Dead, can be interpreted as warning of the dangers of drugs. To what extent are popular songs an effective means to get people to change their behavior?

3 In a broader sense, to what extent does popular culture change or reflect, society?

During the 1970s, cocaine use among the wealthy and the upper middle class rose. Cocaine was expensive and word-of-mouth spread the view that it was not addictive. (People had forgotten the cocaine epidemic that began a century before in the United States.) Use among the wealthy and college educated rose in the early 1980s, with persistent use peaking in 1983. There were indications of addiction problems as emergency room admissions for cocaine increased in the first years of the decade. Usage dropped quickly thereafter as stories of friends and co-workers emptying bank accounts and losing their jobs circulated. Comedian George Carlin remarked that, "Cocaine is God's way of telling you that you have too much money." Use of cocaine among high school graduates rose until 1985 before beginning to decline, but among the least educated, cocaine use (originally quite low in comparison to the aforementioned groups), rose slowly until surpassing college graduates in 1990 and high school graduates two years later. At its peak, cocaine users made up an estimated 5% of people aged 19–50.

The rise in cocaine use among the poor and less educated came with a dramatic drop in price. A new form of cocaine, crack—a rock that was smoked rather than a powder usually ingested through the nose—brought the price to $5 a dose in New York City. Nevertheless, the first reported consumers of the new form of cocaine were the same upper-class cocaine users. It was after the low price created a demand for larger markets for cocaine that the use of crack spread significantly. Most reports record crack spreading quickly into poorer neighborhoods with large minority populations in the mid-1980s. As cocaine entered city neighborhoods, and left the privacy of living rooms and businesses, its use became more visible. Violence accompanied the new markets as gangs competed for turf, shooting and sometimes killing rivals. Between 1987 and 1989 firearm fatalities among black males increased by 71%. Unlike crimes linked with heroin in earlier decades, in which junkies committed robberies to get money to support their addiction, the majority of cocaine-related homicides were committed by dealers protecting or trying to increase their sales in "turf wars." As the shootings escalated, so did news coverage. The increase in crack cocaine and violence also occurred at the same time as a rise in sexually transmitted disease and an increase in babies born exposed to illegal drugs in the womb. Furthermore, the epidemic gave rise to an increase in incarceration rates for African American men. In the late 1980s, many people in the United States saw cocaine use as a significant problem worthy of government internvention.

The federal government responded with increased action by the Drug Enforcement Agency (DEA). The DEA also funded state and local task forces. The Comprehensive Crime Control Act (1984) included a provision that allowed the seizure of assets. The 1986 Anti-Drug Abuse Act provided $8 million specifically for cocaine enforcement. The First Lady, Nancy Reagan, began her "Just Say, 'No,'" campaign. Many private groups formed to fight drug use. Among the best known was the Partnership for a Drug-Free America. Numerous news broadcasts featured stories and schools included cocaine in all forms in drug education programs. The effectiveness of public outreach was

Activity

What is the effect of criminal penalties?

Research the debate over disparity in criminal penalties awarded for powder and crack cocaine.

1 How much of a difference was there in sentences for powder cocaine possession vs. crack cocaine possession?

2 What were the reasons given for the different sentencing rules?

3 What were the effects of those laws?

4 Were the sentencing laws just?

7 ● Into the 21st century, 1980–2000

questioned as cocaine use, while at a lower level that its peak, remained constant into the latter half of the 1990s. Law enforcement efforts may have been more effective as crime levels dropped, but incarceration rates remained high, especially for minority males. The cocaine epidemic that cost upper class people money and careers in 1980 continued to burden communities across the country as the century ended.

Concerns about the environment

Concerns about the environment were numerous. Air pollution, water pollution, radiation leaks, and chemical waste were among the environmental hazards. However two places, the Love Canal and Three Mile Island, and two global environmental topics, ozone depletion and global climate change, became major topics for concern. While there are numerous problems, including declining fisheries, home pollutants (like asbestos) these places and topics demanded a great deal of attention and action in the United States.

The Love Canal

The Love Canal was constructed in the 1890s near the Niagara River in New York to provide hydroelectric power. It was never used. Instead, beginning in the 1920s, the site was used to dump chemical waste until its closure in 1952. The following year the disposal site was covered and sold for one dollar to the Niagara Falls Board of Education. The school board was informed that chemical waste was buried under the ground by the Hooker Chemical Company. Despite the warnings, or because of a misunderstanding of the dangers, an elementary school was built on the site and in 1955 the 99th Street School opened. Homes were built as well, but homebuyers were not provided with information about the site's potential hazards. From the 1950s to the1970s, residents complained about odors and strange substances oozing out of the ground. The response of the school board was to cover the areas with soil or clay. In 1976, the city investigated and found that the soil and water was contaminated with **PCBs** and other toxins. Two years later, the State of New York investigated and found health problems, including reproductive problems in women, and high levels of air-borne and soil-borne toxins. In 1980, the federal government and New York State announced the temporary relocation of approximately 700 families. The Environmental Protection Agency (EPA) agreed to clean up the site with Superfund dollars. The EPA covered a 40-acre area with a cap and a series of devices monitored the air and ground water. By the end of the cleanup and purchase of homes, more than 1,000 families were relocated and $100 million was spent. A debate on the effectiveness of the EPA's response, and the safety of homes outside the cleanup area, continued into the 1990s. The Love Canal served to make Americans aware of the dangers of toxic waste and created continuing questions about the best ways to prevent and respond to chemical waste.

Polychlorinated Biphenyls (PCBs) are considered be an environmental toxin and are a possible carcinogen.

Superfund is the common name for the Comprehensive Environmental Response, Compensation, and Liability Act of 1980

484

Three Mile Island

Three Mile Island (TMI) is a nuclear power plant in Pennsylvania. On March 28, 1979, due to design deficiencies, equipment failure, and human error, there was a severe meltdown of the core of Reactor 2. Within hours, all non-essential personnel were evacuated. The containment dome was not breached. By the evening the core had cooled and was considered stable. But on March 30 a significant amount of radiation from an adjoining building was released into the atmosphere. Pennsylvania governor, Richard Thornburgh, and the chairman of the Nuclear Regulatory Commission, Joseph Hendrie, decided to advise pregnant women and young children within a five-mile radius to leave the area. The order caused some panic and confusion. Reactor 2 was decommissioned permanently, but the other reactors at TMI continued to operate.

TMI had mixed effects. Studies by numerous federal agencies as well as private studies revealed few residual health problems caused by the release of radiation. Average exposures were found to be one millirem, less than a quarter of the radiation in a chest x-ray. Maximum exposure was less than 100 millirem. The effect on the Nuclear Power Industry appears straightforward. While plants under construction at the time of Three Mile Island were completed, no new nuclear plants have been approved and built since the accident. Many industry observers blame overreaction to the dangers of nuclear power plants for the halt in construction, but others point to high initial construction costs requiring huge amounts of up-front investment capital compared to coal and natural gas power generators. Three Mile Island did make the public suspicious of nuclear power and ask questions, not only about operational safety, but also about nuclear waste disposal.

Global environmental concerns in the United States

In 1987, President Ronald Reagan sent the Montreal Protocol Treaty to the Senate for ratification. The treaty committed nations to reduce emissions of **CFCs**. The treaty took effect on January 1, 1989, and began the phase out of ozone-depleting chemicals. In the 1990s, new coolants for refrigeration were used, requiring some redesign of equipment. Seven international meetings took place in the 1990s to revise the pact, and by 2000 enough progress was made to allow scientists to predict that the ozone layer would recover by the middle of the century. By 2000, the United States had reduced CFC emission to close to zero. The Secretary General of the United Nations, Kofi Annan, called the Montreal Protocol "Perhaps the single most successful international agreement to date."

A second global concern that gained significant public attention, especially in the 1990s, was global climate change. In the 1890s, some scientists predicted the possibility that pollution could cause climate change, but it was in the 1970s and 1980s that reports of global climate change began to receive public attention. In 1977, the National Academy of Sciences released a report that discussed the possibility of global warming. It also reported that 40% of man-made

Chlorofluorocarbons (CFCs) are chemicals that are known to deplete the ozone layer. The ozone layer protects the earth's surface from radiation. A common source of CFCs was Freon, used as a coolant in refrigerators and air conditioners.

(anthropogenic) carbon dioxide (CO2) remained in the atmosphere. The panel urged the scientific community to continue research to examine the issues. The chairman of the National Academy Panel that reported on global warming was Roger Revelle. Al Gore, a congressman from Tennessee, and a former student of Revelle's became a co-sponsor of the first hearings on global climate change. Late in the decade, NASA climate scientist James Hansen reported that global warming would become manifest in the following decade and would have a major impact on the environment. With concerns mounting, the United Nations established the Intergovernmental Panel on Climate Change (IPCC) in 1988.

At the same time as awareness of climate change was increasing, the United States was experiencing an expanding economy and rising expectations. US voters had rejected President Jimmy Carter's call to lower expectations and conserve resources in favor of Reagan's optimism and a culture that celebrated consumption and enjoying the many material benefits of a high standard of living. The world's largest economy also emitted the largest share of greenhouse gasses. With 5% of the world's population the United States emitted 25% of its CO_2. As the economy grew, people purchased larger homes, more appliances, and bigger automobiles, including **SUVs.** As a result, energy consumption increased as did emissions of gasses that contributed to global warming.

A sports utility vehicle (SUV) is a generic term for a vehicle similar to a station wagon, but built on a light-truck chassis. Since SUVs are considered light trucks, they are regulated less strictly than passenger cars under the US Energy Policy and Conservation Act for fuel economy, and the Clean Air Act for emissions.

The economic gains did not take climate change off the agenda. At the beginning of the new decade the Global Change and Research Act of 1990 became law. It established the Global Change Research Information Office to provide information to foreign countries to help mitigate and prevent the effects of global climate change. It became active after the 1992 Rio de Janeiro Earth Summit. By 1997, there was still mixed opinion on the amount and effects of anthropogenic greenhouse gasses, but consensus was moving scientists and governments to explore ways to slow down or halt climate change. Representatives of more than 160 nations met in Kyoto, Japan, in December 1997 to negotiate an agreement to limit the emissions of greenhouse gasses for more developed nations (MDCs). The Kyoto Protocol was the result and in it the Clinton administration (Al Gore, the former student of Roger Revelle, was vice president) agreed that the United States would reduce its greenhouse gas emissions to seven percent below 1990 levels. The reductions were to be achieved between 2008 and 2012. By the time Clinton had left office, the Senate had not ratified the treaty, and in 2001 President George W. Bush took ratification off the agenda.

Objections to the Kyoto Treaty were many. Aside from concerns that measures to meet the commitment would hurt the economy and discussion that the rapidly growing economies of India and China made any United States actions futile, doubts about the accuracy of the models used to predict the amount of climate change became louder. Skeptics, including George Easterbrook and Roger Bailey, cast doubts on the accuracy of the conclusions of the IPCC regarding climate change and the need for immediate action. Climate change skeptics explained that models, no matter how advanced, could not include most of the variables. Climate was an interaction of oceans, land, the atmosphere, and sun cycles, each having many sub-factors. Even among those who accepted that global warming was occurring, and that human activity was a major cause, it was debated whether adaptation was preferable to mitigation. In a 1999 NBC/ Wall Street Journal opinion poll only 11% agreed that concerns about global climate change were without justification and a 2000 Harris poll revealed that 72% of US citizens believed that greenhouse gasses caused global warming. Despite public opinion against skeptics' arguments, action to reduce greenhouse gas emission was a voluntary practice among environmental organizations, individuals, and businesses.

Over the two decades the environmental issues in the United States provoked a variety of responses. Problems that had local impact received action, even if slower and below the standards of critics, but often with lengthy litigation and debate. Concerns that involved the entire planet received mixed responses. Reasons for the differences may be due to political climate, economic well-being, political leadership, the immediacy of a local, visible problem vs. a global one in the indefinite future, or perceptions of costs and benefits that affected national interests.

Activity

Assessing public opinion polls

Visit www.americans-world.org to find summaries of polls on a variety of issues discussed in this chapter.

1 To what extent do the actions of political leaders coincide with public opinion?

2 How often do polls asking similar questions have results that differ significantly? Why?

3 Math link: What is margin of error? How many people should be polled for accurate results? What does "random" mean? (For an interesting perspective on randomness, read *The Drunkard's Walk: How Randomness Rules our Lives* by Leonard Mlodinow (2008).

Activity

Global climate change

The following sources discuss or provide information about global climate change:

Source A

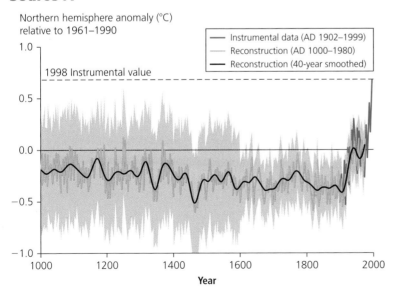

Millennial Northern Hemisphere (NH) temperature reconstruction (blue: tree rings, corals, ice cores, historical records) and instrumental data (red) from AD 1000 to 1999. A smoother version (black), and two standard error limits (grey) are shown.

Source: IPCC Third Assessment Report.

Source B

Using tree rings as a basis for assessing past temperature changes back to the year 1,000 AD, supplemented by other proxies from more recent centuries, [Michael] Mann completely redrew the history, turning the Medieval Warm Period and Little Ice Age into non-events, consigned to a kind of Orwellian "memory hole" … (the hockey stick graph) shows Mann's revision of the climatic history of the last millennium …

At that point, Mann completed the coup and crudely grafted the surface temperature record of the 20th century (shown in red and itself largely the product of urban heat islands) onto the pre-1900 tree ring record. The effect was visually dramatic as the 20th century was portrayed as a climate rocketing out of control. The red line extends all the way to 1998 (Mann's "warmest year of the millennium"), a year warmed by the big El Niño of that year. It should be noted that the surface record is completely at variance with the satellite temperature record. Had the latter been used to represent the last 20 years, the effect would have been to make the 20th century much less significant when compared with earlier centuries.

Source: Daly, John L. "'The Hockey Stick': A New Low in Climate Science." November 12, 2000. http://www.john-daly.com/hockey/hockey.htm.

Source C

The 1997 Kyoto Protocol, which calls for industrialized nations to reduce their CO_2 emissions to 95% of 1990 levels by 2012, is itself considered a difficult target to achieve. Yet the climate simulations lead to the conclusion that the Kyoto reductions will have little effect in the twenty-first century, and "30 Kyotos" may be needed to reduce warming to an acceptable level.

We suggest equal emphasis on an alternative, more optimistic, scenario. This scenario focuses on reducing non-CO_2 GHGs and black carbon during the next 50 years. Our estimates of global climate forcings indicate that it is the non-CO_2 GHGs that have caused most observed global warming. This interpretation does not alter the desirability of limiting CO_2 emissions, because the future balance of forcings is likely to shift toward dominance of CO_2 over aerosols. However, we suggest that it is more practical to slow global warming than is sometimes assumed.

Source: Hansen, James, et al. "Global warming in the twenty-first century: An alternative scenario." Proceedings of the National Academy of Sciences. August 29, 2000. https://www.pnas.org/content/97/18/9875.

Source D

They (many scientists) warned, too, of the related danger of global warming, a rise in the earth's temperature as a result of emissions from the burning of fossil fuels (coal and oil). These problems—and such others as the pollution of the oceans and the destruction of rain forests—required international solutions, which were much more difficult to produce. International conferences … produced some broad agreements on several global environmental problems. But there was no way to enforce compliance with them; and the United States government, during the Bush administration, publicly rejected some of the accords.

Source: Brinkley, Alan. 1999. *United States History: A Survey*, 10th edn. p. 1153.

Questions

1 What are two main points of source D?

2 Compare and contrast sources A and B.

3 To what extent and in what ways does source C support source B? To what extent does it support source A?

4 Using your own knowledge and the documents, discuss the international response to global warming during the 1990s.

Popular culture in the 1980s and 1990s

A case study of the popular culture of a country is an attempt to understand the aggregate trends of various cultural **memes** as an object for study. As cultural historian Robert Darnton wrote, "Historians have always taken what a society writes, publishes, and reads as a guide to its culture, but they have never taken all its books as guidebooks. Instead, they select a few works as representative of the whole and settle down to write intellectual history." In any nation the identification and assessment of the most significant trends in popular culture is problematic due to geographic, socio-economic and ethnic diversity; consequently, the task falls first to the selection of cultural products which collectively best serve as a "guide to its culture." Thus, expanding Darnton's point to include other forms of cultural media, a study of popular culture in the last two decades of the 20th century needs to include music, television, and film, as well as the printed word.

Television

In the United States, while major networks dominated television show production and audience share, the rise of cable television channels (cable had been available in some areas for decades, but the proliferation of satellite-based cable-only channels was a new development) significantly affected what people watched. The most successful challengers to broadcast networks were stations such as Music Television (MTV) which began broadcasting in 1981, the Entertainment and Sports Network (ESPN) which debuted in 1979 and became a 24-hour network in 1980, and Cable News Network (CNN) which began as a 24-hour news station in 1980. Spanish language stations used cable to expand their audience reach. By 1980, stations including Home Box Office (HBO) and Cinemax broadcast full length, commercial-free movies via cable as well. The rise in television offerings challenged the traditional entertainment venues, creating unease among broadcast television stations, the movie theater industry, and even booksellers, as more options competed for the entertainment dollar. The three national networks, ABC, CBS, and NBC, began to feel the pressure of this new competition.

The popular network shows reflected general societal trends. In the era of Ronald Reagan, comedies such as *Family Ties* reflected the conflict between old liberalism, represented by the parents, and the young, energetic conservatism of their son, Alex. Another, even more successful 1980s comedy was *The Cosby Show*, starring comedian

Activity

Historical analysis

Write one or two paragraphs to answer the following questions.

1 For what reasons did the United States government officially support and take supportive action on the Montreal Protocol and not the Kyoto Treaty?

2 Why did the Love Canal and Three Mile Island have national importance, even though the immediate effects were local and somewhat limited?

Memes Richard Dawkins first coined the term *meme* in the 1976 book *The Selfish Gene*. Dawkins writes: "Examples of memes are tunes, ideas, catch-phrases, clothes fashions, ways of making pots or of building arches. Just as genes propagate themselves in the gene pool by leaping from body to body via sperms or eggs, so memes propagate themselves in the meme pool by leaping from brain to brain via a process which, in the broad sense, can be called imitation."

TOK Link

Link to science

Read Richard Dawkins' definition of *meme* above. Do you think that ideas are evolutionary as are genes? In other words, are the longevity, proliferation, and influence of cultural ideas determined by the "survival of the fittest?"

489

Bill Cosby. Both shows illustrated a trend celebrating the idealized nuclear family. The 1980s was also the era of prime-time soap operas, shows dominated by themes of power, betrayal, and wealth, the most famous of which was *Dallas*. Detective shows continued to be popular, led by *Murder, She Wrote*, starring Angela Landsbury as a middle-aged amateur detective and writer. Shows centered around women characters were among the most-watched half-hours on television, including *Golden Girls* and *Rosanne*. The 1980s also saw continued success of *Monday Night Football*, the only continuing prime-time sports program. However, the show that wielded real power to set agendas was the CBS news magazine, *60 minutes*, which drew more viewers than any television show during the 1980s.

In the early part of the decade shows about women, mostly comedies, were among the most watched. *Rosanne*, starring Rosanne Barr as an outspoken, often abrasive lead character, began a trend of more edgy comedies. The decade also featured a shift away from traditional and largely content families solving universal problems, to dysfunctional families with dim-witted and incompetent fathers. Two such shows were both on the emerging fourth major network, Fox: *Married With Children* and *The Simpsons*. *The Simpsons* created by Matt Groening, was a consistently clever and topical cartoon that addressed a broad range of social issues. Debuting at the end of 1989, *The Simpsons* continued into the 21st century and became the longest-running sitcom (situation comedy) in United States' television history. While *The Simpsons* featured a loving, but imperfect, family, *Married With Children* portrayed, often crudely, the Bundy family as four confused, morally suspect, and overwhelmingly self-centered people. The 1990s also featured the rise of New York as the setting for television comedies. *Living Single*, was set in Brooklyn, while *Friends*, featuring four **yuppies**, and *Seinfeld*, an influential show in which stand-up comedian Jerry Seinfeld became famous for playing a semi-fictional version of himself, were both set in Manhattan. The end of the decade brought HBO's *Sex in the City*, also set in Manhattan, and based on the book by columnist Candace Bushnell. It focused on female lifestyle issues, discussing sexuality and the obsession with fashion in a frank and up-beat semi-documentary/fictional mode. More risqué offerings were also featured in the animated series *Beavis and Butt-head* created by Mike Judge for MTV. Two gritty dramas with a more criminally violent edge were HBO's *Oz* and *The Sopranos*. The confronting nature of these dramas pushed the four major broadcast networks to examine their offerings as the decade came to a close.

Film

As cable television expanded and the 1990s saw the rise of Internet use, some experts within the entertainment industry questioned the viability of the film industry based on the significant decline of movie theater attendance, a phenomenon already evident from the 1970s as television became more ubiquitous. However, movie-going, while not growing during the 1980s, did not decline either. Needing to offer a better and different experience than home viewing, theater owners offered enhanced features including stadium-style seating and dynamic sound systems, which helped attendance increase in

Activity

Race and television

Many 1980s and 1990s TV shows featured mainly people of one race. For example, *Living Single* had African American main characters, while the casts of *Cheers*, *Friends*, and *Seinfeld* were overwhelmingly Caucasian. Others, including an action show, *The A Team*, and several Steven Bochco dramas (*Hill Street Blues*, *NYPD Blue*, *LA Law*) had mixed casts.

1 Research the characters of television shows and audience appeal.

2 Were there identifiable settings or environments that favored racial/ethnic diversity?

3 What does the casting say about the television industry and its perception of its viewers?

4 What does the racial/ethnic characterization say about US popular culture and society?

5 Additional exploration: Observe the racial/ethnic, gender and age group make-up of current television shows. Record the advertisements. To what extent does advertising correlate with program demographics?

Yuppies is an extended acronym for Young Urban Professionals.

the 1990s, even as more entertainment options became available. The increased attendance brought the rise of the movie complex, multiple screens in a single facility, offering movie-goers a broad selection of films. Additionally, the double feature disappeared as studios sold their lesser films directly to cable movie stations, and later through mass-market sales as commercially produced video cassettes when the video cassette player/recorder became an increasingly popular home-viewing option. As the 1980s progressed, studios looked to blockbusters to make money, often choosing safe formulas, popular actors and sequels to big hits to insure profitability. But the broader distribution options also made room for independent film-makers to make a variety of more daring films addressing contemporary issues, and extended more innovation and style to traditional genres.

Studios often did well with low risk sequels, conventional formulas and proven movie stars. The original 1976 hit about an underdog boxer, *Rocky*, starring Sylvester Stallone, was followed by *Rocky II* in 1979, *Rocky III* (1982), *Rocky IV* (1985), and *Rocky V* (1990). Another theater-filler was Steven Spielberg's *Raiders of the Lost Ark*, the first of several films featuring Harrison Ford as Indiana Jones. Ford became the middle-aged male action hero of the 1980s and 1990s, starring in more than a dozen action hits from science fiction to techno-thriller. The science fiction genre proved popular with Arnold Schwarzenegger as the *Terminator* (1984) and Michael J. Fox as teenager Marty McFly in *Back to the Future* (1985), and in the multiple sequels that followed each film.

Buddy films were quite popular, especially the mixed-race buddy action/comedy. These films appeared to combine the tight drama of Tony Curtis and Sidney Poitier in the *The Defiant Ones* (1958) with the humor of Paul Newman and Robert Redford in *Butch Cassidy and the Sundance Kid* (1969). Three pairings of actors began successful series of films: Eddie Murphy and Nick Nolte in *48 Hours* (1982), Mel Gibson and Danny Glover in *Lethal Weapon* (1987), and Will Smith and Tommy Lee Jones in *Men in Black* (1997). A significant new direction in the buddy genre were female protagonists, as celebrated in *Thelma and Louise* (1991), starring Geena Davis and Susan Sarandon, which became a huge hit for director Ridley Scott.

Science fiction films, often a male-dominated genre, featured strong female characters in *The Terminator* (1984), featuring Linda Hamilton as the savior of mankind, and Sigourney Weaver as Ellen Ripley in *Alien* (1979) and the three sequels. Other important movies that featured female leads were *Fried Green Tomatoes* (1991), *The Joy Luck Club* (1993), and *The First Wives Club* (1996). Women took the lead behind the camera as well. Directors Susan Sondheim (*Desperately Seeking Susan*, 1985), Penny Marshall (*Big*, 1988), Nora Ephron

Double feature The showing of two films for the price of one ticket.

buddy film A long Hollywood tradition, usually featuring two mismatched and antagonistic men who, through facing adversity together, learn to respect each other and become friends.

A scene from *Rocky IV* directed by Sylvester Stallone in 1985.

(*When Harry Met Sally*, 1989) and Kathryn Bigelow (*Point Break*, 1991) were responsible for many critically-acclaimed and successful films.

Films by and about minorities were an important part of US film culture in the 1980s and 1990s. African American themes came to the forefront. For example, director Spike Lee's *School Daze* (1988) took a look at student life in a historically black college. Other well regarded Spike Lee films of the era include *Do the Right Thing* (1989) and *Malcolm X* (1992). *Boyz N the Hood* (1991), based in South Central Los Angeles, brought director John Singleton an Academy Award nomination for Best Director, the first such honor for an African American. Ramón Menédez's film *Stand and Deliver* (1988) was a movie portrayal of math teacher Jaime Escalante. The film detailed how Escalante led high school students in East Los Angeles to success in Advanced Placement calculus while fighting against the teaching staff, school administration and even some of their parents.

Literature

The 1980s and 1990s brought changes in the book retail industry. The proliferation of other forms of entertainment did not bring a decline to retail book sales. The 1980s featured yearly sales increases averaging 8%. However, how readers bought their books evolved over the two decades. In 1980, independent book stores dominated sales, but the rise of chain book stores, including E. Dalton and Crown, began to challenge the independents. Able to strike better deals with publishers, the chain stores discounted the retail prices of books, but often stocked only 15,000 to 20,000 titles, half that of the average independent, causing fear that the US book market would cater to the major publishers and well-known authors leaving little room for new writers. Many independent sellers did close, but by the early 1990s the book superstores Borders and Barnes & Noble challenged the discount sellers by offering many more titles, often well over 100,000, in a single store. By the end of the 1990s, the online bookseller Amazon, which offered more than a million different titles, challenged the dominance of the retail store.

The mainstay of sales continued to be the traditional genres. Spy novels by writers like Robert Ludlum and Ken Follett were frequently on best-seller lists. The romance genre remained perennially popular among women readers, with authors Judith Krantz and Danielle Steele, who wrote 20 bestsellers in 20 years, selling hundreds of millions of copies. James Michener, a prolific writer of historical fiction, published *Space* (1982) and *Poland* (1983) among other works. The horror novels of Stephen King were also popular. As the 1980s wore on, thrillers continued to be read by millions. New writers included Scott Turow and Sara Paretsky, whose novels revolved around corrupt lawyers and attorneys fighting ethical battles against a corrupt society. John Grisham, a popular writer of the legal thriller genre, sold over 60 million books in the 1990s, the most of any fiction writer. Vampires were a developing theme, as championed by Anne Rice, author of *Interview with the Vampire* (1973) the most popular vampire novel since Bram Stoker's *Dracula*. The technothriller further extended the genre, and its

Activity

Genre and gender

Gender often forefronts different points of view in its application to genre. Compare and contrast two US films from 1980–2000 of a similar theme or genre to highlight the different points of view represented through male and female characters. Your analysis might also want to include, the point of view of the director or screenwriter, and an analysis of gender roles and models.

Activity

Teen movies

Watch a selection of US teen movies from the 1950s (for example, *Rebel Without a Cause* or *Blackboard Jungle*).

Then compare them with US teen films from the 1980s.

1 Create a table of characters, conflicts, themes.

2 How do the movies reflect continuity across the decades?

3 How to the films demonstrate the changes that occurred over the 1960s and 1970s in the United States?

potential for adaptation, as demonstrated in the work of Tom Clancy, whose *The Hunt for Red October* was subsequently made into a video game and a film.

Many different categories of non-fiction found readers. Self-help books filled many store shelves. Diet books were quite popular, often two or three appearing on bestseller lists at the same time. Leo Buscaglia's books were widely read. Biographies and autobiographies of Ronald Reagan, Nancy Reagan, Princess Diana, and other well-known public figures came out every year. Science books were popular: Carl Sagan's *Cosmos* stayed on the bestseller list in 1980 and 1981, along with Alvin Toffler's *The Third Wave* in 1980. Books about successful business practices became a significant genre, with titles such as *In Search of Excellence* (1983) by Thomas J. Peters and Robert H. Waterman. Conservative and values books began appearing on the bestseller lists in the latter years of the Reagan administration, including *The Closing of the American Mind* by Allan Boom and *Cultural Literacy* by E. D. Hirsh, Jr. In the 1990s, books by conservative media stars such as Bill O'Reilly and Rush Limbaugh began a trend that continued into the next decade. The books of John Gray, including *Men are From Mars, Women are From Venus*, reflected a fascination of many Americans with the differences in male and female communication patterns. The exploration of men and women's innate behaviors also found expression in Rob Becker's *Defending the Caveman*, which began its decades-long run in 1991.

Popular music

Charismatic personalities, ethnicity, geography, and technology have influenced American popular music for more than a century. The end of the 19th and the first decades of the 20th century brought the first mass-production sound-playing devices, the Edison Phonograph and the Victrola, into homes in the United States. John Philip Sousa's band played to huge crowds and, according to the Dallas Wind Ensemble, "Before the Rolling Stones or the Beatles … they were the first musical act to travel more than a million miles and perform for more than a million people." Regional and ethnic influence in the forms of the Blues of Mississippi and Chicago, Appalachian Bluegrass, Nashville Country, soul, the Tejano sounds of Texas, Dixieland Jazz, and surf tunes from Southern California, have continually illustrated the variety of popular music. Despite the variety of forms, by the 1960s and 1970 rock was the dominant form of popular music. Perhaps the most prominent development in popular music during the 1980s and 1990s was the decline of Rock in relation to other musical styles.

The two decades saw decentralized musical development. Scores of locations, from the large metropolitan areas of New York and Los Angeles, to the traditional country music center of Nashville, to Seattle and dozens of college towns became starting points for a variety of musical forms. Hip Hop, Techno, Rockabilly, Heavy Metal, Christian Contemporary, Punk, Grunge, College Pop, Teen Pop, Roots Rock, and combinations of the aforementioned types all commanded significant audiences. Rappers, boy bands, girl bands, and pop

Activity

Analyzing best-seller lists

Research US best-seller book lists from the 1980s and 1990s to find out what books people read. A good starting point is the *New York Times* adult best-seller lists that are archived by year on the Hawes Publications Website: http://www.hawes.com/pastlist.htm. Identify trends in publishing and or particular themes or genres in research and writing that captured the popular imagination in 1980–2000. Discuss your findings in relation to current events and social issues discussed in this case study.

Activity

The Oprah effect

Oprah's Book Club is a popular segment of her TV talk show. Oprah Winfrey started the book club in 1996, selecting a new novel for viewers to read and discuss each month. Because of the book club's wide popularity, many obscure titles have become best-sellers, increasing sales in some cases by as many as several million copies. This occurrence is widely known as the Oprah effect. Select some examples from her lists in 1996–2000 and discuss why you think she chose to give them her influential seal of approval.

megastars filled television screens and blasted from automobile speakers during the era. Among the most important developments was the changing delivery of popular music, represented by music television channels, and the rise of hip hop from a local style to a national and then international form.

Music video channels, such as Music Television (MTV), did not invent music videos, but made them mainstream and available in the home 24 hours a day. Prince, an artist who at one time changed his name to a symbol, had several enormous hits including *Little Red Corvette* (1983), and a popular movie with its own hit song by the same name, *Purple Rain* (1984). Madonna's music videos featured provocative visuals and costumes, and captured one view of the commercialism of the decade with her song *Material Girl* (1984). Teen pop star Britney Spears' 1999 debut album *Baby One More Time* attracted millions of devoted fans, but was also the subject of criticism for her Lolita-like video rendition of the title tune. But, the biggest musical star of the era was Michael Jackson. Jackson's videos, among them *Thriller* (1982), featured elaborate choreography, costumes and sets, and catchy music. Jackson's productions became so much a part of pop culture that people who had never watched a music video or heard a song of his knew of the "King of Pop's" "moon walk" dance step and his signature glove. The visualization of pop music created a music-video industry of producers, writers, directors, and actors and made the video an indispensible part of popular music.

Some musicians and audiences rebelled against the elaborate production and easily accessible music rifts. A rockabilly revival, punk, new wave, and Seattle-based grunge provided alternatives to top Billboard Magazine charts pop. Additionally, a number of musicians jumped from style to style, often combining different musical themes while never settling on one. Texas's Michelle Shocked, who referred to herself as a "skateboard punk rocker" in her song *Anchorage* (1988), recorded songs ranging in style from big band, to folk, to punk, to blues, to country, and seemed to personify the rebellion against fitting into a predetermined musical label.

Perhaps the biggest musical development was rap, a genre that not only influenced music, but culture as well. Rap is the music of the hip hop culture. The music follows earlier African American music, but moved into a new form. Rap's beginning is said to have originated in 1970s in the Bronx (one of five boroughs that comprise New York City), when disc jockeys (DJs) took their turntables, amplifiers and loudspeakers onto the street and spun records, adding commentary and rhymes in rhythm. The DJs "scratched" records to make new sounds. "Rapper's Delight," a song by Sugarhill Gang, released in 1979, was the first rap single to get airtime on mainstream music radio. Run-DMC gained national fame in the early 1980s and rap took off quickly after that. Rap artists also included women, including Queen Latifah, whose work dealt with a variety of issues and provided a strong woman's voice.

Rap music, with lyrics that spoke of rebellion, violence, sex, poverty, and politics, mostly in "street language," became a major force in popular music, reaching more than 10% of all music sales by the end

TOK Link
Ethics

With the invention of digital music (first CDs, then mp3 files), the duplication of music became easy. Internet music-sharing services such as Napster appeared, facilitating the free distribution of music tracks without permission from the copyright holder.

Discuss the concept of ownership of creative products.

1 Who owns a song?
2 When a recording is purchased, what rights of use does the owner of the recording possess?
3 Examine the issue of copyright using the ethical reasoning of Jeremy Bentham and Immanuel Kant. How would each ethical system resolve the issue?

Activity
Applying cultural theory

Malcolm Gladwell's *The Tipping Point* (2000) explained his theory that social phenomena spread like disease epidemics. Gladwell came up with three rules—the law of the few, the stickiness factor, and the law of context—to explain why certain cultural products become popular. Read a summary of Gladwell's theory, then, choosing one musical form or performer, research the rise to popularity of your subject.

1 Who or what was responsible for spreading the form or performer?
2 What factors of the music/artist made people pay attention and desire more?

What environmental factors (context) were critical to the growth in popularity?

of the 1990s. According to author and Professor Renford Reese, in the year 2000 the audience for rap was three-quarters non-black: the influence of the hip hop culture had grown into many segments of US society. The sometimes menacing movements and rough language of rappers upset some members of mainstream society. While rap songs dealt with many issues and, similar to rock and roll, heavy metal, and other forms of popular music, ranged in tone from gentle to aggressive, and subject from love to war, rap and hip hop culture did evoke continual criticism as offensive, especially to women. However, when the Parents Music Resource Center formed in 1985 over concerns about explicit music lyrics, most of the group's original list of 15 "filthy" songs were heavy metal bands, and none were rappers. But as awareness of rap grew, so did criticism. West Coast rapper Ice T and the group Body Count provoked heated condemnation from the Bush administration with the 1992 song "Cop Killer." The controversies regarding rap lyrics continued throughout the decade, as did its popularity.

As the 20th century came to a close, there was no dominant musical style. The two decades featured genres that evolved, combined, disappeared, or grew to absorb other styles. Rap music was just one of many genres that included country, metal, and techno, along with songs from both pop princesses and maturing rock legends.

Conclusion

Popular culture continued traditions and evolved in form during the 1980s and 1990s. If examined for trends, television, film, and literature continued many previously popular themes, but brought diverse new material to new audiences. Hundreds of new musical artists appeared and sold millions of records, but, several artists, including Michael Jackson, Madonna, and Britney Spears dominated sales. Perhaps the most important musical development was rap, which significantly influenced both music and culture across the country. The popular culture of the period reflected broader social change, while also illustrating the desire for escapist entertainment and, for some, a wish for a return to previous, more comfortable and better-understood values.

Pop group Menudo featuring Ricky Martin (left) in 1987.

Queen Latifah performs at KMEL Summer Jam 1994 at Shoreline Amphitheatre in Mountain View California, August 13, 1994.

Activity

TOK Link

Language

Language is one of the Ways of Knowing.

1 What are the purposes of offensive language?

2 Who owns words?

3 Can an offensive word be rendered harmless by changing its meaning?

Find examples to illustrate your point, and discuss in your group.

Exam practice and further resources

Sample exam questions

1 Evaluate the successes and failures of the domestic policies of US presidents Ronald Reagan and Bill Clinton.

2 Analyze the main developments in the foreign policies of any two US presidents in 1980–2000.

3 For what reasons and with what results was democracy established in any two Latin American countries in 1980–2000?

4 Examine the social and economic impact of the Internet on one country in the Americas.

5 To what extent can it be said that globalization has benefitted North America to the detriment of South America?

Recommended further reading

Latin America

Lael Brainard & Leonardo Martinez-Diaz. 2009. *Brazil as an Economic Superpower?* Washington DC : Brookings Institution Press.

Jorge I. Domínguez & Michael Shifter (eds). 2008. *Constructing Democratic Governance in Latin America.* Baltimore: The John Hopkins University Press.

Fernando Henrique Cardoso . 2007. *The Accidental President of Brazil: A Memoir.* New York: PublicAffairs.

Flavia Fiorucci & Marcus Klein (eds). 2005. *Argentine Crisis of the Millennium: Causes, Consequences and Explanations.* Amsterdam: Aksant Academic Publishers.

Lois Hecht Oppenheim. 2007. *Politics in Chile: Socialism, Authoritarianism, and Market Democracy.* 3rd edn. Boulder: Westview Press.

Alfonso W. Quiroz. 2008. *Corrupt Circles: A History of Unbound Graft in Peru.* Woodrow Wilson Center Press/ The Johns Hopkins University Press.

United States

Thomas L. Friedman. 1999. *The Lexus and the Olive Tree: Understanding Globalization.* New York:Farrar, Straus and Giroux.

James Livingston. 2010. *The World Turned Inside Out: American Thought and Culture at the End of the 20th Century.* Lanham: Rowman & Littlefield Publishers, Inc.

Henry Raymont. 2005. *Troubled Neighbors: The Story of US–Latin American Relations from FDR to the Present.* Boston: Westview Press.

Richard Rhodes. 2007. *Arsenals of Folly: The Making of the Nuclear Arms Race.* New York: Alfred A. Knopf.

Online resources

"The Age of AIDS." *PBS-Frontline*. (The program online and supplementary information).
http://www.pbs.org/wgbh/pages/frontline/aids/view.

Globalization 101. The Levin Institute: The State University of New York.
http://www.globalization101.org.

GlobalSecurity.Org.
http://www.globalsecurity.org.

The National Security Archive. The George Washington University.
http://www.gwu.edu/~nsarchiv/index.htm.

Index

A

Aberhart, William 218, 222
able despotism 42
Acheson, Dean 250, 342, 346, 356
Acquired Immune Deficiency
  Syndrome (AIDS) 397, 399, 405,
  468, 480–2
Adams, John 23, 31, 52, 66, 68
Adams, John Quincy 49, 98, 117, 118
Adams, Samuel 23, 53
Adams–Onís Treaty 48–9
affirmative action 261
Afghanistan
  Soviet invasion 387, 406, 407, 410
African Americans 54, 190, 248, 253,
  435, 492
    Black Cabinet 189
    British colonies 20
    Civil Rights Act 259, 261, 262,
      418–19
    civil rights movement 242, 243,
      246, 251, 254–5, 257–9, 265, 267,
      373–4
    Digital Divide 474–5
    education 254–5, 258
    franchise 251, 254, 261, 262
    Great Depression 189–90, 192, 204
    Great Migration 189–90, 192
    Harlem Renaissance 189
    HIV/AIDS 480–2
    labor movement 190
    military draft 373–4
    NAACP 189, 190, 251, 345
    segregation 243, 251, 254–5, 257–
      9, 262, 267
    slavery 12, 20, 24, 54–5
    women 192
Agosti, Orlando Ramon 332–4
agrichemicals 479
agriculture
    Brazil 228–9, 230
    Dust Bowl 187–8, 191, 198, 205,
      206, 212, 214
    Great Depression 189, 197, 198,
      199, 205, 206, 211–12
    Latin America 225–6
Alamo, Battle of the 96, 97
Alaska 107, 479
Albanian-Serbian conflict 439, 442
Alberta 210
Albright, Madeleine 435
Alessandri, Jorge 389–90
Alfonsín, Raúl 457–8
Algeciras Conference 135
Algerian War 327, 332
Ali, Muhammad 374
Allen, Paul 469
Allende, Salvador 310, 312, 332,
  384–7, 391–3
Alliance for Progress 310–11, 379–80,
  384, 390

Alma-Ata Protocol 431
Alphabet Agencies 196–7
Álvarez, Gregorio 460, 461
Alvear, Marcelo Torcuato de 234, 239
Alves da Silva, Darly 465
American Anti-Imperialist League
  130, 131
American Civil Liberties Union (ACLU)
  345
American Exceptionalism 118, 406
American Relief Administration 186
American War of Independence 22–6,
  30–4, 51, 63, 89
    African Americans 54–5
    foreign intervention 33–4, 66
    guerrilla warfare 30, 34
    Native Americans 33–4, 54
    objectives 31
    scorched-earth policy 34
    Treaty of Paris 24, 34, 52, 54
Amish 21
amnesty, political 334
anarchism 117, 156
Andropov, Yuri 407–8
Annan, Kofi 485
Apache 100
Aquinaldo, Emilio 132
Arab-Israeli conflict 39, 268, 414–16
Arbenz, Jacobo Guzmán 298, 361,
  365–6
Arévalo Bermejo, Juan José 365
Argentina 60, 62, 142, 310, 311, 366,
  447
    Austral Plan 457
    Beagle Channel Islands 456, 458
    Catholic church 77, 325
    caudillos 62–3, 75, 76–7, 449
    Concordancia 236–8
    de Güemes 75
    de Rosas 63, 75, 76–7, 449
    Dirty War 331–2, 333, 455–6, 458
    the disappeared 333, 455–6
    economy 175, 177, 178–9, 226,
      227, 234–40, 320–2, 323, 332,
      333, 445, 449, 455, 456–7
    Ejército Revolucionario del Pueblo
      (ERP) 331, 333
    foreign investment 226, 235, 237
    franchise 239, 324
    Great Depression 227, 234–8, 240
    immigration 235
    independence 43–6
    indigenous population 60, 77
    industrialization 234–5, 236–8, 320,
      321, 325, 457
    Infamous Decade 320
    Justicialismo 320–2
    labor movement 178, 235, 320, 333
    Madres de la Plaza de Mayo 333, 334,
      455–6
    Malvinas (Falkland) War 333, 456

    military budget 321
    military regimes 227, 234, 236–9,
      325, 328, 331–4, 394, 447, 455–6,
      458
    nationalization 321
    neoliberalism 455–8
    New Argentina 321–2
    Operation Condor 327, 461
    Perónism 11, 313, 314, 320–7, 331,
      455, 457, 459   slavery 56
    social welfare program 321, 324
    Tragic Week 178
    United Officers Group 238
    US aid withdrawn 388
    US intervention 338
    women 323–5
    World War I 175, 176, 177, 179,
      235
    Yrigoyen 178, 234–6, 239
Aristide, Jean-Bertrand 443–4
Arizona 61, 95, 99, 148
arms race 383, 406–7
arms reduction talks 387, 407–10, 430
Arnold, Benedict 348
Arras, Battle of 163
Arthur, Chester 117
Artigas, José 63, 75
arts
    book retailing 492
    Cold War 348–55
    Cuba 306–7
    Depression era Canada 223–4
    literature 492–3
    McCarthyism 348–50
    New Deal 203–6
    Quiet Revolution 292
atomic weapons *see* nuclear weapons
Austin, Stephen 96
Austral Plan 457
Auto Pact 278–9
Avro Arrow Project 276
Aylmer, Colonel William 41

B

Bailey, Roger 486
Baker, James 411, 427
balkanization 38
Balkans conflict 439, 442
Baltimore 85
banana republics 361, 367
Barral, Countess de 76
Baruch, Bernard 151
Bassols Garcia, Narciso 338
Batista, Fulgencio 295, 297–9, 301,
  308, 368
Batlle Ibáñez, Jorge 462
Bay of Pigs invasion 298, 302, 371,
  380–1
Beagle Channel Islands 456, 458
Begin, Menachim 414
Belaúnde Terry, Fernando 451–2

Belgrano, General Manuel 43
Belzú, Manuel Isidoro 63
Bemis Heights, Battle of 33
Bennett Buggies 215
Bennett, R.B. 182, 208, 213–15, 220–1
Bennett's Boroughs 213, 220–1
Benton, Thomas Hart 204
Berlin blockade 256, 347, 379
Berlin Wall 371, 422, 426, 430
Bermúdez, Francisco Morales 451
Bernades, Artur 228
Bethune, Mary McLeod 189
Beveridge, Albert 131
Big Stick diplomacy 133–9, 144
bimetallism 124–5
Bishop, Maurice 311–12, 413–14
Black Hawk Down 439
Black Tuesday 184
Bladensburg, Battle of 85
Blossett, Colonel John 41
Bogotá 27
Bogota, Act of 380, 381, 382
Bogota Conference 339, 343
Boland Amendment 410, 416
Bolívar, Simón 41–4, 49, 56
Bolivia 63, 310, 311, 327, 446
    coca production 453
    franchise 340
    Guevara 298
    military coup 328
    Paz Estenssoro 340
    US intervention 338, 340
    World War I 175, 176
boondoggles 199
Bordaberry, Juan María 459, 460
Borden, Robert 161, 162, 166–71, 208
Bosnian-Serbian conflict 334, 399, 439, 442
Boston 13, 30
Boston Tea Party 26, 31
Bourassa, Henri 165, 168
Bourassa, Robert 283, 284
Bourbon monarchy 27, 29, 38–40
Bourbon reforms 22, 27–9, 38
Boves, José Tomás 40
Boxer Rebellion 133
Boyaca, Battle of 41
Braddock, General Edward 24
Brain Trust 195
branch plants 210
Brannan Plan 249
Brazil 49, 142
    Abertura 464, 465
    Afro-Brazilians 316
    Catholic church 47, 317, 465, 467
    caudillos 76, 315
    coffee production 175, 179, 227, 228–9, 230, 232, 234, 315, 317, 449
    Communism 316, 317, 338
    Constitution 46–7
    cruzado 465–6
    economy 175, 177, 178, 179, 227, 228–31, 316, 317, 329–31, 449, 464–5
    Estado Novo 231–3, 314–16

Great Depression 227, 229–31, 239
    immigration 176
    independence 9, 45–7, 62
    industrialization 178, 229–30, 231–4, 315–16, 319, 325
    land ownership 465, 467
    military dictatorships 328–31, 334, 383, 394, 464–5
    monarchy 46–7, 59, 62, 76
    native peoples 465
    neoliberalism 466
    October Coup 316–17
    Paulistas 317, 319
    Plan Real 466
    Portuguese colonial rule 9, 46–7
    posseiros 465
    poverty 330–1, 465
    Samba 316
    slavery 46, 60, 62, 76
    US treatment of 317
    Vargas 230–3, 314–19, 325, 329, 445
    World War I 175, 177, 178, 179–80
    World War II 231, 232, 233, 315
Brest Litovsk, Treaty of 153
Brezhnev Doctrine 387, 430
Brezhnev, Leonid 393, 408
brinkmanship 362, 382
Britain *see* United Kingdom
British colonies 59, 61
British East India Company 25–6
British Guiana 123
British Legions 41
British North America 9, 13–14, 63–4, 88
    administration and political control 12, 13, 15
    American Revolution *see* American War of Independence
    boundary 61, 86, 97–8
    clergy reserves 91
    Coercive (Intolerable) Acts 26
    congresses 25, 26, 30, 31
    Constitution Act 89–90
    Durham Report 64, 88, 93–4, 104
    economic system 15–17
    Fenian raids 86, 107
    Florida 27
    franchise 15
    French and Indian War 12, 22, 23–5, 27, 29, 89
    geography 13
    Loyalists (Tories) 52, 89, 90–1
    Middle colonies 20
    migration to 12, 17, 19–20
    native population 13–14, 19–20, 24, 33–4
    Navigation Acts 16
    New England 20
    Oregon boundary settlement 61, 95
    Oregon territory 86
    Parti Rouge 92
    Proclamation Line 24, 52
    rebellions of 1837 89–93, 104

    religion 20–1
    salutary neglect 16, 25
    slavery 13, 20, 24, 54–5
    social system 17, 19–20, 29
    Southern colonies 20
    taxation 25
    Ten Resolutions 91
    Townshend Acts 25
    Treaty of Paris 24, 34
    War of 1812 48, 63, 80–7, 105
    western frontier 24, 61
    see also Canada
broadband 472
Brock, Sir Isaac 84, 86, 87
Brown, George 104
Brown vs. Board of Education 254
Bryan, William Jennings 124–5
Brzeshinski, Zbigniew 387
Bubley, Esther 205
Buchanan, Patrick 478
Buck, Tim 219
Buenos Aires 27
Bull Moose Party 134, 140
Burgess, John 119
Burgoyne, General John 30, 33
Bush, George H.W. 398, 411, 417–31, 432, 434, 439
Bush, George W. 418, 425, 486
Bush, Jeb 418

C
cabildos 15, 29
California 61, 95, 98, 99, 100, 205
Calvo, Carlos 136–7
Cambodia 369, 370, 375, 376
Canada
    African Americans 55
    armed forces 161–3, 167, 169–71, 270, 271, 279
    Bennett's New Deal 214–15, 216
    boundary 61, 86, 95, 97–8
    British colony *see* British North America
    British North America Act 166, 212, 215, 274
    Chanak Affair 174, 208
    civil rights movement 282
    Clear Grits 104
    Cold War 271, 279
    confederation 88, 104–8
    Crown corporations 272
    Dominion status 64, 88, 104–8, 115, 160, 161, 172, 212
    East 104
    economy 165–7, 173–4, 209–12, 242, 271, 272, 288–9
    First Nations 13–14, 109, 222, 243–4, 273, 275, 282
    flag 281
    franchise 169–70, 222, 275
    French Canadians 63, 64, 88, 91, 104, 106, 107, 208, 218, 225, 242, 273, 282–7, 291–2
    Great Coalition 104
    Great Depression 208–25
    Grits 271

hockey 224–5
immigration 92, 169–70, 212, 243–4, 273, 281, 292
independence 11, 63–4, 88–9
Indian Act 222
industrialization 210, 243
internment 244, 283
Korean War 279, 358, 359
labor movement 173, 174, 219–21, 273
languages 63, 64, 88, 92, 107, 282, 292, 293
Lower 63–4, 89, 90, 92–3, 104
Loyalists (Tories) 52, 89, 90–1, 271
Maritimes Rights Movement 208, 209
"militia myth" 87
monarchy 11, 273
nationalism 281
NATO 279
Newfoundland 243, 271
NORAD 271, 363–4
October Crisis 282–7
Parti Bleu 104
political system 59, 88, 271–2, 273–4, 288, 290
population 243–4, 272, 273
post-World War II 242, 243–4, 270–1
provinces 63
Quebec see Quebec
rebellion 64
Regina Manifesto 216–17
Rupert's Land 104
social welfare program 209, 243, 271, 272, 278, 279, 280–1, 288
Statute of Westminster 88
Upper 63, 89, 90–1, 104
US independence 34, 63
US regional dominance 11, 88, 105, 119, 210
Vietnam War 374, 377
War of 1812 48, 63, 80–7, 92, 105
War Measures Act 283–4
West 104
women 169
World War I 160–74, 208, 283
World War II 244, 270, 283
Canadian Patriotic Fund 161
cancion de protesta 306
Capra, Frank 206
Carabobo, Battle of 41
Caracas Declaration 366
Cárdenas, Lázaro 314, 318, 445
Cardona, José Miró 299
Cardoso, Fernando Henrique 464, 466–7
Cardwell, Edward 106
Caribbean 11, 57, 61
Carnegie, Andrew 131
Carranza, Venustiano 142
Carrera, Rafael 63, 75–6
Carter, Jimmy 329, 361, 387–8, 399, 400, 405, 406, 410, 411, 444, 486
Cartier, George Étienne 104
Caseros, Battle of 77
Casey, William 416

Cass, Lewis 111
castas 18, 38
Castelo Branco, Humberto 329–30
Castillo Armas, Carlos 366
Castillo, Ramón 234, 320
Castro, Fidel 11, 242, 244, 284, 296–312, 327, 334, 368, 379, 380–2, 392
Castro, Raúl 297, 298, 299
caudillos 62–3, 74–9, 95, 96, 449
Cavallo, Domingo 458
Cedras, Raoul 439, 444
cell phone 475–6
censorship
    Argentina 320, 323, 324
    Chile 394
    military regimes 328, 393–5
Central Intelligence Agency (CIA) 361, 363, 384, 407
    Chile 385
    CIA assets 424
    contra insurgency 311, 410–11, 416–17
    Cuba 298, 368, 381, 382
    El Salvador 412–13
    Guatemala 361, 363, 364–6
    Honduras 366
    plausible deniability 363
    Vietnam 370
Cervera, Admiral Pascual 129
Chacabuco, Battle of 43, 44–5, 46
Chaing Kai-shek 345
Chambers, Whitaker 249, 342
Chamorro, Violeta 424
Chamoun, Camille 414
Chanak Affair 174, 208
Chaplin, Charlie 350
Chapultepec, Act of 338
Charlottetown Conference 105–6
Château Clique 64, 90, 92
Cheney, Richard 411
Chernenko, Konstantin 408
Cherokee 109–10, 112
Chesapeake incident 80, 81
Chiang Kai-shek 360
Chibas, Eduardo 297
Chicago Boys 446
Chickasaw 109
Chile 60, 142
    abolition of slavery 56
    Allende 310, 312, 332, 384–7, 391–3
    Beagle Channel Islands 456, 458
    Catholic church 392, 395, 456
    CIA operations in 385
    Cold War 389–95
    Communism 338, 384–5, 389
    constitution 445
    Dirty War 333, 334, 394–5
    the disappeared 394–5
    economy 175, 177, 179, 226, 389–90, 446, 449
    education 393
    franchise 74, 388, 391
    immigration 176
    independence 43–6, 62
    indigenous population 60
    industrialization 178
    left/right division 386–7, 389–93

military regimes 227, 328, 334, 385–7, 393–5
Mothers Centres 391
nationalization 392
neoliberalism 446
Operation Condor 327, 461
Pinochet 328, 332, 334, 385–7, 393–5, 445, 446, 456
Portales 75
US aid, withdrawal 388
US intervention 338, 384–5
World War I 175, 177, 178, 179
China 141–2, 347, 376, 384, 422
    Communist Revolution 345, 360
    Korean War 346, 355, 357–8, 360
    Tiananmen Square massacre 418, 431
    trade with 441
    US policy towards 133, 141
    Vietnam War 369
chlorofluorocarbons (CFCs) 485
Choctaw 109–10, 111
Christopher, Warren 443
científicos 226
civil rights movement
    Canada 282
    United States 242, 243, 246, 251, 254–5, 257–9, 265, 267, 291, 373–4
Clark, Charles Joseph 270, 282, 288–9
Clausewitz, Carl von 244
Clay, Henry 80, 83
Clemenceau, Georges 155
Cleveland, Grover 117, 123–4, 126, 127
clientism 447, 449
Clinton, Bill 398–9, 418, 420, 432–44, 478, 479, 480, 482, 486
Clinton Doctrine 439, 440, 443, 444
Clinton, Henry 69
Clinton, Hillary 432, 433
Cohn, Roy 346, 347
Cold War 242, 336–7, 387–8, 410, 430, 468
    Afghanistan 387, 406, 407, 410
    Alliance for Progress 310–11, 379–80, 383, 384, 390
    anti-americanism 367–8
    arms expenditure 243, 279, 406–10
    arms race 383, 406–10
    arts 348–55
    Bay of Pigs invasion 302, 303, 371, 380–1
    Berlin blockade 256, 347
    Chile 389–95
    CIA operations 311, 361, 363, 364–6, 370, 381, 412–13
    Cuban Missile Crisis 256, 276, 277, 298, 362, 379, 390
    Cuban Revolution 368
    détente 406
    espionage 249–50, 344–5, 347, 382, 407
    Federal Loyalty Program 342
    film industry 350–1, 468

HUAC 249–51, 337–40, 348–9, 351
Justicialists 322
Kennedy Doctrine 379, 382
Korean War 337, 339, 346, 355–60, 361, 369
Latin America 325, 328, 338–50, 361–7, 383–95, 410–14, 445, 450
Latin American military regimes 328–34, 361, 380, 383–5, 388
McCarthyism 253–4, 266, 338, 341–55
Middle East 414–17
military expenditure 339, 388
nuclear weapons 356, 362–3, 406–10
popular culture 337, 350–2, 353, 355
PSYOPS 407
religious groups 350, 353
space race 353
United States 243, 245, 246, 249–51, 266, 336–7
US aid 368
US policy of containment 329, 337–50, 361, 362, 370, 379, 388, 406
Vietnam War 337, 360, 369–78, 379, 383, 384
Collor de Mello, Fernando 466
Colombia 49, 60, 451 175 170 171 356
Bogota revolution 343
constitution 63
independence 38–9, 41, 42
Korean War 359–60
monoculture economy 449
Panama Canal 135–6
slavery 56
World War I 175, 178, 179
colonies, European 9–14, 57, 61
British see British colonies; British North America
economic systems 15–17
emigration to 12, 17–20
Enlightenment 22–3, 35, 42
independence see independence movements
political control 12, 15
religion 20–1
slavery see slavery
social systems 17–20
Spanish see Spanish colonies
Colorado 61, 95, 99
Columbus, Christopher 12
Cominform 364
Comintern 219, 350, 364
Committee of Five 31
Communism
Argentina 333
Bolshevik revolution 153, 156, 173, 178, 341
Brazil 316, 317, 338
Canada 218, 219, 220, 223
Chile 338, 384–5, 389

China 344, 345, 346, 431
Cold War see Cold War
Comintern and Cominform 219, 350, 364
Cuba 296, 297, 298, 300, 302–12, 338, 368, 410
domino theory 364, 365, 370, 388
El Salvador 406, 410, 411–13, 445
Grenada 410, 413–14
guerrilla movements 328, 333
Latin America 333, 364, 366, 384–5, 406, 410–13, 451–2
McCarthyism and HUAC 253–4, 266, 338, 341–55
New Deal 202
Nicaragua 329, 406, 410–11, 445
North Korea 355–6
padlock law 218, 219
Popular Front 350
Red Scare 156, 337, 341, 344
Shining Path 451–2
Soviet bloc 426, 430–1, 442
Truman 245, 246, 248, 249–51
US anti-Communism 341–55
US policy of containment 329, 337–50, 361, 362, 370, 379, 388, 406
see also Korean War; Vietnam War
compact disc (CD) 468, 476
comparative advantage 478
computer 468–75, 476
Comuneros 28
Comunidades Eclesiásticas de Base 411
Concord, Battle of 30
Condor, Operation 327, 461
Conference of Security and Cooperation in Europe (CSCE) 430
Connally, John 255, 268
Connecticut 20, 54
conservatism 62, 63, 75
Constitutional Convention 24, 65–7
consultas 446–7, 458, 461, 462, 466
consumerism 223, 354
containment, US policy of 329, 362, 370, 379, 388, 406
Continental Congress 24, 26, 30, 31, 33, 64, 68
Continentalism 118
Continentals 51
contras 311, 410–11, 416–17, 422–4
Coolidge, Calvin 117, 184
Cooper, James Fennimore 98
Cooperative Commonwealth Federation 216–17
Córdoba, Treaty of 40
Cornwallis, Lord 34
Corporatism 313
Cortiñas, Nora Morales de 455
Costa Rica 62, 140, 364, 412
World War I 175
Cotton, Joseph 204
Coughlin, Father Charles E. 202–3
counter-culture 373–4, 375
court packing 199–201
Creeks 109
creoles 15, 18, 27, 38–9, 55–6, 62

Haitian Revolution 37
independence movements 27, 28, 29, 39, 40
Crerar, Thomas 209
crimes against humanity 334
criollos 15
Cronkite, Walter 374
Crosby, John 289
Cross, James 284
cruzado 465–6
Cuba 411, 412, 413, 445
bastistadaros 301
Bay of Pigs invasion 302, 303, 371, 380–1
Castro 11, 242, 244, 284, 296–312, 368, 380–2
Castro's personality cult 304–5
Catholic church 304
CIA operations 368, 381, 382
Communism banned 338
dissidents 301, 304, 306
economy 227, 295, 301–2, 449
emigration from 301, 304, 306
Fidelistas 300, 301, 304, 309, 310, 328
healthcare and education 296, 297, 304, 307–8
independence 130–1, 295, 296
isolation 310, 312
land reform and nationalization 303–4
national militia 300, 304
Platt Amendment 130–1
population 295–6, 300, 308
racial segregation 296, 308
rectificación 304
regional impact of revolution 310–12, 325, 327, 334, 390, 450
Revolution 242, 244, 295–9, 325, 327, 334, 368, 379, 390
slavery 60, 62, 295
Soviet support 302–3, 305, 309, 312, 379, 382, 410
Spanish-American War 118, 126–32, 295
Spanish colonial status 61, 126–8, 295
sugar cane industry 295–6, 301–2, 303–4, 449
US domination and control 295, 296, 297, 298, 301–2, 303
US occupation force 130
women 307
World War I 175
Cuban Missile Crisis 256, 276, 277, 298, 362, 379, 390
Curaçao 61
Currie, Sir Arthur 167, 172
cyberspace 472

D
D'Abuisson, Roberto 412
Dancing Rabbit Creek, Treaty of 110
Darwin, Charles 118, 119
Dawes, Charles 160
Dawes Plan 160

Dawkins, Richard 489
Dayton Accords 442
De Gaulle, Charles 293
death squads
    Argentina 331–2, 333, 455–6, 458
    Brazil 330
    Chile 332, 394–5
    El Salvador 413
Debs, Eugene 152
Deep-throat 269
Delaware 20
democracy 59, 66
    Latin America 445–67
    see also franchise
Deng Xiaoping 431
dependency theory 449
deregulation 400–1, 434
Desbiens, Jean-Paul 292
descamisados 323–4
Desert Shield, Operation 426, 428
Desert Storm, Operation 426–30
Desha, Joseph 82
Dessalines, Jean-Jacques 37–8
détente 406
DEW Line 271
Dewey, George 128–9
Díaz, Porfirio 142
dictatorships 59, 63, 242, 244, 310, 314
    Argentina 227, 234, 236–9, 325, 328, 331–4, 449, 455–6, 458
    Brazil 230–1, 314–19, 325, 328–31, 334, 383, 464–5
    Chile 227, 328, 385, 393–5
    Cuba 304–5
    foreign support 314
    Guatemala 227, 328, 365–6
    Haiti 383, 439, 443–4
    Latin America 327–34, 365–6, 380, 397, 445, 449–57, 459–65
    Panama 424–5
    Perú 450–1
    Uruguay 459–64
    US support 244, 328–9, 361, 366, 380, 383–5, 388, 445, 450
Diefenbaker, John George 270, 271, 275–8, 280, 289
Diem, Ngo Dinh 370–9
Digital Divide 473–5
digital video disc (DVD) 476
diplomacy 244
Dirty War 331–2, 333, 394–5, 455–6, 458
the disappeared 333, 394–5, 455–6, 464
Dixiecrats 245, 251
Dobrynin, Anatoly 408
Dollar Diplomacy 140–1, 144, 176, 339
domestic policy 244
Dominican Republic 61
    military coup 328
    US military aid 383
    US occupation 142
Dominicans 75
domino theory 364, 366, 370, 388
dot-com bubble 473
Douglas, Thomas C. 271

Douglas, Tommy 216, 222, 284
Drago Doctrine 137
Drago, Luis 137
drugs, illegal 480, 481, 482–4
    production and trafficking 405, 424, 443, 451, 452, 453
Duarte, José Napoleón 411–13
Dukakis, Michael 417
Dulles, Allan 363, 365–6
Dulles, John Foster 362, 363, 364, 365–6, 368, 381
Duplesis, Maurice 218–19, 290
Dupuy de Lôme, Henri 128
Durham, John Lambton, Earl of 93
Durham Report 64, 86–7, 88, 104
Dust Bowl 187–8, 191, 198, 205, 206, 212, 214
Dutch colonies 12, 59, 61
Dutra, Eurico Gaspar 231, 316–17
Duvalier, François 383

E
early adapter 476
Earned Income Tax Credit (EITC) 435
Easterbrook, George 486
Echota, Treaty of 110, 112
economics
    Brazilian miracle 330–1
    buying on the margin 184
    Chicago School 332, 445–6
    currencies pegged to US dollar 228
    dot-com bubble 473
    European colonies 15–17, 46
    Fair Deal 246, 249, 252
    free-trade 59, 62, 278
    globalization see globalization
    gold standard 121, 123–5, 228, 268
    Great Depression 182–240
    inflation 206
    ISI 182, 227, 233, 236–8, 239, 244, 301, 313, 315, 325, 332, 364, 445
    Keynesian 196, 215, 268, 272, 402
    laissez-faire 62
    Latin America 55
    Long Depression 116, 121
    mercantilism 15–16, 46, 52, 449
    monetary policy 116, 185–6
    neoliberalism 445–6, 466
    New Deal 182, 191, 192, 195–207, 246
    panics 183, 184
    price fixing 197
    price gouging 268
    protectionism 16, 62, 186, 210, 213, 227
    Reaganomics 399–403, 420
    recessions 183
    social cost 400
    stagflation 288, 332, 333
    supply-side 332, 399–402
    tariffs 186
    trickle-down 400
    valorization 229
Ecuador 60
    constitution 63
    franchise 74

independence 41, 42
    military coup 328
    slavery 56
    Velasco 313, 314
    World War I 175
education
    Argentina 321, 324, 325
    Canada 278, 291–2
    Cuba 296, 297, 304, 307–8
    populist regimes 313
    United States 249, 258, 261, 262, 352, 420
    US racial segregation 254–5, 267
Eisenhower Doctrine 414
Eisenhower, Dwight David 250, 252–5, 271, 345, 348, 352, 358–68, 370, 380–1
Ejército Revolucionario del Pueblo (ERP) 331, 333
El Salvador 422, 445
    communist insurgency 406, 410, 411–13
    Duarte 411–13
    military dictatorships 328, 383–4, 388, 445
Elders, Jocelyn 435
Ellison, Ralph 204
email 471, 473
enlargement, doctrine of 439
Enlightenment 22–3, 35, 42, 59, 66
environmental issues 440, 441, 468, 479, 484–9
    acid rain 468, 480
    Amazon region 465
    climate change 397, 468, 479, 480, 484, 485–9
    globalization 479, 485–9
    Kyoto Treaty 479, 486, 488
    Montreal Protocol 405, 479, 485
    ozone depletion 405, 468, 479, 480, 484, 485
    pollution 419–20, 479–80, 484–5
    Rio de Janeiro Earth Summit 486
    US measures 262, 267–8, 387, 398, 405, 419–20, 479–80, 486
Equal Rights Amendment 267
Erlichman, John 269
Espin, Vilma 307
espionage 249–50, 344–5, 347, 382, 407
ethnocentrism 141
eugenics 119, 120
Evans, Arthur "Slim" 221
Evans, Walker 205
executive branch of government 150
extraterritoriality 136–7
Exxon Valdez oil spill 419–20

F
Fair Deal 246, 249, 252
Falkland War 333, 456
Falwell, Jerry 481
Family Compact 63–4, 89–91
fascism 202, 309–10, 313, 320, 324
Fathers of the Confederation 104
Federal Bureau of Investigation (FBI) 342, 346, 352
federal government 61, 64–6, 67–73

Federal Loyalty Program 342
Federalist Papers 69, 71–3
Fenian raids 86, 107
Ferreira Aldunate, Wilson 461
Fidelistas 300, 301, 304, 309, 310, 328
Figueiredo, Joao 331, 464–5
film industry 468, 490–2
    Cold War 350–1, 468
    HUAC investigations 250, 341, 344, 351
fisheries 479–80, 484
Fiske, John 119
flexible response 379
Florida 23, 27, 48–9
Ford, Gerald 385, 406
foreign legions 41
foreign policy 244
Fort Henry 86
Fort McHenry 85
Fort Michilmackinac 84
Fort Pitt 34
Fort Ticonderoga 33
Fortunato, Gregório 318
Foster, Vince 433, 435
Fourteen Points 154
France 49
    American War of Independence 33, 34, 66
    colonies see French colonies
    French and Indian War 23–4, 89
    French Indochina 360, 369–70
    Napoleonic Empire 29, 35, 38
    Napoleonic Wars 22, 29, 36, 37
    Revolution see French Revolution
franchise 62
    Argentina 239, 324
    Bolivia 340
    British colonies 15
    Canada 169–70, 222, 275
    Chile 74, 388
    Latin America 74
    Native Americans 74, 222
    United States 152, 251, 254–5, 261, 262, 267
    women 152, 169–70, 389
Francia, José Gaspar Rodríguez de 63
Franco, Itamar 466
Franklin, Benjamin 23, 31, 66, 67
Free Trade Area of the Americas (FTAA) 444
Freeman's Farm, Battle of 33
Frei, Eduardo 390–1, 392
French colonies 9, 12, 23, 59, 61
    French Indochina 360, 369–70
    Louisiana 23
    North American 23
    race and social hierarchy 35–6
    Saint Domingue 9, 35–8
    slavery 35–8
French and Indian War 12, 22, 23–5, 27, 29, 89
French Revolution 23, 31, 34, 35, 36
Friedman, Milton 269, 332, 445–6
Frondizi, Arturo 367
Front de Libération du Québec (FLQ) 273, 283–7

Fuchs, Karl 344, 347
Fujimori, Alberto 451–4

G
Gadsen Purchase 100
Gairy, Eric 311
Gaitán, Jorge Eliecer 297, 339
Galbraith, John Kenneth 264, 354
Galtieri, Leopoldo 333, 456
Galton, Francis 119, 120
Gamayel, Bashir 415
García, Alan 452
Garfield, James 117
Gates, Bill 469, 471
Gates, Major General 33
Geisel, Ernesto 331, 464
General Agreement on Tariffs and Trade (GATT) 440, 441
Geneva Accords 370, 373
gens de coleur 35–6, 37–8
Georgia 20
German reunification 430, 442
Ghent, Treaty of 85, 86
Giap, General Vo Nguyen 372
Gingrich, Newt 434
Glass-Steagall Banking Reform Act 197
Glassco Commission 279
globalization 115, 116, 175, 397, 446, 468, 475
    effect on US 476–9
    environmental issues 479–80, 485–9
    multinational corporations 465
    opposition to 441, 477, 478
    popular culture 477
gold standard 121, 123–5, 228, 268
Goldwater, Barry 261
Gompers, Samuel 130
Good Neighbor policy 338
Gorbachev, Mikhail 407, 408–10, 426, 430–1
Gore, Al 479, 486
Goulart, Joao 317, 329, 383
Gozenko, Igor 250
Gran Colombia 41, 42–6, 49
grand blancs 35
Grant, General Ulysses S. 116
Great Compromise 61, 68–9
Great Depression 182–240
    Argentina 227, 234–8, 240
    Brazil 227, 229–31, 239
    Canada 208–25
    causes 183–4, 197, 209–11
    Federal Reserve monetary policy 185–6
    Latin America 225–40
    National Recovery Administration 197
    popular culture 205–6, 223, 224–5
    protectionism 186, 210, 213, 227
    recession of 1937 206–7
    role of religion 222–3
    social effects 186–94, 212
    stock market crash 184–5, 210–11, 229–30
    United States 183–207

US banking reforms 197
Great Lakes 13, 86
Great Migration 189–90, 192
Great Mississippi Flood 186
Great Railway Strikes 116
Great Society 257, 260–5, 266, 371, 373
Great White Fleet 134–5
greenhouse gases 480, 486
Greenland 11
Grenada 445
    New Jewel Movement 310, 311–12, 413–14
    US invasion 312, 398, 410, 413–14
Grito de Dolores 39
Group of Seven 223–4
Group of United Officers (GOU) 320
Guadalupe-Hidalgo, Treaty of 95, 99, 100–1, 103
Guam 127, 128, 130
Guatemala 63, 75–6, 140, 298, 412, 446, 447
    CIA covert operations 361, 363, 364–6
    military dictatorship 227, 328, 365–6
    US aid withdrawn 388
    war of independence 11
    World War I 175
Güemes, Martín Miguel de 75
guerrilla warfare
    Brazil 47
    Cuba 126, 297, 298
    El Salvador 411–13
    Guevara's handbook 310
    Haitian Revolution 36, 37
    Latin American guerrilla movements 328, 330, 331–2
    Perú 451–2
    Philippines 132
    Spanish colonies 28
    Uruguay 460, 461–2
    Vietnam 369–78
    War of American Independence 30, 34, 39
Guevara, Ché 297, 298–9, 301–3, 309, 310, 392
Gulf of Tonkin Resolution 369, 371
Gulf War 418, 426–30
Guthrie, Woody 193, 223
Guzmán, Abimael 451

H
Habbib, Philip 414
habeas corpus 330
Habsburg monarchy 15, 22, 27
Hague Conference 137
Haig, Alexander 411, 414, 415
Haiti 445
    dictatorships 383, 439, 443–4
    French colonial rule 9, 35–8
    Haitian Revolution 11, 35–8
    independence 37–8
    monarchy 37, 62
    slavery 35–8
    Toussaint L'Oveture 11, 36–7
    US occupation 142, 444

Venezuelan Revolution 41, 42
World War I 175
Haldeman, H.R. 269
Halibut Treaty 174
Halifax, Nova Scotia 30
Halle, Louis Joseph 339
Hamilton, Alexander 65, 67, 68, 72
Hansen, James 486
Harding, Warren G. 117, 186, 195
Harkness, Douglas 276
Harlem Renaissance 189
Harrison, Benjamin 117
Hastie, William 189
Havana 27
Hawaii 122–3
Hawley-Smoot Tariff Act 186
Hay Bunau-Varilla Treaty 388
Hay, John 133
Hayes, Rutherford B. 117
healthcare
    Argentina 321, 324
    Canada 243, 272, 278, 279, 281
    Cuba 296, 297, 304, 308
    populist regimes 313
    United States 249, 256, 257, 260,
        261, 262–3, 268, 432–3, 480
Hearst, William Randolph 126
Hellman, Lillian 349
Henry, Richard 72
Hepburn, Mitchell 219
Hepburn's Hussars 219
Herrera, José de 98, 102
Hezbollah 416
Hidalgo, Father Miguel 38, 39
Hinkley, John 401
Hispanic Americans 190–1
Hispaniola 35
    see also Haiti; Saint Domingue;
        Santo Domingo
Hiss, Alger 249, 266, 341–2, 354
HIV 480; see also Acquired Immune
    Deficiency Syndrome (AIDS)
Ho Chi Minh trail 373
Hollywood Ten 250, 341, 350–1
Honduras 412, 423
    CIA operations in 366
    dictatorship 227, 366
    US intervention 140, 366
    World War I 175
Hoover, Herbert 117, 150, 151, 182,
    183, 185–7, 195, 197, 202, 203
Hoover, J. Edgar 342, 346, 352
Hoovervilles 187
Hopkins, Harry 197–8
horizontal integration 117
House Un-American Activities
    Committee (HUAC) 249–51, 253–4,
    341–2, 344, 348–9, 351
Howe, Joseph 107
Hudson, Rock 481
Hudson's Bay Company 89
Huerta, General Victoriano 142
Hughes, Sam 161, 162, 165, 169
human rights 388, 394–5, 410, 412
Humphrey, Hubert H. 266
Hunter Patriots 91
Hunter's Lodges 86
Hussein, Saddam 426–30, 439

I
Ibáñez del Campo, Carlos 321, 389
impeachment 266, 269, 435–7
Imperial War Cabinet 168, 172
Imperial War Conference 168
Import Substitution and
    Industrialization (ISI) 182, 227,
    233, 236–8, 239, 244, 301, 313,
    315, 325, 332, 364, 445
impressment 80, 81
independence movements 9, 61–2
    economic and social effects 51–7
    the Enlightenment 22–3, 35, 42
    foreign intervention 33–4, 41, 42,
        48–9, 52
    foreign volunteers 41
    Haiti 9, 11, 35–8
    origins 22–6
    Spanish colonies 9, 11, 27–9,
        38–46, 48, 52
    United States see American War of
        Independence
Indian tribute 39
indigenous populations 12–13, 60,
    109, 248
    American War of Independence 34
    British North America 24
    Bureau of Indian Affairs 109
    Canada 13–14, 109, 243–4, 273,
        275, 282
    Canada's Indian Act 222
    European colonies 13–14, 17,
        18–19, 28
    franchise 74, 222
    French and Indian War 12, 22, 24
    Indian removals 109–12
    Latin America 55–6, 74, 77, 109
    Tecumseh 81, 82, 85
    Trail of Tears 109–10
    United States 53–4, 81, 82, 88,
        109–12
Industrial Workers of the World
    (IWW) 153
industrialization
    Argentina 234–5, 236–8, 320, 321,
        325, 457
    Brazil 178, 229–30, 231–4, 315–
        16, 319, 325
    Canada 210, 243
    Latin America 16, 178, 225–6,
        228, 229–30, 231–5, 236–8, 313,
        445
    United States 51, 52, 61, 68, 96
Infamous Decade 320
inflation 206
infrastructure 117
integrated circuit (chip) 471, 476
intendancy system 27
Inter-American Development Bank
    368
Inter-American Military System 328
Inter-American Reciprocal Assistance
    and Solidarity Agreement 338
Inter-American Treaty of Reciprocal
    Assistance 338–9
Intermediate Nuclear Force Treaty
    410
International Court of the Hague
    334
International Criminal Court 478
International Labour Organization
    174
international law 137–9, 478
    crimes against humanity 334
International Monetary Fund (IMF)
    434, 459
internationalism 147
Internet 468, 471–5, 476, 477, 490
internment 244
interstate highway system 253
Inuit 273
Iran 414
    CIA operations in 363
    hostage crisis 387–8, 406,
        416–17
    Iran-Iraq War 414
    Iran–Contra affair 411, 416–17
Iraq
    Gulf War 418
    invasion of Kuwait 398, 426–30
    Iran-Iraq War 414
Irish immigrants 19, 96, 144, 255
    Mexican-American War 99
Irish legion 41
Iroquois Confederation 19
Irreconcilables 159
isolationism 130, 147, 155, 156,
    160
Israel, Arab-Israeli conflict 268,
    414–16, 439
Iturbide, Augustín de 40

J
Jackson, General Andrew 85–6, 87,
    91, 109–10
Jamaica 62
Japan 141–2, 156
    Russo-Japanese War 134, 140
Jay, John 64, 67, 69
Jefferson, Thomas 30, 31–2, 52, 53,
    61, 65–6, 68, 69, 71
    War of 1812 80–2, 83, 84
Jeffersonian democracy 265
Jesuits, expulsion 28, 75
Jim Crow laws 251, 262
Jiménez, Tucapel 395
jingoism 124
Joao VI, King of Portugal 46–7
Jobs, Steve 470, 471
Johnson, Daniel 292
Johnson, General Hugh 197
Johnson, Lyndon Baines 190, 257,
    260–5, 279, 329, 360, 369, 371–3,
    374, 380, 383–4
Johnson, Magic 482
Johnson Treatment (Way) 261
Joseph Bonaparte, King of Spain 29,
    38, 42
Junín, Battle of 42
juntas 38, 39, 236, 310
Just Cause, Operation 425
Justicialismo 320–2
Justicialists 322
Justo, General Augustín 234,
    236

K

Kazan, Elia 341, 351
Kelly, John 415, 416
Kennan, George 338, 339
Kennedy Doctrine 379, 382
Kennedy, John Fitzgerald 244, 253, 255–60, 261, 266, 276, 360, 368, 370–1, 372, 379–83
Kennedy, Robert 258, 374, 384
Kent State shootings 375–6
Key, Francis Scott 85
Keynes, John Maynard 196, 215, 272, 402
Khmer Rouge 376
Khrushchev, Nikita 371, 382
Kim Il-Sung 356
King, Martin Luther 257, 258, 262, 374
King, William Lyon Mackenzie 182, 208–9, 212–13, 214–16, 219, 243, 270–1, 283
King-Byng Affair 208
Kipling, Rudyard 120
Kissinger, Henry 373, 376, 385
Knights of Columbus 353
Korean War 279, 337, 339, 346, 347, 355–60, 361, 369
Kosovo 442
Kosygin, Alexei 393
Ku Klux Klan 258, 262
Kubitschek, Juscelino 329
Kuwait, Iraqi invasion 398, 426–30
Kyoto Treaty 479, 486, 488

L

La Plata viceroyalty 27
labor movement
    African Americans 190
    Argentina 178, 235, 320, 331, 333
    Brazil 233, 330, 465
    Canada 173, 174, 219–21, 273
    Chile 391, 395
    CIA operations 363
    Latin America 177–8
    military regimes 328, 329, 330, 333
    Red Scare 156, 337, 341
    Taft-Hartley Act 248–9
    United States 116, 117, 152–3, 190, 199, 243, 245, 246, 248–9, 252, 341, 342, 402, 404, 434, 440
    Wagner Act 199, 246, 248
    World War I 152–3
Lacalle, Luis Alberto 462
Laffer, Arthur 401
Lake, Tony 440
lame duck presidency 420
Lancaster, Burt 204
Lange, Dorothea 205, 206
Laos 369, 370, 376
Laporte, Pierre 283
latifundias 225
Latin America
    agriculture 225–6
    Alliance for Progress 310–11, 379–80, 383, 384, 386

American United Fruit Company 297, 361, 365
anti-americanism 367–8, 384, 450
authoritarian tradition 449
banana republics 361, 367
Catholic church 59, 62, 63, 75–6, 77, 313, 450, 456
caudillos 62–3, 74–9, 95, 96, 449
CIA operations in 298, 311, 361, 363, 364–6, 368, 410–11, 412–13, 416–17
clientism 447, 449
Clinton Doctrine 443, 444
Cold War 325, 328, 338–50, 361–8, 383–95, 412–13, 445, 450
Communism 39, 364, 366, 410–13, 451–2
consultas 446–7, 458, 461, 462, 466
creoles 55–6, 62
Cuban revolution, impact of 310–12, 325, 327, 333, 450
democracy 445–67
dependency theory 449
dictatorships 59, 63, 295, 397, 445, 449–57, 459–65
Dollar Diplomacy 140–1, 176
economic policies 55, 175–9, 226–7, 244
fascism 202, 313, 315–16, 320, 324
foreign investment 175–7, 226–7, 235
forms of government 59–60
franchise 74, 239, 340
geography 13, 61, 449
global integration 175
Great Depression 225–40
indigenous population 56, 60, 74, 77, 109
industrialization 16, 178, 225–6, 228, 231–5, 313, 445
Inter-American Reciprocal Assistance and Solidarity Agreement 338
ISI 182, 227, 233, 236–8, 244, 301, 313, 315, 325, 332, 364, 445
labor movement 177–8
Mann Doctrine 383, 384
mestizos 60
migration to 119, 176
military regimes 227, 239, 242, 244, 310, 314, 325, 327–34, 361, 380, 383–5, 388, 393–5, 397, 445, 449–57, 459–65
military training 328–9, 364, 370, 450
monoculture economies 175, 227, 228–30, 232, 234, 244, 295–6, 301–2, 315, 317, 449
neoliberalism 445–6, 455–8
neopopulism 446–7, 458
Nixon's visit 366–8, 379, 384
populist leaders 313–27, 449
post-World War II 242, 244
regionalist divisions 62, 75
slavery 56, 60, 76
social structure 55–6, 62

socialism 244, 364
Summit of the Americas 444
US aid 338, 339, 362, 368, 380, 383, 388, 434
US economic importance 178–9
US economic interests 361, 364, 365, 384–5, 391
US foreign policy 135–40, 244, 338
US Good Neighbor policy 338
US intervention 295, 298, 311–12, 328–9, 338–9, 361, 364–6, 380–1, 398, 410–14, 416–17
US military aid 338, 339, 383, 450
World War I 175–80
Lattimore, Owen 346
Laurier, Wilfred 160–1, 162, 164, 167, 168–9, 208
Lausanne Conference 174
Lawrence, Jacob 204
Lead belly 206
League of Nations 156–9, 172, 173, 174
Lebanese civil war 398, 414–16
Lee, General Robert 116
Lee, Spike 482, 492
Lee-Enfield rifle 161, 172
Lesage, Jean 290, 294
Levesque, Rene 273, 289, 291
Lewinsky, Monica 438
Lewis and Clark expedition 31
Lexington, Battle of 30
liberalism 62, 63, 75
Liberia 140–1
liberty tree 65
limited war 355, 371
Lincoln, Abraham 82, 98
Liverpool, Lord 83
Livingston, Robert 31
Llosa, Mario Vargas 452
Lloyd George, David 155, 167–8, 172
lobos 18
Locke, John 23
Lodge, Henry Cabot 120, 157–9
Lomax, John 206
London Conference (1866) 107
London, Treaty of 155, 156
Long Depression 116, 121
Long, Huey P. 202, 203
Long Telegram 338
Louisiana 23
Louisiana Purchase 31, 61, 96
Love Canal 484
Loyalists (Tories) 52, 89, 90–1
Lugar, Richard 442
Luis, Washington 228, 229–30
Lusitania, RMS 145–6

M

MacArthur, General Douglas 356, 357–9
McCarthy, Joseph 246, 249–51, 253–4, 266, 337, 343–4, 345–52
McCarthyism 253–4, 266, 338, 341–55
McCurran Internal Security Act 344
Macdonald, Sir John A. 104, 105, 106, 107
McFarlane, Robert 416

McGovern, George 263, 269
MacKenna, Colonel Juan 45
MacKenzie, William Lyon 83, 90–1
McKinley Tariff 121–2
McKinley, William 117, 123, 127–8, 130, 131–2, 133, 135
Madero, Francisco 142
Madison, James 65, 67–9, 71, 80, 82–3, 85
Madres de la Plaza de Mayo 333, 334
Magaña, Álvaro 412
Mahan, Alfred Thayer 120, 134
Mai Lai massacre 374–5
Maipú, Battle of 43, 45
Malvinas War 333
Manhattan project 250, 344
Manifest Destiny 95, 96, 97–9, 105, 118
Manila 27
Manila Bay, Battle of 129
manipulated democracy 329
Mann Doctrine 383, 384
Mann, Thomas 383
Mao Zedong 345, 356, 360, 369
Maritimes Rights Movement 209
Marsh Report 272
Marshall, George C. 250, 345, 346
Marshall, Thurgood 258
Martí, José 126, 297, 298
Martínez de Hoz, José Alfredo 455, 456
Marxism 117
Maryland 20
Massachusetts 20, 30, 53, 54, 64–5
Massera, Emilio Eduardo 332–4
Matos, Hubert 301
Matthews, Herbert 299
May Day 317
medical care *see* healthcare
Medici, Emilia Garrastazu 330
Meighen, Arthur 208
meme 489
Mendes, Chico 465
Menem, Carlos 334, 458
Mennonites 21
mercantilism 15–16, 46, 52, 449
MERCOSUR 459
mestizos 18, 28, 39, 60
Métis 273
Mexican-American War 61, 95–103, 105
Mexico 49, 410, 412
  abolition of slavery 39, 56, 97
  Cárdenas 314, 445
  Catholic church 39, 95
  caudillos 95, 96
  científicos 226
  Constitutional Decree for the Liberty of Mexico 39
  economy 175, 227, 441, 443, 451
  geography 13
  government 59
  independence 95
  indigenous population 56
  Mexican-American War 61, 95–103, 105
  Mexican Revolution 142, 178
  monarchy 40, 59, 62, 95
  Monroe Doctrine 118

NAFTA 441
Peso Crisis 443, 459
population 51
Porfiriato 11
Revolution 40
Santa Anna 96, 97, 98, 100
territorial losses 61
US economic aid 434
war of independence 11, 38, 39–40, 62
Zapatista 441
Zimmerman Telegram 148–9
Mexico City 13
Middle East
  US intervention 268, 398, 414–17, 418, 426–30
migration
  Cuban dissidents 301, 304, 306
  effect of globalization 477
  from Europe 12, 17–18, 19–20, 116, 119, 121, 176
  Great Migration 189–90, 192
  Hispanic Americans 190–1
Miles, General Nelson 129
Miller, Arthur 349, 351
Milosevic, Slobodan 442
Minh, Ho Chi 360, 369–70
Miranda, Francisco de 40, 45
Mitchell, Charles 184
monoculture economies 175, 227, 228–30, 232, 234, 244, 295–6, 301–2, 315, 317, 449
Monongahela, Battle of 24
monopoly ports 16
Monroe Doctrine 49–50, 101, 117–18, 123–4, 136, 144, 379, 456
Monroe, James 49, 101, 117–18
Montcalm, Marquis de 89
Montesquieu 23, 66
Montojo, Admiral Patricio 128–9
Montreal 13, 30, 84, 86, 92, 293
Montreal Protocol 405, 479, 485
Moral Diplomacy 141–2, 155
moral hazards 186
Moral Majority 481
Morales, Carlos 136
Morelos, Father José Maria 39
Morgan, J.P., Jr. 184
Moroccan Crisis, First 135
mp3 player 493
Mujica, José 460
mulattos 18, 39
Müller, Lauro 180
Murrow, Edward R. 352
Mussolin, Benito 313, 320
Mutually Assured Destruction (MAD) 362–3, 407

N
Napoleon I 36, 37, 42, 83, 84, 85
Napoleonic Code 62
Napoleonic Wars 22, 29, 36, 37, 43, 45–7, 48, 80, 81, 83–4, 85, 117
  Spanish colonies 22, 29, 38, 41
A Nation at Risk 420
National Association for the Advancement of Colored people 189, 190, 251, 345

national debt 25
National Recovery Administration (NRA) 197
nationalism 30
Native Americans *see* indigenous populations
Naval Club Pact 461
Navigation Acts 16
Nebraska 187
neoliberalism 445–6, 455–8, 466
neopopulism 446–7, 458
Netherlands
  American War of Independence 33
  colonies *see* Dutch colonies
Nevada 61
Neves, Tancredo 465
New Brunswick 63, 89, 104, 106, 107
New Deal 182, 191, 192, 195–207, 246
  the arts 203–6
  opposition to 202–3
New Deal, Bennett's 214–15
New England 54, 83
New Federalism 265–9
New Frontier 255–6
New Granada 27, 41
  Comuneros 28
  War of Independence 38–9, 40–1, 42
New Hampshire 20
New Jersey 20, 54
New Jewel Movement 310, 311–12
New Look 361–7
New Mexico 61, 95, 99, 100
New Orleans, Battle of (1815) 85–7
New Republicanism 252–3
New Spain
  War of Independence 38–40
  see also Mexico
New World 12
new world order 431, 439
New York 20, 30, 54
Newfoundland 63, 106, 212, 243, 271
Nicaragua 135, 445
  Catholic church 311
  Communism 329, 406, 410–11, 412
  contras 311, 410–11, 416–17, 422–4
  Iran–Contra affair 411, 416–17
  monoculture economy 449
  Sandinistas 310, 311, 384, 388, 410–11, 422–4
  Somoza regime 383, 384, 388, 410
  US intervention 140, 311, 384, 398, 416–17, 422–4, 445
  World War I 175
Nixon, Richard Milhous 255, 265–9, 341, 342, 348, 366–8, 369, 370, 373, 375–6, 384–5, 387, 406
noble savage, concept of 19
Noriega, Manuel 417, 424–5
North American Aerospace Defense Command (NORAD) 271, 363–4
North American Free Trade Agreement (NAFTA) 434, 440–1
North Atlantic Treaty Organization (NATO) 279, 399, 442, 443

North Carolina 20
North Korea 439
    see also Korean War
North, Oliver 416
Nova Scotia 63, 89, 104, 105–6, 107
NSC-141 and NSC-68 documents 340
nuclear accidents 484, 485
nuclear weapons 247, 250, 347, 352, 356, 362–3, 379, 439, 442
    arms reduction talks 387, 407–10, 430
    Cuban Missile Crisis 256, 276, 277, 362, 379, 390
    FCDA 353–4
    limited war 355
    Mutual Assured Destruction 362–3, 407
    nuclear holocaust literature 354
    Strategic Arms Limitation Talks (SALT) 376
nueva trova 306
Nunn, Sam 442, 444

O
O'Connor, Sandra Day 405
October Crisis 282–7
O'Donojú, Juan 40
O'Higgins, Bernardo 43–5, 46
oil crisis 288, 331, 406
Oklahoma 109, 187
Old Three Hundred 96
O'Leary, Hazel 435
Olney, Richard 123–4
On To Ottawa Trek 219, 220–1
O'Neil, Tip 401, 402
Onís, Luis de 48–9
Ontario 63, 89, 107, 271
Open Door Policy 133
Oregon territory
    boundary settlement 61, 95
    US annexation 88, 97–8, 100
Oregon Treaty 98
Organization of American States (OAS) 310–11, 339, 381, 382, 424, 425
Organization of Petroleum Exporting Countries (OPEC) 268, 331, 406
Ortega, Daniel 410, 424
Ortiz, José María 234
Oswald, Lee Harvey 259
Ottawa 107, 270, 274
Our Lady of Guadalupe 40
Oval Office 269

P
Padilla, Herberto 306, 307
padlock law 218, 219
Páez, José Antonio 75, 79
Paine, Thomas
    Common Sense 22–3
País, Frank 299
Palestinians 415
Pan American Financial Conference 178
Panama 41, 388, 417
    Noriega 424–5

US invasion 398, 418, 424–5
World War I 175
Panama Canal 120, 126, 135–6, 366, 388, 412, 449
Papineau, Louis Joseph 91–3
Paraguay 63, 327
    Stroessner 383
    World War I 175, 176
Paredes, General Mariano 98
Parent Commission 292
Paris Peace Accords 373
Paris Peace Conference 154–9, 179
Paris, Treaty of (1783) 24, 34, 52, 54
Paris, Treaty of (1898) 130
Parks, Gordon 205
paternalism 132
Patriote Rebellion 91–3, 104
patronage 165
Paulistas 317, 319
Paz Estenssoro, Victor 340
Peace Corps 257
peace dividend 431
Peace Progressives 160
Pearson, Lester Bowles 270, 278–81, 294
Pedro I, Emperor of Brazil 47
Pedro II, Emperor of Brazil 76
Peña, Manuel de la 99
Peninsular War 29, 41, 43, 46–7
peninsulares 15, 18, 27, 28, 38, 39
Penn, William 21
Pennsylvania 20–1, 54
pension provision
    Canada 209, 243, 272
    United States 199, 202, 402
peons 75
Perkins, Frances 192
Perón, Evita 320, 323–4, 327
Perón, Isabel 331, 455
Perón, Juan 11, 313, 314, 320–7, 331
Perot, Ross 432, 441
Pershing, General John Joseph 153
Perú
    coca production 451, 452, 453
    constitution 63
    dictatorships 227, 328, 450–1
    economy 179, 452–4
    Fujishock 452–4
    independence 42, 43, 44
    rebellion of Túpac Amaru II 28
    Shining Path 451–2
    slavery 56
    World War I 175, 178
Peso Crisis 443, 459
Pétion, Alexandre 41, 42
petit blancs 35
Philadelphia 13, 30
Philadelphia Convention 59–66
Philadelphia Plan 267
Philby, Kim 347
Philippines
    anti-US rebellion 132
    independence 132
    US annexation 127, 128–30, 132
Pinkney, William 81
Pinochet, Augusto 328, 332, 334, 385–7, 392, 393–5, 445, 446, 456
piracy 17

Plains of Abraham, Battle of 89
Plan de Iguala 40
Platt Amendment 130–1
plausible deniability 363
plebiscite 460
Plessy vs. Ferguson 251, 267
Podgorny, Nikolai 393
Point Four programs 339
Pol Pot 376
Polk, James Knox 95, 96, 97–8, 100, 102
Pollock, Jackson 204
polychlorinated biphenyls (PCBs) 484
popular culture
    Brazil 316
    Cold War 337, 350–2, 353, 355, 468
    Cuba 306
    globalization 477
    Great Depression 205–6, 223, 224–5
    music 468, 493–5
    protest songs 392, 457
    United States 468, 489–95
Popular Front 350
populist regimes, Latin American 313–27, 449
Porfiriato 11
Pork Chop Hill, Battle of 359
Portales, Diego 75
Portuguese colonies 12, 450
    Brazil 9, 46–7
    mercantilism 46
    Napoleonic invasion 46–7
    political control 15
Portuguese Revolution 47
posseiros 465
Powell, Colin 410, 416, 425, 444
Prats, General Carlos 393
Prebisch, Raúl 237–8
Prestes, Júlio 228, 230, 230
Prevost, Sir George 84
Prince Edward Island 63, 89, 104, 105–6
prohibition 295
the Prophet 81, 82
protectionism 16, 62, 186, 210, 213, 227
protectorates 122–3
Prussia
    American War of Independence 33
PSYOPS 407
Public Works Administration 189, 198
Puerto Rico 60, 61, 127, 128, 130
Pulitzer, Joseph 126

Q
Quakers 20–1
Quebec 63, 88, 89, 92, 106, 107, 242, 271–2
    Catholic church 163, 222–3, 291–3
    October Crisis 282–7
    Quiet Revolution 243, 273, 290–4
    separatists 168, 218, 273, 282–7, 288, 289, 292–4
    World War I 163, 165, 168, 170–1

Quebec Conference 106
Queenston Heights, Battle of 84, 86–7
Queremistas 316
Quiet Revolution 243, 273, 290–4
Quito 13

R

racial segregation 243, 251, 254–5, 257–9, 262, 267, 296, 308
radio 202, 203, 205–6, 218, 225
 McCarthy era 351
 Radio Free Europe 363
 US public broadcasting 262
Rafael, Jorge 332
railways
 Canada 166
 Great Railway Strikes 116
 United States 116, 248
Randolph, A. Philip 190
Randolph, John 82
Reagan, Nancy 483
Reagan Revolution 398, 418
Reagan, Ronald 265, 306, 311, 397, 398, 399–417, 425, 430, 479, 486, 490, 493
Red Scare 156, 337, 341, 344
refrigeration 226
Regina Manifesto 216–17
Regina Riot 221
Rejón, Manuel 100–1
religious dissenters 20–1
Reno, Janet 433, 435
republicanism 59, 62
Reservationists 156
responsible government 64, 86–7
Revelle, Roger 486
Rhee, Syngman 356
Rhode Island 20, 54
Rideau Canal 86
Ridgway, General Matthew 358
Rio de Janeiro 46
Rio Conference 338
Rio Earth Summit 486
Rio Treaty 338–9
Roberts, Justice Owen 199
Roca-Runciman Pact 236
Rochambeau, Comte de 34
Rockefeller Report 385
Rodriquez, Carlos Rafael 302
Rolling Thunder, Operation 371
Roman Catholic church
 Argentina 77, 325
 assassination of Romero 388
 Bourbon reforms 27, 28
 Brazil 47, 317, 465, 467
 British colonies 19
 Canada 63, 88, 91, 106, 163, 222–3, 291–3
 Chile 392, 395, 456
 Cold War 353
 Comunidades Eclesiásticas de Base 411
 Cuba 304
 Jesuits 28, 75
 Latin America 59, 62, 63, 75–6, 77, 313, 388, 450, 456
 liberal and conservative thinkers

 62
 Mexico 39, 40, 95
 Nicaragua 311
 Spanish colonies 20, 27, 28
Romero, Oscar 388
Rooke, James 41
Roosevelt Corollary 118, 136, 140
Roosevelt dime 202
Roosevelt, Eleanor 189, 192, 195, 203–4
Roosevelt, Franklin Delano 182, 183, 194, 195–207, 245, 256, 338
Roosevelt, Theodore 118, 119, 120, 124, 127, 129–30, 133–6, 138–9, 140, 144
Rosas, Juan Manuel de 63, 75, 76–7, 449
Rose, Fred 219
Rosenberg, Ethel and Julius 249–50, 344–5, 347
Ross, Chief John 112
Ross rifle 161, 169, 172
Rothko, Mark 204
Rough Riders 129–30
Rousseau, Jean-Jacques 23, 66
Royal Twenty Centers 213, 221
Rúa, Fernando de la 459
Rubin, Robert 434
Rupert's Land 89, 104
Rush-Bagot Treaty 86
Rusk, Dean 362
Russia 12, 49, 117, 141, 442
 Bolshevik revolution 153, 156, 173, 178, 341
 Russo-Japanese War 134, 140
 World War I 153
 see also Soviet Union
Rust Belt 478
Rwandan civil war 439, 440

S

St. Alban's raid 106
Saint Domingue 35–8
 economy 35
 race and social hierarchy 35–6
 see also Haiti
St. Lawrence Seaway 243, 253, 271
St. Patrick's Battalion 99
Saint-Laurent, Louis Stephen 270, 271, 275
Salinas, Carlos 441, 444
salons 74, 76
salutary neglect 16, 25
Samoan Islands 121–2
San Francisco 98
San Lorenzo, Battle of 43
San Martín, José de 42–5, 49, 56
Sandinistas 310, 311, 384, 388, 410–11, 422–4
Sanguinetti, Julio María 461–2
Santa Anna, Antonio López de 96, 97, 98, 99, 100
Santa Fe Ring 101
Santa Fe Trail 100
Santo Domingo 35, 61
 Haitian Revolution 36
São Paulo 13
Saratoga, Battle of 30, 33
Sarkis, Elias 414

Sarney, José 465
Saudi Arabia 416, 426
savings and loan associations 421
Schine, David 346, 347
School of the Americas 364, 394, 450
Schultz, George 408, 411, 415, 416, 417
Schwarzkopf, General Norman 427
scorched-earth policy 34
Scott, General Winfield 99
Seeger, Pete 348
Seminoles 109
Seregni, Líber 461
Seven Years' War *see* French and Indian War
Seward, William 106
Shafter, General William 129
Shallala, Donna 435
Shawnee 82
Shay's Rebellion 53, 64–5, 67
Sherman, Roger 31, 68
Shining Path 451–2
Sierra Madre 13
Silva, Lula da 467
Singletary, Amos 73
slavery
 abolitionists 38, 39, 76, 97
 Brazil 46, 60, 62, 76
 European colonies 9, 12, 13, 19
 Haiti 9, 35–8, 62
 Latin America 56, 60, 295
 Mexico 39, 56, 97
 New Spain 39
 rebellions 35–8, 62
 Texas 97–8
 United States 20, 24, 51, 54–5, 60, 68–9, 96, 97, 98, 105, 205
 Venezuela 40–1, 51
Slidell, John 98
Smith Act 342
Smith, Goldwin 119
social cost 405
Social Credit 218
social Darwinism 118–20
Social Gospel movement 222–3
social welfare programs
 Argentina 321, 324
 Canada 209, 220–1, 243, 272, 278, 279, 280–1, 288
 Cuba 297, 304, 307–8
 military regimes 329
 populist regimes 313
 United States 199, 202, 207, 249, 252, 261, 262, 268, 402, 434–5, 480
socialism
 Canada 173, 216
 Latin America 244, 364
 Red Scare 156, 337, 341
 United States 117, 152–3, 156, 199, 202
Soler, General Miguel Estanislao 44–5
Somalian civil war 399, 431, 439–40
Somoza regime 383, 384, 388
Sons of Liberty 25
South Carolina 20, 30, 34
Southeast Asia Treaty Organization (SEATO) 370, 377

Soviet Union
  Afghanistan 387, 406, 407, 410
  arms reduction talks 387, 407–10,
    430
  Brezhnev Doctrine 387, 430
  Cold War 336–7, 364, 369, 410,
    430
  Cuba 302–3, 305, 309, 312, 379,
    382, 410
  Cuban Missile Crisis 379
  dissolution 398, 418, 422, 431
  expansionism 356, 369
  Korean War 358
  Latin America 333, 392, 393
  Middle East 414–15, 426
  nuclear weapons 356
  perestroika and glasnost 422
  space race 353
  see also Russia
space race 353
Spain
  American War of Independence 33
  Bourbon restoration 38–40
  colonies see Spanish colonies
  Constitution of Cádiz 62
  Joseph Bonaparte 29, 38, 42
  Peninsula War 29, 41, 43
Spanish-American War 118, 126–32,
  295
Spanish colonies 12, 13–14, 59, 61,
  450
  administration and political control
    13, 15, 20, 27
  Bourbon reforms 22, 27–9, 38
  cabildo 15, 29
  castas 18, 38
  Catholic church 20, 27–8, 40
  Comuneros 28
  creoles 15, 18, 27, 38
  Cuba 61, 126–8, 295
  divisions between 13, 38
  economic system 15–17, 27–8
  Florida 23, 27, 48–9
  geography 13, 38
  Gran Colombia 41, 42–6
  Guatemala 11
  Havana 27
  independence 9, 11, 13, 15, 23,
    27–9, 38–45, 48–9
  Indian tribute 39
  juntas 38, 39
  Louisiana 23
  Manila 27
  Mexico 11, 38, 39–40, 95
  migration to 12, 17–18
  military defense 28–9
  monopoly ports 16
  Napoleonic Wars 22, 29, 38
  native population 13–14, 17, 18–
    19, 27, 28, 39
  peninsulares 15, 18, 27, 28, 38, 39
  Perú 28
  Philippines 127, 128–9
  Puerto Rico 127, 128, 130
  race and social hierarchy 17–19,
    28, 29, 38

Santo Domingo 35, 36
slavery 13, 19, 39, 40–1
social system 17–19, 38
taxation 27
Texas 48–9
Treaty of Córdoba 40
Venezuela 40–4
viceroyalties 27, 38
Spanish Succession, War of 27
Spencer, Herbert 118–19, 120
sport 224–5
Springfield rifle 129
Sputnik 353
Stalin, Josef 219, 300, 345, 356, 358
"Star Spangled Banner" 85
Star Wars see Strategic Defense
  Initiative
Starr, Kenneth 437–8
Steinbeck, John
  The Grapes of Wrath 188, 206, 351
Stevenson, Adlai 252, 342, 346, 359
Strategic Arms Limitation Talks
  (SALT) 376, 407
Strategic Arms Reduction Treaty
  (START) 430
Strategic Defense Initiative (SDI) 407,
  408–9
Stroessner, Alfredo 383
Strong, Josiah 119, 120
suburbs 243, 248
suffrage see franchise
Sullivan, John L. 118
survivalist entrepreneurship 192
Swamp Fox 30
System of Central American
  Integration (SICA) 423

T
Taft, Robert 247, 248, 348
Taft, William Howard 117, 132,
  140–1
Taft-Hartley Act 248–9
Taylor, General Zachary 98
Taylor, Paul 205
Tea Act 25–6
technological revolution 468–76
Tecumseh 81, 82, 85
Tela Accords 423
television 468, 476, 489
  McCarthy era 253, 347, 350,
    351–2
  news coverage 258, 372, 374, 411
  presidential debates 255, 266
  US public broadcasting 262
Teller Amendment 128, 130
Terkel, Studs 204
terrorism 444
  9-11 attacks 439
  Quebec (FLQ) 273, 282–7
Tela Accords 422
Tet offensive 372, 374
Texas 48–9, 96–7, 187
  independence 97–8
  US annexation 61, 88, 95–7, 100,
    118, 148
Thailand 369
Thames, Battle of the 85

Thatcher, Margaret 408, 427
Three Mile Island 484, 485
Thurmond, Strom 251
Tiananmen Square massacre 418,
  431
Tippecanoe, Battle of 82
Titans of Wall Street 184
Tocqueville, Alexis de 111
Toledo, Alejandro 454
Topolansky, Lucía 460
Tories see Loyalists
Torrijos, Omar 388
torture, Latin American military
  regimes 328, 333, 334, 395
Toussaint L'Oveture 11, 36–7
Tower Commission 417
Towers, Colonel James 41
Townsend, Francis E. 202
Townshend Acts 25
trade
  globalization 441, 476–9
  mercantilism 15–16, 449
  monopoly ports 16
  Navigation Acts 16
Trafalgar, Battle of 81
Tragic Week 178
Trail of Tears 109–10
Trudeau, Pierre Elliot 270, 273,
  282–9, 377
Truman Doctrine 342, 343–4
Truman, Harry S. 115, 245–51, 337–
  50, 356–9, 361, 369, 380
Túpac Amaru II 28
Tupamaros 460, 461–2
Tupper, Sir Charles 106
Twain, Mark 130
26th July Movement 295, 298,
  299–300
Tyler, John 97, 98

U
Ubico, Jorge 365
Union Nationale 218
United Fruit Company 297, 361, 365
United Kingdom
  colonies see British colonies; British
    North America
  Falkland War 333, 456
  French and Indian War 12, 22,
    23–5, 27, 29, 89
  Haitian Revolution 36, 37
  Napoleonic Wars 36, 37, 41, 80,
    81, 83–4, 85
  national debt 25
  War of 1812 48, 63, 80–7
United Nations 356–7, 442, 443, 478
United Provinces of Central America
  75
United States of America
  African Americans see African
    Americans
  Alaska 107
  Alliance for Progress 310–11, 379–
    80, 383, 384, 386
  armed forces 67, 129, 134–5, 144,
    146–7, 156, 373–4, 398, 407, 438
  arms sales 387

Articles of Confederation 61, 64–70
banking reforms 421
Big Stick diplomacy 133–9, 140, 144
Bill of Rights 61, 65, 67, 69, 259
British colony see British North America
civil rights legislation 259, 261, 262, 418–19
civil rights movement 242, 243, 246, 249, 251, 254–5, 257–9, 265, 267, 373–4
civil war 104, 105, 106, 116, 118 ??? some p cap c and w ?????????
Clinton Doctrine 439, 440, 443, 444
Cold War see Cold War
Constitution 53, 61, 62, 64, 66, 67–70
consumerism 354
court packing 199–201
Declaration of Independence 9, 30, 31–2
deregulation 402, 404–5, 434
Digital Divide 473–5
Dollar Diplomacy 140–3, 144, 176, 339
Dust Bowl 187–8, 191, 198, 205, 206
economic aid 388
economy 51–2, 53, 115, 116–17, 120–1, 145–6, 150, 159–60, 183, 209, 243, 252–3, 257, 268–9, 420–1, 433, 477–9
expansionist foreign policy 115, 117–32, 136
Fair Deal 246, 249, 252
Federalist Papers 69, 71–3
Federalists and Anti-Federalists 61, 64–9
Florida 48–9
foreign policy 117–43, 338; see also Cold War
franchise 152, 251, 254–5, 261, 262, 267
Gadsden Purchase 100
geography 13
Good Neighbor policy 338
Great Compromise 61, 68–9
Great Depression 183–207
Great Society 257, 260–5, 266, 371, 373
Hawaii 122–3
health and social welfare provision 199, 202, 207, 249, 252, 261, 262–3, 268, 402, 432–3, 434–5, 480
Hispanic Americans 190–1, 435, 474–5, 492
immigration 96, 116, 121, 144, 261, 477
independence 34, 64
Indian Removal Act 109–12
industrialization 51, 52, 61, 69, 96,

116–17
Irish Americans 16, 144, 255
isolationism 130, 147, 155, 156, 160
Japanese Americans 205
Kennedy Doctrine 379, 382
Korean War 337, 339, 346, 355–60, 361, 369
labor movement 116, 117, 152–3, 190–1, 402, 404, 434, 440
Latin American wars of independence 47–9, 52
Long Depression 116, 120
Louisiana Purchase 31, 61, 96
McCarthyism 249–51, 253–4, 266, 336–51
Manifest Destiny 95, 96, 97–9, 105, 118
Mann Doctrine 383, 384
Mexican-American War 61, 95–103, 105
Mexican Revolution 142
Middle East 268, 398, 414–17, 418, 426–30
military aid 388
military draft 373–4
military expenditure 243, 339, 362, 388, 406–10
military regimes supported by 328–9, 361, 380, 383–5, 388, 445, 450
Monroe Doctrine 49–50, 117–18, 123–4, 136, 144, 379, 456
Moral Diplomacy 141–2
Native Americans see indigenous populations
New Deal 182, 191, 192, 195–207, 246
New Economic Policy 268
New Federalism 265–9
New Frontier 255–6
New Look 361–7
New Republicanism 252–3
northern states 51, 54, 68–9
Open Door Policy 133
Oregon 88, 97–8, 100
Philadelphia Convention 59–66
Point Four programs 339
political system 59, 61, 64–73, 420, 432
population 144
post-World War II 242, 243
poverty 248, 253, 259–60, 262–3, 266
Progressive Era 136, 140
protectorates 122–3
racial segregation 243, 251, 254–5, 257–9, 262, 267
railways 116
Reagan Revolution 398, 418
reconstruction 116
regional dominance 11, 57
Revolutionary War see American War of Independence
Rust Belt 478
Shay's Rebellion 53, 64–5, 67

slavery 20, 24, 51, 54–5, 60, 68–9, 96, 97, 98, 105, 205
social system 52–4
southern states 51, 54, 68–9
Spanish-American War 118, 126–32
technological revolution 468–76
Texas 61, 88, 95–7, 100, 118, 148
Trail of Tears 109–10
Truman Doctrine 342, 343–4
unification 13, 23, 31
urbanization 117, 121
Vietnam War 261, 265, 266, 337, 360, 369–78, 379, 383, 384, 406
War of 1812 48, 63, 80–7, 105
War of Independence see American War of Independence
westward expansion 49, 52, 53–4, 61, 69, 81, 82, 85, 88, 95–6
World War I 134, 144–60, 209
World War II 183
urbanization 117, 121, 225, 230, 445, 480
Urgent Fury, Operation 413–14
Uriburu, General José Félix 234, 236, 236
Urrutia, Manuel 297, 299
Uruguay 62
    caudillos 62–3, 75
    military dictatorship 459–64
    Naval Club Pact 461
    Operation Condor 327, 461
    World War I 175
    Utah 61, 95, 99

V
Valley Forge, Battle of 24
valorization 229
Vance, Cyrus 387
Vargas, Getúlio 228, 230–3, 313, 314–19, 325, 329, 445
Vargas Swamp Battle 41
Vásquez, Tabaré 462, 463
Végh Villegas, Alejandro 460
Velasco Alvarado, Juan 450–1
Velasco, José María 313, 314
Velasco, Treaty of 97
Venezuela 310, 311
    crisis of 1902 136, 138–9
    independence 40–2, 61, 62, 79
    Páez 75, 79
    population 51, 60
    slavery 56
    US boundary dispute 118, 123–5
Veracruz, Battle of 96
Vermont 54
Verona, Operation 249–51
Versailles, Treaty of 155–6, 159, 172, 174
vertical integration 117
viceroyalties 27, 38
Videla, Jorge Rafael 331, 332–3, 455–6
video-cassette 468, 476
Vienna, Congress of 117
Viet Cong 371–2
Viet Minh 360, 369–70
Vietnam War 261, 265, 266, 337,

360, 369–78, 379, 383, 384, 406
  anti-war movement 265, 372,
    374–5
Vietnamization 369, 373
Villa, Pancho 142
Vimy Ridge, Battle of 163, 172
Viola, Roberto 334, 456
Virginia 20, 24, 31, 34
Virginians 65, 67–8
Volcker, Paul 402
Voltaire 66

W
Wagner Act 199, 246, 248
Walker, Margaret 204
Wall Street Crash 184–5, 211, 227
Wallace, George 258, 266
Wallace, Henry J. 245
War of 1812 48, 63, 80–7, 105
War Hawks 80, 82–3
Warren, Earl 254
wars of attrition 30, 34, 37, 39, 371
Warsaw Pact 442
Washington DC, British capture 85
Washington, George 24, 30, 34, 44,
    53, 65–6, 67, 68, 69
Washington state 98
Washington Treaty 160
water supply 479–80, 484
Watergate scandal 265, 266, 269,
    373, 385
Waterloo, Battle of 83
Wayne, John 349–50, 351
weapons of mass destruction 429
Weathermen 375
Weinberger, Caspar 415, 416, 425
Welles, Orson 204
Wellington, Arthur Wellesley, Duke
    of 83–4
West Indies *see* Caribbean
Westmoreland, General William 372
Weyler, General Valeriano 126, 128
White, Thomas 166
Whitewater scandal 437–8
Whitman, Walt 98
Wilson, Woodrow 117, 134, 141–60,
    172, 195
Windmill, Battle of the 91
Winnipeg General Strike 173
Wolfe, General James 89
women
  African American 192
  Argentina 317–19
  Canada 169–70, 282, 293
  Chile 391, 393–4
  contraception 293
  Cuba 307
  employment 191–2
  franchise 152, 169–70, 324, 389,
    391
  Great Depression 191–2
  Latin America 76
  military draft 373–4
  United States 151–2, 267, 373,
    374, 435, 490, 491–2
  women's movement 267, 373
  World War I 151–2

Wood, Grant 204
Woodsworth, J.S. 209, 216, 222
Works Progress Administration 189,
    199
World Trade Organization (WTO)
    434, 440, 441, 478
World War I 115
  Allied blockade 145–6
  Canada 160–74, 208
  Canadian economy 165–7, 173,
    209
  Canadian government agencies
    166
  German submarines 145–6, 147,
    150, 151
  Imperial War Cabinet 167, 172
  industrialization 178
  Latin America 175–80
  Latin American economy 175–9
  Quebec 163, 165, 168, 170–1
  reparations 185
  statistics 155
  Treaty of Brest Litovsk 153
  United States 134, 144–60
  US armed forces 146–7
  US economy 145–6, 150, 159–60,
    209
  US government agencies 150–1
  US neutrality 144–6, 147
  US Selective Service Act 150
  women and 151–2
  Zimmerman Telegram 148–9
World War II 242
  Brazil 231, 232, 233, 315
  Canada 270
  post-war economy 242
  United States 183
World Wide Web 468, 471–3
Wozniak, Steve 470, 471
Wright, Richard 206
Wyoming 61, 95, 99

Y
Yaqui Indians 56
yellow press 126, 127, 128
Yeltsin, Boris 431, 442
Yemen 439
Yom Kippur War 268
Yorktown, Battle of 24, 34
Young, Neil 375
youth movement 374, 375
Ypres, 2nd Battle of 172
Yrigoyen, Hipólito 178, 234–6, 239
yuppies 490

Z
Zapata 40
Zelaya, José Santos 140
Zimmerman Telegram 148–9

Acknowledgements

We are grateful for permission to reprint from the following copyright material:

Bill Albert & Paul Henderson: Table from *South America and the First World War: The Impact of War on Brazil, Argentina, Peru and Chile* (Cambridge University Press, 1988), copyright © Cambridge University Press 1988, reprinted by permission of the publishers.

Elena H Alvares: Table from 'Economic development, restructuring and the illicit drug sector in Bolivia and Peru: Current Policies', 37: 3 *Journal of Interamerican Studies & World Affairs*, 1995, reprinted by permission of the publishers, John Wiley & Sons Ltd.

David Beckwith, with Neil MacNeil & James Kelly: extract from 'Reaganomics: Too Many Voices', *Time*, 19.10. 1981, copyright © TIME Inc 1981, reprinted by permission via Copyright Clearance Center. TIME is a registered trademark of Time Inc. All rights reserved.

Alan Brinkley: extracts from *American History: A Survey* (10e, McGraw Hill, 1999), copyright © Alan Brinkley 1999, reprinted by permission of The McGraw-Hill Companies.

Canadian Press reporter: 'Canadian on Death Row in US down to last legal remedy', *The Canadian Press*, 17.5.2010.

Arlo Guthrie: 'Do Re Mi', copyright © 1961 Ludlow Music, Inc, USA, assigned to TRO Essex Music Ltd, Suite 2.07, Plaza 535 Kings Road, London SW10 0SZ. International Copyright Secured. All Rights Reserved. Reprinted by permission of TRO Essex Music Ltd.

Richard Warren Lewis: extract from an interview with John Wayne, Playboy Magazine, 1.5.1971, copyright © *Playboy Magazine* 1971.

Arthur Miller: extract from 'Why I wrote "The Crucible"', *The New Yorker*, 21.10.1996, copyright © Arthur Miller 1996, reprinted by permission of The Wylie Agency (UK) Ltd. All rights reserved.

The Miller Center of Public Affairs: extracts from *American President: An Online Reference Resource*, miller.center.org/president; 'George Herbert Walker Bush', Consulting Editor: Stephen Knott, Associate Professor, National Security Decision Making Department, United States Naval War College; and 'Domestic Affairs: William Jefferson Clinton', Consulting Editor: Professor Russell J Riley, Co-Chair of the Presidential Oral History Program and Project Director of the William J Clinton Presidential History Project, Miller Center of Public Affairs, reprinted by permission of The Miller Center of Public Affairs.

Edmund Morris: extract from ' "A matter of extreme urgency": Theodore Roosevelt, Wilhelm II, and the Venezuela Crisis of 1902', *Naval War College Review*, Spring 2002, reprinted by permission of the author and Naval War College Press.

National Telecommunications and Information Administration: extract from 'Falling Through the Net II: Data on the Digital Divide' (NTIA, US Department of Commerce, 1998) available at http://www.ntia.doc.gov/ntiahome/net2/falling.html.

James T Patterson: extracts from *Restless Giant: The United States from Watergate to Bush vs Gore* (OUP. 2005), reprinted by permission of Oxford University Press.

Murray N Rothbard: 'The Great Society: A Libertarian Critique', copyright © 2003 Ludwig von Mises Institute, first published in The Great Society Reader: *The Failure of American Liberation* (Vintage, 1967), reprinted under the Creative Commons Licence.

Claude Ryan: extract from his editorial, *Le Devoir*, 17.10.1970, reprinted by permission of Le Devoir.

John Steinbeck: extract from *The Grapes of Wrath* (Penguin, 2001) copyright © John Steinbeck 1939, renewed © John Steinbeck 1967, reprinted by permission of Penguin Books Ltd, and Viking Penguin, a division of Penguin Group (USA) Inc.

Chris Taylor, with Ann Blackman & Anne Moffett, Sarah Dale, & Collette McKenna: extract from 'Digital Divide', *Time*, 4.12.2000, copyright © TIME Inc 2000, reprinted by permission via Copyright Clearance Center. TIME is a registered trademark of Time Inc. All rights reserved.

Time Magazine Reporter: extract from 'Canada: '"This very sorry moment"' *Time*, 26.10.1970, copyright © TIME Inc 1920, reprinted by permission via Copyright Clearance Center. TIME is a registered trademark of Time Inc. All rights reserved.

Mark A Uhlig: extract from 'Contras: Lost Cause?', *New York Times*, 10.8.1989, copyright © The New York Times 1989. All Rights Reserved. Used by permission of PARS International Corp and protected by the Copyright Laws of the United States.

Jordan M Young: extract from *The Brazilian Revolution and Aftermath* (Rutgers University Press, 1967), reprinted by permission of the author.

We have tried to trace and contact all copyright holders before publication. If notified, the publishers will be pleased to rectify any errors or omissions at the earliest opportunity.